Italy

FODOR'S TRAVEL PUBLICATIONS

are compiled, researched, and edited by an international team of travel writers, field correspondents, and editors. The series, which now almost covers the globe, was founded by Eugene Fodor in 1936.

OFFICES
New York & London

Fodor's Italy

Editor: Richard Moore
Area Editor: Barbara Walsh Angelillo
Editorial Contributors: Robert Brown, Leslie Gardiner, Mark Lewes, Peter Nichols, Pamela Vandyke Price, Tom Szentgyorgyi
Drawings: Beryl Sanders
Maps: C.W. Bacon, Brian Stimpson, Swanston Graphics
Cover Photograph: Charles C. Place/Image Bank

Cover Design: Vignelli Associates

Fodor's 89 Italy

FODOR'S TRAVEL PUBLICATIONS, INC.
New York & London

ISBN 0–679–01663–5

MANUFACTURED IN THE UNITED STATES OF AMERICA
10 9 8 7 6 5 4 3 2 1

CONTENTS

FOREWORD

Italy is a country of striking contrasts, from its snow-covered borders with Switzerland to the sun-drenched rocks of Sicily. It is a country rooted deeply in the history of Western civilization. A country where atavistic memories are stirred by the sight of a statue in a town's ornate square, by a religious procession winding through a vine-clad countryside, by a Roman temple etched against the evening sky. It is a country incredibly rich in remembrance of the past, in supreme works of the imagination, and in the still-lovely landscapes from which those works sprang.

But Italy is not a country living solely on treasured memories of past glorics, vibrant though those may be. It is one of the great success stories of modern Europe, a leading nation in many fields—especially in the arts of film and fashion, and in industrial design. In fact, Italy now ranks as the fifth industrial nation in the developed world, having overtaken Britain. The Italian way of life is a richly varied one, sophisticated metropolitan society happily coexisting with its deep country roots. The visitor, too, can enjoy both the urbane delights of city hotels and superb food, and the simpler pleasures of country living. The price ranges available are likewise broad, with many opportunties for a genuinely budget vacation.

Unfortunately, there is a catch in Italy being such a desirable destination—it is no secret! Michelangelo's *David,* in Florence's Accademia, rises above a sea of jostling admirers that would put a football crowd to shame. At the height of the season, Venice seems to be in extra danger of sinking under the weight of visitors. The press of people on Capri sometimes threatens to force those nearest the edge to have to swim for the mainland. (There's a good deal to be said for finding out on the spot when museums are at their busiest—do the bus trips all arrive at more or less the same time every day, for example?—and planning your visit around these times.) But there is something for everyone in Italy, and the fortitude needed for a swift visit to the most famous highlights, can be more than compensated for by finding the fascinations of the country's byways—the beauty of hidden Tuscan towns; that Signorelli fresco which is all the more effective because you don't have to jostle to see it; the lunch in the little trattoria on a village square, where you can get happily drowsy on local wine. We hope that you will find help in this edition of *Fodor's Italy* for whatever kind of visit you plan.

For those of our readers who may be interested in a different approach to their visit to Italy, we also publish a *Fodor's Rome* and *Fodor's Florence and Venice,* dealing with these cities in greater detail than we can in this guide, and a *Budget Italy* for those who wish to watch their pocketbooks.

*

We would like to express our thanks to all those who have assisted us in the preparation of this edition: to the staff of the Italian State Tourist Office in London; the

Italian Tourist Office in New York; the directors and staff of ENIT in Rome and AAST and regional tourist offices throughout Italy.

Finally, we would like to thank Barbara Walsh Angelillo for all the hard work and skill which she has once more brought to her task as Area Editor. Her knowledge of, and love for, Italy remains one of the main supports of our enterprise.

*

While every care has been taken to assure the accuracy of the information in this guide, the passage of time will always bring change, and consequently the publisher cannot accept responsibility for errors that may occur.

All prices and opening times quoted in this guide are based on information available to us at press time. Hours and admission fees may change, however, and the prudent traveler will avoid inconvenience by calling ahead.

Fodor's wants to hear about your travel experiences, both pleasant and unpleasant. When a hotel or restaurant fails to live up to its billing, let us know and we will investigate the complaint and revise our entries where the facts warrant it.

Send your letters to the editors of Fodor's Travel Publications, 201 East 50th Street, New York, NY 10022. European readers may prefer to write to Fodor's Travel Publications, 30–32 Bedford Square, London WC1B 3SG, England.

FACTS
AT YOUR
FINGERTIPS

FACTS AT YOUR FINGERTIPS

Planning Your Trip

SOURCES OF INFORMATION. The major source of information for anyone planning a vacation to Italy is the *Italian National Tourist Office.* **In the U.S.** the addresses are—630 Fifth Ave., New York, N.Y. 10111 (212–245–4822); 500 North Michigan Ave., Chicago, IL 60611 (312–644–0990); 360 Post St., Suite 801, San Francisco, CA 94108 (415–392–6206).

In Canada—3 Place Ville Marie, Montreal, Quebec H3B 2E3 (514–866–7667). **In the U.K.**—1 Princes St., London W1R 8AY (01–408 1254).

They can supply information on all aspects of travel to and about Italy, from which type of vacation is best suited to your needs and purse, to the most economical ways of getting around. They also have a wealth of material on hotels, restaurants, excursions and museums and will produce copious amounts of information, much of it free and all of it useful.

PACKAGE TOUR OR INDEPENDENT TRAVEL? Time, convenience, cost and the type of travel that most interests you are the factors to consider when it comes to choosing an all-inclusive, fully-escorted tour, a loose plan-your-own-itinerary package tour, or totally independent travel.

Package tours are the easiest to arrange, and probably the most economical and efficient way for a first-time traveler to Italy to get an overview of the most famous sights. The operator will arrange for all plane, rail, motorcoach and other transportation; transfers wherever needed; tour guides; and generally commodious accommodations. Flight-plus-lodging for many such tours often works out to be less expensive than the flight alone would be if booked as a regular economy fare. Thus, even if you prefer arranging for accommodations at someplace other than that offered by the tour operator, and even if you have no intention of participating in any group sightseeing or other package activities, it may still be in your best interest to buy the entire package.

Among the general items to check when considering any package are:
—Does the price quoted cover air as well as land arrangements? If air fare is not included, does the tour operator have a special rate available?
—How many meals are included?
—If an overnight stopover is involved prior to the formal start of the tour (or at its conclusion), are accommodations handled by the tour operator or are you on your own? Is there an extra charge for such "additional" nights?
—How tied to the tour are you? If it is a motorcoach tour, for example, must you stay with the tour city-by-city or can you leave and re-join it at will?
—Does the rate for an automobile included in the package carry an additional per-mile fee or is mileage unlimited? Is the car in the base rate exactly what you need (air conditioning may or may not be necessary for you, but there is a substantial difference in charges for standard and automatic shifts in Italy—can you drive a standard)?
—What is the tour operator's responsibility for getting you home on time (within reason of weather delays, etc.)?

Traveling independently allows for greater freedom than does tour travel, but it is also almost always more expensive (assuming you desire comparable accommodations and services). In contrast, you will almost always get better value for your money (that does not necessarily mean it will be cheaper) when dining on your own. Tour operators have arrangements with particular establishments that can handle busloads of tourists at a time; in order to serve them simultaneously and at a reduced rate, there will usually be a fixed menu offered, or a limited selection from the full menu. The food in such places also tends to play on stereotypes; both your options and the quality of the food you get are likely to be better if you go it on your own. Specific suggestions will be offered in the individual regional sections throughout this book.

If you have not tied yourself to a tour and do not require en route assistance in finding accommodations within your budget, go directly to the information kiosk at rail, ship or air terminals in the city or town where you wish to stay. The people manning these kiosks are among the most helpful and reliable sources of information concerning available hotel, hostel, pension, bed-and-breakfast and tourist-home rooms. During peak tourist periods they may suggest some surprisingly viable—and fascinating—alternatives, either one town away, or at a local university, or even a monastery that rents rooms out to the public! But during peak periods there are long lines at these kiosks.

In booking a package tour it is best to go through a travel agent; indeed, except for the likes of American Express, Thomas Cook and the airlines, most packagers do not handle their own reservations.

TRAVEL AGENTS. The critical issues in choosing a travel agent are how knowledgeable that person is about travel and how reliable his or her bookings are, regardless of whether you are looking for a package tour or planning to go it independently. The cost will be substantially the same whether you go to a major tour operator such as *Maupintour, American Express, Thos. Cook & Son* and *Olson's* or to the small agency around the corner. Most commissions are paid by airlines, hotels and tour operators. In Europe there may be a small general service charge for fee-per-reservation; in the U.S. only out-of-the-ordinary telephone or telex charges are ever paid by the client.

The importance of a travel agent is not merely for the making of reservations, however. A good travel agent booking a flight for a customer will know what general discounts are in effect based on how long your stay will be, how far in advance you are able to make your reservations, whether you are making a simple round trip or adding extra stops and other factors. He or she should also be able to suggest suitable accommodations or packages that offer the kind of services you want.

In the case of package tours, you want to be sure that the tour operator can deliver the package being offered. Here again, a travel agent can be helpful. Certainly the organizations named above have established their reputations based on reliability—the inevitable occasional foul-up notwithstanding.

Not all U.S. travel agents are licensed, as the laws vary from state to state, but membership in the American Society of Travel Agents (ASTA) is a safeguard. Similarly, U.K. agents belong to the Association of British Travel Agents (ABTA). Members prominently display ASTA or ABTA shields.

TOUR OPERATORS. Full details of the many operators offering trips to Italy are available from the *Italian National Tourist Office,* Alitalia and other international airlines and, of course, travel agents. But such is the range of tours available from both North America and the U.K. that a summary of some of the more typical is of interest. (All our examples are meant to be representative of typical offerings that are regularly available. Details are as of mid-1988; check for current information.)

From the U.S.—*CIT* is one of the most active tour operators in Italy—with 40 offices in the country, 80 worldwide. It offers several options, including "All That Italy," a comprehensive tour that costs between $1,839 and $2,177, and "The Etruscan" which takes you through Rome, Florence, Venice, and many of the smaller cities in the region, costing from $1,199 to $1,849. City packages for independent travelers are also available. CIT Travel Service, 666 Fifth Ave., New York, N.Y. 10103 (212–397–2666); 2055 Peel St., Suite 102, Montreal, Quebec H3A 1V4 (514–845–9101).

Among other tour operators, *Cosmos/Globus Gateway* offers a land-only 13-day major cities tour, "Italian Mosaic," costing around $850, and a 16-day jaunt,

"Grand Tour of Italy and Sicily," including an overnight cruise from Naples to Palermo for around $1,100. Cosmos/Globus Gateway, 150 S. Los Robles Ave., Suite 860, Pasadena, CA 91101 (818–449–0919 or 800–556–5454).

Maupintour's top-of-the-line Italian tour, "Italy—Alps and Lakes," takes 23 days, costs about $5,098 but runs all the way from the northern Alp and lake regions right down to Naples, Sorrento and Capri. Maupintour, Box 807, Lawrence, KS 66044 (913–843–1211 or 800–255–4266).

Wilderness Travel, 1760 Solano Ave., Berkeley, CA 94707 (415–524–5111), has a country walking tour of the medieval Hilltowns of Italy. Land cost $1,790.

Other tour operators with lively Italian programs are—

Alitalia, 666 Fifth Ave., New York, N.Y. 10103 (212–903–3300).

American Express, 822 Lexington Ave., New York, N.Y. 10021 (212–758–6510 or 800–241–1700).

Cortell Group, 770 Lexington Ave., New York, NY 10022 (212–751–4200).

Olson Travelworld, P.O. Box 92734, Los Angeles, CA 90009 (213–670–7100).

Pan Am, Pan Am Bldg., New York, N.Y. 10017 (212–687–2600).

Perillo Tours, 30 N. William St., Pearl River, N.Y. 10965 (800–431–1515).

From the U.K.—Again, *CIT* is a leader in the Italian market. They have a huge range of offers available from Britain, from beach vacations, motoring and self-catering holidays to 2- and 3-center holidays. In the latter category you can mix Florence with Elba, or Venice, or Viareggio, Rome with Amalfi, Florence, Venice or at least 4 other towns, and so on in a chain of possibilities. With such a wide range of offerings, the costs are naturally wide ranging too. CIT, Marco Polo House, 3–5 Lansdowne Rd., Croydon CR9 1LL (01–686 5533).

Naturally, one of the most prominent reasons for visiting Italy is her art treasures, and there are plenty of tours which are for this purpose alone. One of the longest-serving companies in the field is *Swan Hellenic,* 77 New Oxford St., London WC1A 1PP (01–831 1616). In the States their address is 500 Fifth Ave., New York, N.Y. 10110 (212–719–1200 or 800–221–1666). Their coverage of Italian art includes Lombardy and the Lakes, the Hill Towns, and Sicily. Every Swan Hellenic tour is accompanied by a selected guest lecturer, all of them specialists in their field. As an example, their 15-day Renaissance Italy tour takes in Venice, Padua, Ravenna, Urbino, Borgo San Sepolcro, Arezzo, Siena, San Gimignano, Florence, Pisa, Lucca, Verona, Bergamo and Milan. . . which is a lot of ground to cover in 15 days. Cost is around £1,790.

Two other operators in the field are *Serenissima,* 21 Dorset Sq., London NW1 6QG (01–730 9841); in the U.S., *The Serenissima Travel Group,* 41 East 42nd St (Suite 2312), New York, N.Y. 10017 (800–358–3330), whose Villas and Gardens of Northern Italy lasts for 10 days and costs from around £1,795.

Prospect Art Tours Ltd., 10 Barley Mow Passage, London W4 4PH (01–995 2163/4), with several Italian ventures, including an antiquities tour that takes in Pompeii and Herculaneum, 7 days for about £550.

If you want to rival Raphael yourself, *Voyages Jules Verne,* 21 Dorset Sq., London NW1 6QG (01–723 6556), will give you the chance. They run a painting holiday by Lake Orta, near Lake Maggiore; 10 days for approximately £590, expert tuition included. They also run a popular Botany and Wild Flowers tour to the Dolomites, 15 days based in Selva, from around £620.

WHEN TO GO. The main tourist season in Italy runs from mid-April to the end of September, when the weather is best. Spring and early autumn (through October) are good for sightseeing everywhere. Keep in mind that at Easter foreign tourists crowd the cities, while Italians flock to the resorts and to the country. During April and most of May cities of historic and artistic interest may be invaded by busloads of eager schoolchildren on excursion.

If you can avoid it, don't travel at all in Italy during August, when much of the population is on the move, crowding all transportation; cities are deserted, many restaurants and shops closed. With the exception of such places as Taormina and the Italian Riviera, coast resorts usually close up tight from October or November to April; they're at their best in June and September.

You will find more detailed *When to Go* sections in each *Practical Information,* to help you on a regional basis.

Climate. Average maximum afternoon temperatures in degrees Fahrenheit and centigrade.

Rome	Jan.	Feb.	Mar.	Apr.	May	June	July	Aug.	Sept.	Oct.	Nov.	Dec.
F°	54	56	62	68	74	82	88	88	83	73	63	56
C°	12	13	17	20	23	28	31	31	28	23	17	13
Milan												
F°	40	47	56	66	72	80	84	82	76	64	51	42
C°	4	8	13	19	22	27	29	28	24	18	11	6

SEASONAL EVENTS. You will find all the most interesting regional festivals listed in the *Practical Information* sections at the end of each chapter. We should warn you to check on dates of festivals on the spot, as some events are liable to change from year to year and the very local nature of many of them makes them variable. Local Tourist Offices (see the *Practical Information* sections again) have up-to-date lists of all events and will be happy to help.

January, the Roman Catholic Epiphany celebrations and decorations in Rome's Piazza Navona; the Greek Catholic Epiphany rites at Piana degli Albanesi, near Palermo.

February (sometimes March), pre-Lenten carnivals in many places, particularly in Venice and Viareggio, during the ten days before Shrove Tuesday. Almond Blossom Festival at Agrigento; the Saint Agatha Festival at Catania; the Flower Show at San Remo.

March, nationwide mid-Lent festivals, feasts for the poor, usually on St. Joseph's Day, the 19th. Florence's traditional Scoppio del Carro Easter Sunday (sometimes falls in April).

April, Florence's traditional Scoppio del Carro; the International Trade Fair at Milan; International Handicrafts Fair, Florence.

May, Musical Festival at Florence; Feast of Sant' Efisio in Cagliari; Annual Fish Festival at Camogli (near Genoa); the Festa dei Ceri, Gubbio; the Sardinian Costume Cavalcade at Sassari.

June, Tournament of the Bridge, Pisa; the Festival of the Two Worlds, at Spoleto (month long); nationwide celebration of Feast of St. John, with the most important observances in Rome and Florence.

July, the Palio at Siena (repeated in August); the Feast of the Redeemer, Venice; International Ballet Festival, Nervi; the Madonna del Carmine festival, Naples, Noantri festival, Rome. Macerata opera festival, in the Arena Sferisteiro, to mid-Aug. Assisi Festa Musica Pro. Opera at Caracalla in Rome.

August, Feast of the Assumption of Mary, throughout Italy; Tournament of the Quintana, Ascoli Piceno; Palio of the Gulf, La Spezia; the final of the Palio at Siena. Feast of the Redeemer, Nuoro (Sardinia).

September, The Joust of the Saracen, Arezzo; Joust of the Quintana, Foligno; Historic Regatta, Venice; Festival of Santa Rosa, Viterbo.

October, Celebrations in honor of Columbus, Genoa; Annual Truffle Fair, Alba. Autumn music festivals in Como, Naples.

November, Feast of the Madonna della Salute, Venice.

December, traditional Christmas celebrations throughout the country.

Pilgrimages. The first goal of Catholic pilgrims to Italy is, of course, Rome and its four major churches, and the favored times to go there are Easter and Christmas. Important Easter ceremonies are held also in Florence, Sulmona and during Holy Week in Taranto, Trapani and Marsala.

Special pilgrimage days for Loreto are 25 March, 15 August, 8 September and 8 and 10 December. 13 June is the day to visit the tomb of St. Anthony in Padua.

The Black Madonna of Tindari, in Sicily, is visited especially on 8 September, and the Madonna of Trapani, on the same island, on 25 March.

Information may be obtained from ENIT (see *Sources of Information* earlier).

WHAT TO PACK. The first principle is to travel light. If you plan to fly across the Atlantic, airline baggage allowances are now based on size rather than weight. Economy class passengers may take free two pieces of baggage, provided that the sum of their dimensions is not over 106 inches and neither one singly is over 62 inches-height, width and length. For first class the allowance is two pieces up to 62 inches each, total 124 inches. The penalties for oversize are severe; to Western Europe around $50 per piece.

These restrictions also apply to Alitalia's domestic flights. One piece may be carried as cabin baggage, maximum size 18x14x7 ins.

Do not take more than you can carry yourself; it's a lifesaver if you go to places where porters are hard to find. It's a good idea to pack the bulk of your things in one large bag and put everything you need for overnight, or for two or three nights, in another. This obviates packing and repacking at every stop. If you plan to be traveling by train, take smallish or medium-sized bags, easier to get on and off trains and into overhead racks.

The weather is considerably milder in Italy than in the north and central United States or Great Britain all the year round. In the summer season, make your clothing as light as possible—but women should have a scarf, light stole or jacket handy to cover bare shoulders and arms when visiting churches, where pants suits are acceptable but shorts are taboo (they can be very strict about this in Italy). It's no longer necessary for women to cover their heads in churches, however. A sweater or woolen stole is a must for the cool of the evening, even during the hot months. In the summer, brief afternoon thunderstorms are common in Rome and inland cities, so carry a plastic folding raincoat. And if you go into the mountains, you will find the evenings there quite chilly. During the winter, a medium-weight coat will stand you in good stead, while a raincoat is essential. You'll probably need an umbrella, too, but you can pick it up on the spot (or invest in a good folding one).

The deluxe spots are still dressy, but not formal. Men aren't required to wear ties or jackets anywhere, especially in the summer, except in some of the grander hotel dining rooms and top-level restaurants. Formal wear is very definitely the exception rather than the rule at the opera nowadays. For the huge general papal audiences, no rules of dress apply except those of common sense. For other types of audience, the Vatican Information Office will illustrate requirements.

If you wear glasses, take along a spare pair or the prescription and if you have to take some particular medicine regularly, especially if it is made up only on prescription, better bring a supply. Its exact equivalent may be difficult for the average pharmacist to identify, although it undoubtedly exists.

WHAT IT WILL COST. Prices in Italy have been climbing steadily for several years. The simplest way to budget your money is to choose one of the many prepackaged trips. They will be more expensive than formerly, but still offer good value and a wide variety of costs, depending upon the degree of luxury provided.

Naturally, the main bulk of your expenditure will be on hotel and restaurant bills. We suggest price ranges in these two categories further on under the relevant sections, the price ranges tied in to our system of grading. You should keep in mind that costs in Italy are increasing at a rate of about 10% each year. Our estimate of hotel and restaurant prices tries to take this rate of increase into account, but—crystal balls being notoriously unreliable gadgets—you may well find that the costs of transportation and other services are higher by the time you get to Italy.

Costs. We deal with the prices of hotels and restaurants under the relevant sections below. Standing at a bar, a cup of espresso costs from 700 to 1,000 lire, triple that for table service. A bottle of beer costs from 1,600 to 3,000 lire, a Coca-Cola costs 1,500 lire. A small sandwich *(tramezzino)* costs about 1,200 lire, a more substantial one about 2,000. You will pay about 5,000 lire for a short taxi ride in Rome, less in Florence, more in Milan. Admission to a major museum is about 5,000 lire; a three-hour sightseeing tour, about 25,000 lire.

Off-Season Travel. This has become more popular in recent years as business houses have finally recognized the many advantages of staggering vacations throughout the year and as tourists have come to appreciate the advantages of avoiding the crowded periods. Plane fares are cheaper and so are hotel rates. Italy is ideally suited for off-season vacationing, since its mild climate makes it an outdoor country all year round. The winter is of course the season to hear the famous La Scala Opera at Milan, as well as the operas of Venice, Naples, Rome and other cities. The Italian Riviera and Sicily are attractive in winter. Sicily, Sardinia and the Deep South are good in April, May and early autumn. June is best for islands such as Capri, Ischia and Elba.

TAKING MONEY ABROAD. Traveler's checks are still the standard and best way to safeguard your travel funds, as most companies will replace them quickly and efficiently if loss occurs. You should always keep a note of the check numbers separate from the checks themselves to help with the replacement process. You will usually get a better exchange rate in Italy for traveler's checks than for cash.

In the U.S. many of the larger banks issue their own traveler's checks, which are almost as well recognized as those of the longer established firms, American Express, Cook and Barclays. Many banks will carry one or other of those brands of check as well as their own.

The best known British checks (in this case cheques!) are Cook's, Barclays, Lloyds, Midland and National Westminster banks'—as well as American Express, of course.

It is always a good idea to have some local currency on arrival for taxis and tips. Some banks provide this service; alternatively contact Deak International, 630 Fifth Ave., New York, N.Y., 10011 (212–757–6915—call for other locations).

Britons holding a Uniform Eurocheque card and cheque book can cash cheques for up to £100 a day at banks, and write cheques in restaurants, hotels, etc.

Credit Cards. Credit cards are now an integral part of the Western Financial Way of Life, and, in theory at least, are accepted all over Europe. But, while the use of credit cards can smooth the traveler's path considerably, they should not be thought of as a universal answer to every problem.

Firstly, there is growing resistance in Europe to the use of credit cards, or rather to the percentage which the credit card organizations demand from establishments taking part in their schemes. Not so long ago, 200 restaurants in Paris refused to accept credit cards—and some of them still refuse—simply because they felt that the benefit credit cards bring is all on the side of the customer. There are also many thrifty Italian restaurateurs who are damned if they see why they should turn over any part of their hard-earned money to credit card companies, and stoutly refuse to accept plastic payment. A great many of these are the more atmospheric, regional establishments, most likely the very ones you will want to eat in. So keep an eye open for those little signs in the window; you could easily find yourself in an embarrassing situation otherwise.

Another point that should be watched with those useful pieces of plastic is the problem of the rate at which your purchase may be converted into your home currency. If you want to be certain of the rate at which you will pay, insist on the establishment entering the current rate onto your credit card charge at the time you sign up—this will prevent the management from holding your charge until a more favorable rate (to them) comes along, something which could cost you more dollars than you counted on.

We would advise you, also, to check your monthly statement very carefully indeed against the counterfoils you got at the time of your purchase. It has become increasingly common for shops, hotels or restaurants to change the amounts on the original you signed, if they find they have made an error in the original bill. Sometimes, also, unscrupulous employees make this kind of change to their own advantage. The onus is on you to report the change to the credit card firm and insist on sorting the problem out.

We have included in this edition credit card information for as many establishments as we have been able to verify. There are some surprising omissions of hotels or restaurants that you would think would accept credit cards, but don't. The initials we use for this information are AE, DC, MC and V—which stand for American Express, Diner's Club, MasterCard (alias Access and Eurocard) and Visa (Barclaycard in Britain).

PASSPORTS. All travelers require a passport for entry into Italy. **In the U.S.,** apply in person at U.S. Passport Agency Offices, local county courthouses or selected Post Offices. If you have a passport not more than eight years old you may apply by mail; otherwise you will need:

—proof of citizenship, such as a birth certificate;

—two identical photographs two inches square, in either black and white or color, on non-glossy paper and taken within the past six months;

—$35 for the passport itself plus a $7 processing fee if you are applying in person (no processing fee when applying by mail) for those 18 years and older, or if you are under 18, $20 for the passport plus a $7 processing fee if you are applying in person (again, no extra fee when applying by mail);

—proof of identity that includes a photo and signature, such as a driver's license, previous passport, or any governmental ID card.

Adult passports are valid for 10 years, others for five years; they are not renewable. Allow four to six weeks for your application to be processed, but in an emergency, Passport Agency offices can have a passport readied within 24–48 hours, and even the postal authorities can indicate "Rush" when necessary.

If you expect to travel extensively, request a 48- or 96-page passport rather than the usual 24-page one. There is no extra charge. When you receive your passport, write down its number, date and place of issue separately; if it is later lost or stolen, notify either the nearest American Counsel or the Passport Office, Department of State, 1425 K St. NW, Washington, DC 20524, as well as the local police.

British subjects must apply for passports on special forms obtainable from main post offices or a travel agent. The application should be sent or taken to the Passport Office according to residential area (as indicated on the guidance form) or lodged with them through a travel agent. It is best to apply for the passport 4–5 weeks before it is required, although in some cases it will be issued sooner. The regional Passport Offices are located in London, Liverpool, Peterborough, Glasgow and Newport. The application must be countersigned by your bank manager or by a solicitor, barrister, doctor, clergyman or justice of the peace who knows you personally. You will need two full-face photos. The fee is £15; passport valid for 10 years.

British Visitor's Passport. This simplified form of passport has advantages for the once-in-a-while tourist to most European countries (Yugoslavia and Eastern Europe countries presently excepted). Valid for one year and not renewable, it costs £7.50. Application may be made at main post offices in England, Scotland and Wales, and in Northern Ireland at the Passport Office in Belfast. Birth certificate or medical card for identification and two passport photographs are required—no other formalities.

Canadian citizens apply in person to regional passport offices, post offices or by mail to Bureau of Passports, Complexe Guy Favreau, 200 Dorchester West, Montreal, P.Q. H2Z 1X4 (514–283–2152). A $25 fee, two photographs and evidence of citizenship are required. Canadian passports are valid for five years and are non-renewable.

Visas. Not required by passport holders of the U.K., Eire, the U.S.A., and Canada for stays of up to 3 months, but visas are required for citizens of some Commonwealth countries.

INSURANCE. The different varieties of travel insurance cover everything from health and accident costs, to lost baggage and trip cancelation. Sometimes they can all be obtained with one blanket policy; other times they overlap with existing coverage you might have for health and/or home; still other times it is best to buy policies that are tailored to very specific needs. Insurance is available from many sources, however, and many travelers unwittingly end up with redundant coverage. Before purchasing separate travel insurance of any kind, be sure to check your regular policies carefully.

Generally, it is best to take care of your insurance needs before embarking on your trip. You'll pay more for less coverage—and have less chance to read the fine print—if you wait until the last minute and make your purchases from, say, an airport vending machine or insurance company counter. If you have a regular insurance agent, he or she is the person to consult first.

Flight insurance, which is often included in the price of the ticket when the fare is paid via American Express, Visa or certain other major credit cards, is also often included in package policies providing accident coverage as well. These policies are available from most tour operators and insurance companies. While it is a good idea to have health and accident insurance when traveling, be careful not to spend money to duplicate coverage you may already have . . . or to neglect some eventuality which could end up costing a small fortune.

For example, basic Blue Cross-Blue Shield policies do cover health costs incurred while traveling. They will not, however, cover the cost of emergency transportation, which can often add up to several thousand dollars. Emergency transportation *is* covered, in part at least, by many major medical policies such as those underwritten by Prudential, Metropolitan and New York Life. Again, we can't urge you too strongly that in order to be sure you are getting the coverage you need, check any policy carefully before buying. Another important example: Most insurance issued specifically for travel do not cover pre-existing conditions, such as a heart condition.

Travel Assistance International, the American arm of Europ Assistance, offers a comprehensive program providing medical and personal emergency services and offering immediate, on-the-spot medical, personal and financial help. Trip protection ranges from $35 for an individual for up to eight days to $220 for an entire family for a year. Full details from travel agents or insurance brokers, or from Europ Assistance Worldwide Services, Inc., 1133 15th St. N.W., Suite 400, Washington, D.C. 20005 (800–821–2828). In the U.K., contact Europ Assistance Ltd., 252 High St., Croydon, Surrey (01–680 1234).

Carefree Travel Insurance, c/o ARM Coverage Inc., 120 Mineola Blvd., Box 310, Mineola, N.Y. 11510 (516–283–0220 or 800–645–2424), offers insurance, legal and financial assistance, and medical evacuation arranged through InterClaim. Carefree coverage is available from many travel agents.

International SOS Assistance Inc., P.O. Box 11568, Philadelphia, PA 19116 (215–244–1500 or 800–523–8930), does not offer medical insurance but provides medical evacuation services to its clients, who are often international corporations.

IAMAT (International Association for Medical Assistance to Travelers), 736 Center St., Lewiston, N.Y. 14092 (716–754–4883) in the U.S.; or 188 Nicklin Road, Guelph, Ontario N1H 7L5 (519–836–0102) in Canada.

Baggage. It is possible, though often a complicated affair, to insure your luggage against loss through theft or negligence. Insurance companies are reluctant to sell such coverage alone, however, since it is often a losing proposition for them. Instead, it is most often included as part of a package that would also cover accidents or health. Remuneration is often determined by weight, regardless of the value of the specific contents of the luggage. Should you lose your luggage or some other personal possession, be sure to report it to the local police immediately. Without documentation of such a report, your insurance company might be very stingy. Also, before buying baggage insurance, check your homeowners policy. Some such policies offer "off-premises theft" coverage, including the loss of luggage while traveling.

Trip Cancellation. The last major area of traveler's insurance is trip cancellation coverage. This is especially important to travelers on APEX or charter flights. Should you get sick abroad, or for some other reason be unable to continue your trip, you may be stuck having to buy a new one-way fare home, plus paying for space on the charter you're not using. You can guard against this with "trip cancellation insurance," usually available from travel agents. Most of these policies will also cover last minute cancellations.

STUDENT AND YOUTH TRAVEL. All student travelers should obtain an *International Student Identity Card,* which is in most instances needed to get student discounts, youth rail passes, and Intra-European Student Charter Flights. Apply to *Council on International Educational Exchange,* 205 East 42 St., New York, NY 10017 or 312 Sutter St., San Francisco, CA 94108. Cost is $10. Canadian students should apply to the *Association of Student Councils,* 187 College St., Toronto, Ont. M5T 1P7. Cost: $10.

The following organizations can also be helpful in finding student flights, educational opportunities and other information. Most deal with international student travel generally, but materials for those listed cover Italy.

American Youth Hostels, PO Box 37613, Washington, DC 20013. Members are eligible for entree to the worldwide network of youth hostels. The organization publishes an extensive directory to same.

Council on International Educational Exchange (CIEE), 205 East 42 St., New York, N.Y. 10017, and 312 Sutter St., San Francisco, CA 94108, provides information on summer study, work/travel programs and travel services for college and high school students, and a free Charter Flights Guide booklet. Their *Whole World Handbook* ($8.95 plus $1.00 postage) is the best listing of both work and study possibilities.

Institute of International Education, 809 United Nations Plaza, New York, NY 10017, is primarily concerned with study opportunities and administers scholarships and fellowships for international study and training. The New York office has a visitor's information center; satellite offices are located in Chicago, Denver, Houston, San Francisco and Washington.

Also worth contacting is *Educational Travel Center,* 438 North Frances, Madison, Wisconsin 53703. Specific information on rail and other discounts are listed in the appropriate sections hereafter.

In Canada: AOSC *(Association of Student Councils),* 187 College St., Toronto, Ont. M5T 1P7, 416–979–2604, is a non profit student service cooperative owned and operated by over 50 college and university student unions. Its travel bureau provides transportation tours and works camps world wide. Try also *Tourbec,* 535 Ontario East, Montreal, Quebec H2L 1N8, 514–288–4455.

HANDICAPPED TRAVEL. *Access to the World: A Travel Guide for the Handicapped,* by Louise Weiss, is an outstanding book covering all aspects of travel for anyone with health or medical problems; it features extensive listings and suggestions on everything from availability of special diets to wheelchair accessibility. Order from Facts On File, 460 Park Ave. South, New York, N.Y. 10016 (212–683–2244). The guide costs $14.95.

Tours specially designed for the handicapped generally parallel those of the non-handicapped traveler, but at a more leisurely pace. For a complete list of tour operators who arrange such travel write to the *Society for the Advancement of Travel for the Handicapped,* 26 Court St., Brooklyn, NY 11242, 718–858–5483. Travel Information Center of *Moss Rehabilitation Hospital,* 12th St. and Tabor Road, Philadelphia, PA 19141, 215–329–5715, answers inquiries regarding specific cities and countries as well as providing toll-free telephone numbers for airlines with special lines for the hearing impaired and, again, listings of selected tour operators.

Also helpful is the *Information Center for Individuals with Disabilities,* 20 Park Plaza, Rm. 330, Boston, MA 02116 (617–727–5540).

From the U.K.: The *Air Transport Users' Committee,* 129 Kingsway, London WC2B 6NN, publish a very useful booklet, *Care in the Air,* free, which includes advice for handicapped passengers.

LANGUAGE. There is no problem for a non-Italian speaker in the main tourist cities; you will always find someone who speaks English. But it would be a pity not to try to acquire at least a useful smattering of Italian, it is a very beautiful and expressive language. A combination of a phrase book and close attention to the Italians' astonishing pantomime of gestures will go a long way. If you happen to be an opera buff you will be amazed what a short compendium of operatic words and phrases can accomplish. You will hear words coming back at you that you thought were the private territory of Tosca and Rigoletto.

But the best preparation for getting the most out of your trip is to take an evening class in Italian the previous winter. You do not need a lot—just enough to help you in your day to day contact, and to be able to disentangle the signs and labels in some of the world's finest museums. Who knows, you might get a taste for it and embark on Dante.

TIME. Italian summer time operates from the last weekend of March to the last weekend of September, it is then one hour ahead of Britain and six ahead of New York. As the U.S. changes its clocks at a slightly different date, there will be a couple of weeks when the system is out of sync.

Getting to Italy

FROM THE U.S. By Air. Air fares are in a constant state of flux, and our best advice is to consult a travel agent and let him or her make your reservations for you. Agents are familiar with the latest changes in fare structures—ever more confusing despite "deregulation" among U.S. carriers who now allegedly base prices on distance traveled—as well as with the rules governing various discount plans. Among those rules: booking (usually) 21 days in advance, minimum stay requirements, maximum stay allowances, the amount that (sometimes) must be paid in advance for land arrangements. Lowest prices overall will, of course, be during the off-season periods.

Generally, on regularly scheduled flights, you have the option, in descending order of cost, of First Class, Club or Business Class, APEX or Stand-by tickets. APEX is by far the most used and the most useful of these categories. Some charter service is still available; again, an agent will be able to recommend which ones are reliable. Sometimes it is also worth investigating package tours even if you do not wish to use the tours' other services (hotels, meals, etc.); because a packager can block book seats, the price of a package can be less than the cost when air fare is booked separately.

If you have the flexibility, you can sometimes benefit from last-minute sales tour operators have in order to fill a plane. A number of brokers specializing in such discount sales have also sprung up. All charge an annual membership fee, usually about $35–45. Among these: *Stand-Buys Ltd.,* 311 W. Superior, Ste. 414, Chicago, IL 60610 (312–943–5737); *Moments Notice,* 40 E. 49th St., New York, N.Y. 10017 (212–486–0503); *Discount Travel Intl.,* 114 Forrest Ave., Narberth, PA 19072 (215–668–2182); and *Worldwide Discount Travel Club,* 1674 Meridian Ave., Miami Beach, FL 33139 (305–534–2082). Sometimes, tour and charter flight operators themselves advertise in Sunday travel supplements, as well. Do try to find out whether the tour operator is reputable and whether you are tied to a precise round trip or whether you will have to wait until the operator has a spare seat in order to return.

Airlines specifically serving Italy from major U.S. cities (usually via New York) include:

Alitalia, 666 Fifth Ave., New York, N.Y. 10103 (212–582–8900).

Pan Am, Pan Am Bldg., New York, N.Y. 10017 (212–687–2600).

TWA, 605 Third Ave., New York, N.Y. 10016 (212–290–2141).

Typical round trip fares as of mid-1988: New York to Rome first class, $4,200; APEX $889 to $939. Charter fares were about the same as (or slightly lower than) APEX.

By Boat. For details on the possibility of freighter travel to or from Europe, consult *Air Marine Travel Service,* 501 Madison Avenue, New York, N.Y. 10022 (212-371–1300), publisher of the *Trip Log Quick Reference Freighter Guide.*

you are really sold on bucking the modern world you can, of course, take the liner still crossing the Atlantic on a regular schedule, the *QE2,* Cunard's great ship. They have sail one-way—fly the other schemes which mean that you can considerably cut the travel time involved. The snag is that she does not sail to Italy and you will have to find your own way down through France.

FROM THE U.K. By Air. The two major Italian cities, Rome and Milan, are well served by air from the U.K. by the major airlines, including *Alitalia, British Airways* and *British Caledonian.* In addition there are a multitude of charter operators selling flights to a wide range of holiday destinations at reduced prices. These surplus seats can be obtained very cheaply—scan the "classified" columns in newspapers such as *The Times, Sunday Times, Mail on Sunday* and also the weekly magazines such as *Time Out.* However, be careful, always ring up and work out the total price, i.e., fares + tax + surcharges etc.—not all are quite as cheap as they seem at first glance. The rule of thumb is that the cheaper the fare, the more likely it is to carry a burden of restrictions. *Always* make sure you know what these are— ask the airline or travel agent before you buy the ticket.

Nearly all the direct flights to Italy go from London Heathrow. The capital Rome has a minimum of 4 flights a day by British Airways/Alitalia, with flying time of just under 2½ hours. Milan has the best service with at least 6 flights daily taking just 1 hour 50 minutes. The airport serving Pisa/Florence has 2 flights a day by British Airways/Alitalia which take a little over 2 hours. Naples, the most southerly main airport, has a direct flight four days a week, with a flying time of 2 hours 35 minutes.

British Caledonian operate a daily (except Tuesdays) service from London Gatwick to Genoa. The flight takes about 3 hours. There are also 4 flights a week from Dublin to Rome during the summer and 3 flights a week from Dublin to Milan via Genoa. Both of these latter services are run by Aer Lingus.

The domestic Internal Services run by Alitalia are very good and connections are available from the international flights to regional airports including Cagliari in Sardinia, Palermo in Sicily, Naples, Venice and Brindisi.

By Train. Getting to Italy by train presents no problem whatsoever, and whether a pauper or a prince it is possible to travel in style and comfort. For princes and princesses, or simply for those who only want the best, there is the *Venice–Simplon Orient Express,* which is privately owned and run by Sea Containers. This train, using beautifully restored Pullman carriages in Britain and immaculate interwar Wagonlits coaches from Boulogne to Venice, runs twice a week from end March through October from London to Venice via Paris and Milan. Fares start at around £680 (sharing a double cabin) for a one-way trip, including all meals (but not drinks). However VSOE offer a wide range of inclusive packages based on the train journey and these are excellent value for money. Ask for the *Individually Arranged Holidays* brochure from Orient Express, Suite 1235, One World Trade Center, New York, N.Y. 10048 (800–223–1588; in N.Y., 212–938–6830) or Sea Containers House, 20 Upper Ground, London SE1 9PF (01–928 6000).

However, if you are not ready for the train trip of a lifetime, there are several other routes to Italy. The simplest way is to use one of the through trains from the Channel ports since this cuts the toting of heavy bags to a minimum. One of the most convenient departures in this respect is the 10.45 from London (Victoria), which connects with the lunchtime sailing from Dover to Calais. At Calais (Gare Maritime) join the main train leaving at 15.56 for the overnight run through to Italy. Milan is reached at 07.03 the following morning, Bologna at 09.06 and finally Rome at 12.58. A portion of the train also serves Genoa. Couchettes are available from Calais and sleeping cars are attached en route at Thionville. There is also a convenient overnight train from Calais (Maritime) to Venice. For this leave London (Victoria) just after lunch and then travel by Sealink ferry from Folkestone. The main train departs from Calais (Maritime) at 19.32 and pulls into Venice just before three the following afternoon. The train runs via Paris where sleeping accommodation is attached—sleepers are available as far as Milan (arrives 10.55) and couchettes through to Venice itself. A self-service restaurant facility is provided as far as Paris. There is also a useful connection from this train for Bologna at Milan.

If the idea of traveling overnight doesn't appeal, many Italian destinations can be reached quickly from Paris. The City Link Service, rail–hovercraft–rail, run by *Hoverspeed,* will take you to Paris in under 5½ hours. Stay overnight in the city, and then next morning continue by the fabulous 168 m.p.h. TGV to Lausanne (advance reservation obligatory and on occasions a supplement). At Lausanne change to a waiting EuroCity express to Milan. The journey along the banks of Lake Geneva and the Rhone valley is well worth the detour. An early morning (07.14) departure from Paris on the *Lutetia* gives a 14.50 arrival in Milan, and the lunchtime train (12.28), the *Cisalpin,* allows an evening arrival (19.50). For travelers using the *Lutetia* there is a connection at Milan by the *rapido,* the Tergeste, to Venice which is reached at 19.00. Also Genoa can be reached by 17.42 using the 16.05 departure from Milan.

Now a few words of advice. Firstly, due to the popularity of these trains it is essential to book well in advance, especially if any form of sleeping accommodation is required, but this is no problem as the reservation system of European railways is very efficient.

Secondly you must claim your seats since some travelers—especially Italians and Inter-Railers—do not respect the reserved notices, so make sure of your places.

Thirdly, how to claim a reserved seat. Look for the coach number or letter, displayed on the side of each vehicle. Do not walk up inside the trains because they are *very* long. Once the correct carriage has been located look for the seat number, either on the headrests or on the side of the compartments.

Fares. At press time (fall '88) the adult single fare in 2nd class from London to Rome worked out at around £105. The under 26s can travel more cheaply to a wide range of Italian destinations by buying BIGE—details from Eurotrain, 52 Grosvenor Gdns., S.W.1 (01–730–8579) or Transalpino, 71–75 Buckingham Palace Rd., London S.W.1 (01–834–9656). As a guide, a single to Rome will be about £80. **Note**—on these student services a wide choice of routes is available, and also break of journeys is allowed, so work out what you want to visit en route and enquire at time of booking.

For further information: The *Thomas Cook Continental Timetable* provides invaluable planning data. Note that the summer schedules (May–Sept) of the European railways are very different from those in winter, so it is essential to obtain the timetable closest to the time of the proposed visit. The timetable is published monthly and can be bought in the U.S.A. from *Forsyth Travel Library,* P.O. Box 2975, 9154 West 57th St., Shawnee Mission, KS 66201, or in the U.K. over the counter at any branch of Thomas Cook or by post from *Thomas Cook Timetable Publishing,* PO Box 36, Peterborough.

Long-distance tours. From the U.K. CIT operate a special holiday express composed of the most modern coaches. This is run in conjunction with their CITALIA holidays and is a delightful introduction both to Italy and long distance rail travel. Places served include Rome, Pisa, Bologna and Rimini. Everything is arranged and tour escorts travel with you.

By Bus. International bus travel in Europe has been bedeviled with many problems in recent years, with several operators going under. The most reliable firms are promoted under the banner of International Express, the operator in this case being *Eurolines.* During the summer (July to September) there is a service on three days a week to Turin and Milan. The coach leaves London Victoria Coach Station in the evening and arrives in Turin at 9.30 P.M. the following evening. Milan is reached just before midnight. The Monday and Friday departures are extended to Bologna, Florence, Rome and Brindisi. The Friday service also offers a connection to Venice—arriving there at four in the morning! Arrival times can be somewhat inconvenient. Coach prices are not very competitive, an adult return to Rome costing about £130. Passengers holding open return tickets must book the return run at least four days in advance. Refreshment stops are made en route, usually at motorway service stations. Details from *International Express,* The Coach Travel Centre, 13 Regent St., London SW1Y 4LR (01–439 9368), or from any National Express appointed travel agent. Central enquiries on 01–730 0202.

FERRY SERVICES SUITABLE FOR TRAVEL TO ITALY FROM BRITAIN

	HOVER SPEED	NORTH SEA FERRIES	SALLY VIKING LINE	SEALINK BRIT. FERRIES	TOWNSEND THORESEN	THORESEN/ RTM	BRITTANY FERRIES
DOVER – ZEEBRUGGE					●		
– OSTEND						◆	
– CALAIS	●			◆	●		
– BOULOGNE	●				●		
FOLKESTONE – BOULOGNE				◆			
HARWICH – HOOK OF HOLLAND				◆			
PORTSMOUTH – CAEN							●
– CHERBOURG				+	●		
RAMSGATE – DUNKIRK			●				
FELIXSTOWE – ZEEBRUGGE					●		
POOLE – CHERBOURG							+
WEYMOUTH – CHERBOURG				+			
HULL – ZEEBRUGGE		●					

+ Operate in Summer only.

◆ Recommended for Rail travellers – easy rail/ship interchange.
Through services operate from the Hook of Holland, Ostend, Calais and Boulogne (Maritime) to destinations in Italy during the Summer months.

● Only really suitable for car-borne travellers. Several of the Operators provide bus services between the local railway stations and the port terminal buildings. They are only suitable for passengers with light luggage.

By Car. It is a long way to Italy! To give you an idea, from Calais to Rome is around 1,690 Km. (1,050 miles) and to Venice is around 1,370 Km. (850 miles) depending on the exact route taken. The quickest overall journeys can be made by using one of the short-sea crossings (see ferry chart) from Dover to Calais and then driving down through France, entering Switzerland at Basel, then via the Gottard tunnel to Milan. The roads on this route are of a good standard and most of the run can be completed without using toll motorways. Alternatively, use one of the crossings to the Belgian ports of Ostend and Zeebrugge as these plug directly into the free Belgian motorway/dual carriageway network and offer a very speedy get-away—but remember that the sea crossing will take longer. The total driving time, calculated from the ferry port, will work out at around 20 hours.

On the motorways in Italy tolls have to be paid. These can be reduced by contacting the Italian National Tourist Office for up-to-date details of their special reductions for car-borne tourists visiting Italy. For this purpose the country is divided into three regions: **Northern** for visits as far south and including Rome, **Central,** and **Southern** Italy. The packs, which can be bought in advance or at the offices of the Italian Auto Club (ACI) at frontier crossings, contain vouchers for super-grade gasoline and reductions on motorway tolls. The saving on petrol prices is around 20%. Also included is a card which gives access to the free breakdown assistance service for tourists run by the Italian Automobile Club. The cost of the schemes ranges from £75 to £210 according to the region. Passport and logbook must be carried.

An additional bonus is that you also get free breakdown service from the ACI. The Italian Tourist Office publishes a guide to motorway tolls which is very useful for costing/planning purposes. Details from Italian National Tourist Office: in the U.K.—1 Princes St., London, W1; in the U.S.—630 Fifth Ave., New York, N.Y. 10111.

Motorail. This is a good idea if you wish to take your own car but avoid the long drive and overnight stops. French Railways run a summer Motorail service from Boulogne to Milan. During the peak period (mid-July–early Sept) there are 2 trains a week. Both run overnight and take some 15 hours. Sleeping berths and couchettes are available. The return fare for a car, driver and passenger in second class with couchettes each way works out at around £450. Information and bookings in the U.K. from *French Railways,* 179 Piccadilly, London W1V OBA (tel. 01–409 3518).

To get you even closer to your final destination, Italian Railways run connecting Motorail services from Milan to many destinations including Rome, Naples, Villa S. Giovanni (Calabria) and Brindisi. Details, including dates of operation, can be obtained in the U.K. from *Italian State Railways,* 50–51 Conduit Street, London W.1 (01–434–3844) and the U.S.A. from *CIT Travel Service,* 666 Fifth Ave., New York, N.Y. 10103 (212–397–2666).

Fly-Drive. Alitalia offers a fly-drive service from Britain, and great value it is. When you pay for scheduled airfares for 2 or more people you can get an Avis group 'A' car (that's the small one); if it's 2 adults the unlimited mileage is for 7 days, if it's 3 adults 9 days, if it's 4 adults 11 days. The offer holds good for 18 airports in Italy and there is no need to return the car to the starting point. You can get larger cars and extra days for a supplementary payment. The minimum stay has to be 7 days, maximum one month.

Arriving in Italy

CUSTOMS ON ARRIVAL. Two still cameras and one movie can be brought in duty free by each person entering Italy. Ten rolls of still-camera film and 10 rolls of movie film may be brought in duty free, along with binoculars, a portable phonograph and 10 records, a tape recorder, tapes and a portable radio. Visitors from non-European countries may bring in up to 400 cigarettes, two bottles of wine and one of spirits per person. European-based visitors are limited to 300 cigarettes, one bottle of wine, and a pint of alcoholic spirits. Other items intended for your personal use are admitted without question as long as quantities are reasonable. There is a restriction on the amount of Italian lire which may be brought in or out of the country.

Although there are technical limitations to what you may export from Italy on your departure they do not apply to ordinary tourist purchases. Any major purchase will likely be shipped to your home directly by the store you bought it from, which will obtain any necessary licenses.

MONEY MATTERS. Travelers may bring into, or out of, Italy a maximum of 400,000 lire in lire banknotes. However, unlimited amounts of travelers' checks or foreign currencies may be brought in. Tourists are required to provide an official record of all their currency and travelers' checks. When leaving the country, they may not take out more money than they brought in. Purchases of Italian currency have to be recorded.

Money can be changed in Italy not only at banks, travel agencies, and hotels, but, in effect, by anyone. That is to say, you may pay any bill or make any purchase in your own currency as well as in lire. To avoid misunderstandings, be sure to check the exchange rate you are getting; it will be more favorable at banks and exchange and American Express offices, probably less so in hotels, restaurants and stores.

One warning about exchanging money must be writ large. The lire is a currency that runs into thousands at the drop of a hat, so it is extremely easy to misplace the odd nought at the end of a number. There are many sorry stories of people changing $200 and coming away with $20 in lire without noticing. Similarly, always check your change. This applies not just in banks but restaurants, rail stations, hotels and shops to name only the most obvious places.

As we go to press, in mid-1988, the long-heralded possibility that Italy will drop a few noughts from its currency seems to be moving within the bounds of action. This would probably mean that 6,000 lire would turn overnight to 6 lira—if that is the system decided upon. The currency would become, in the economists' jargon, "heavy." Life would be greatly simplified if it does happen, but it could well mean that the Italian economy would go through a tricky phase.

The exchange rate varies these days. As we go to press, the rate is around 1,360 lire to one U.S. dollar, 2,320 to the pound sterling.

SECURITY. In large cities, especially Rome and Naples, purse-snatching is a hazard. Along with the anger and inconvenience it's bound to cause, this latter-day scourge has sent many a tourist to the hospital after being dragged or pushed to the ground. It's far better to relinquish the booty rather than be battered. Some precautions: wear a shoulder bag, crossbelt style. Carry your handbag on the side away from the curb and keep a firm grip on it. Don't rest your purse or camera on a table or chair at a sidewalk café or restaurant; keep it on your lap, with the strap around your wrist. Beware of pickpockets on buses and at such tourist attractions as papal appearances in St. Peter's Square.

Watch your luggage in stations or airports, where it may be snatched from right under your nose. Don't leave luggage in cars; if this is unavoidable, on sightseeing or meal stops, lock everything in the boot out of sight; don't leave cameras or valuables even there. Whenever possible park in daytime on guarded parking places, it is well worth the small fee; at night in a garage. Reports of smashed windows and windscreens are increasing, on top of a high rate of car-thefts.

Don't carry all your cash, travelers' checks and passport with you; leave what you don't need in the hotel safe, along with any other valuables. *Don't* leave valuables in your hotel room.

Be very wary of pickpockets in main railway stations and on trains, especially in the hectic moments of departure and arrival. If you think you might doze off on the train, secure your valuables first. Politely decline offerings of food or beverages by traveling companions on trains, especially on long-distance runs; in some instances the refreshments have been drugged and the travelers have turned out to be thieves. This may sound like a bad movie script—but Italian life is full of bad movie scripts.

Finally, whenever you buy something—a rail ticket, a meal, a theater seat, a souvenir—always check your change carefully—*very* carefully.

Staying in Italy

HOTELS. Italian hotels are officially classified on a star system, from 5 stars on the deluxe level, 4 corresponding to our grading of Expensive, 3 to Moderate and 2 stars to Inexpensive. Pensions are listed as hotels but are usually smaller and more informal. Conventional tourists will probably prefer not to go below the Moderate grade in Italy, except in large, tourist-oriented cities. This, in fact, gives them a very wide choice of hotels because, while ceilings are established by law for the prices which hotels in any particular category may charge, no establishment is obliged to be placed in a higher category. Some very good establishments prefer to be classified as Moderate for fiscal reasons.

Breakfast is optional, but is usually quoted with room rate, and can be pricey. A service charge of about 15%, in addition to general and sojourn taxes, is usually included in the room rate. You may find a charge for airconditioning, varying from 3,000 to 15,000 lire per day per person, in hotels in which this feature is optional.

In all hotels you'll find a rate card on the back of the door to your room, or inside the closet door—it tells you exactly what you will pay for that particular room. Any discrepancy between this rate and that on your bill should be cause for complaint and should be reported to the local tourist office.

Credit Cards. The letters AE, DC, MC and V in our hotel listings refer to the credit cards accepted by each establishment: American Express, Diner's Club, MasterCard (incorporating Access and Eurocard) and Visa (incorporating Barclaycard) respectively.

Hotel Chains. Among the reliable hotel chains and groups in Italy are the *Compagnia Grandi Alberghi* (CIGA), which operates some of the most luxurious establishments, and the *Relais and Châteaux* group, catering to those who prefer small, quiet and posh hotels. *Atahotels, Italhotels* and the *Space* group all include top-drawer places, some in the Moderate range. The *Jolly Hotels* are consistently good four-star establishments. *AGIP* chain is dependable, good for motorists.

Hotel Prices. The following prices are for a double room with bath. A single room with bath will work out around two-thirds the double rate. On request, an extra bed may be placed in a double room of adequate proportions, for an additional charge of 35% of the double room rate.

	Deluxe	*Expensive*	*Moderate*	*Inexpensive*
Major Tourist City	400,000	200,000	112,000	75,000
Major Resort	300,000	180,000	90,000	60,000
Art City/Budget Resort	—	125,000	90,000	50,000

Tourist Villages. In the wake of the *Club Méditerranée*, tourist villages are springing up throughout Italy. They offer bungalow accommodations, centralized dining and entertainment services, shops, hairdressers, babysitting and medical services, pools, private beaches and sports facilities. As a rule these villages are isolated and off the beaten track. All-inclusive costs make them a good vacation buy. The best are the *Valtur* villages at Ostuni, Pollino, Brucoli and Capo Rizzuto, and the *Forte* village at Santa Margherita di Pula in Sardinia.

Villa Rental. Also ideal for families is a villa vacation. Through CIT or your travel agent you can rent a fully equipped villa for 2–8 persons, some with maid service included, on the Adriatic or Tuscan coasts, in Sardinia, at Baia Domizia or at Rosa Marina village (see Ostuni). The London based *Villas Italia Ltd.*, 227 Shepherds Bush Rd., W6 (740 9988), offers villas in Tuscany, Rome and Positano. Insist on seeing photos of the villa and get a clear idea of what services are included in the price. *CV Travel,* 43 Cadogan St., London SW3 2PR (01–581 0851), has property to rent in Tuscany and Porto Ercole, with a palazzo in southern Italy on their books, luxurious apartments on the sea. Further information on renting villas, farmhouses from Cuendet, 53030 Strove (Siena) or ENIT offices.

In the U.S., *Villas International,* 71 W. 23 St., New York, N.Y. 10010 (800–221–2260; 212–929–7585 in New York), has villas and apartments in major cities, many in the Tuscany area; and *At Home Abroad, Inc.,* 405 E. 56 St., New York, N.Y. 10022 (212–421–9165) have properties all over Europe including Italy.

CAMPING. Camping is just about the cheapest way to travel, and Italy has plenty of beautifully located campsites, many with bungalows, many open all year. Italians themselves have taken to camping as an inexpensive vacation alternative; consequently seaside and mountain resort campsites are overcrowded in July and August. At all times, camping on public or private land other than camping grounds is usually frowned on by local authorities and isn't recommended except for overnights. Obtain an international camping carnet from your local camping association before you leave home. In Italy you can apply for a camping license or for the carnet, both of which are valid in the other European and Mediterranean countries; write to the *Federazione Italiana del Campeggio,* Casella Postale 649, 50100 Florence. Send several passport photos with your application. The Federazione publishes a multilingual official *Guida Camping Italiana,* campsite directory—costs about 8,000 lire. Camper rental agencies operate throughout Italy; for details inquire at travel agents. You can fly to either Sardinia or Sicily, pick up a fully equipped camper on arrival and explore the island as you please. Camp rates for two persons, with tent, average about 15,000 lire a day.

YOUTH HOSTELS. There are about 155 hostels in Italy, some in such beautiful settings as the 14th-century castle of Rocca degli Alberi at Montagnana, near Padua, the Castle of Murat at Pizzo in Calabria, and the Castle of Scilla on the straits of Messina. Headquarters in Italy is the *Associazione Italiana Alberghi per la Gioventù,* Piazza Civiltà del Lavoro, Quadrato della Concordia, 00144 Rome, a member of the International Youth Hostels Federation. Hostel rates are about 10,000 per person per night, including breakfast—but it's not easy to find accommodation, especially in the main tourist centers, unless you book well in advance.

Ample information about this type of traveling can be obtained **in the US and Canada** from *American Youth Hostels, Inc.,* PO Box 37613, Washington, D.C. 20013; and the *Canadian Hostelling Association* national office, Tower A, 333 River Road, 3rd Floor, Ottawa, Ontario K1L 8H9.

In England the addresses are: *Camping and Caravan Club Ltd.,* 11 Lower Grosvenor Place, London SW1 (828 1012); the *Youth Hostels Association,* 14 Southampton St., London WC2 (836 8541); *The Cyclists Touring Club,* Cotterel House, 69 Meadrow, Godalming, Surrey GU7 3HS (04868–7217).

FARM VACATIONS. *Agriturist,* 6 Piazza Sant' Andrea della Valle, Rome, can provide information on staying with a farm family in the Italian countryside. Or you can rent a farmhouse in Tuscany; information from local tourist office, *Azienda Soggiorno,* Via Banchi di Sotto, Siena.

RESTAURANTS. Long ago, you could predict the clientele and prices of an eating place according to whether it called itself a *ristorante, trattoria* or *osteria.* Now these names are interchangeable, and a rustic-looking spot that calls itself an osteria may turn out to be chic and expensive. Generally speaking, however, a trattoria is usually a family-run place, simpler in decor, menu and service than a ristorante, and slightly less expensive. A true osteria is a wine-shop, very basic and down-to-earth, where the only function of food is to help keep the clients sober.

If you have any doubts about what you may be getting into, check the menu that's always on display in the window or just inside the door. It will give you an idea of what your meal will cost. In all but the simplest places, there's always a cover charge (*pane e coperto*) and usually a service charge (*servizio*). These will increase your bill by 15 to 20 percent. The *menu turistico* includes taxes and service, but beverages are usually extra.

In Rome, lunch hour usually lasts from 1 to 3 P.M., dinner from 8 to 10 P.M. Service begins a little earlier in the north, where dining rooms close punctually at the appointed hour. Mealtimes in the south are much more flexible, usually starting a bit later than in Rome and continuing until quite late, especially in the warm season.

Nearly all restaurants close one day a week. Closing days are listed here, but they do sometimes change; it's best to have your hotel *portiere* phone ahead if your heart's set on any one place. It's wise to book in luxury and expensive spots; you may find it advisable in the moderate ones, and in inexpensive places you'll probably have to share or wait for a table unless you get there early.

As the pace of Italian life quickens along Northern European lines, more and more fast-food places are opening, offering tourists a wider choice of light meals. A *Tavola Calda* or *Rosticceria* displays a selection of hot and cold dishes. Here you pay only for what you eat; some items are priced by the portion, others by weight. You usually select your food, find out how much it is, then pay the cashier and get a stub that you must give to the counter man when you pick up your meal.

Many bars have snack counters where you can get a cold or toasted sandwich. If you choose to concoct your own sandwiches for an impromptu picnic, go to any *alimentari* store.

Prices. Restaurants here are divided according to price, giving an approximate charge per person for a full meal, with wine. In moderate and inexpensive places you may find the carafe wine a pleasant surprise; in expensive restaurants you'll have to order from the wine list. The price categories are: *Expensive* 70–95,000 lire up per person for dinner; *Moderate* 30–55,000; *Inexpensive* 20–30,000; including cover and service. Restaurants are required by law to give you a receipt, which you in turn are required to take with you.

If you're budgeting closely, don't order fish or expensive cuts of meat. Prosciutto, truffled dishes and mushrooms also are pricy items. Beware items such as fish on *à la carte* menus or Florentine steaks and filets that are priced "SQ" (according to quantity) or "L. 4,000 hg"—this means that you'll be charged according to the weight of the item you've ordered and, in the second case, that the charge will be 4,000 lire per hectogram (3½ oz).

Credit Cards. The letters AE, DC, MC and V in our restaurant listings refer to the credit cards accepted by each establishment: American Express, Diner's Club, MasterCard (incorporating Access and Eurocard) and Visa (incorporating Barclaycard) respectively.

Drinking Water. Drinking water is safe in all important towns; for tap water in restaurants, ask for *acqua semplice*. Off the beaten track, drink mineral water; many prefer the uncarbonated type, known as *non-gassata* or *minerale naturale*. Think twice about ordering milk, cream and custard-filled pastries in out-of-the-way places.

TIPPING. Charges for service are included in all hotel bills and generally appear as a separate item on restaurant checks. In restaurants, a 15% service charge is usually added on to the total, but it doesn't all go to the waiter. In large cities and resorts it is customary to give the waiter a 5% tip in addition to the service charge made on the check.

In general, chambermaids should be given about 1,000 lire per day, 3–4,000 per week; bellboys 1–2,000 lire for carrying your bags; doormen about 500 lire for calling a cab; give the concierge about 15% of his bill for services, or from 5,000 to 15,000 depending on how helpful he is; tip a minimum of 1,000 lire for room service and valet service.

Checkroom attendants and theater ushers expect 500 lire per person. Washroom attendants get from 200 lire. A 100-lire tip for whatever you drink standing up at a café, 500 or more for table service in a smart café, less in neighborhood bars. At a hotel bar, tip 1,000 for cocktails. Give a barber or hairdresser from 3–5,000 for a tint or perm depending on the type of establishment.

These are average figures. In deluxe hotels and restaurants you should increase these amounts up to half, in accordance with the service given.

Railway and airport porters charge a fixed rate per suitcase. Tip an additional 500 lire per person, more if the porter is very helpful.

Service station attendants are tipped a few hundred lire if they are especially helpful.

Taxi drivers expect about 10%. Tip guides about 1,000 lire per person for a half-day tour, more if very good.

CONVENIENT CONVENIENCES. All hotels, restaurants and bars have public WCs, and in most cases they're much less grim than they used to be. *Alberghi Diurni* have sparkling clean conveniences, for a modest charge, along with baths, showers, dressing rooms, barbers and anything else you may need to freshen up during the day. They're usually located near the railway stations. You'll find public (municipal) toilets, in varying stages of neglect, in most towns. Railway station and airport conveniences are generally good. In smaller towns WCs are known by their Italian name: *gabinetti* or as *toelette*. If there's an attendant, a tip of 100 lire is customary.

MAIL. Mail rates change frequently, following the upward trend in prices. For current rates ask your hotel *portiere* or inquire at the post office or tobacconist where you buy stamps. Postcards pay full letter rate if they contain more than greeting and signature. Mail service is generally slow; keep this in mind if arranging to receive mail along your way (allow up to 14 days for mail from the U.K., 21 days from the U.S.). Correspondence can be addressed to you c/o the Post Office by adding *Fermo Posta* to the name of the locality. Delivery will be made at the local Central Post Office, where you must present your passport and pay a small fee. Special delivery (*Espresso*) gets your outgoing mail on its way faster, and is relatively expensive. In Rome, for fast processing of outgoing mail use the Vatican City post office, to the left of St. Peter's.

Telegrams and cables can be sent from any post office or from *Telegrafo* offices; they also may be dictated over the telephone.

TELEPHONES. Pay phones operate with a token (*gettone*), which you get for 200 lire from a token machine next to the telephone or from the nearest cashier. The newer pay phones also take coins. For *teleselezione* (long-distance direct dialing) have a handful of tokens or coins ready. In all cities the phone company has service bureaux (ask for *Telefoni*), where the operators will place your call for you.

Hotels frequently add several hundred percent to charges for long-distance calls; we advise you to use the public *Telefoni* service. Calls to London and to the U.S. are relatively inexpensive, and lower rates are in effect during evening and nighttime hours. The rate to the U.S. is lowest during the 24 hours of Sunday and between 11 P.M. and 8 A.M. Italian time on weekdays.

The emergency number is 113, for ambulance, fire and police.

CLOSING TIMES. National Holidays in Italy are New Year's Day, Jan. 6 (Epiphany), Easter Sunday and Monday, April 25 (Liberation Day), May 1, June 2 (Republic Day), August 15 (Assumption, known as Ferragosto), November 1, December 8, December 25 and 26. There are also local saints' days and festivals which the traveler must allow for if he wants to visit shops, post offices or banks. There are also long pauses in the middle of the day.

Normal business hours are about as follows, with individual variations: stores are open from 9 to 1 and from 4 to 8. Banking hours are usually from 8.30 to 1.30 and from 3 or 3.30 to 4 or 4.30 in the afternoon. Banks are closed on Saturdays. Exchange (*cambio*) offices, however, have store hours. The Central Post Office is open until 9 P.M. for some operations. Branch offices open from 8 to 2. Barbers open from 8 to 1, 4 to 8 and are closed Sunday afternoons and Mondays. Women's hairdressers are open 8 A.M. to 8 P.M., but most close all day Sunday and Monday.

Streetcars (trams) and buses stop running at about half an hour after midnight and recommence about 5 A.M. There are, however, skeleton services all night on the chief routes in large cities. The *EPT* or *AAST* information office, or the hall porter, for that matter, can give you the precise details for each city.

MUSEUMS AND PLACES OF INTEREST. Italian museums have short hours, are closed on at least one day a week, often Mondays, and have free admission for one day a week. They are open on some holidays, but closed on others. Check at the local tourist information office for up-to-date details of opening times as they tend to fluctuate from even the sparse announced details.

Fees for entrance are generally in the 3,000 to 4,000 range, but there are some major exceptions. For example, the Medici Chapels and the Accademia in Florence are 3,000, the Uffizi, the Pompeii excavations, the Villa d'Este and the Palatine and Forum in Rome are all 5,000.

Churches are open at odd hours, generally from early morning to noon, when they close for a couple of hours or so, opening again in the afternoon until sunset. Be careful if you want to prowl around on a Sunday—don't try it during mass.

Be sure to keep a fistful of 100-lire coins in your pocket for the *luce* (light) machines that illuminate the works of art hidden in the perpetual dusk of ecclesiastical interiors. You will miss a great deal if you aren't prepared. Also carry a pair of binoculars with you. They are enormously helpful in getting a good look at painted ceilings, church domes and out-of-the-way frescos, which you have lit up with your 100-lire coin.

Sightseeing. The local Tourist Information offices (EPT or AAST) will provide you with lists of all the sights, and from then on it's up to you. You can book sightseeing tours through travel agencies, sometimes through your hotel. We recommend that you shop around—as much as you have time for—to see which tour suits your taste, and that you try to do at least some sightseeing on your own, setting your own pace and itinerary.

SHOPPING. "Made in Italy" has become synonymous with style and quality craftsmanship whether it refers to high fashion or Maserati automobiles. Good buys are usually listed as leather goods, silk ties and dressing gowns, knitwear, gold jewelry, ceramics, straw goods and other handicrafts.

The most important thing to keep in mind when traveling and shopping in Italy is that every region has its local specialties—Venice for glassware, lace and velvet; Naples for coral, cameos and tortoiseshell articles; Vietri for ceramics; Florence for leather goods, straw and raffia products and embroideries; and Milan and Como for silks, to mention but a few.

In general, the idea that bargaining is the rule in Italy is mistaken. There is no universal policy, but for the most part prices are fixed in the better shops. Where you see the sign *prezzi fissi* you can be sure that there is no bargaining to be done. There may be occasions when you will get a discount on a large purchase, however, and it is always worthwhile to ask, but don't expect the final price to be one-half of what the shopkeeper asks.

A warning is sounded against buying antiques in this country renowned for its skilled imitators. There are fascinating shops in all of the major cities, but unless you really know your antiques, don't buy without the advice of an expert or you may be throwing away money on a copy. Also, when buying fine jewelry, be sure to go to a store with a sound reputation.

There are a few general things about shopping abroad that knowledgeable shoppers will always take into account.

—Wherever possible carry your purchases home with you, especially if they are valuable or fragile.

—Find out all about custom regulations. You could be stung for a small fortune and turn a bargain into a very expensive commodity indeed.

—If you are shipping goods home, be very sure you have understood the terms, how the shipment will be made, when it should arrive . . . and get it all in writing.

SPORTS. Both spectator and participant sports facilities exist throughout Italy. The Italians are keen motor-racing, horse-racing, bicycle-racing and football fans, and they have considerable interest in bowling. Winter sports and mountaineering opportunities abound as, naturally, do all water sports around Italy's vast coastline. Golf and tennis, fishing and hunting, are also popular.

For the equestrian-minded tourist, the *Associazone Nazionale per il Turismo Equestre,* Largo Messico 13, Rome, can furnish information on riding parties and tours of the Italian countryside.

Those interested in a golfing holiday might like to contact *Eurogolf,* 3B London Rd., St. Albans, Herts AL1 1LA (0727–42256), who have programs taking in some of the best courses in Europe, including two in Italy.

BEACHES. Italy isn't the place to go for an exclusively beach holiday. With the exception of Sardinia, you'll find better beaches and cleaner water at better value in other parts of the Mediterranean. But nowhere else will you find the Italian combination of great art, marvelous monuments, tempting cuisine and attractive seaside resorts.

Sea bathing in the immediate area of Rome, Venice, Naples, Genoa, Salerno and Palermo is forbidden—if not always by the authorities, at least by good sense. One expert says that 70% of all Italian beaches are a health hazard. The best swimming is in Sardinia (except around Cagliari, Arbatax and Porto Torres), off portions of the coasts of Calabria and Apulia, and off the islands of Elba, Capri, Ischia, Ustica, the Aeolians and western Sicily.

Generally, the beaches near Italian tourist capitals and major art cities are occupied by bathing establishments, where you pay a daily (or weekly or monthly) fee for the use of the facilities such as changing cabin, shower, and pool and rental of deck chair and umbrella. Charges average from 10 to 20,000 lire for two and are well worth it, for untended public beaches are usually unkempt and crowded.

At beach resorts, the hotels we list almost always are equipped with private beach facilities and/or swimming pool. The reason for the monumental investment that so many beach hotels have had to make in building pools is, quite simply, the pollution of the Mediterranean. This is so important a factor in coastal vacation life that we now offer a Pollution Report to keep you abreast of the full nasty situation.

POLLUTION REPORT. Italy has the worst pollution problem in the Mediterranean, and you would be wise to avoid certain areas if you are looking for clean beaches, clean water or clean air. Here is a thumb-nail reading of the places most likely to be unpleasant.

The entire Ligurian coast is a 'black spot,' from San Remo in the west all along the Gulf of Genoa down south past Livorno, including the most famous Rivieras, Ponente, Levante and della Versilia, but with the honorable exception of the Cinque Terre. Needless to say, mouths of rivers have to be given the widest possible berth, as for instance Marina di Pisa near the Arno, or the beaches of Lazio near Ostia, where the Tiber deposits its filth. Between these two larger-than-life sewers, however, the Etruscan Riviera, Elba where the Ligurian and Tyrrhenian Sea meet, and the coast south to Civitavecchia are pleasurably clean. Not much can be said against the Riviera of Ulysses, roughly from Anzio to Felice Circeo, nor very much in its favor. Then the Gulf of Gaeta blends waste from a nuclear power plant to the usual open sewers, while the adjoining Bay of Naples makes do with ancient sewers without nuclear frills. Forget about it, except for the west coasts of Capri and Ischia—though there the crowds enjoying the open sea tend to create their own pollution. The Gulf of Salerno is an improvement, except near Salerno itself.

The Deep South—Calabria on the Tyrrhenian, Apulia, Lucania and the Gargano peninsula on the Adriatic Sea—offers the only truly enjoyable beaches, though not, of course, round major towns like Reggio Calabria, Taranto, Brindisi and Bari. The Tyrrhenian shore is on the whole rockier and the sea a more inviting bluegreen than the grey of the flatter Adriatic coast. Continuing north after the relatively unspoilt Gargano, the obnoxiousness is proportionate to the size of the endless string of beach resorts, only interrupted by larger towns, like Pescara and Ancona, where swimming is a memory of the past. An effort has been made to clean up the Adriatic Riviera, excessive seaweed and all, from Cattolica to Milano Marittima, and even the beach of Rimini is not out of bounds. But that's for all practical purposes the end of beach life for the tourist.

The northern part of the Italian Adriatic has few fans left, as the natural muddiness of the greybrown water has been fouled by industrial pollution, from Ravenna across the Po delta and the Venetian Lagoon, probably the least wholesome stretch of water in the Mediterranean, including the famed Lido. The resorts from Caorle to Grado are a possibility, but hardly worth an extra trip. Trieste's water has the consistency expected in busy ports.

The sea round Sardinia, except near Cagliari, Arbatax and Porto Torres, is cleaner than round Sicily, where only the west and south coast are recommendable, except near Gela's refinery.

Not even the most foolhardy would risk the rivers, which seem to flow mainly with detergents. They are clean at the source in the mountains, but the icy cold is no less lethal than the warmer brew further down. This cold is likewise the proof of ecological health in the numerous small lakes high up in the Alps. As for the large Lakes of Lombardy, they are crowded with bathers without any fatality having been proved yet.

In air pollution Milan and Turin are the undisputed leaders, being the main industrial centers, but Rome and Venice produce quite respectable smogs when the weather is right. The Po plain is highly industrialized in Lombardy, but the gray pall thins out over the lush farmland of Emilia Romagna.

Noise is a corollary of the traffic pollution problem. Italians generate noise and have learned to live with it—loud talking, loud music, loud motors. They're used to it, but you may not be, so give a thought to buying a set of ear plugs, at least for your sleeping hours.

Getting Around Italy

BY AIR. Because of the length of the Italian peninsula in comparison with its width, it is peculiarly suited for air travel in the north-south direction. The country is well served by *Alitalia* and its domestic associates *ATI* and *Aermed.* There are youth fares and some night flight reductions. However, one-way fares are relatively inexpensive, especially when bought locally at the favorable exchange rate. Sample one-way fares (all economy) from Rome in the fall of 1988 were Milan 153,500 lire; Venice 136,500 lire; Palermo 136,500 lire; Catania 156,000 lire; Cagliari 82,500 lire; Bari 118,000 lire.

Getting into Town from the Airport. All main Italian airports have regular bus connections into the center of the city, usually dropping passengers off near the main rail station. The cost varies from town to town, of course, but is usually around 2,500–4,000 lire. Taxi fares may be 10–15 times as much. Which you choose depends on whether economizing is important, whether you divide the taxi fare among the members of the party, and whether you will have another long taxi or bus ride from the town terminal to your hotel.

As there are some maverick airports—for Florence the airport is at Pisa, for example—we have put extra data in the relevant sections in most of the *Practical Information* sections at the end of the chapters.

BY TRAIN. Although not endowed with the best conditions to start with—a mountainous terrain over much of the country, political divisions, economic imbalance between north and south—Italy nevertheless has a remarkably good railway system. In recent years there has been a marked improvement not only in speed but also in comfort and frequency of trains. The main lines are largely electrified, the others diesel operated. Indeed Italy has always been in the vanguard of electrification and other technical advances. Several sections of the new high speed "Diretissima" are now in use. The outdated TEE trains have been replaced by modern airconditioned EuroCity and IC express trains.

Among the inconveniences of the system are seasonal crowding (we strongly advise reserving seats in advance), lack of multilingual personnel and luggage carts at stations; and complicated ticketing system which makes it extremely difficult to change tickets or get refunds on unused tickets.

What to look for. The majority of Italian trains, both expresses and local, have both 1st and 2nd class carriages. However, several of the top trains are 1st-class only and at the other end (mainly local, suburban and stopping trains) are 2nd-class only.

Trains are classified as *Intercity* (fast services with a supplement charge dependent on the class and distance), *espresso* (fast long distance expresses), *diretto* (medium fast trains with more stops than an express but quicker than a local) and *locale* (which live up to their name, making all stops).

Most long distance overnight trains have 1st- and 2nd-class sleeping cars and 2nd-class couchettes, some with couchettes only. Of course they all have ordinary coaches as well. The sleeping cars are operated by *Wagons-Lits* and the couchettes by the railway.

2nd-class travel in Italy, particularly at weekends and on holidays of which the Italians have a large number, is often crowded. It is advisable to get there early especially if the train starts at that station. 1st class is less crowded and on limited accommodation trains where seat reservations are obligatory, standing is not permitted.

Tickets and seat reservations. Tickets are sold not only at stations, where lines may be long, but also at authorized travel agencies (look for the FS insignia), where you can also make seat reservations on long distance and international trains.

Catering on Italian railways is done by the restaurant division of *Wagons-Lits.* Increasingly, buffet cars are being introduced although all EuroCities and a selected number of other *Intercities* have full restaurant service. Mini-bar and trolley services are found on many long distance trains and all stations (other than the smaller ones) have buffets or bars, usually privately operated. However, it can be a good idea to take your own provisions with you on long journeys. There are no drinking-water fountains on trains.

Note in some Italian cities (e.g. Milan, Turin, Genoa, Naples and Rome) there are two or more main line stations although one is usually the principal terminus or through station. *Always* check which your train will arrive at or depart from.

Fares. Italian Railways are among the cheaper in Europe, particularly if you use the reduced rate tickets. For those planning to do a lot of traveling by train—much more than, say, a Rome–Naples–Florence–Venice–Milan itinerary—*Travel at Will* tickets (a.k.a. Italian Tourist Ticket) are the best as they cover the whole system including Sicily and Sardinia. They are also valid on the ferry services between Italy and Sicily but *not* on those to Sardinia or on buses or on privately owned railways. They can be used on all *Intercities* and EuroCity trains without extra charge. They can be bought outside Italy (advisable) up to 60 days before date of departure and first use. We recommend strongly that you obtain these tickets before going to Italy as trying to get them there involves fighting through a considerable and time-consuming bureaucratic maze. In the U.S., passes may be purchased from the *Italian State Railways,* 666 Fifth Ave., New York, N.Y. 10103. In the U.K., from *CIT,* 51 Conduit St., London W1.

The Travel at Will ticket (*Turistico de Libera Circolazione*) can be obtained for both first and second class. In 1988 the U.K. prices in second class were as follows—8 days £65, 15 days £79, 21 days £92, 30 days £112; in first class the prices for the same periods were £102, £123, £148, and £178. All but the 8 day ticket can have their validity extended if required.

It is often advantageous to enquire at the main offices of both Thomas Cook/Wagons-Lits and American Express in Italy if you're after rail tickets. Italian stations are often very crowded.

In Italy there are also *kilometric tickets* for 3,000 km (1,875 miles) of travel priced at £107 in 1st class, £60 in 2nd, and valid for 30 days. In addition there are *Family Tickets* where four or more of the same family traveling together get 30% off both the adult and the children's fares. Proof of identity (eg passport) must be shown. Costs £5.

Italian Railways are constantly changing the numbers and conditions of *special excursion* tickets and you should inquire either from your travel agent before you leave home or at main line stations in Italy on arrival about these.

Eurailpass. If you plan to do a lot of traveling around not just in Italy but in Western Europe generally, we suggest that you get a *Eurailpass.* This is a convenient, all-inclusive ticket that can save you money on over 100,000 miles of railroads and railroad-operated buses, ferries, river and lake steamers, hydrofoils, and some Mediterranean crossings in 15 countries of Western Europe (excluding the United Kingdom, and Ireland). It provides the holder with unlimited travel at rates of: 15 days for $298; 21 days for $370; 1 month for $470; 2 months for $650; 3 months for $798; and 2nd-class Youthpass (anyone up to age 26) fare of 2 months for $420. Children under 12 go for half-fare, under 4 go free. These prices cover first-class passage for the EuroCity expresses and other services. Available only if you live outside Europe or North Africa. The pass must be bought from an authorized agent in the Western Hemisphere or Japan before you leave for Europe. Apply through your travel agent; or the general agents for North America: *French National Railroads,* Eurailpass Division, 610 Fifth Avenue, New York, N.Y. 10020; 1500 Stanley St., Montreal, Quebec H3A 1R3; or 4009 Granville Street, Suite #452, Vancouver, B.C. V6C 1T2; the *German Federal Railroad,* 747 Third Ave., New York, N.Y. 10017 or 1290 Bay St., Toronto, Ontario M5R 2C3, Canada. Also through the *Italian State Railways,* 666 Fifth Ave., New York, N.Y. 10103. To get full value from your pass, be sure not to have it date-stamped until you actually use it for the first time. For complete details, write to Eurailpass, c/o WBA, 51 Ridgefield Ave., Staten Island, N.Y. 10304.

BY BUS. Within Italy there are a number of express bus services linking some of the main cities. These are either part of the Europabus network or are operated by Italian companies, and are excellent alternatives to train travel on secondary lines; e.g. there is a daily service from Rome to Siena or L'Aquila. *ANAC,* Piazza Esquilino 29, Rome, publishes a complete timetable. Some lines offer sight-seeing along the way, such as—

Florence–Siena–Perugia–Assisi–Spoleto–Rome
Rome–Naples–Pompeii–Sorrento–Positano–Amalfi (early June–early Sept.)
Both the above can be used for intermediate stops on prior notice.

Other tours are available, several on themes such as the *Burchiello Tour,* which mixes bus and boat on a tour of the Veneto villas. April to October, 1 day, 100,000 lire which includes lunch.

Buses in major towns and cities have a flat fare of about 600 to 700 lire. Buy tickets at newsstands or tobacconists beforehand. Big tourist cities offer good-value tourist tickets.

BY CAR. (You will find regional information on road travel in the *Practical Information* sections at the end of each chapter.) In most Italian towns the use of the horn is forbidden in certain if not all areas. A large notice *Zona di Silenzio* indicates where. Other regulations are largely as in Britain and the US, except that the police have power to levy on-the-spot fines. Parking in *Zona Disco* is for limited periods. Discs can be bought at petrol stations. Outside built-up areas parking is permitted on the righthand side of the road. Fines for driving after drinking are heavy, with the additional possibility of 6 months' imprisonment. There is however no fixed blood/alcohol level and no official test. One drives on the right side of the road.

The *Automobile Club of Italy (ACI),* with headquarters at Rome, Via Marsala 8, has branch offices in all major towns, and information offices at most of the frontier posts. A few small ones, to which access is over a mountain pass, are closed during the winter.

A Green Card insurance is required by non-EEC members for driving in all European countries, plus a valid US or UK driving license supported, for Italy, by an Italian translation. These may be had free from the *AA, RAC* or *Italian State Tourist*

Office. Motorists should also have with them their car registration papers and a red warning triangle.

Auto Fuel. Gasoline (petrol) costs about 1,200 lire per liter for super, a bit less for normal, but vouchers giving tourists a discount of around 15% together with five 2,000 lira motorway vouchers and free breakdown service are now available as a package from the *AA* or *RAC.* Both clubs have a handling charge for both members and non-members. Only a few gas stations are open on Sundays and most close for a couple of hours at lunchtime and at 7 P.M. for the night. Those on autostrade are open 24 hours. Check when you arrive, as new speed limits will be in effect in 1989.

Car-Sleeper Express. Because of the long distances to be covered in Italy, motorists may wish to use one of the car-sleeper trains available within the country. These operate from Milan to Rome, San Remo, Viareggio, Bari or Brindisi (connecting with the car-ferry service for Greece); from Turin, Genoa, Bolzano or Calalzo (Cortina) to Rome; and from Rome, Naples, Milan or Turin to Villa San Giovanni (for Sicily car-ferry).

Car Hire. There are many firms from which cars can be rented. In most big cities there is a branch of *Avis, Hertz* or *Maggiore* rental agencies, which also rent chauffeur-driven and self-driven cars—reservations may be made through travel agencies or directly. Cars may be rented at airports and railway stations (Rome, Milan, Naples, Genoa, Florence, Turin, etc.).

There is an agreement between the Italian government and the auto rental firms to limit the age range for drivers renting cars to between 25 and 70.

Emergency Service. Thanks to the *Automobile Club of Italy,* breakdown service is free to foreign tourists traveling by car. It includes minor repairs of a stalled car and towing. In case of major trouble, repair charges are strictly controlled by the ACI. By dialing 116 from any telephone, any motorist whose car is disabled even on remote roads, will reach a central service station: give approximate location and, if possible, the source of the mechanical trouble, and assistance will come within a short time. Also, information is obtainable on the location of the nearest service station and where replacement parts for a particular make of car are available. In case of a road accident, this number will also reach a medical station and aid will promptly be dispatched.

Classification of Roads. The extensive network of *autostrade* (toll motorways) connecting all major towns, is complemented by equally well maintained but nonpaying *superstrade* (highways), *strade di grande communicazione* (main trunk roads), *strade di interesse regionale* (regional highways), *strade importanti* (main roads) and *altre strade* (other roads). All are clearly signposted and numbered. The ticket issued on entering an *autostrada* must be returned on leaving, along with the toll. On some shorter *autostrade,* mainly connections, the toll is payable on entering.

The *Autostrada del Sole,* A1, A2 and A3, crosses the country from North to South, connecting Milan to Reggio Calabria. A4 from west to east connects Turin to Trieste.

Kilometers into Miles. This simple chart will help you to convert to both miles and kilometers. If you want to convert from miles into kilometers read from the center column to the right, if from kilometers into miles, from the center column to the left. Example: 5 miles=8 kilometers, 5 kilometers=3.1 miles.

miles		km	miles		km
0.6	1	1.6	37.2	60	96.5
1.2	2	3.2	43.4	70	112.2
1.8	3	4.8	49.7	80	128.7
2.4	4	6.3	55.9	90	144.8
3.1	5	8.0	62.1	100	160.9
3.7	6	9.6	124.2	200	321.8
4.3	7	11.2	186.4	300	482.8
4.9	8	12.8	248.5	400	643.7
5.5	9	14.4	310.6	500	804.6
6.2	10	16.0	372.8	600	965.6

12.4	20	32.1	434.9	700	1,126.5
18.6	30	48.2	497.1	800	1,287.4
24.8	40	64.3	559.2	900	1,448.4
31.0	50	80.4	621.3	1,000	1,609.3

BY BOAT. The waters around Italy are crisscrossed by a network of ferries, some of them quite large boats and most of them diesel—no longer the attractive steamers. You can sail from Genoa, Livorno (Leghorn), Civitavecchia (north of Rome) and Naples to Sardinia; from Naples to Palermo and Messina and Catania (in Sicily) and between Sardinia and Sicily. And on the Italian Lakes—Maggiore, Como, Garda and Lugano there are numerous services. Full information locally.

Car ferries operate to the two islands of Sicily and Sardinia as well as from Piombino to Elba and from Anzio and Formia to the island of Ponza. In addition there are regular ferries from Naples to both Capri and Ischia.

Leaving Italy

CUSTOMS ON RETURNING HOME. U.S. residents may bring in $400 worth of foreign merchandise as gifts or for personal use without having to pay duty, provided they have been out of the country more than 48 hours and provided they have not claimed a similar exemption within the previous 30 days. Every member of a family is entitled to the same exemption, regardless of age, and the exemptions can be pooled. For the next $1,000 worth of goods a flat 10% rate is assessed.

Included in the $400 allowance for travelers over the age of 21 are one liter of alcohol, 100 non-Cuban cigars and 200 cigarettes. Only one bottle of perfume trademarked in the U.S. may be brought in. However, there is no duty on antiques or art over 100 years old. You may not bring home meats, fruits, plants, soil or other agricultural products.

Gifts valued at under $50 may be mailed to friends or relatives at home, but not more than one per day of receipt to any one addressee. These gifts must not include perfume costing more than $5, tobacco or liquor.

If you are traveling with such foreign-made articles as cameras, watches or binoculars that were purchased at home or on a previous trip, either carry the receipt or register them with U.S. Customs prior to departure.

Canadian residents. In addition to personal effects, and over and above the regular exemption of $300 per year, the following may be brought into Canada duty-free: a maximum of 50 cigars, 200 cigarettes, 2 pounds of tobacco and 40 ounces of liquor, provided these are declared in writing to customs on arrival. Canadian Customs regulations are strictly enforced; you are recommended to check what your allowances are and to make sure you have kept receipts for whatever you may have bought abroad. Small gifts can be mailed and should be marked "Unsolicited gift, (nature of gift), value under $40 in Canadian funds." For other details, ask for the Canada Customs brochure, "I Declare."

British residents except those under the age of 17 years, may import duty-free from *any* country the following: 200 cigarettes or 100 cigarillos or 50 cigars or 250 grams of tobacco; 1 liter of alcoholic drink over 22% volume (i.e. whiskey and other hard liquor), *or* 2 liters of alcoholic drink under 22% volume plus 2 liters of still table wine. Also 50 grams of perfume, 9 fl. oz. of toilet water and £32 worth of other normally dutiable goods (not to include more than 50 liters of beer).

Returning from any *EEC country* (and remember that Italy is in the EEC), you may, *instead* of the above exemptions, bring in the following, provided you can prove they were *not* bought in a duty-free shop: 300 cigarettes or 150 cigarillos or 75 cigars or 400 grams of tobacco; 1½ liters of alcoholic drink over 22% volume, *or* 3 liters under 22% volume plus 4 liters of still table wine (it would be wise to check the latest position regarding wine allowance, as EEC are considering an increase); 75 grams of perfume and 13 fl. oz. of toilet water and £250 worth of other normally dutiable goods.

DUTY FREE. Duty free is not what it once was. You may not be paying tax on your bottle of whiskey or perfume, but you are certainly contributing to somebody's profits. Duty-free shops are big business these days and mark ups are often around 100 to 200%. So don't be seduced by the idea that because it's duty free it's a bargain. Very often prices are not much different from your local discount store and in the case of perfume or jewelry they can be even higher.

As a general rule of thumb, duty-free stores on the ground offer better value than buying in the air. Also, if you buy duty-free goods on a plane, remember that the range is likely to be limited and that if you are paying in a different currency to that of the airline, their rate of exchange often bears only a passing resemblance to the official one.

GREAT EXPECTATIONS

Life at the Crossroads of the Mediterranean

by
PETER NICHOLS

Peter Nichols has spent practically all his working life as a journalist with
The Times *of London, first in London, then in Berlin and Bonn and from
1957 to the present in Rome. He has written six books, including a study
of modern Italy,* Italia, Italia, *which won the coveted* Book of the Year *prize
in Italy. His most recent book,* The Pope's Divisions, *was published in 1984.
He lives in Rome with his wife, the Italian actress Paola Rosi.*

Expect a great deal from Italy. That is the golden rule, because there
is no other country in Europe with as much to give as Italy and to ask
too little is to miss the whole point of going at all. But there are obstacles
to a full enjoyment of the Italian experience which the wise traveler will
find ways to circumvent, ignore or somehow or other remove, so that the
greatest expectations are rewarded.

Some of the romance has gone for ever—the moment of arrival is a good
example. One of the most memorable excitements before the days of modern travel, of aircraft and of Alpine tunnels, must have been that descent
from the Alps down the valleys to a new world washed by the Mediterranean, a world stocked with the greatest treasures of Western civilization.
Nowadays that surge of emotion is replaced by a curt message from the

pilot that Mont Blanc is on the right and in another hour we shall be in Rome. Even for the motorist, a line-up to enter one of those long, dark tunnels—however great they may be as engineering feats—is daunting more than a thrill. Not much can now be revived of the physical contact of arriving on the plains of Lombardy, but it would be foolish to let the moment of arrival go by unnoticed.

The fact that Italy is an industrialized country and reached the status of sixth among the world's industrial producers in a short space of time, does not help to preserve the magic either. The sudden expansion which followed the period of postwar reconstruction changed an economy which had been predominantly agricultural to one based largely on industry. It swelled the towns and cities, denuding the land in the process. Italy for the first time knew the problem of urban conglomerates—Milan, Turin, Rome itself and Naples all faced a flood of immigrants in the '60s without the necessary administrative machinery to cope with them. As a result the drive from the airport, or the arrival on the outskirts by car from the motorway, necessarily takes one through ugly, unplanned suburbs, through nightmares of traffic (Naples is the worst in this respect, with traffic problems both shattering and hilarious) and dreadful moments of self-doubt arise about the wisdom of having decided to come to Italy at all.

This is the moment to hang on grimly to that rule of great expectations and not be discouraged. A British writer defined one of the three joys in life as "traveling in Italy with someone you love"—so, with luck, you can look at your companion and cheer up. Or you could remember Samuel Johnson's dictum that the object of travel was to reach the Mediterranean. By the time you have thought these comforting thoughts you should have arrived at the town center where there is a touch more discipline and a good deal more obvious beauty.

The Psychology of Locale

Much damage has been done to Italian cities and even more to city life. Over the centuries the classic Italian style of living was in small—or medium—sized towns and, perhaps more than any other people, the Italians are suited to that form of urban background which could be summed up as an ability to be provincial in the best sense of that term. Once the shock of arrival has passed, this provincialism is worth underlining as it has remained a continuing characteristic of the country, despite the upheavals of economic expansion. Regional diversity is one of Italy's greatest charms.

To talk first of the extremes of diversity. You can eat an excellent kouskous with fish in the traditional Arab style on the island of Lampedusa, which is farther to the south than the northernmost tip of Tunisia, just as you can eat sauerkraut in the Teutonic areas of the Bolzano province. Sicily not only has more imposing Greek ruins than the Greeks have themselves (with the exception of the Acropolis), but offers its own unique amalgam of Norman and Arab cultures. Sicily provides one explanation of the curious truth that in Italy the south is more south than its latitude would suggest, just as the north is more northern than its geographical position would warrant. Marseilles is unmistakably a Mediterranean port, while Genoa—which is on the same latitude—is temperamentally a northern city. The Genoese are frequently compared to Scots, but no one would ever make such a comparison between the northernmost inhabitants of the British Isles and the Marseillaises.

The reason for this stretching of extremities to make them even wider apart is both historical and psychological. The series of occupations and foreign dynasties which the south has known have enhanced its southern nature; Arabs, Spaniards and the Byzantine influence all marked it deeply. The evidence of one's own eyes is sufficient in Naples to tell that the wonderful Norman remains are totally out of place down there and have, indeed, never appealed to the Neapolitans, who found that rather cold dignity quite at odds with their own temperament. And so it never fitted as a style into the architectural development which ran in a line from Greek—for the Greeks founded the city—through Roman to Spanish and Baroque. At the other end of the scale of extremes, the north still bears the sobering touch of Austrian administration or, in the case of Piedmont, the heavy hand of a militaristic domination by a succession of remarkable rulers who brought that strategically vital little region to being as near to the Prussian mentality as any people south of the Alps could get.

The psychological factor is due to another trick played by history, apart from foreign occupation. Italy is almost entirely a Mediterranean country, in the sense that its coasts are long and all of them are washed by that sea which has been by far the greatest single source of Western civilization. Yet a part of the Italian mind looks north, because its history brought it directly into the affairs of northern and western Europe—largely because of the presence in Rome of the greatest center of Christendom. When the Roman Empire in the west fell, the popes were left without a civil protector and so looked to the north for allies. First the Franks and then the Germans became the secular protectors of the papacy. Inevitably, Italy's interests were forced northward in a way which the peninsula's geographical situation would hardly have warranted.

This same pull exists today. Italian membership of the European Community, and the status of the country as a leading industrial democracy, exert this stimulus to look northward, over the Alps, towards the industrial democracies of the north. The other pull, southward, is also a constant, but more fitful. For years during the period of economic expansion, it tended to be forgotten, but it is now back strongly because of the renewed strategic importance of the Mediterranean area, as well as the enlargement of the Community to include Greece, Portugal, and Spain.

An Embarrassment of Riches

To return, so to speak, to ground level. These fitful historical shifts move across a peninsula that is without rival in the contribution it has made to Western culture. Italy's museums contain about three million exhibits. Many of them are not on show because of the parsimony successive Italian governments have exhibited towards their vast heritage. What there is to see, however, imposes an essential task of selection. The great summits are relatively easy to list.

The Sistine Chapel is a reasonable candidate to be first, with its splendors by Michelangelo and an array of Renaissance painters in the less prominent spaces. There is only one way to see it. Go to the entrance of the Vatican Museums at opening time. Buy a ticket and run all the way to the chapel without looking at any of the tantalizing exhibits on the way. They can be looked at later. You should then arrive a good ten minutes before the first of the unwieldy guided groups who effectively destroy the atmosphere.

While en route around Italy, look at Michelangelo's three magnificent versions of the *Pietà*—one in St. Peter's, another in the cathedral museum in Florence and the third in the Castello Sforzesco in Milan. While in the Castello, look at the ceiling attributed to Leonardo, and from there go on to find the work of restoration in hand on the *Last Supper*, which is his most famous painting after the *Mona Lisa* housed in the Louvre.

The Renaissance comes to full splendor in Florence. Apart from the Uffizi Gallery, which possesses Italy's richest collection, look in the Brancacci Chapel in Santa Maria del Carmine to see the frescos painted there by Masaccio who, with the great sculptor Donatello, breathed the spirit of humanism into Italian art. Imagine those frescos freshly painted when Leonardo, Michelangelo, Fra Angelico and Botticelli all went to see them and study them and sketch these—for their times—revolutionary works. And, for the summit of humanistic thinking expressed with the maximum delicacy and grace, there are Botticelli's three pagan allegories in the Uffizi, *The Birth of Venus*, his *Primavera* and *Pallas Subduing a Centaur*.

In Venice, the greatest joys are the discoveries of masterpieces not only in the museums—the Titians, Tintorettos, Giovanni Bellinis and Veroneses—but discovering the places for which they were painted. Frescos are one thing, because they are put where they are supposed to stay: pictures are not. Yet look at Titian's *Madonna* and the *Assumption of the Virgin* in the Venetian church of Santa Maria Gloriosa dei Frari, and the full force of a picture hanging in the place the painter had in mind for it when he did the painting is clear. And go to the Accademia Museum, if for nothing else then to see Giorgione's *The Tempest*, which, with its half-naked woman, a soldier and a baby, delights and perplexes, as it always has and was presumably intended to do.

Atavistic Images

Mark Twain made a disgruntled remark after having been told that Michelangelo's hand was behind so much of what he saw and admired in Rome—"Lump the whole thing! Say the Creator made Italy from designs by Michelangelo!" His jibe was not far from a certain truth. One of the delights of visiting Italy is to see landscape, architecture, faces even, which are familiar from one's previous knowledge of Italian art and architecture. This element of *déja vu* adds to the impact. The Tuscan hills, with their seemingly planned designs of olive groves, cypresses and vines, the rhetorical church facades of Rome, the Venetian canals, the walled towns on their hilltops, are all part of an image that we carry with us—or rather back with us—when we go to Italy.

The same can be said for Pompeii, the greatest of the southern archeological sites. So much is familiar about the extraordinarily-preserved example of a provincial town which flourished in the comparatively early days of Roman expansion. Even the Gulf of Naples, despite the destruction of much of its beauty by brutal building speculation, retains a very clear idea of that sumptuous beauty which made it famous from antiquity onward. Virgil, who came from Mantua, chose to live in Naples and to die there. The brooding volcano and the mixture of grace and squalor in the old city still recall Gibbon's famous remark that Neapolitans appeared to live between paradise and hell. The archeological discoveries at Pompeii and Herculaneum towards the end of the 18th century provided the impetus for the style known as neo-Classicism that ruled the visual arts for decades. Capri, across the water, is over-built and, in season, overcrowded, yet it still manages to exhale that sense of having given pleasure for centuries and still being intent on doing so.

These are not random choices, even if a great many more would be easy to find. They are meant to make the point that the aim in Italy should not be to collect sights, but experiences. And this is where the distinction comes between Italy and other European countries. It can still summon up a degree of magic which is unique. That magic can be analysed, enjoyed but never fully comprehended.

One of the reasons why it exists is because it plays on chords within us. It is conjured up by so many influences which have their origins in Italy and which helped form the society in which we live, and its values. In a sense a journey to Italy is a return to one's roots. That would also include the religious element, which has been powerful for many centuries. Rome in particular offers this aspect of pilgrimage. Even to the most sceptical mind, the highpoints of this experience equal what the remains of the Roman Forum must mean to a classicist. In fact, the most thrilling archeological visit to be made in Rome is to the area under the main altar of St. Peter's. This means going down into the crypt (the burial place of some of the best-known popes, including John XXIII), down below the level of the first basilica built by the Emperor Constantine, through some of the tombs which formed part of a Roman cemetery buried by Constantine when he excavated a part of the Vatican Hill to construct his church. There one sees a modest monument to St. Peter which was arguably his tomb after he was—so the tradition goes—crucified upside down near the present site of Christendom's greatest church. It is then clear that the first Christian emperor at least felt that the moment was of such importance that part of a hill and part of a cemetery had to be removed to give it the place of honor.

Pros and Cons

Forget the magic for a moment. What does the traveler find both in his favor and against his interests in this still somewhat bewildering country?

For the motorist, the system of highways is superb, but the tolls are high on the main motorways and petrol is the most expensive in Europe. The fear of a breakdown is a little diminished by the thought that in the smallest village it is almost certain that you will find a mechanic with instinctive flair for his work and—as most Italians have a passionate attachment to their cars in a much more intense way than other races—there will be ample sympathy for your predicament.

The trains are adequate, but it is wise where possible to pay extra for an express train, or a super-express, which are more likely to be punctual. Country bus services are a good standby but the main problem, in small places, is to discover who has the timetables—it may be the newspaper stall, or the local real estate agent, or pinned up in a shop window.

If you plan to have one restful day make it Monday; museums and archeological sites are almost all closed and, for much of the year, the shops on a Monday morning, too.

Do not despise the small-scale pleasures. To eat an ice-cream or drink a coffee sitting down may cost you twice as much as it would standing at the counter of a bar—which is probably the explanation of why Italians look more at their ease on their feet in the subway or on a bus than seated—but it gives you the chance to watch a fascinating world go by. Italians tend to act in a way that suggests they know they are being looked at, even when no one is doing so; hence there need be no shyness about staring. You will not embarrass them. A warm evening in one of Rome's animated squares, a walk in Venice in the quiet of the night, a table outside some bar in a country town are places from which to watch, in miniature, a whole world go by.

Enjoy the surprises as well. Italians have a flair for putting together entertainments of a very varied kind in the smaller towns and villages, and they are very bad at publicizing them. You may well simply walk into an exhibition or a concert of high level quite unexpectedly, or a local festival in honor of the patron saint, a traditional form of folk culture which is returning strongly. Or it may be an improvized exhibition of beautifully embroidered tablecloths from Florence in a little town hall, or a special market which most country towns celebrate—there is no other word for it—once a year, a spectacle in itself and, once again, something which is increasing in importance rather than diminishing.

One of the special properties of magic, if it is real magic, is that it can never leave one bored. Italy can be exhilarating, worrying, highly annoying, perplexing, sad, comical, inspiring—but it is difficult to be bored in Italy.

Trouble is not always avoidable. In the big cities in particular it is as well to keep a close eye on handbags and not to leave baggage in cars. Bag-snatching and pickpocketing are listed as petty crimes, but there is nothing petty about the shock which can ruin a visit. It is best to take every precaution against an unpleasant surprise. Be sure at airports or rail stations to take officially licensed taxis, and never listen to the hisses of little men who work the taxi queues, offering to drive you to your destination for a good price.

If you have a mishap while driving, remain very restrained whatever dramatic gestures the other person is making in your direction. The apparent violence of these protests tends to increase when the other person is in the wrong, roughly in equal proportion to the degree of the fault. The rule is—do not react, especially if you are in the right, because your sense of complacency will be taken as an even worse affront than having allowed yourself to be struck by the other car.

It is mainly on the roads that these difficulties occur, because there is something which transforms an Italian when he steps into a car. You will certainly notice that courtesy is extreme in some situations. You may well have difficulty in getting in and out of elevators because the other people will want you to go first, and insist on this respect towards a guest. But once behind the wheel of a car and the same person will practically knock you off the road in order to move one car ahead of you—and snarl angrily at you as he passes.

Pasta Masters

Italian food is back in fashion. It used to be the case that traditional Italian food, meaning mainly *pasta* dishes, had either to be eaten with a certain sense of holiday guilt, or avoided where possible because of its alleged propensity to give one added pounds. Italians knew better, instinctively, but were also impressed by the theories that held that their diet was essentially one of a poor nation and that its improvement with meat, in particular, was necessary for an advanced Western country. The Mediterranean diet, based on pasta and olive oil, is now basking in the praises of the dietologists, especially because of its lack of animal fat.

It would, however, be a shame to eat Italian food just because it is good for you. Its real virtues are something more than the comparatively little cholesterol which it forms. It is basically simple. Spaghetti is flour ripened in strong sun, mixed with water and dried. There is a great variety of types of pasta, and of the sauces to go with them, but the secret of them all is that the Italian kitchen depends on the freshness and quality of its ingredients, rather than on elaborate preparation, and on the instincts of the people who prepare and cook it.

Italy has great restaurants. The travel magazines regularly make their choice of the top ten or the best dozen in the peninsula, and their recommendations can be safely followed—as we hope can ours! In some regions the cooking is superior to others. Emilia-Romagna is normally regarded as the best culinary area of Italy, but others—Tuscany, for instance, the Veneto, Piedmont—all rival it closely.

The same may be said for wines. There are great wines to be found and there are also perfectly good carafe wines produced locally. These wines are best drunk in smaller towns in the areas where they are made. They taste better; they complement the local food. In the last few years the classification of wines by locality and quality has been greatly improved. The enjoyment of wine can be greatly enhanced by being drunk in the right place and at the right time. Those heavy dessert wines in Sicily, for instance, have a special blend of flavors when drunk at the foot of Etna, with the scent of lemon blossom in the air. A light Venetian sparkling wine will add elegance even to one of Palladio's villas, or romance to the Grand Canal. Brunello, now perhaps Italy's most famous wine, seems made to be drunk while looking at the Siena landscape, while the weightier Barolo goes well with the view of some mist-enshrouded Piedmontese castle guarding one of those vital Alpine passes.

Which brings us back to those points of entry where the Italian experience begins. But need not end. Much has changed since Italy was the magnet which drew the fashionable elite on the Grand Tour. The reasons for going there have changed much less. They just need seeking out with greater diligence.

ITALY'S HISTORY AND ART

A Young Nation—An Ancient Heritage

Italian art flows as naturally as its wine, its sunshine, and its *amore,* and it has been springing from the Italian spirit for nearly as long. Perhaps nowhere in the world has such a vital creative impulse flourished for almost three millennia with such variety within the noble sweep of its classical tradition. Perhaps no other country's cultural life has been so inextricably interwoven with its history.

And yet, Italy lives comfortably in the midst of all her accumulated treasures. She accepts them casually and affectionately as she does her children and her flowers. True, some of her precious store has been gathered into world-famous museums, but the Italian knows best and loves most intimately the art which surrounds his every day to day activity. He goes to church among thousand-year-old mosaics, buys his groceries in a shop which has been open since the time of Columbus, picnics on the steps of a temple which was old when Christ was born, attends the opera in the same theaters where Rossini and Verdi saw their works premiered, and falls asleep in a high rise built by one of today's major architects.

Italy wears the raiment of her heritage with a light and touching grace. She must: it is the very fabric of her life.

Greeks and Etruscans

B.C.
753   Legendary founding of Rome by Romulus
mid-700s   Greeks began colonizing Southern Italy and Sicily

710	Taranto founded by Sparta
510	Last of the Etruscan kings, Tarquin the Proud, expelled from Rome. Republic founded, headed by 2 annually-elected consuls
498	Tarquin killed at the Battle of Lake Regulus
494	Latin League of 30 Latium cities started, led by Rome
471	First Plebeian magistrates elected in Rome
456	Aeschylus, the dramatist, killed at Gela (Sicily) when an eagle dropped a tortoise on his bald head
450	Twelve Tables of Law, Rome's written codex, based on Greek models
396	Rome captures Veii (Etruscan city) after 10-year siege
390	Gauls invaded Italy, sacked Rome except for the Capitol
390–367	Camillus re-established supremacy in central Italy, reconquered Etruria and rebuilt Rome
mid-300s –mid-200s	Last century of Etruscan power

Its very geographical position, thrusting out into the Mediterranean as it does, made the South of Italy a prey for every passing conqueror and colonizer. It was a natural landing zone for the Greeks when they were looking for *lebensraum* in the 8th century B.C. They founded settlements around the shores of Southern Italy and in Sicily and called their new-won lands Magna Graecia—Greater Greece. In Sicily at Agrigento, Syracuse, Selinute and Segesta, and especially at Paestum near Naples, there are still some of the best-preserved Doric temples in the world, standing sharp and proud against the cobalt sky. These monuments shape the fact that this colonization was no fly-by-night operation, but a significant part of the Greek world for centuries, until internal dissension, external pressure from Carthage and the growing might of Rome itself, brought about their downfall. By 200 B.C. the days of Magna Graecia were over.

A mere hint of the fabulous treasures that must have decorated the homes and temples of Magna Graecia can be seen in the two superb bronze statues which were found off the coast of Calabria in 1972. Called the *Warriors of Riace* they can now be viewed in the Archeological Museum of Reggio—though they have been on tour. Dating from the 5th century B.C. they are among the finest early bronze pieces remaining to us from the ancient world.

But the most important and at the same time mysterious of pre-Roman inhabitants of Italy were the Etruscans—"the long-nosed, sensitive-footed, subtly-smiling Etruscans," as D.H. Lawrence calls them. It used to be thought that they were a central Italian tribe, confined to the area called Etruria just north of Rome, where the great tomb-cities of Tarquinia, Cerveteri and Chiusi were discovered. But recent excavations have shown that the Etruscans controlled nearly all the peninsula, from Salerno to Mantua, and that—far from being hostile to the Roman settlers—they lived in perfect amity with them for a long period.

They held Italy when Rome was a collection of mud huts. They were an artistic and a bulldog breed and in their painted wooden villas they maintained a relaxed if superstitious society, keeping their children round them while they dined in chambers adorned with frivolous ornaments.

Their art speaks boldly of a garish and sensual life style. Etruscan towns were massively fortified mountain tops linked by roads which skimmed the highest ridges. Their temples were wooden with clay sculpture embellishments, all painted in vivid red, blue and yellow. Those few clay deities which survive are often giants whose fierce grins inspire an alarmed respect. It is, however, the careful provision for the afterlife of their dead which gives the clearest picture of Etruscan life. Their earth mound tombs were embellished with murals of lavish banquets, ecstatic dancers, cunning hunters and lusty warriors. In the center of the chamber stood the life size terracotta image of the dead man and his wife reclining on a banquet couch, partaking with a wry delight of their silent and eternal farewell party. Rome was to adopt the Etruscans' religious ceremonies (vestal virgins and household gods), their arts of divination (sheep's liver, thunder, the flight of birds) and their theatrical entertainments (from the flute-and-dance routine of Etruscan sacrificial captives, Roman comedy was born).

For a hundred years, until the abdication of Tarquin the Proud in 510 B.C., Etruscan kings ruled Rome. After that, history speaks of another hundred years of civil war, and legends embroider it. Yet the Etruscans left nothing of their civilization above ground, no clue to the language they spoke apart from a few cabalistic tablets, no clue to where they came from (some say mainland Greece, others the shores of the Black Sea) and no clue to where they disappeared to. Blind superstition and devotion to soothsayers were the Etruscans' undoing. The last of them vanished 2,300 years ago, but you cannot tour Italy today without being aware of them. The finest of medieval hilltowns are built on Etruscan foundations. The most admired objects in the archeological museums are Etruscan statuettes and lamps and earrings.

The Republic

312	Appius Claudius begins construction of the Appian Way and Aqua Appia, Rome's oldest aqueduct
283	Rome seizes Corsica
280–275	War against Pyrrhus, King of Epirus
266	Rome conquers Calabria
260–241	*First Punic War*—Rome v Carthage, struggle for the upper hand in central Mediterranean. Rome wins Sicily
220	Flaminian Way (Rome to Rimini) finished (started 299)
219–202	*Second Punic War*—218 Hannibal invades Italy over the Alps with elephants; 216 he wins the battle of Cannae, Roman army wiped out in a "carnival of butchery"; 207–3 Romans led by Scipio Africanus carry the war back to Spain and to Carthage itself; 203–2 Hannibal recalled to Carthage and defeated by Scipio at Zama
196–147	Eastward expansion of Rome
149–146	*Third Punic War*—Carthage totally destroyed
133	Asia Minor becomes a province; Rome now governs the whole Mediterranean basin—Egypt excepted
106–78	*Period of Gaius Marius and Sulla*—112–105 together they win war against Jugurtha, king of Numidia (modern Algeria); 102–1 Marius beats Germanic tribes and halts invasion from the north; civil war between the two ends with death of Marius in 86; 82 Sulla becomes sole Dictator; 78 Sulla dies
71	Slaves revolt under Spartacus; defeated by Pompey and Crassus
67–44	*Period of Pompey and Caesar*—67 Pompey beats Mediterranean pirate fleets; 66–63 Pompey in the East wins Syria and Palestine; 60 First Triumvirate (Rule of Three), Pompey, Caesar and Crassus; 58–49 Caesar wages the Gallic Wars (and writes about it 51); 55 and 54 invasions of Britain; 49 Caesar crosses Rubicon and starts civil war; 48 Caesar defeats Pompey at Pharsalia; 47 Cleopatra has Pompey murdered; 46 Caesar returns to Rome as Dictator; 44 Caesar murdered on the Ides of March (March 15)

43	*Second Triumvirate*—Octavius (Caesar's heir and nephew), Mark Antony and Lepidus
42	The Triumvirate hunts down Caesar's assassins; victory at Philippi
40–31	Power struggle between Octavius and Antony; 31 Battle of Actium, deaths of Antony and Cleopatra
27	Octavius becomes Augustus Caesar—beginning of the Empire

The Romans were great borrowers—they borrowed gods and ideas with equal gusto, but managed to convert their wholesale plagiarism into a positive virtue by the sincerity with which they adopted their acquisitions. Their genuinely innate talents lay not in the creation of ideas, but in the organizing of them; in engineering, in architecture, in building roads, in anything that needed intelligence, skill and a capacity for taking infinite pains. They were no strangers to sweat—imagination came harder.

Starting from a small village of mud huts they rose through five-and-a-half centuries to become masters of the whole Mediterranean region, a feat accomplished by a genetic combination of backbone and brain that has never been equalled in recorded history. As Pliny said, of a time after Rome had won its wide territories—"Prior to this, Rome knew nothing of these exquisite and refined things . . . rather was it full of barbaric weapons and bloody spoils; and though it was garlanded with memorials and trophies of triumphs there was no sight which was joyful to refined spectators."

The size and scope of their engineering feats grew with their wealth and power. From the very beginning it was phenomenal, and usually showed a breathtaking breadth of vision. No one who has followed a vestigial Roman road across the European landscape could fail to be impressed. The monumentality of the works undertaken entered a new phase with the Empire.

The often quoted remark of Augustus, that he found Rome brick and left it marble, omits a vital ingredient of Roman building—concrete. The use of concrete was one of the Romans' greatest contributions to the history of architecture, for it enabled them not only to create vast domes and vaults, undreamed of before, but also to build such tricky structures as underwater jetties to extend vital port installations. Perhaps the earliest concrete dome was in Pompeii, that of the Stabian Baths (2nd century B.C.), while the Tabularium in Rome has the earliest great concrete vault (78 B.C.). Baths were often the most lavish buildings in any town, and all the imperial Baths in Rome—those of Caracalla and Diocletian especially, had superb vaulted roofs. The concrete dome at its most impressive can be seen in the Pantheon in Rome (around 125 A.D.), a massive construction 43 m. (141 ft.) across. It is a fascinating feat of both design and engineering, for it is modeled on a sphere, the height of the supporting walls being equal to the radius of the dome—the whole creating an awesome feeling of the imaginative use of space, which could accommodate a great globe, of which the dome would be the top portion.

Though most of the largest and most impressive architectural undertakings were the work of the Empire, all the early work done in the Republic laid, as it were, the foundations on which the emperors and their hordes of architects and workmen could build.

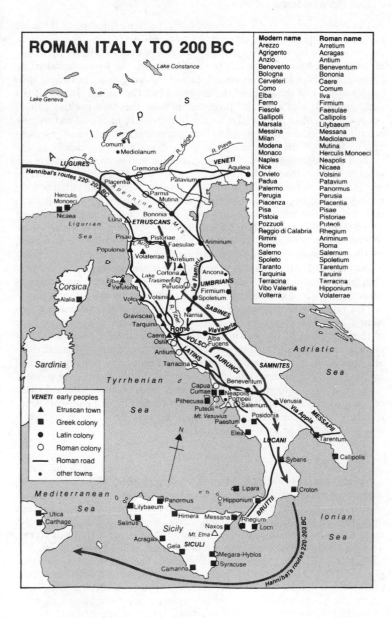

ROMAN ITALY TO 200 BC

Modern name	Roman name
Arezzo	Arretium
Agrigento	Acragas
Anzio	Antium
Benevento	Beneventum
Bologna	Bononia
Cerveteri	Caere
Como	Comum
Elba	Ilva
Fermo	Firmium
Fiesole	Faesulae
Gallipolli	Callipolis
Marsala	Lilybaeum
Messina	Messana
Milan	Mediolanum
Modena	Mutina
Monaco	Herculis Monoeci
Naples	Neapolis
Nice	Nicaea
Orvieto	Volsinii
Padua	Patavium
Palermo	Panormus
Perugia	Perusia
Piacenza	Placentia
Pisa	Pisae
Pistoia	Pistoriae
Pozzuoli	Puteoli
Reggio di Calabria	Rhegium
Rimini	Ariminum
Rome	Roma
Salerno	Salernum
Spoleto	Spoletium
Taranto	Tarentum
Tarquinia	Taruinii
Terracina	Tarracina
Vibo Valentia	Hipponium
Volterra	Volaterrae

VENETI early peoples
▲ Etruscan town
■ Greek colony
● Latin colony
○ Roman colony
— Roman road
• other towns

The Roman Face

The reverse side of the Roman coin from the representation of the great building is, naturally, the one with the portrait. A six-century-long tradition of portraiture was in full swing by the end of the 3rd century B.C. Possibly stemming from the practice of the Etruscans, the Romans started by keeping deathmasks of their ancestors and carrying them in funeral processions, not just the mask of the deceased but the collected faces of the past family. It was a natural progression from this to a positive cult of portraiture. Unlike the Greeks, whose portraits are idealized and usually beautiful, the Romans belonged to the "warts and all" school of representation. Many of the busts that have come down to us are nearly savage in their relentless portrayal of the subject. Men and women alike stare out at us from faces that might well be the real thing after being petrified by one glance from Medusa. This was not merely a Republican cult, the long history of portraiture continued right down through the Empire until well into the 3rd and 4th centuries A.D. Indeed some of the most brilliant and psychologically revealing heads are those of emperors. To see the very look of Romans to the best advantage, visit the Capitoline Museum in Rome, where there are dozens of heads in serried ranks staring stonily at the passers-by. But, indeed, almost every museum in Italy, and a great many outside, have examples of this extraordinary national art. Certainly the wildernesses of wrought stone in Rome's great galleries are full of them.

This relentless realism is a very important facet of the mentality of ancient Rome. It was part of the general Roman belief in the importance of the individual, of the worth and dignity of the unique personality that is each man's birthright while, at the same time, recognizing that individual's responsibility to all the other personalities around him that go to make up the totality of society. The consequence of this centuries-long concern with the cult of personality is that we now have an unparalleled gallery of faces, from the lowest Roman tradesman to the chain of emperors, tracing the history of a civilization through the very people who created it and—in the final analysis—destroyed it.

The Empire

From Augustus (died A.D. 14) to Theodosius (died 395) there were 48 Roman emperors, many of them eminently forgettable, some of them men of genius, quite a few who added nothing to the Roman way of life except new ways of death. Here are some, chronologically arranged, who did leave behind something that contributed to the grandeur that was Rome. The date following the emperor's name is that of his taking power.

Augustus (27 B.C.). Republican Rome was badly planned, in fact not planned at all, and the great contribution of Augustus was to commence serious town planning, even more than the miracle of turning bricks into marble. It was in his reign that Rome began to turn from being a glorified provincial capital and became a great city. He was in every way a great ruler, with a clear sense of what was needed to cure the chaos left behind by the civil wars. He created an administrative structure which was only minimally corrupt and fairly efficient, he set up ministries to look after the state's highways, manage public works, repair temples and import food. He built all over the place, inside and outside Italy.

This was the greatest period of literature Rome knew, with Virgil, Horace, Livy, Ovid, Seneca and Propertius all writing and Maecenas (a name that entered many languages) as patron to the arts and friend of the emperor. Augustus' influence extended to every corner of Roman life. The laws were completely reshaped, morals were cleaned up—and not before time, and he used his long life (he ruled for 41 years) to the advantage of a Rome which he found in chaos and left in order.

Claudius (41 A.D.). An indefatigable builder, who constructed aqueducts for Rome and the port of Ostia which was joined by canal to the Tiber. An enthusiastic patron of circuses and gladiatorial combats, he comes vividly to life in the two famous historical novels of Robert Graves, *I Claudius* and *Claudius the God*.

Nero (54). Most notorious of the emperors, but by no means the worst, his domestic and foreign policies were popular and successful at first. He built the Temple to Jupiter at Baalbeck in Lebanon and started a canal across the isthmus of Corinth in Greece, among many other undertakings around the empire. In Italy he completed, or re-shaped, projects that had been started by his uncle Claudius, but is probably best remembered by the Baths he built in Rome (62) and the great Domus Aurea, the Golden House, so huge that the cry went up "All Rome has become a villa." Unfortuntately, this magnificent palace lasted less than 40 years, disappearing under the massive Baths of Titus and Trajan. But the subterranean corridors and rooms that remained hidden provided an inspiration for Raphael, 14 centuries later, when he created the "grottesque" decorations (the word comes from "grotto") based on the Neronian frescos he had seen by lamplight in recently-revealed parts of the Domus Aurea. Nero was the last descendant of Augustus to be emperor, after him the office was held by men nominated by the all-powerful armies—usually power-hungry generals.

Vespasian (69). Born in Rieti, Vespasian was the first of the new, military, emperors. A down-to-earth countryman, with a realistic sense of humor, his dying words "I think I am in the process of becoming a god" have lived on. He started the building of the Colosseum (which was completed by his son, Titus), reconstructed the temple of Capitoline Jove and generally restored the city which had burned down under Nero.

Titus (79). Apart from completing the Colosseum, Titus continued his father's program of public works around Italy, notably with the Arch that bears his name, celebrating the virtual annihilation of the Jewish nation, and the magnificent public baths that helped to obliterate Nero's Golden House—both in Rome.

Trajan (98). A great soldier who brought Romania and the Middle East into the empire. He sorted out Rome's finances, as well as improving the city's water supply and drainage. His official architect from 97–117 was Apollodorus of Damascus, one of the most influential early builders, who worked extensively for his patron in Italy—not only in Rome, where he built among other things the Baths and Forum of Trajan, but also in Ancona, Civitavecchia and Benevento. He also worked under Hadrian, but fell out with him eventually, was exiled in 130 and finally condemned to death. His main contribution, which was crucial at this point in history, was to fuse together Greek and Roman approaches to the problems of architecture to produce a coherent and totally new style.

Hadrian (116). The greatest imperial builder of them all. He was responsible for a marvelous villa at Tivoli, just outside Rome, where you may still wander among the ruins of replicas of the grandest monuments of the ancient world. He also finished the great Pantheon in Piazza della Rotonda (126), and constructed his own huge mausoleum which afterwards became the papal fortress of Sant'Angelo near the Vatican. To explore both Tivoli and the Castel Sant'Angelo is to understand a great deal about the way the Roman builders went to work, and to see how they used fantastic quantities of both brick and stone in their gigantic undertakings. Hadrian also imported shiploads of sculpture and other decorative furnishing from Rome's client states, and it was this incredible wealth of art that remained in Italy, above and below ground, ready to fire the imagination of the Renaissance.

Margaret Yourcenar's historical novel *The Memoirs of Hadrian* provides an excellent study of this complex emperor who carried his building schemes to far corners of the Empire, from the north of Britain to Greece and the Middle East.

Marcus Aurelius (161). The philosopher-emperor. His death at Vienna in 180 caused Gibbon to write that with him had ended "the period in the history of the world during which the condition of the human race was most happy and prosperous." His two main monuments in Rome—his equestrian statue in the piazza of the Campodoglio and his column in the Piazza Colonna—are both under restoration after the severe attacks of the city's pollution.

Septimus Severus (193). Born in Africa and died in England, this was the first non-Roman emperor. His arch by the Forum in Rome is one of Italy's most elaborate.

Caracalla (217). One of the baddies, in fact a dangerous psychopath, he created Rome's most beautiful and luxurious baths—now the venue for summer opera.

Diocletian (284). Son of a freed slave, who worked his way up through the ranks of the army, Diocletian was the man who first divided the empire, so that there was a ruler for both east and west, thus reorganizing the almost impossible task of administering a structure which had grown impossibly large. He was of Illyrian birth—from the region which now straddles Albania/Yugoslavia—and his near-eastern origins made him the first of the truly imperial emperors, laying the foundations for the royal mystique which was to reach its apotheosis in Byzantium. He was, in a way, more Persian than Roman. His reign saw the stepping-up of Christian persecution, and became an age of martyrs. Among his extra-Italian building projects was the huge fortified palace on the Dalmatian coast, which now forms the nucleus of Split.

Constantine (312). Called "the Great." He built some of the first churches in Rome, including old St. Peter's, and completed the magnificent basilica of Maxentius in the imperial fora. Having ordered the erection of his triumphal arch and other buildings near the Colosseum, he left the city and spent nearly all his life at Byzantium, which he renamed Constantinople. Constantine reunited the empire divided by Diocletian, believed that Rome's future lay with the Catholic church although he was unlikely to have been a Christian himself, and presided over the Council of Nicaea (325) which decided the future course of orthodox beliefs.

Theodosius (379). In 380 Theodosius finally made Christianity the state religion. Rome now became the seat of the most important Christian bishop, but the center of real power moved eastwards to Constantinople.

Italy's reign as the spider at the heart of a vast web was nearly over. The Dark Ages loomed ahead.

The Dark Ages

354–430	St. Augustine—wrote *The City of God* after Alaric's sack of Rome in 410
401	Visigothic invasions begin; 410 Alaric sacks Rome; legions withdrawn from Britain to defend Italy
452	The Huns under Attila invade Northern Italy; turned back by Pope Leo I, the Great, at the gates of Rome
455	Rome sacked by the Vandals, nominally Christians, under the lame Gaiseric
476	Odoacer proclaimed Emperor of the Gothic Kingdom of Italy
488	Ostrogoths invade Italy; 493 Theodoric proclaimed king, but subject to Byzantium; 526 death of Theodoric
536–40	Justinian, the Byzantine Emperor, invades Italy; 553 final defeat of the Goths, Italy again part of the Byzantine empire
568	Mass-migration of Lombards into Italy; attained control by 570; rule lasted until 774
590–604	Pope Gregory I, the Great; discovery of relics of St. Peter
609	Pantheon consecrated as church (Santa Maria ad Martyres), by Pope Boniface IV
643	Lombards annexed Liguria
751	Aistulf, king of the Lombards, seizes Ravenna from Byzantine rule
774	Charlemagne (742–814), son of Pepin, invades at the request of Hadrian I; with the fall of Pavia in 774 Lombardy becomes a Papal State and Lombard rule is ended in Italy
800	Charlemagne is crowned emperor by Leo III in Rome; 814 death of Charlemagne; the dissolution of his empire over the next century created chaos out of which the rival Italian states were born
962	Otto I becomes emperor, founds Holy Roman Empire
1036	The Normans commence the conquest of Southern Italy

These six hundred years, give or take the odd decade, were the Dark Ages for Italy, a period when the northern barbarians surged in and out, the Visigoths, the Huns, the Vandals, the Ostrogoths and finally the Lombards, all drawn to the southern honeypot that lay temptingly on the other side of the frozen Alps. Byzantium lost its hold on its birthplace, for some time keeping just the area around Ravenna and losing that finally in 751. The popes slowly improved the shining hour, on a "two steps forward, one step back" basis, filling the vacuum of continuity in civic rule to extend their power further and further over the face of the land.

This was not a period of growth or one in which any kind of culture could flourish. The arts of Byzantium, of course, were the great exception. The imperial court was transferred to Ravenna from Rome in about 402 and the city began a period of great if short-lived prosperity under Honorius and his sister Galla Placidia, whose tomb is still one of the city's treasures. When the city was briefly recaptured from the Lombards by Count Belisarius in 540, the Empress Theodora and her husband Justinian set out to restore the now-faded splendor of the place with even more sumptuous buildings and decorations.

The mosaics which enrich the great churches of Ravenna are among the most beautiful in the world—a natural progression from those of ancient Rome, though far surpassing them in skill. Nor did the artistic glories of Ravenna stop at mosaics. Lustrous silk woven into ceremonial garments for church and court; ivory carvings which often echoed their Roman origins, replacing pagan with Christian motifs, shaped with enormous skill and creating objects of hieratic dignity; gold jewelry and superb ivory furniture such as the throne of Maximian—all bring down to us the luxurious world that replaced ancient Rome with an eastern softness and opulence. It would be nearly a thousand years before Italy saw wealth so conspicuously allied to artistic genius again.

The Middle Ages—Growth of the City States

1154–90	1154 Frederick I (Barbarossa) crosses the Alps from Germany; struggle between papacy and emperor (Ghibellines on side of emperor, Guelfs on side of pope); Milan is main Guelf center; 1155 Barbarossa crowned emperor in Rome; 1158 and 1162 emperor sacks Milan; 1177 Barbarossa humbles himself to Pope Alexander III at Canossa; 1189 Barbarossa goes on the 3rd Crusade, drowns 1190
1198–1216	Innocent III, one of the greatest popes; 1209 he sanctioned the Order of St. Francis of Assisi (1181–1226)
1212	Venice annexes Crete
1233–50	Frederick II wages war first against the Lombard League (grouping of the northern cities), then against the pope; Innocent IV has to flee to France; Frederick (*Stupor Mundi*) dies 1250
1265–1321	Dante Alighieri; 1314 Divine Comedy
1282	"Sicilian Vespers", massacre of the French in Sicily at Easter
1298	Marco Polo's *Travels*
304–74	Petrarch; poet who perfected the sonnet
1313–75	Giovanni Boccaccio, originator of the novel
1309	Popes transfer to Avignon
1348–49	BLack Death rages
1347	Cola di Rienzo attempts to restore Rome as capital of a "Sacred Italy"; murdered 1354
1347–80	Catherine of Siena, Italy's patron saint; canonized 1461; 1377 helped to bring about the return of the popes from Avignon

Gradually, and taking almost as many forms as there were towns, the city states began to rise. Some started on the road of statehood early— Venice, for example, had its doge (a version of the same word that gives us "duke") as early as 697. In every way Venice was a law to itself. Genoa did not gets its doge until 1339, though the city was well organized much sooner, being run by seven consuls until about 1191, then by mayors, with brief breaks for foreign domination.

In even the smaller towns the ancient Roman traditions of city life slept, until they were reawakened by the increasing trade of the 10th and 11th centuries. Local craft groups and corporations joined together for the well-being of their towns, channeling their increasing wealth into civic buildings and defense. The Church itself was a leader in commerce and, strange to say, one of the biggest of the newly opening markets for Italian trade was the world of the infidel, the Saracens, also the object of increasing military attention as the Crusades got under way. A brilliant picture of what was happening along the trade routes of the known world comes down to us in the writings of Marco Polo, whose great journeys, made towards the end of the 13th century, show just how far and through what hardships the businessmen of the time were prepared to go in pursuit of a fast ducat.

But even as Italy was gradually building the basis for its next period of greatness, so it was also in the grip of internal strife. Sides were chosen as between pope and emperor, the Guelfs and the Ghibellines—both words are corruptions of German names, Welf and Waiblingen, rival parties north of the Alps. In Italy they were given to supporters of the pope—Guelphs, and the emperor—Ghibellines. (If you have a job remembering which was which, the trick is that one has one syllable, the other three. It is especially helpful in Florence.) Even in the middle of the resulting confusion and the slow fragmentation of Italy into city states, the glorious past was never entirely forgotten, but it took a foreigner, the half-Norman half-German Emperor Frederick II—von Hohenstaufen—(1194–1250) to give nostalgia tangible form. His starkly geometric Castel del Monte not far from Andria in Apulia, and the broken fragments of his triumphal arch (1247) in Capua, are fleeting reminders of this remarkable poet-emperor's dream of a revival of antique purity in southern Italy, but from this seed sprang a startlingly vigorous classical style in the sculpture of the Tuscan Nicola Pisano.

Within the complex of Pisa cathedral, with its famous tower and handsome round baptistery, Nicola (1220–84) created the cool but deeply-felt sculpture of the Baptistery pulpit in 1260 and followed it with a similar pulpit in Siena. His son Giovanni created pulpits in Pistoia (1301) and in Pisa cathedral (1310), replacing his father's classic concerns with a ferocious intensity of spirit which proclaims the emergence of the Gothic style in Italy.

The architecture of Pisa is only one aspect of the Romanesque in Italy. From the massy, squat brick of Sant'Ambrogio in Milan in the north to the sunny facets of Bari cathedral in the south, Romanesque's stolid logic dominates the peninsula. Unexpected relief from this sobriety comes in Florence, where the crisp shade and dark-green and snowy marble of the Baptistery and the serene harmony of San Miniato hold a promise of the coming of the Renaissance.

No development proclaimed the new humane mood of the Italian Church in the 12th century more clearly than St. Francis (1181–1226) and his order of Franciscan friars. Their gentle concern for the welfare of man and for his place in the natural order of things lent a warmth to the art of the Gothic era. As a memorial to the beloved saint, a curious two-level church was built in his native Assisi and consecrated in 1253. Each level was a barn-like hall destined for mural paintings rather than as a frame for stained glass as it would have been in French churches of the period.

Soon the major painters from various cities came to Assisi to decorate its walls. The excitable Cimabue (1240–1302) came from Florence; the urbane and courtly Simone Martini (1284–1344) from Siena; perhaps even the young Giotto (1266–1337) came, fresh from the experience of Rome, but it is more likely that the most famous of the mural scenes, the epic cycle of the Life of St. Francis in the upper church, is the work of an imitator of the precocious Giotto. The master himself traveled northward to Padua where he decorated the interior of the Scrovegni Chapel (Madonna dell'Arena) with scenes from the lives of the Virgin and Christ (1306), which, in their simplicity, clarity and faultless sense of human drama, changed the direction of Italian painting and placed it on an equal footing with its sculptural prototypes.

Siena stirred to life with the ambitious plan for the cathedral, so large that less than a quarter of it was ever built. Its boisterous and colorful facade teems with Giovanni Pisano's animated sculptures and its high altar was adorned with the jewel-like, multipaneled altarpiece by Duccio

(1308), now hanging in the cathedral museum. With it Sienese painting shook off the now decadent Byzantine style.

Rome slept out the Gothic era: the pope was now a virtual prisoner in Avignon in Southern France and almost nothing was happening among the sordid slums and the crumbling ruins of antiquity. About the only artistic claim Rome could make during the Middle Ages was the work of the Cosmati—the marble and mosaic craftsmen who created pavements, tombs and pulpits, inlaid with colored stones and glass.

Milan flexed its military muscle but fumbled the arts in the later Middle Ages, concentrating its energies on the colossal muddle which would eventually become its cathedral five hundred years later.

After Giotto's death in 1337, Florentine artists were largely occupied with the progress of the stately cathedral for which the master had provided the design for a campanile, or bell tower. Few painters could match his achievement and most chose to concentrate on isolated aspects of his work. Furthermore, Florence was racked by financial depression and a series of virulent attacks of the Black Death which wiped out more than half of the population. Orcagna (1370–1427) reflected the desperate mood of the time in his grim and angry sculpture and painting. Only gradually, around 1400, did art recover its equilibrium with the richly naturalistic painting of Gentile da Fabriano (1370–1427), the iridescent pictorial fantasies of Lorenzo Monaco (1370–1425), and the lyrical bronze sculptures of Lorenzo Ghiberti (1378–1455), especially his magnificent doors for the Baptistery.

The Renaissance

1379–1402	Gian Galeazzo Visconti, Duke of Milan, attempts to conquer Italy; pushes southwards to surround Florence but dies of a fever in 1402
1404	Verona and Vicenza acquired by Venice
1406	Florence overthrows Pisa
1407	The Republic of Genoa takes over Corsica
1423–54	War between Florence and Venice against Milan; this opens the era of the great *condottieri,* mercenary army commanders
1433	Cosimo di Medici exiled from Florence; 1434 returns and rules until 1464
1434	Revolt in Rome; Pope Eugenius IV (1431–47) takes refuge in Florence; 1443 returns to Rome
1450	Pope Nicholas V (1447–55) founds Vatican Library
1455	The Italian League, defensive grouping of Milan, Florence, Venice, Alfonso of Naples and the pope, against external attack; Fall of Constantinople in 1453 emphasized Turkish menace, plus danger of French invasion; this was the nearest Italy came to unification in this century
1469	Lorenzo the Magnificent (1449–92) inherits the Florentine leadership; 1478 Pazzi conspiracy, Giuliano di Medici murdered
1458–64	Pope Pius II (Aeneas Silvius) great humanist and diplomat; dies waiting to go on a Crusade against the Turks
1471–84	Pope Sixtus IV (Francesco della Rovere) tries to reinforce the Papal States and to secularize the papacy
1492	Columbus crosses the Atlantic; Roderigo Borgia (1492–1503) becomes Pope Alexander VI; 1493 he divides the newly discovered territories between Spain and Portugal
1494	Charles VIII of France invades; 1495 he takes Naples
1498	Death of Savonarola
1500	Louis XII of France gains Milan

The Renaissance—which means rebirth, the rebirth of the classical spirit of the ancient world—began in Florence. But why in Florence, a city which could boast fewer Roman buildings and sculptures than many another Italian town? Perhaps it was her distinguished literary heritage which prided itself not only on the epic poetry of Dante, but the lyrics of Petrarch and the ribald prose of the father of the novel, Boccaccio. More important, however, was the long artistic tradition for a clear-sighted humanism, a drive to enquire into the nature of man and his place in the universal order. Florentines saw the world as a coherent whole and envisioned man as its heroic master.

As always in Florence, sculpture showed the way. Ghiberti, creator of the *Doors of Paradise,* stood as the link between the Gothic and the Renaissance, his workshop acted as a training ground for the next generation of masters and his own work deepened as he matured, taking on a new logic and drama with his studies of antiquity. It was Donatello (1386–1466) who explored a vital naturalism, first with his impudent, spring-fresh bronze *David* and later with the calmly alert *St. George* for one of the outside niches of the Church of Orsanmichele, a veritable showcase for the new sculptural style. By turns gently equivocal as in the bronze *David,* and explosively eccentric as in the *Cantorie* (choir gallery) for the cathedral, Donatello's forceful and original sculpture won him a widespread fame and led to the Paduan bronzes for the Basilica of Sant'Antonio and the equestrian monument to the general Gattamelata in the square outside, a reworking of an ancient Roman form and a milestone in this branch of sculpture. His late years saw an hysterical religious conversion best exemplified by the dessicated horror of the *Penitent Magdalen* in the Florentine Baptistery and the tremulous emotion of the bronze panels of the San Lorenzo pulpit. These last were finished after his death by his pupil Bertoldo, who in his turn became an early master of Michelangelo. The Renaissance is threaded through by these interlinked relationships.

Architecture entered a new era with Filippo Brunelleschi (1377–1446) who is traditionally supposed to have invented a new system of linear perspective which enabled him to prepare the ground plan, elevation and overall proportional balance of a building in advance instead of working piecemeal as had most medieval masterbuilders. Although his impressive engineering feat in raising the vast dome over Florence Cathedral is his most conspicuous achievement, his elegant, peaceful churches of San Lorenzo and Santo Spirito, the refined Pazzi Chapel and the powerful original part of the Pitti Palace best represent his new ideas.

In the generation which followed, Leone Battista Alberti (1404–72) developed these new ideas in design and wrote the first major theoretical treatises on architecture, as well as books on sculpture and painting. He was, in fact, that rare bird, the Renaissance ideal of the "complete man", for he dabbled in the theater, mathematics, music and athletics as well, and single-handedly steered the Renaissance into a new era.

Painting caught up and added a new dimension with the work of Masaccio. Although he died in 1428—aged about 27—after only six years of mature activity, this rustic genius brought a pungent naturalism and profoundly human sobriety to painting with his deeply expressive frescos of the *Life of St. Peter* in the Brancacci Chapel of the Carmine Church in Florence. He applied Brunelleschi's classic architectural style and the de-

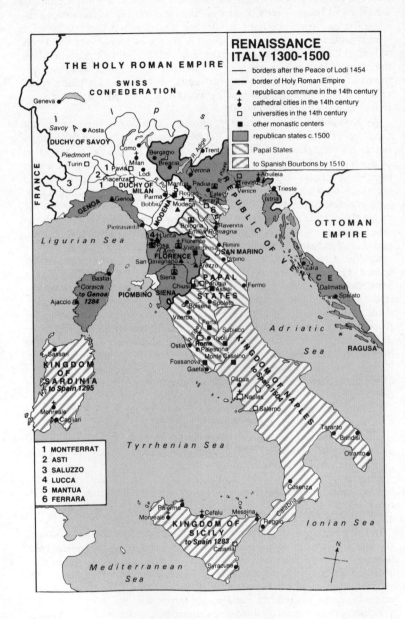

RENAISSANCE ITALY 1300-1500

— borders after the Peace of Lodi 1454
— border of Holy Roman Empire
▲ republican commune in the 14th century
✝ cathedral cities in the 14th century
□ universities in the 14th century
■ other monastic centers
▨ republican states c.1500
▨ Papal States
▨ to Spanish Bourbons by 1510

THE HOLY ROMAN EMPIRE

SWISS CONFEDERATION

Geneva

Savoy ● Aosta

DUCHY OF SAVOY

Piedmont
Turin □

FRANCE

1 Pavia
Como
Milan
Lodi
Bergamo
Brescia
Trent
R. Adige
Verona
R. Po

2 Piacenza
DUCHY OF MILAN
Parma
Bobbio
Modena
MODENA
Mantua
Padua
Este
Ferrara
Treviso
Venice
Aquileia
Trieste
Istria

3 Genoa
GENOA
Pietrasanta

Ligurian Sea

REPUBLIC OF VENICE

OTTOMAN EMPIRE

Bologna
Emilia Romagna
Ravenna
Rimini
SAN MARINO
Urbino
Zara
Dalmatia
Spalato

4 Lucca
Pisa
Vallambrosa
FLORENCE
San Gimignano
Arezzo
Siena
Chiusi
PAPAL STATES
Perugia
Assisi
Fermo

Bastia
Corsica
to Genoa
1284
Ajaccio

Sassari
KINGDOM OF SARDINIA
to Spain 1295

PIOMBINO
SIENA

Bolsena
Spoleto
Viterbo
Farfa
Subiaco
Tivoli
Rome
Ostia
Palestrina
Monte Cassino
Fossanova
Gaeta
Capua

KINGDOM OF NAPLES
to Spain 1504

Adriatic Sea

RAGUSA

Monreale
Cagliari

Tyrrhenian Sea

Naples
Salerno

Taranto
Brindisi
Otranto

1 MONTFERRAT
2 ASTI
3 SALUZZO
4 LUCCA
5 MANTUA
6 FERRARA

Cosenza

Calabria

Palermo
Cefalu
Messina
Reggio
Monreale
KINGDOM OF SICILY
to Spain 1283
Catania
Syracuse

Ionian Sea

Mediterranean Sea

N

vice of linear perspective to project a convincing three-dimensional illusion in the noble *Trinity* mural in Santa Maria Novella.

After Masaccio a generation of highly individual painters in Florence brought variety to his example. Fra Angelico (1387–1455)—more properly Fra Giovanni da Fiesole—was a delicate colorist and a reticent spokesman for religious sentiment in his work at the Monastery of San Marco, the same monastery that was to see the excesses of Savonarola a few decades later; Andrea del Castagno (1421–57) brought an explosive drama to his murals in Sant'Apollonia, turning Donatello's sculpture into the language of paint; Paolo Uccello (1396–1475) had a fanatical mania for the pure geometry of perspective which dominates the dreamy *Battle of San Romano* in the Uffizi; Domenico Veneziano (d. 1461) integrated pliant line and radiant color in his *St. Lucy* altar, parts of which are in England, the U.S. and Germany, while the main section, the *Maddona and Child*, is in the Uffizi, too; and Fra Filippo Lippi's eccentric individuality (1457–1504) lends a wistful pathos to the frescos in Prato cathedral that took him 12 years to complete, during which time he was tried for fraud and abducted a nun!

Elsewhere in Italy the lessons of the Florentine Renaissance were absorbed, though slowly. In Northern Italy Mantegna (1431–1506) developed the new idiom in Mantua through his antiquarian obsessions, developing what Vasari called his "stony manner." One of his works, the ceiling of the *Camera degli Sposi* in the Mantua Castello, is an early forerunner of the illusionist vaults the Baroque painters were to perfect. Mantegna's style, which seemed to be fashioned from marble and bronze, was to be softened and humanized by the glowing nature poetry of his brother-in-law, Giovanni Bellini (1430–1516), who revitalized Venetian painting.

Other regional centers blossomed into often vividly independent creative activity. Cosmé Turà (d. 1495) brought craggy design and fruity color to Ferrara; Piero della Francesca (d. 1492) left his silently enigmatic images in Arezzo, Urbino and especially in his native Borgo San Sepolcro (now called Sansepolcro) in Tuscany, where they can be seen in the town museum; Sassetta (1400–50) and his Sienese followers developed the exquisite mysticism of the local tradition; Antonello da Messina (1430–79) in remote Sicily, refined a meticulous style resembling that of the Flemings.

Through all the rich developments of the *quattrocento* Rome remained an artistic backwater, dependent for what episodic activity there was on imported talent.

Leonardo, Michelangelo and Raphael

By 1475 the lessons of the new style had become second nature in Florence and artists began to explore personal byways, such as the elusive linear grace of Sandro Botticelli (1445–1510); the everyday prose of Domenico Ghirlandaio (1449–94); the fastidious decoration of Filippino Lippi (1457–1504), the progeny of Fra Filippo and his nun, Lucrezia; and the fierce energy of the nude in action as studied by Antonio Pollaiuolo (1432–98), the better of two brothers.

None, however, could match the intelligent curiosity of the young Leonardo da Vinci (1452–1519). When he was only about twenty years old he assisted his master, the powerful sculptor Verrocchio, in painting a picture of the Baptism of Christ; the angel head and landscape added by the youth at once eclipsed all competition in delicate loveliness.

Leonardo's restless mind ranged over experiments and inventions of every kind. As his inspiration raced ahead of his hand an impatience with the craft of painting led to the cascade of ideas which he poured forth in the *Adoration of the Magi,* only to leave the picture an incomplete sketch when he abruptly departed for Milan in 1482 to concentrate on science and technology. In this alien and unsophisticated environment he painted only occasionally but none the less produced the first masterpiece of the High Renaissance, his great mural of the *Last Supper.*

Back home art remained almost untouched by Leonardo's enigmatic new style. But its revitalizing force had begun to stir a new spirit, a potential which would soon startle Florentines when a daring young sculptor named Michelangelo Buonarroti (1475–1564) produced a sequence of energetic statues which culminated in the giant figure of *David,* the traditional symbol of heroic Florence confronting its barbaric neighbors. Leonardo's return home in this same year engendered a fierce rivalry between the now aging master and his young challenger, a confrontation which produced big plans but few tangible results. Soon the third of the great masters of the High Renaissance, Raphael Santi of Urbino (1483–1520), joined them and injected his cooly ideal images into the contest.

Meanwhile the warrior Pope Julius II had determined to renew the glories of Papal Rome. His first project was to raze old St. Peter's and replace it with a colossal domed church designed by Donato Bramante (1444–1514) whose ingenious Milanese buildings such as Santa Maria presso Santo Satiro had set a forceful new course for architecture. Although few of his Roman projects were to be realized as planned, Bramante's perfectly balanced Tempietto at San Pietro in Montorio best exemplifies his aims.

In 1508 Julius called Michelangelo and Raphael to Rome. Leonardo soon followed, but his dilatory attention to painting and absorption with science produced few significant works. Julius set the reluctant Michelangelo the herculean task of covering the vast Sistine ceiling with a complex of scenes from the Creation. After four years of protean labor the mighty achievement was unveiled to the astonishment of Pope and public. Raphael's simultaneous fresco cycle in the *Stanze* of the Vatican in which he enobled the Papacy seems by comparison a modest achievement, but its wealth of invention, superb control, and classic poise were to exert an even more powerful influence in the centuries to follow.

Within but a few years Bramante and Raphael were dead, Leonardo had retired to die in France and Michelangelo was frustrated with the work on a monumental tomb for Julius, a bothersome project which was to leave scattered components in various collections but little more than the *Moses* on the stunted monument today in San Pietro in Vincoli. The Golden Age was passing and already stirrings of discomfort, seismic vibrations from the impending Reformation across the Alps, disturbed the ordered optimism of the Renaissance.

Mannerism—The Cinquecento

1503	Death of the Borgia pope, Alexander VI; collapse of his son, Cesare Borgia's, power; election of Julius II (Giuliano della Rovere)
1509	Venice loses Faenza, Rimini and Ravenna to the battling pope
1513	Giovanni di Medici becomes Pope Leo X; Niccolo Machiavelli's (1469–1527) *The Prince,* textbook for Renaissance rulers

1516	Ludovico Ariosto's *Orlando Furioso,* a hugely popular epic poem
1520	Martin Luther excommunicated; 1521 the Diet of Worms marks the beginning of the Reformation
1525	Capture of Francis I of France by Charles V, the Holy Roman Emperor, at Pavia effectively ends France's adventures in Italy until Napoleon
1534	Ignatius of Loyola (1491–1556) founds the Society of Jesus (the Jesuits), to become the main weapon in the Counter Reformation, the struggle against Protestantism
1559	Spain's hold on Italy (especially Naples and Milan) confirmed by the Treaty of Château-Cambrésis; domination lasts until 1713
1564–1642	Galileo, physicist and astronomer holds to his beliefs in the teeth of the Inquisition
1567–1643	Claudio Monteverdi—lays foundation of Italian opera
1571	Battle of Lepanto—great victory of Christian navies over the Turks, but Italian (especially Venetian) rule in the eastern Mediterranean is in decline. Venice loses Cyprus in 1573
1585	Vicenza's *Teatro Olimpico,* first permanent playhouse since classical times, opens with *Oedipus Rex*

Florence, where it had begun, was to see the crisis of Renaissance style. Two young painters led the way in a revolt in which a vibrant and overheated emotionalism created the restlessly expressive—almost neurotic—style we call Mannerism.

Jacopo Pontormo (1494–1556) painted his *Descent from the Cross* in 1525. It now hangs in Santa Felicità in Florence, a florid tangle of writhing form and incandescent color which rotates slowly in a pin-wheel of tormented anguish. His friend Giovanni Battista Rosso's (1494–1540) treatment of the same theme in Orvieto cathedral is a brutal hallucination of abstracted horror. Later in Borgo San Sepolcro he painted the subject once again, this time as a ghastly nightmare haunted by demonic masks. In Siena, Domenico Beccafumi (1484–1551) explored a manner of ethereal and ghostly beauty. Introverted and highly personal, Mannerist experiment suggests anxiety and alienation in a key familiar to modern man.

Michelangelo himself created a thunderous vision of apocalyptic *Judgement* on the altar wall of the Sistine Chapel and his restless *Medici Tombs* in Florence mirror the spiritual turmoil of the times, but his heroic challenge grew deeper with old age and concluded with the profoundly moving *Pietàs* in Florence cathedral museum and at the Castello Sforzesco in Milan.

In time Mannerism lapsed itself into formula and pedantry from which only the most talented could forge a personal idiom. Giulio Romano (1492–1546), one of Raphael's chief assistants, exploited ingenious illusionistic tricks at the Palazzo del Te in Mantua; Francesco Salviati (1510–63) festooned the Sala del Udienza of Florence's Palazzo Vecchio with ceremonial narrative histories, and Agnolo Bronzino's (1503–72) coldly brilliant portraits in the Uffizi exemplify the proud formality of the era. In sculpture the rhetoric of Benvenuto Cellini (1500–71), whether in large scale works such as his *Perseus,* or in small, such as his superb salt cellar, or even in his celebrated *Autobiography,* is impressively daring—as are the spiraling contortions of Giambologna (1529–1608).

As the Church Militant embarked on the Counter Reformation, Vignola (1507–73) gave it an appropriate architectural setting with the Church of Il Gesù in Rome, but an even more enduring model was created by the fecund inventiveness of Michele Sanmicheli (1484–1559) in Verona, with his penchant for fortress-like structures and strong ornament, and the lovely villas and the festive churches which Andrea Palladio (1508–80) built in Vicenza, Venice and the surrounding countryside.

In Venice the unfathomable mystery of Giorgione (1476–1510), by turns austere and remote—in the Castelfranco *Madonna*—or pastoral and intimate—in the *Tempesta* in Venice's Accademia—parallels the ideal forms of the High Renaissance in Central Italy, but in the softly inflected cantilena of the Venetian dialect. When his brief decade of creativity was cut short by the plague in 1510, Giorgione's leadership was assumed by Titian (Tiziano Vecelli, 1487–1576), whose extroverted sensuality gave a dynamic propulsion to Venetian painting, most evident in the buoyant swirl of the *Assumption of the Virgin* (1518) in the Frari Church. Although the impact of Mannerism is perceptible in Titian's powerful ceiling paintings in the Church of the Salute, his healthy naturalism avoided stereotypes to arrive at a new depth of feeling in the Accademia *Pietà*, a glowing farewell, left unfinished at his death, by one of the supreme and most productive masters of painting.

Among the painters of the younger generation Paolo Veronese (1528–88) conserved the classical spirit, enriching it with a sumptuous display of physical beauty and radiant color. His decorative ensembles in Venice's San Sebastiano and the airy Palladian Villa Barbaro at Maser are serenely festive, and other of his huge canvasses can be seen in most of the world's national galleries. Jacopo Bassano (1510–92) gave biblical themes the touching realism of everyday life and immortalized the country landscape of the Venetian Arc, his native region. Jacopo Tintoretto (1518–94) climaxed—and in effect ended—the Venetian Renaissance with his volcanic explosions which engulf the ornate interiors of the Palazzo Ducale and the Scuola di San Rocco. By 1600 the routine acres of canvas scattered throughout the churches of Venice by Palma il Giovane (1544–1628) had suffocated the tradition.

Art and architecture seemed to have sunk into lethargy in the later years of the 16th century. Only a fresh view of traditional values and a thoroughgoing reform could restore the artists' confidence. This came with the Caracci family in provincial Bologna. Annibale (1560–1609); its greatest member, migrated to Rome where, with such epic works as the frescoed ceiling of the Palazzo Farnese, he returned a fresh and tasteful buoyancy to the legacy of Raphael and Michelangelo. By contrast the roistering and unruly life style of Michelangelo Merisi da Caravaggio (1571–1610) produced an art which, in its unflinching truthfulness, came to influence realist painting throughout Europe, and has made him one of the most popular painters to modern eyes.

Baroque and Beyond

1600s	*Period of nepotistic popes*—the Barberini, Borghese etc.— playing at family favorites. Also the century of *bravos* (professional thugs) and *banditi* (troops of brigands), usually for hire
1645–69	Venice versus the Turks—Venice loses Crete
1647	Naples—Masaniello's abortive revolt against Spanish rule
1691–1700	Innocent XII cleans up the papacy
1713	House of Savoy gets Sicily at Treaty of Utrecht; 1720 exchanges it for Sardinia
1734	Bourbons take over Kingdom of Naples and rule, with interruptions, until 1860

1796–1814   *The Napoleonic Period*—1796, Napoleon (aged 27) campaigns in Lombardy; 1797 Venice surrenders to France; Napoleon creates a series of republics in Italy—the Ligurian Republic (Genoa), the Cisalpine Republic (including Lombardy, Emilia, Romagna, and western Venetia. Naples was the only part of Italy to defy Napoleon, but became the Parthenopean Republic in defeat. 1799 Pius VI taken to France where he died; 1808 Napoleon occupies Rome and Murat becomes King of Naples; 1809 France annexes the Papal States; 1812 Pius VII also taken to France, but lives to return. During the Napoleonic period Italy was comparatively well governed, with new roads, canals, the Code Napoléon. For the first time since the ancient Romans, Italy assumed—though by force—a unity.

Baroque sculpture owes its impetus to Gianlorenzo Bernini (1598–1680). His *Apollo and Daphne,* today with several other of his masterpieces in Rome's Borghese Gallery, exploits an unmatched technical facility to project a dazzlingly expansive effect of motion and emotion. As an impresario of all the arts he combined media to spectacular effect in the altar tabernacle and throne shrine in St. Peter's and the emotionally volatile *Ecstasy of Santa Teresa* in Santa Maria della Vittoria. His fountains lend a festive and cooling note to many of Rome's piazzas. Unlike Bernini, his contemporary Francesco Borromini (1599–1667) is intimate and convoluted in style, delighting in the intricate spatial effects of San Carlo alle Quattro Fontane and Sant' Ivo. He spawned an active school, especially in far off Turin where Guarini (1624–83) carried on his picturesque ideas.

For a century the operatic spectacle of Baroque art enriched the peninsula with such splendors as the Versailles-like palace and gardens at Caserta, the bubble domes of the Salute church in Venice, and the acrobatic ceilings of Guercino (1591–1666), Guido Reni (1575–1642), Pietro da Cortona (1596–1669) and a host of other inspired decorators. But like the Renaissance, the Italian Baroque gradually wound down and underwent a metamorphosis in the early 18th century. In place of civic grandeur and religious fervor Italians began to prefer a quieter and more sophisticated elegance better suited to their restricted finances and diminished international influence.

Charm and leisure were turned to accommodate the hordes of travelers for whom Italy was the goal of the fashionable Grand Tour. No city outdid Venice in permissiveness. In this pre-postcard era her view painters, Canaletto (1697–1768) and Guardi (1712–93), caught the nostalgic aura of the pink and blue sea-washed city in paintings to be brought home as souvenirs. Artificial and perhaps a bit tawdry in its sunset glow, Venice was still to produce one last burst of creative brilliance in Tiepolo (1696–1770). His magical transformations dissolved the walls of Rococo interiors into cloud buoyed visions of lovely goddesses and untroubled heroes.

But the modern world was knocking in the person of Napoleon, and it was almost with relief that the weary princedoms left the stage and returned the darkened theater to its memories. Legend has it that Italian art ceased about 1800. Like most legends this one is only partly true. With most of Europe Italy embraced the stern principles of French Neo-Classicism, but the sculptor Antonio Canova (1757–1822) gave it a frigidly voluptuous tone best seen in the Borghese *Venus,* surprisingly, a portrait of Napoleon's sister, Pauline Bonaparte. Canova designed a new type of tomb of which his own monument in Venice's Frari church is typical, chaste and austere in its mock pyramid and marble mourners, yet uneasily realistic and sexual in its oblique implications. His clay models, largely preserved in his studio in Possagno near Venice, are more spontaneous and inspired. A parallel with his style can be found in the severe architecture of Japelli (1783–1852), Valadier (1762–1839) and Quarenghi (1744–1817). Painters of the time such as Andrea Appiani (1754–1817), Napoleon's court painter in Italy, and Francesco Hayez (1791–1882), Italy's leading Romantic painter, are perhaps less inventive.

The Risorgimento

1815	Congress of Vienna splits Italy again; Austria gets Lombardy-Venetia, but controls most of Italy. For three decades various parts of the country revolt against foreign rule
1840s	Arrival of the railway, forging new inter-regional links
1848	The Year of Revolutions all over Europe and especially in Italy (Venice, Rome, Milan and Naples)
1849	Pius IX restored by French troops; Austria beats Garibaldi and regains Venice; Vittorio Emanuele II becomes king
1854	Under Cavour, Piedmont joins the Crimean War
1856–60	France and Piedmont unite against Austria; 1860 much of Italy joins them; Garibaldi and his 1,000 invade Sicily and Naples
1861	Kingdom of Italy declared, capital in Turin
1865	Florence becomes the capital
1867	Garibaldi defeated in a march on Rome
1870	Rome becomes the capital and the final unification of Italy is achieved
1882	Garibaldi dies
1883	Benito Mussolini is born

Although the overstuffed rhetoric of the mid-19th century endowed Italy with its share of outsized white elephants, such extravaganzas as Rome's shimmering Vittorio Emanuele Monument have taken on an affectionate aura in our no-nonsense time. Victorian painters were more clear-sighted and a group called the *macchiaioli* (spatterers) produced frank and handsome landscapes, especially those of the Florentine Giovanni Fattori (1825–1908). The gently impressionist sculpture of Medardo Rosso (1858–1928) provides a foil to the chic dash of Giovanni Boldini's (1845–1931) society portraits.

Modern Italy

1880s	Italy joins scramble for colonies in Africa, gets Somaliland and Eritrea. 1896 Italian army annihilated at Adowa trying to take Ethiopia
1900	King Umberto assassinated; Vittorio Emanuele III becomes King
1900s	Period of strikes; 1907 general strike in Milan
1911	War with Turkey; Italy gains Libya, Cyrenaica and the Dodecanese Islands
1915	Italy signs secret Treaty of London and then openly enters World War I on the side of Britain, France and Russia
1917	Defeat of Italians at Caporetto followed by rout of 400,000 Italian troops; heroic stand reverses situation.
1919	d'Annunzio seizes Fiume; Mussolini founds Fascists (23rd March) in Milan

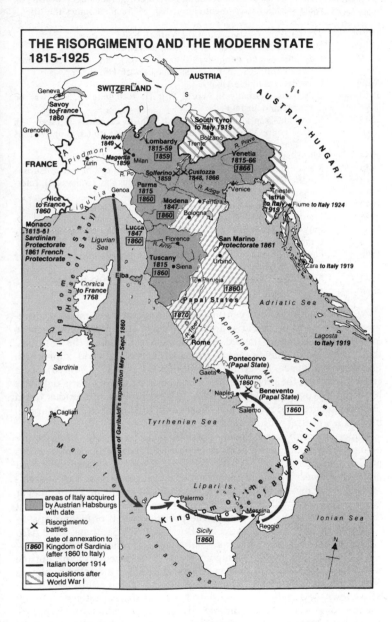

THE RISORGIMENTO AND THE MODERN STATE
1815-1925

areas of Italy acquired
by Austrian Habsburgs
with date

× Risorgimento
battles

1860 date of annexation to
Kingdom of Sardinia
(after 1860 to Italy)

Italian border 1914

acquisitions after
World War I

1922	National strike broken by the Fascists; Mussolini's March on Rome; he becomes head of coalition government; in the next few years all democratic government eliminated; Mussolini assumes the title of *Il Duce*
1929	The Lateran Treaty creates the Vatican State
1934	Hitler and Mussolini's first meeting in Venice
1935	Italy attacks and conquers Ethiopia; Vittorio Emanuele II assumes title of Emperor of Ethiopia; alliance with Hitler
1939	Mussolini occupies Albania
1940	Italy joins Germany in World War II; 10th June declares war on France and Britain
1943	Mussolini's son-in-law, Ciano, and Vittorio Emanuele II (aged 74), stage coup; Mussolini arrested on 25th July; Italians now victims of their German allies
1944	Allied landings at Anzio; Rome surrenders 4th June
1945	Mussolini captured and killed by anti-Fascists; end of war in Europe
1946	Vittorio Emanuele III abdicates in favor of his son, Umberto II; referendum votes for a republic
1947	Allied peace treaty with Italy; she loses all her colonies
1954	Trieste area divided between Italy and Yugoslavia
1957	Italy becomes one of the founder members of the EEC, established by the Treaty of Rome
1966	Floods in northern and central Italy, especially Florence, destroy many art treasures
1978	Aldo Moro kidnapped and assassinated by the Red Brigade
1980	Naples and the Campania hard-hit by severe earthquakes.

At the beginning of our century, as Cubism and other modern movements were emerging in Paris, another group of Italian painters began to experiment in depicting the old theme of movement. Called the Futurists, they explored a dynamic range of sequential action and vivid color which had a wide influence. Severini (1883–1966), Boccioni (1882–1916), Balla (1871–1958) and their associates can best be seen at the Galleria dell'Arte Moderna in Rome. De Chirico (1888–1978) depicted a mysterious world of empty squares and mannequin figures akin to Surrealism, and Morandi imbued his neutral still life pictures with a tender life.

Under Fascism experimental painting declined, but architecture bloomed into a pompous official style which survives in the desolate vistas of Cinecittà near Rome. Stylistically vapid, Fascist architecture at least indulged engineering and in the postwar period spawned such great architects as Pier Luigi Nervi (b. 1891). His exposition halls in Turin, hangar at Orbetello, sport palaces in Rome and the new Papal Audience Hall at the Vatican are a dizzying ode to the poetic potential of technology.

A small number of painters such as Burri (b. 1915), Santomaso and Afro (1912–76) have attracted international attention in the past few decades, while the work of Pietro Annigoni (b. 1910) represents to the outside world a kind of Renaissance man reborn. A group of attractive sculptors of which Manzù (b. 1908), Greco (b. 1913) and Marini (1901–80) are the best known—especially because they have had some prestigious church commissions—and widely admired. By and large Italian contemporary artists have become more cosmopolitan, and the greater mobility of the young has resulted in an exodus of talent to other artistic centers of Europe, notably Munich, London, Paris and Amsterdam; while the gulf they have left is filled to overflowing with young foreign artists irresistibly attracted to Italy, their spiritual home. Op Art, Pop Art, Minimal Art . . .

all have had their day in the Italian avant-garde, as in progressive circles the world over. Ask the Italian-in-the-street who represents the purest traditions of his country today and he will probably answer: "Henry Moore" (the British sculptor whom Florence adores).

Painters young and old, conventional and aggressively "modern", are found in most Italian towns and villages, inhabiting gaunt medieval tenements, ramshackle farmhouses, mountain eyries and seaside chalets. One group of four has lived and worked for some years in a boat, propelling it from harbor to harbor and setting up floating exhibitions. Schools of painters have taken over remote islands, and their canvases are the whitewashed walls of fisherman's cottages. On a summer Sunday you can scarcely drive a dozen miles in Italy without coming to a painting exhibition in a community hall, devoted to local talent, much of it genuine peasant work in the primitive style of Grandma Moses.

There, as in the great galleries, you are aware of the strong color sense, the adventurousness of Italian art. The tradition is widely diffused, perhaps diluted, but it is certainly too early to write its obituary. That has been done periodically over the past twenty centuries, inevitably to the chagrin of the mistaken commentator. In the midst of the burgeoning vitality which charms and occasionally maddens the visitor the arts are not long to be neglected. Italians live the tradition too deeply.

ITALIAN OPERA

Passion on the High C's

by
LESLIE GARDINER

Italian music, fully as much as Italian art, has become part of the common cultural heritage throughout the world. It is not only the international staple of hundreds of opera companies, but the unconscious possession of all who whistle a Neapolitan folk song or tap their feet to the Grand March from *Aïda*. And it is no accident that one of those examples is from opera—Italian music is synonymous with what Dr. Johnson called "that exotic and irrational entertainment."

Opera had its origin in Florence where a group of Humanists who called themselves the Camerata hoped to revive classic Greek and Roman drama by combining theater and music in Peri's *Dafne*, first heard in 1597. From this primitive beginning it was only a decade until Claudio Monteverdi (1567–1643) created the first operatic masterpiece, *Orfeo*, an entertainment for the Gonzaga court at Mantua. The new fashion spread rapidly and found an enthusiastic public in pleasure-loving Venice where by mid-century at least eleven opera houses were in simultaneous operation. Monteverdi had moved there in 1613 and produced a long series of masses, motets, madrigals, ballets and operas. His powerfully dramatic *Incoronazione di Poppea,* one of the scant three of his operas for which we have a surviving score, was premiered in 1642, the year before his death. Monteverdi's followers, especially the talented Cavalli (1602–76), rode an international wave of popularity which carried opera throughout Europe and gave every Italian city its enthusiastic fans, in particular Naples which supplanted Venice as the opera capital in the 18th century.

Composed for intimate theaters, Baroque opera stages badly when performed, as it usually is in Italy, in a house seating several thousand people. Aside from an occasional reverent essay in archeological restoration which misses the fire and drama of the original, Monteverdi and his heirs are too often heard in performances tainted by the more strenuous performance tradition of later music-drama.

By the mid-18th century the opera craze had placed such emphasis on lavish spectacle and the vocal pyrotechnics of the fashionable *castrati* that musical values tended to become superficial and routine. A fresh breath of humor was introduced by the comic interlude played between the acts of the ponderous classic dramas. These *opera buffa* short diversions increased in scale with Pergolesi (1710–36), Cimarosa (1749–1801) and Paisiello (1740–1816) to become full length comedies in their own right. The best place to hear these delightful romps as well as other small-scale Baroque operas is Milan's small auditorium, the Piccola Scala, named after its great neighbor.

The Lifeblood of Italy

But opera in the present-day sense, the opera of the past 180 years—the opera that people, rightly or wrongly, call "grand" opera—is even more naturally associated with the Italians than was the Baroque kind. They invented it. It is an art form peculiarly suited to their temperament. Sung in Italian, with Italian orchestras, conductors, designers and above all producers, it has achieved its truest expression. For the most blasé theatergoer, a visit to the Italian opera is a unique experience. (And an expensive one: at La Scala in Milan you may pay fifty dollars for a seat.)

Italian opera is not to every non-Italian's taste. Some think stylized acting and great singing a bad mixture esthetically; some are embarrassed by the naked emotion of it and the cliché sentimentality or incomprehensibility of the plots; and some ridicule the conventions which permit a dying heroine to rise and sing a powerful aria and perhaps an encore before lying down again to die, or a tenor to waste precious minutes (as he does in *Trovatore*) singing over and over again to his companions that mother is burning to death and there is not a moment to lose. In fact, *Trovatore* has taken more than its share of abuse for the sheer absurdity of its plot, but daft or not it contains some of the most spine-tingling music in all opera.

Riding on stirring or syrupy music, the stories are frequently violent and sexual and it has been pointed out that, if the censor dealt with opera as he does with motion pictures, only one well-known work (not an Italian one) would be passed for universal exhibition.

But, whatever foreigners may think, opera is the Italian's cultural lifeblood, a reflection of the drama of his existence, a sublimation of his personal mythology; his melodrama, burlesque, pantomime, circus and celebrity concert rolled into one. It is an art medium which grows neither old nor old-fashioned. Unfortunately, what it does is grow more expensive. If anything will kill opera it is economics. The sheer size of the production costs, added to the expense of orchestra, chorus and grotesquely inflated star fees will almost certainly spell the deathknell of the art.

Bel Canto and the Prima Donna

For the ordinary music-lover, Italian operatic history begins with the melodious trio of Rossini (1792–1868), Bellini (1801–1835) and Donizetti (1797–1848). There is a tendency to sneer at the naïve plots and barrel-organ choruses of these pioneer composers and their librettists. It is hard to recapture the mid-19th century's passionate enthusiasm for spotless village maidens, noble prigs and unconvincing villains, the stock characters of the opera. We are more sophisticated now. Yet the sparkle of Rossini, the melodious tenderness of Bellini, the perennially rich lyricism of Donizetti, the arias crystal-clear, the recitative natural and sweet . . . these qualities, applied to the hackneyed little dramas of the times, immortalized them and can still touch the heart. The *bel canto* style—in which libretto and dramatic tension are sacrificed to virtuoso singing, and strict convention gives a certain number of set-piece arias to each singer, depending on the importance of the role—slowly passed out of fashion. The arias survive and, on the techniques those singers developed to cope with them, later composers were able to build.

Bel canto, a strictly Italian phenomenon, produced a typically Italian human being: the prima donna, haughty, tempestuous, temperamental, singer and actress combined, a despot in all her glory before whom even principal tenors (themselves a byword for pride and vanity) had to bow. Other lands acclaimed their Edmund Keans and Henry Irvings . . . Italy had her Giulia Grisi, Giuditta Pasta, Emma Nevada and Adelina Patti; and, among great 19th-century tenors, Giovanni Rubini, Luigi Lablache, Antonio Tamburini and the ever-memorable Cavaliere Mario. Operas were sometimes written for a particular diva: Bellini designed *Sonnambula* for Madame Pasta, for example, and afterwards transposed the whole thing to suit Maria Malibran, with whom he was in love.

The prima donna as a specimen of humankind in full, overblown excess is virtually an extinct species. Leading singers' voices are almost certainly every bit as good, and probably better, than they were in the high and holy days of Patti and Melba, but the behavior which theater staff and audience alike were prepared to stomach has more or less disappeared. There are still heavyweight tenors who can cancel appearances on a whim, but in modern circumstances it is not a ploy that they can get away with too often. Also the present-day demand for singers who can both act and look the part of the characters they are representing has bred a generation of divas and leading men whose intelligence predisposes them to avoid the old-fashioned, over-the-top emotional excesses.

Viva Verdi

On the heels of Giuseppe Verdi (1813–1901), a new class of operagoer arrived. Intellectuals suddenly decided that this mass spectator entertainment was no longer to be despised. Verdi introduced nobler themes and a grander style. His librettists told more credible stories. Verdi's strong plots and sincere emotions, sincerely and artistically handled, illuminated Italian opera with a brilliance which eclipsed anything that had gone before. Early Verdi is characterized by rhythmic ingenuity and splendid orchestration. The operas of his middle period—*Rigoletto, La Traviata, Il Trovatore, La Forza del Destino, Aïda*—have been for more than a hundred years the dazzling epitome of what we think of as "grand" opera, Italian style. His later work is notable for its dramatic vocal melodies and its prophetic vision of the modern principle that musical instruments, as well as voices, should have their full share in interpreting the moods and emotions of the opera. His last, and possibly greatest, opera, *Falstaff,* written when he was 79, exemplifies the concepts of music drama every bit as well as the more bombastic works of Wagner who died ten years before *Falstaff* appeared.

Verdi's "tunes" (many are no more than that) are simple and catchy. The original cast of *Rigoletto* was warned not to hum *La Donna è Mobile* in public, in case the public tired of it before they heard it. But those simple tunes are not weak or banal; they have the glamor of genuine feeling in them, and Verdi is at his most impressive when embroidering them vocally and instrumentally. *La Donna è Mobile* has survived for more than a century, and we are not tired of it yet.

No composer, perhaps, has been more acclaimed in his lifetime. The word Verdi happened to be an acronym for the name of the future monarch of a united Italy, and "Verdi! Verdi!" at the opera house was both a call for the maestro and a battle cry of the Risorgimento: "*V*ittore *E*manuele, *R*e *D'I*talia".

Realism

As the great sun of Verdi set, a constellation of new stars ascended. (We are now at the end of the 19th century.) Leoncavallo (1858–1919) and Mascagni (1863–1945) were one-opera men—the short but perennially popular *Pagliacci* and *Cavalleria Rusticana* respectively. Boito (1842–1918), who wrote several of Verdi's libretti, is best known for *Mefistofele.* Cilea (1866–1950), a Calabrian, had the southerner's yearning for strong effects, but handled his tragic themes with restraint and delicacy. Of his five "gracious sisters", *Gina, Tilda, Arlesiana, Gloria* and *Adriana Lecouvreur* (all tragedies of hopeless love), only the last-named is more or less regularly revived.

These composers ushered in *verismo,* "realism", against violent diehard opposition. Giordano brought bicycles on stage in his opera *Fedora;* Leoncavallo introduced a live donkey in *Pagliacci.*

The newcomer whose picturesque and confident treatment of unlikely themes from legend, biography and stage tragedy earned him (after some initial resistance) a fame almost equal to Verdi's was Giacomo Puccini (1853–1925). It was in their Puccini roles that our fathers and grandfathers remembered the household names of yesterday—Caruso, Melba, Geraldine Farrar, Emmy Destin, Tetrazzini, Gigli—and in the same operas we have acclaimed the great singers of our own times—Callas, di Stefano, Tito Gobbi, Sutherland, Renata Scotto, Placido Domingo. Operas such as *La Bohème, Madame Butterfly, Tosca* and *Turandot* are the firmest of favorites in Italy and abroad, and with Puccini's freshness and sureness of romantic touch they continue to mediate in the conflicting storms of changing taste.

Opera Today

Italians are conservative about their opera, and no living composer has been elected to the pantheon which Verdi and Puccini knew in their lifetimes. There are few likely candidates. One possibility is the American Giancarlo Menotti (b. 1911), whose immensely successful *The Medium* and *The Consul,* first performed in New York just after the war, seemed to give Italian opera new vigor.

Menotti represents the contemporary Italian maestro-of-all-trades: composor, conductor, impresario. And perhaps his fame to posterity will rest as solidly on his organization of the "Two Worlds" music festival at Spoleto as on his musicianship.

The music festivals enable visitors to Italy to see authentic opera, with star singers under the batons of internationally famous conductors—the heirs of Toscanini—such as Muti, Abbado, Giulini and Alberto Erede. The most prominent opera festivals are the "Two Worlds" mentioned above (June, July at Spoleto, also includes ballet, drama, etc.) and the Maggio Musicale Fiorentino (May and June, Florence).

The official opera season is early December to mid-April. The principal opera houses are La Scala (Milan), Teatro dell' Opera (Rome), La Fenice (Venice), Teatro Comunale (Florence) and San Carlo (Naples). The audience's dress and jewelry on première nights matches the extravagant internal décor and, under huge clusters of candelabra, a full house resembles an overflowing basket of flowers—a sight to remember, even before the curtain has gone up.

Performances last all evening, with lengthy intervals. Despite the formality of the occasion, audiences are noisy and uninhibited, especially in the "second league" of opera houses, which includes the Teatro Comunale of Genoa, Teatro Regio of Parma, Teatro Massimo of Palermo, Teatro Bellini of Catania and Teatro Giuseppe Verdi of Trieste. As with old provincial music-halls, each opera house has its tradition of critical appreciation; of the Parma opera house (where Toscanini was schooled) many tales are told concerning young hopes blighted and promising careers wrecked.

Nowadays the tourists keep opera alive financially, chiefly at the summer openair spectacles, done with typical *floridezza* at the Arena of Verona (July, August), the Baths of Caracalla in Rome (July, August), the Arena Flegrea in Naples (July), the Sferisterio at Macerata (July) and intermittently in the Castello Sforzesco of Milan.

At that season the "grand" opera houses are under dust-sheets, looking forlorn, and their exuberant Baroque facades cast shadows on workmen playing cards; but you can visit them, and try out the acoustics from their vast sloping stages, and return home boasting that you've sung at La Scala or the San Carlo. Occasionally, strolling the back streets of old towns, you hear pouring out from a hundred radio sets in a hundred tiny houses the well-loved passages from *Rigoletto, Butterfly* and *Lucia di Lammermoor.* Such is the commitment of the middle-aged and elderly to their beloved Verdi, Puccini and Donizetti. It must be said that you don't hear this when there are young people in the house, when there are football matches or quiz shows on the television channels.

ITALIAN FOOD

And—It's Good for You!

Gourmets and dieticians are getting all the credit for what tourists have known all along: *la cucina italiana* is a remarkable blend of fresh ingredients and straightforward culinary techniques that is not only tasty and tempting to look at but is healthful, too.

If you really want to experience the joys of authentic Italian food, don't limit yourself to hotel restaurants, some excellent, most rather dull. With the help of the restaurant lists, seek out the places that serve a hard-to-please local clientele.

Starting the Day

Italians start the day with their usual breakfast of *cappuccino* and *cornetto* (brioche) at the local bar. Then, when mid-morning hunger pangs strike, they go to the nearest bakery for crisp pizza hot from the oven. Pizza recurs throughout the day as a quick snack; there are literally thousands of *pizzerie* where you can buy squares of crusty pizza to carry you through from one meal to another.

On their coffee breaks the Italians take strong *espresso*. They consider the *cappuccino*, half coffee and half frothy milk, strictly for early morning consumption. If they want their coffee diluted, they'll ask for *caffè lungo*, made with more water, or *caffè macchiato* (*espresso* with a splash of milk added at the last minute). *Caffè Hag* is decaffeinated coffee. *Caffè freddo* has little in common with iced coffee; it's more like a coffee syrup served cold, not iced. *Thè freddo*, similarly, is pre-sweetened and not iced. Ice is something Italians use very little of. Except in top hotels and restaurants, if you ask for ice you're likely to get two tiny, oddly-shaped pieces grudgingly pried from the establishment's single ice tray. It's for your own good, the Italians would say: iced drinks are harmful, they upset the all-important digestion and can cause collapse. It's not easy to get a really cold beer, either.

If you have continental breakfast at your hotel, it will consist of *caffè latte* (coffee with hot milk), or *thè* (tea) or *cioccolato* (hot chocolate) if you prefer, with bread or rolls, butter and jam. Top-rank hotels may also offer a full breakfast menu, à la carte.

Pasta, Polenta and Rice

In theory, the main meals, lunch and dinner, consist of several courses. They start with *antipasto (hors d'oeuvre).* In its simplest form, *antipasto* usually consists of a few slices of *salame* and *prosciutto* with olives, pickled mushrooms or vegetables and a butter curl (butter isn't served with bread anywhere in Italy, except in the most tourist-conscious places). Some restaurants are famed for their *antipasto* tables, where there may be as many as sixty varieties of tantalizing treats. In such places even some Italian customers prefer to make a meal of the *antipasto* and leave it at that. One summertime delicacy is *melone* (chilled melon) or *fichi* (ripe figs) with *prosciutto.*

An important part of the menu is the entrée. It may be *minestra* (soup), either thick vegetable soup such as minestrone, or broth with rice or *pastina* (tiny forms of *pasta);* or it may be *asciutta* (dry entrée). This could be risotto, rice cooked in broth with one of many different condiments. Or it could be *pasta,* which along with *pizza,* has conquered the palates of the Western world—and beyond.

Pasta comes in infinite varieties and is served with an equally varied range of sauces. *Spaghetti* and *linguine* are long, thin types; *rigatoni* and *penne* are short and tube-like in form; *fettuccine* and *tagliatelle* are ribbon-like and are generally made with eggs. Green pasta, such as *tagliatelle verdi,* is egg pasta to which chopped spinach is added for color and flavor. The more complicated forms include *ravioli, agnolotti, cannelloni* and *cappelletti* or *tortellini;* all are shaped in different ways but are always stuffed with a meat or cheese mixture. Try any kind of egg pasta (especially *tortellini) alla panna,* that is, in a delicate sauce of fresh cream. *Gnocchi* are tiny dumplings of semolina and potatoes, served as a first course with a rich sauce and lots of cheese.

In the north, people prefer *polenta,* a cornmeal mush, to pasta. *Polenta* is good, too, if it's cut when cold then toasted on the grill. Northerners also prefer *risotto,* which should be served steaming hot and thick with generous amounts of whatever its special condiment may be—saffron for *risotto alla milanese,* mushrooms for *risotto ai funghi,* chicken livers for *risotto alla finanziera.* Venice has its own variation on the theme: *risi e bisi,* a dense risotto with peas.

Butter is widely used in northern Italian cooking, while olive oil is favored in the south. If you get a chance, try *bruschetta,* a thick slice of country-style bread toasted on the grill, rubbed with garlic and doused with olive oil and salt. Many rustic restaurants serve *bruschetta* as an appetizer. It's simple but delicious, especially with local wine.

With pasta as its staple, southern Italian cooking relies heavily on tomatoes as a condiment; vegetables such as artichokes and eggplant are added to give distinctive flavor.

By the way, parmesan cheese isn't usually served with pasta *alla puttanesca, alla marinara, al pesto,* or with any kind of fish sauce. You'll find it used in abundance, however, in the specialties of the Bolognese cuisine, which is recognized as the best in Italy and one of the world's finest. Parmesan is a natural accompaniment to *pasta al ragù alla bolognese;* ragù is a thick meat sauce, knowingly flavored. Parmesan is also used in the mixture that goes into Bologna's famous *tortellini* and *agnolotti.*

What's known abroad as "romano" cheese is really *pecorino,* a hard sharp cheese produced in the area around Rome. It's used to enhance the stronger flavors of *amatriciana* and *carbonara* sauces. Cheese-lovers should search the menu for pasta dishes *ai quattro formaggi,* a sauce that blends four cheeses into a delectable creaminess. Especially popular during the summer months is a spaghetti sauce made of chopped, uncooked tomatoes with a hint of garlic and a touch of basil, light and refreshing; it may be called *spaghetti alla checca* or *al pomodoro crudo.*

Meat Dishes and Pizza

Next comes the main course, either *pesce* (fish) or *carne* (meat). Ready-to-serve dishes are listed as *piatti del giorno* (the day's special). Although good beef is hard to come by in Italy there are some exceptions, and many restaurants are known for their top-quality meat. Florentine steaks are tender and tasty. Italian cooks do wonders with veal, pork, poultry and lamb, all of which you may order *alla griglia* (grilled or charcoal-broiled), *arrosto* (roasted) or in a variety of sauces. A *cotoletta alla milanese* is a breaded veal chop, while a *cotoletta alla bolognese* is a breaded veal cutlet served with tomato sauce and melted *mozzarella. Pollo* or *coniglio* (chicken or rabbit) *alla cacciatora* is sautéed in red or white wine with garlic and rosemary; some cooks add a splash of vinegar. *Pollo alla diavola* is grilled chicken. *Petto* (breast) of chicken or *tacchino* (turkey) appears on menus in a number of versions. Save for the exceptions mentioned above, a *bistecca* is usually a tough and disappointing slice of meat that has nothing whatsoever to do with a steak as you know it. In some areas a pork chop is called a *bistecca di maiale; lombata* or *braciola* are more specific terms for a chop. Some flavorful variations on the meat menu are *brasato* (braised meat), *spezzatino* (stew), and *involtini* or *bauletti* (roulades).

Strictly speaking, pizza is an entrée, though most tourists find it quite satisfactory as a one-dish meal. The commonest type is *pizza alla napoletana,* with tomatoes, mozzarella cheese, anchovies and a sprinkling of oregano. *Pizza alla margherita* has more mozzarella and no anchovies. *Pizza ai funghi,* with mushrooms, and *pizza alla capricciosa,* with a topping of prosciutto, egg, and olives, are other favorites. (Similar dishes to order at a *pizzeria* are *crostini,* rounds of bread topped with mozzarella and baked in the oven, and *calzone,* an oven-baked envelope of thin dough containing mozzarella and prosciutto.

Fish, Vegetables, Fruit and Cheese

From the Mediterranean and the lakes come fish of all kinds. Try *gamberi* (shrimp) or *scampi* (prawns) and *polipo* (octopus). *Triglie alla li-*

vornese, (mullet in tomato sauce), *pesce spada* (swordfish), and *calamari* (squid) appear on most menus. *Spigola* (bass) and *dentice* (bream) can be expensive choices. Sadly, it has to be admitted that you would be wise to think very carefully before launching into an appetizing-looking dish of shellfish. The days are well past when Mediterranean shellfish was totally safe, and—especially when on vacation—this is one area where discretion is the better part of valor.

Vegetables range from showy red *peperoni* (peppers) and *carciofi* (artichokes) to tiny fresh *piselli* (peas) and *cipolline* (little onions). Greens are served *all'agro* (boiled and dressed with olive oil and lemon), *al burro* (sautéed in butter) or *passati in padella* (sautéed in oil, sometimes with garlic). Salads are usually simple; in season, from June through September, tomatoes can be sublime.

Italians like to finish off their meals with fruit; a full dinner would also include cheese and a sweet. Among the best-known cheeses are *groviera,* *fontina* and *caciotta,* all mild; *provolone,* either mild (*dolce*) or sharp (*piccante*); caciocavallo, a mild cheese found in the South; *gorgonzola,* a soft blue cheese; and the ubiquitous *parmigiano. Mozzarella,* by the way, appears as an antipasto, never at the close of a meal.

If the prospect of eating this much appalls you, you'll take comfort in the fact that not even the Italians eat this way any more, except on special occasions. Some exponents of *la nuova cucina,* the Italian version of *nouvelle cuisine,* have gone so far as to eliminate pasta from their menus, arousing the ire and disdain of traditionalists.

The Finishing Touch

One thing everyone agrees on is the excellence of *gelato* (Italian icecream), often served *affogato*—literally, "drowned" in whisky—as a dessert. As a between-meals treat you may order your *gelato con panna* (with whipped cream) in a *cono* (cone) or *coppa* (cup). A *cassata* is the familiar ice-cream bomb made of frozen whipped cream, candied fruit and *gelato,* while a *semifreddo* can be anything from a frozen mousse to an ice-cream cake. Not strictly an ice-cream, a *granita* is composed of fine crystals of ice, either coffee or lemon-flavored, and is served in a glass.

You will find sections on each regional cuisine at the beginning of the Hotel and Restaurant listings in the *Practical Information* sections at the end of every chapter. The variations you will encounter as you travel around Italy are considerable and fascinating. The one thing that does not vary is the unswerving loyalty that regional cooks show to the use of fresh ingredients and traditional methods of preparation, many of which go back at least to the Middle Ages.

ITALIAN WINE

History in Your Glass

by
PAMELA VANDYKE PRICE

Pamela Vandyke Price is a noted British writer on wine. She has published twenty-one books on the subject, her latest being The Penguin Wine Book. *Her writing, broadcasting, and lecturing on wine and wine-related subjects has won her several awards, both French and British.*

Italy and its islands constitute one great wine-flask! Not only is wine made in every province—a wide range of wines—but a wide variety of spinoff delights, vermouths, spirits and liqueurs, are also available. It's a country where, as Italians will tell you, they thank God for wine—and they make so much of it that they jostle France for being the world's top producer and are in the major league of exporters. France, the U.S., West Germany, Canada and the U.K. are taking more and more from Italy and those lucky enough to travel in the country will treasure many delightful experiences of the wines.

Don't, however, expect most Italians to be too serious about wine. They've been lucky enough to enjoy its pleasures since very early times; the poets of Imperial Rome wrote drinking songs, neatly-turned verses inviting a patron to dinner often included mentions of the wines to be offered. Columella, in the first century A.D., wrote what is still an important

67

work of reference on wine cultivation. Down the ages the nobility and high-ranking ecclesiastics—including the Popes—and the middle classes who made the arts and crafts of Italy world-renowned have all revelled in wine, either the produce of their own estates or, as far as humbler people are concerned, the wines bought "down the road" from a neighboring grower. Today, the wine you enjoy in a top restaurant may also come from "my brother/cousin/friend . . . who has a holding in the best region of . . . ", and it will be presented with as much pride as the well-known and famous names.

Regulations and Controls

Only quite recently did the Italians realize that their wines are capable of competing in world markets, not merely of giving pleasure to Italian communities overseas or tourists. The system of regulation by which their wines are now controlled and labeled is directed from the Italian Ministry of Agriculture in Rome. You are likely to hear the proud assertion that so-and-so is a "DOC" wine: this means that it has achieved the category of *Denominazione di Origine Controllata*—being produced in a defined area, according to the traditional methods established there. If a wine bears the letters DOCG the categorization is even prouder, for the final "G" means *e Guarantita,* signifying that it is a wine produced according to all the previous conditions, plus agreed quality. There are not many of these and, as you might expect, they are unlikely to be cheap! *Barolo, Barbaresco, Brunello di Montalcino* and *Vino Nobile de Montepulciano* were the pioneers of the *DOCG* nobility.

But if a wine hasn't got the DOC this may simply be because there hasn't yet been time for the various procedures involved to be gone through—so don't assume that it isn't a first-rate drink.

One of the most important developments in the Italian wine world has been the way in which many large firms, including many of those engaged in the making of vermouth, have acquired interests in various wine regions; because of their vast technical resources and, often, international links, they have enabled many wine areas and small-scale producers to make excellent wines, suited to world markets. In some parts of Italy, too, the way in which non-Italians have fallen in love with the country and settled there, making wine, has greatly influenced local trends. The British have loved the Chianti country for well over a century, as witness the writers, poets and painters living there and now many Americans are also sharing the enthusiasm for well-made Italian wines by "doing it themselves."

Drink as You Please

There are few conventions surrounding Italian wines. If you enjoy a red wine with fish or white wine with game, go ahead and order it—you'll see plenty of people around you in any restaurant choosing whatever they feel like. The fruity, slightly sparkling red *Lambrusco* is, traditionally, served in its homeland with delectable *zampone*—a stuffed pig's trotter, hot or cold; and *Lacryma Christi,* the white wine made near Naples, can be served at room temperature! Often the very grapey sparkling wines of Asti are offered with rather richly-sauced dishes—first courses with mayonnaise, *vitello-tonnato* and, certainly, with ices and cassata.

It's not usual to decant even the finer Italian red wines but, for the very top examples, it may well be worth while opening them several hours ahead of time. There are some—admittedly, the more special and expensive wines—that may seem disappointing when first poured after the cork is drawn, but then, after twenty-four hours, they develop superbly and impressively. For these delights you should ask advice and, if possible, order well ahead of drinking time.

In most eating-places you can order a single glass of wine, or a carafe or half-carafe, so don't hesitate to ask. And it's also easy to enjoy a glass of one of the many vermouths made in Italy or one of the numerous liqueurs while you rest your feet after some expedition to a museum or art gallery or simply want to enjoy the scenery and the world going by from a cafe table in the sun. Even if you already know and love Italian wines, try to explore the local drinks that, maybe, are not exported—you've many pleasant surprises in store!

Regional Variations

Because of the hundreds of wines made in Italy, space permits mention of only the main regions, where the traveler is likely to find many of great interest. You will find further notes in the *Practical Information* sections together with food for each region under *Regional Specialties.* The more you wander off the beaten track in Italy, the more unusual local wines you will find to enjoy. Never hesitate to adventure an unknown bottle. Here, however, are some of those that are better known.

Piedmont—This is one of the greatest wine regions: the fine sparkling wines of Asti are made here, the noble reds—Barolo, Barbaresco, the various wines with the prefix *Barbera, Gattinara, Ghemme, Grignolino* and others named for the grapes making them, such as *Moscato, Nebbiolo, Pinot, Dolcetto, Riesling, Cortese.* The wines of *Gavi* are among the most prized of Italy's whites.

Among the sparkling wines, note those made by the Champagne method—used for their finer wines by many firms—and those making sparkling wines by what is known as the *metodo classico* process; all Piedmont sparklers are of varied character, not necessarily sweet. On the spot, try the sparkling red *Brachetto.*

Lombardy—Around Milan and the beautiful lakes vast quantities of charming wines are made—*Chiaretto, Franciacorta, Lugana, Oltrepò Pavese, Valtellina;* where, too, wines with the evocative names of *Grumello, Inferno,* and *Sassella* come from. Because of the northern situation, delightfully fresh white and red wines are produced. (In Oltrepò Pavese, the most famous producer founded a vineyard based on that of the great Château Lafite of Bordeaux).

Trentino–Alto Adige—This delightful region is becoming known for its fine and most interesting wines, many using classic grape varieties—*Pinot Grigio, Müller Thurgau, Sylvaner, Cabernet, Gewüztraminer, Pinot Bianco, Merlot, Pinot Nero* and many others. One of the most rewarding local wines is the Lagrein, but there are many others and an exploration of the area is rewarding—it combines the charm of the Italian lake scene, plus the fascination of the more northern countryside. But it's individual—neither Austrian, as the name *Sud-Tirol* might imply, nor wholly Italian, even if the ampler charm of more southern wine areas is involved. Red and white wines can attain high quality. The sparkling wines, made in varying degrees of sweetness according to the Champagne method, are also of special quality.

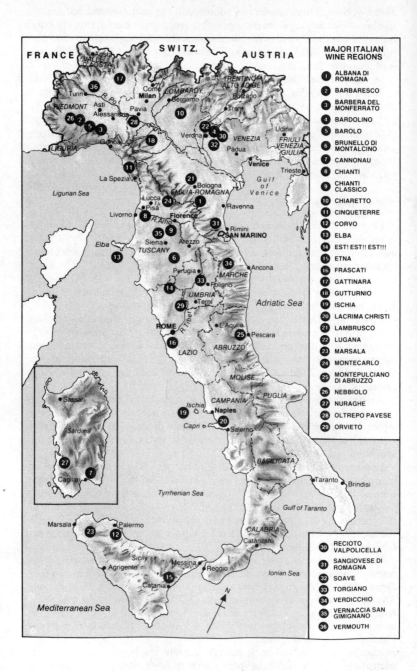

MAJOR ITALIAN WINE REGIONS

1. ALBANA DI ROMAGNA
2. BARBARESCO
3. BARBERA DEL MONFERRATO
4. BARDOLINO
5. BAROLO
6. BRUNELLO DI MONTALCINO
7. CANNONAU
8. CHIANTI
9. CHIANTI CLASSICO
10. CHIARETTO
11. CINQUETERRE
12. CORVO
13. ELBA
14. EST! EST!! EST!!!
15. ETNA
16. FRASCATI
17. GATTINARA
18. GUTTURNIO
19. ISCHIA
20. LACRIMA CHRISTI
21. LAMBRUSCO
22. LUGANA
23. MARSALA
24. MONTECARLO
25. MONTEPULCIANO DI ABRUZZO
26. NEBBIOLO
27. NURAGHE
28. OLTREPO PAVESE
29. ORVIETO

30. RECIOTO VALPOLICELLA
31. SANGIOVESE DI ROMAGNA
32. SOAVE
33. TORGIANO
34. VERDICCHIO
35. VERNACCIA SAN GIMIGNANO
36. VERMOUTH

Veneto—Some delightful and famous wines come from here: *Bardolino, Soave, Valpolicella, Prosecco di Coneglicano, Amarone, Venegazzù* and many named for the well-known classic grapes that make them. You may not, however, find more than a few of them in the big hotels in Venice, where a more general selection tends to cater for an international clientele. The word *Recioto* on a label of some means that the "ears" or shoulder clusters of the overall bunch of grapes have been used—as these get riper than the main part of the bunch because they catch more sun. The resulting wine will tend to be richer and more "special."

Friuli-Venezia Giulia—This north-east region produces a wide variety of wines, many bearing the names of classic grapes—*Merlot, Pinot Bianco, Traminer, Tocai, Pinot Grigio, Cabernet, Sauvignon, Riesling Renano (Rheinriesling)* being only a few. They are only gradually becoming known on export lists, so visitors should profit by being on the spot to try them, especially, perhaps, those known simply as *Collio,* from the various hills where the vineyards are picturesquely situated. It is here that the very famous *Picolit* is made, formerly Italy's most prized white dessert wine, now rare, but still made by some dedicated producers—and, inevitably, expensive. It should certainly be tried—note the curious inner flavor and almost mineral after-taste, although it is essentially a flowery, full, soft wine.

Emilia-Romagna—This is the gutsy gastronomic region, and, as a natural concomitant to the food, there is the fizzy red *Lambrusco,* red *Barbera, Gutturnio* and a range of wines from many different grapes, also some *Picolit.* Although these wines for years tended to be rather underrated even by Italians, they are now emerging as interesting and often very good.

Tuscany—Together with Piedmont, this is the most famous wine region—here you find all the Chiantis from different areas, *Vino Nobile di Montepulciano,* the Elba wines, the "Etruscan" red and whites of *Parrina, Montecarlo Bianco* and the much-praised *Sassicaia* (an impressive red), the pleasantly fruity *Tignanello,* the powerful *Brusco dei Barbi,* aromatic white *Vernaccia di San Gimignano* and many, many more. The enchanting countryside, the historic old towns and villages, the delectable local gastronomy give the vineyards, the simple country houses and the great estates a setting for truly fine and individual wine. The local *Vin Santo,* made from semi-dried grapes, is produced in dry and sweet versions. If you can treat yourself to a very special wine meal, order one of the *Brunello di Montalcino* reds well in advance, so that the wine can be opened and breathe to delight you hours later.

Umbria—Although many different wines are made here, two are specially notable: *Orvieto,* white and either dry or sweet, enjoys a long reputation in wine history. The Torgiano wines, thanks to an inspired contemporary maker, are newcomers but already enjoy world fame—red *Rubesco,* white *Torre di Giano* are only two of the range. *Vin Santo* is also widely produced in this region.

Marche—The east-coast wines are represented on many lists by dry white *Verdicchio,* but there are many others, red and white, *Vin Santo* and *Vernaccia.* Even the tiny republic of San Marino has its own wines, worth sampling.

Latium—Around Rome, the well-known wines are those of *Frascati,* both sweet and dryish, and the *Est ! Est ! ! Est ! ! ! di Montefiascone;* this gets its odd name because a bishop, traveling to Rome, sent his servant ahead to mark places where the wine was good, with an "Est !" At Montefiascone, the wine got a triple "Est !" and the good bishop actually settled down and eventually died there. This area makes more wine than any other in Italy, however, and the range is huge, the various wines of the Castelli Romani offering all sorts of quality, in white and red.

Campania—The volcanic soils around the Bay of Naples contribute to the minerally *Lacryma Christi* whites—supposedly named because Christ, looking down on the beautiful bay, wept at the sins of the people. *Greco di Tufo* is another white dry wine worth attention, and both Ischia and Capri have a range of their own wines.

Sardinia—Often with odd names—*Cannonau, Monica, Nuraghe, I Piani, Nasco*—Sardinian wines are not often seen outside their homeland. The grapes are often unusual too. The white *Torbato* is highly regarded and a *Vernaccia* from Oristano is a multi-purpose drink, higher in strength than a table wine, sometimes sweet and full.

Sicily—Very much an island of wine, Sicily produces a wide range in addition to *Marsala* and there is even wine made on the Lipari Islands. Modern installations have enabled light dry wines to be made, in addition to the rosé and fairly full-bodied reds. *Corvo,* both white and red, is a non-vintage, representing typical Sicilian style. Other wines are named for the grapes and the Vallelunga estate of Conte Tasca d'Almerita makes *Regaleali,* highly respected, as does the Barone di Villagrande on his Etna estates.

As Well as Wine . . .

Vermouth—Italy is the birthplace of vermouth—at least, as we know it today. Wine has been flavored with herbs and spices since before records were kept, according to what was available and to the taste of the drinkers. Turin—easy of access to plenty of wine, with the herbs of the nearby Alpine pastures, and spices coming in via the great trade routes from the east—is still the commercial centre of vermouth. Today, the mighty companies making vermouth bring in wine from many other regions, including Sicily and the south.

Each vermouth house will have an individual style and most make a wide range: light and dry *bianco,* which can be slightly sweet; the tawny-reddish sweet vermouth, very much the after-work refresher of the Italian; and, nowadays, some put out a pink or rosé vermouth. Traditionally, Italians drink vermouth neat, chilled for preference, but, as you'll know, it features in many mixes. Because barmen are well aware of this—and have evolved some delicious cocktails—it's probably wise, if you order a '*Martini*' and want straight vermouth, to specify "Without gin" (*senza gin*), so that you don't get served a cocktail. *Punt e Mes* is a bittersweet vermouth from Carpano, oldest of the vermouth houses.

Bitters—Campari, herby and with a quinine-based bitterness, is a world-famous drink. In Italy it can be bought as a pre-prepared mixed version in a single glass bottle. It may also be used for various cocktails.

But there are many bitter drinks, useful to "settle" the digestion after a heavy meal. *Cynar,* based on artichokes, is one; *Averno,* from Sicily, is another; *Chinamartini, Amaro 18* are others; but possibly the most famous is *Fernet Branca,* renowned as a "morning after" settling beverage—and believed by many Italians to be an aphrodisiac—which is in fact drunk as an aperitif as well as a digestive.

Liqueurs—There are so many Italian liqueurs that you've simply got to sample whatever is available where you are! Some of the better-known include: herby *Strega,* which is said to be a type of love charm for those who share it; almond-flavored *Amaretto di Saronno; Menta* or *Mentuccia,* flavored with mint; *Centerbe,* flavored with the "hundred herbs" from which it gets its name; *Fior d'Alpi,* which is also marketed under the name *Millefiori,* being a sweetish yellow liqueur with a sprig in each bottle, on which blobs of sugar crystallize; *Cerasella,* a cherry liqueur; *Aurum,* made from brandy and oranges and *Rosolio,* flavored with rose petals. The most famous of all is possibly *Maraschino,* named for the type of cherry that is used. *Galliano* is herby and medium-to-sweet in flavor.

Most manufacturers of liqueurs also make anise, orange, caraway and similar styles of liqueurs that are popular everywhere. *Sambuca* is a famous aniseed version.

Brandy—There are many Italian brandies—Stock Original 84 VSOP is one of the top selling brandies in the world, but there are many others. Buton's *Vecchia Romagna* is another famous brand.

Grappa—This is not to be confused with Italian brandy. It's made from the final mass of skins, pips and stalks after the grapes have been pressed. It can be a somewhat tough beverage, but, when matured, it does attain a smoothness. Try it as a digestive—and it may also be added to your black coffee.

Marsala—This is one of the great fortified wines of the world, first made in the south of Sicily—in and around Marsala—by John Woodhouse of Liverpool, who began exporting it in 1773. Other Englishmen followed him into this trade but today the Marsala establishments of Ingham, Woodhouse, Whitaker are all under the control of the firm of Florio, which in fact belongs to Cinzano. There are many other firms there, making the wine.

Marsala is a complex wine, blended and matured in a solera system, somewhat akin to sherry. It undergoes considerable maturation in the huge wooden casks—don't miss a chance to see round any Marsala establishment—and, it will surprise you to know, there are a wide range of wines, very dry, sweet—as used for *zabaglione*—*Marsala all'uovo* enriched with eggyolks, and flavored Marsalas, which can be of chocolate, almonds, banana, strawberry and so on. If you've never tried a fine dry Marsala as an aperitif, perhaps on a chilly evening, you're in for a pleasant surprise!

Some Useful Facts and Handy Words

For those who think of European wines in terms of the classic French names Italy will come as quite a surprise. The Italians' attitude to wine is closer to the Americans, freer of the snobbery that sometimes hangs around the French wine scene. Also, you should not associate the vintages of Italian fine wines with those of France—some years that were a disaster across the frontier were triumphs in Italy, as witness the wonderful Chiantis of 1968. Remember, too, that in many regions the wines will be drunk while quite young, only the very finest being put down to improve with age.

Many Italian grapes will be familiar to those who already know California wines, because so many are cultivated there. But don't expect them to possess more than a passing family resemblance! Many wines are named for the grapes that make them: *Barbera, Cortese, Nebbiolo, Moscato, Malvasia*—and others bear names familiar because of their contribution to other classic wines: *Riesling, Merlot, Cabernet, Pinot, Tocai.* Sometimes, however, a grape that makes rather humble wines in one region will achieve greatness in Italy, as witness the *Trebbiano* (the *Ugni Blanc* of France).

Italy has a whole vocabulary of words associated with wine. *Cantina* is a cellar or winery; *azienda agricola, podere, fattoria, tenuta* all signify an agricultural holding. *Vigneto* is a vineyard, an *enoteca* is, in theory, a wine museum—but it may be more in the nature of a shop with extensive stocks of wine.

The words *annata* and *vendemmia* both signify vintage. *Vecchio* means old, *stravecchio* very old; *riserva* tells you that a wine has been aged longer than usual, *superiore* that it has satisfied various criteria of production.

Rosso, bianco and *rosato* (red, white, rosé) are easy enough to understand; *secco* and *asciutto* mean dry, while *amabile, abboccato,* and *pastoso* all mean sweet or sweetish, although this term can vary considerably. *Dolce* also means sweet, but *passito* signifies that the grapes have been slightly dried prior to pressing so that the resulting wine tends to be intense and sweet; *liquoroso* is usually a dessert fortified wine—sweetish anyway.

Don't assume that the term *Classico* has anything to do with the way the wine is made—it means that the wine comes from a particular region denoted as Classico, notably Chianti.

Labels attached to the necks of bottles may bear various symbols and names, often showing that the wine maker belongs to one of the region's *consorzii* or associations (consortia). One of the most famous of these is the *Gallo nero* or black rooster of Chianti Classico. But it is not obligatory to belong to a *consorzio,* so some famous firms do not put the seal on their wines.

Wine Museums

Many important Italian installations have museums devoted to wine, although these can sometimes be more in the nature of archives of the particular establishment. Perhaps the most impressive and rewarding museum is at Pessione, outside Turin, where Martini & Rossi exhibit the whole history of wine, in addition to their own products. The other famous vermouth makers, Cinzano, have a museum in Turin.

The Bersano establishment at Nizza Montferrato in Piedmont has a good wine museum; so does Giorgio Lungarotti, with the Museo del Vino at Torgiano in Umbria. There is another enoteca in the enchantingly colonnaded little town of Greve in the Chianti district of Tuscany. At Siena, in Tuscany, there is a fine enoteca, with a restaurant. You can order samples of wines to taste from the hundreds of bottles kept here as if in a library.

ROME, THE ETERNAL

Treasurehouse of Western Culture

A lifetime isn't enough to see everything that is beautiful or historic or curious in Rome, so don't worry if you have only a few days, and, above all, don't try to crowd too much into them. Tired eyes can't appreciate paintings or sculptures, and tired feet are a serious distraction from even the loveliest scenes.

For a first, overall notion of Rome and its riches, it might be advisable to take a half-day sightseeing tour. But then pick up a good street map and do at least some sightseeing on your own. Decide what interests you about the city—then wander out and see it. Take a taxi, bus or the Metro (which is very easy to use) from one vital point to another, then branch out on foot.

Ancient Rome

A good starter might be one beginning at the city's center, in Piazza Venezia, where even the Romans still orient themselves. Stand in the middle of this square, facing the biggest thing in front of you. That's the "Wedding Cake," the monument to King Victor Emmanuel II, a comparatively modern work (1911) for Rome. It holds Italy's Tomb of the Unknown Soldier and a statue of Victor Emmanuel II on horseback. Turn your back to it and look at the handsome Palazzo Venezia on the left of the big square. Over the main portal is the balcony from which Benito Mussolini once harangued his fellow countrymen.

Your first tour starts from a point that embodies some of Rome's earliest and greatest moments: the Campidoglio, on the Capitoline Hill just behind the Piazza Venezia. The majestic ramp and the beautifully-proportioned piazza are Michelangelo's handiwork. After 400 years the fine equestrian statue of Marcus Aurelius that was the focal point of the piazza was so menaced by air pollution that it had to be removed from its pedestal for restoration; Marcus and his steed won't be back in place for a long time.

While the Palazzo Senatorio at the center is still Rome's City Hall, the palaces flanking it are given over to fine museums: the Museo Capitolino on the left contains some fine classical sculptures, including the *Dying Gaul,* the *Capitoline Venus,* and a fascinating series of busts of ancient philosophers and emperors. In the Palazzo dei Conservatori (your ticket is good for both) on the right of the piazza, you'll find some splendid salons, one of which contains Bernini's large and masterful marble effigy of Urban VIII. Farther along you'll see the *Capitoline Wolf,* an Etruscan bronze of the 6th century B.C. (the twins were added during the Renaissance), and the graceful *Boy with a Thorn.* Upstairs, the picture gallery displays Caravaggio's *Young St. John,* among other fine paintings.

Off to the side of the Campidoglio, the red-brick church of the Aracoeli (stairs at far side of Museo Capitolino) is worth a visit for its medieval pavement, a Renaissance gilded ceiling that commemorates the victory of Lepanto, some Pinturicchio frescoes, and a much-revered wooden statue of the Holy Child.

The Campidoglio gardens offer some good views of ancient Rome; Caesar's Forum, below the garden to the left of the Palazzo Senatorio, is the oldest of the Imperial Fora, built when the original Roman Forum became too small for the burgeoning city's needs. Half-hidden by the trees, across the Via dei Fori Imperiali—the broad avenue created by Mussolini—are Trajan's Forum on the left, with its huge semicircular market building, and Trajan's Column, under which the emperor was buried. On the right of Trajan's Market are the ruins of the Forum of Augustus. The entire area may eventually become an archeological park; the various digs you see underway are part of that plan.

The Roman Forum, once nothing more than a marshy hollow, became the political, commercial and social center of Rome, studded with public meeting halls, shops, temples and shrines. As Rome declined these monuments lost their importance and eventually were destroyed by fire or barbarian invasions. Rubble accumulated, much of it was carted off by medieval home-builders as construction material, and the site reverted to marshy pastureland; sporadic excavations began at the end of the 19th century.

From the Campidoglio garden descend the Via San Pietro in Carcere, a ramp of stairs that leads down to the Mamertine Prison, two gloomy cells where Rome's vanquished enemies were finished off in short order. Tradition has it that St. Peter himself was held prisoner here and that he miraculously brought forth a spring of water in order to baptize his jailers.

You don't really have to try to make sense of the mass of marble fragments scattered over the area of the Roman Forum. Just consider that 2,000 years ago this was the center of the then-known world, and that much of the history you studied at school happened right here. You can distinguish some of the better-preserved monuments—among them, the Arch of Septimius Severus, the Basilica of Maxentius and the Arch of Titus—some now protected by scaffolding and green netting from further deterioration due to air pollution. Walk up to the Palatine Hill, where the emperors had their palaces. From its belvedere you can see the Circus

Maximus; here more than 30,000 spectators at a time attended horse and chariot races.

Now turn to the Colosseum, stupendous monument of ancient Rome. Originally known as the Flavian Amphitheater, it was begun in 72 A.D. and inaugurated in the year 80 with a program of games and shows lasting a hundred days. On opening day alone 5,000 wild beasts perished in the arena. Its 524 m. (1,719 ft.) circumference could contain more than 50,000 spectators. In later centuries it came to be called the Colosseum, after a colossal gilded-bronze statue of Nero that stood nearby. It served as a 13th-century fortress, a quarry from which materials were filched to build sumptuous Renaissance churches and palaces, and was finally declared sacred by the popes in memory of the many Christians believed martyred there. Climb to the first level, where you can see a scale model of the Colosseum as it was in its heyday, with its marble facings and ingenious system of awnings.

Just beyond the Colosseum stands the Arch of Constantine, built to commemorate Constantine's victory over Maxentius at the Milvian Bridge. If you continue down the Via San Gregorio and turn left through the Porta Capena Park you'll come to the Baths of Caracalla, ancient Rome's most beautiful and luxurious. Now towering ruins, their magnificent halls and libraries were lovely places in which to stroll and gossip. You can see the *frigidarium* and its vast rectangular pool used for bathing, the *tepidarium* with two flanking exercise halls, and the *calidarium,* a huge circular room with a ruined apse. On the Celian Hill, between Caracalla and the Colosseum, there are a number of very old and interesting churches; Santa Maria in Domnica, Santi Quattro Coronati, Santi Giovanni e Paolo and San Gregorio are all well worth a visit.

The Spanish Steps and the Fountain of Trevi

From Largo Goldoni on the Via del Corso you get a head-on view of the Spanish Steps and Trinità dei Monti as you start up the Via Condotti, Rome's most elegant and expensive shopping street. The Piazza di Spagna and the Spanish Steps get their name from the Spanish Embassy to the Holy See, opposite the American Express Office, though they were built with French funds. This was once the core of Rome's bohemian quarter, especially favored by American and British artists and writers. At the center of the piazza is Bernini's Fountain of the Barcaccia (the Old Boat), around which Romans and tourists love to cool themselves on hot summer nights. Behind it, sloping gently upwards, the famed 200-year-old flight of 137 Spanish Steps begins at a brightly-laden flower stall, between an English tea room on the left and, on the right, the house in which Britain's illustrious poet, John Keats, died in 1821. The stairs ascend gracefully to a square on the top dominated by the Church of Trinità dei Monti, begun only a few years after Columbus discovered America.

Then, from the narrow end of the Piazza di Spagna take the Via di Propaganda and continue along into the Via Sant'Andrea delle Fratte. Turn left into the Via del Nazareno, cross busy Via del Tritone to the Via delle Stamperia and follow it along. By now you can probably hear the rushing waters of the Fountain of Trevi, just around the corner of Palazzo Poli. One of Rome's most spectacular fountains, it was ordered by Pope Clement XII, designed by Salvi and completed in 1762. It features a couple of lusty marble tritons leading a chariot bearing Oceanus, through spurts and

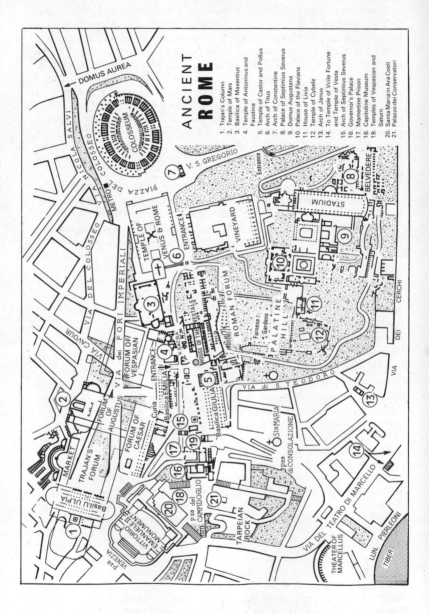

ANCIENT ROME

1. Trajan's Column
2. Temple of Mars
3. Basilica of Maxentius
4. Temple of Antoninus and Faustina
5. Temple of Castor and Pollux
6. Arch of Titus
7. Arch of Constantine
8. Palace of Septimius Severus
9. Domus Augustana
10. Palace of the Flavians
11. House of Livia
12. Temple of Cybele
13. Arch of Janus
14. To Temple of Virile Fortune and Temple of Vesta
15. Arch of Septimius Severus
16. Governor's Palace
17. Mamertine Prison
18. Temples of Vespasian and Saturn
19. Capitoline Museum
20. Santa Maria in Ara Coeli
21. Palazzo dei Conservatori

cascades of water that play among a maze of scenic effects when the fountain labors at full capacity. Legend has it that you can ensure your return to Rome by tossing a coin in the fountain, but legend doesn't say what you should do to fend off the army of souvenir vendors looking for a share of your small change. The fountain is undergoing restoration, but you can still see it behind a special transparent enclosure.

From here you can trace your steps back to the Via del Tritone, turn right and climb up to the Piazza Barberini to see the Fountain of the Tritone (Triton), designed by Bernini in 1640, less showy than Trevi, but very graceful indeed, with its triton blowing a high arc of water out of a conch shell. A short way up the Via Quattro Fontane, Palazzo Barberini's Galleria Nazionale offers some fine works by Raphael (the *Fornarina*) and Caravaggio and a salon with gorgeous ceiling frescos by Pietro da Cortona. Upstairs, don't miss the stunning suite of rooms decorated in 18th-century fashion.

Santa Maria Maggiore and San Giovanni in Laterano

Not far from Termini Station on the Via Cavour, Santa Maria Maggiore (St. Mary Major) was built on the spot where a 3rd-century pope witnessed a miraculous mid-summer snowfall. Inside there are precious mosaics and a handsome carved wood ceiling supposed to have been gilded with the first gold brought from the New World. Now follow the Via Cavour to Largo Venosta and the Via San Francesco da Paola, which is really a street staircase that passes under the old Borgia palace and leads to the square in front of San Pietro in Vincoli (St. Peter in Chains). The church was reportedly founded in 442 by the Empress Eudoxia to hold the chains (still there) that bound St. Peter. Inside is Michelangelo's masterful statue of Moses, which he described as "the tragedy of my life" and which was destined for the unfinished tomb of Julius II. Crass commercialism has ruined the starkly majestic effect of this memorial, for the place is besieged by guided tours and the monument itself is a front for a large souvenir shop crammed with ugly rubbish.

With the help of your street map, cut through the Colle Oppio park to the Via Labicana and the Church of San Clemente on the Via di San Giovanni Laterano. San Clemente is composed of three churches, one on top of the other. At street level today is the 12th-century basilica; below it is a 4th-century basilica, and below that is a pagan shrine of the time of Nero.

Now you can proceed straight on to San Giovanni in Laterano (St. John Lateran), which is the cathedral of Rome, where the pope officiates as bishop of Rome. Its towering facade and Borromini's cool, tense Baroque interior emphasize the majesty of its proportions. Across the street, opposite the Lateran Palace, a smallish building houses the Scala Santa (Holy Stairs); circle the palace to see the 6th-century octagonal baptistery and Rome's oldest and tallest obelisk, brought from Thebes and dating to the 15th century B.C.

One more church awaits you just down the Viale Carlo Felice. Santa Croce in Gerusalemme, with a pretty Rococo facade and Baroque interior, shelters the relics of the True Cross found by St. Helena, the mother of Constantine. The chapel on the lower level gleams with brilliant 15th-century mosaics.

ROME
Points of Interest

1) Arch of Constantine
2) Arch of Titus
3) Augustan Forum
4) Baths of Caracalla
5) Baths of Diocletian
6) Castel Sant' Angelo
7) Chiesa Nuova
8) Colosseum
9) Column of Marcus Aurelius
10) Fontana di Trevi

11) Galleria Borghese
12) Galleria d'Arte Moderna
13) Giardino Zoologico
14) Il Gesù
15) Mamertine Prison
16) Marcellus Theater
17) Mausoleum of Augustus
18) Museo Capitolino
19) Museo Napoleonico
20) Museo Nazionale Romano

21) Nero's House of Gold
22) Palazzo Barberini
23) Palazzo Corsini
24) Palazzo Doria
25) Palazzo Farnese
26) Palazzo Margherita U.S. Embassy
27) Palazzo di Montecitorio
28) Palazzo Quirinale
29) Palazzo Venezia
30) Pantheon
31) Roman Forum
32) S. Andrea delle Valle
33) S. Carlo alle Quattro Fontane;
    S. Andrea al Quirinale
34) S. Cecilia
35) S. Giovanni in Laterano
36) S. Luigi dei Francesi
37) S. Maria Maggiore
38) S. Maria sopra Minerva
39) S. Maria del Popolo

40) S. Maria in Trastevere
41) S. Pietro in Vincoli
42) S. Prassede
43) S. Pudenziana
44) S. Stefano Rotondo
45) SS. Apostoli
46) SS. Giovanni e Paolo
47) Scala Santa
48) Spanish Steps
49) Tarpeian Rock
50) Temple of Manly Fortune
51) Temple of Vesta
52) Tiberina Island
53) Trajan's Column
54) Trajan's Forum
55) Trajan's Markets
56) Trinita dei Monti
57) Villa Farnesina
58) Villa Giulia
59) Villa Medici

Ⓜ Metro Stations

Scale
0 — 400 — 800 yds.
0 — 500 — 1000 ms.

(All streets not shown)

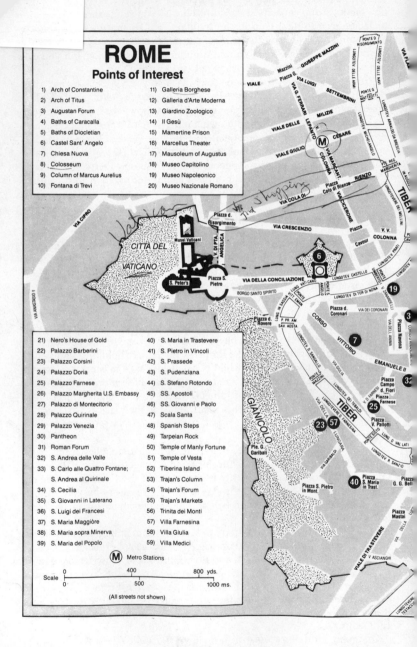

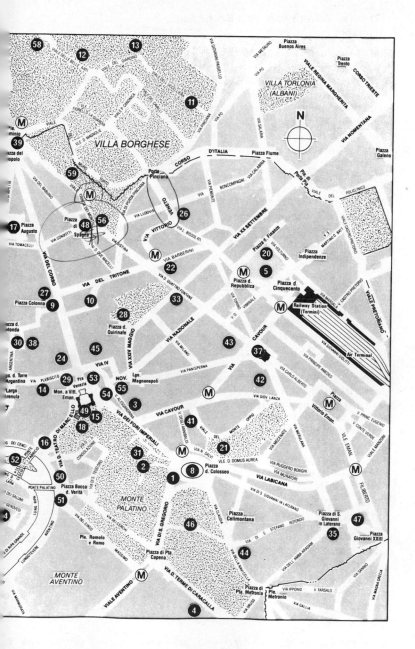

The Via Veneto and Villa Borghese

The Via Veneto winds its way upwards from the Piazza Barberini past
Santa Maria della Concezione, a Capuchin church famous for its crypt,
where the skeletons and assorted bones of 4,000 dead monks are artistically arranged in four macabre chapels. The street curves past the U.S. Embassy at Palazzo Margherita and the Consulate next door passing luxury
hotels, big cafes and chic shops before coming to the Porta Pinciana, gateway to Villa Borghese.

Inside the park, tree-shaded paths to the right lead to one of Rome's
leading art galleries, the 17th-century Galleria Borghese. The gallery was
built expressly to house the Borghese family's fabulous art collection,
which includes Canova's nude of Pauline Borghese, sister of Napoleon,
reclining on her couch. Among other remarkable works are Bernini's incomparable *Rape of Proserpine, Apollo and Daphne, David Drawing the
Sling* and the *Aeneas and Anchises* on which, at 15 years of age, he assisted
his father. The upstairs picture gallery remains closed for restoration. This
is unfortunate because it features works by Caravaggio, Cranach, Correggio and Rubens; treasure of the collection is Titian's *Sacred and Profane
Love.*

A stroll through the park takes you past the botanical garden, with its
pretty little lake, to the Pincio, a portion of the gardens planned by Valadier and completed in 1814 as part of his overall plan for the Piazza del
Popolo. The Pincio terrace offers a superb view of central Rome, absolutely spectacular when there is a fine sunset. Below, the Piazza del Popolo
is Rome's largest square and traditional gathering place for mass meetings
at election time. This spacious square, an oval formed by two great semi-
circles, has in its center four fountains with lions and, among them, an
obelisk telling about Rameses II, one of Egypt's top men in the 13th century B.C. Next to the 400-year-old Porta del Popolo, stop in at the Church
of Santa Maria del Popolo to see the pair of striking paintings by Caravaggio and some Bernini sculptures, all in a rich Baroque setting.

Not far away is the Villa Giulia, former papal summer palace set in lovely gardens; it houses one of the world's great Etruscan collections. This
is the place to study that strange, half-understood civilization, for here
are not only magnificent terracotta statues, but also jewelry, household
implements, sarcophagi—a whole way of life on display. Gold, silver and
ivory, cups and dishes, dancers and satyrs, cosmetic boxes, figures smiling
that eternally mysterious smile . . . it is an embarrassment of riches, among
which the most precious gems are the *Apollo of Veio* and the *Sarcophagus
of the Sposi.* When you have had your fill of such lovely treasures, you
can step out into the lovely nymphaeum, with its cool recesses, lily pools
and fern-softened fountains and then take a close look at a full-scale reconstruction of an Etruscan temple in the garden.

Vatican City

Vatican City covers 108 acres sprawled over a hill west of the Tiber
River, separated by a thick, high wall from the city of Rome that surrounds it. Inside that wall, about 1,000 people live as residents, printing
their own newspaper, issuing their own stamps, striking their own money.
The little state has its own flag, print shops, mosaic workshop, observato-

ry, model railway station, post office, power plant, even barracks for its armed forces. Radio Vatican, a powerful transmitting station, broadcasts in 14 different languages twice daily to six different continents. In Rome itself, outside the Vatican wall, 13 buildings enjoy extraterritorial rights; many other Papal properties within the Eternal City are exempt from taxes.

The Lateran Treaty of February 11, 1929, signed by the Holy See and the Mussolini Government, established the Vatican City as an independent and completely sovereign state, to which diplomatic representatives are accredited from many nations.

The sovereign of this little state is Pope John Paul II, till his election after a two-day conclave on October 16 1978, Cardinal Karol Wojtyla, Archbishop of Cracow. The 264th Pope of the Roman Catholic Church, the first non-Italian for 456 years and the first Pole ever, possesses full legislative, judicial, executive and military powers within his own state and is authorized to live in or move through Italian territory whenever he so desires. Pope John Paul, one of the youngest Supreme Pontiffs, heads the Roman Catholic Church and its followers throughout the world, being assisted in this capacity by the College of Cardinals, which functions somewhat like a kind of senate. The Cardinals, currently 111, are nominated and chosen by the Pope and, upon his death, elect a successor, as the world witnessed in the dramatic sequence of events that led to the election of John Paul II.

The Pope reigns over 700 million Catholics, for whom a papal audience is the highlight of a trip to Rome. The intricate rules of etiquette that were once characteristic of the Vatican have been greatly relaxed by recent Popes, especially under Pope Paul VI, and much of the Apostolic Palace has been redecorated in severely simple style. The Swiss Guards, however, still wear the colorful dress uniforms designed by Michelangelo.

A tour through this smallest state in the world should start with St. Peter's and might include a visit to the gardens. Save the museums and the Sistine Chapel for another day.

For some practical details of visiting the Vatican, see page 102 in the *Practical Information* section at the end of this chapter.

St. Peter's

The Via della Conciliazione approach to St. Peter's, created by the order of Mussolini, gives your eye time to become accustomed to the enormous dimensions of the square and basilica. But look at the people on the broad steps in front of the church and you'll be struck by the contrast between their size and the immense dimension of the building dwarfing them.

The piazza is Bernini's masterpiece, completed in 1667 after 11 years' work, a relatively short space of time for those days, considering the vastness of the job. This enormous space has held as many as 400,000 people at one time; it's surrounded by a pair of quadruple colonnades, topped by a balustrade and 140 statues of saints.

St. Peter's had its beginnings about the year 319, when the Emperor Constantine built a basilica here over the tomb of St. Peter. The original basilica remained for 1,100 years, until it threatened to collapse towards the middle of the 15th century. Reconstruction work began in 1452—but it was not until 1626, or almost 200 years later, that the masterpiece stood complete as you see it today. No less than five of Italy's greatest artists—

ST. PETER'S

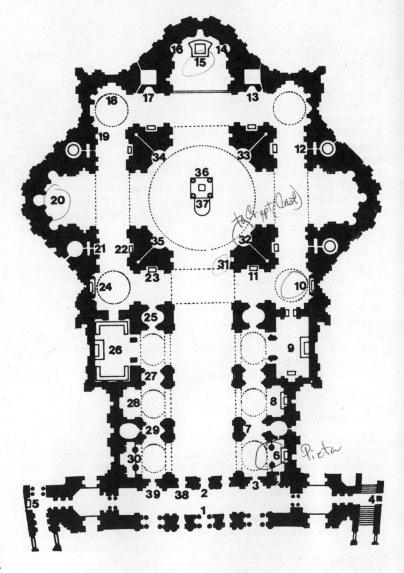

KEY TO PLAN OF ST. PETER'S

1 Vestibule—The Ship, restored *Giotto* mosaics
2 Central Door—reliefs *Filarete c 1440*
3 Holy Door
4 Emperor Constantine—*Bernini*
5 Charlemagne—*Comacchini 1725*
6 Chapel of the Pietà; Pietà— *Michelangelo 1500*
7 Christina of Sweden monument—*Fontana*
8 Chapel of St. Sebastian— mosaic after *Domenichino;* under altar, Innocent XI tomb; on left Pius XII monument; on right, Pius XI monument
9 Chapel of the Holy Sacrament—gate des. by *Borromini;* Ciborium—*Bernini;* The Trinity—*Da Cortona*
10 Gregorian Chapel—*Michelangelo* and *Della Porta* (to left, Entrance to Cupola)
11 Altar of St. Jerome—mosaic after *Domenichino*
12 Clement XIII monument— *Canova c 1790*
13 Clement X monument; opp. in floor, tombs of Sixtus IV and Julius II
14 Urban VIII monument— *Bernini*
15 Gloria—*Bernini*, with St. Peter's Chair
16 Paul III monument—*Della Porta*
17 Alexander VIII monument
18 Chapel of the Column; right, altar and tomb St. Leo the Great; over, Meeting of Attila and Leo—*Algardi c 1648;* opp., ancient Image of the Virgin; under altar, tombs of Leos II, III and IV; in center Leo XII

19 Alexander VII monument— *Bernini*
20 St. Joseph's Altar; right, Altar of St. Thomas the Disbeliever; left, Altar of St. Peter's Crucifixion
21 Pius V monument—*Tenerani;* (below, Entrance to Sacristy)
22 Altar of the Lie
23 Altar of the Transfiguration —mosaic after *Raphael*
24 Clementine Chapel—*Della Porta;* under altar, St. Gregory the Great tomb; left, Pius VII monument— *Thorwaldsen*
25 Leo XI monument—*Algardi c 1648;* opp., Innocent XI monument—*Monnot*
26 Chapel of the Choir
27 Pius X monument; opp., Innocent VIII monument— *Pollaiolo 1498*
28 Chapel of the Presentation; under altar, Pius X tomb; right, John XXIII monument —*Greco;* left, Benedict XV monument—*Canonica 1928*
29 Clementina Sobieski monument, opp., Pillar of the Last Stuarts—*Canova c 1820;* (Exit from Cupola)
30 Chapel of the Baptist, Font
31 St. Peter—prov. uncertain
32 St. Longinus—*Bernini;* (Entrance to Crypt)
33 St. Helen—*Bolgi*
34 The Veronica—*Mochi*
35 St. Andrew—*Duquesnoy*
36 Bronze Baldachino—*Bernini*
37 Confession—*Maderno*
38 1977 Bronze Door/*Minguzzi*
39 Bronze Door—*Manzu*

Bramante, Raphael, Peruzzi, Antonio Sangallo the Younger, Michelange-lo—died while striving to erect the new and greater St. Peter's.

The first architect was Alberti and then came Bramante, who was put in charge of the plans. It was Bramante's Greek Cross that was chosen as the basic design. But Bramante died in 1514. Raphael, Antonio, Sangal-lo and others followed him in the growing work until 1547, when Michel-angelo took charge of the work at the age of 72. He returned to Bramante's plan, but did not live to see its realization. The most beautiful cupola in the world was completed by Della Porta and Fontana.

During all this time, the plans were significantly altered. Under the iron hand of Paul V, the Greek Cross (with four equal arms) was abandoned and the plans returned to the Latin Cross. The eastern arm was extended by 165 feet. The effect of this change was to block the view of the wonder-ful cupola. And now we come to the optical illusions. Maderno and Berni-ni went to work on the square and the columns. They faked their construc-tion: Maderno flattened the façade to free the cupola, and Bernini made the square appear to be a circle, though its real form is elliptical.

Now climb the steps and enter the portico—you'll be barred from the basilica if you're wearing shorts, a sleeveless dress or revealing clothing—where you get a sampling of what's awaiting you in Filarete's 15th-century bronze doors, salvaged from the old basilica. Once inside the basilica, pause a moment to judge its approximate size. It is difficult at first to real-ize just how huge it is. But walk over to the cherubs clinging to a column at the left, place your arm across the sole of a cherub's foot and you will discover that it is as long as the distance from your fingers to your elbow. It is because all the proportions of this giant building are in such perfect harmony that its vast scale escapes you at first. Each of the bronze inscrip-tions in the marble floor indicates the approximate ground-floor dimen-sions of the principal Christian churches in the world; the relative length of each is measured from St. Peter's great portals, and the longest falls far short of the apse of the basilica. That should give you a vague idea of the vastness of the place, along with figures that show St. Peter's covers about 18,100 square yards, runs 212 yards in length, carries a dome which rises 435 feet and stands 138 feet across its base.

Four massive piers support the cupola at the crossing, where the mighty Bernini baldacchino rises high over the papal altar. The pope celebrates his mass here, over the crypt holding the tombs of many of his predeces-sors including, it is believed, St. Peter's. The antique casket in the niche below the altar holds the episcopal *pallia,* white wool stoles that are a sym-bol of authority.

Notice the elegant bronze throne above the main altar in the apse. It is Bernini's work (1656) and it covers a wooden and ivory chair that St. Peter himself is said to have used. However, this throne cannot be older than medieval times. We come to these contradictions often. Faith far out-weighs authenticity when it is a question of sacred objects. Can the remains of a "vigorous man" discovered beneath St. Peter's and recently exposed in the *tropaion* really be those of the Apostle? Does the head—most likely added in the 5th century, to a very old statue of St. Peter—actually repro-duce the features of the Saint? Again it will be faith rather than reasonable argument. But see how the adoration of a million lips has completely worn down the bronze on the right foot of the statue, fixed to the last pillar on the right at the crossing.

But could you question whether Michelangelo's *Pietà* (in the first side chapel on the right), sculpted when he was only 22, owes more to man's art than to an artist's faith? As we contemplate this masterpiece we are able to understand a little better that art and faith sometimes partake of the same impulse. (Tragically damaged by a maniac in 1972, the statue has been masterfully restored and screened off with shatterproof glass.)

Stroll up and down the aisles and transepts, noting well many of the world's finest works of art in mosaic, in sculpture, and designed with stucco. Names like Bernini, Michelangelo, Canova and Della Porta are commonplace here.

Perhaps at this point you have come to the conclusion that St. Peter's doesn't seem to be a church at all—and you're right. It's not just a church, but was designed as the setting for all the pomp and panoply of ecclesiastical ceremony. Indeed, only when it's the brightly-lit scene of a great gathering do its vast dimensions find their true measure.

What you should see in St. Peter's and what you will see are two entirely different things, for it's quite possible to spend the best part of a week inside without covering the whole. However, try not to miss the Treasury, wherein, among numerous other priceless objects, there's a chalice of pure platinum presented by Spain's King Charles III to Pope Pius VI, the massive and beautiful bronze tomb of Sixtus V by Pollaiuolo, and an ancient cloak they say Charlemagne might have worn for his coronation.

For one of the most impressive sights, take the elevator up to the roof of the basilica, interesting in itself, whence you climb a short interior staircase to the base of the dome for a dove's-eye view of the interior of the basilica. Only if you are stout of heart and sound of wind should you attempt the very taxing climb up the narrow stairs—there's no turning back!—to the balcony of the lantern, where the view embraces the Vatican gardens as well as all of Rome.

From the heights of St. Peter's turn now to the depths of the Crypt. As the only exit from the Crypt leads outside St. Peter's it is best to leave this visit to the last. The Crypt is lined with marble chapels and tombs and occupies the area of the original basilica, over the Grottoes. You can book special tours of the Grottoes. Apply in advance at the Ufficio Scavi, under the Vatican gate on the left of St. Peter's.

Coming out of St. Peter's, the building on your left—the Vatican Palace—has been the residence of Popes since 1377. Actually, it represents a collection of individual buildings covering more than 13 acres, with an estimated (no one has ever bothered to count them!) 1,400 rooms, chapels and galleries. Interestingly enough, the Pope and his papal court occupy an infinitesimal part of the Vatican Palace; the rest is occupied by huge libraries, museums, and rooms filled with art and relics.

Vatican Museums

The Vatican collections are immense, covering about 4½ miles of displays. Special posters at the entrance and throughout the museum plot out a choice of four color-coded itineraries for you, the shortest taking approximately 90 minutes, the longest 4½–5 hours, depending on your own rate of progress. You can rent a taped commentary in English explaining the Sistine Chapel and the Raphael Rooms, and you're free to photograph what you like, barring use of flash, tripod or other special equipment, for which permission must be obtained.

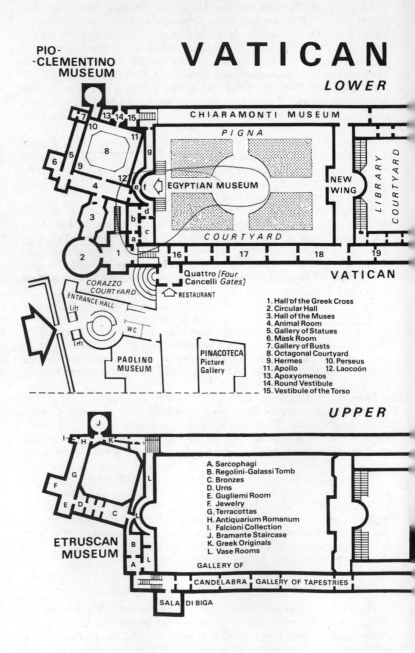

VATICAN

LOWER

PIO-
-CLEMENTINO
MUSEUM

CHIARAMONTI MUSEUM

PIGNA

EGYPTIAN MUSEUM

NEW WING

LIBRARY COURTYARD

COURTYARD

16   17   18   19

VATICAN

Quattro [*Four*]
Cancelli *Gates*]

RESTAURANT

CORAZZO COURTYARD

ENTRANCE HALL

Lift

Lift

WC

PAOLINO MUSEUM

PINACOTECA Picture Gallery

1. Hall of the Greek Cross
2. Circular Hall
3. Hall of the Muses
4. Animal Room
5. Gallery of Statues
6. Mask Room
7. Gallery of Busts
8. Octagonal Courtyard
9. Hermes   10. Perseus
11. Apollo   12. Laocoön
13. Apoxyomenos
14. Round Vestibule
15. Vestibule of the Torso

UPPER

A. Sarcophagi
B. Regolini-Galassi Tomb
C. Bronzes
D. Urns
E. Gugliemi Room
F. Jewelry
G. Terracottas
H. Antiquarium Romanum
I. Falcioni Collection
J. Bramante Staircase
K. Greek Originals
L. Vase Rooms

ETRUSCAN MUSEUM

GALLERY OF

CANDELABRA   GALLERY OF TAPESTRIES

SALA DI BIGA

MUSEUMS

FLOOR

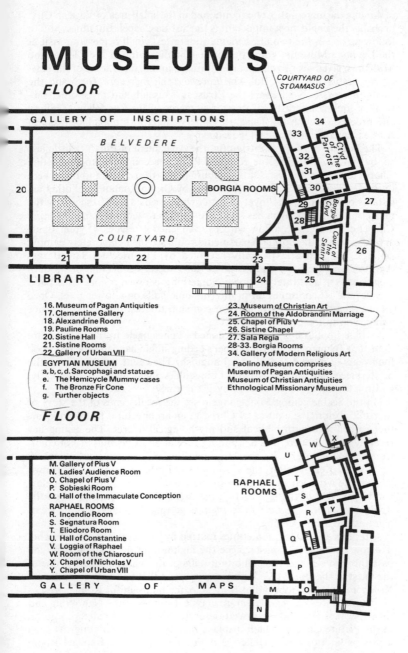

COURTYARD OF ST DAMASUS

GALLERY OF INSCRIPTIONS

BELVEDERE

34

33

Ctyd of the Parrots

32

31

30

BORGIA ROOMS

29

Borgia Ctyd

27

20

28

COURTYARD

Court of the Sentry

26

21   22

23

LIBRARY

24   25

16. Museum of Pagan Antiquities
17. Clementine Gallery
18. Alexandrine Room
19. Pauline Rooms
20. Sistine Hall
21. Sistine Rooms
22. Gallery of Urban VIII

EGYPTIAN MUSEUM
a, b, c, d. Sarcophagi and statues
e.   The Hemicycle Mummy cases
f.   The Bronze Fir Cone
g.   Further objects

23. Museum of Christian Art
24. Room of the Aldobrandini Marriage
25. Chapel of Pius V
26. Sistine Chapel
27. Sala Regia
28-33. Borgia Rooms
34. Gallery of Modern Religious Art

 Paolino Museum comprises
Museum of Pagan Antiquities
Museum of Christian Antiquities
Ethnological Missionary Museum

FLOOR

V

W   X

U

M. Gallery of Pius V
N. Ladies' Audience Room
O. Chapel of Pius V
P. Sobieski Room
Q. Hall of the Immaculate Conception
RAPHAEL ROOMS
R. Incendio Room
S. Segnatura Room
T. Eliodoro Room
U. Hall of Constantine
V. Loggia of Raphael
W. Room of the Chiaroscuri
X. Chapel of Nicholas V
Y. Chapel of Urban VIII

RAPHAEL ROOMS

T

S

R

Y

Q

P

GALLERY   OF   MAPS

M   O

N

Among the incredible riches contained in the small area of Vatican City, probably the single most important is the Sistine Chapel. But unless you're following one of the two abbreviated itineraries, you'll begin your visit at the Egyptian Museum, going on to the Chiaramonti and Pio Clementino Museums, given over to classical sculptures, among them some of the best-known statues in the world—the *Laocoön,* the *Belvedere Torso* and the *Apollo Belvedere.* Next come the Etruscan Museum and three other sections of limited interest. All itineraries merge in the Candelabra Gallery and proceed through the Tapestry Gallery, hung with magnificent tapestries executed from Raphael's designs.

The Gallery of Maps is intriguing, the Apartment of Pius V a little less so, but now you'll enter the Raphael Rooms, second only to the Sistine Chapel in artistic interest. Of these four rooms, the second and third were decorated mainly by Raphael, the others by Giulio Romano and other assistants of Raphael. The lovely Loggia was designed and frescoed by the master himself. Next, you pass through the Chiaroscuro Room to the tiny Chapel of Nicholas V, aglow with Fra Angelico's frescoes. If your itinerary takes you to the Borgia Apartments you'll see their elaborately painted ceilings, designed and partially executed by Pinturicchio. The Borgia Apartments have been given over to the Vatican's collection of Modern Religious Art, accurately termed "something between a pork barrel and a junk pile." It continues on in interminable halls on a lower level. Once you've seen the Borgia Rooms you can skip the rest in good conscience and get on to the Sistine Chapel.

In 1508 Pope Julius II commissioned Michelangelo to fresco the more than 10,000 square feet of the chapel's ceiling single-handed. The task took four years of mental and physical anguish. The result, however, was the masterpiece that you see. A pair of binoculars, incidentally, helps greatly, and try to beat the tour groups by going early.

On the Sistine ceiling Michelangelo set the focal scenes of the story of humanity before the coming of Christ in an architectural framework further embellished with biblical and mythological figures. The ceiling has recently been cleaned; it is a stunning revelation of his mastery of color. Commissioned to execute the large painting of the *Last Judgement* 20 years later, over the altar, the aged and embittered artist painted his own face on the wrinkled human skin in the hand of St. Bartholomew, below and to the right of the figure of Christ, which he clearly modeled on the *Apollo Belvedere.* The *Last Judgement* is getting the same cleaning treatment as the Sistine ceiling.

After this experience, sometimes marred by the crowds of tourists who, like you, consider this masterpiece the highlight of their Rome visit, you pass through some of the exhibition halls of the Vatican Library, one of the finest in the world. We highly recommend that you look in on Room X, Room of the Aldobrandini Marriage, for its beautiful Roman frescos of a nuptial rite. You can see more classical statues in the New Wing and then (perhaps after taking a well-deserved break at the cafeteria) go on to the Picture Gallery, which displays mainly religious paintings by such artists as Giotto, Fra Angelico and Filippo Lippi. The Raphael Room holds his exceptional *Transfiguration, Coronation,* and *Foligno Madonna.*

In the Pagan Antiquities Museum modern display techniques enhance a collection of more Greek and Roman sculptures. The Christian Antiquities Museum has Early Christian and medieval art, while the Ethnological Museum shows art and artifacts from exotic places throughout the world.

The complete itinerary ends with the Historical Museum's collection of carriages, uniforms and arms.

Old Rome

A district of narrow streets with curious names, airy Baroque piazzas and picturesque courtyards, old Rome occupies the horn of land that pushes the Tiber westward toward the Vatican. Start this itinerary at the Piazza Venezia and take the Via del Plebiscito to the huge Church of the Gesù, epitome of Baroque churches, encrusted with gold and precious marbles and topped by a fantastically painted ceiling that flows down over the pillars to become three-dimensional, merging with painted stucco figures to complete the illusion.

At Largo Argentina take the Via dei Cestari past the Church of Santa Maria Sopra Minerva, a Gothic church built over a Roman temple, with some beautiful frescos by Filippo Lippi. The enormous brick building in front is the Pantheon, one of Rome's most perfect, best-preserved—and perhaps least appreciated—monuments of antiquity. The Pantheon was built in 27 B.C. by Augustus' general Agrippa and completely rebuilt by Hadrian, who deserves the credit for this fantastic feat of engineering. The interior of the Pantheon is infinitely more spectacular than the outside suggests. You pass through the original bronze door into a truly majestic hall covered by a dome 142 feet high that rises mightily to a round opening at the top from which the Pantheon receives its only light. Once walls and dome were covered with rich decorations of gilt-bronze and marble, plundered by later emperors and popes. The bronze for Bernini's baldacchino in St. Peter's came from the Pantheon.

From the Piazza della Rotonda in front of the Pantheon, take the Via Giustiniani into the Via della Dogana Vecchia to the Church of San Luigi dei Francesi, where there are three stunning Caravaggios in the last chapel on the left. The inevitable coin machine provides the illumination and Caravaggio's mastery of light effects takes it from there.

Just behind San Luigi is the Piazza Navona, a beautiful 17th-century piazza that traces the oval form of the underlying Circus of Diocletian. At the center is Bernini's lively Fountain of the Four Rivers, with an enormous cave-pierced rock squared off by four statues of rivers representing the four corners of the world.

Leaving the piazza by way of the Via della Cuccagna you pass Palazzo Braschi, a museum containing interesting paintings and objects documenting Rome's history from medieval times. Right across the Corso Vittorio are the Baracco Museum of ancient sculpture on your left and Palazzo della Cancelleria, imposing Renaissance palace, property of the Vatican, on your right. Just a block or two to the left on Corso Vittorio looms the mighty Sant'Andrea della Valle, where Puccini set the first act of *Tosca*.

Take the Via dei Baullari through Campo dei Fiori (Field of Flowers). This was once the site of public executions; now one of Rome's busiest, most popular daily markets is held here. You can poke among the stalls, with their mountains of fruits and vegetables, and listen to the bickering and shrieking of both sellers and buyers as they haggle over everything from artificial flowers to live snails. Continue on into the Piazza Farnese, where Sangallo, Michelangelo and Della Porta all had a hand in constructing the magnificent Palazzo Farnese, now the French Embassy. The twin fountains in the piazza are formed of Egyptian granite basins from the

Baths of Caracalla. Behind Palazzo Farnese, turn right onto the Via Giulia, where you'll see some elegant palaces, old churches and a number of antique shops.

At the end of Via Giulia, just across the river is the old Borgo district, in the shadow of St. Peter's, that was once populated by high dignitaries of the storied 15th-century Papal Court who lived in fabulous luxury until their time passed with the end of the Papal State in 1870.

Look to the right along the river. That enormous round structure, with its cylindrical tower and tremendously thick walls, is the Borgo's outstanding historical monument today—Castel Sant'Angelo. Emperor Hadrian started building it as his tomb about the year 135 and Antoninus Pius finished it six years later. According to legend, the castle got its name during the plague of 590, when Pope Gregory the Great, passing by in a religious procession, saw an angel sheathing his sword appear atop the stone ramparts to predict, correctly, the plague's immediate end. Here it was, too, that Pope Clement VII took refuge in 1527 from the German mercenaries of Charles V. Outside, in a cleared enclosure around the castle, the city has laid out a public park; it provides an excellent opportunity to make a circuit of the castle, thus permitting you to judge for yourself just how immense the architectural work is and why, during the Middle Ages, it became the citadel of Rome. Inside, for a small fee, you may wander through most of Castel Sant'Angelo's many rooms, over its courtyards, and along the high-ceilinged hallways; don't fail to climb the stairs leading to the upper terrace, where you have all Rome at your feet. You get a good view, too, of the Passetto Vaticano, a 15th-century arcaded passageway inside the castle grounds that links the old fortress directly with the Vatican.

The Ghetto and Trastevere

Wander into that gloomy part of old Rome bounded by Piazza Campitelli and Lungotevere Cenci, into the city's least visited but most interesting area—the ancient Jewish ghetto. The same ghetto you see today existed even in the time of Emperor Titus, who brought so many Jews out of Palestine to Rome. Within this cramped area, until 1847, all Jews of Rome were confined under a rigid, night-long curfew; at the little church opposite Quattro Capi Bridge, they were forced to attend sermons converting them to Catholicism at their own expense. Now, of course, with the old gates of the ghetto torn down and social barriers removed, Rome's Jews live where they please, and the ghetto today is a ghetto only in name.

Among the most interesting sights here are the pretty Fountain of the Tartarughe (Turtles) on the Piazza Mattei, the Via Portico d'Ottavia—where medieval inscriptions and ancient friezes testify to the venerable history of these buildings—and the Teatro di Marcello, hardly recognizable as a theater now, but built at the end of the 1st century B.C. by Julius Caesar to hold 20,000 spectators.

Cross the Tiber over the ancient Ponte Fabricio to the Isola Tiberina, where a city hospital stands on a site dedicated to healing ever since a temple to Aesculapius was erected here in 291 B.C. Continue across Ponte Cestio into Trastevere, a maze of narrow streets that—along with the Monti district between the Roman Forum and Santa Maria Maggiore—constitute the city's most authentically Roman neighborhoods. Here you should see the Church of Santa Maria in Trastevere, one of Rome's oldest, with 12th- and 13th-century mosaics shining on its facade and interior. Find your way to the beautifully frescoed Villa Farnesina on the Via Lungara, where extravagant host Agostino Chigi delighted in impressing his guests by having his servants clear the table of precious silver dinnerware by casting it into the Tiber. Naturally, none of the guests knew of the nets he had stretched underwater to catch it all.

Trastevere's population has become very heterogeneous, as lots of foreigners, rich and poor, have moved into the district. And popular tradition has been distorted into false folklore for the benefit of tourists in some of its big restaurants. But the real *Trasteverini* are still there, hearty and uninhibited, much chagrined at the name their quarter has justifiably acquired for purse-snatching and petty thievery. Their goodwill can't help once the damage has been done, so intensify your security measures as you stroll these byways.

The Quirinal and Some Churches

The Quirinal, highest of Rome's seven hills, regales you with a splendid view of the city. In the square, the fountain shows Castor and Pollux reining in their unruly horses; the statues are Roman replicas of old Greek works, the obelisk came from the Mausoleum of Augustus, and the basin was salvaged from the Roman Forum itself. The largest building on the square is Palazzo Quirinale, residence—in chronological order—of popes, kings and the president of Italy.

Along the Via Venti Settembre are two very interesting little churches, each an architectural gem. The first you'll come upon is Sant'Andrea, a singularly harmonious work designed and decorated by Bernini. The second is the Church of San Carlo, by Bernini's rival, Borromini, who created an intricate exercise in geometrical perfection in a space no larger than one of the piers of St. Peter's. Farther on, at the Piazza San Bernardo, the Church of Santa Maria della Vittoria is known for Bernini's sumptuous Baroque decoration of the Cornaro Chapel, an exceptional fusion of architecture, painting and sculpture, where the conversation piece is the *Ecstasy of St. Theresa,* which represents a mystical experience in what some regard as very earthly terms.

Still another church—this one of much greater dimensions—awaits you down the Via Orlando at the Piazza della Repubblica, where the pretty Fountain of the Naiadi (Naiads) displays voluptuous bronze ladies wrestling happily with marine monsters. The Church of Santa Maria degli Angeli, together with the Museo Nazionale behind it, are only part of the remains of the colossal Baths of Diocletian, built in the 4th century A.D., largest and most impressive of the ancient baths. During the Renaissance Michelangelo converted the vast central chamber of the baths into a church; the museum occupies a part of the baths that was later made into a monastery. The museum's vast collections of archeological finds, mainly sculptures, have been on view only sporadically in the past, but radical restorations are underway and parts of the museum will be progressively opened to the public.

The Via Appia Antica, the Catacombs, and EUR

An excursion to the Via Appia Antica makes a pleasant change from museum-going. Do it on a fine day and take along a picnic or plan to have lunch at one of the restaurants near the catacombs. (The 118 bus from San Giovanni Laterano takes you to the Catacomb of San Callisto.)

Called "Queen of Roads," the Via Appia was completed in 312 B.C. to connect Rome with the south. Not far beyond the Porta San Sebastiano, which gives you a good idea of what 5th-century Rome's fortifications looked like, you'll come upon the little church of Domine Quo Vadis, where tradition says that Christ appeared to St. Peter, inspiring him to return to Rome and face martyrdom.

There are two important catacombs on the Via Appia. The first you'll come upon is that of San Callisto (closed Wednesday), one of the best-preserved underground cemeteries. A friar will guide you through its crypts and galleries. Just beyond is the 4th-century church of San Sebastiano, named for the saint who was buried in the catacomb (closed Thursday) that burrows underground on four different levels. This was the only Christian cemetery to remain accessible during the Middle Ages, and it gave origin to the term "catacomb." It's located in a spot where the road . dips into a hollow, known to the Romans as *catacumbas* (Greek for "near the hollow"). The Romans used the name to refer to the cemetery that had existed there since the 2nd century. The term came to be applied to all the underground cemeteries discovered in Rome in later centuries.

On the other side of the Via Appia are the ruins of the Circus of Maxentius, where the obelisk now in Piazza Navona was found. A bit farther along is the Tomb of Cecilia Metella, a Roman noblewoman, contemporary of Julius Caesar. The monument was turned into a fortress in the 14th century. The tomb marks the beginning of the most interesting and evocative stretch of the Via Appia, lined with remains of tombs and fragments of statuary. Cypresses and pines stand guard over ruined sepulchers and ancient paving stones trodden by triumphant Roman legions.

EUR lies just outside the city on the road to Ostia and was begun by Mussolini to house the Universal Exposition of Rome (hence the initials) in 1942. This world's fair never took place because of the war, and EUR was abandoned, to be reappraised in post-war years as an ideal building site for the expanding city. Strikingly modern government ministries and skyscrapers have been shooting up here, in a setting of landscaped gardens, lush parks and broad avenues.

At EUR the architect Nervi built his circular Palazzo dello Sport for the 1960 Olympics. The section is also the site of several museums, among them the Pigorini Museum, with its important prehistoric and ethnological collections. Another, the Museum of Roman Civilization, displays a very impressive plaster model, in scale, of what Rome looked like during its heyday of empire. EUR is easily reached from downtown Rome by means of the Metropolitana (Line B), which runs from Termini railway station. The EUR-Marconi stop is handiest for museums, about 10 minutes' walk away.

PRACTICAL INFORMATION FOR ROME

WHEN TO GO. Peak of the tourist season in Rome is Easter, when the greatest number of visitors crowd into the city. Spring and fall are the best seasons; the weather is usually good from mid-April through October. If you visit Rome in July and August you must do as the Romans do; get up early, do your sightseeing, then

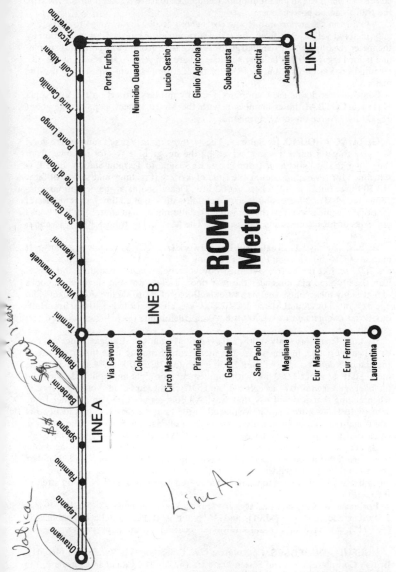

take refuge from the early-afternoon heat, resuming your activities later in the day
when the evening breeze cools things off. But remember that many shops and restaurants are closed in August. Roman winters are relatively mild, with some persistent rainy spells.

GETTING INTO TOWN FROM THE AIRPORT. Fiumicino Airport is around
31 km. (19 miles) from the city. The **ACOTRAL** bus that stands just outside the
exit of the Arrivals Terminal takes you directly to the Via Giolitti, on one side of
the Termini rail station. The fare is 5,000 lire, and you buy your ticket at the booth
inside the Arrivals Terminal before you board the bus. The same applies in reverse

before you leave Rome for Fiumicino. Remember to leave a good hour for the trip, the traffic can be horrendous.

A taxi from the airport into Rome costs about 50,000 lire as we go to press. Use only metered yellow cabs from the stand just outside Arrivals Terminal. You pay the meter reading plus a fixed charge for service to or from the airport, plus supplements for luggage, night, holiday services. There are yellow taxi stands at the city terminal on Via Giolitti and in front of the Termini station—insist they use the meter.

Some charter flights use Ciampino, a scruffy military airport on the Via Appia Nuova. ACOTRAL buses connect it with the Metro system; taxis charge about 35,000 lire. Agree on fare beforehand.

GETTING AROUND. By Subway. The *Metropolitana*, Rome's subway, is a good fast way to get around the area served by the newer Line A—for instance, from the center to the Vatican, or from Piazza di Spagna to Termini Station. Line B is scheduled for revamping, but at the time of writing it is dingy and slow. All fares are 700 lire. Books of 10 tickets, 6,000 lire. Ticket booths at major stations; machines take 100 or 50-lire coins. Carry a clutch with you at all times, they are useful for other machines too (like the coin-operated illumination in churches). Buy books of tickets at tobacconists and newsstands. The Metro runs from 5.30 A.M. to about 11.30 P.M.

By bus. The city has an extensive bus network (ATAC). You can buy a transport map at *ATAC* information booths (Termini, St. Peter's), or at newsstands. Fares are 700 lire, like the metro; you must buy your ticket before boarding and cancel it in the little red machine near the rear door. Tickets are sold singly or in books of 5 at many tobacconists and newsstands. Books of 10, 6,000 lire. *BIG* ticket valid one day on all buses and Metro costs 2,800. Weekly tourist ticket 10,000 lire. Half-day ticket *(biglietto orario)*, 1,000 lire. Avoid rush hours (8–9, 1–2 and 7–8) if you possibly can.

By taxi. Taxis—use only yellow cabs—wait at stands in strategic points and can be called by phone, in which case the meter runs from the time the driver leaves the stand. *Radiotaxi* also will send you a cab (38.75; 35.70; 49.94 or 84.33). The meter starts at about 3,000 lire, with supplements for night and holiday service and for baggage. *Radiotaxi* accepts AE and DC credit cards, but you must specify when calling that you will pay that way. All charges are listed on an official rate card (with English translation) displayed in the taxi; the driver should justify any additional requests by producing some kind of official notification of the increase. In case of a dispute insist that he drive you to find the nearest *Vigile* (city cop).

By car. Once you're in Rome, the best way to get around is on foot, using public transportation for longer distances. Driving in Rome isn't recommended, unless you are thirsty for the wilder forms of experience; traffic is heavy, parking impossible and many of the streets so narrow that no self-respecting donkey would attempt them.

For excursions outside the city, *Hertz* is at Via Sallustiana 28 (51.712); *Avis* is at Piazza Esquilino 1/c (47.01); and *Maggiore* is at Piazza della Repubblica 57 (463.715). All have airport and additional locations in the city.

USEFUL ADDRESSES. Consulates: U.S. Consulate, Via Veneto 121 (46.741). British Consulate, Via Venti Settembre 80/a (475.5441). Canadian Consulate, Via Zara 30 (855.341).

Tourist Information: EPT, written enquiries to Via Parigi 11; information office at Via Parigi 5 (463.748), and at the Termini Station and Fiumicino Airport. American Express Company, Piazza di Spagna 35 (67.641). CIT, Piazza della Repubblica 64 (47.94); Piazza Cola di Rienzo 33 (388.057); and Termini Station (474.0923). ENIT (National Tourist Board) Via Marghera 2 (497.1222).

Automobile Club of Italy, Via Marsala 8 (49.981).

Main Post Office, Piazza San Silvestro.

Telephones for long-distance, international and intercontinental calls: service offices at Piazza San Silvestro next to main post office; Termini Station, main lobby; Viale Mazzini post office; Viale Porta Angelica near St. Peter's; Fiumicino Airport.

SEASONAL EVENTS. January. The toy fair at Piazza Navona has its joyful conclusion on the eve of the Epiphany, January 6.

February. Carnival brings informal costumed merriment to the streets and some organized entertainment to the piazzas.

April. The Pope presides over the solemn rites of Holy Week and the impressive Easter celebrations in St. Peter's. Piazza di Spagna bursts into bloom late in April when the Spanish Steps are covered with azaleas. The International Horse Show begins at Piazza di Siena in Villa Borghese.

May. There's an antiques fair in Via dei Coronari and a rose show at Valle Murcia, above the Circus Maximus. The Foro Italico is scene of an international tennis tournament.

June. On the eve of June 24, feast of San Giovanni, the district of the same name bursts with festive doings, mainly gastronomic.

July. From July 16–31, the Festa di Noantri enlivens Trastevere, one of the city's oldest quarters, with a rousing mixture of worship and carnival. The summer opera opens at the Baths of Caracalla, continuing into August. Santa Cecilia's summer season of symphonic music is held in the Piazza di Campidoglio, and there are performances of classical and contemporary theater at Ostia Antica's Roman Theater.

August. The events of the *Estate Romana* continue with outdoor cinema, theater and music in the city's parks and piazzas.

December. Rome's concert season gains momentum under the aegis of the Academy of Santa Cecilia, the Philharmonic Academy and several other music societies. The Teatro dell'Opera opens its season. The Pope participates in observances of the feast of the Immaculate Conception at Piazza di Spagna on December 8.

TELEPHONE CODE. The area code for Rome is 06.

HOTELS. It is always advisable to book in advance, but if you get into Rome and have to find a hotel, the EPT Information Offices at Via Parigi 5, Termini Station and Fiumicino Airport will help you, at no charge. You may have to wait, as they're chronically short of personnel. Students can try the *Protezione Giovane* office at Termini Station, which specializes in finding low-cost convent accommodations for girls, but will help anyone if they are not too busy, or the *CTS,* a student tourist center, at Via Genova 16 (tel. 46.791), fairly near the station. *Don't* rely on the official-looking men who approach tourists at Termini Station, offering to get them a room. They tout for the less desirable hotels in the station area.

Noise is a problem in many hotels and pensions. The best places are soundproofed, but in the moderate and inexpensive range you should ask for an inside room if you're a light sleeper.

Deluxe

Ambasciatori Palace, Via Veneto 70 (47.493). Palatial; bright spacious rooms and suites. AE, DC, MC, V.

Bernini Bristol, Piazza Barberini 23 (463.051). Excellently located for everything from shopping to sightseeing; bedrooms and suites in contemporary or period fashion. AE, DC, MC.

Cavalieri Hilton, Via Cadlolo 101, Monte Mario (31.511). With a spectacular view of the city, this sleek, modern hotel makes up in efficiency and comfort what it lacks in atmosphere; several restaurants; park and pool. Minibuses to the center of town. AE, DC, MC, V.

Eden, Via Ludovisi 49 (474.3551). Near the Via Veneto; reputation for quiet comfort and good service; superb view from penthouse bar/restaurant. AE.

Excelsior, Via Veneto 125 (47.08). CIGA. Magnificent white palace with plush suites and rich decor. Two restaurants and a piano bar. AE, DC, MC, V.

Grand Hotel, Via Orlando 3 (47.09). Crown jewel of the CIGA chain, between Termini Station and the Via Veneto. This solid old hotel has an atmosphere of refined elegance and a tradition of discreet service. AE, DC, MC, V.

Hassler-Villa Medici, Piazza Trinità dei Monti 6 (678.2651). At the Spanish Steps, it rivals the Grand Hotel for sheer luxury and top prices. Lovely rooms and impeccable service. AE.

Expensive

Atlante Star, Via Vitelleschi 34 (656.4196). Near St. Peter's. Smart modern decor, roof garden. Free airport pick up. AE, DC, MC, V.

Boston, Via Lombardia 47 (473.951). Quiet location near the Via Veneto; nicely decorated, comfortable with a good restaurant. AE, DC, MC.

Colonna Palace, Piazza Montecitorio 12 (678.1341). Very central; smallish rooms, clubby ambiance in handsome old palace. Breakfast only. AE, DC, V.

De La Ville, Via Sistina 69 (67.33). Excellent location cheek by jowl with the deluxe Hassler. Lovely garden. AE, DC, MC, V.

D'Inghilterra, Via Bocca di Leone 14 (672.161). Breakfast only. In the heart of the shopping district; atmosphere and charm of a private club. AE, DC, MC, V.

Flora, Via Veneto 191 (497.821). Dated decor, but bedrooms comfortable, and service is attentive. AE, DC, MC, V.

Forum, Via Tor dei Conti 25 (679.2446). Near Piazza Venezia, a fine hotel; rooms are quiet and elegant. Rooftop dining terrace overlooking the Roman Forum. AE, DC, MC, V.

Giulio Cesare, Via degli Scipioni 287 (310.244). In Prati district, an elegant, beautifully kept, very quiet hotel with garden; gourmet buffet breakfast; no restaurant. AE, DC, MC, V.

Jolly, Corso d'Italia 1 (84.95). At the top of the Via Veneto overlooking the Villa Borghese. A strikingly modern, burnished glass and steel building; completely sound-proofed; modern and functional furnishings. AE, DC, MC, V.

Lord Byron, Via de Notaris 5 (360.9541). A *Relais* hotel. The relaxed, intimate atmosphere of a posh town house. On the edge of the Villa Borghese and the Parioli district, a bit out of the way, but in delightful surroundings. Book well in advance. AE, DC, MC, V.

Plaza, Via del Corso 126 (672.101). Excellent central location, handy to everything; solid old hotel with good atmosphere. AE, DC, MC, V.

Quirinale, Via Nazionale 7 (47.07). Central, with an air of solid comfort. Posh salons and pleasant bar. AE, DC, MC, V.

Regina Carlton, Via Veneto 72 (476.851). The usual advantages of a convenient location together with tastefully-cheerful decor and attentive service make this a good choice. AE, DC, MC, V.

Valadier, Via della Fontanella 15 (361.0592). Near The Spanish Steps. A sumptuous small hotel. Understated luxury. Recently renovated. A restaurant is planned for 1989. AE, DC, MC, V.

Victoria, Via Campania 41 (473.931). Considerable luxury, solid comfort, impeccable management. Near the Via Veneto. Bar, restaurant, and elegant public rooms. AE, DC, MC, V.

Moderate

Arcangelo, Via Boezio 15 (318.851). Near St. Peter's; quiet, good-sized rooms, attentive service. AE, DC, MC, V.

Britannia, Via Napoli 64 (465.785). Breakfast only. Small, very modern; near the Opera House and Termini Station. AE, DC, MC, V.

Carriage, Via delle Carrozze 36 (679.4106). Breakfast only. Quite small but very well located near the Piazza di Spagna. AE, DC, MC, V.

Columbus, Via della Conciliazione 33 (656.4874). Large, well-furnished; in handsome palace near St Peter's. AE, DC, MC, V.

Delle Legazioni, Via Barberini 11 (475.1616). On several floors of a well-kept building in a very central location. DC, MC, V.

Esperia, Via Nazionale 22 (487.245). Breakfast only. Good-size; on a main thoroughfare, handy to everything. V.

Fontana, Piazza di Trevi 96 (678.6113). At Trevi Fountain; small, well-furnished, with roof garden and good atmosphere. DC, V.

Gregoriana, Via Gregoriana 18 (679.4269). Breakfast only. Only 19 rooms in this delightful hotel near the Spanish Steps. Book well in advance.

Internazionale, Via Sistina 79 (679.3047). Breakfast only. Smallish, well-furnished, near Trinità dei Monti. Book ahead. AE, DC, MC, V.

Locarno, Via della Penna 22 (361.0841). Right behind Piazza del Popolo; solid, older hotel with 38 good-sized rooms, all with bath. AE, V.

Mozart, Via dei Greci 23/b (678.7422). Very central, small and quiet. Popular with musicians.

La Residenza, Via Emilia 22 (679.9592). Buffet breakfast, no restaurant. Cordial and comfortable, with garden. Near the Via Veneto.

Sant'Anna, Borgo Pio 134 (654.1602). Ample rooms. Soothing and welcoming atmosphere. AE, DC, MC, V.

Sistina, Via Sistina 136 (475.8804). Very central location. Tasteful decor and good atmosphere.

Sitea, Via Vittorio Emanuele Orlando 90 (475.1560). Central location near Termini Station, spacious and well-decorated rooms. Exceptional management. Bar; restaurant. AE, DC, MC, V.

Sole al Pantheon, Via del Pantheon 63 (679.3329). Very centrally located; historic landmark hotel with smallish rooms, steeped in atmosphere.

Tea, Via Sardegna 19 (679.9387). Near the Via Veneto; with restaurant, garage and garden.

Inexpensive

(all without restaurant)

Ausonia, Piazza di Spagna 35 (679.5745). Great location; helpful management. Simple but clean.

Croce di Malta, Via Borgognona 28 (679.5482). Small, clean and comfortable; in the shopping district near the Piazza di Spagna. V.

Dinesen, Via di Porta Pinciana 18 (475.3501). A few steps from the Via Veneto. 20 rooms, 18 with bath, and an immaculate Nordic air. AE, V.

Farnese, Via Alessandro Farnese 30 (386.343). Near Tiber, handy to metro and buses. Villa with good rooms on top floor.

Portoghesi, Via dei Portoghesi 1 (686.4231). On a picturesque little piazza in old Rome. Reliable accommodations, good atmosphere. MC, V.

Sant'Anselmo, Piazza Sant'Anselmo (573.547). A pension in the Aventine district. Comfortable old villa with garden. AE.

Scalinata di Spagna, Piazza Trinità dei Monti (679.3006). Popular small pension near the Spanish Steps. Warm atmosphere; top rates.

Sicilia Daria, Via Sicilia 24 (493.841). Clean, cordial, good-sized pension near the Via Veneto.

Suisse, Via Gregoriana 56 (678.3649). Unbeatable location near Spanish Steps. Clean, comfortable rooms; relaxed atmosphere.

CAMPING OUT. There are several camping grounds on the outskirts of Rome; most are connected with the center by bus, and some have bungalow facilities. Handiest to the city are *Flaminio,* on Via Flaminia Nuova at km. 8; *Seven Hills,* Via Cassia 1216; *Nomentano,* on Via Nomentana at km 12. From April through October, the *Internazionale* camping ground is open on the beach at Castelfusano; it's a short bus ride away from the Metro station.

For information on all camping facilities, write to *Federazione Italiana del Campeggio,* Casella Postale 649, 50100 Firenze.

MUSEUMS AND GALLERIES. The city's museums and galleries are divided into state *(nazionale),* city *(communale)* and private. State museums now charge from 1,500 to 4,000 lire, with top fees of 5,000 lire for the Roman Forum and Villa D'Este at Tivoli; entrance is free at least one day a week.

State and city museums and monuments in Rome are closed Mondays and on January 1, Easter, May 1, August 15 and December 25. State museums are usually open from 9 A.M. to 2 P.M. on weekdays, 9 to 1 on Sundays. Double-check opening hours with the Rome EPT office. The best time to visit the more important museums is either at opening hour or toward closing (but ticket offices close from 60 to 30 minutes before).

Gabinetto Nazionale delle Stampe, Via della Lungara 230. Important collection of prints from the 15th to 19th centuries in beautiful Villa Farnesina.

Galleria Borghese, in the Villa Borghese. Some extraordinary Berninis and Canova's *Pauline Borghese.* Upper floor closed in 1987.

Galleria Colonna, Via della Pilotta 17, near Piazza Venezia. Sat. only, from 9 A.M. to 5 P.M. The once-powerful Colonna family's own art collection. Contains some masterpieces, overshadowed by the sumptuosity of the salons.

Galleria Doria-Pamphili, Piazza del Collegio Romano 1/a, near Piazza Venezia. Open Tues., Fri., Sat., Sun., 10 A.M. to 1 P.M. In another princely residence, an extraordinary collection that includes works by Velásquez, Titian and Caravaggio. Take guided tour of magnificent Apartments.

Galleria Nazionale dell'Arte Antica (in two locations): **Palazzo Barberini,** Via Quattro Fontane 13. A rich collection of 13th–16th century paintings, including Raphael's famous *Fornarina;* **Palazzo Corsini,** Via della Lungara 10, lovely 18th-century palace; later sections of the collection.

Galleria Nazionale di Arte Moderna, Viale delle Belle Arti 131. Important collection of modern art. Large sections closed for redecoration so check. Has useful coffee shop. Early 20th-century art in new wing.

Keats and Shelley Memorial House, Piazza di Spagna, on the right of the Spanish Steps. A collection of Keatsiana and a good library.

Museo Barracco, Corso Vittorio 168. This 16th-century palace, built for a French cardinal, contains a fine collection of ancient sculptures.

Museo Capitolini, Piazza del Campidoglio. In two elegant palaces, designed by Michelangelo, an extraordinary collection of Greek and Roman antiquities. Open Tues. and Sat. 9–1.30 and 5–8; Wed.–Fri. 9–1.30; Sun 9–1.

Museo della Civiltà Romana, Piazza Giovanni Agnelli 10, at EUR. An interesting collection on ancient Rome.

Museo di Goethe, Via del Corso 17. Relics and documentation of Goethe's visits to Italy are on display in the rooms in which he lived.

Museo di Palazzo Venezia, Piazza Venezia (entrance on Via del Plebiscito). A 15th-century palace with collection of Renaissance arts and crafts.

Museo di Roma, Piazza San Pantaleo. The 18th-century Palazzo Braschi houses material illustrating the history of Rome from the Middle Ages.

Museo Napoleonico, Via Zanardelli 1. A rather specialized but rich collection of mementos of Napoleon, his family and times.

Museo Nazionale delle Arti e Tradizioni Popolari, EUR, Piazza Marconi 10. Italian folk art and traditions. Several sections temporarily closed.

Museo Nazionale di Villa Giulia, Via Borghese Piazza di Villa Giulia 9. The fabulous villa of Pope Julius III houses one of the world's great Etruscan collections.

Museo Nazionale Romano, Villa delle Terme di Dioclenziono, near Termini Station. A vast collection of classical sculpture and art, mostly closed while being rearranged.

Museo Pigorini, EUR, Piazza Marconi 10. An extensive collection of prehistoric remains, it documents early man's development in the Latium area.

PLACES OF INTEREST. Ara Pacis, Via Ripetta. A handsome white marble altar erected to celebrate Augustus's victories in Spain and Gaul. It's enclosed in what is best described as a glass box, and was painstakingly reconstructed from fragments. Open weekdays 9 A.M. to 1.30 P.M. Sun. 9 A.M. to 1 P.M. Closed Mon.

Baths of Caracalla, Via delle Terme di Caracalla. Inaugurated by Caracalla in the 2nd century A.D. The Rome Opera's summer season is held here. Open 9 A.M. to one hour before sunset. Sun. and hols. 10 to 1 P.M. Closed Mon.

Castel Sant' Angelo (Hadrian's Tomb), Lungotevere Castello. Built by Hadrian in the 2nd century A.D. as his family tomb, it was later converted into a fortress and was used by the popes. There's a museum of arms and armor, a collection of paintings and some beautiful frescos in its salons and a marvelous view from the terrace. Children love it; it's a fairy-tale castle come true. Open 9 A.M. to 1 P.M. Sun. 9 A.M. to noon. Closed Mon.

Colosseum, Piazza del Colosseo. Ancient Rome's most famous monument. Built in the 1st century A.D. it could hold 50,000 spectators and was faced with marble as model upstairs shows. Open 9 A.M. to one hour before sunset.

Domus Aurea, Via Labicana at Colle Oppio. Nero's fabulous palace has been excavated only in part. On its walls were found the delicate painted decorations that inspired Raphael and other Renaissance artists. It is usually closed to the public to prevent further deterioration.

Forum. The Roman Forum and Palatine Hill were the center of public life in ancient Rome; one of the world's most remarkable monuments. Open 9 A.M. to one hour before sunset. Sun. and holidays 10 to 1 P.M. Closed Tues.

Mamertine Prison, Via dei Falegnami, at Roman Forum. This was the state prison of ancient Rome where St. Peter was perhaps jailed. Open 9 A.M. to 4 P.M. Closed Tues.

Monument to Vittorio Emanuele, Piazza Venezia. An enormous white marble confection which contains the Instituto per la Storia del Risorgimento and the Tomb of the Unknown Soldier.

Pantheon, Piazza della Rotonda. This magnificent construction was built in the 1st century B.C., rebuilt by Hadrian and consecrated as a church in 609. Open 9 A.M. to 2 P.M. Sun. 9 A.M. to 1 P.M. Closed Mon.

Piazza del Quirinale. Definitely one of the "must" sights of Rome. Surrounded by palaces on three sides, including the Palazzo del Quirinale, with a magnificent view over the city on the fourth. In the middle stand colossal equestrian statues of Castor and Pollux.

Temple of Vesta, Piazza Bocca della Veritá. One of the holiest shrines of ancient Rome, where the sacred fire of Vesta burned. The present building dates from the 2nd century though its architectural origins are much older.

Tomb of Cecilia Metella, Via Appia Antica. This cylindrical tomb was built for a Roman noblewoman of the Republican era. Open 9.30 A.M. to 1.30 P.M. closed Mon.

Trajan's Market, Via IV Novembre 94. Vast complex of shops and market places overlooking Trajan's Forum and Trajan's Column, famous for spiral reliefs, now shrouded in protective coverings.

VISITING THE CATACOMBS. Of the 40 catacombs, eight are open to the public. Visitors are always accompanied by a guide, usually one of the friars charged with custody of the catacombs. The catacombs usually close at noon, reopen at 2.30 or 3. Hours vary in winter and summer.

On the Via Appia Antica. *Catacomb of San Callisto* (Via Appia Antica 110; Closed Wed.), one of the most important; many 3rd-century popes are buried here.

Catacomb of San Sebastiano (Via Appia Antica 132; Closed Thurs.), originally a pagan burial ground that had previously served as a rock quarry.

On the Via Ardeatina. *Catacomb of Domitilla* (Via delle Sette Chiese 282; Closed Tues.), one of the oldest and most extensive of Rome's catacombs; named for Flavia Domitilla, who belonged to the imperial family and who donated the land for the cemetery.

On the Via Nomentana. *Catacombs of Sant' Agnese* (Via Nomentana 349, entrance in the left nave of the basilica; Closed Mon.), on three levels.

On the Via Salaria Nuova. *Catacombs of Priscilla* (Via Salaria Nuova 430; apply to the Benedictine Sisters at the Casa di Priscilla; Closed Mon.), dates to the 2nd century and extends on two levels, with many well-preserved frescos.

CHURCHES. As the center of the Christian world, Rome is naturally bursting at the seams with churches. Their interest-quotient varies—some are historically important, some interesting for their art treasures, some as works of superb architecture. Below are only a few of the dozens of visitable possibilities.

One or two points to bear in mind are that Roman churches have erratic and unpredictable opening times and they are emphatically not open all the time. But generally they are open from about 7 A.M. to noon, and from 3 to 7 P.M. These times, however, can be no more than approximate. Many churches that are shut up tight during the week can be visited on Sundays. Also, they are places of worship and though women no longer have to cover their heads, appropriate dress and behavior are required.

Sant'Agnese, Piazza Navona. Across from Bernini's sensational fountain, one of Rome's monumental churches dominates the square with its Borromini facade, dome and twin towers.

Sant'Andrea al Quirinale, Via del Quirinale. A lovely small Baroque gem by Bernini.

Sant'Andrea della Valle, Corso Vittorio Emanuele. 2nd-largest dome in Rome and powerful frescos by Lanfranco and Domenichino.

San Carlo alle Quattro Fontane, at the Quattro Fontane intersection. The most unusual Baroque church in the city—tiny and exciting.

Il Gesù, Piazza del Gesù. 1560 and one of the world's most influential church buildings. Gloriously frescoed vault.

San Giovanni in Laterano, Piazza San Giovanni in Laterano. Rome's chief church from Constantine to the Renaissance and still Rome's Cathedral. Full of historic and artistic interest—beautiful Baptistry.

Sant'Ignazio, Piazza Sant'Ignazio. The Jesuit church with a brilliantly tricky illusionistic dome painting.

Sant'Ivo all Sapienza, Corso Rinascimento. A Borromini masterpiece, using a very difficult site. Lovely dome.

San Luigi dei Francesi, Piazza San Luigi dei Francesi. Not so much for the church, but for its treasures, especially three superb Caravaggios.

Santa Maria degli Angeli, Piazza della Repubblica. A conversion from Roman Baths, transformed by Michelangelo, though altered in the 18th century.

Santa Maria del Popolo, Piazza del Popolo. Another artistic treasure house. Two powerful chapels, the Chigi—with Bernini sculptures—and one dominated by two marvelous Caravaggios.

Santa Maria della Vittoria, Via Venti Settembre. Early Baroque, renowned for Bernini's *Ecstasy of St. Theresa.*

Santa Maria in Vallicella (Chiesa Nuova), Piazza della Chiesa Nuova. Especially notable for the ceiling frescos by da Cortona and paintings by Rubens.

Santa Maria Maggiore, Piazza di Santa Maria Maggiore. A truly fabulous interior, starting with the 5th-century mosaics. Full to bursting with interest.

Santa Maria Sopra Minerva, Piazza Minerva. Rome's only Gothic church. Michelangelo's *Risen Christ,* frescos by Filippo Lippi, tombs of St. Catherine of Siena and Fra Angelico.

Oratory of St. Filippo Neri, Piazza della Chiesa Nuova. Chiefly for Borromini's elegantly curving facade.

San Pietro in Vincoli, Piazza San Pietro in Vincoli. The chains which bound St. Peter and Michelangelo's astonishing *Moses,* nearly ruined by the intrusive souvenir shop.

Trinità dei Monti, Viale Trinità dei Monti. At the top of the Spanish steps, not so much for itself as for its position and view.

VATICAN CITY. Entry Formalities. Though the Vatican City is a sovereign state, there are no formalities governing entrance. When you step into the great square of St. Peter's you are on Vatican territory. You can enter all the museums as well as the church itself without showing any papers. Men or women in shorts are not allowed into St. Peter's or the Vatican Museums, and women must also cover bare upper arms.

Information. There is an information office (698 4466) on the lefthand side of the piazza, just in front of the facade of St. Peter's. Apart from obtaining general information about the Vatican, you may also book guided tours here. This can be done up to two days in advance. One tour includes the gardens and the Sistine Chap-

el, another takes in the gardens and St. Peter's. The tours are held from
through October and cost about 15,000 and 10,000 lire respectively. O
year-round, garden only, except Wed., Sun., 8,000 lire.

Opening Times. The Vatican Museums, which include the Sistine Chapel, are
open Monday to Saturday. Hours during the Easter period and from July through
September are from 9 to 5 (no admission after 4 P.M.). In all other months they're
from 9 to 2 (no admission after 1 P.M.). The museums are closed on Sunday, except
for the last Sunday of the month, when admission is free unfortunately making them
very crowded. Otherwise they are closed on Sundays and on religious holidays: Jan.
1, Feb. 11, March 19, Easter Sunday and Monday, May 1, Ascension Thursday,
Corpus Christi, June 29, August 14 and 15, November 1, December 8, December
25 and 26. The admission fee is 8,000 lire. There's a snack bar and reasonably-priced
cafeteria for lunch, a post office and bank. There are four color-coded routes
through the museums, each taking a different length of time to cover. The longest,
which is by far the best if you have the time, can take up to five hours to do properly.
The shortest, just covering the highlights, can be done in around 1½ hours if you
hurry.

Bus Service. A shuttle bus runs every half hour on the half hour from the Information Office on St. Peter's Square through the Vatican Gardens to a secondary
entrance to the Vatican Museums. Service mornings only until 12.30 P.M. No service
Sun. or Wed. Fare 1,000 lire.

Papal Audiences. Pope John Paul appears in mass audiences on Wednesday
mornings; during the winter they are held in Italian architect Nervi's soaring modern audience hall (entrance from the left-hand colonnade), and from March to October in St. Peter's Square. For tickets to an audience, apply to the Papal Prefecture
(*Prefettura*) which you reach through the Bronze Door at the end of the right-hand
colonnade. The office is open from 9 to 1 on Mondays and Tuesdays and from 9
until shortly before the audience on Wednesdays. On Sunday at noon the Pope appears at his third-floor study window to address the crowd gathered in St. Peter's
Square. Many kneel as he imparts the papal blessing and there's much applause
and cheering as he waves goodbye.

Pope John Paul retires to the cool of Castel Gandolfo for brief periods during
the summer, but continues to receive pilgrims there or in the Vatican.

For public audiences, when any number of persons up to 10,000 might be on
hand, dress conservatively, modestly, without worrying about details. However, for
the *baciamano* (ring-kissing) audience, at which the Pope greets from 20 to 40 persons at a time, it's mandatory for men to wear dark suits and women to dress in
black or white, with long sleeves, high neck and black veil for the head. Invitations
to these audiences are extended only on special recommendation from local ecclesiastical authorities.

Vatican Post Office. You may buy Vatican-issued stamps and coins at the Vatican Post Office, next to the Information Office.

PARKS AND GARDENS.
Rome's public gardens are remnants of the vast parks
created by Renaissance princes in imitation of ancient Roman "villas" or country
estates. They provide a pleasant diversion from more formal sightseeing. What's
more, in good weather they're perfect for picnic lunches.

Colle Oppio. On the Esquiline Hill overlooking the Colosseum, this land was
confiscated by Nero as site of his fabulous palace, the *Domus Aurea* (Golden
House). Its fire-razed ruins disappeared under the foundations of the public baths
built later by Titus and Trajan.

The Janiculum (Gianicolo). The view from the terrace is superb. The park was
laid out after 1870 in honor of the Italian patriots who fought here in 1849 in a
desperate attempt to dislodge French troops defending Vatican rule over Rome.
A bronze Garibaldi looks out over the capital from a marble pedestal.

Villa Ada. A large, rambling park between the Via Salaria and the heights above
the Tiber, the villa once belonged to the Italian royal family. The Catacombs of
Priscilla lie within its walls.

Villa Borghese, most famous of Rome's parks; created in the 17th century by Cardinal Scipione Borghese and opened to the public in 1902. Among its most appealing corners are the Lake Garden, a botanical garden with a café and a small lake where you can rent a boat; the Piazza di Siena, pine-shaded amphitheater where an important horse show is held in May each year; the approaches to the Casino Borghese art gallery; and the Pincio, a 19th-century addition to the park and a favorite vantage point overlooking Rome. The terrace of the Casina Valadier on the Pincio is a lovely (but pricey) spot for lunch. The Villa Borghese offers puppet shows, occasional outdoor concerts on the Pincio, a children's cinema, and riding at the Galoppatoio near Porta Pinciana. On its fringes are Rome's Zoo, the magnificent Etruscan museum of the Villa Giulia, the National Gallery of Modern Art.

Villa Celimontana. This lush walled park covers the western slopes of the Celian Hill, between the Colosseum and the Baths of Caracalla. The main entrance is at the Piazza della Navicella.

Villa Doria Pamphili. One of Rome's largest and most recently acquired public parks, its vast expanse of meadows and pine woods is studded with statues, fountains and gardens. It lies behind the Janiculum and is a favorite spot for Sunday outings.

Villa Glori. Handsome pines cover a hillside overlooking a bend in the Tiber in this park set aside in honor of Italian patriots.

Valle Murcia, Via di Valle Murcia, on the Aventine Hill above the Circus Maximus. The *Roseto* is open to the public in May for the Rose Show, and for other flower shows in season.

Villa Sciarra. Quiet and rather old-fashioned, like the Monteverde Vecchio district in which it's located, this is a pleasant little park with lots of statues and curious fountains.

THEATERS. Much of what you ordinarily see and do during a visit to Rome constitutes impromptu entertainment, but if you want to schedule your diversions, you have quite a choice. Do you want to dance yourself or watch Carla Fracci do it? Care to watch showgirls or puppets? Mozart or jazz? You're sure to find something for your tastes.

If you want to go to the opera, ballet or a concert, it's best to ask your hotel *portiere* to do the difficult job of getting tickets for you. They go on sale at the box office only, just a few days before performances, and there's usually a line.

Theaters and cabarets, both of which are enjoying increased attention from the Roman public, are not listed here. You would need a good command of Italian to enjoy either. If you care to try, the season runs from late fall to early spring, engagements are short, and the offerings consist mainly of classic or repertory theater. But you don't have to understand Italian to enjoy the beautiful setting of the openair performances of classical drama in the Roman Theater at Ostia Antica, held in July every year.

City authorities have undertaken a program of musical, artistic and just plain fun events that are injecting new life into Rome's piazzas, parks and palaces, especially in the summer months. Look for posters announcing events. The famous Roman carnival has been revived and enlivens the pre-Lenten period.

Ballet. Unlike New York or London, Rome hasn't caught ballet fever. The few occasions to see ballet here are the series at the *Teatro dell'Opera* and an occasional engagement at the *Teatro Olimpico* (see Concerts below). Nonetheless, Rome has contributed such names as Elizabeth Terabust and Diana Ferrara to the international ballet scene.

MUSIC. Concerts. Always a center for good music, Rome has burgeoned with a great number of new concert series, which for lack of proper auditoria have taken temporary haven in churches and historic palaces. The principal concert series are those of the *Accademia di Santa Cecilia* (offices at Via Dei Greci, box office 654.1044), the *Accademia Filarmonica Romana* (Teatro Olimpico, Via Gentile da Fabriano 17; 396.2635), the *Instituzione Universitaria dei Concerti* (San Leone Magno auditorium, Via Bolzano 38, 853.216), and the *RAI Italian Radio-TV* series at Foro Italico (368.65625). The *Gonfalone* series concentrates on Baroque music (Via del Gonfalone 32; 687.59527). The *Associazione Musicale Romana* (656.8441) organizes music festivals and concerts in churches and palaces throughout the year. Many are free, as are concerts of sacred music proffered by ecclesiastical authorities. The introduction of the vernacular in Roman Catholic rites has limited occasions to hear splendid executions of sacred music by church choirs. The Santa Cecilia Symphony Orchestra's summer season (July) has moved to the magnificent setting of Piazza del Campidoglio.

Only way to keep tabs on *all* the concerts scheduled for any one day is to buy the *Messaggero* or the *Repubblica* (or pick up one of the copies always available for customers' consultation at neighborhood bars) and check the list of *Spettacoli* for the day. *Ingresso gratuito* means that it's free. Depending on the venue, concert tickets can cost anything from 6–20,000 lire, for unreserved seats.

Opera. The opera season runs from November to May in the *Teatro dell'Opera* on the Via del Viminale (461.755). Tickets go on sale two days before performances, and the box office is open from 10 A.M. to 1 P.M. and 5 to 7 P.M. Prices range from 8,000 to 44,000 lire, and up to 64,000 lire for first nights. Often plagued by strikes and lack of funds, the Rome Opera always manages to come up with a respectable season, and sometimes an excellent one.

The summer season at Caracalla stages spectacular performances in the Roman baths. Tickets are on sale in advance, at the Teatro dell'Opera box office or at the box office at the Baths of Caracalla from 8 to 9 P.M. on the evening of the performance. Carry a warm wrap and something to cover bare legs, as it gets very cool and damp as the evening wears on.

MOVIES. There's one English-language cinema in Rome, the *Pasquino*, Vicolo del Piede, just off Piazza Santa Maria in Trastevere (580.3622). Film clubs sometimes present English-language films in the original version; consult the Rome newspapers or *This Week in Rome*.

SHOPPING. Shopping in Rome is part of the fun, no matter what your budget. You're sure to find something that suits your fancy *and* your pocketbook. It's a good idea to windowshop for a while before you buy, easy enough to do as you sightsee your way through the center of town. Italians have a way with their display windows that makes them minor works of art, a pleasure to behold. Jot down the names and addresses of the shops that interest you and note the prices, too, so that you'll have a basis for comparison.

The best buys in Italy are still leather goods of all kinds—from gloves to bags to jackets—and then there are silk goods and knitwear. We would add fashions to the list, for this is the homeland of fine boutique fashions for men and women. A fairly well-trained eye will find some worthy old prints and minor antiques in the city's interesting little shops, while full-fledged collectors can depend on the prestigious names of some of Italy's top antique dealers. Genuinely Italian handicrafts aren't so easy to find in these days of oriental imports, though some of the better shops offer Italian pottery and handwoven textiles.

It's always a good idea to carry a comparative size chart with you, especially if you wish to buy gifts of clothing for others. A rule of thumb that may help you orient yourself in the realm of sizes is that your Italian shoe size would be your American size, plus 31 (a U.S. size 7 is an Italian 38); your Italian dress size would be your American size, plus 32. Sizes aren't uniform, however, and vary greatly from one item to another. If you're buying for someone else, you'd be wise to come forearmed with a tape measure and a list of the person's measurements. In general you'll find Italian fashions well-made, often hand-finished, with generous hems and seams. Fabrics in ready-made clothing are usually good but often are not machine washable or shrink-proof.

In any case, remember that Italian stores generally will not refund your purchases, and that they often cannot exchange goods because of their limited stock. Always take your purchases with you, as having them shipped from the shop can cause unlimited grief. *Saldi* are sales, sometimes very satisfactory, but you have to be discerning. *Prezzi fissi* means just that: the prices are fixed and it's a waste of time to ask for a discount unless you're buying a sizeable quantity of goods or a particularly costly *objet d'art*. Most shops in Rome honor a variety of credit cards and will accept dollars or pounds at the current exchange rate. Ask for a receipt for your purchases; you may need it at customs on your return home.

The most elegant and expensive shops are concentrated in the Piazza di Spagna area. The Via Margutta is noted for its art galleries, the Via del Babuino for its antique shops, and the Via Gregoriana for its high fashion ateliers. Bordering this top-price shopping district is the Via del Corso, which—with the Via Frattina and Via del Gambero—is lined with shops and boutiques of all kinds where prices and goods are competitive. The Romans themselves like to shop here.

Up from the Piazza Colonna, the Via del Tritone has medium-priced shops featuring everything from fashion fabrics to sleek, modern kitchens. And still farther up, on the Via Veneto, you'll find a few more high-priced boutiques and shoe salons. Down in Old Rome, the Via dei Coronari is famed as an antique-dealers' row, the Pantheon area has a number of slipper purveyors, and the Via dei Giubbonari attracts budget shoppers. You'll come across many interesting little boutiques and crafts shops in the district's narrow, winding streets.

Rome has few department stores. There's a *Rinascente* at Piazza Colonna (clothing and accessories only) and another at Piazza Fiume (with a well-stocked housewares and gadgets department in the basement). *Coin* on the Piazzale Appio at San Giovanni in Laterano is good for fashion. The *UPIM* and *STANDA* chains are similar to Mark's and Spencer's, with a wide range of medium-quality, low-priced goods. They're the place to go if you need a pair of slippers, a sweater, a bathing suit or such to see you through until you get home. In addition, they carry all kinds of toiletries and first-aid needs. And for emergencies, most *STANDA* and *UPIM* stores have an invaluable while-you-wait shoe repair service counter.

Once you have window-shopped the center, it may be worthwhile to stroll down the Via Cola di Rienzo, where much of what you've seen—same brands, same quality—is on sale for less. The Via Ottaviano, which you take to get to St. Peter's from the last stop on Metro Line A, offers low-priced fashions and bags of medium quality.

Religious articles overflow from the shops around St. Peter's, on the Viale Porta Angelica and the Via della Conciliazione—and, indeed, from the nun-run souvenir shop tucked away in the side of St. Peter's itself.

Young Romans and bargain-hunting matrons love to go to the openair market at the Via Sannio, near San Giovanni, where they find second-hand U.S.-made clothing at unbeatable prices. On Sunday morning there's a flea market at Porta Portese, now stocked mainly with new or second-hand articles of clothing. However, there are still a few dealers in old furniture and just plain junk that attracts the attention of eternally optimistic Romans, who remember the eagle-eyed fellow who walked out of Porta Portese with a masterpiece worth millions for which he had paid a few thousand lire. Everybody bargains, it's part of the fun, and you should, too, if you see something you like.

Shop hours in Rome vary greatly, but in general you'll find the shops open from 9 to 1 and from 4 to 7, with half-hour variations, many of the centrally located, tourist-oriented shops stay open during the lunch hour, and the *Rinascente* department stores and *UPIM* stores in the center of town remain open throughout the day. All shops close on Saturday afternoon during the summer months (July and August) and on Monday morning during the rest of the year. (Food shops, by the way, close on Saturday afternoon in summer, on Thursday afternoon from September through June). Window-shopping can be frustrating at midday, evenings and holidays, for most shops have heavy blinds hiding them from view when they're closed.

RESTAURANTS. Rome can boast restaurants representative of the cuisine of many parts of Italy, but also there is a brand of Roman restaurant with a quality all its own. You will find general points under *Restaurants* in the *Facts at your Fingertips* section, but here are a few more local comments.

The lunch hour in Rome lasts from 1 P.M. to about 3, though you won't be turned away if hunger strikes shortly after noon. Dinner is served from 8 or 8.30 P.M. until about 10.30; some restaurants stay open very late, especially in the summer, when they spread their tables out along the sidewalks so that their patrons can enjoy the cool of the evening while lingering over a *quartino* (quarter-liter) of wine.

If you're in the habit of going over your restaurant check carefully, you had better take a quick course in Sanskrit, for that's the only writing used by Roman waiters.

Roman Specialties. Authentic Roman cuisine isn't so well known abroad, largely because it is based on local ingredients, many of which are found only at certain times of the year - milkfed lamb, globe artichokes from the sandy coastal plains, tender vegetables. Queen of Roman pastas is *fettuccine,* golden egg noodles, usually topped with a rich tomato and meat sauce, a dollop of butter and a dusting of *parmigiano. Fettuccine* are best when they are freshly made; by all means order them if you see these flour dusted yellow ribbons of pasta displayed along with the daily offerings of your chosen restaurant. *Spaghetti alla carbonara* is served with raw egg, chunks of *guanciale* (unsmoked bacon) and lots of freshly-ground black pepper; *spaghetti all' Amatriciana* has a piquant sauce of tomato, unsmoked bacon and hot red pepper. *Gnocchi,* a Roman favorite for Thursday dinner, are tiny dumplings of semolina and potato.

Abbacchio, baby lamb, is at its best in spring; during the summer you will find *pollo alla diavola* (grilled chicken), or *pollo coi peperoni* (chicken with peppers) on local menus. *Baccalà* (codfish) is most popular in the form of crunchy fillets fried in batter.

Artichokes *alla romana* are sautéed whole with garlic and mint, and *carciofi alla giudia* are masterfully fried, with each petal crisp and light enough to melt in your mouth.

Local cheeses include the mild *caciotta* and sharp *pecorino.* Roman cooks also use *ricotta* in a number of dishes.

Typical wines of Rome are those of the Castelli Romani—*Frascati, Colli Albani, Marino* and *Velletri.*

Deluxe

ABC, Via Veneto 66 (474.0950). Always open. Posh atmosphere, smart clientele and good food. AE, DC, V.

Casina Valadier, at the Pincio in Villa Borghese (679.2083). The surroundings and view more than make up for uninspired but acceptable cuisine. AE.

La Cupola, Hotel Excelsior, Via Veneto 125 (47.08). Always open. Classic Italian cuisine served with style in elegant ambience. Perfect pasta dishes, are good reasons for eating here. AE, DC, MC, V.

Eden Hotel, Via Ludovisi 49 (474.3551). Closed Sat. and Sun. Panoramic dining room; good food, service.

Hostaria dell'Orso, via Monte Brianzo 93 (656.4250). Closed for lunch. In unique and historic premises, a Roman tradition for elegant evenings, now largely usurped by tourists. So-so food. AE, DC, MC, V.

Le Jardin, in the Lord Byron Hotel, Via de Notaris 5 (360.9541). Closed Sun. One of the best in Rome, presenting a select menu of beautifully prepared dishes and fine wines. AE, DC, MC, V.

Le Pergola, Hotel Cavalieri Hilton, Via Cadlolo (31.51). Evenings only. Imaginative menu; marvelous view. AE, DC, MC, V.

Le Restaurant, Via Vittorio Emmanuele Orlando 3 (47.09) Closed Aug. A discreet haunt of Rome's classiest crowd, this is the ultimate in elegance. Delicious meat specialities. DC, MC, V.

El Toulà, Via della Lupa 29/b (687.3750). Closed Sat. lunch, Sun. and Aug. Absolutely tops for ambience; cuisine and service generally fine. AE, DC, MC, V.

Expensive

Albérto Ciarla, Piazza San Cosimato 40 (581.8668). Evenings only. Closed Sun. and three weeks in Aug. In Trastevere, a fish restaurant *par excellence.* AE, DC, MC, V.

Al Chianti, Via Ancona 17 (861.083). Closed Sun. and two weeks in Aug. Near the Piazza Fiume. Cordial host and range of well-prepared food. AE, DC, V.

Andrea, Via Sardegna 28 (493.707). Closed Sun. and two weeks in Aug. Near the Via Veneto, finest classic cuisine. AE, DC, MC, V.

Apicio, Via Principe Amedeo 3 (461.446). Closed Sun. In the Hotel Metropole near the station; fine Italian regional dishes. DC, V.

Dal Bolognese, Piazza del Popolo, 1 (361.1426). Closed Mon., Sun. in June, July, Aug. 5–20. Long a favorite of people in the arts. DC.

Il Buco, Via Sant'Ignazio 8 (679.3298). Closed Mon. A smart little place for Tuscan cuisine. Some items in (M) range. AE, DC.

Cicilardone, Via Merulana 77 (733.806). Closed Sun. eve. and Mon. Near S. Maria Maggiore. Small, friendly place; very good food and wines. Reserve.

L'Eau Vive, Via Monterone 85 (654.1095). Closed Sun. In old Rome, beatific atmosphere, French cuisine, run by Catholic lay missionaries. AE, DC, V.

Fortunato, Via del Pantheon 55 (679.2788). Closed Sun. Popular with politicos and Romans. AE.

Galeone, Piazza San Cosimato 27 (581.8668). Closed Wed. Sailing-ship decor; fish specialties. AE, DC, MC, V.

Giovanni, Via Marche 64 (493.576). Closed Sat. and Aug. Off the Via Veneto, behind the Excelsior; a straightforward, very good trattoria. AE, V.

Leon d'Oro, Via Cagliari 25 (861.847). Closed Sun. and mid-day. In the Salario district; fish with flair, some rather pricey. DC, MC.

La Maiella, Piazza Sant'Apollinare 45 (656.4174). Off Piazza Navona. Abruzzese specialties; summer terrace. AE, DC, MC, V.

Osteria dell'Antiquariato, Piazza San Simeone 27 (659.694). Closed Sun. Near Piazza Navona; especially nice in summer.

Passetto, Via Zanardelli 14 (659.937). Closed Sun. Near Piazza Navona; a Roman classic serving favorites such as canelloni and baby lamb. AE, DC, MC, V.

Pianeta Terra, Via Arco del Monte 94 (656.9893). Closed Mon. and end July–Aug. Small, elegant. Excellent and inventive cuisine. AE.

Pino e Dino, Piazza Montevecchio (656.1319). Near Piazza Navona. Tiny, delightful, excellent food.

Piperno, Monte dei Cenci 9 (654.0629). Closed Sun. evening, Mon. and Aug. Interesting specialties of Old Rome's Jewish Ghetto.

Quinzi e Gabrieli, via delle Coppelle 5 (687.9389). Closed lunch and Sun. Small sophisticated oyster bar. AE, DC.

Ranieri, Via Mario dei Fiori 26 (679.1592). Closed Sun. Italian-international cuisine in Belle Epoque ambience. AE, DC, MC, V.

Regno di Re Ferdinando, Via Banchi Nuovi 8 (654.1167). Closed Sun. In Old Rome; inconspicuous entrance, attractive Neapolitan tavern. AE, DC.

La Rosetta, Via della Rosetta 9 (656.1002). Closed Sun., Mon. lunch and Aug. One of Rome's best for fish. AE, DC.

Sabatini, Vicolo Santa Maria in Trastevere 18 (581.8307). Closed Wed. In historic setting, the usual Roman dishes.

Tana del Grillo, Salita del Grillo 6 (679.8705). Closed Sun. and Aug. Near the Forum; popular with excellent pastas.

Taverna Giulia, Vicolo dell'Oro 23 (656.9768). Closed Sun. and Aug. In Old Rome; consistently good Northern Italian specialties. AE, DC, MC, V.

Il Tentativo, Via della Luce 5 (589.5234). Closed Sun. and Aug. Intimate, sophisticated ambience and exquisite gourmet cuisine; must reserve. AE, DC, V.

Il Veliero, Via Monservato 32 (654.2636). Closed Mon. One of Rome's top seafood restaurants; in Old Rome, near Piazza Farnese. AE, DC, V.

Moderate

Aquila, Via Rasella 138 (461.214). Closed Sun. and hols. Near Piazza Barberini. Classic Roman restaurant, good daily specials.

Archeologia, Via Appia Antica 139 (788.0494). Closed Thurs. Rustic trattoria.

Archimede-Santa Chiara, Via Santa Chiara 31 (655.216). Closed Sun. Superlative fried dishes. DC.

La Campana, Vicolo della Campana 18 (656.7820). Closed Mon. and Aug. Off Via della Scrofa; one of the oldest and best trattorias.

Cannavota, Piazza San Giovanni in Laterano (775.007). Closed Wed. and 1–20. Aug. Excellent Roman cooking. AE, V.

Cecilia Metella, Via Appia Antica 125 (513.6743) Closed Mon. Garden; good food.

Checco er Carrettiere, Via Benedetta 10 (581.7018). Closed Sun. evening and Mon. Behind Piazza Trilussa in Trastevere; a colorful trattoria. AE, DC.

Ciceruacchio, Via del Porto (580.6046). Closed Mon. and Aug. A Trastevere cellar restaurant with summer garden. AE, DC, V.

Colline Emiliane, Via degli Avignonesi 22 (475.7538). Closed Fri. and Aug. Just off the Piazza Barberini; homemade pasta, truffles.

Da Amato, Via Garibaldi 62 (580.9449). Evenings only. Closed Sun. Italo-Spanish oasis in Trastevere for *paella* and other interesting dishes.

Da Elda al Senato, Corso Rinascimento 71 (654.2982). Closed Sun. and Aug. Near the Piazza Navona; popular place.

Dal Bolognese, Piazza del Popolo 1 (361.1426). Closed Mon. Long a favorite with the arty crowd. Perfect for people-watching. AE, V.

Fortunato al Pantheon, Via del Pantheon 55 (679.2788). Closed Sun. Boasts a faithful and demanding clientele, varied menu. AE.

Giggetto, Via Portico d'Ottavia 21 (656.1105). Closed Mon. and July. In the heart of the Ghetto, this spot is famous for Roman Jewish specialties.

Il Gladiatore, Piazzale del Colosseo 15 (736.276). Closed Wed. Facing Colosseum, attracts tourists and Romans, too, with good food. AE, DC, V.

Massimo d'Azeglio, Via Cavour 18 (460.646). Closed Sunday. Near Termini station, excellent restaurant in hotel of same name. AE, DC, MC, V.

Da Meo Patacca, Piazza dei Mercanti (581.6198). Evenings only. In Trastevere, outrageously fake and lots of fun. AE, DC, V.

Orso 80, Via dell'Orso 33 (686.1710). Closed Mon. Good Roman dishes, lively evenings. AE, DC, V.

Pancrazio, Piazza del Biscione 92 (656.1246). Closed Wed. and Aug 1–18. In Old Rome, near Campo dei Fiori. Fascinating cellar restaurant. AE, DC, MC, V.

Piccola Roma, Via Uffici del Vicario 36 (679.8606). Closed Sun. and Aug. Central, thoroughly satisfactory.

Pierluigi, Piazza Ricci (686.8717). Closed Mon. Popular with foreign residents of Rome.

Quattro Mori, Via Santa Maria delle Fornaci 8/a (632.609). Closed Sun. and Aug. Located near Vatican; best Sardinian restaurant in town.

La Rampa, Piazza Mignanelli 18 (581.8284). Closed Sun., Mon. lunch and Aug. Attractive marketplace decor and vast menu in this favorite near Spanish Steps. AE.

Romolo, Via di Porta Settimiana 8 (581.8284). Closed Mon. and 15 days in Aug. A Trastevere favorite. AE, DC, V.

Santopadre, Via Collina 18 (489.405). Closed Sun. and Aug. Near Piazza Fiume. Small classic restaurant.

Severino a Santa Croce, Via Santa Croce in Gerusalemme 1 (750.112). Closed Thurs. and 20 July to 5 Aug. Trattoria, near San Giovanni.

Tempio di Bacco, Via Lombardia 38 (475.4625). Closed Sat. Near Via Veneto; reliable for classic dishes. AE, DC, MC, V.

Val di Sangro, Via Alessandria 22 (861.134). Closed Fri. and July 15–Aug. 16. Neighborhood favorite featuring fish and country-style pasta.

Vecchia Roma, Piazza Campitelli 18 (656.4604). Closed Wed. and two weeks in Aug. Near Piazza Venezia; good atmosphere.

Inexpensive

Baffetto, Via del Governo Vecchio 114 (686.1617). Closed lunch; Sun., Aug. Rome's best-known inexpensive pizzeria; plainly decorated.

Da Enzo, Vicolo dello Scavolino (679.0974). Closed Sun. and two weeks in Aug. Small, homely trattoria, near Trevi Fountain.

Da Umberto, Piazza San Giovanni della Malva (581.6646). Closed Wed. and Sept. Trastevere trattoria, behind Piazza Trilussa.

Fiammetta, Piazza Fiammetta 8 (685.5777). Closed Tues. Near Piazza Navona; order carefully to stay in price range.

Gioia Mia, Via Avignonesi 34 (462.784). Closed Wed. Near Piazza Barberini; a popular place.

Hostaria Farnese, Via dei Baullari 109 (654.1595). Closed Thurs. Home cooking in tiny trattoria in the heart of Old Rome. AE, V.

Hostaria del 104, Via Urbana 104 (484.556). Closed Wed. Near S. Maria Maggiore. Interesting choices.

Luigi, Piazza Sforza Cesarini. Closed Mon. Friendly, crowded; known for good food; pleasant outdoor tables in summer.

Matricianella, Via del Leone 4 (678.3870). Closed Sun. and Aug. Just off Via del Corso, good pasta and pizza.

Nello e Franco, Via del Pellegrino 107 (656.9361). Closed Mon. Sturdy Roman favorites; different specials each day.

Otello alla Concordia, Via della Croce 81 (679.1178). Closed Sun. Old favorite in the center of the shopping district.

La Pentola, Piazza Firenze 20 (654.2607). Closed Sat. and 15 July to 15 Aug. DC, V.

Pierluigi, Piazza Ricci (656.1302). Near Piazza Farnese; popular trattoria.

Polese, Piazza Sforza Cesarini 40 (656.1709). Closed Tues. Straightforward Italian cuisine; good *fettuccine;* outdoor dining in summer.

Tavernetta, Via del Nazzereno 3 (679.3124). Closed Mon. and Aug. Between the Trevi Fountain and Spanish Steps; good-value tourist menu. AE, DC, MC, V.

Tulipano Nero, Via Roma Libera 15, Piazza San Cosimato (581.8309). Closed Wed. A bright and noisy Trastevere pizzeria. Youthful clientele.

CAFES. A fine art in Rome, cafe-sitting offers a comfortable perspective for people-watching. Remember that you pay double or more for table service, but you're welcome to sit as long as you like.

Babington's, Piazza di Spagna. Historic English tearoom. Pricey. AE.

Bacaro, Via degli Spagnoli 27. Off Via della Scrofa. Delightful wine bar.

Café de Paris, Via Veneto. The original *dolce vita* café. Pricey. AE, DC.

Caffè Greco, Via Condotti. Old-world atmosphere. Table service costly.

Casina Valadier, on the Pincio. Terraces with marvelous view. AE.

Doney, Via Veneto. Traditional tourist favorite.

Fassi, Corso d'Italia at Piazza Fiume. Shaded garden, delicious ice cream.

Giolitti, Via Uffizi del Vicario. Near Pantheon. Best ice cream in Rome.

Rosati, Piazza del Popolo. Rendezvous of artists and literati.

Sant'Eustachio, Piazza Sant'Eustachio. Near Pantheon. Famous *espresso.*

Tre Scalini, Piazza Navona. Grandstand view. *Tartufo* specialty.

NIGHTCLUBS AND DISCOS. Rome has never been a great city of nightlife. There are a few good clubs and discos though, and many others that enjoy a brief season of popularity before closing in oblivion. Nightclubs are open until about 4 A.M.; many close in August. You may have to pay a small membership fee in addition to the entrance charge. Most discos open about 10:30 P.M. and charge an entrance fee of around 20,000 lire, which sometimes also includes the first drink. The prices quoted cover the entrance fee (if any) and the first drink at a table. Additional drinks usually cost from 8–10,000 lire.

Acropolis, Via Luciani 52, in the Parioli district (870.504). For the young; crazy psychedelic lights and deafening decibels. 15,000 lire.

Blue Bar, Hostaria dell'Orso, Via dei Soldati 25 in Old Rome (656.4221). This ground-floor piano bar is a popular haven for a quiet drink. 25,000 lire.

Cabalà, Hostaria dell'Orso, Via Soldati in Old Rome (656.4221). A lovely place to dine and dance; closed on Sat. 45,000 lire.

Club 84, Via Emilia 84, just off the Via Veneto (475.1538). Been going strong since the days of *La Dolce Vita;* live and disco music. 25,000 lire. AE, MC.

Easy Going, Via della Purificazione 9, near Piazza Barberini (474.5578). An uninhibited club for gays. 15,000 lire.

Gilda, Via Mario dei Fiori, near Piazza di Spagna (678.4838). The place to spot Italian actors and politicians. Hot new nightspot with two restaurants and live disco music.

Hysteria, Via Giovanelli 12 (Largo Benedetto Marcello), (964.587). Frenetic disco for a glamorous crowd.

Jackie-O, Via Buoncompagni 11 (461.401). Disco playground for the smart international set and extravagant cinema types. 40,000 lire. AE.

Open Gate, Via Sau Nicolo da Tolentino 4 (475.0464). Smart, art-deco supper club. 30,000 lire. AE, DC.

Piper, Via Tagliamento 9 (854.459). First of Rome's discos, it's still going strong, mainly with a young crowd. 15,000 lire. MC.

Scaraboccio, Piazza Ponziani 8 (580.0495). Loud music and video screens make this another popular spot.

Veleno, Via Sardegna 27 (493.583). Good disco music and up-market clientele. 25,000 lire.

THE ENVIRONS OF ROME

Roman Villas and Etruscan Tombs

A breath of country air and a change of scenery can enhance your enjoyment of Rome and give you a new perspective on its disparate delights. It's a good idea to intersperse city sightseeing with jaunts *fuori porta* (outside the gates), as the Romans would say. Below we list and describe some of the most interesting day trips to be had from Rome.

We have started close in, to the east, with Tivoli, the goal of all who love Rome's past, and then move clockwise through Subiaco, Palestrina and the Castelli Romani; southwards towards Monte Cassino, famous for its devastation in the last World War and subsequent restoration; towards the coast with Anzio and Ostia Antica; and finally north, to visit the strongholds of Rome's early rival civilization, the Etruscans, at Cerveteri, Bracciano, Tarquinia and Viterbo.

Try not to schedule your excursions for Sundays, which is when the Romans conduct their weekly exodus, creating enormous traffic jams and filling up every decent trattoria for miles around. During the week you'll probably have Frascati or wherever pretty much to yourself, to be savored and enjoyed along with a draught of the local wine. While tour agencies run guided bus tours to many of the spots mentioned here, you may prefer the freedom and flexibility of doing them on your own. They're all well-connected with the capital, though it's a good idea to check timetables for your return trip and to double-check opening hours of museums and archeological sites with the Rome EPT offices.

Tivoli

Tivoli is a five-star draw for a jaunt outside Rome, its attraction being its two villas—an ancient one in which Hadrian reproduced the most beautiful monuments in the then-known world, and a Renaissance one, in which Cardinal Ippolito d'Este put a river to work for his delight. Ancient Tibur, as it was then called, has been a pleasure resort for a long time. The ancient Romans came here to take cures in the sulfureous waters of the Acque Albule springs on the plain and then ascended the hill to their fine country villas.

It's advisable to visit the Villa Adriana (Hadrian's Villa) first, especially in the hot months, to take advantage of the cool morning hours, as there's very little shade. Then you can take the bus up to town, have lunch and enjoy the cool terraces of the Villa d'Este and the refreshing waterfalls of the Villa Gregoriana.

Hadrian built his villa over a vast tract of land below ancient Tibur; he needed the space, for he had a project in mind, inspired by journeys all over the empire. A man of great genius and intellectual curiosity, he was fascinated by the accomplishments of the Hellenistic world, and he decided to re-create this world for his own enjoyment. From 118 to 130 A.D., architects, laborers and artists worked on the villa, periodically spurred on by the emperor himself, newly returned from a trip abroad and full of ideas for even more daring constructions. After Hadrian's death in 138, the fortunes of his villa declined; it was sacked by barbarians and Romans alike, and many of its decorations ended up in the Villa d'Este. Still, it's an impressive complex of the most varied architectural forms. A fascinating new museum at the entrance proposes nine itineraries through the villa, images of the most important statues found there, and exhibits illustrating materials and techniques used in its construction.

One of the most beautiful parts of the whole huge complex is the Canopus, an artificial valley in which Hadrian reproduced an ancient Egyptian canal on the Nile. Columns and arches are reflected in the still water, and a few statues still stand to evoke the time when the villa was full of them. On the hill to the side of the Canopus, a museum contains the more recent finds made in the excavations. Wander among intriguing ruins of great halls, libraries and baths.

After this walk you'll be glad to get the bus up to Tivoli. It stops in the main square, just a few steps from the entrance to the Villa d'Este. Ippolito d'Este also happened to be a cardinal, thanks to his grandfather, Pope Alexander VI. To console himself for his seesawing fortunes in the political intrigues of the time, Ippolito tore down part of a Franciscan monastery that occupied part of the site that the cardinal had chosen for his villa. Then the determined prelate deviated the Aniene river into a channel that runs under the town to provide water for the Villa d'Este's fountains—and what fountains: big, small; noisy, quiet; rushing, running and combining to create a late-Renaissance masterpiece in which sunlight, shade, water, gardens and carved stone create an unforgettable experience. If you can, see it when it's illuminated on summer evenings.

Tivoli offers yet another spectacle, the Villa Gregoriana, where artificial waterfalls created by order of Pope Gregory XVI in 1835 look as if they had always existed in this savagely beautiful setting. You can follow a pretty footpath down through the villa. Some of Tivoli's restaurants have terraces overlooking this sight.

Subiaco

Mountains and monasticism characterize this itinerary into the mystic past of Rome's rugged hinterland. Subiaco is now a modern town built over World War II rubble, overlooking the Aniene valley. Here Nero built himself a villa, said to have rivaled that of Hadrian at Tivoli, and dammed the river to create three lakes and a series of lovely waterfalls. Beyond Subiaco the valley narrows to an almost impassable gorge, and that's the direction you take to see two famous monuments of Western monasticism. The first you come upon is the convent of Santa Scholastica, the only one of the hermitages founded by St. Benedict and his sister Scholastica to have survived the Lombard invasion of Italy. Of its three cloisters, the first has been largely rebuilt, the second is of the 15th century and the third is a beautiful example of 13th-century Cosmatesque decoration. The library contains some precious volumes, for this was the site of the first printshop in Italy, set up in 1464.

A twenty-minute walk up the valley takes you past wild scenery to the monastery of St. Benedict, built over the grotto where the saint meditated upon his Rule. Clinging to the cliff with its nine great arches, the monastery has resisted the assaults of man and nature for almost 800 years. Every inch of the upper church is covered with frescos by Umbrian and Sienese artists of the 14th century. In front of the main altar a stairway leads down into the lower church, carved out of the living rock, with yet another stairway down to the grotto or cave where Benedict lived as a hermit for three years. The frescos here are even earlier; look for the portrait of St. Francis of Assisi, painted from life in 1210, in the Chapel of St. Gregory, and for the oldest fresco in the monastery in the Shepherds' Grotto.

Back in town, if you've got the time, stop in at the 14th-century church of San Francesco to see the frescos by Il Sodoma, and climb up to the fortified abbey to see the frescoed apartments of Pius VI, who was abbot of Subiaco before he became pope.

Palestrina

This interesting town on the slopes of Monte Ginestro, 38 km. (24 miles) outside Rome, has remained surprisingly obscure outside Italy, except to students of ancient history and music lovers. Its most famous native son, Giovanni Pierluigi da Palestrina, born here in 1525, is the renowned composer of 105 masses, along with sundry madrigals, magnificats and motets. But the place was celebrated long before his lifetime. In fact, Palestrina, the ancient *Praeneste,* was founded much earlier than Rome. It was site of the Temple of Fortuna Primigenia, which dates from the beginning of the 2nd century B.C., one of the vastest, richest, and most frequented temple complexes of all antiquity. People came from afar to consult its famous oracle. It's interesting to note that no one had any idea of the extent of the complex until World War II bombings exposed ancient foundations that extend way out onto the plain below the town. Now you can make out the four superimposed terraces that formed the main part of the temple; they were built up on great arches and were linked by broad flights of stairs. The whole town sits on top of what was once the main part of the temple. There are reminders of this everywhere, from the huge foundation stones that you see on your left as you approach the town on the Via degli Arcioni, to the large hall and mosaic-paved grotto off the Piazza Regina Margherita, where the 12th-century cathedral itself was built over an ancient edifice.

But to get a better idea of what this famous temple looked like, climb up to the Palazzo Barberini at the top of the town. The palace was built in the 17th century along the semicircular lines of the original temple. Its museum contains a wealth of material found on the site, some of it going back to the 4th century B.C., and a scale model of the temple. Its treasure is the 1st-century B.C. mosaic of the *Nile in Flood*.

When you've absorbed as much as you can of the museum-temple, make your way down the street staircases and explore the town. There's a monument to composer Pierluigi, of course, and there are some rather good, simple restaurants and shops selling local embroidery work in what else but *punto Palestrina*.

The Castelli Romani

The *castelli* aren't really castles, as their name would seem to imply. They're little towns that are scattered on the slopes of the Alban Hills, near Rome. And the Alban hills aren't really hills, either, but extinct volcanoes. There *were* castles here in the Middle Ages, however, when each of these towns, feuds of rival Roman lords, had its own fortress to defend it. The Castelli make a pleasant excursion with fine views and good restaurants at less than an hour from Rome.

Among the most interesting of the towns is Frascati, queen of the Castelli, famous for its dry golden wine and patrician villas. About 5 km. (3 miles) above the town are the remains of ancient Tusculum, supposedly founded by Telegonus, son of Ulysses and Circe. It probably dates back to the Etruscans, or even earlier, and it became a summer colony of such wealthy Romans as Cicero and Lucullus, who had villas here. In the Middle Ages the counts of Tusculum were strong enough to threaten Rome itself, at that time in a precarious state. When Pope Celestine III settled the matter by having Tusculum destroyed in 1191, its inhabitants moved down the hill and founded Frascati. Tuscolo, as it's now known, offers a beautiful view of the countryside and the sea, some picturesque Roman remains of a theater, and lovely walks over ruin-studded meadows and through groves of chestnut trees. It's a good spot for a picnic, but a car is essential, as public transport is nil.

Getting to Frascati is no problem; the bus drops you off in the main piazza, where you can begin your exploration of this interesting town, where important Renaissance families summered in luxurious villas to escape the heat and malaria of the city.

Most impressive of these villas is Villa Aldobrandini, built in the late 16th century and adorned with frescos by the Zuccari brothers and Cavalier d'Arpino. The park is a marvel of baroque fountains and grottos. The splendid villa, with its majestic box-shaded avenue, dominates the hillside, within view of the sea shining in the distance. Still owned by the Aldobrandini family, it can usually be visited in the mornings, but only upon application to the Frascati Tourist Office in the Piazza Marconi.

Frascati is a town to wander in, up and down its hilly streets, coming to the Baroque cathedral and formidable medieval fortress, and stopping off at some of the many wine shops to sample the local brew.

From Frascati you can catch the bus to Grottaferrata, where there's an 11th-century Abbey of Basilian monks that was transformed into a fortress by Sangallo in the 15th century for Cardinal Giuliano della Rovere. It's a fascinating mixture of sacred and military; in the first courtyard the cardinal's palace houses a collection of illuminated manuscripts and Byzantine objets d'art. In the second courtyard there is the Romanesque Church of Santa Maria, with some beautiful 13th-century mosaics and 17th-century frescos by Domenichino in the Chapel of St. Nilus. Services are held in the Byzantine Greek Catholic rite.

Another itinerary through the Castelli starts out on the Via Appia Nuova, passing through an interminable forest of apartment dwellings that stretch as far as the lower slopes of the Alban Hills where you are confronted with the acres and acres of vineyards that supply Rome with its wine.

You might make Castel Gandolfo your first stop. The town was built on the site of legendary Alba Longa, founded by Ascanius, son of Aeneas, and birthplace of Romulus and Remus. The Gandolfo family of Genoa became its overlords in the Middle Ages and gave the *castello* their name. Now it's famous as the summer residence of the popes, whose papal palace was built in the 17th century by Carlo Maderno; latest addition to the beautiful park is a papal swimming pool. Under the town lie the ruins of Domitian's fabulous villa. Just off the main piazza with its imposing entrance to the papal palace, there's a terrace that gives you a fine view of Lake Albano, of volcanic origin. The Church of San Tommaso di Villanova and the fountain on the piazza are both by Bernini.

Next stop is Albano, a pretty little town, best known for its wine and its view of the lake. In the 3rd century A.D., Septimius Severus had a large military camp built here, where earlier emperors had created pleasure villas; a 1944 bombardment laid bare the remains of the camp, which have since been excavated and in part reconstructed. The Porta Pretoria was the main entrance to the camp, which was furnished with a cistern, at the end of the modern Via Saffi, that could hold as much as 10,000 cubic liters of water. Not far away are the remains of a Roman amphitheater, and on Borgo Garibaldi there's a 1st-century Roman tomb.

Genzano overlooks the Lake of Nemi, where two of Caligula's warships were recovered from the bottom only to be burned by the Germans during their retreat in World War II. Genzano has the usual Baroque fountains and princely palace (this one belonged to the Sforza-Cesarini family), and lots of wine, of course, but it's celebrated for its feast of the *Infiorata,* on Corpus Christi each year, usually in May. The tradition began in the late 18th century, and it's one of the most unusual sights you'll see in the Rome area. The entire length of a broad street that slopes up the hill to the church of Santa Maria della Cima is covered with a series of decorative motifs and religious effigies made entirely of flower petals.

Another of the Castelli, Marino, has an ancient Colonna fortress and palace, a few old churches and a famous wine festival, the Sagra dell'Uva. It's usually held on the first Sunday in October when Marino's fountains flow with wine, and it's all free.

Ninfa, Norma and Sermoneta

Ninfa is an enchanted spot, a dream garden of lush vegetation, running streams so pure that you can drink from them, medieval ruins blanketed with flowering vines. Along with the little hill towns of Norma and Sermoneta it constitutes an unusual excursion to the foothills of the Lepine mountains southeast of Rome. Unfortunately, local transportation is inadequate, so we can recommend this itinerary only to those who are traveling by car. And there's another reservation: the garden at Ninfa is open only on the first Saturday and Sunday of the month from April through October. You must get tickets in advance in Rome at the Caetani office at Via Botteghe Oscure 32 or at WWF, Via Mercadante 10 (tel. 844.0108). *If* you can get it all together, you'll surely find it worth the trouble.

Ninfa should be your first stop. It's the site of a town that prospered in medieval and Renaissance times only to succumb to the deadly assaults of malaria in the 17th century. Abandoned by its population, Ninfa languished for centuries until one of the Caetani heirs in the early 1900s decided to create a botanical garden in this exceptional setting. Visits are guided by volunteers recruited by the World Wildlife Fund, which assists the Caetani Foundation in administering the garden; some of the guides speak a little English.

Next you'll drive up interminable hairpin curves to Norma, about 1,200 feet directly above Ninfa, on a site founded by Hercules, or so the legend goes.

Sermoneta, next town on the itinerary, has more character, thanks mainly to the stunning Caetani castle that dominates the town. The castle was built in the 13th century, fell into the grabby Borgia hands of Pope Alexander VI and was transformed into a fortress by Sangallo. Its handsome grey-and-white stone walls set the medieval tone that most of the old town has maintained. The cathedral, with a handsome Romanesque belltower, was built on the ruins of a pagan temple.

Montecassino

You can see the Abbey of Montecassino from far away, squat and ponderous on the crest of a hill, and you can imagine what a perfect target it made for the Allied air and artillery bombardment that reduced it to rubble in 1944. The old town below the abbey also was destroyed in a concerted effort to oust German troops from their Gustav Line stronghold. It was a tragic mistake, of course, for the abbey sheltered monks and refugees and not the German observation post, as believed. In the forty-or-so years since then, the abbey has been rebuilt, stone upon stone, a monument to the Benedictine Order's motto *Ora et Labora* (Pray and Work).

Benedict of Norcia had come to Montecassino in 529, leaving the tiny monasteries he had founded at Subiaco to a handful of followers. On a piece of mountainous land donated to him by a patrician, Benedict founded his abbey on the site of a pagan temple to Apollo. Here he lived, gave his Rule to his monks, and died in 543. He was buried together with his twin sister Scholastica, who had died only 40 days earlier in a convent on the plain below. Postwar reconstruction brought to light the urn containing their remains.

Benedict's Abbey was one of the beacons of civilization and culture throughout the troubled centuries; it became a center of political, economic and spiritual power. It has been destroyed many times in its history—by the Lombards in the 6th century, by the Saracens in the 800s, and it was severely damaged in 1349 by an earthquake. Now it has risen again. The marbles, stuccos and rich wood carvings of the main church, the simplicity of its courtyards and crypt have been reproduced and conscientiously reconstructed. There remains the task of replacing the wealth of paintings and frescos that once covered its walls. A first step in this direction was taken in 1979 with the unveiling of a large fresco executed by Pietro Annigoni. Fortunately, the abbey's archives and library escaped destruction; they had been moved to the safety of Rome's Castel Sant'Angelo during the war and so are visible again at the abbey, an incredible collection of precious illuminated manuscripts and ancient volumes, a compendium of Western culture.

On the hill above the abbey thousands of graves in the Polish military cemetery are a constant reminder of the inferno that Montecassino endured, finally to rise again like the phoenix from its ashes. The British military cemetery is a few kilometers away at S. Giorgio al Liri, near Sora.

Anzio, Nettuno and Ponza

Names that evoke memories of dramatic wartime bulletins: the beachhead at Anzio, "fierce fighting," "heavy losses." These terrible moments are remembered still in the seemingly infinite rows in the military cemeteries. There are four of these—it was an operation extremely costly in lives—and they bring many visitors from the U.S.A., Britain and Germany. Tours for military veterans are a local industry.

The German cemetery is at Pomezia on SS148, the road to Rome. There are two British cemeteries, one near the beachhead and another two miles inland. The very large American cemetery is at Nettuno, two miles from Anzio. It is arranged round an artificial lake and dominated by the massive columns and colonnades of the Memorial to the Missing. In these landings the American Ranger battalions were prominent.

Modern Anzio and Nettuno have settled down again to their role as seaside resorts for the Romans; in the summer months they're an uninterrupted series of brightly colored villas; crowded seafood restaurants and pizzerias, and packed bathing establishments. They regain some of their melancholy charm off-season.

At Anzio Nero built an important circular port and a luxurious villa that later yielded such archeological treasures as the statues of the *Belvedere Apollo,* the *Gladiator* and the *Anzio Maid.* Now there's not much left of Anzio's former glory: a few remains of the port, some grottos carved out of the rock to serve as storerooms for Nero's villa, and the ruins of the villa itself at the end of the shore promenade. Modern Anzio hasn't much to recommend it except its strategic location as jumping-off point for the island of Ponza.

Ponza is a gem, best off-season, for in July and August it's overcrowded and self-conscious. At other times of the year it's lovely, with rocky coasts and a few exceptionally beautiful beaches, such as the Chiaia di Luna, long stretches of white sand and transparent water. The town of Ponza, where the boat docks, is a succession of stairways and ramps leading up from the port to the church; it's well worth making the climb for the view from the top.

Ostia Antica

The wind from the sea whispers through tall pines at Ostia Antica, over the ruins of ancient Rome's port. Founded sometime around the 4th century B.C., Ostia Antica gives you a glimpse of what Rome itself must have been like. Here there are no medieval or Baroque encrustations to distract

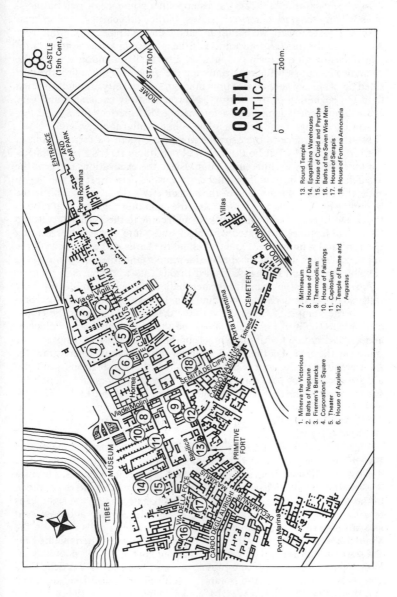

OSTIA ANTICA

0 — 200 m.

1. Minerva the Victorious
2. Baths of Neptune
3. Firemen's Barracks
4. Corporations' Square
5. Theater
6. House of Apuleius
7. Mithraeum
8. House of Diana
9. Thermopolium
10. House of Paintings
11. Capitolium
12. Temple of Rome and Augustus
13. Round Temple
14. Epagathiana Warehouses
15. House of Cupid and Psyche
16. Baths of the Seven Wise Men
17. House of Serapis
18. House of Fortuna Annonaria

you from the sight of the ancient city's streets, baths, theaters and dwellings. Oleanders and creepers grow along mellow brick walls, as they did when the city was inhabited by a cosmopolitan populace of rich businessmen, wily merchants, sailors and slaves. In the 2nd century A.D. the great *horrea,* or warehouses, were built to handle huge shipments of grain from Africa, and the *insulae,* forerunners of the modern apartment house, provided housing for a growing population. Eventually abandoned under the combined assaults of the barbarians and the *Anopheles* mosquito, the port silted up: wind-borne sand and tidal mud covered the city, and it lay buried until the beginning of this century. Now extensively excavated and very well-maintained, it makes for a fascinating visit, perfect for a mild day in winter, spring or fall, or for a late summer afternoon.

Near the entrance to the *Scavi* (excavations), there's a fortress built in the 15th century by Baccio Pontelli for Pope Julius II. It's a model of Renaissance military architecture. Your visit to the excavations starts at the Via delle Tombe, lined with sepulchers of various periods, from which you enter the Porta Romana, one of the ancient city's three gates. This is the beginning of the *Decumanus Maximus,* the main thoroughfare that crosses the city from end to end. On your left you'll come to the Terme di Nettuno (Baths of Neptune), decorated with black-and-white mosaics representing Neptune and Amphitrite. Directly behind the baths is the barracks of the fire brigade, which must have played an important role in a town where valuable goods and foodstuffs passed through its warehouses.

Now you'll see the beautiful theater, built by Augustus and completely restored by Septimius Severus; behind it in the vast Piazzale delle Corporazioni is the Temple of Ceres. Next to the theater you can visit the House of Apuleius, built in Pompeian style, and the Mithraeum, with balconies and a hall decorated with the symbols of the cult of Mithras, whose statue stands at the rear. On the Via dei Molini there's a mill, where grain for the warehouses next door was ground. Along the Via di Diana you'll see a *thermopolium,* or bar, with a marble counter and a fresco depicting the fruit and foodstuffs that were sold here. At the end of the Via dei Dipinti, where a large building conserves the original mosaics and painted decorations, the Museo Ostiense displays much of the interesting material found among the ruins.

Retracing your steps along the Via dei Dipinti you'll come to the Forum, with monumental remains of the city's most important temple, dedicated to Jupiter, Juno and Minerva, and other ruins of baths, a basilica and smaller temples. There's a Round Temple that was a kind of pantheon of the emperors. At the crossroads the Via Epagathiana on the right leads to a large warehouse building erected in the 2nd century and now used as a storehouse for archeological material. Off the Via della Foce, on the Via del Tempio di Ercole, the House of Cupid and Psyche is named for the statue found there; you can see what remains of a large pool and enclosed garden and marble and mosaic decorations. On the Via delle Foce you'll also see the House of Serapis, a 2nd-century multi-level dwelling, and the Baths of the Seven Wise Men, named for a fresco in the east room. On the left, atop the stairs, there's a belvedere. Take the Via del Tempio di Serapide and the Cardo degli Aurighi, where you'll pass another "apartment building," back to the *Decumanus Maximus* and follow it to the Porta Marina. Off to the left, on what used to be the seashore, are the ruins of the Synagogue, one of the oldest in the Western World. On your return, go right at the Bivio del Castrum past the slaughterhouse and the large round temple to the Cardine Massimo, a road lined with interesting remains. From here turn left to see the Casa della Fortuna Annonaria, the richly-decorated dwelling of a wealthy Ostian.

The EPT publishes an excellent pamphlet with map and guide to Ostia Antica, available free at EPT offices.

The Etruscan Heartland—Cerveteri, Bracciano, Tarquinia and Viterbo

The nucleus of the old town of Cerveteri stands on the site of the Etruscan city of Caere, a thriving commercial center in the 6th century B.C. Now the zone is overbuilt with unattractive vacation villas, but ignore them and concentrate on the serene beauty of the famous Necropolis of the Banditaccia, a lovely green park in which the Etruscan residents of Caere left a heritage of great historical significance. This was their "city of the dead," a monumental complex of tombs in which they laid their relatives to rest, some in simple graves, others in burial chambers that faithfully reproduce the characteristics of Etruscan dwellings. In the round tumulus tombs you'll recognize the prototypes of the Augusteum and Hadrian's Mausoleum in the Castel Sant'Angelo and the Tomb of Cecilia Metella. The most interesting of the tombs are the Tomba dei Capitelli, the Tomba dei Vasi Greci, in which a great number of Greek vases were found, and the Tomba dei Rilievi, packed with detailed reliefs of household objects. The Necropolis is a short walk from the center of town.

You'll be able to see some of the material found in the tombs in the Museo Nazionale Cerite, which is in the 12th-century castle on the town's main piazza.

Not far from Cerveteri, the lake of Bracciano is an almost perfect circle of deep blue water in the green countryside. Like so many of Latium's lakes, its bed is the smooth crater of an extinct volcano. It's favored by Romans for its camping and sailing facilities and especially for its lakeside restaurants. Facing each other across the lake, the towns of Anguillara and Trevignano were probably founded by the Etruscans; each has a smallish medieval castle in ruins and not much else to recommend it but some picturesque views and a generally tranquil air. Anguillara is famous for its eels (the town's name probably derives from *anguilla,* eel), which are plentiful in the lake, particularly at its mouth behind the promontory.

Bracciano's greatest attraction is the mighty castle that dominates the town. A 15th-century marvel of sturdy towers and massive walls, the Odescalchi castle is acknowledged to be one of the finest and best-preserved examples of Renaissance military architecture. The castle's ceremonial apartments and living quarters are remarkably well-preserved and fully furnished with a fine collection of original pieces from various periods of its history. Some rich stuccos and frescos by the Zuccari brothers contribute to the overall air of grandeur. From the battlements you get a stunning view of the lake and the old town nestling at the castle's base. In all it's a dream castle, and in this case the dream can come true, for if you've got aristocratic references and a lot of money the Odescalchi family will rent it out to you for an unforgettable party or reception.

From June to September a little excursion boat makes the rounds of the lake.

Once a powerful Etruscan city and later an important medieval center, Tarquinia sprawls atop a hill overlooking the sea north of Rome, beyond

Civitavecchia. This charming town offers unexpected visual delights as its narrow medieval streets suddenly open onto quaint squares dominated by lovely palaces and churches. You should see the church of San Francesco, with a Romanesque rose window and massive 16th-century campanile, and find your way to Santa Maria di Castello, a majestic Romanesque church, impressive in its simplicity. Walk down the Via delle Torri and then climb the hilly streets to the churches of San Martino and Santissima Annunziata.

Next make your way to the beautiful Palazzo Vitelleschi, a splendid 15th-century building that contains a wealth of Etruscan treasures. One, perhaps the greatest, strikes you as you enter the main hall—the marvelous golden terracotta horses, a frieze that once decorated an Etruscan temple. If you needed any proof of the degree of artistry the Etruscans attained, this is it. But there's more: upstairs are some more of the precious frescos from the necropolis, detached to keep them from deteriorating. Examine the sarcophagi that were found in the tombs. The figures of the deceased recline casually on their stone couches, mouths curved in enigmatic smiles, in one hand a plate containing a few beans, ancient symbol of afterlife.

Now for the highlight of this trip; the painted tombs of the necropolis, which lie under rolling farmland just outside town. Regularly scheduled guided visits start from the museum at the Palazzo Vitelleschi, where a motorcade forms. A new ticket booth near the necropolis area makes entrance easier for those who are under their own steam. If you haven't got a car, hitch a ride with someone who does or hire a taxi for a fixed fee. A well-informed guide will show you through the underground tombs, which date from the 7th to the 2nd century B.C. and are decorated with lively frescos depicting aspects of Etruscan life. Although scores of tombs have been identified and excavated, you'll likely visit only three or four of the most famous.

Of the thousands of tombs that exist throughout the territory of Etruria, only a small percentage have been excavated by government experts and authorized scholars. Many, instead, are found and plundered by local "experts," called *tombaroli*. They dig illegally, sometimes locating tombs that have eluded even the archeologists. The valuable objects that they find stock a thriving clandestine market.

In the heart of Tuscia, which is the modern name for the Etruscan dominion of Etruria, lies Viterbo, a lovely old medieval city, beautifully preserved and extremely picturesque. Like every other center in this area, it was founded by the Etruscans and later taken over by the Romans. Its moment of glory came in the 13th century, when it became seat of the papal court. The old town still nestles within 12th-century walls. The houses are made of dark volcanic stone giving Viterbo a uniformly-gray aspect that heightens the sensation of age and makes such notes of color as flowered windowboxes all the more striking. Viterbo is a marvelous place to take pictures.

If you come by train you'll start your visit just outside the town walls, while the bus takes you right to the center of town. In any case, make your way to the Piazza San Lorenzo, where the Gothic Palazzo Papale was built in the 13th century as a worthy residence for the popes who chose to sojourn here. During a conclave in 1271 that dragged on for months without getting down to the business of electing a new pope, the people of Viterbo lost patience with the college of cardinals. After all, it was the townsfolk who had to foot the bill for the prelates' room and board. In order to hasten the decision and send the cardinals packing, the inhabitants of Viterbo tore the roof off the great hall and put the churchmen on bread and water. Sure enough, Pope Gregory X was elected within a very short time. There's also a Romanesque church on the piazza, to which a Renaissance facade has been added. On the left of the cathedral is a 15th-century house.

Now walk down the Via San Lorenzo and take the Via San Pellegrino through the medieval quarter, one of the best-preserved in Italy. It's a delightful vista of arches, vaults, towers, exterior staircases, worn wooden doors on great iron hinges, tiny hanging gardens, all in that lovely dark stone, occasionally accented with warm rose-coloured brick. Look in at the many antique shops along the way, but don't buy unless you're an expert. At the end of the Via San Pellegrino turn left toward the Via delle Fabbriche and the Piazza della Fontana Grande, where the largest and most original of Viterbo's curious Gothic fountains bubbles away. There's a good small museum and a pretty cloister at Santa Maria della Verità, and you should also see the Gothic church of San Francesco.

From the center of town you can catch a bus for the ten-minute ride to Bagnaia, a quaint hamlet and site of the Villa Lante, a 16th-century palace in a jewel-like garden. On your way to Bagnaia you'll pass the handsome Renaissance church of Santa Maria della Quercia.

If you've come by car, drive over to see the strange Monster Park at Bomarzo, populated by weird and fantastic sculptures of mythical monsters and eccentric architecture, created at the order of Prince Vicino Orsini in the 16th century for his wife Giulia Farnese, who is said to have taken one look and died of heart failure.

Other gems in this area are the medieval abbey of San Martino al Cimino, the Palazzo Farnese at Caprarola and the Borgia fortress at Civita Castellana.

PRACTICAL INFORMATION FOR
THE ENVIRONS OF ROME

WHEN TO GO. If you can avoid it, don't visit this region in the hottest months, both because of the climate and because the entire area, especially along the coast, is crowded with vacationing Romans. April, May, end-September and October are the best months. Winters are mild, though places like Subiaco and Cassino are at altitudes where the cold can become intense.

TOURIST INFORMATION. Anzio: AAST, Via Pollastrini 3, 984.6119. **Cassino:** AAST, Corso delle Repubblica, 21.292. **Civitavecchia:** AAST, Viale Garibaldi 42, 25.348, and at port, 29.985. **Fiuggi:** AAST, Via Gorizia 4, 55.446, and Piazza Frascara 4, 55.019. **Formia:** AAST, Viale Unita d'Italia 30, 21.490. **Frascati:** AAST, Piazza Marconi 1, 942.0331. **Gaeta:** AAST, Piazza 19 Maggio, 461.165. **Tarquinia:** AAST, Piazza Cavour 1, 856.384. **Terracina:** AAST, Via Lungolinea 156, 727.759. **Tivoli:** AAST, Piazzale Nazioni Unite, 20.745. **Viterbo:** AAST, Piazza Verdi 4a, 34.776; EPT, Piazzale dei Caduti 16, 30.092.

SEASONAL EVENTS. In **February** carnival festivities at Frascati, Ronciglione (near Viterbo) and Tivoli are especially colorful.

The feast of St. Benedict on 21 **March** is celebrated at Subiaco and, especially, Cassino.

Usually in **April,** Holy Week is the occasion of a procession of hooded penitents at Civitavecchia and a dramatic Passion Play at Sezze, near Latina.

On the feast of Corpus Christi, usually in **May,** Genzano stages its Infiorata, when its main street is covered with elaborate decorations made entirely of flower petals.

In **July** there are peach festivals at Palestrina and Castel Gandolfo.

Gaeta celebrates the Feast of the Sea on 14 **August,** and on 15 August Tivoli is scene of the Inchinata, a religious observance and folkore festival all in one.

The Feast of Santa Rosa at Viterbo, 3 **September,** is one of the most important in the region; there's a spectacular procession and colorful fair.

The **October** grape harvest inspires wine festivals in Tivoli and Marino, where the fountains spout wine instead of water during the festivities.

HOTELS AND RESTAURANTS. This is essentially an area that we expect you will want to explore on the basis of day-trips from Rome, to vary the metropolitan experience. For this reason the following lists concentrate mainly on places to have lunch during—or dinner after—a relaxed day's sightseeing. There is a scattering of hotels in the list for those who wish to overnight in any particular spot that may have caught their fancy.

Regional Specialties. Many of the dishes on Roman menus originated in the towns and countryside around the capital city. The ubiquitous *Amatriciana* sauce, of tomatoes, bacon and hot red pepper, is the specialty of Amatrice, near Rieti. In Viterbo homemade *fettucine* are cut into fine strands and are known as *fieno* (hay). The region's soups range from the *imbracata* (pasta and beans) of Viterbo to the exquisite *zuppa di pesce* for which Anzio, Gaeta and Civitavecchia are famous. Sermoneta and Priverno produce creamy fresh mozzarella, and the farmlands both south and north of Rome are known for the quality of their green vegetables, especially artichokes.

Locally produced meat is principally lamb; *abbacchio* (baby lamb) is roasted with plenty of garlic and rosemary or is grilled *alla scottadito* (to burn your fingers as you pick it up to savor its good-to-the-bone taste). Prepared throughout the region, *porchetta* (whole roast pig) appears not only at table but also at roadside stands, where it's served with generous slices of dark *Genzano* bread. The same type of bread is toasted, slathered with garlic and doused with olive oil to make bruschetta, unrivaled accompaniment of a glass or two of local wine.

Along with the wines of the Castelli (especially Frascati, Marino and Velletri), the region produces the fine white *Est Est Est* of Montefiascone, the sweetish red *Cannaiola* of Marta on Lake Bolsena, the reds and whites of *Vignanello* and the other towns around Viterbo, and the *Cesanese* and *Falerno* of the southern coastal areas.

Albano Roma (06). *Il Falcaccio* (M), Via Cavour 99 (932.1209). Closed Sat. Central trattoria. *Delle Scalette* (M), Corso Matteotti 30 (932.3993). Closed Sat. Similar. *La Paranza* (M), Corso Matteotti 37 (932.3444). Closed Mon.

Anzio Roma (06). Beach resort, port. *Dei Cesari* (M), Via Mantova 3 (947.4751). Open Feb. 15–Dec. 15. AE, DC, MC, V.

Restaurants: *Da Alceste-Buongusto* (M), Piazza Sant'Antonio 6 (984.6744). Seaside veranda; fine seafood. Closed Tues. V. *Garda* (M), Riviera Zanardelli 5 (984.6058). Near port. Closed Wed. AE, DC, V. *Romolo* (I), Via Porto Innocenziano 19 (984.4079). On port; tempting seafood antipasto. Closed Wed. and in Dec. V.

Bracciano Roma (06). **Restaurants:** The best restaurants are on the lake shore: *Argenti* (M), Via Lungolago, *Casino del Lago* (M), Via del Lago 4 (902.4025). Closed Tues. This one also has 12 (M) rooms.

In town try *Sora Tuta* (M), Via Fausti 18.

Cassino Frosinone (0776). Celebrated abbey. **Restaurants:** *Forum Palace* (M), Via Casilina Nord, km. 136 (481.211). Local and international dishes. AE, DC, V. *K2* (M), Via Montecassino 1 (481.366). In archeological zone. Closed Tues. *Nuovo Pavone* (M), on Formia road (480.397). Closed Mon.

Castel Gandolfo Roma (06). Pope's summer residence. **Restaurants:** *Cacciatori* (M), Via Zecchini 1 (932.0993). Veranda overlooking lake. Closed Tues. *Pagnanelli* (M), Via Gramsci 4 (936.0004). Nice view and good food. Closed Tues. AE, DC, V. *La Panzanella* (M), on lakeshore (936.0049). Closed Wed. and 15–30 Aug.

Cerveteri Roma (06). **Restaurants:** *Dei Cacciatori* (M), on the main piazza. **La Necropoli** (M), Via Mura Castellane 54 (995.0123). Shellfish specialties, pleasant Etruscan decor. *Pattacchino* (M).

Civitavecchia Roma (0766). Port of Rome; boats for Sardinia. *Mediterraneo* (M), Viale Garibaldi 38 (23.156). On seafront promenade, handy to steamer dock. **Restaurants:** *Villa dei Principi* (E), Borgo Odescalchi 11 (21.220). Spacious and attractive, overlooking sea. Closed Tues. and in July. AE.
La Cambusa (M), Calata Principe Tommase 6 (23.164). Good seafood at reasonable prices. Closed Mon. off-season. *Del Gobbo* (M), Lungoporto Gramasci 29 (23.163) Tasty *zuppa di pesce*. Closed Wed. *Taverna della Rocca* (M), Calata della Rocca 3 (29.764). On the sea at port. Closed Wed.

Fiuggi Frosinone (0775). Important spa. *Palazzo della Fonte* (L), Via dei Villini (55.681). Handsome large building in park; posh but old-fashioned.
Silva Splendid (E), Corso Nuova Italia 40 (55.791). Tastefully modern; outdoor pool. AE, DC, MC. *Vallombrosa e Majestic* (E), Via Vecchia Fiuggi 209 (55.531). Central and very comfortable; pool; gardens. AE, DC, MC, V.
Imperiale (M), Via Prenestina 29 (55.055). Central; attractive contemporary furnishings. AE, DC, V.
Restaurants: At **Fiuggi Fonte**—*Hotel Tripoli* restaurant (M), Via Quattro Giugno 13 (55.136). Open April–Nov. Very good local cuisine in pleasant surroundings.
At **Fiuggi Città**—*Tre Abruzzi* (M), Via Garibaldi 5 (55.945). Closed Thurs. *Pozzo della Vergine* (M), Via Umberto (55.885). Closed Mon.

Formia Latina (0771). Beach resort. *Castello Miramare* (E), at Pagnano (24.238). On hillside; only 10 rooms, but an oasis of peace and quiet. AE, DC, MC, V. *Miramare* (E), Via Appia 44 (267.181). On the sea; large villa and cottages in park; pool, beach. AE, DC, MC, V.
Restaurants: *La Conchiglia* (M), Via Colombo 13 (21.068). Unpretentious and pleasant. Closed Mon. and in Nov. AE, DC, MC. *Da Italo* (M), Via Unità d'Italia (21.529). Fish specialties *in cartoccio* (cooked in paper bag). Closed Mon. and in Dec. AE, DC, V. *Sirio* (M), Via Unità d'Italia (21.917). Closed Tues. and the last two weeks in Nov. AE, DC, V.

Frascati Roma (06). Roman Castles town. **Restaurants:** *Cacciani* (M), Via Armando Diaz 13 (942.0378). Central, excellent dining, lovely view. Closed Tues. AE, DC. *La Frasca* (M), Via Lunati 3 (942.0311). Central, pleasant trattoria, very good food and wines. Closed Wed. and 15 days in Jan. MC, V.
On road to Colonna—*Richelieu* (M), (948.5293). Exceptional cuisine, interesting menu, fine house Frascati. Closed Tues. DC, MC, V.

Gaeta Latina (0771). Naval station and beach resort; medieval quarter. *Le Rocce* (M), at San Vito (460.606). On beach; attractive, with good views. Open April 1–Oct. 31. *Summit* (M), a little way out on SS213 (680.333). Modern resort hotel on beach; terraces, pool. Closed Jan. and Feb.
Restaurants: *La Salute* (M), Piazza Caboto (460.050). On old port; fish specialties. Closed Tues. AE. *Sciamm* (M), Via Mazzini 25 (465.216). Home-cooked local

dishes. Closed Mon off-season. *Taverna del Marinaio* (M), Via Faustina 43 (461.342). Near the old port; good fare. Closed Wed. AE.

Grottaferrata Roma (06). Roman Castles town. Byzantine abbey. **Restaurants:** *La Bazzica* (M), Viale Kennedy 60 (945.9947). Known for its good food. Closed Tues. *Al Fico* (M), Via Anagnina 134 (945.9214). Country house, dining terrace; fine cuisine. Closed Wed. AE, DC. *Squarciarelli* (M), at Bivio Squarciarelli (945.9580). Classic Roman dishes; popular with tourists. Closed Fri. V.
On the road to **Montecompatri**—*Castagneto* (M), Via Tuscolana (946.8289). Favorite with Romans for good food and pretty gardens. Closed Wed. AE, DC, MC, V.
On the road to **Roccapriora**, *Casal Molara* (M), Via Tuscolana (945.8272). Old country house, local cooking and wines. Closed Tues. AE, V.

Ostia Roma (06). Rome's beach, to be avoided during summer and Sundays. **Restaurants:** *Ferrantelli* (M), Via Claudio 7 (562.5751). Roman cuisine. Closed Mon. AE, DC, MC. *Santa Barbara* (M), Piazza Anco Marzio (560.1327). Mostly seafood and very good indeed. Closed Wed. AE, DC, V.
At **Ostia Antica**—*Al Monumento* (M), Piazza Umberto (565.0021). Near castle, good seafood. Closed Mon. DC. *Allo Sbarco di Enea* (M), Via Romagnoli 675 (565.0034). Near entrance to excavations; outdoor summer dining. AE, MC. Closed Mon., Feb.

Palestrina Roma (06). Temple town. **Restaurants:** *Baficchio* (M), Via Prenestina Nuova (995.8948). Home-style. Closed Fri. V. *Coccia* (M), Piazza Liberazione 3 (995.8172) Good restaurant of the Hotel Stella. AE, DC, V. *Scifa* (M), Piazza Regina Margherita 19 (955.8391). Rustic dishes; reasonable prices. Closed Mon. and in July. *La Pergola* (I), Corso Pierluigi 61 (955.8204). Simple trattoria. Closed Tues.

Ponza Latina (0771). Town on the main island of Pontine archipelago, off Terracina. High season, Easter, Jul. 1–Aug. 31. *Chaia di Luna* (E), (80.113). High above beautiful beach, overlooking sea; modern, attractive villa complex; pool. Open May 15–Sept. 30. AE.
Torre dei Borboni (M), on promontory (80.109). Atmosphere, excellent views; partly in old tower above sea. Open May 1–Oct 31. V. *Ponzio Pilato* (M), (80.053). Delightful small pension with garden; views of port. Open June 1–Sept. 30.
Restaurants: All open every day during season. *Gennarino a Mare* (M), on port (80.071). AE, DC, V. *La Kambusa* (M), Via Pisacane (80.280). Very good, try pasta *alla Kambusa* or *alla sicula*. Open June 1–Sept. 30. AE, DC, V. *Mimi* (M), (80.338). Best, pricey. *Torre Borboni* (M), (80.109). Very good terrace restaurant of hotel (see above). Open May 1–Oct. 30. V.

Sabaudia Latina (0773). Site of smart Baia d'Argento resort colony. High season, Easter, July 1–Aug. 31. *Le Dune* (E), Lungomare (55.551). Modern white shore hotel; terraces; pool, tennis; on large private beach. Open Apr.–Oct.
Restaurants: *La Pineta* (M), Corso Vittorio Emanuele III (55.551). Closed 20 Dec.–20 January, Tues. *Saporetti* (M), Lungomare Torre Paola (536.024). Seafood specialties, some pricey. Open June 1–Sept. 30.

San Felice Circeo Latina (0773). Summer colony, beach resort. High season, Easter, July 1–Aug. 31. *Maga Circe* (E), Via Bergamini (527.821). Splendidly located with flowered terraces overlooking the sea; pool, beach. AE, DC, MC, V.
Punta Rossa (M), at Quarto Caldo (528.069). Quiet location on sea, pretty bungalows; pool, beach. Open Mar. 14–Oct. 15. AE, DC.
Restaurants: *Da Alfonso* (E), at Torre Cervia lighthouse (528.019). Typical seafood specialties. AE, DC, MC. *Trattoria Serena* (M), Via Sabaudia 184 (536.249). Pleasant spot with good food. Closed Tues. off-season and in Oct.

Sperlonga Latina (0771). Picturesque old town overlooking good sandy beaches. High season, Easter, July 1–Aug. 31. *Parkhotel Fiorelle* (M), at Fiorelle (54.092). Quiet location in garden oasis on beach; pool. Open Mar. 1–Oct. 31.

Restaurants: *Grotta di Tiberio* (E), Via Flacca (54.027). Fine seafood menu. Closed Tues. DC, V. *Laocoonte* (E), Via Colombo 4 (54.122). Closed Mon. AE. *Fortino* (M), Via Flacca (54.337). Family-run; fish specialties. Closed Wed. *Sombrero* (M), Via Flacca (54.124). Beach restaurant; Spanish and Italian dishes. Open daily from Easter to Sept. 30.

Subiaco Roma (0774). Ancient monastery. **Restaurants:** *Aniene* (M), Via Cadorna (85.565). In center of town. *Roma* (M), Via Petrarca 38 (85.239) Closed Tues. *Belvedere* (I), Via dei Monasteri 33 (85.531). Good hotel restaurant near monastery. *Mariuccia* (I), Via Sublacense at km. 20. (84.851). On Affile–Fiuggi road. Closed Mon. and Nov.

Tarquinia Viterbo (0766). Etruscan treasures. *Tarconte* (M), Via Tuscia 19 (856.585). Modern, comfortable hotel with good views. AE, DC, V. **Restaurants:** *Il Bersagliere* (M), Via Benedetto Croce 2 (856.047). Below town, on road to station. Closed Sun. night, Mon. AE, DC, V. *Giudizi* (M), near museum (857.190). Central. Closed Mon. *Solengo* (M), Via Tuscia 19 (856.141). Good restaurant of Hotel Tarconte. AE, DC, V. *Velcamare* (M), Via degli Argonauti at Tarquinia Lido (88.024). Excellent local dishes, *risotto alla pescatore*. Closed Tues. off-season, Nov.–Dec. V.

Terracina Latina (0773). Medieval town, beach resort. High season Easter, July 1–Aug. 31. *L'Approdo* (E), Viale Circe (727.671). Modern beach hotel. **Restaurants:** *Hostaria Porto Salvo* (E), Via Appia (75.251). Seaside restaurant, good food. Closed Mon. and Oct. AE, DC, V. *La Capannina* (M), Via Appia (752.539). Veranda overlooking sea. Closed Thur. and Nov. AE, DC, MC, V. *Grappolo d'Uva* (M), lungomare Matteotti 2 (752.585). Book ahead for this small trattoria near main piazza. Closed Mon. and Jan. AE, DC, V.

Tivoli Roma (0774). **Restaurants:** Both a 15-minute walk from Villa D'Este at the entrance to Villa Gregoriana—*Cinque Statue* (M), Via Quintili Varo 1 (20.366). Excellent local dishes; attractive setting. Closed Fri. and Sun. evening. *Falcone* (I), Via del Trevio 34 (22.358). Closed Mon.

Viterbo Roma (0761). *Mini Palace* (M), Via Santa Maria Grotticella 2 (239.742). Low modern building; functional rooms. AE, DC, MC, V. **Leon d'Oro** (I) Via della Cava 36 (344.444). A historic inn with simple, old-fashioned accommodations. AE, DC, V. **Restaurants:** *Ciro* (M), Via Cardinale La Fontaine 74 (234.722). In medieval quarter; good food. Closed Fri. AE, DC, V. *Scaletta* (M), Via Marconi 45 (30.003). Central, longtime favorite. Closed Mon. AE, DC, V. *Spacca* (M), Via della Pace 9 (34.650). Local cuisine. Closed Mon. At **Bagnaia**—*Biscetti* (M), Via Generale Gallin 11 (288.252). Fine food. Closed Thurs. and July AE. *Checcarello* (M), Piazza Venti Settembre (288.255). Atmosphere and rustic specialties. Closed Wed. AE. At **La Quercia**—*Aquilanti* (M), (31.701). Classic cuisine. Closed Tues. and in July. AE, DC, V.

GETTING AROUND. Rome is the hub of a public transportation network that extends in every direction to even the smallest towns of the region, providing essential connections for commuting workers and opening up the whole area for interested visitors.

By train. Civitavecchia, Tivoli, Cassino and Formia are on main rail lines; secondary lines connect the capital with Viterbo, Fiuggi, the Castelli towns and Anzio.

By car. Roads are excellent, though often heavily trafficked. Superhighways provide fast, direct connections to Civitavecchia and Tarquinia (A12), about 90 mins.; to Tivoli (A24), about 40 mins.; to Cassino (A2), leave at the Montecassino exit; and to Viterbo via Orte (A1), around 90 mins.

By bus. Acotral buses connect Rome terminals (Viale Castro Pretorio behind Termini Station and Via Lepanto at Metro Station) with such places of interest as Tivoli, Subiaco, Palestrina, Cerveteri, Tarquinia and Viterbo. In many cases, trains duplicate the bus routes, providing faster service but making it necessary to transfer to a local bus in order to get from the train station into the center of town, as at Cerveteri and Tarquinia. But be warned, the buses are not the fastest way of doing these "days out" trips.

PLACES OF INTEREST. Among the sites of great interest in this area are the following. Check before setting off to explore them in case the hours of opening have changed. See also the items under *Museums* in the *Facts at Your Fingertips* section.

Cerveteri. Necropolis, get directions from the Museum, Castello Ruspoli. The Necropoli della Banditaccia is a magnificent example of the Etruscan cemeteries. Summer: Tues. to Sun., 9 until one hour before sunset. Closed Mon. Entrance fee 4,000 lire. **Museo Cerite,** Tues. to Sat. 10–4. Closed Sun. and Mon.

Ostia Antica. Scavi di Ostia Antica, the Ostia Antica excavations, as described in our text. Entrance to the site, Tues. to Sun., 9 to an hour before sunset, closed Mon. Entrance fee, 4,000 lire. Museum of finds at the site, open Tues. to Sun., 9–2, closed Mon.

Palestrina. Museo Nazionale Archeologico Prenestino, Palazzo Colonna Barberini. Interesting collection, especially for the *Nile Mosaic.* 9–1.30 weekdays, 9–12.30 Sun. and hols. Closed Mon. 3,000 lire.

Subiaco. Convent of St. Scholastica. Open 9–12.30, 4.30–8 in summer; 9–12.30, 4–7 in winter. During services only the church is open. The archives and library are open on weekdays for those wishing to study.

Monastery of St. Benedict. Open 8.30–11.30, 3–8 in summer, to 7 in winter.

Tarquinia. Museo Nazionale Tarquinese, Palazzo Vitelleschi, Piazza Cavour. Excellent collection of Etruscan art, with frescos as well. Tues.–Sun. May–Sept., 9–6.30; Oct.–Apr., 9–2. closed Mon. **Necropolis,** reached from the Museum. Plenty of tombs and frescos to see. Entrance fee, including museum admission, 4,000 lire.

Tivoli. Villa Adriana, Hadrian's Villa. An enormous and fascinating archeological site. Open 9.30–an hour before sunset, closed Mon. (or Tues. when the Mon. is a holiday). Entrance fee 4,000 lire.

Tivoli. Villa d'Este. The magnificent cascades and fountains can be seen daily from 9 to 90 mins. before sunset. Entrance fee 5,000 lire.

Viterbo. Museo Civico, Piazza Crespi. Etruscan finds and other art. Summer: Mon. to Sat., 8–1.30; 3.30–6 (Apr., Oct.) or 7.30 (May–Sept.); winter: Mon. to Sat., 9–1.30. Closed holidays. Entrance fee, 1,000 lire.

FLORENCE

Birthplace of a New World

If all you know of Florence (Firenze) comes from books, from art history, you might be led to imagine the city as a kind of out-size museum, a place apart from contemporary life. If so, the minute you arrive in Florence, this impression will be promptly, even brutally dispelled. If you come by train, you will step off into one of Italy's finest modern buildings, the so-called "new" station, built before the last war, for many years a textbook touchstone for young Italian architects. If you come by automobile, you will arrive along the sweeping new super-highway, the Autostrada del Sole. True enough, one of the exits leads you past the 14th-century Certosa, the handsome Carthusian Monastery, but another exit leads you straight to the supermarket. The shops in the center of the city, the stands in the open-air markets, still sell traditional Florentine products like straw mats and little tooled leather boxes or book-covers, but in other shops you can buy the latest creations of high fashion or the universal jean machine.

An official Italian guidebook says of Florence: "It enjoys universal fame because of its natural beauty, the aristocratic elegance of its appearance, the richness and high quality of its monuments and art collections . . ." The beauty and elegance are all there, but, along with them, the foreign visitor must be prepared for the bustle and racket of everyday life, which goes on in Florence as it does in Buffalo or Leeds or anywhere. The bustle and racket are exacerbated by the thousands, literally thousands, of tourists who flood in for a few hours on bus tours from other large Italian cities, take in the main sights and flood out again. There are times when it is virtually impossible to get into the most famous buildings. If you can spare

129

several days to see Florence, it is wise to try to do your visiting of these most celebrated spots at off-peak hours.

Everyone, including the inhabitants of Florence themselves, agrees that there is a special Florentine character, though it is harder to find agreement on just what it is. Ideally, the Florentine is cultivated, urbane, witty. But he can also be a *becero,* "a low blackguard, a cad", according to the Cambridge Italian Dictionary, or he can be a *grullo,* "fool or chump". He is most likely to have, as a classic author said, "sharp eyes and a bad tongue". Florentine wit has been famous from the time of Boccaccio at least; along with their Madonnas and their saints, the great painters also left a store of biting caricatures. And beside the loftiest achievements of Italian literature, the Florentines produced some searing satire and rich anthologies of jests and practical jokes. Waiters in Florence, by the way, are notoriously rude, especially in the small, typical trattorias called *bucas.*

Florentine History

Florence began as a small Roman village, graduating through the centuries to a fair-sized metropolis, handily placed on the Via Flaminia and with its bridge over the Arno. By the year 1000 it had already become a fair-sized city, sometimes housing a central administration for Tuscany and in a useful location to control trade and gather taxes. During the 13th century the city took its stand as a Guelph community, siding with Rome's popes against the emperors attempting to usurp their power, and rapidly—with the ultimate victory of the popes—it grew into an important city-state, constantly striving for supremacy over all Tuscany. Local factions fought among themselves in Florence; but, led by a circle of shrewd banking families, the city drove ahead to exert its influence in much of civilized Europe.

In the 15th century, a prospering, ever-expanding Florence passed under the sway of the powerful Medici family. The golden foundations of the Medici fortunes were laid down by Giovanni di Bicci de'Medici (1360–1429) and his father, though they were both content to concentrate on their business affairs rather than dabble too much in politics. The Medici's greatest son, Lorenzo the Magnificent (1449–92), combined political wisdom with an artistic leadership that soon sent Florence skyrocketing to the top position of Italy's Renaissance in art—the culmination of a period of artistic and cultural growth that had begun as far back as the 13th century.

The work of those three centuries can be seen all over Florence: the architecture of Brunelleschi, Giotto, Alberti, Sangallo, Ammannati; the sculpture of Pisano, Donatello, Cellini, the Della Robbias; the painting of Ghirlandaio, Fra Angelico, Fra Filippo Lippi, Botticelli, Leonardo da Vinci, Fra Bartolomeo; the combined genius of Michelangelo, Rossellino and Benedetto da Maiano. They gave to Florence in those illustrious years a depth and power never attained anywhere else.

The surge of influential creativity was not confined to the realms of painting, sculpture and architecture alone. The court of Lorenzo was also the seat of an intellectual gathering of scholars and poets, called the Platonic Academy—a name which, in itself, gives the clue to the rebirth of interest in the classical world. It is notable that Lorenzo, a man of enormous ability and talent, was as much a part of the deliberations of the Academy as he was its host. The subjects that interested the assembled intellectuals covered a wide field—not only Platonic philosophy, but architecture and esthetic theory (especially with the work of Alberti), translations and commentaries (particularly of great classical texts), and general theorizing on the arts. The Academy acted as a conduit through which ideas firmly based on the world of Greece and Rome flowed into the general reservoir of European thought.

But this period of Florentine history was not all enlightenment and progress. It also saw the rise and fall of one of the world's great ascetic fanatics, Savonarola (1452–98). A Dominican monk in the monastery of San Marco, he became a reformer and scourge of luxury and humanism. Enormously popular with the poorer populace, his crusade reached its climax in 1497, when he masterminded a great burning of "vanities"—wigs, paintings, books, clothes, mirrors, everything that fitted with his ideas of worldly laxity. This great bonfire was held in the Piazza della Signoria—and within a year he himself was hanged and his body then burned on the same spot.

During the 16th century, Florence became the capital of the Grand Duchy of Tuscany, which passed, on the extinction of the Medici family in 1737, to Francis of Lorraine. His descendants ruled till 1860 when Tuscany joined a united Italy, for which the city of art and culture was the capital from 1865 to 1871.

In the summer of 1944, Florence—like all of Tuscany—found itself a roaring battlefield. Allied troops ranged along the south bank of the city's bisecting Arno River; Hitler's German legions occupied positions along the north bank. Inevitably, it happened. The Germans, resisting furiously for 18 terror-packed days, blew up all of Florence's dearly loved, world-famed bridges, excepting only the Ponte Vecchio (Old Bridge), which they blocked on either side with the ruins of demolished buildings. Reconstruction began immediately after the German retreat.

Two decades later, a new catastrophe befell the city. In the terrible floods of the late fall of 1966, countless art treasures of inestimable worth were destroyed or damaged. It is difficult to visualize the extent of the devastation, as mud-laden water, 15 feet deep or more, roared through the streets. Again the Florentines pitched in, aided from all over the world, and all the museums and monuments have been restored. Because of pollution, much outdoor sculpture is being moved into museums (e.g. Donatello's *Judith*).

Exploring Florence

Florence hugs the banks of the Arno River where it cuts through north-central Tuscany, tucked in a bed of surrounding hills. Elegant, somewhat aloof, as if physically conscious of a past greatness, this historic center of European civilization that once represented Italy's peak in art, thought and culture, still shares with Rome the honor of first place among all Italian cities for the wealth and importance of its artistic works. Every street, every square and winding alley is a show-window of Romanesque, Gothic, and especially Renaissance architecture in churches, palaces, towers, statuary, galleries, ornate museums.

For the most cursory tour of Florence, five days are indispensable. Consider all but the fact that this city holds at least 13 monumental palaces, 19 of Italy's most beautiful churches, no less than 22 individual museums, 5 major gardens and public parks. You should see its Cathedral, Baptistery, Piazza della Signoria and Palazzo Vecchio, Uffizi Art Gallery, Bargello (or National) Museum, Pitti Palace, Gallery of the Academy, the Medici Tombs, Piazzale Michelangelo, Medici-Riccardi Palace, churches like Orsanmichele, Santo Spirito, the Carmine, Santa Maria Novella, San Lorenzo, Santa Croce and the Pazzi Chapel, San Marco (the museum, too), San Miniato, the Badia, Santissima Annunziata, and drive along Viale dei Colli. But how? Obviously, you won't have time to glance over more than a maximum one-half of these—even in five days—without some planning and organization.

Seven Independent Tours

Specific, detailed trips around Florence begin from the city's center at Piazza del Duomo. In seven comparatively short tours branching away from this monumental square, you can see most of Florence as completely as you wish. Another promenade along Viale dei Colli—and you have covered the city. As every item on your visiting list is likely to have different opening hours, make sure of them when you are planning your tours. Arriving just after a building has shut is deeply frustrating. We would, also, suggest that you equip yourself with a pair of binoculars. Many of the most fascinating frescos are high up on the walls of churches and almost impossible to make out in detail without some kind of help. Naturally, this is true all over Italy, but nowhere more so than in Florence.

First Tour

First, explore the Piazza del Duomo itself, around which stand the great Duomo (Cathedral), the Campanile (Bell Tower) of Giotto, and the Baptistery.

The lofty Cathedral of Santa Maria del Fiore, its official name, is one of the longest in the world. Begun by the great master, Arnolfo di Cambio, in 1296, work continued on the church until 1436—some 140 years—after which it was finally consecrated. Gothic architecture predominates, with a 19th-century facade blocked in white, green and dull red marble, looking for all the world like a huge vertical marble floor. Inside, the church stands as one of the most stupendous examples of Gothic architecture in Tuscany; its works and monuments of art are priceless. Over your head, a gigantic octagon-shaped dome decorated by the immense fresco, *The Last Judgement,* by Vasari and Zuccari, is hidden while restoration work continues. From the outside of the cupola you will get a magnificent view of Florence and the surrounding countryside. You reach the cupola gallery by a fatiguing climb up 463 steps between the two skins of the double dome—a fascinating way of finding out how the building was done.

Scattered through both dome and church below are numerous sculptures, frescos and paintings by such artists as Ghirlandaio, Donatello, Benedetto da Maiano, Luca della Robbia, Mino da Fiesole, Andrea del Castagno, Paolo Uccello and Nanni di Banco. Important ancient remains, discovered during repair work after the 1966 flood, have been excavated beneath the cathedral's nave. Brunelleschi's superb dome is still shrouded inside by scaffolding as the restoration proceeds apace.

Beside the cathedral, Giotto's 14th-century Campanile, regarded as the most beautiful bell tower in the world and one of the greatest creations of Gothic art, towers 85 m. (292 feet) above ground. Two rows of low-

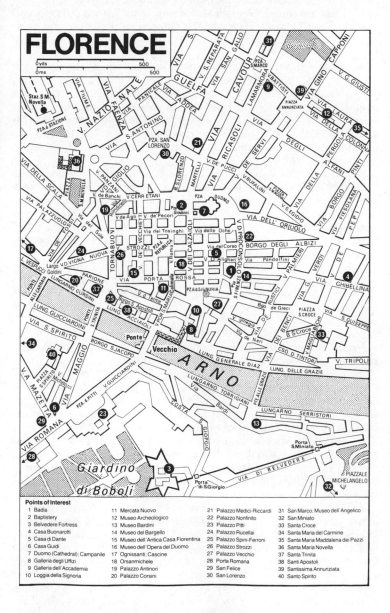

Points of Interest

1 Badia	11 Mercata Nuovo	21 Palazzo Medici-Riccardi	31 San Marco: Museo dell'Angelico
2 Baptistery	12 Museo Archeologico	22 Palazzo Nonfinito	32 San Miniato
3 Belvedere Fortress	13 Museo Bardini	23 Palazzo Pitti	33 Santa Croce
4 Casa Buonarotti	14 Museo del Bargello	24 Palazzo Rucellai	34 Santa Maria del Carmine
5 Casa di Dante	15 Museo dell'Antica Casa Fiorentina	25 Palazzo Spini-Ferroni	35 Santa Maria Maddalena dei Pazzi
6 Casa Guidi	16 Museo dell'Opera del Duomo	26 Palazzo Strozzi	36 Santa Maria Novella
7 Duomo (Cathedral): Campanile	17 Ognissanti; Cascine	27 Palazzo Vecchio	37 Santa Trinita
8 Galleria degli Uffizi	18 Orsanmichele	28 Porta Romana	38 Santi Apostoli
9 Galleria dell'Accademia	19 Palazzo Antinori	29 San Felice	39 Santissima Annunziata
10 Loggia della Signoria	20 Palazzo Corsini	30 San Lorenzo	40 Santo Spirito

reliefs line the first floor, done by Luca della Robbia and Andrea Pisano (first row) and Arnoldi and students of the Pisano-Orcagna school (second row). These are copies: the originals are now in the Museo dell'Opera del Duomo. The Campanile is crowned by three more stories of magnificent windows; to reach the top, climb the 414 steps for a marvelous view of Florence.

Across the square from the cathedral, you find the Baptistery of San Giovanni, featuring its three world-famous sets of bronze doors. This octagonal marble baptistery was erected in the Romanesque style in the 11th–12th centuries upon the ruins of an ancient pagan temple. Inside, below the splendid mosaics of the cupola, stand the mighty baptismal font and Donatello's tomb (1427) of the anti-Pope John XXIII. The eye-catching many-paneled bronze doors deserve a brief description:

East Door—This is the door facing the Duomo, the one Michelangelo called *The Gate of Paradise,* done by Ghiberti in the 27 years between 1425 and 1452 and the scenes from the Old Testament represent his greatest work. Around the frame of the doors are 24 statuettes of prophets and Sibyls, plus a further 24 small portraits in medallions, one of which (the fourth down on the right-hand side of the left-hand door) is a self-portrait of Ghiberti, balding and with a secret smile.

South Door—The work of Andrea Pisano in 1326 (but finally hung in its current location in 1424), showing his *Scenes From the Life of St. John the Baptist* and the *Theological (Faith, Hope and Charity) and Cardinal Virtues.*

North Door—This earlier result of Ghiberti's efforts (1403–1424) represents his *Life of Christ* and *Evangelists and Doctors.*

The doors are being dismantled and placed in the museum at No. 9, behind the cathedral. Known officially as the Museo dell'Opera del Duomo, it contains a wealth of art works, mainly sculpture, including statues by Arnolfo da Cambio, moved here from the cathedral. On the mezzanine is a *Pietà* by Michelangelo, begun about 1550 and originally intended for his own tomb. It was finished after his death by Tiberio Calcagni, who restored sections that Michelangelo was reputed to have smashed in irritation. The Museum also has some superb works by Donatello and Luca della Robbia, including their sculptured *cantorie,* or choir decorations.

Trip No. 1 out of Piazza del Duomo takes you along Via Calzaioli to a two-storied oratory, the church of Orsanmichele, one of Florence's most interesting constructions, built between 1337 and 1404 on the former site of a storehouse for corn. Interestingly enough, this church functioned at first only on the ground floor, with the upper story being still used as a granary. Its most noteworthy architectural decorations are those running around the outside. Under them are niches holding statues by Nanni di Banco, Donatello, Ghiberti and Verrocchio that constitute some of the most representative examples of Renaissance sculpture in Florence. Inside the church, see the tabernacle, a really priceless 14th-century work of art by Andrea Orcagna.

Continuing along Via Calzaioli, you soon find yourself in Piazza della Signoria, the city's largest square, with a round slab in its center marking the spot where the Dominican monk Savonarola was hanged and then burned in 1498 as a heretic. It was on the same spot a year earlier that this 15th-century version of the Ayatollah Khomeni intimidated the citizens of Florence into burning pictures, wigs, musical instruments—any outward sign of vanity. The square itself is overshadowed by Palazzo della Signoria, better known among Florentines as Palazzo Vecchio (the Old Palace), beside which you can't miss Ammannati's huge *Fountain of Neptune.*

The Old Palace, once the home of the Medici family's Cosimo I and later a united Italy's seat for its Chamber of Deputies, when Florence was briefly the Italian capital (1865–71), is probably the most important civic building in the city. Built in rusticated stone in the 16 years between 1298 and 1314 by Arnolfo di Cambio, then added to in subsequent centuries by artists like Buontalenti and Vasari, it is now occupied by the municipality of Florence. The figures on the steps, from the left to right, are the *Marzocco,* heraldic lion of Florence; *David,* a copy of Michelangelo's original which is in the Accademia; and *Hercules and Cacus,* by Bandinelli. Donatello's restored *Judith and Holofernes* is now inside. The five-centuries-old courtyard holds a copy of Verrocchio's cherub with a dolphin (the original is upstairs in the Cancelleria). Vasari's staircase will lead you up to the floors above which are crowded with works of art displayed in a wide range of period rooms, varying from the overwhelming to the intimate, for this was both a center of government and a palace. Far and away the grandest of the rooms is the great Sala dei Cinquecento, called after the 500 deputies who deliberated there from 1865–71. It was also the scene of the famous battle of the frescos, when Leonardo and Michelangelo created two huge masterpieces in competition with each other. Neither fresco survived and their place is now taken by huge historical studies by Vasari and others. In fact, Vasari's hand can be seen all over the palace, both as an architect and as a painter. The great hall also has Michelangelo's *Victory,* a two-figure sculptural group which may have been yet another piece left over from the ill-fated tomb of Pope Julius. On the other floors are lovely ceilings, most painted and some coffered as well, such as that in the Sala dei Gigli on the 2nd floor. Don't miss Francesco de' Medici's Studiolo (little study) which was richly decorated by Vasari, Bronzino and others. In fact, try to find time to wander through all these rooms, which are redolent with the fascinating history of the city.

Next to the Old Palace, the 14th-century Loggia della Signoria, with its three semi-circular Gothic-Florentine arches, features two rows of statues known the world over. Among them are: *The Rape of the Sabines,* by Giambologna; *Rape of Polyxena,* by Fedi; *Perseus,* Cellini's masterpiece in bronze; *Ajax With the Body of Patroclus,* copied from a 4th-century B.C. Greek original; and *Hercules and Nessus,* by Giambologna. At press time the Loggia was undergoing structural repairs, with some statues slated for restoration when the main job is finished.

Beyond the Old Palace and this Loggia della Signoria is the Piazza degli Uffizi, a long, narrow square almost entirely surrounded by the Palazzo degli Uffizi, which houses the most important collection of paintings in Italy and one of the richest in the world. This fabulous collection, beautifully arranged in the Uffizi Gallery, was opened by the Medici to the public in the 17th century and is thus the first art gallery of modern times, continuing the antique tradition of museums. Most of the Italian (and some foreign) schools of painting are represented, with particular stress on Tuscan schools. Every one of the gallery's innumerable windows affords splendid views of the Duomo, the Palazzo Vecchio, or the Arno River, with San Miniato Hill above and Ponte Vecchio on your right.

You could spend days here, and enjoy every minute, but if you are pressed for time, here is a brief list of the highlights:

The *Adoration of the Magi* and *The Annunciation* by Leonardo da Vinci; *Portrait of Leo X* and *The Madonna of the Goldfinch* by Raphael; the *Urbino Venus* by Titian; *The Rest on the Flight to Egypt* by Correggio; *Portrait of Jacopo Sansovino* and *Christ and the Woman of Samaria* by Tintoretto; *Medusa, Bacchus* and the *Sacrifice of Isaac* by Caravaggio; Botticelli's *Spring* and *The Birth of Venus,* both recently restored; Michelangelo's *Holy Family;* and three self-portraits by Rembrandt, from youth to old age. At the end of the seemingly infinite series of rooms, high above the Piazza della Signoria, is a very welcome coffee bar with a view of Florentine towers and domes.

The Corridoio Vasariano (Vasari Corridor), a passage that once linked Palazzo degli Uffizi with Palazzo Pitti and which includes the upper level of Ponte Vecchio, is hung with fascinating self-portraits of the great Renaissance artists. You get a special ticket from the Uffizi ticket counter, which will admit you for the hour-long guided tour.

Second Tour

Another, shorter trip out of Piazza del Duomo leads along Via Roma to the somewhat modern Piazza della Repubblica, in the heart of old Florence, at the far end of which you take Via Calimala to the Mercato Nuovo (New Market), covered by a portico. This is one of the places in Florence where you can buy craft work and other souvenirs. At one side is Tacca's bronze copy of the *Wild Boar,* commonly called *Il Porcellino* (Little Pig) by Florentines. Branch off Via Calimala now, moving into Via Por' Santa Maria, where, in the single night of August 3–4, 1944, German troops mined and blew up every house on the street.

Follow Via Por' Santa Maria up to and over the 14th-century Ponte Vecchio (Old Bridge), the oldest bridge in the city, which is lined on both sides with shops of goldsmiths, silversmiths and many of Florence's best jewelry firms. Then, on the other side of the bridge, head down Via Guicciardini, now rebuilt, into Piazza de' Pitti, which takes its name from Palazzo Pitti, a 15th-century palace once occupied by the Grand Dukes of Tuscany and from 1866 to 1870 by the first King of Italy. It was begun in 1458 to a design by Brunelleschi, left unfinished, then brought up to its present size in the mid-1600s. Its long facade, fronting the piazza, is much as Brunelleschi must have imagined it, solid and severe—not unlike a Roman aqueduct turned into a palace.

The severe early-Renaissance exterior of this monumental palace hides a wealth of artistic treasures. Below is the Museum of Works in Silver, on the second floor the Gallery of Modern Art, and on the first floor the magnificent Palatine Gallery, this last a collection of splendid paintings that fills 28 rooms, interspersed by several halls draped and decorated with priceless tapestries, portraits, sculptures, and frescos. Some of the ceilings here are pure marvels. Among the highlights, a brief list among thousands of important works of art, we can mention these: *Donna Gravida* and *Madonna del Granduca* by Raphael; *La Bella* and *The Concert* by Titian; *The Three Ages of Man* by Bellini. If you can schedule your visit to the Pitti Palace when the sun is out you will be in luck, for many of the rooms have virtually no artificial light, and the pictures are very hard to see on an overcast day—a fact which is not helped by the protective glass now covering some of the pictures, turning them into excellent mirrors.

Beside the Pitti Palace is an entrance to the Boboli Gardens, a typical Italian-style arrangement designed in 1550 by Tribolo for Eleanor of Toledo. Be sure to see the amphitheater; the Viottolone, a wide path descending to gardens between groves of laurel, cypress, oaks and pines, and with lots of fascinating side paths; Neptune's Fish Pond, with its huge bronze statue of the sea god himself; and the Piazza dell'Isolotto, centered with Giambologna's Fountain of Oceanus. The Belvedere Fortress at the top of the rising terraces gives a magnificent view across the city and its surroundings. Some of the surroundings, in the shape of olive groves and vineyards press close up to the fortress, and there—so close to the heart of the city—you can feel yourself instantly in the depths of Tuscany.

In the far corner of the Piazza de' Pitti you will find the medieval church of San Felice, with some interesting paintings inside. At no. 9 Piazza San Felice is the Casa Guidi, once the home of the poets Robert and Elizabeth Browning. Slated to become an office building, it was saved at the last moment by funds collected in America and Britain by the Browning Society and is open in the early evening (4–7, Tues. to Fri.). Now follow the Via Romana past the Museum of Physics and Natural History to its end at Porta Romana, a massive tower dated 1326. Way up, on the inner side, is a Madonna by Giotto's school.

Third Tour

A third trip could lead from Piazza del Duomo along Via de' Cerretani, past the Church of Santa Maria Maggiore, left into Via Rondinelli and into Piazza Antinori. Here is a palace of the same name, that was built during the 15th century on a design by Giuliano da Sangallo. Continuing out of Piazza Antinori along Via Tornabuoni, one of Florence's swankiest streets, you finally reach an intersection, on the left of which stands Palazzo Strozzi, built for one of the main banking families by Benedetto da Maiano in 1489, continued 17 years later by Cronaca. One of the most beautiful buildings of the Renaissance, a formidable blend of castle and palace, the building now contains artistic and cultural institutes.

It's a short walk off the intersection down Via della Vigna Nuova to Palazzo Rucellai, another and even greater Renaissance masterpiece. The palace is perhaps the finest work Leon Battista Alberti ever did. It was his plans, the first ever to attempt to apply purely classical characteristics to the facade of a palace, that Bernardo Rossellino followed to construct Palazzo Rucellai between 1446 and 1451. This time the money did not come from banking but from cloth, for the Rucellai family were yard goods merchants.

Back on Via Tornabuoni again, amble along it to the end at Piazza Santa Trínita. In the center of this square is a Column of Justice brought here in 1560 from the Baths of Caracalla in Rome; on the left stands Baccio d'Agnolo's 16th-century Palazzo Bartolini-Salimbeni; to the right, you have the Church of Santa Trínita. This latter is perhaps Florence's most beautiful Gothic church, rebuilt near the end of the 13th century, enlarged during the next 100 years and given a Baroque facade in the 1590s. Inside are precious works of art, among which those you must see first are the Sassetti Chapel frescos on *The Life of St. Francis* by Ghirlandaio, damaged in the 1966 flood and masterfully restored, and Luca della Robbia's Federighi tomb.

Outside the church, just opposite it in Borgo Santi Apostoli, you find one of Italy's oldest Romanesque churches, the 11th-century Church of Santi Apostoli, which has been enlarged and restored. And if you continue down the street a bit, there are the Palazzo Rosselli del Turco (no. 19), done in 1517, and a group of medieval homes that are typical of the structures of those days.

Then back to Piazza Santa Trínita, crossing it to the 13th-century Palazzo Spini-Ferroni, built like a massive fortress and the city's most representative private palace during the Middle Ages, you come upon the reconstructed Bridge of Santa Trínita, a copy replacing Ammannati's 16th-century masterpiece, which was destroyed by German mines in 1944.

Cross over the bridge into Piazza Frescobaldi, continue down Via Maggio, lined with 16th-century palaces, then turn right along Via Michelozzi into Piazza Santa Spirito. There, on the right, is the Church of Santo Spirito, one of Brunelleschi's best creations; he began it in 1444 and worked on it until his death two years later, after which the construction was continued by Manetti among others and finished in 1487. As in all Florentine churches, there are lovely paintings here in 40 arched niches, including a *Madonna* by Filippino Lippi.

Walk to the end of Piazza Santo Spirito, down Via Sant' Agostino, then Via Santa Monaca to reach the Church of Santa Maria del Carmine, built in 1268 and restored after a fire almost burned it to the ground in 1771. Architecturally, this church has no particular importance. The reason visitors from all over the world come to its doors is to look upon one of the few parts of the building to escape the fire, the Brancacci Chapel, containing one of the most celebrated series of frescos in Italian art. Done by Masaccio, who left such a tremendous impression upon Italian painting, Masolino da Panicale and Filippino Lippi, the series is divided into one upper and one lower group showing episodes in the lives of St. Peter, St. Paul, and St. John. The rest of the church is well worth wandering through, with frescos and fragments of frescos, attractive cloisters and a fine Corsini Chapel. It is sometimes possible to hear concerts here.

If you wish, you can combine this tour with Tour No. 2 to the Pitti Palace and the Boboli Gardens.

Fourth Tour

Tour No. 4 runs from Piazza del Duomo along Via Cerretani and Via Panzani into Piazza della Stazione, where you take Via degli Avelli, beside the church, to its end in Piazza Santa Maria Novella. Here is the entrance to the Church of Santa Maria Novella, begun by the Dominican friars, Sisto and Ristoro, in 1278 and finished by Talenti in 1360; part of the facade is to designs by Alberti. It's a Tuscan interpretation of Gothic art, with an interior rich in precious paintings, among which some of the more famous are frescos by Ghirlandaio in the chancel, executed with the help of assistants (among whom legend places the young Michelangelo) of scenes of the life of the Virgin, John the Baptist, St. Dominic and so on. They are full of contemporary detail and are vibrant with realistic portraits of the people of his time—the Medici, artists and members of the Platonic Academy. Other frescos by Nardo di Cione are in the Strozzi Chapel, and a really imposing *Trinity* by Masaccio can be seen in the north aisle. To the left of the church is the entrance to the cloisters which are well worth visiting, though as they are under restoration they may be difficult to get into; among the things to see there are the restored Paolo Uccello frescos.

Across the square from this church is the Loggia of San Paolo, along the left of which runs Via de' Fossi. Follow it into Largo Goldoni. Make a short side trip here up Lungarno Corsini to Palazzo Corsini, one of the best examples of Baroque architecture in Florence.

Back at Largo Goldini, take Lungarno Vespucci along the river across Piazza Ognissanti, noting well at the end of this square the magnificent Church of Ognissanti (All Saints) which, although originally dating from 1239, was restored in the 18th century. Inside are some outstanding frescos by Botticelli and Giovanni da San Giovanni; but the most important work of all stands in the adjoining convent (to the left of the church)— Ghirlandaio's masterpiece, *The Last Supper* (9–12, 4–6 every day).

Continue along Lungarno Vespucci, past a number of swank hotels, to its end at the entrance of the Cascine, once the ancient farm lands of Tuscany's Grand Dukes, but laid out in the second half of the 18th century as a public park stretching two miles along the banks of the Arno River. To cover the park well, you need a horse-carriage for about an hour, taking one of the main avenues (Viale degli Olmi) and returning by the other (Viale dei Lecci). The Cascine runs about 2½ miles through thick woods, ending at a monument dedicated to the Indian prince Rajaram Cuttraputti, who died in Florence in 1870 and was cremated on this spot by order of relatives who knew how much he loved the city. This park, incidentally, is a favorite rendezvous for young Florentine couples, in addition to being a natural locale for picnics, hikes, tennis matches and the ever-popular bicycling runs.

Fifth Tour

A fifth tour takes you north from Piazza del Duomo along Via Martelli into Via Cavour, with the Medici-Riccardi Palace, built by Michelozzo between 1440 and 1460 for the Medici family, who lived there until 1540. Now a headquarters for the Florence Prefecture, its most distinctive characteristics are the beautiful Tuscan Renaissance courtyard and a series of windows designed by Michelangelo. It houses the Medicean Portrait Museum and a tiny but memorable chapel, its walls decorated with Benozzo Gozzoli's glorious frescos, representing the *Journey of the Magi* (1459). It's a spectacular cavalcade showing the lush Florentine countryside, Lorenzo the Magnificent (on a charger) and the artist himself. This small room is frequently missed by visitors, but is one of the most lovely works of art in the city. The Palace also contains a large hall, the Gallery, with sumptuous, airy ceiling paintings. (Closed when official meetings are in progress.)

Continue to the left of the palace along Via dei Gori to Piazza San Lorenzo (another busy marketplace, with dozens of stalls offering both gimcrack rubbish and interesting craftwork), and here inspect the Church of San Lorenzo, one of Brunelleschi's most valuable works, which he did in the years between 1425 and 1446. The interior, shaped like a Latin cross, is a monumental classic in harmony. Adjoining it are the Old Sacristy, another Brunelleschi masterpiece, and behind it (on Piazza Madonna degli Aldobrandini) is the New Sacristy, by Michelangelo, with its beautiful tombs of Giuliano Duke of Nemours, and Lorenzo, Duke of Urbino, near the burial place of Florence's famed Lorenzo the Magnificent. Note the intent expression of the statue called *The Thinker* and the perfect anatomy of *Dawn* and *Twilight,* and of the figures representing *Night* and *Day.* Famous from innumerable reproductions, these funerary monuments create an indelible impression when seen in their original setting.

Return now to Via Cavour and walk up to Piazza San Marco—to the Church of San Marco, which contains numerous 16th-century works of art. Just to the right of the church is its museum, set up in an ancient monastery built by Michelozzo in 1437 for Dominican friars. Visit this place even if you must sacrifice time elsewhere. The most important works of Fra Angelico are painted on the walls of monks' bare cells and brighten the timeworn corridors, to form an art collection rare in Italy for its interest and unity. It's a really fabulous place, with illuminated choir books, cloisters, crucifixes, and the gloomy cells in one of which the monk Savonarola once lived. Among the fascinating details is the telltale black halo of Judas Iscariot. Make certain, too, that you see Fra Angelico's famous masterpiece, *The Annunciation.*

Just below the Piazza San Marco, on the Via Ricasoli, is the Gallery of the Academy (the Accademia). Though there are some interesting primitive paintings here, it is for Michelangelo's original *David* and his *Captives* that it is most visited. The exhibition halls leading up to the *David* are often so jam-packed with bus tours that you may have literally to fight your way. Try to get there early. Taken with the tombs in the New Sacristy and the small works in the Bargello, these massive pieces create an understanding of just why Michelangelo has exercised such a hypnotic fascination for succeeding ages.

If you like, continue out of Piazza San Marco on Via Arazzieri to Via San Gallo, then follow it into Piazza della Libertà. Here take a streetcar or bus along the Via Vittorio Emanuele to Via Stibbert, where, at No. 26, you can visit the Stibbert Museum. The place has a magnificent collection of armor and Oriental objects presented by Frederick Stibbert to the Commune of Florence—things like a set of 15th-century Italian armor mounted on a horse, a series of 14 cavaliers of the 16th century in full-dress armor, Italian costumes of the time of Napoleon I, arms and costumes of various periods from India, Persia, China and Japan.

Sixth Tour

Off Piazza del Duomo again for Tour No. 6, take Via dei Servi into Piazza Santissima Annunziata, in the center of which is Giambologna's statue of Ferdinand I, two rather curious fountains by Tacca, and a portico by Brunelleschi.

The Church of Santissima Annunziata was built in 1250, then rebuilt entirely in the mid-15th century by Michelozzo and his helpers. The first two chapels on the left hold important frescos by Andrea del Castagno; in the lunette over the cloister entrance is a Madonna by Andrea del Sarto.

Continue along Via Colonna, past the Convent of Santa Maria Maddalena dei Pazzi. *Pazzi,* the plural of *pazzo,* means lunatic. It was also the name of a famous Florentine family, belonging to the Ghibelline party, rivals of the Medici. We know about it from the history of the Pazzi Conspiracy which terminated in Giuliano de' Medici's assassination in the cathedral. We also know that Giacomo and Francesco Pazzi were caught and hanged by Lorenzo de' Medici, who had escaped being assassinated.

A war followed, called the Pazzi War. The Pope (whose banker was a Roman Pazzi), Naples and Siena attacked the Medici in Florence. You may be interested to learn the origins of these family names. The Medici, for example, get their name from the word for "doctor", and from the traditional symbol of the pharmacist—his globes—that decorated their coat of arms.

But, after leaving Santa Maria Maddalena dei Pazzi whose Chapter House boasts the celebrated Perugino fresco, *Crucifixion and Saints,* turn right into Via Farini, on which you will find the Florence Synagogue.

Seventh Tour

The last of these quick jaunts through Florence is, perhaps, one of the most eye-filling. This time leave Piazza del Duomo by way of Via del Proconsolo, passing Palazzo Nonfinito, where the National Museum of Anthropology and Ethnology is housed, and the rather elegant 15th-century Palazzo Pazzi, with its artistic courtyard. About here, Via del Proconsolo intersects with Via Dante Alighieri, where you find the house in which Dante was born. Farther along, the street passes the Church of Badia, a Benedictine establishment founded by Marquis Ugo of Tuscany, with an interior shaped like a Greek cross; inside, the valuable works of art include a tomb of the Marquis Ugo (died 1001), considered Mino da Fiesole's masterpiece, and a *Vision of St. Bernard* by Filippino Lippi.

On the other side of Via del Proconsolo is the cold, fortress-like Palazzo del Podestà, otherwise known as the Bargello, built in three parts between 1254 and 1346, with a high tower and picturesque courtyard. The palace today houses Florence's National Museum and its three floors are dedicated to the works of Florentine sculptors famous during the Renaissance. Here are masterpieces by Donatello, Settignano, Verrocchio, Michelangelo, and many other great names in the world of art. It is one of those museums which reveals exciting new surprises at every turn quite apart from being an historically interesting building in its own right. There is a mixture of display styles, too, some of the works on show being mounted in a thoroughly modern manner.

Beyond the museum, through Piazza San Firenze and into Borgo dei Greci leading away from it, you come to Piazza Santa Croce, dominated by the Church of Santa Croce, largest and most beautiful of all Italy's Franciscan churches and one of the nation's most perfect examples of Gothic architecture.

Probably built from designs by Arnolfo di Cambio, it dates back to 1294. It was one of the worst damaged buildings in Florence during the horrendous floods of 1966 which rose to 5 meters (16½ ft.) in parts of the building. Somehow, it has become customary to bury Italy's historic greats in the Church of Santa Croce, with the result that it now resembles a sort of Pantheon for Italian glories of the past. Here are the remains of illustrious personages like Galileo, Michelangelo, Machiavelli, Foscolo, Alfieri, and others. Inside, too, you find some of the city's most treasured art works; for example, Giotto's frescos in the Bardi and Peruzzi Chapels, along with those by Maso di Banco, Taddeo and Agnolo Gaddi. The famous Cimabue crucifix, badly damaged in the flood, is on view in the museum housed in the former refectory after the exceptional restoration it underwent at Fortezza di Basso. Be sure to see Brunelleschi's architectural gem, the Pazzi Chapel in the cloister next to Santa Croce.

A View of the City

Aside from these seven short tours—but necessarily included in any visit to Florence—is a walk (about four miles) or ride along Viale dei Colli, opened in 1877 as one of the most lovely promenades in the city. (This visit could be tacked on to the end of the Pitti Palace and Boboli Gardens tour.) If you have no car and still hesitate about hiking it all the way, take a bus from Lungarno Serristori. Best time to go is in the morning or late afternoon. The road winds outside and above Florence to a height of 340 feet at Piazzale Michelangelo where, in the middle, there is a bronze reproduction of his *David*. The view here from the railing covers all of Florence, the plain beyond, Fiesole, and the highest peaks of the Apennine Mountains in the far distance. Sadly, the view nearer at hand isn't such fun as the piazza is always crammed to the gunwales with tourist buses.

Turning away from the railing, take the stairway on your left or the road on your right up through rows of giant cypress trees to the Church of San Salvatore al Monte, built by Cronaca about 1500, then continue higher to the top of the hill. There you will find the Church of San Miniato al Monte, one of the most beautiful and famous of Florence's many churches and a masterpiece of Romanesque architecture. It was built in 1013, during the time of Emperor Henry II, and finished later in the 13th century. The interior is floored in marble and covered with frescos by Spinello Aretino and the 14th and 15th-century Florentine school; there's a tabernacle by Michelozzo and a Chapel of the Cardinal of Portugal by Manetti, with Rossellino's sepulcher of the cardinal done in 1461 and ceiling plaques by Della Robbia.

Environs of Florence

Anyone remaining in Florence for a reasonable length of time should try to alternate visits to its scattered environs with tours throughout the city itself, thus breaking the inevitable monotony derived from a surfeit of too many churches, art, palaces, and museums. This is rather important in most Italian cities; in Florence particularly it may mean the difference between thorough enjoyment of your visit and cultural indigestion.

See Fiesole first. It's only 20 minutes out of Florence's Piazza San Marco by bus no. 7 over a route lined with moss-grown garden walls, olive trees, cypresses, sumptuous villas, and beds of geraniums and irises.

Fiesole, on the top of a hill and still surrounded by ramparts, was an important Etruscan town, whose tombs are now being excavated all over the countryside. Briefly dominating the region in the Middle Ages, it finally succumbed to Florence. Things to see: the cathedral, built in 1028, with works by the Della Robbias, Mino da Fiesole, Nicodemo di Michelangelo, among others; the 2nd-century B.C. Roman amphitheater, uncovered in 1809; the Bandini Museum, with Della Robbia terracottas, Byzantine icons and paintings of the 13th–15th centuries; and, above all, the Monastery of San Francesco, built over an Etruscan acropolis, a Roman temple, and a medieval castle. Fiesole's sights are scattered; to see them all involves a lot of walking.

Next, visit the "villa towns"—three out of four of which are within 8 km. (5 miles) of Florence. There's Settignano (bus from Piazza San Marco, in the city), and its world-famous Italian garden outside the superb 17th-century Villa Gamberaia, which can be visited by arrangement a week in advance. Inquire at Florence tourist office about visiting villas as closing times are very variable—and several are in the grip of the restorers. Nearby Villa I Tatti was American art critic Bernard Berenson's home; it now houses the Harvard Institute for Renaissance Studies. Visit Villa di Castello (bus from Station Square), with another beautiful, terraced garden beside the villa once owned by the Medici family; and nearby Villa Petraia, boasting a magnificent fountain by Giambologna.

At Sesto Fiorentino, the Museo di Doccia displays examples of the magnificent porcelain created at the Richard-Ginori factory from the early 18th century.

A little farther out (21 km., 13 miles, by SACA bus line from Piazza Santa Maria Novella, or by Lazzi coach from Piazza Adua), the Villa Poggio a Caiano, bought by Lorenzo the Magnificent and decorated by artists like Sangallo and the Della Robbias, was the scene of a 16th-century tragedy when both Grand Duke Francesco Medici and his wife (and formerly mistress) Bianca Capello, died there on the same night in 1578.

Closer to Florence (about 6½ km., 4 miles) by bus from Piazza Santa Maria Novella) is the Certosa del Galluzzo, a Carthusian monastery founded in the 14th century. Its subterranean chapels and convent hold priceless works of art. Guided tours are available, 9–12, 4–7, which last around three-quarters of an hour. There's also a "pharmacy" where you can buy the Florentine version of Chartreuse. The liqueur comes in attractive bottles and makes an excellent and reasonably-priced souvenir.

Some 26 km. (16 miles) outside Florence, perched high on Montesenario, another monastery should be given a place on your itinerary. Originally a hermitage, it has a chapel dating back to the 15th century with lovely views from the surrounding woods.

Impruneta is a delightful hill town about half-an-hour south from Florence by bus, famous for its Della Robbia terracottas and pottery workshops.

PRACTICAL INFORMATION FOR FLORENCE

WHEN TO GO. Weather-wise, the best seasons in Florence are spring and fall, which is when the city is most crowded with tourists. July and August are not much better as far as crowds are concerned, and they are much hotter. Therefore, you might consider an off-season visit, in late fall or early spring, or even in winter. Since most of what you will want to see is indoors, the weather need not be the overriding factor—and off-season vacationing means usually better service in hotels and restaurants, as well as avoiding the crowds.

USEFUL ADDRESSES. U.S. Consulate, Lungarno Vespucci 38 (298.276); British Consulate, Lungarno Corsini 2 (284.133); AAST, Via Tornabuoni 15 (216.544); EPT, Via Manzoni 16 (247.8141); main post office (for long-distance and intercontinental phone calls), Via Pellicceria 1. Other *Telefoni* offices on Via Cavour, 21r, and at the railway station.

SEASONAL EVENTS. February to March: important couture and boutique fashion shows (by invitation only).

April: the Scoppio del Carro—literally, "Explosion of the Cart"—takes place Easter Sun. morning in the Piazza del Duomo; toward the end of the month, International Handicrafts Show opens.

May: on the first Sun.—also on Jun. 24 and 28—costumed pageants provide the setting for the historic Gioco del Calcio, a fantastic 16th-century forerunner to the game of football; a display of prize irises (the Florentine lily is really an iris, symbol of the city since the Middle Ages) can be seen at Piazzale Michelangelo; the Feast of the Ascension sees the locals flocking to the Cascine park for the Festa del Grillo, when crickets in tiny cages are sold as good-luck charms; and the Maggio Musicale festival of opera, ballet and concerts commences, continuing into June.

September: the 28th sees a bird fair at Porta Romana; and an important antiques fair is held in odd-numbered years, continuing into Oct.

December: the winter opera season gets underway.

TELEPHONE CODE. The telephone code for Florence is 055.

HOTELS. As an important tourist center, Florence naturally has many good hotels, but you will be well advised to make reservations well in advance any time of year, even in Jan.–Mar. (fashion shows) and from Easter through Sept. Knowledgeable tourists have learned to stay away from Florence at Easter and during the peak summer months of July and August. There is an information office and hotel reservation service at the railway station; ITA, in station lobby (282.893).

Deluxe

Excelsior Italie, Piazza Ognissanti 3 (264.201). CIGA. On the Arno, in imposing and historic palace; beautifully furnished and eminently comfortable rooms; assiduous service. Roof terrace for dining in good weather. Excellent *Cestello* restaurant. AE, DC, MC, V.

Regency, Piazza d'Azeglio 3 (245.247). A *Relais* hotel. A gem, in a quiet residential zone; luxuriously furnished villa, where you're coddled and spoiled by an attentive staff. Quiet rooms overlooking the garden. AE, DC, MC, V.

Villa Cora, Via Macchiavelli 18 (229.8451). Above Boboli gardens, 18th-century villa, beautifully furnished in period pieces; good atmosphere, pool. Suburban. AE, DC, MC, V.

Villa Medici, Via del Prato 42 (261.331). Between station and Cascine park. Contemporary and classic public rooms, spacious bedrooms. Pretty garden with swimming pool; terrace restaurant. AE, DC, MC.

Villa San Michele, Via di Doccia, Fiesole (59.451). About 15 minutes outside of town, on a hillside providing fabulous views over the city. One of the most desirable and expensive hotels in Italy, set in a converted monastery. AE, DC, MC, V.

Expensive

Augustus, Vicolo dell'Oro 5 (283.054). Near Ponte Vecchio. Understated elegance, modern comfort. AE, DC, MC, V.

Baglioni, Piazza Unità d'Italia 6 (218.441). Near station; large, comfortable rooms; Renaissance decor in public rooms; roof garden. AE, DC, MC, V.

Bernini Palace, Piazza San Firenze 29 (278.621). Behind Palazzo Vecchio, a newly opened (1987) hotel on historic premises. Decor is luxurious simplicity. No restaurant. AE, DC, MC, V.

Croce di Malta, Via della Scala 7 (282.600). Facing Santa Maria Novella; 120 compact, functional rooms, half overlooking garden; pool. AE, MC, V.

Kraft, Via Solferino 2 (284.273). Solid look, modern comforts. 66 small, well-appointed rooms; rooftop terrace restaurant; pool. AE, DC, MC, V.

Loggiato dei Servi, Piazza Annunziata 3 (219.165). In Renaissance setting, tastefully furnished in 19th-century style. Comfortable; low rates for category.

Lungarno, Borgo San Jacopo 14 (264.211). Superior, quiet, with 71 smallish, nicely-decorated rooms, many facing Arno with view of center, some with balcony. AE, DC, MC, V.

Majestic, Via del Melarancio 1 (264.021). Near station; very comfortable, modern rooms in pseudo-16th-century Florentine decor; a fine hotel. AE, DC, MC, V.

Monna Lisa, Borgo Pinti 27 (247.9751). Near cathedral. In patrician palazzo; fine antique furnishings, modern baths, quiet rooms on courtyard. A gem. AE, DC, MC, V.

Plaza Lucchesi, Lungarno della Zecca Vecchia 38 (264.141). In handsome old palace on the Arno; elegant ambience, contemporary decor. Bar and restaurant. AE, DC, MC, V.

Principe, Lungarno Vespucci 34 (284.848). Relaxed, private-home atmosphere. 22 bright, tastefully furnished rooms, many overlooking river, others on tiny garden. AE, DC, MC, V.

Rivoli, Via della Scala 33 (216.988). Near station. 62 smallish spotless rooms; pleasant public rooms, garden courtyard.

Villa Villoresi, at Colonnata, Sesto Fiorentino (448.9032). Pension in handsome 17th-century edifice. 27 rooms, many with frescos, period furnishings; pool in large park on outskirts. Restaurant.

Moderate

(Without restaurant unless specified)

Annalena, Via Romana 34 (222.402). Near Pitti Palace. Small; period decor; all rooms on garden courtyard. Book ahead. MC, V.

Aprile, Via della Scala 6 (263.147). In the 15th-century Palazzo del Borgo, a former Medici residence. Ask for a room overlooking Santa Maria Novella or the quiet garden. AE, DC, MC, V.

Beacci Tornabuoni, Via Tornabuoni 3 (212.645). Central, famous pension with old-fashioned comfort; roof terrace. Restaurant; half-board preferred. Book ahead. AE, DC, V.

Byron, Via della Scala 49 (tel. 216.700). Near train station. Pleasant, filled with antique furniture and fittings.

Cavour, Via del Proconsolo 3 (287.102). Very central; blend of modern and antique. Offers wonderful views of the cathedral. AE, DC, MC, V.

Continental, Lungarno Acciaiuoli 2 (282.392). Hard by Ponte Vecchio; 71 small, but well-appointed rooms; bright, cheery ambiance; roof garden; some traffic noise. AE, DC, MC, V.

Hermitage, Vicolo Marzio 1 (287.216). At Ponte Vecchio. Bright, tastefully furnished, small; with terrace overlooking Arno.

Montebello, Via Montebello 60 (298.051). Fairly central, town house; smart, modern decor; small garden. AE, DC, MC, V.

Pitti Palace, Via Barbadori 2 (282.257). Near Ponte Vecchio, combining Old World charm with modern comfort. Helpful American owner. Roof terrace. AE, V.

Porto Rossa, Via Porta Rossa 19 (287.551). Very central; lots of old-fashioned charm and atmosphere. Spacious rooms, those on street are noisy. AE, DC, MC, V.

Rapallo, Via Santa Caterina d'Alessandria 7 (472.412). Fairly central, attractive; restaurant. AE, DC, MC, V.

La Residenza, Via Tornabuoni 8 (284.197). Central, small, with elegant touches. Front rooms noisy. Half-board preferred.

Villa Azalee, Via Fratelli Rosselli 44 (214.242). Just outside center of town; intimate, tasteful atmosphere in small villa with large garden. DC, MC, V.

Villa Le Rondini, Via Bolognese Vecchia 224 (400.081). Attractive old country house in huge park in suburbs; very quiet; pool. Restaurant. AE, DC, MC, V.

Inexpensive

Alessandra, Borgo SS. Apostoli 17 (283.438). Central, old-fashioned pension; clean and simple. Ask for a room overlooking the Arno.

Cristallo, Via Cavour 27 (215.375). Rooms overlooking the courtyard are best bets here. Aristocratic old palace, some rooms with casement ceilings, frescoes, or balconies. AE, DC, MC, V.

Palazzo Vecchio, Via Cennini 4 (212.182). 18 rooms in immaculate 19th-century villa. Around the corner from train station, but like staying in a country home. AE, DC, MC, V.

Rigatti, Lungarno Diaz 2 (213.022). Near Uffizi. Charming rooms, new baths; rooms on garden quieter. Book ahead.

Royal, Via delle Ruote 52 (483.287). Near San Marco museum; smallish; all private baths; very good. AE, MC, V.

CAMPING. *Italia & Stranieri* at Viale Michelangelo 80 (681.1977), overlooking the city, and *Mugella Verde* on S. Piero a Sieve (848.511), farther out but offering pool, tennis courts, riding, and bungalows.

RESTAURANTS. At restaurants, remember that dinner hours are earlier here than in Rome, starting at 12.30 for the midday meal, in the evening from 7.30 P.M. on. Many of Florence's best restaurants are very small, especially the various Bucas, so get there early and be prepared to share a table.

Florentine Specialties. Cooking in Florence has a special character of its own— simple, tasty, with few spices or sauces, but based heavily on Tuscan olive oil, which is perhaps Italy's best. Meat, poultry and vegetables become the foundation of most dishes here, while *macaroni* is a favorite in soups. Some of the city's specialties— served in most restaurants—include *minestrone* or *ribollita* (a vegetable soup) and *zuppa alla Certosina* (breaded vegetable soup). Other dishes strictly Florentine: *triglie o baccala alla Livornese* (rock mullet or dried codfish with tomato sauce), *bistecca alla Fiorentina* (grilled steak, Florentine-style—big, thick steaks, a bit tough by U.S. standards), *stracotto alla Fiorentina* (stewed beef with sauce), *tortino di carciofi* (eggs with artichokes), *trippa e zampa alla Fiorentina* (tripe and calf's leg with sauce), *manzo o agnello girato al fuoco di legna* (beef or lamb roasted on a spit) and *funghi alla Fiorentina* (mushrooms served Florence-style). Roast chicken, pigeon or veal is especially well done in Florence, as are *fagioli* (beans).

Tuscany is the home of *Chianti,* and every table holds a bottle of it. The name has become an Italian trademark throughout the world; sample a glass or two of the red with your meals to understand why. There are also excellent whites from the Chianti region. And most restaurants have in stock another delightful—if a bit strong—sweet white wine answering to the name of Vin Santo, which is made of old dried grapes and, they say, will bring the dead back to life! Good dry wines from this part of the country include *Rufina, Montalbano* and *Montepulciano.* An exceptional dry pink wine, if properly chilled, can challenge anything France has to offer; ask for *Vinrosa di Torre de Passeri.*

Expensive

Cestello, Hotel Excelsior, Piazza Ognissanti 3 (294.301). Fine dining, many Florentine specialties, in a very pleasant setting, on roof terrace in summer. AE, DC, MC, V.

Enoteca Pinchiorri, Via Ghibellina 87 (242.777). Closed Sun., Mon. noon, Aug. and 25–27 Dec. One of Italy's best for superb blending of exquisite food and wines in beautiful setting in old palace; dining in lovely garden court in good weather. AE, DC, MC, V.

Relais Le Jardin, Piazza Massimo d'Azeglio 5 (587.655). Closed Sun. By reservation only. Intimate, refined atmosphere and cuisine offering both international and regional specialties; beautifully served. AE, DC, MC, V.

Sabatini, Via dei Panzani 9/a (282.802). Closed Mon. A classic for fine Tuscan cuisine in attractive ambiance. AE, DC, MC, V.

Terrazza Brunelleschi, Piazza dell'Unita Italiana 6 (215.642). Rooftop restaurant of the Hotel Baglioni with elegant Empire decor, outdoor dining in summer. Reserve. AE, DC, MC, V.

Il Verrocchio, Hotel Villa La Massa at Candeli (630.051). In an elegant setting, a Pinchiorri-trained chef proffers refined cuisine. AE, DC, MC, V.

Moderate

Angiolina, Via Santo Spirito 36r (298.976). On the "other" side of the Arno; superbly cooked Florentine dishes in spectacularly vaulted interior.

Antico Fattore, Via Lambertesca 1r (261.215). Closed Sun., Mon. and July. Near the Uffizi. Friendly and relaxed dining. AE.

Buca dell'Orafo, Via dei Girolami 28/r (213.619). Closed Sun., Mon. and Aug. Typical, tiny cellar restaurant; fine *bistecca.*

Camillo, Borgo San Jacopo 57r (212.427). Closed Wed., Thurs. and Aug. Charming and popular; varied menu. AE, DC, MC, V.

Cantinetta Antinori, Piazza Antinori 3 (292.234). Closed Sun. Attractive wine cellar serving snacks or full meals and famous house wines. Closed Sat., Sun., and Aug. AE, MC, V.

Celestino, Piazza Santa Felicita 4/r (296.574). Closed Sun. and Aug. Between Ponte Vecchio and Palazzo Pitti, handy and good. AE, V.

Il Cibreo, Via dei Macci 118/r (234.1100). Closed Sun., Mon., and Aug. 1 to Sept. 10. Reserve. Interesting trattoria, unusual menu. AE, DC, MC, V.

Coco Lezzone, Via del Parioncino 26/r (287.178). Closed Tues. dinner and Sun. (Sat. and Sun. in summer). Earthy trattoria with whitewashed walls, red-checked tablecloths. Classic Florentine fare.

Da Noi, Via Fiesolana 46/r (242.917). Closed Sun., Mon., and Aug. Reserve for this small, relaxing place serving seasonal specialties creatively prepared.

Dino, Via Ghibellina 51/r (241.452). Closed Sun. evening, Mon. and Aug. Near Santa Croce, a quiet wine cellar where you dine on fine Tuscan cuisine or sample a great variety of cheeses and wines. AE, DC, MC, V.

Le Fonticine, Via Nazionale 79/r (282.106). Closed Sat. and Aug. Excellent homemade pasta and one of the best *bistecca Fiorentina* in town. AE, V.

Leo, Via Torta 7r (210.829). Closed Mon. and two weeks in Aug. Near Santa Croce. Tasty specialties. Try the *grancrostone alla piercapponi:* mozzarella, mushrooms, tomato and truffles served *au gratin* on a chunk of bread. AE, DC, MC, V.

Maria da Ganino, Piazza Cimatori 4 (214.125). Closed Sun. Central, rustic, small and lively. Good country cooking. AE, DC.

Paoli, Via dei Tavolini 12/r (216.215). Closed Mon. evening, Tues. and July. Central, lots of atmosphere, pseudo-Gothic decor; good food. AE, DC, MC, V.

La Sostanza, Via del Porcellana 25/r (212.691). Closed Sat. evening, Sun., holidays and Aug. Typical, small, popular with residents and tourists for genuine atmosphere and cuisine, characteristically brusque waiters.

Tre Jolly-Bibò, Piazza Santa Felicita 6/r (298.554). Closed Tues. Good lunch stop between Ponte Vecchio and Palazzo Pitti. Try the spaghetti *algranchio* (with crab). AE, DC, MC, V.

Inexpensive

Acqua al Due, Via dell'Acqua 2r (284.170). Closed Mon. and Aug. Near Bargello, popular with young crowd for mixed pasta dishes.

Buca Poldo, Chiasso degli Armagnanti 2/r (296.578). Closed Thurs. and Jan. Tiny, top-value trattoria near the Signoria.

Da Cesarino, Via dei Pepi 12 (241.756). Closed Thurs. Near Santa Croce. Small, simple, good pastas. AE, DC, V.

Del Carmine, Piazza del Carmine 18/r (218.601). Closed Sat. evening, Sun. and Aug. Near famous church. Try *cremino* for dessert.

Di Fagioli, Corso dei Tintori 47/r (244.285). Closed Sun. and Aug. Small and friendly, with a great *antipasti* table. Near Santa Croce.

Quattro Leoni, Via Vellutini 1/r (218.562). Closed Sun. and Aug. Near Pitti Palace. Cozy neighborhood eatery, with open fireplace blazing in winter.

San Niccolò, Via San Niccolò 60/r (282.836). Closed Sun. and two weeks in Aug. Delightful, tiny osteria, simple and delicious food. A great bargain.

WINESHOPS. In addition, there are many wineshops where you can have a snack or sandwich. Of these, **Le Cantine,** Via dei Pucci, is smart and popular. As is **Cantinone del Gallo Nero,** Via Santo Spirito 6, which also serves meals in brick-vaulted wine cellar. More modest are **Fiaschetteria,** Via dei Neri 17/r between the Uffizi and Santa Croce; **Piccolo Vinaio,** Via Castellani, behind Palazzo Vecchio, closed winters; and the wineshop at Borgo San Jacopo 19r.

GETTING THERE AND GETTING AROUND. By air. The first thing to remember about getting to Florence by air is that you can't do it very easily. Peretola, the local airport, provides daily connections with Milan and Rome, and regular flights to and from Paris, as well as other cities in Italy and southern Europe. The next nearest airport is at Pisa—Galileo Galilei—80 km. (50 miles) away. There are regular flights into Pisa from the U.K., and, of course, linking flights from Rome and other major Italian cities which have transatlantic arrivals. But the trip from Pisa to Florence is not a breeze: there is now no regular bus service so you have to take the train (an hour's trip) from the Pisa airport rail station. The service is badly scheduled and you could find yourself waiting around for quite a time. Unfortunately, the only alternative is a vastly expensive taxi which could set you back around $100. It is difficult to see why such a tourist-intensive spot as Florence is so badly served.

By train. Florence is on the main line from Milan, Venice and, via Rome, the south. The main station is close to the downtown area.

By car. Forget it. Florence is mainly a town to walk in. Taxi rides will be fairly short and there are lots of buses. And anyway a lot of the historic center is a pedestrian zone.

By bus. There's an extensive network of city buses (ATAF). For a small fee you can buy a booklet with routes and timetable at the ATAF office at Piazza Duomo 57/r, or pick it up free at the AAST office on Via Tornabuoni. Buy ticket (600 lire for one ride; 700 lire for a ticket valid for one hour) at tobacconists or newsstands *before* you get on the bus.

Bus Tours. Half-day bus tours of the city are offered by travel agencies. Inquire at AAST and EPT offices about bus tours to suburban villas (April–June) and the wine country (Sept.–Oct.). You can also visit Pisa in an afternoon, Siena and San Gimignano on a one-day tour.

Agriturist, Via del Proconsolo 10 (287.838) arranges day trips out into the surrounding countryside to see farms and vineyards; spring through fall.

By taxi. Taxis wait at stands located in strategic points of the city; they can be called from the stands, or through Radiotaxi 47.98 or 43.90.

MUSEUMS. Below we list some of the most outstanding museums, galleries and palaces in Florence. Check with tourist offices for hours, in case they have changed. You would be wise to plan your museum itinerary well in advance, say the day before, so as to see as many places as possible grouped together. Also, try to start as early as you can to avoid the floods of tourist buses that descend on the city and follow a fairly circumscribed route in order to take in the highlights. Thus the Accademia will be like a demented Central Station while the Medici-Riccardi chapel will be almost deserted. See also our comments in *Facts at Your Fingertips* under *Museums.* Note that all the following have entrance fees of around 2,000 to 4,000 lire.

Casa Buonarotti (Michelangelo's House), Via Ghibellina 70. Wed. to Mon., 9–1, closed Tues.

Galleria dell'Accademia, Via Ricasoli 60. Florentine primitives plus famous works by Michelangelo, including the original of his *David* and *The Captives.* Tues. to Sat., 9–2, Sun. 9–1, closed Mon. Entrance fee 3,000 lire.

Galleria degli Uffizi, Piazzale degli Uffizi 6. One of the world's great collections, particularly rich in Italian and Flemish paintings—many of the most famous recently cleaned. It includes the collection of artists' self-portraits in the Vasari corridor over Ponte Vecchio (Admission by appointment only, on Tues. and Sat. at 9.30 A.M.). Cafeteria overlooking the Piazza della Signoria. Tues. to Sat., 9–7, Sun. 9–1, closed Mon. Entrance fee 5,000 lire.

Medici Chapels, Church of San Lorenzo, Piazza Madonna. The tombs by Michelangelo, one of Italy's greatest treasures. Tues. to Sat., 9–2, Sun. 9–1, closed Mon. Entrance fee 3,000 lire.

Museo Archeologico, Via della Colonna (Palazzo della Crocetta). Important Etruscan collections, Greek and Roman sculpture. Some attractive displays. Tues. to Sat., 9–2, Sun. 9–1, closed Mon.

Museo Bardini, Piazza de'Mozzi. Outstanding private collection, though not much visited; works by Tiepolo, Pollaiuollo, Uccello, etc. Mon., Tues., Thurs. to Sat. 9–2, Sun. 8–1. Closed Wed.

Museo del Bargello, Via del Proconsolo 4 (in the Palazzo del Podestà). Sculptures by Donatello, Bellini, Verocchio and other decorative arts. Tues. to Sat., 9–2, Sun. 9–1, closed Mon.

Museo dell'Angelico, Piazza San Marco. Large number of works by Fra Angelico collected from all over Florence. Tues. to Sat., 9–2, Sun. 9–1, closed Mon.

Museo dell'Antica Casa Fiorentina (Museum of the Old Florentine House) Palazzo Davanzati, Via Porta Rossa 13. A home furnished as it would have been in olden times, 14th–17th centuries. Lots of interest and atmosphere. Tues. to Sat. 9–1.30, Sun. 9–12.30, closed Mon.

Museo dell'Opera del Duomo, Piazza del Duomo 9. Collection of outstanding works from the Cathedral, Baptistery and Campanile, with Michelangelo's *Pietà* in the lead. Mon. to Sat. 9–6, Sun. 9–1. Closed Tues.

Palazzo Medici-Riccardi, Via Cavour 1. Two especial points of interest; the Gozzoli chapel and a Rococo hall, though the latter is sometimes closed for meetings. Daily 9–12, 3–5, Sun. 9–12. Closed Wed. Free.

Palazzo Pitti, Piazza Pitti, with the Galleria Platina, Galleria d'Arte Moderna and Museo degli Argenti. One of Italy's most renowned galleries. Site also of the Boboli Gardens. Tues. to Sat., 9–2, Sun. 9–1, closed Mon.

Palazzo Vecchio (Palazzo della Signoria), Piazza della Signoria. Works by Vasari (who masterminded much of the interior), Michelangelo, Ghirlandaio and many others, frescos and much else. Mon. to Fri., 9–7, Sun. 8–1, closed Sat. Free on Sun.

Santa Maria Novella, Piazza Santa Maria Novella. Not only the interior of the church itself, but the chapels and the cloisters are overflowing with magnificent works of art. Cloisters open Mon. to Thur. and Fri., 9–2, Sun. 8–1, closed Fri.

SHOPPING. Florence is the best place to buy leather goods, linens, gold jewelry and straw. Its very atmosphere is ideal for wandering and window-shopping in tiny side streets that meander off at odd angles and the central district can be happily and thoroughly explored by foot.

The most fashionable streets in Florence are Via Tornabuoni, which runs from the Arno to Via Cerretani, and Via della Vigna Nuova which angles it midway. But the most characteristic part is the medieval Ponte Vecchio, the charming bridge over the Arno River, which is crowded with small shops. It is here that the city's jewelers and silversmiths are gathered, even as they were hundreds of years ago.

Florentine jewelry has a particular quality of satin finish which characterizes it. In English it is commonly called brushed gold and in Italian *satinato.* Much of Florence jewelry is also filigree.

Cameos are another specialty of the Florentine workshop which has the trained artisans to do the intricate carving. The orange and dark shells come from Cuba and the lovely pink ones from Madagascar, but it is the artist's labor which turns these simple sea animals into delicate works of beauty. Depending on workmanship, therefore, cameos vary widely in price. Some shops will even show you the cameo being worked, and you'll understand more about this charming shell.

Florence is one of the best cities in which to buy shoes. The quality is superb, and the price range wide enough to suit every pocket. Another attractive specialty of Florence is marbled paper, from which a wide variety of small items are made, diaries, masks, bookmarks, and boxes—all of which make very buyable presents.

Also, be sure to save time for a visit to the outdoor markets, either the one at Loggia del Mercato Nuovo or the much larger one that fills the Piazza San Lorenzo. There you will find a wild mixture of plastic rubbish, cheap jeans, leather work that will bear investigation, and lots of other craft products. If you have the urge to bargain, you can certainly try, but you are not likely to come out on top. The market at Loggia del Mercato Nuovo is open all day except Sunday and Monday morning. The market at San Lorenzo is closed Sunday and Monday.

TUSCANY

Where Nature Rivals Art

Tuscany, shaped like a rough triangle, has its base along a broad stretch of Italy's west coast some miles north of Lazio and Rome, with the apex pointing inland across more than half the width of the peninsula. Along the main roads very unattractive ribbon development has encroached on the wooded hills, snow-crested peaks, vineyards, stands of cypress and olive groves, but the lovely "green valleys of Tuscany" can still be found off the beaten track. Artistically and historically, its towns are showplaces of the centuries-old Tuscan culture that brought forth masters like Michelangelo, Dante, Leonardo da Vinci, Boccaccio, Petrarch.

Tuscany is a happy blend of mountains, valleys and beaches. High mountains like the Apennines and Apuan Alps; broad valleys like those of the Arno and Serchio Rivers, emerald green in their fertility. Long, sandy stretches of beach curve along the coast through Forte dei Marmi, Viareggio, Leghorn into the pine woods of Maremma. No lakes to speak of, but plenty of streams and bubbling, fresh-water springs.

Behind this scenic wealth lie agricultural areas that pay off in livable dividends to hard-working peasants and mountaineers. The soil of Tuscany is not as rich as neighboring Emilia, for example, but its wheat, wines, oil, chestnuts and livestock help make for a reasonable prosperity. Shipping and fishing predominate through the coastal reaches; arts and crafts originate higher, in mountain hamlets. Tuscany's laborers work at steel, iron, machinery, textile and chemical plants fed from considerable natural resources such as iron on the island of Elba, pyrites, tin, copper and antimony in the Maremma area, marble from Apuania, borax out of Larderello.

But the history, the art of Tuscany, the culture that has drawn educated people to this region for centuries—these are responsible for its position as a leader in the field of Italy's tourist trade. Florence symbolizes best the Tuscan pride in grace and refinement, and its deathless masterpieces of architecture, painting, sculpture and literature make it a storehouse of artistic wealth. They help create in other Tuscan cities like Siena, Pisa, Lucca, Volterra, Pistoia and Arezzo an atmosphere of the Middle Ages somehow preserved almost intact.

That, perhaps, remains the permanent characteristic of Tuscany today—a stubborn, proud refusal to change its natural beauty and way of life, so that in many of the smaller cities, in the towns and villages and isolated monasteries tucked far back through the rolling hills and valleys, you still catch something of the feeling that someone has turned the clock back.

Much of Tuscany had its origin before the dawn of history under the Etruscans, who left their art, fortified ruins and obscure civilization scattered across the region's most fertile valleys and strategic hills. The conquering Romans came next, and the lords and barons of the tempestuous Middle Ages. This combination of three distinct cultures makes itself evident wherever you wander through the Tuscan hinterland.

Unlike its southern neighbor Lazio, where Rome dominates the entire region, Tuscany is not merely Florence, but rather a sprawling chain of cities and towns rivaling each other for the right to be classified as most distinctive of the area. Florence—and possibly Siena—may have a better claim to that title; but it is impossible to consider the whole without its parts.

Central Tuscan History

The northern Tuscan cities have a somewhat similar background. Pistoia, flourishing through the 14th century, when the Guelph communes were all-powerful, went on to fall under the incredible Medici family's rule; it was severely damaged during the 1944 German retreat and has since been rebuilt. Lucca, once a Roman city that later fought for—and won—her independence from 1370 to 1799, when Napoleon I handed it over to his sister, Elisa Baciocchi, eventually became the capital of a Tuscan duchy under Maria Luisa of the Bourbons in 1815. And Livorno (Leghorn) subjected to Florence's rule in 1421, proudly saw her famous port begun in 1571 under the rule of the Medici Duke Cosimo I—to watch it smashed by German troops and Allied bombers four centuries later and then laboriously regain its commercial position.

Pisa preserves proud memories of the 11th century, when she was the leading maritime republic holding undisputed power over Sardinia, Corsica, even the far Balearic Islands. The city, losing her sea supremacy to Genoa's fleet after the battle at Meloria in 1284, found herself forced under the rule of a succession of feudal barons, the last of whom passed her along to Florence in 1405. The astronomer Galileo Galilei, and the physicist Antonio Pacinotti, inventor of the electromagnetic ring were born here. Pisa's Romanesque architecture, which later developed a "Pisan style" of its own, spread through much of Tuscany and as far off as the Island of Sardinia.

Central Tuscany's history is best discovered in places like Volterra, first one of 12 Etruscan city-states, then a Roman municipality and finally a free and independent community from the 12th to the 15th century, with innumerable Etruscan ruins and medieval walls still evident as proof of its past. Or San Gimignano, a hilltop village right out of the Middle Ages; it flourished from the 12th century through 1357, when—like a lot of other Tuscan municipalities—it submitted to the rule of Florence's Medici family.

Of all central Tuscany, however, Siena preserves its medieval glory on the grandest scale. An Etruscan town became the Roman Sena Julia, of little importance until the barbarian invasions made the coastal road too hazardous. Seat of a bishop since the 8th century, Siena found its vocation in the 12th as a money-lending center for most of Europe. The next century brought the city to its zenith with the rise and fall of the Buonsignori family, bankers who handled the papal finances, among other things. In 1260 Siena won a stunning victory over its bitter rival Florence at Montaperti, securing predominance for the rest of the century. But in 1298 the Buonsignori went bankrupt, which disrupted the finances of the city and marked the beginning of its decline.

In 1348 Siena was decimated by a devastating plague, and 51 years later bowed to the rule of Florence. A few years later she won back her liberty for a brief period; but in 1559 Siena was officially annexed to the Duchy of Tuscany. Its architecture, an adaptation of the Gothic style to Italian taste, is still the most distinctive characteristic of the old town.

To the south, most indicative of Tuscany's history are Grosseto and Orbetello, along with Arezzo. Orbetello, too, can be traced back to the ancient Etruscans, who left the amazingly well-preserved ruins you see about three miles north of the town; in 1557, Philip II of Spain made it the capital of a short-lived military state. And Arezzo, likewise starting as an Etruscan village, subsequently became the ally of Rome, to evolve into a free community during the Middle Ages. Arezzo too made the fatal mistake of competing with Florence, under whose sway it fell in 1384.

Exploring Tuscany

Tuscany, as one of Italy's larger regions, demands time and considerable planning to sample its variety. A trip along its coast fits easily into the itinerary of anyone traveling through Florence to or from Rome. But the remainder of the region—north, south, and southeast—is best visited by making side trips out of Florence.

Visiting the Tuscan coast by car allows one to make several interesting trips inland from A12 or the Via Aurelia. The former bypasses, the latter passes through, the interesting localities, mainly parallel to the coastal railway. But before following the coast south from La Spezia, Liguria's southernmost town, A15 provides a very scenic yet comfortable crossing of the Apennine Mountains of northern Tuscany to Parma in Emilia, over the 1,042 m. (3,419 ft.) La Cisa Pass and through the lush Taro Valley. The densely wooded mountains, slashed by torrents rushing down from towering peaks, have not yet fallen victims to tourism.

Sadly, this cannot be said for the coast. Slightly inland from A12, Carrara is an attractive town at the foot of the Apuan Alps, where the famous marble has been quarried since antiquity for some of the greatest sculpture. In Massa, a 13th-century castle guards the lovely cathedral and ducal palace. Crossing the mountains from here and following the Serchio Valley via Barga is an original and picturesque approach to Lucca. Another interesting inland village is Pietrasanta, from which Michelangelo built a road up to Monte Altissimo to quarry the lovely white marble, "holy stone" indeed, used to advantage in the pretty village churches.

The beach resorts of Marina di Massa, Forta dei Marmi, Marina di Pietrasanta and Lido di Camaiore have coalesced into the overcrowded ribbon development of the Riviera della Versilia, 21 km. (13 miles) between a lovely sandy beach and pine woods dying of pollution to Viareggio, the largest and most crowded bathing resort on the Tyrrhenian coast. From late January to March, Italy's annual carnival time is better-evidenced here than anywhere in the country, with flower-decked parades and almost continuous weekend masquerade balls. Puccini wrote many of his hugely successful operas at nearby Torre del Lago. The great composer is buried in the park of his villa, now a museum, next to Lake Massaciuccoli.

Pisa

The forest of Migliarino has withstood the encroachment of holiday development, mainly because the mouths of the Serchio and the Arno make bathing highly problematic, though Marina di Pisa has some pretensions towards being a popular resort.

Higher up the Arno is Pisa. Between the Borgo Stretto and the Via 29 Maggio, the maze of old streets and little squares has been closed to traffic. The famous Quadrilateral, within the imposing ramparts, is best entered by the Porta Nuova (of Santa Maria), which opens on the four principal landmarks of Pisa. The ensemble is strangely lit at night by a rather green spotlight that falls on it like unreal moonlight.

The Cathedral dates back to at least the 11th century, when the architect Buscheto supervised the laying of the cornerstone. Work on it continued through the 12th and 13th centuries. Many little columns give the Rainaldo facade an airy, light look. The folding doors opposite the bell tower are especially noteworthy. Perhaps you will be surprised, after the delicacy of the exterior, by the majestic scale of its interior. Notice particularly the astonishing pulpit attributed to Nicolo and Giovanni Pisano. Across from the pulpit is the hanging lamp which inspired Galileo with his theories about the motion of pendulums. Visit, too, the Baptistery (12th-century) designed on a circular plan and covered with marble. Look up at the pointed cupola and be sure to see the Pisano pulpit—another carved masterpiece.

The third landmark in the Quadrilateral is one of the best-known in the world, the Leaning Tower. Begun in 1173, the Leaning Tower cants about 14 feet off center because of a slight slip of land during its construction. Some 294 steps spiral up to a terrace on top, where the view of all Pisa is worth the hike. The delicately columned exterior is often disfigured by top-to-bottom posters.

Nearby, the Camposanto is a small cemetery, enclosed by four galleries that contain priceless but badly faded old frescos and some disgracefully dirty sculptures. A wartime shell hit the North Gallery, damaging the world-famous frescos of *The Triumph of Death,* which inspired Liszt's composition *The Dance of Death.* Expertly restored in a former chapel, they alone convey the somber magnificence of the original decorations.

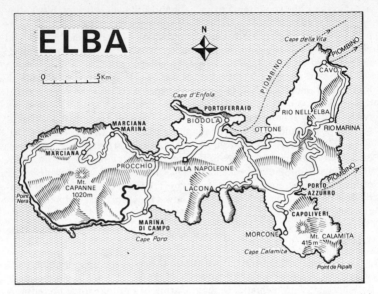

Another site you will want to see among the many in Pisa is Piazza dei Cavalieri, one of Tuscany's finest squares architecturally, around which cluster a huge palace of the same name and the curiously named Palazzo dell'Orologio (Palace of the Clock).

Livorno and Volterra

Moving farther south along the coast, the A12 and the main north-south railroad line reach Livorno (Leghorn), home of the Italian Naval Academy but little else of interest. The crowded Via Aurelia hugs the Etruscan Riviera south through Castiglioncello to Cecina. Turn 29 miles inland to Volterra, one of the richest and most interesting of Tuscany's art cities and one-time rival of Florence. Center of this formidable town is the Piazza dei Priori, to one side of which is the Palazzo Pretorio, with an art gallery worth visiting. The nearby cathedral has some lovely frescos by Benozzo Gozzoli. Volterra's famed fortress is now a prison; its Etruscan Museum holds some 600 highly artistic alabaster cremation urns; Via Roma and Via Bicciarelli provide a genuine medieval atmosphere within the walls, which even boast an Etruscan gate. Outside the town, the *balze,* a huge ravine, has swallowed up numerous Etruscan tombs through the centuries. Alabaster is still being worked in Volterra (some of its streets are covered with fine white dust coming from the workshops) and constitutes one of the typical products of Italian craftsmanship. The Cyclopean blocks of stone at Porta all'Arco are likewise Etruscan.

The Via Aurelia continues south via the fine beach of San Vincenzo for the 35 km. (22 miles) to medieval Campiglia-Marittima—and another notable side trip of 13 km. (8 miles) to Piombino, ferrying point for the Island of Elba.

Elba

Even off season, the 19-km. (12-mile) crossing is assured at least once a day from Piombino to Portoferraio, biggest town on Elba. The island is 29 km. long (18 miles), about 19 km. (12 miles) wide, and best known for the historical part it played as Napoleon's place of exile for ten months in 1814–15, enshrined in the famous example of palindrome "Able was I ere I saw Elba". You will still be able to see Napoleon's house—the Villa dei Mulini—located at the top of the town, as well as furnishings and other mementos kept there. He seems to have lived a rather spartan existence. His "country house" lies 5 km. (3 miles) away in San Martino. It contains an Egyptian room that is decorated with optical illusions showing scenes from the Egyptian campaign. The exile himself added a strange handwritten inscription that reads: "Napoleon is happy everywhere". Most likely he wasn't dreaming of the Hundred Days at that moment! He might have been looking out on the beautiful view from the terrace.

Other points of interest on the island are: Monte Capanne, which can be ascended in a *cabinovia* (a rather scary small cage)—the views from the top, especially on a clear day, are worth every effort; the thermal baths at San Giovanni; the sanctuary of Madonna di Monserrato, a pretty, mountain setting; the churches at Santo Stefano, Poggio and Marciana Alta, all with attractive interiors and placed in scenically lovely spots.

Until recently Elba was an almost unspoiled paradise, where prices were low and the visitor in some sections a curiosity; it is secluded no more. Still: thick wooded slopes, isolated beaches, and a round-the-island drive by car or bus that takes you from tremendous scenery along the edge of high, seaside cliffs to tiny towns where the sweet white wine of Elba (it's delicious, but be careful after the second glass!) comes cold and sparkling at restaurants and roadside inns. In short, it's an intimate kind of island and good for a family holiday, but an awful lot of families have discovered the fact.

Back to the mainland at Piombino, and then the main north–south railway line and highway at Campiglia-Marittima, you continue south over the Maremma, a vast expanse of reclaimed flats frequented by hunters out for the wild boar that still live there, through towns like Follonica and Grosseto to Orbetello Station, 5 km. (3 miles) from the town itself and last stop before Tuscany runs into the Lazio region and Rome. Orbetello, without monuments worth mentioning, is a possible jump-off point for a variety of scenic trips. It's built between two salt lakes on a tongue of land running out from the coast; by car or by bus, try visiting Porto Santo Stefano and Port'Ercole—two fishing villages on the Argentario peninsula's tip, "in" spots for the international set—and Ansedonia, with the impressive Etruscan remains at Cosa.

Prato, Pistoia and Lucca

The autostrada (A11), which runs from Florence to the west coast, bypasses three major cities—Prato, Pistoia, Lucca—all of them remarkable for their fabulous collections of art and beauty of architecture.

Inland, as already noted, north, south, and southeast Tuscany may be visited best by trips out of Florence in those general directions. It's also possible, of course, to see inner Tuscany by branching away from the various cities and towns along the coastal route from north to south, or from Siena or Arezzo. However, since most travelers come to Florence first, the city is a more natural headquarters for side trips.

Prato, only 19 km. (11 miles) outside Florence, features numerous works by many of the great artists who enriched Tuscany. The cathedral, off Via Mazzoni, and the area around Piazza del Comune are representative of what the city has to offer. It is an 11th-century Romanesque work, enlarged three centuries later by Giovanni Pisano, who succeeded with amazing skill in combining the original primitive style with the then-dominant Gothic style. A roll-call of Italian artists who put their time and efforts to this immense church reads like a listing of Tuscany's most illustrious names in the history of art: frescos by Filippo Lippi, especially notable is that of Herod's feast and Salome's dance; sculptures by Donatello, Mino da Fiesole, Rossellino, Benedetto da Maiano, stained-glass windows by Lorenzo da Pelago; and the exquisite bronzes of Bruno di Ser Lapo, Pasquino da Monpulciano, Giambologna, Ferdinando Tacca. To the left of the entrance is the Chapel of the Holy Girdle, supposedly the girdle of the Virgin, given to Doubting Thomas to tighten his faith. It was brought to Italy in 1141 and is shown to the faithful from a special pulpit several times a year.

Or wander through Prato's many other churches; you shouldn't miss San Domenico, San Francesco, the magnificent Santa Maria delle Carceri by Sangallo, San Agostino, San Vincenzo, the paintings by Lippi in the Church of Spirito Santo, and the beautiful doorway of Santa Maria della Pietà.

Pistoia more than rivals what you have just seen at Prato, with its centers of artistic culture scattered about the city from Piazza del Duomo to the area near the Church of Sant' Andrea. The cathedral or Duomo itself is of Pisan style, flanked by a 13th-century tower and housing some of the town's best works of art. Opposite stands a Gothic baptistery, built in alternating layers of black and white marble; elsewhere around Piazza del Duomo are the Palazzo del Podestà, adorned with coats of arms, and the rather gloomy Palazzo Comunale, now serving as a museum. Among Pistoia's churches you should try to see the two oldest—Sant'Andrea and San Giovanni, each with a priceless pulpit, Sant'Andrea's being by Giovanni Pisano, representing a mass of New Testament scenes and rising on seven slender red-porphyry pillars—San Francesco, dating back to the 13th century, and San Paolo, a 14th-century Pisan-style building.

About eight miles past Pistoia and halfway to the sea is Montecatini Terme, which, with some 200 hotels and pensions open April through November, is Italy's leading—and one of Europe's largest—spas. Eight thermal establishments in the shady hot-spring park dispense waters to drink and bathe in for a wide variety of ailments. Funicular to Montecatini Castle, one of numerous medieval fortresses crowning the surrounding hills.

Then beautiful Lucca, where tree-planted 16th-century ramparts are now used as delightful promenades. The Romanesque and Gothic cathedral is considered by some experts as the most spectacular monument in Tuscany today. And the Church of San Michele, with works by Lippi, Luca della Robbia and others, provides a perfect example of Pisan-Luccan architecture. Outside the old town walls are ever-expanding suburbs of beautiful private villas and gardens.

Napoleon made his sister Elisa, Princess of Lucca and of Piombino in 1805. She held court at Lucca with her Corsican husband Baciocchi. Although she had some of Pauline's traits—she liked artists just as much as the works they produced—she was serious in the way she tackled her responsibilities, repairing the highways and policing them against the all-too-numerous robbers, as well as helping to improve the city and promoting local farming. Napoleon's abdication in 1814 forced her to move to Bologna, and, after Waterloo, to the Austrian provinces.

The art gallery—formerly the Ducal Palace—contains some remarkable paintings and sculptures. But the real beauties of Lucca are found in more out of the way places. Take a walk through the old city, for example, following this itinerary: Via Roma, Piazza del Mercato, the Church of San Frediano, Piazza San Pietro, and, particularly, Via Guinigi, bordered by superb little palaces, as well as the Piazza dei Servi.

The second outing we recommend you make by car. You will reach the gardens of the Villa Reale very quickly, it's only 8 km. (5 miles) out of town. There are guided tours of the superb 17th-century gardens every hour, 9–12, 3–6, Tues., Thur. and Sun. in summer; Nov. to June, 9–12, 3–6 every day except Mon. There's a music festival in August.

Barga, to the north, has a magnificent 11th-century cathedral, and from there you can embark on excursions into the Apuan Alps and to Lake Santo, 1,500 meters (5,000 ft.) above sea-level. Camaiore also possesses an interesting church, while the spring waters of Bagni di Lucca have been taken since antiquity, and were especially favored by British writers, including Shelley and Browning.

Empoli, Certaldo and San Gimignano

Instead of taking the superstrada (A1) south from Florence to Siena, you might detour west along the Pisa road to Empoli, turning south to include Certaldo, San Gimignano and Poggibonsi.

First stop, 34 km. (21 miles) out of Florence, may be at Empoli, a thriving market for its excellent works in glass. The town, also important agriculturally, has rich works of art that include the Church of Santo Stefano and, in particular, the Collegiata, a Florentine-Romanesque building erected in 1093. Inside it, a small gallery holds paintings and sculptures by Rossellino, Fra' Bartolomeo, Botticini, the Della Robbias, and Mino da Fiesole.

Up the Elsa Valley from Empoli, some 58 km. (36 miles) from Florence, you reach Certaldo, the home of the writer Giovanni Boccaccio, on a flat plain backed by a hill on which the ancient Castle of Certaldo commands a view of the entire valley. This castle, incidentally, is considered one of Tuscany's best examples of a medieval stronghold. The town is dominated by the episcopal palace, also on the hill, feudal seat of the vicars, who numbered 650 down through history.

Continue southeast to Poggibonsi, famed for its wine; then take the 11-km. (7-mile) branch to San Gimignano, the most remarkable of all the Tuscan medieval hill towns. Time seems to have stood still there since the Middle Ages. Out of some 79 defensive towers thirteen—of various heights—are still intact and give San Gimignano a uniquely photogenic silhouette. It also has its fair share of Tuscan art treasures: beautiful frescos decorate the walls of its two churches and the *pinacoteca* houses some outstanding paintings. The pride of the Civic Museum, located in the Palazzo del Popolo, is a *Virgin with Saints* by Pinturicchio, and twin paintings by Filippino Lippi depicting *The Annunciation*. Down the hill from the cathedral, the little church of San Agostino contains some stunning frescos by Benozzo Gozzoli. You shouldn't neglect the countryside around San Gimignano either.

Siena

29 km. (18 miles) past Poggibonsi, set beautifully on three hills, rich in works of art, is one of Italy's best-preserved medieval towns—Siena, which amply justifies a visit of two or three days at least. Many will go to Siena drawn by the memory of St. Catherine (1347–1380), the remarkable woman who helped to bring back the popes from their exile in Avignon. The daughter of a Sienese dyer (the 21st child) she is remembered for her faith and holiness and for her deep concern for Man's salvation.

The people of Siena, noted for their cordiality and their pure Italian speech—hence the Summer School of Italian Language and Culture in the 700-year-old university—are proud of the town's monumental high points: the immense unfinished cathedral, with its intarsia pavement and its stunning striped black-and-white marble exterior, and the Palazzo Pubblico on the Piazza del Campo, flanked by the Mangia Tower, which offers a splendid view.

Siena was in the forefront of the impressive artistic movement initiated by the Emperor Frederick II which led to the Tuscan renewal of the 13th century. The Gothic device of narrative figuration in which the same people are shown simultaneously in different parts of the picture, thus telling a story in sequence, came to a climax in the Siena School of Painting, brilliantly represented in the Art Gallery. In fact, almost all public or church buildings in town command enough historical or architectural interest to warrant personal inspection. In particular, see Pinturicchio's animated early 16th-century frescos in the Piccolomini Library, in a wing of the cathedral whose facade is one of the masterpieces of Italian art.

Jacopo della Quercia, Siena's most famous architect-sculptor, is responsible for the superb font in the Baptistery of San Giovanni. The Church of San Domenico is known for its frescos and paintings. This is the church closely associated with St. Catherine, who performed some of her miracles and had visions here. Her experiences are commemorated in a chapel called after her, with frescos by Il Sodoma. Some fine Sienese painting is in the art gallery of the Buonsignori Palace, notably works by Duccio, Simone Martini, Giovanni di Paolo and Il Sodoma.

Siena explodes in a frenzy of local rivalries on July 2 and on August 16 each year. On those two days the town celebrates its historic *Corsa del Palio* (Parade of the Banner), consisting of a full-blown, all-day festival in which representatives of Siena's 17 individual districts parade in medieval costume, compete in a horse race at Piazza del Campo, then hold openair banquets after the district winning the race has been awarded the year's *palio* (banner) of Siena as a prize. This has been going on for years, possibly since the 13th century, with one district alone already having won some 60 individual banners in keen competition that finds the entire town divided 17 different ways each year.

Sienese are also music-lovers. The Accademia Chigiana sponsors a famous international music summer-school and a brief, excellent festival, the "Sienese Week", at the beginning of September.

Worthwhile detours to the southeast are the historic townships of Montalcino, granted in 814 by the Emperor Ludovicus the Pious to the remarkable Abbey of Sant'Antimo, 8 km. (5 miles) south, and last mountain redoubt of the Sienese in their struggle against Florence; Pienza, built by Pope Pius II between 1459 and 1462 round the village of Corsignano, where he had been born Enea Silvio Piccolomini; Montepulciano, entirely Renaissance except for the severe Gothic Communal Palace; the mighty monastery of Monte Oliveto Maggiore in a dramatic setting, with its magical series of 36 frescos by Signorelli and Il Sodoma showing the life of the monastery's patron saint, St. Benedict, in the cloisters; and to the south, the no less impressive Romanesque Abbey of San Salvatore above an 8th-century crypt.

The Southeast

On the last of these suggested tours through Tuscany's interior, both railroad and the Autostrada del Sole lead to Arezzo and Cortona, with three or four notable side trips, including one to the mountaintop sanctuary of La Verna.

The most scenic road follows the Arno River to Pontassieve. Farther east, amidst the heavily-forested hills, Consuma, a village of Etruscan origin, stands on the watershed of a mountain with wide panoramic views over the nearby valleys. Neat little inns along the way serve good, wholesome food—including the delicious *Casentino* ham—washed down with *Chianti* wine, served cold. One day by car will take you into any number of old villages and ancient castles straight out of storybooks.

Higher than Consuma, on the same road, the mountains spread into a succession of meadows and hills forming the Pratomagno, on the western side of which lies the magnificent forest of Vallombrosa, at 962 meters (3,152 ft.) with a 10th-century monastery perched even higher above it. Along the southern side of the Pratomagno is Saltino, also at 926 meters famous throughout all Europe for its view over the Arno River Valley, Florence, the Apuan Alps, the Adriatic Sea, mountains around Pistoia, and the Chianti Hills, covered with woods, vineyards (from which come the grapes that produce Chianti wine) and castles.

Poppi, the ancient fief of the Guidi Counts, is the point of departure for visiting the Camaldoli Hermitage at 816 m. (2,677 ft.), by way of Maggiona through striking countryside of great contrasts. A modern monument marks the site of the battlefield of Campaldino where the Guelphs routed the Ghibellines in 1289. The La Verna monastery—tradition attributes its origins to St. Francis of Assisi—lies east of Poppi, across a landscape of harsh beauty. From Bibbiena you can continue on directly to Arezzo.

Arezzo and Cortona

Arezzo rises on the gentle slope of a hill to the Duomo and the Medici Fortress, built by Etruscan settlers hundreds of years before the ancient Roman Empire. Here, in one of Tuscany's principal towns, is the birthplace of the Italian poet Petrarch, and the home of Guido d'Arezzo, 11th-century inventor of the musical scale, to whose memory a monument has been erected in Piazza Guido Monaco. Vasari, whose talents enhanced painting, sculpture and architecture, had a beautiful house close to the Church of San Domenico in his native town, which you can visit. You will also become acquainted with the name of another of Arezzo's famous sons, Aretino, a highly gifted and somewhat scabrous writer. But first and foremost, Arezzo is a storehouse of Tuscan art treasures.

Make certain you see the town's 14th-century Church of San Francesco, in which Piero della Francesca left a series of his frescos, entitled *Story of the Cross,* that must be listed among the most outstanding examples of Italian painting, and visit the Pieve di Santa Maria, a 12th-century Romanesque church, with its five-story belfry pierced by no fewer than 40 double windows. Three stories of narrow columns adorn a most unusual façade. Walk through the Museum of Medieval Art and its neighboring art gallery, especially if medieval art is one of your interests; or, not far off, the Archeological Museum features some really fine works in ancient Arezzo pottery. A bit farther ahead is a Roman amphitheater built in the 2nd century.

Marcillat, a 16th-century glassmaker from Bourges, spent several years in Arezzo; as a result the Church of San Francesco and the Duomo contain beautiful stained-glass windows.

The annual festival called the Joust of the Saracen (Giostra del Saraceno), which is held in Arezzo on the first Sunday in September, commemorates the town's fighting ancestors. It is a tilting competition, favorite sport of the medieval world, with four teams charging with lowered lance at a big dummy of a Saracen. It isn't without its perils as the swinging figure carries a flail tipped with lead balls that can inflict an unpleasant wound.

Sansepolcro contributed its fair share to Italy's artistic wealth. This town, on the way to the Adriatic, was the home of Piero della Francesca in the 15th century. If you wish to see his works, and those of his disciples, stop to visit the art gallery.

South of Arezzo, 101 km. (63 miles) from Florence, Cortona, of Etruscan origin but medieval appearance, stands on a hill towering over broad, flat stretches of the Val di Chiana plain. Cortona boasts the work of a remarkable number of Italy's artistic greats, including Sangallo, Fra Angelico, Pietro Lorenzetti, Luca Signorelli, and others. It was the birthplace of Pietro da Cortona, whose brilliant work as an interior decorator enriched the Pitti Palace in Florence and the ceiling of the great hall of Rome's Barberini Palace. The small Diocesan museum across from the Duomo contains a strikingly rich collection of canvases, including works by Fra Angelico and Signorelli. The Palazzo Pretorio houses a representative collection of Etruscan bronzes, including a fifth-century B.C. lamp, as well as Roman objects excavated in the region.

Outside the town gates, in the Church of Santa Margherita, patron saint of Cortona, there's a beautiful 14th-century Gothic tomb; and above the church, at 650 meters (2,132 ft.), stands the village's ancient fortress, with an excellent view over the entire countryside.

The road along Lake Trasimeno leads to Chiusi, ancient Etruscan capital and paradise for archeologists. The museum, near the cathedral, houses a priceless collection of Etruscan objects; the Etruscan tombs all round the town outskirts are not easy to find, so it is best to ask at the museum for directions. Normally a guide will accompany you.

PRACTICAL INFORMATION FOR TUSCANY

WHEN TO GO. The best month is May—which is why Florence holds its music festival then. June too is a good month. Avoid central Tuscany in mid-summer. It can get very hot in the hill towns. The beach resorts are predictably overcrowded through July and August.

TOURIST OFFICES. Abetone: AAST, Piazza delle Piramidi (60.231). **Arezzo:** EPT, Piazza Risorgimento 116 (23.952). **Castiglioncello:** AAST, Piazza della Vittoria 644 (752 333). **Castiglione della Pescaia:** AAST, Piazza Garibaldi (933.678). **Chianciano Terme:** AAST, Via Sabatini 7 (63.538). **Cortona:** AAST, Via Nazionale 72 (603.056) and Piazza Signorelli 10 (63.056). **Elba:** AAST, Calata Italia 26, at Portoferraio (92.671). **Fiesole:** AAST, Piazza Mino da Fiesole 45 (598.720). **Grosseto:** EPT, Via Monterosa 206 (22.534). **Livorno:** EPT, Piazza Cavour 6 (33.111) and at rail station (401.193). **Lucca:** EPT, Piazza Guidiccioni 2 (49.187) and Via Vittorio Veneto 40 (43.639). **Montecatini Terme:** AAST, Viale Verdi 66 (70.109). **Pisa:** EPT, Piazza Archivescovo 8 (501.761). **Pistoia:** Palazzo dei Vescovi (21.622). **Prato:** AAST, Via Muzzi 51 (tel. 35.141). EPT, Via Cairoli (24.112). **Siena:** AAST, Piazza del Campo 56 (280.551); EPT, Via di Citta 5 (47.051). **Viareggio:** AAST, Viale Carducci 30 (48.881). **Volterra:** Via Turazza 2 (86.150).

SEASONAL EVENTS. Arezzo: the 13th-century Battle of the Saracens is re-enacted on the first Sun. in Sept. with armored knights.

Lucca: the Festival of the Holy Cross on Sept. 13.

Montecatini Terme: the annual horse show takes place Jul.

Pisa: Jun. 5 sees the historic Games of the Bridge; Jun. 16—the feast day of Pisa's patron saint, San Ranieri—illuminated boat processions; and Jun. 17, other events.

Pistoia: a traditional festival—the Giostra dell'Orso—harking back to the 14th century, takes place in Sept.

Siena: the Feast of St. Catherine is celebrated from Apr. 28–30; Jul. 2 heralds the first race of the exciting Palio. Feelings run high through Aug. 16, when the final race is run, preceded by the traditional historical pageant.

Viareggio: the Feb. carnival is the most important in all Italy, with a procession of grotesque gigantic papier-mâché figures and fantastic floats.

TELEPHONE CODES. You will find the telephone area code for each town against its name in the Hotel and Restaurant listings (after the province name). If there is a different area code from the majority of the establishments—say when a hotel or restaurant is in an outlying place—then the code is given in front of the telephone number.

HOTELS AND RESTAURANTS. As you can tell by scanning the following listings, Tuscany is superbly served with both hotels and restaurants. Indeed, in some of the older-established watering holes there are luxury establishments second to none. It is a settled, fairly prosperous region and you will find yourself well looked after. Prices in the busier vacation spots will be slightly higher than average.

Regional Food and Drink. Florentine dishes are, of course, to be found all over Tuscany, but some of the other cities also have specialties of their own. Livorno and Viareggio have an answer to the *bouillabaisse* of southern France in *cacciucco*, a fish soup of the same general type. Pisa likes elvers (young eels) cooked in oil, with a suspicion of sage—ask for *cieche*. Siena will give you its own special pastries for dessert—*panforti, cavallucci* and *ricciarelli*, while you will find *castagnaccio* in many parts of Tuscany—a sweet whose basis is flour made from chestnuts. Also throughout Tuscany you will find that delicious form of pasta called *pappardelle con la lepre*, noodles doused in a wild hare sauce.

In addition to the wines of the Chianti district, we might call your attention to the dry red *Brolio* and the somewhat similar *Brunello di Montalcino*. Among white wines, there are two of quite distinctive flavors, that of the Island of Elba, *Bianco dell'Elba*, slightly sweet, and the *Vernaccia di San Gimignano*, which is pleasantly dry when young, quite sweet when aged. *Montepulciano* is a robust red.

Abetone Pistoia (0573). Important winter sports center and summer resort. High season Easter, 15 July to 31 Aug., Christmas. *Palazzaccio* (M) (60.067). Open 15 Dec. to 31 March and 1 July to 31 Aug. Little atmosphere; modern comforts and good view. AE, DC, MC. *Regina* (M) (60.007). Open 20 Dec. to 15 April and 25 June to 15 Sept. Comfortable, old-fashioned, small. DC, V.

Restaurants. *La Capannina* (M) (60.562). Closed Tues. evening, Wed. and 1–15 June. Local specialties. AE, DC, MC, V. *Pierone* (M), Via Giardini (60.068). Closed Thurs. and 15–30 June. Small; reserve. DC, MC.

Just outside town, *Bizzino* (I), Via Secchia 70 (60.195). Rustic; good country-style home cooking.

Arezzo Arezzo (0575). Art city. *Continental* (M), Piazza Guido Monaco 7 (20.251). Central; spacious rooms. AE, DC, MC, V. *Etrusco* (M), Via Fleming 39 (381.483). Newish, modern; on outskirts. AE, DC, MC, V. *Europa* (M), Via Spinello 43 (357.701). Modern, near railway station. No restaurant. AE, V. *Minerva* (M), Via Fiorentina 6 (27.891). On outskirts, good for motorists. AE, DC, V.

Restaurants. *Buca di San Francesco* (M), Piazza San Francesco 1 (23.271). Closed Mon. evening, Tues. and July. Cellar restaurant where the atmosphere is up to the food. AE, DC, MC, V. *Il Cantuccio* (M), Via Madonna del Prato 76 (26.830). Closed Wed. and June. Very central; vaulted ceilings, modern decor, fine food. DC. *Cecco* (M), Corso Italia 215 (20.986). Closed Mon. and Aug. Central, good. AE, DC, MC, V. *Tastevin* (M), Via de Cenci 9 (28.304). Closed Mon., Sun. in summer; and Aug. New sights, attractive place, fine local cuisine. AE, MC, V.*Spiedo d'Oro* (I), Via Crispi 12 (22.873). Closed Thurs. and 1–18 July. *Simpatico,* good local dishes.

At **Madonna di Torrino,** 8 km. (5 miles) outside town, *Torrino* (M), (360.264). Closed Mon. Large, very efficient, with very good food. AE, DC, MC, V.

Castiglioncello Livorno (0586). Beach resort. High season 15 June to 15 Sept. *Miramare* (M), Via Marconi 8 (752.435). Open 1 April to 30 Sept. Pleasant location in pine grove; unpretentious decor; 64 rooms, some with sea view. V. *Mon Hotel* (M), Via Aurelia 963 (752.570). Open 1 April to 30 Sept. Overlooking sea; smallish, with lift to private swimming area. DC, MC, V. *Villa Saint Vincent* (M), Via Aosta 3 (752.445). Open 1 April to 31 Dec. Pleasant, small, with garden. MC.

Restaurants. *Poggetto* (M), Via del Poggetto at Quercetano (752.754). Closed Mon. Very good food and view from dining terrace. AE, DC, V. *Rugantino* (M), Via del Quercetano (752.707). Closed Tues. and Nov. *Simpatico;* good pastas, fish and steaks. AE. *Le Spianate* (M), Via di Campofreno 15 (752.671). Closed Tues. Nice view.

Castiglione della Pescaia Grosseto (0564). Citadel town and lively beach resort. High season, Easter and 15 June to 15 Sept. *L'Approdo* (M), Via Ponte Giorgini 29 (933.466). Overlooking port; comfortable, nice views.

At **Riva del Sole,** outside town, lovely beach and pinewoods, *Riva del Sole* (E) (933.625). Large, resort hotel on beach. MC, V.

At **Poggiodoro,** above town, *David* (M) (939.030). Attractive, small, with good views. V.

At **Roccamare,** on road to Punta Ala, *Roccamare* (E) (941.124). Open 1 April to 31 Oct. Modern holiday village with hotel and bungalows in pinewoods, on beach.

Restaurants. *Il Gambero* (M), Via Ansedonia (933.737). Closed Wed. Seafood specialties. *Romolo* (M), Via delle Libertà (933.533). Closed Tues. and 1 Oct. to 30 Nov. Some dishes pricey.

At **Tirli,** in hills 16 km. (10 miles) away, *Tana del Cinghiale* (M) (945.810). Closed Wed. and Jan. Fine for game.

Certaldo Firenze (0571). Hill town, Boccaccio's birthplace. *Osteria del Vicario* (M) (668.228). Closed Wed. In pretty medieval building with garden, good local cuisine.

Chianciano Terme Siena (0578). Important spa. High season 15 April to 31 Oct. *Excelsior* (E), Via Sant'Agnese 6 (64.351). Open Easter to 31 Oct. Large; very comfortable and efficient; thermal pool, park. AE, DC, V.
Ambasciatori (M), Viale della Libertà 512 (64.371). Central, large, in park, thermal pool. AE, DC, V. *Capitol* (M), Viale della Libertà 492 (64.681). Open 15 April to 31 Oct. Striking, modern decor; pool on rooftop terrace. AE, DC, V. *Fortuna* (M), Via della Valle 76 (64.661). Open 15 April to 5 Nov. Just outside town; quiet, attractive modern decor; pool, tennis. AE, DC. *Michelangelo* (M), Via delle Piane 146 (64.004). Open 1 May to 31 Oct. Very quiet, on hillside overlooking resort; park, pool, tennis. AE, DC, V.
President (I), Viale Baccelli 260 (64.131). Open 15 April to 31 Oct. Superior in category; elegant modern appointments.
Restaurants. *Casanova* (E), Strada della Vittoria 10 (60.449). Closed Wed. Open 1 April to 9 Jan. Good food in rural setting just outside town. AE, DC, V. *Al Casale* (M), Via Cavine 36 (30.445). Closed Tues. off-season. Open 16 March to 31 Dec. Rustic; good country cooking. AE, DC, V.
At **Cetona:** *La Frateria di Padre Eligio* (E), Convento di San Francesco (238.015). Closed Tues. In renovated Franciscan monastery, rehabilitation community operates excellent restaurant.

Cortona Arezzo (0575). Art city. *San Luca* (M), Piazza Garibaldi 1 (603.787). Simple, bedrooms with fine view.
At **Sant'Egidio,** above town, *Villa Guglielmesca* (M) (603.365). Open 1 April to 31 Oct. In pretty park, small, comfortable. AE, DC, MC, V.
Restaurants. *La Loggetta* (M), Piazza Pescheria 3 (603.777). Closed Sun. evening (except in summer), Mon., Jan 5–Feb 10. Truly excellent food, mainly local cuisine, in antique ambiance. AE, DC, MC, V. *Tonino* (M), Piazza Garibaldi (603.100). Closed Mon. evening and Tues. Large, can be good, but unsatisfactory when crowded. AE, DC, MC, V.

Elba Livorno (0565). Largest island of Tuscan archipelago.
At **Biodola,** *Hermitage* (E) (969.932). Open 9 May to 30 Sept. Smart, modern, bungalows in pinewood, right on sandy beach; indoor/outdoor pools; terraces. AE. *La Biodola* (M) (969.966). Open 19 April to 20 Oct. Modern building on beach; indoor/outdoor pools; tennis. AE.
At **Capoliveri-Naregno,** *Elba International* (M) (968.611). Open 1 May to 30 Sept. Big, modern, impersonal; lift to beach, salt water pool. DC, V. *Le Acacie* (M) (968.526). Open 1 May to 30 Sept. Arranged in several villas on beach; pool, tennis; attractive lounge and flowered dining terrace. DC, V.
At **Cavoli,** *Bahia* (M) (987.055). Open 1 April to 31 Oct. Bungalows on lovely beach; essential to reserve way ahead for this exceptional spot. V.
At **Fetovaia,** enchanting spot off the beaten track, *Lo Scirocco* (M) (987.060). Open 1 April to 20 Oct. Tiny, 15-room haven overlooking cove. DC, MC.
At **Lacona,** *Lacona* (M) (964.050). Very large, modern, in extensive grounds on beach with terraces, buffet-style restaurant.
At **Magazzini,** *Fabricia* (M) (966.181). Open 4 April to 30 Sept. Low-slung, modern, in olive grove, 5 minutes through garden to beach; saltwater pool. AE, DC.
At **Marciana Marina,** *La Primula* (E), Viale Cerboni (99.010). In town, 5 minutes from beach; pleasant, attractive. DC, V. *Gabbiano Azzurro* (M), Viale Amedeo 94 (99.226). Bright, friendly, 10 minutes from beach. AE, MC, V.
Restaurants. *Rendez-Vous* (M), Piazza della Vittoria (99.251). Closed Wed. off-season. Open 20 Feb. to 7 Jan. Seafood and game, very good. AE, DC, MC. *Da Sauro* (M), at port (99.027). Closed Mon. Open 1 April to 15 Oct.

At **Marina di Campo**, *Montecristo* (E) (976.861). Open 1 April to 31 Oct. Smart, attractive and comfortable; pool. AE, DC, MC, V.

Restaurants. *Bologna* (M), Via Firenze 27 (97.105). Closed Mon. Open 1 April to 15 Oct. AE, MC. *Da Gianni* (M), at La Pila (976.965). Closed Fri. off-season. Open 1 March to 31 Oct. Southern Italian cuisine. *La Triglia* (M), Via Roma (97.059). Closed Thurs. off-season. Open 10 March to 31 Oct. Exclusively seafood. AE, DC, MC, V.

At **Ottone**, *Villa Ottone* (E) (966.042). Open 1 April to 2 Oct. Mediterranean-style with loggias, gardens, pool and tennis; water sports on bay. AE, DC, MC, V.

At **Picchiae**, *Picchiaie Residence* (M) (966.072). Open 12 May to 23 Sept. Quiet hillside location; handsome building with beautiful view; tennis, pool. AE, DC.

At **Porto Azzurro**, *Cala di Mola* (M) (95.225). Open 15 May to 15 Oct. Modern, well-equipped, resort-style, with pool, beach.

Restaurant. *Lanterna* (M), on port (95.026). Closed Mon.

At **Portoferraio**, *Garden* (M), at Schipparello (966.043). Open 1 May to 30 Sept. Quiet, resort-type; all rooms with balcony and sea view; gardens, beach.

Restaurants. *La Ferrigna* (M), Piazza Repubblica (92.129). Central and large; seafood. Efficient service. *Stella Marina* (M), Via Vittorio Emanuele (92.302). Closed Tues. Open 1 April to 31 Oct. Seafood only and very good. DC.

At **Procchio**, *Desirée* (E) (907.502). Open 20 April to 2 Oct. Spacious, modern, on private beach; airy comfortable rooms; pool. AE, DC, MC, V. *Del Golfo* (M) (907.565). Open 19 April to 14 Oct. Large building contains attractive public rooms, nicely decorated bedrooms; ample grounds, large saltwater pool; private sandy beach. AE, MC, V.

Empoli Firenze (0571). Art town, glass manufacturing center. **Restaurant.** *Bianconi* (M), Via Romagnola 70 (90.558). Closed Wed. and 25–31 July. Unpretentious lunch stop. AE, V.

Fiesole Firenze (055). Art town, Florence suburb. *Villa San Michele* (L), Via Doccia 4 (59.451). Open 20 March to 5 Oct. One of Italy's most distinguished; in converted 15th-century monastery, partly designed by Michelangelo. *Relais* hotel, top-level comfort and service. AE, DC, MC, V.

Aurora (M), Piazza Mino da Fiesole (59.100). Small, with terraces, good view. AE, DC, MC, V. *Bencistà* (I), on Maiano road (59.163). Open 15 March to 31 Oct. Old family villa in olive grove; peaceful; good views.

Restaurants. *Le Lance* (M), Via Mantellini (599.090). Closed Mon., Tues, and Jan. Summer terrace with view of city. AE, DC, V.

At **Maiano**, 3.5 km. (2 miles) away, *Trattoria Le Cave* (M) (59.133). Closed Sun. evening, Thurs. and Aug. Attractive old place, summer terrace; good local cuisine. Reserve. AE, DC.

Forte dei Marmi Lucca (0584). Important, very smart beach resort. High season Feb., Easter, 15 June to 15 Sept. and Christmas. *Augustus* (L), Viale Morin 169 (80.202). In lush park, main building and attractive bungalow contain 60 tastefully furnished rooms; smart clientele, beach club, disco. AE, DC, MC, V. Open 20 May to 30 Sept.

Alcione (E), Viale Morin 137 (89.952). Open 1 June to 30 Sept. Comfortable rooms, pretty garden. AE, DC, V. *Byron* (E), Viale Morin 46 (80.087). Open 15 May to 15 Sept. Small, attractively decorated villa with pool. AE, DC, MC, V. *Hermitage* (E), Via Cesare Battisti (80.022). Open 1 June to 15 Sept. Modern, quiet, in park short walk from beach; spacious rooms; pool; minibus to beach. AE, DC, MC, V.

Adams Villa Maria (M), Viale Italico 110 (80.901). Open 1 June to 30 Sept. Overlooking sea in shady park; pool. AE, DC, MC, V. *Astoria Garden* (M), Via Leonardo da Vinci 10 (80.754). Open 15 May to 30 Sept. Quiet, pleasant, small. AE, DC, MC, V. *Pleiadi* (M), Via Civitali 51 (881.188). Open 15 May to 30 Sept. Smallish, quiet, with garden. DC. *Raffaelli-Villa Angela* (M), Via Mazzini 64 (80.652). Open 20 May to 30 Sept. Very good atmosphere; tennis, private beach, pool and gardens. AE, DC, V.

Restaurants. *La Barca* (E), Viale Italico 3 (89.323). Closed Tues. and Dec. Classic coastal cuisine. AE, DC, MC, V. *Bistrot* (E), Viale della Repubblica (89.879). Closed Mon. and Nov. AE, DC, V. Pleasant for both seafood and meat dishes. *Lorenzo* (E), Via Carducci 61 (84.030). Closed Mon. and 15 Nov. to 15 Dec. Reserve. Unpretentious décor; one of the best fish restaurants in the area. AE, DC, MC, V.

Tre Stelle (M), Via Montauti 6 (80.220). Closed Mon. and 10–25 Oct. Good *risotto* and seafood. *Al Fosso* (M), Via della Barbiera 42 (83.365). Closed Mon. off-season. Attractive, good food.

Giglio Grosseto (0564). Island hideaway in Tuscan archipelago. High season Easter and 15 June to 15 Sept.

At **Giglio Porto,** *Castello Monticello* (M) (809.252). Open 15 April to 30 Sept. Smallish; pool, tennis. *Arenella* (M) (809.340). Open 1 June to 24 Sept. Small, quiet. Good views of coastline.

Restaurants. At Giglio Porto, *Da Meino* (M), Via Umberto (809.228). Closed Wed. and Nov. Veranda overlooking sea. *La Vecchia Pergola* (M) (809.080). Closed Tues. Open 1 March to 31 Oct. Summer dining terrace.

At **Giglio Castello** (bus service), *Donna Rosa* (M), Piazza Gloriosa (806.019). Very good food.

Grosseto Grosseto (0564). Commercial center. **Restaurants.** *Buca San Lorenzo* (M), Viale Manetti 1 (25.142). Closed Mon. Attractive ambiance, good food. AE, DC, MC, V. *La Casereccia* (M), at Poggione, Via Senese 202 (451.470). Closed Wed. and Aug. Very good trattoria, can be pricey. *Maremma* (M), Via Paolucci 7 (21.177). Closed Tues. Good. AE, DC, V.

Lido di Camaiore Lucca (0584). Beach resort. High season Easter, 15 June to 15 Sept. and Christmas. *Ariston* (E), Viale Colombo 355 (66.333). Open Easter to 15 Oct. Small, quiet, in large park, with pool; tennis, beach facilities. AE, MC, V. *Caesar* (M), Viale Colombo 325 (64.841). Open 6 Feb. to 31 Oct. Good, small, with sea view, pool, tennis and garden. *Colombo* (M), Viale Colombo 161 (66.051). Small. AE, DC, MC, V.

Restaurants. *Bertocca* (M), Viale Pistelli 128 (64.941). Closed Tues. Another fine seafood restaurant. *Da Clara* (M), Via Aurelia 289 (904.520). Closed Tues. evening, Wed. and Nov. Very good seafood, mushrooms in fall. AE, DC, MC, V.

Livorno Livorno (0586). Important port, of minor interest to tourists.

Restaurants. *La Banditella da Cappa* (E), at Ardenza, Via Angioletti 3 (501.246). Closed Sun. and 20 July to 20 Aug. At beach suburb, family-run, attractive, attentive service, excellent seafood. DC. *Norma* (E), Via Provinciale Pisana 60 (401.032). Closed Sun. and 15–31 Aug. Small, *simpatico,* very good. V. *La Barcarola* (M), Viale Carducci 63 (402.367). Closed Sun. and Aug. Big, busy and good. AE, DC, MC, V. *Giardino* (M), Viale Italia 103 (807.002). Closed Thurs. V. *Oscar* (M), at Ardenza, Via Franchini 78 (501.258). Closed Mon. and Aug. Tops for seafood, can be pricey. V. *La Parmigiana* (M), Piazza Orlando 8 (807.180). Closed Sun. and July. Classic seafood cuisine.

Lucca Lucca (0583). Picturesque art city. *Napoleon* (M), Viale Europa 1 (53.141). Outside bastions, modern, comfortable. No restaurant. AE, DC, MC, V. *Universo* (M), Piazza del Giglio 1 (49.046). Central; traditional furnishings; good restaurant. AE, DC, MC, V. *Ilaria,* (I), Via del Fosso 20 (47.558). Small, family run, recently renovated. No restaurant. AE, DC, MC, V.

At **Massa Pisana,** 5 km. (3 miles) away, *Villa La Principessa* (E) (370.037). Open Mar. 1–Nov. 15. Exquisitely decorated, exclusive villa; all creature comforts, vast park, large pool. AE, DC, MC, V.

Restaurants. *Buca di Sant'Antonio* (M), Via della Cervia 1 (55.881). Closed Sun. evening, Mon. and 8–30 July. Very good food and atmosphere. AE, DC, MC, V. *Da Giulio in Pelleria* (M), Via San Tommaso 29 (55.948). Closed Sun., Mon. and Aug. Small trattoria, popular for good local dishes. *Il Giglio,* (M), Piazza del Giglio 2

(44.058). Closed Tues. eve., Wed. Quiet, turn-of-the-century charm; classic cuisine. AE, DC, MC, V. *Il Punto* (M), Piazza San Quirico (46.264). Closed Fri. and Oct. Varied menu. DC, V. *Sergio* (M), Piazza dei Bernardini 7 (49.944). Closed Mon. evening and Tues. Good. AE, DC, MC, V.

At **San Macario in Piano,** 6.5 km. (4 miles) away on Viareggio road, *Solferino* (M) (59.118). Closed Wed., Thurs. lunch; Aug. 2–21; Jan 7–15. Very pleasant, excellent food, both local and international; ingredients from family farm. AE, DC, MC, V.

At **Ponte a Moriano,** 9.5 km. (6 miles) away, *La Mora* (M), at Sesto (57.109). Closed Wed. evening, Thurs. and 2 weeks in July. Reserve. Well worth going out of your way for this old way-station; authentic local cuisine. AE, DC, MC, V.

Marina di Massa Massa-Carrara (0585). Beach resort. High season Easter, 1 June to 31 Aug. *Excelsior* (E), Via Battisti 1 (240.141). Large, beachfront hotel with pool. DC, MC, V.

At **Poveromo,** *Nedy* (M), Via del Fescione 32 (309.206). Open 15 March to 31 Oct. Quiet, small, with garden. AE, V. *Villa Irene* (M), Via delle Macchie 125 (309.310). Open 15 May to 30 Sept. Attractive, small, with ample grounds, beach facilities.

Restaurants. *Il Grotto* (M), Via delle Pinete 2 (201.200). Closed Tues. Inviting, good food. *Da Riccà* (M), Lungomare di Ponente (201.070). Closed Mon. and 15 Oct. to 15 Nov. Seafood only. AE, DC, V.

Marina di Pietrasanta Lucca (0584). Beach resort. High season Feb., Easter, 15 June to 15 Sept. and Christmas. *Palazzo Spiaggia* (E), at Focette, Viale Roma 303 (21.195). Open 15 May to 15 Oct. Smart, modern resort hotel; pool in attractive garden; private beach. AE, DC, MC, V.

Battelli (M), at Motrone, Viale Versilia 189 (20.010). Open 26 May to 30 Sept. In smart section of resort; garden, tennis, beach facilities. *Esplanade* (M), at Tonfano, Viale Roma 235 (21.151). Open 1 April to 31 Oct. On shore boulevard. AE, MC.

Montalcino Siena (0577). Medieval fortress town near Siena, famous Brunello wine. **Restaurants.** *Edgardo* (M) (848.232). Closed Wed. Jan. 10–30. Reserve. AE, DC, MC, V. *Il Giglio* (M) (848.167). Modest inn, excellent fare. *Taverna dei Barbi* (M), at Fattoria Barbi (848.277). Closed Wed. and Feb. Rustic; good country cooking.

Monte Argentario Grosseto (0564). Popular, picturesque peninsula, linked to mainland by three tongues of land enclosing two saltwater lagoons. Main towns on the peninsula are Porto Santo Stefano and Port'Ercole, both mere fishing villages years ago, but today smart resorts. At the base of the peninsula, 16 km. (10 miles) apart, are Fonteblanda and Ansedonia.

At **Ansedonia,** on Aurelia highway. **Restaurants.** *Pitorsino* (E), Via Aurelia (862.179). Closed Wed. off-season. Open 5 March to 9 Jan. Gourmet-level dining. *Il Pescatore* (M), Via della Tagliata 13 (881.201). Closed Tues. Fish specialties, some pricey.

At **Cala Piccola,** *Torre di Cala Piccola* (E) (825.133). On secluded cliff-top site on the peninsula's extreme western tip; private beach, pool, gardens; also residential.

At **Fonteblanda,** *Corte dei Butteri* (E) (885.547). Open 20 May to 20 Sept. Very smart, elegant and well-furnished haven with pool, fine beach.

At **Orbetello,** at little town in the middle of the central isthmus. **Restaurants.** *Egisto* (M), Corso Italia 190 (867.469). Closed Mon. off-season and Nov. *Osteria del Lupacante* (M), Corso Italia 103 (867.618). Closed Wed. and 15 Jan. to 15 Feb. Attractive, seafood specialties, some pricey. AE, DC, MC, V.

At **Port'Ercole,** *Pellicano* (E) (833.801). Open 10 March to 10 Jan. Small, quietly posh, informal and very expensive. Set apart in large park with heated pool, private beach, tennis. AE, DC, MC, V. *Don Pedro* (M) (833.914). Open 1 April to 31 Oct. Modern, with good views. MC. *Villa Letizia* (M) (833.995). Open 20 Dec. to 10 Jan. and 15 Feb. to 31 Oct. Small, with pool in garden. AE, V.

Restaurants. *La Ribotta* (M), at Terra Rossa (814.473). Closed Tues. off-season. Good fish dishes. *La Lampara* (I), Lungomare Doria 50 (833.024). Closed Tues. and 1 Dec. to 28 Feb. At center of port; good pasta and pizzas.

At **Porto Santo Stefano**, *Filippo II* (E), Poggio Calvello (812.640). Open 1 May to 30 Sept. Attractive, pricey, on promontory; private beach, gardens. *Vittoria* (M), Strada del Sole 65 (818.580). Small, overlooking town and port. MC, V.

Restaurants. *Armando* (M), Via Marconi 1 (812.568). Closed Wed. and 1–20 Dec. AE, DC. *La Formica* (M), at Pozzarello beach (814.205). Closed Wed. and 15 Oct. to 15 Nov. Popular, on beach, open fire in winter. AE.

Montecatini Terme Pistoia (0572). Most important spa in Italy. High season 15 July to 30 Sept. *Grand e La Pace* (L), Via delle Torretta 1 (75.801). Open 1 April to 31 Oct. Large, handsome, in extensive park; pool, cure facilities and tennis. AE, DC, MC, V. *Bellavista* (E), Viale Fedeli 2 (78.122). Closed Jan. Large, attractive, with garden terraces; indoor and outdoor pools; tennis. AE, MC, V. *Croce di Malta* (E), Viale Quattro Novembre 18 (75.871). Very comfortable, with heated pool, all amenities. AE, MC, V. *Tamerici Principe* (E), Viale Quattro Novembre 2 (71.041). Open 1 April to 30 Nov. Facing lovely park, large, well-appointed, with terraces and pool. AE, MC, V.

Astoria (M), Viale Fedeli 1 (71.191). Open 1 April to 6 Nov. Good, medium-sized, with pool and garden. AE. *Capelli-Croce di Savoia* (M), Viale Bicchierai 139 (71.151). Open 1 April to 15 Nov. Traditional furnishings; pool, garden. AE, DC, MC, V. *Terme Pellegrini* (M), Piazza del Popolo 34 (71.241). Open 1 April to 31 Oct. Central, nicely furnished.

Restaurants. *Lido's* (E), Via Guermani 2 (766.378). Closed Mon. and Nov. At upper terminal of funicular, with splendid views; excellent food and atmosphere. DC, V. *Da Giovanni* (M), Via Garibaldi 25 (71.695). Closed Mon. At No. 25 up-market cuisine and atmosphere; at No. 27 less expensive, rustic specialties. Both AE, DC, V.

Montepulciano Siena (0578). Art city, wine center. *Marzocco* (I), Piazza Savonarola 25 (77.262). Unpretentious, small—reflecting atmosphere of town. AE, DC, V.

Restaurant. *Cantuccio* (M), Via delle Cantine (757.870). Closed Mon. and 1–15 July. Rustic atmosphere.

Montesenario Firenze (055). Noted monastery near Florence. Reader suggests *Gli Scoiattoli* (M) (406.610); in town of Bivigliano. Neat, modern inn with good views. English-speaking owners; good alternative for motorists; frequent buses into city. Good restaurant. V.

Restaurant. *La Giulia* (M) (406.602). Fine lunch stop; summer dining on terrace; winters beside huge hearth.

Piombino Livorno (0565). Jumping-off point for Elba. *Centrale* (M), Piazza Verdi 2 (32.581). Adequate overnight. MC, V.

Restaurants. *Orazio* (M), Via Lombroso 55 (33.297). Closed Mon. *Piave* (M), Piazza Niccolini (33.050).

Pisa Pisa (050). Famous art town. *Dei Cavalieri* (E), Piazza Stazione 2 (43.290). CIGA. On station square; best in town, with elegant, attractive bedrooms and salons in contemporary decor. AE, DC, MC, V. *Duomo* (E), Via Santa Maria 96 (27.141). A few steps from famous tower; large, modern; comfortable rooms. DC, MC, V. *Arno* (M), Piazza della Repubblica (22.243). Fairly central, smallish; good restaurant. *La Pace* (M), Via Gramsci 14 (502.266). Near station, comfortable. DC, MC. *Royal Victoria*, (I), Lungarno Pacinotti 12 (50.2130). Old World ambiance; recently renovated. Restaurant. AE, DC, MC, V.

Restaurants. *Ristori dei Vecchi Macelli* (E), Via Volturno 49 (20.424). Closed Wed., Sun. noon. and 10-25 Aug. Elegant, attractive; varied menu of excellent choices. AE, DC, V. *Sergio* (E), Lungarno Pacinotti 1 (48.245). Closed Sun., Mon. noon 2 weeks in July and two weeks in winter. Very good; masterful use of home-grown herbs; delicious *patisserie*. AE, DC, MC, V.

Bruno, (M), Via Luigi Bianchi 12 (55.094). Closed Mon. evening, Tues.; Aug. 1–20. Just outside old city walls; Classic Tuscan dishes. AE, DC, MC, V. *Buzzino* (M), Via Cammeo 44 (27.013). Closed Tues. and Nov. Near tower; pleasant place with garden; good food. Some dishes pricey. AE, DC, MC, V. *Emilio* (M), Via Roma 28 (26.028). Closed Mon. V. *Pergoletta* (M), Via delle Belle Torri 36 (23.631). Closed Mon. and 15-31 Aug. Family-run, relaxed atmosphere; reasonable. *Santa Maria* (M), Via Santa Maria 104 (26.206). Closed Fri. and Nov. Near Leaning Tower, restful, modern, very reasonable. *Schiaccianoci* (M), Via Vespucci 104 (21.024). Closed Sun., evening, Mon. and Aug. Small, excellent, near station; reserve for a chance to dine well. *Spartaco* (M), Piazza Vittorio Emanuele 22 (23.335). Closed Sun. On main piazza near station, classic food, fine wines. AE, DC, MC, V.

Pistoia Pistoia (0573). Art city. *Residence Convento* (M), Via San Quirico 33 (452.651). Just outside town; best for comfort and atmosphere. V.

Restaurants. *Boschetto* (M), Viale Adua 469 (401.185). Closed Mon. On main road skirting town, good food. *Cuccioli della Montagna* (M), Via Panciatichi 4 (29.733). Closed Mon., Aug 1–25. Central, best in town. AE, DC, MC, V. *Rafanelli-Sant'Agostino* (M), Via Sant'Agostino 47 (32.046). Closed Mon. and 1–22 Aug. At-tractive, spacious, very good food. AE, DC, V.

Prato Firenze (0574). Art city. *Palace* (E), Via Pier della Francesca (592.841). On outskirts; large, modern and comfortable. AE, DC, MC, V. *President* (M), Via Simintendi 20 (30.251). Fairly central. AE, DC, MC, V.

Restaurants. *Pirana* (E), Via Valentini 110 (25.746). Closed Sat., Sun. and Aug. Large; very good cuisine emphasizing seafood, steaks and mushrooms. AE, DC, MC, V. *Villa Santa Cristina* (E), Via Poggio Secco 58 (595.951). Closed Sun. evening, Mon. and Aug. Outside town near autostrada exit; lovely centuries-old villa, good ambi-ance and cuisine. AE, DC, MC, V.

Baghino (M), Via dell'Accademia 9 (27.920). Closed Sun. Old-world atmosphere, longtime favorite. *Bruno,* (M), Via Verdi 12 (23.810). Closed Thurs. dinner, Sun., Aug. Near Norman castle, simple decor; traditional dishes with creative touches. AE, DC, MC, V. *Stella d'Italia* (M), Piazza Duomo 8 (27.910). Closed Fri. evening, Sat. and Aug. Central; very pleasant. AE, DC, MC, V. *Tonio* (M), Piazza Mercatale 161 (212.666). Closed Sun., Mon. and 5–30 Aug. Central; good steaks and seafood. AE, DC, MC, V.

Punta Ala Grosseto (0564). Extensive and exclusive beach resort, near Marem-ma reserve. *Alleluia* (E) (922.050). Rustic-chic decor; small, very comfortable, with pool and beach. *Cala del Porto* (E) (922.455). Open 18 May to 30 Sept. At port; good rooms, atmosphere. AE, DC, MC, V. *Gallia Palace* (E) (922.022). Open 25 May to 30 Sept. Best, most luxurious and priciest; posh appointments; very smart clien-tele; all resort facilities. AE.

San Gimignano Siena (0577). Picturesque old hill town near Siena. *La Cisterna* (M) (940.328). Closed Tues., Wed. noon and 11 Nov. to 10 March. On pretty piaz-za, inn with spacious rooms, old-fashioned decor. Fine restaurant overlooking tiled rooftops, very good food. AE, DC, MC, V. *Bel Soggiorno* (M), Via San Giovanni 91 (940.375). Small inn; good restaurant. Closed Mon. and Mar. AE, DC, MC, V. *Le Ter-razze,* (M), Piazza della Cisterna 23 (940.328). Closed Tue., Wed lunch. Time-honored inn. Charming view; Tuscan dishes. AE, DC, MC, V. *Pescille,* (M), Località Pescille, Strada Castel San Giminano (940.186). Closed Feb. Attractive, rambling farmhouse. Contemporary decor blends with country classic. Fine restaurant. AE, DC, MC, V.

Siena Siena (0577). Italy's best preserved medieval city. *Certosa di Maggiano* (L), Strada di Certosa 82 (288.180). *Relais* hotel. Just outside town, only 14 rooms in renovated monastery of 15th-century; exceptional atmosphere, comfort and service; pool, tennis. AE, DC, MC, V. *Park* (L), Via di Marciano 16 (44.803). CIGA. Just outside walls, handsome 15th-century country villa, antique filled lounges; spacious, pleasant rooms; good-sized pool, lovely grounds. AE, DC, MC, V. *Jolly Excelsior* (E), Piazza La Lizza (288.448). Only top hotel within town walls; large, palace-type, all comforts. AE, DC, MC, V.

Athena (M), Via Paolo Mascagni 55 (286.313). Large, just inside bastions; little atmosphere. No restaurant. DC, V. *Minerva* (M), Via Garibaldi 72 (284.474). At San Lorenzo gate. Adequate comforts. *Palazzo Ravizza* (M), Piana dei Mantellini 34 (280.462). Not far from cathedral, within bastions; 17th-century building, fine old furnishings; garden; smallish, reserve well ahead. AE, DC, MC, V. *Santa Caterina,* (M), Via Piccolomini 7 (221.150). Closed Nov 10–Mar. Intimate townhouse; pretty, homey rooms. AE, DC, MC, V.

Restaurants. *Alvaro* (M), Via Massetana 68 (286.110). Closed Sat. and 1–15 Aug. Central, good. *Il Campo,* (M), Piazza del Campo 50 (280.725). Closed Tues. and mid-Jan–mid-Feb. On scenic main plaza; local specialties. AE, DC, MC, V. *Da Guido* (M), Vicolo Pier Pettinaio 7 (280.042). Closed Mon. and 1–21 July. Near Piazza del Campo; typical atmosphere and cuisine. AE, DC, MC, V. *Al Marsili* (M), Via Castoro 3 (47.154). Closed Mon. Handsome ambience, good food, service; excellent wines. AE, DC, MC, V. *Al Mangia* (M), Piazza del Campo 43 (281.121). Closed Mon. Outdoor tables on one of the world's most beautiful piazzas. AE, DC, MC, V. *Nello-La Taverna* (M), Via del Porrione 28 (289.043). Closed Mon. and Feb. Near Piazza del Campo; typical local dishes. AE, DC, MC, V. *Osteria Le Logge* (M), Via Porrione 33 (48.013). Closed Sun. and 1–15 July. Central, good food, fine house wine. AE. *Le Tre Campane* (M), Piazzetta Bonelli 2 (286.091). Closed Tues. and 1 Jan. to 28 Feb. Central, reasonable and good. *Tullio ai Tre Cristi,* Vicolo Provenzano (280.608). Closed Sun. evening, Mon. and Feb. Central, longtime favorite. AE.

Sinalunga Siena (0577). Old town at Valdichiana exit of Autostrada del Sole. *Locanda dell'Amorosa* (M) (69.497). Romantic small inn on country estate; fine restaurant (E). Closed Mon. and Tues. noon, 20 Jan. to 28 Feb. Gourmet-level cuisine in lovely rustic setting. AE, DC, V.

Viareggio Lucca (0584). Beach resort. High season Feb., Easter, 15 June to 15 Sept. and Christmas. *Astor* (E), Viale Carducci 54 (50.301). Elegantly modern, well-furnished, overlooking beach; light, airy. AE, DC, MC, V. *Royal* (E), Viale Carducci 44 (45.151). Huge, Renaissance-style building overlooking seaside promenade; spacious, well-furnished rooms; pool, beach area. DC, V. *Principe di Piemonte* (E), Piazza Puccini 1 (50.122). Open 15 May to 15 Oct. Palace-type, on promenade, many rooms with balcony and sea view; sumptuous public rooms; sidewalk terrace, indoor pool. AE, DC, MC.

American (M), Piazza Mazzini 6 (47.041). Small, modern and well-appointed. No restaurant. AE, DC, MC, V. *Garden,* Via Foscolo 70 (44.025). Attractive, small; short walk to beach. AE, DC, MC, V. *Excelsior* (M), Viale Carducci 88 (50.726). Open 15 May to 15 Oct. Traditional comfort in large hotel on shore. AE, DC, MC, V.

Restaurants. *Delfino Blu* (E), Lungomare Carducci 41 (42.207). Closed Thurs. and 15 Nov. to 15 Dec. Elegant, small. Reserve. DC, MC, V. *Fedi-Da Gianfranco* (E), Via Verdi 111 (48.519). Closed Tues. and 25 Sept. to 15 Oct. *Simpatico,* small, not all dishes pricey. AE, DC, MC, V. *Foscolo* (E), Via Foscolo 79 (44.220). Closed Tues. and Oct. AE, DC, MC, V. *Patriarca* (E), Via Carducci 79 (53.126). Closed Wed. off-season and Nov. Tops in town and in area for seafood and Tuscan specialties. Ample menu and day-to-day offerings. AE, DC, MC. *Romano* (E), Via Mazzini 122 (31.382). Closed Mon. off-season and Jan. *Simpatico* host, very good food. AE, DC, MC, V. *Tito del Molo* (E), Lungomare Corrado del Greco 3 (42.016). Closed Wed. and n. Longtime favorite for seafood; not everything is pricey. AE, DC, MC, V. *Gusmano* (), Via Regia 58 (31.233). Closed Tues. and Nov. Fine choice in lower price range. DC, MC, V.

Volterra Pisa (0588). Art city and alabaster center. *Nazionale* (M), Via dei Marchesi 11 (86.284). Smallish, adequate comforts; unpretentious. *San Lino,* (M), Via San Lino 26 (85.250). Centrally located. Modern comforts in former convent. Restaurant; pool. AE, DC, MC, V.

Restaurants. *Etruria* (M), Piazza dei Priori 6 (86.064). Closed Thurs., Nov. 15–Dec. 31. Tasty local cuisine. AE, DC. *Il Porcellino* (M), Vicolo delle Prigioni 16 (86.392). Closed Tues. Open 25 March to 10 Oct. Simple, good. AE, DC, V.

GETTING THERE AND AROUND. By air.

Tuscany's airport is at Pisa. But as we said in the Florence *Practical Information,* that is not particularly good news if you want to go into Florence by the train.

Travelers using the economical Alitalia Jet-Drive package can fly to Pisa for visiting the north of Tuscany including Florence, Siena and San Gimignano. Alitalia has a tie-up with Jolly Hotels at which Jet-Drive passengers can get up to 20% discount, and there are Jolly Hotels in Florence and Siena.

By train. The main rail line runs past Cortona through Arezzo and Florence to Prato. Another main line connects Florence with Pisa, and the coastal line from Rome to Genoa passes through Pisa and all the beach resorts. There are a few local lines, but buses connect the smaller towns and cities quite well on autostrade and superhighways.

By car. The suggested routes for train and bus travelers do equally well for tourists in their automobiles. The area is well served by three autostrade: part of the A1; the Autostrada del Sole, connecting Florence with Bologna and Rome, passing close to Arezzo; and the A11, leading west from Florence, and meeting the coastal A12 between Viareggio and Livorno. Toll-free superstrade link Florence with Siena and Arezzo. The last is probably the best center from which to explore this charming area, and is within easy reach of Perugia in Umbria, passing Lake Trasimeno en route.

By boat. Boat services link the islands of Tuscany's archipelago with the mainland; passenger and car ferries leave from Livorno and especially from Piombino for Elba. The ferry to Giglio leaves from Porto Santo Stefano on the Argentario.

EMILIA-ROMAGNA

Princely Cities, Princely Food

Bordered on the north by the Po River and on the south by a massive section of the Apennines, the Emilia-Romagna region is really a string of little and big cities, laid out for the most part along that arrow-straight Roman road known as the Emilian Way, which runs from Milan through Piacenza, in the northwest, to Rimini, on the Adriatic. Romagna is the area from Rimini to the outskirts of Bologna, while Emilia refers to that portion between Bologna and Piacenza. The political division of the two parts of this region dates back to the Lombard invasion around 568 A.D. They took possession of the now-called Emilia, while the rest remained under Byzantine control, as its name shows.

Fidenza, Parma, Reggio, Modena, Bologna, Imola, Faenza, Cesena, lie along the Emilian Way which, just short of Rimini, crosses the Rubicon. It was this river which Caesar crossed in defiance of the Fates and the Roman Senate, leading his legions on to Rome.

Rome built Via Emilia, the magnificent arterial way, for military and political purposes. In the centuries which followed it became the principal trade route, and was in large measure responsible for the growth of the region. A leisurely pace along this highway is recommended in order to enjoy the charming communities mellowed with age and containing much of outstanding interest and beauty.

The countryside beyond the cities and towns through which the highway runs is flat and low and often flooded, but it is a rich, fertile land. Its grape vines lacing the fruit trees, its fields of wheat and flax, its pasture for the cattle, contribute heavily to Italy's agricultural resources.

In the mountains, southwest of Bologna, ancient watchtowers still stand on seemingly inaccessible peaks where they were built by feudal lords to guard against forays into their domains. Both the Germans and the Allies used many of them as observation posts during the last war.

From Etruscans to Communists

Emilia-Romagna has dominated the history of Italy in some peculiar ways. Much of it was Etruscan in earliest colonization, even the names of the tribes of its earliest inhabitants being lost in the maze of prehistoric legends. The Etruscans did not last very long, nor did they stamp their impress very deeply on the area. When the Romans came, in the heyday of the Republic, they met little opposition on their expansion northward.

The Romans found at Bologna, for example, the Etruscan community called Felsina. They renamed it Bononia, established a powerful garrison there and moved on to the northwest, building their Via Emilia as they went. Other garrisons were established, similarly, until the long chain from Rome to Rimini, from Rimini to Milan and on to Gaul, was complete.

Discharged legionaries, after 25 years' service, were rewarded by grateful Rome with plots of marshland along the military highway. These they could, if they would, drain, cultivate and make into farms. That so many of them did is one of the major miracles of Rome's 1,000 years. The original discontent of these poor old soldiers, dumped virtually penniless onto a swamp after so much service in Rome's legions, may be the basis of Emilia's traditional unrest. Certainly the discontent has always been there. In the earliest days Hannibal found friends and allies there when he swept down through the Alps on his way to eventual defeat. But Hannibal's rear guard wasn't very popular in Emilia either and his lines of supply did not last long.

When, several hundreds of years later, the Roman Empire, beset from without by barbarian hordes and from within by corruption, disintegrated into the darkness of the Middle Ages, Emilia, in addition to contributing as usual to the fall of the forces then in power, had three distinctions. First, Ravenna became, for as long as it lasted, the capital of that refugee government which proclaimed itself the Western Empire. Second, other cities set up more rapidly than most other parts of erstwhile Rome the free city principalities which lasted for close to 1,000 years. Third, one of these free principalities became the world's oldest existing republic—that of San Marino.

The Este family in Ferrara, the Pallavicini in Piacenza, the Bentivoglio in Bologna, the Da Polenta in Ravenna—after the Byzantine influence began to wane—and the famed Malatesta in Rimini, governed their own and nearby towns, for better or for worse, depending largely upon the incumbent ruler and the temper of the people at the moment, until late in the 16th century, when the Papal States absorbed most of them. Parma and Piacenza went over to Farnese rule instead. And the Este, losing Ferrara, managed to retain their tight hold on Modena and Reggio.

The Habsburgs took the place of the Este family, when Austria moved down into Italy and France's Bourbon monarchs won control from the Farnese. The Napoleonic conquest of Italy aroused Emilia's never dormant revolutionary feeling and turned it towards nationalism. This led to the formation of an alliance with Piedmont and the House of Savoy.

From the birth of the Kingdom of Italy until late in 1944 there is little record of any revolutionary resurgence in the province, athough Emilians will tell you with pride that there was always a resistance movement against Mussolini there. In 1944, with the Allies battering at the Apennine gateways to north Italy, Bologna and the region around it became the center of such violent partisan activity as to elicit the Nazis' most vicious reprisals.

Since the end of the war Emilia has become the showcase for the abilities of the Italian communists' administration. The successful coexistence of a liberal commercial tradition and a communist ideology is one of the main characteristics of this region.

From Piacenza to Parma

We will assume that you are starting your journey in the northwest corner of Emilia, the natural route if you come from the north.

Your first stop, obviously, will be Piacenza. Had you been here in about 1565 you would have seen hordes of workmen laboring on the Palazzo Farnese, begun seven years previously by Vignola for the Farnese dukes, of whose dominions Piacenza was then a part. But it is still unfinished today, a colossal, massive remnant of a glory that is no more. The cathedral would have been there then, as it is today, a 12th-century Lombardian-Romanesque structure with a spectacular façade. So, too, would the Lombard Church of Sant' Antonino, and the Palazzo del Comune, in the square, dating from the 13th century. Little else remains.

Two interesting side trips from Piacenza are to Grazzano Visconti, a modern version of a medieval village, noted now for its craftwork, especially wrought-iron and hand-made furniture; and to Velleia Romana, the Roman remains of a small country town, attractively situated. Both these can be reached by bus or train.

You may stop at Fidenza to see its Romanesque cathedral, and if you like thermal baths, go up to Salsomaggiore, which is Italy's chief inland watering place, with the single exception of Montecatini.

Parma, founded by Roman legionaries on the Via Emilia in 183 B.C., was ruled after the barbaric invasions by count-bishops, who in the 12th century built the Romanesque cathedral, to which the octagonal five-story pink baptistery was added in 1196 after the plans of Antelami. When power passed to the town council, the Mayor, Torello da Strada constructed the municipal palace in 1221, a rival center transformed by the Visconti (1346–1448) into a fortress, still facing the Renaissance governor's palace on the Piazza Garibaldi.

In 1545 Pope Paul III Farnese made his son Pietro—born before his father's ordination—Duke of Parma. In the centuries of Farnese rule, Mannerism dominated the arts—most impressively in the church of the Steccata, influenced by Bramante and Michelangelo, and decorated by Parmigianino, who collaborated with Correggio in the frescos in the Church of San Giovanni Evangelista. Correggio's fresco of the Assumption in the dome of the cathedral is one of the great Renaissance masterpieces.

Duke Alexander Farnese, Viceroy of the Netherlands, modeled the citadel at the town's entrance on the fortifications of Antwerp. In 1602 he began the vast Palazzo della Pilotta, which now houses the National Gallery, a superb collection of mainly Italian paintings; the Museum of Antiquities, Etruscan and Roman; the Bodoni Museum, medieval and Renaissance furnishings; and the Palatine Library, some 40,000 manuscripts, incunabula and books. The famed Farnese Theater, built entirely of wood, on the top floor, was so damaged in World War II that it has had to be rebuilt, piece by piece, with the original wood being utilized as much as possible.

Across the huge Piazza Pilotta, in a former palace, is the Glauco-Lombardi Museum, a collection of objects that once belonged to Napoleon's Empress Marie-Louise, who at the Congress of Vienna received the Duchies of Parma, Piacenza and Guastalla. From 1814 to 1847 she resided across the river in the 18th-century Palazzo del Giardino, whose delightful park was laid out by the French architect Petitot. Marie-Louise built the neo-Classical Teatro Regio, where Italy's most demanding opera fans whistle and hoot a tenor off the stage at the drop of a high C.

Halfway southeast to Modena is Reggio Emilia, the Roman Forum Lepidi, with a 13th-century cathedral, several baroque churches and the Parmeggiani Gallery, containing good examples of the work of Veronese, El Greco and Van Dyck.

For lovers of music there is a pilgrimage northwest from Parma. Verdi, whose very name became the rallying cry for Italian independence, was born in Roncole, near Busseto. Busseto is itself an attractive town, with a castle. Verdi's mansion, Sant'Agata, lies on the outskirts.

A different kind of pilgrimage brings gourmets to this area, for its notable concentration of some of Italy's best restaurants.

Modena

Modena lies 24 km. (15 miles) southeast on A1. The Estes added the city to their principality of Ferrara in 1284, together with Reggio. It became the Este capital in 1598, and remained so until the last Este Duke was overthrown by the French in 1797. His daughter married an Austrian Archduke and thus this last acquisition of the uniquely profitable system of dynastic marriages that the House of Austria carried on for centuries was ruled by a Habsburg until 1859.

Modena is reputed to have Italy's highest per capita income, so that it is sometimes called the "mink capital." This wealth accounts for the grand-scale urban renewal program, including a large park designed by a leading English landscape architect. This will further enhance the medieval town center, tranquil squares where fountains play below the 14th-century bell tower, La Ghirlandina, and arcaded streets round the exceptionally fine Romanesque Duomo. The bas reliefs that decorated the arched buttresses are now on display in the small cathedral museum.

In the Palazzo dei Musei, which houses Modena's most important art collections, you will find of especial interest the Biblioteca Estense, which contains a world-famed collection of illuminated manuscripts, bookbindings, rare engravings and incunabula. Both Italian and foreign works are included. The most notable single object, perhaps, is the Borso d'Este Bible, which contains 1,200 miniatures of the Ferrara school of the 15th century. The Galleria Estense is one of Italy's largest, though not most important, art galleries. (Emilian, Venetian and Tuscan primitives; 16th-century Italian, foreign schools, etc.) The vast Ducal palace provided the setting for a brilliant Renaissance court. It is now the Italian Military Academy. A strikingly realistic terracotta *Pietà,* by Mazzoni, is in the church of San Giovanni Decollato. The cherries of nearby Vignola are justly famous.

Bologna

Your next stop will be Bologna. Italy's "Red capital" it is also an important economic center, a focus for learning (Marconi, the wireless inventor was born here) and has been famous for its artistic achievements throughout the ages. It is hard to say which of all these facets will most attract the visitor. Scientists and students will inevitably be drawn to the university, founded in 1119, where the first lessons in human anatomy were given, and where later Galvani, by mere observations of the twitchings of dissected frogs, learned of the flow of electric current. Within the university's walls can still be seen Lelli's two famous limewood anatomical models, carved to perfection because of the dearth and expense of actual corpses, which at that period had to be stolen.

Gourmets, and Bologna is a city of gourmets, will concentrate on the joys of the table, tasting several dishes *alla Bolognese* and drinking some of the marvelous wines of the region. Lovers of art and architecture will wander through the streets, between the Renaissance palaces, into the magnificent churches, around the famous fountains, exploring the rich monuments to Bologna's treasured past.

Of course the ideal traveler would be a rare composite of all three. He would, of course, visit the university, where he would be thrilled by the memory of the 6th-century scholars who revived the study of Roman law. Then he would lunch, very leisurely, at one of the city's fine restaurants, ordering a Bolognese luncheon, *un pranzo alla Bolognese,* and having eaten well, set forth to visit the great Church of San Petronio, one of Italy's most superb Gothic structures. Although the façade is as yet unfinished (it was only started in 1390) the center portal is adorned by Jacopo della Quercia's truly marvelous bas-reliefs of biblical episodes, the Prophets and the Virgin Mary. Within the cathedral, see the chapels by Costa and Onofri and the Renaissance choir.

Although it was made a free city by the Emperor Henry V in 1116, Bologna nevertheless joined the Lombard league against the Hohenstaufen emperors. The leading families indulged, moreover, in endless and ruthless feuds, depending for their survival on some 200 mighty towers, of which only two remain in the Piazza di Porta Ravegnana—the others having suffered from the neighborly warfare—the Torre degli Asinelli, 350 feet high and 7 feet out of the perpendicular, and the truncated Garisenda tower, which lists a frightening 11 feet. From the top of the Asinelli Tower you will get an excellent vista of Bologna's greatness. Nearby are the palaces of the Drapers' Company and the Loggia dei Mercanti. Then there is the Gothic Palazzo Comunale and Renaissance Palazzo del Podestà, while in the restored Palazzo di Re Enzo the son of Frederick II, King Enzo, was jailed until he died after 23 years. (For entry, enquire at the Bologna EPT.)

And there, between them, is the Piazza del Nettuno, one of Bologna's major attractions for its marvelous and magnificent Fountain of Neptune, designed by Giambologna in 1566. Seen together with the Piazza Maggiore, it forms a harmonious ensemble. The statue of Neptune is undergoing restoration, but can be seen as work progresses in the adjacent courtyard, to which it has been removed. It should be back in place by mid-1990.

The Strada Maggiore, bounded almost entirely by medieval houses with their characteristic porticos designed to keep the fussy Bolognesi dry in the rain, leads to Santa Maria dei Servi, of the 15th century, containing Cimabue's *Madonna*. Nearby the church of Santo Stefano—there are seven noteworthy churches in the immediate vicinity—is one of the finest examples of Romanesque architecture in Italy.

The most beautiful private palaces in Bologna can be found on the Via Santo Stefano and Via Zamboni, which leads to the Church of San Giacomo Maggiore, built in the 13th century. The Renaissance Chapel of the Bentivoglio is connected to their family palace by an underground passage. A church of the same period, San Domenico, contains a very beautiful tomb of the saint, whose life is shown on its bas-reliefs by Michelangelo and Niccolò dell'Arca among others. You will certainly want to see the magnificent altarpiece in the Church of San Francesco. Bologna's Art Gallery (Pinacoteca) has a fine collection of the Bologna School and a few outstanding examples of other works such as Raphael's *The Ecstasy of St. Cecilia*. Visit the Museo Civico Medievale as well; it has a collection of classical and medieval pieces and a famous Etruscan *situle*.

The neo-Classical Sanctuary of San Luca is a must for all visitors to Bologna. A unique uninterrupted 4-kilometer portico (a kind of colonnade of 660 arches) will lead you uphill to where the Church contains a venerated Byzantine picture of the Madonna believed to protect the city.

Crossing the Rubicon

The A14 continues 106 km. (66 miles) southeast to the Adriatic. Imola has a few Renaissance monuments and a restaurant that deserves attention. Faenza is known for its typical majolica ware. Its international Ceramic Museum houses an imposing collection of ancient and modern ceramic pieces, including works by Picasso and Matisse. Also worth visiting is Forlì, with its Romanesque Church of San Mercuriale, its bell tower, the splendid tomb of Barbara Manfredi, the Ravaldino Fortress once defended by Catherine Sforza, and its museums and art gallery.

At Cesena the Renaissance Malatesta Library is famed for its book treasures, priceless manuscripts and miniatures. This is a graceful Renaissance building. The Benedictine monastery and the fortress are of great architectural interest and have rich collections of paintings and old manuscripts. The harbor of Cesenatico, built as a port for Cesena, bears the mark of Leonardo da Vinci's genius.

At Savignano stop for a few moments to catch your historical breath. For here is the Rubicon, that little nearly dried-up stream you are passing almost without notice. But it is of this stream that the Roman Senate, fearing its military leaders' power, proclaimed "General or soldier, veteran or conscript, armed person whoever you may be, stop here, and let not your standards nor your arms nor your army cross the Rubicon."

Julius Caesar, weary of the oligarchic rule of the Roman plutocracy—and heavily loaded with debts and ambition—defied the senatorial edict and crying "The die is cast," led his battle-scarred veterans across the Rubicon and on to take virtual imperial control of Rome.

Sigismondo Malatesta, in the 15th century, is responsible for much of Rimini's artistic fame. He preserved a number of Roman monuments and added its finest Renaissance structure when he built the Malatesta Temple in honor of his then mistress, Isotta degli Atti. In 1450 Alberti designed the Malatesta Temple façade, inspired by Rome's triumphal arches. Sigismondo's Castle is another historic monument of the Renaissance period. The famous Francesca da Rimini lived out her sad destiny in the 13th century and was immortalized by Dante in his *Inferno.* You will recall his line, "And the night we read no further." This contains everything about love's natural conclusion in passion, but the passage has been censored wherever it could be, from Dante's time onward. It was sometimes shown by three dots. But Dante's image of the book being put down and closed is by far the most moving conclusion to this tragic tale of Paolo and Francesca. She had married Gianciotto Malatesta by proxy and had fallen in love with Gianciotto's handsome young brother, Paolo. Her jealous husband killed them both with a single blow of his sword. The episode also provided the inspiration for one of Ingres' finest paintings, and a Tchaikovsky overture.

The Bridge of Tiberius over the Marecchia River, and the Arch of Augustus represent important Roman contributions to Rimini's architecture. In addition, recent archeological discoveries have demonstrated that the Roman Amphitheater, of which little remains, was once the largest in Italy, with a seating capacity of 12,000. It is the only one visible in the Emilia-Romagna region. The Romanesque-Gothic Sant' Agostino Church contains important frescos of the Giotto school.

San Marino—Oldest of Republics

Just a few miles away from Rimini—not in Emilia nor even in Italy actually by definition—is the tiny little Republic of San Marino, a hangover from the Middle Ages, which claims the honor of being the oldest republic in the world—oldest still in existence, that is. Its area is only 23 square miles.

San Marino, on Mount Titano more than 600 meters (2,000 ft.) feet above Rimini's bathing beach, clings to its medieval characteristics with a somewhat pecuniary tenacity, as it is its imaginative conservation which has enabled its people to survive financially, rather than various industries ranging from ceramics to cotton yarn and paint. San Marino city boasts three castles, a Government Palace and a fine church, and it has preserved its medieval pomp and circumstance; two Regent Captains are elected for six months to sit with members of the Grand Council. Huge crowds gather for the picturesque investiture ceremony on April 1 and October 1.

It is said that the Republic of San Marino was founded back in the 4th century by a Dalmatian stone cutter named Marino who settled as a hermit on the slopes of Titano. That it survived through all the medieval and Renaissance conflicts is due not so much to its courage as to its acumen. It never sought to expand. When Napoleon offered it more territory—"preserve a sample of Republic"—its citizens politely refused. They preferred their mountain, and nothing but their mountain. The prosperity of the Republic these days depends on tourism and its multifarious activities, but especially stamp production, the postage stamps of San Marino being considered of high quality by the experts, and fun by the average stamp collector.

The town is frankly touristy. If you're looking for authentic atmosphere, go to San Leo 11 km. (7 miles) away. Atop a sheer cliff, San Leo's fortress is a mighty example of military architecture. You can see the small dark cell in which Cagliostro, the charming charlatan, was walled up to die.

Both the town, which has two exceptional and very old churches, and the fortress offer terrific views.

Ravenna

Through Bellaria, Cervia and other seaside resorts you can go from Rimini to Ravenna, capital of the western half of the Roman Empire in the 5th century. After the murder of the first Germanic king, Odoacer, in 493, Ravenna became the capital of the Ostrogoth Kingdom till its reconquest by the Byzantines in 539. Ravenna was sumptuously embellished by Justinian and Theodora, while under subsequent Byzantine governors, called exarchs, the city was the final link between the Pax Romana and the Middle Ages. With the expulsion of the Byzantines by the Longobards and Franks, Europe plunged into "the thousand years of darkness".

Sadly, Ravenna is suffering from a serious subsidence problem, similar to that which afflicts Venice.

The Churches of San Vitale and Sant' Apollinare and the Cathedral's Baptistery are world-famous examples of early Byzantine Christian art, dating back in some cases to the 5th century. San Vitale's mosaics are both unique and wonderful, their style and workmanship the finest in Byzantine art.

Ravenna's cathedral was rebuilt in 18th-century Baroque, except for the 10th-century cylindrical bell tower and the 5th-century octagonal baptistery, with its two tiers of 8 arcades, which support a dome entirely covered with mosaics.

The Pulpit of St. Maximian, an Egyptian ivory work of the 6th century, is in the Archbishop's Palace behind the cathedral. In the Via Baccarini to the left of San Francesco is the tomb of Dante, who found his final safety and home here after being banished from Florence. It was in the *pineta* (pine woods), toward the sea from here, that Dante meditated on the verses of his *Divine Comedy,* and it was near here that Byron was accommodated by the husband of his love, La Guiccioli.

Lovers of Byzantine art will enjoy the wonderful mosaics in the 5th-century Mausoleum of Galla Placidia and in the Chapel of St. Peter Chrysologus.

Before leaving Ravenna see the Church of Sant' Apollinare Nuovo, built by order of Theodoric, the 6th-century King of the Ostrogoths. Theodoric's tomb, a pile of square stones without mortar, covered by a monolithic dome, stands on Via Cimitero. 5 km. (3 miles) away at Classe (route 19 toward Rimini) is the magnificent Basilica of Sant' Apollinare, completed in 549, with striking 6th- and 7th-century mosaics, and an impressive 9th-century bell tower.

North of Ravenna the vast marshes around the lagoon of Comacchio have been reclaimed and the farmland has been protected by pine forests against the encroaching sand-dunes along the coastal road through the string of beach resorts to Venice. The town of Comacchio itself is interestingly picturesque, with canals, tiny bridges and fishermen whose main catch is eels.

Ferrara

The Este family ruled Ferrara from 1208 to 1598, when it was incorporated into the Papal States by Clement VIII. Until then the ducal court

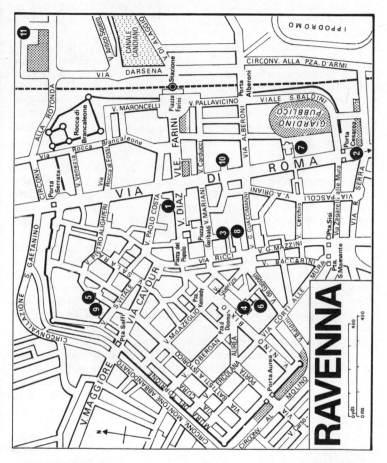

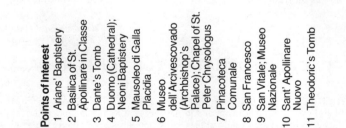

Points of Interest

1 Arians' Baptistery
2 Basilica of St.
 Apollinare in Classe
3 Dante's Tomb
4 Duomo (Cathedral);
 Neoni Baptistery
5 Mausoleo di Galla
 Placidia
6 Museo
 dell'Arcivescovado
 (Archbishop's
 Palace); Chapel of St.
 Peter Chrysologus
7 Pinacoteca
 Comunale
8 San Francesco
9 San Vitale; Museo
 Nazionale
10 Sant' Apollinare
 Nuovo
11 Theodoric's Tomb

had combined culture, elegance and cruelty in the refined Renaissance blend. Niccolò III (1393–1441) killed his wife and her lover. And Ercole I (1471–1505), his successor, tried to poison his nephew, but failed. Niccolò, the nephew, took advantage of his uncle's absence to take over the throne. However, Eleanor of Aragon, Ercole's wife, was not to be taken by surprise and Niccolò was captured and beheaded. Lucretia Borgia, who married Alfonso I, would not seem out of place in the Este family, yet she became the most enlightened and gentlest of princesses. Renée of France became the wife of Ercole (1534–1558). A famous poet, Ariosto (1474–1533), also lived here. His *Orlando Furioso* is still read. Another great writer, Tasso, was a local celebrity as well.

The Castello Estense, still surrounded by its 14th-century moat, is the essence of Ferrara. Four mighty towers protect its halls and salons, which once resounded to the brilliant gatherings of a sophisticated Renaissance court.

The city's 12th-century cathedral is worth a visit. So, too, is the Church of San Francesco. But many appreciate even more the Palazzo Schifanoia, once a pleasure resort for the Este princes. It was finished in 1471 and contains, in its Sala dei Mesi, some remarkable frescos by Cossa. And then there is the Palazzo di Ludovico il Moro, which Rossetti built early in the 16th century. It now contains a very fine archeological museum.

While we are speaking of museums, here are the most important: the Palazzo dei Diamanti, which houses the art gallery, a wealth of works from the Ferrara School (Garofalo, Tura, Roberti); the Museo Civico (in the Schifanoia Palace); and the Cathedral Museum, to which we especially draw your attention because of its two fine paintings by the leading local painter, Cosimo Tura, *St. George Fighting the Dragon* and *The Annunciation.*

You will enjoy visiting two elegant residences, the Casa Romei (15th century, opposite the palace occupied by Renée of France), and the *palazzino* of the Marquis of Este, 16th-century patron of the arts. Not far from the cathedral meanders the medieval Via delle Volte, with its characteristic sequence of awkward arches and river-stone pavement, probably the most picturesque in the city.

The Abbey of Pomposa (48 km., 30 miles, from Ferrara) was originally founded in the 7th century. It has some lovely mosaics and an attractive campanile with a superb view from the top. It is one of those buildings, off the beaten track, which repay a visit by anyone who likes quiet atmosphere.

PRACTICAL INFORMATION FOR EMILIA-ROMAGNA

WHEN TO GO. The weather in Emilia-Romagna comes close to resembling that of Milan. From November through February it is apt to be quite damp and foggy, and July and August are usually unpleasantly hot. Spring and fall are the best seasons.

TOURIST OFFICES. Bellaria: AAST, Via Leonardo de Vinci, at the Palazzo del Turismo (0541–44.108). **Bologna:** EPT, Via Marconi 45 (051–237.414); Via Leopardi 1E (051–236.602); Railway Station (051–372.220); Piazza Nettuno 1/d (051–239.660); CIT, Piazza Martiri 7 (starting point for bus trips) and Central Station; American Express, Via Marconi 45 (051–235.783 and 267.600). **Castrocaro:** AAST, Via Garibaldi 50 (0543–767.162). **Cattolica:** AAST, Piazza Nettuno 1 (0541–963.341). **Cervia:** AAST, Viale Romana 53 (0544–71.781). **Ferrara:** EPT, Largo Castello 28 (0532–21.267 or 35.017). **Forli:** EPT, Corso Repubblica 23 (0543–25.545). **Modena:** EPT, Corso Canalgrande 3 (0543–237.479 or 222.482). **Parma:** EPT, Piazza Duomo 5 (0521–34.735). **Piacenza:** EPT, Via San Sirio 17 (0523–27.398); Piazzetta dei Mercanti 10 (0523–29.324). **Ravenna:** AAST, Piazza San Francesco 7 (0544–36.129); Via Salaria 8 (0544–35.404). **Reggio Emilia:** EPT, Piazza Battisti 4 (0522–43.370). **Rimini:** AAST, Piazzale Indipendenza (0541–24.511); American Express, SIT, Viale Vespucci 127 (0541–271.7 or 237.79). **Salsomaggiore:** AAST, to Viale Romagnosi 7 (0524–78.265). **San Marino:** Ente Governativo del Turismo, Palazzo del Turismo (0541–992.101).

SEASONAL EVENTS. Bologna: The Opera Season starts in February; April sees the International Children's Book Fair; June, a Music Festival; there is a Fashion Show in late Nov.

Parma: Food Fair in Sept.; winter Opera Season.

Piacenza: Opera in Feb.; a traditional pageant in June.

Ravenna: June Musical Summer in Sant'Apollinare in Classe; July–Aug., Organ Festival in San Vitale.

Reggio Emilia: Opera Season Jan. through Mar.; June, streets are decorated for the Flower Display contest; July, the folklore Torneo dei Maggi, repeated in Aug.

Rimini: First half of Sept., Sagra Malatestiana, sacred music festival.

Salsomaggiore: Feb., lively Children's Carnival; June, parade and Battle of the Flowers.

TELEPHONE CODES. You will find the telephone area code for each town against its name in the Hotel and Restaurant listings (after the province name). If there is a different area code from the majority of the establishments—say when a hotel or restaurant is in an outlying place—then the code is given in front of the telephone number.

HOTELS AND RESTAURANTS. The coastal towns of this region are extremely popular as Italian family resorts and are therefore swamped in summer. You would be wise to book well in advance, and even wiser to stay in one of the historic inland cities. In coastal resorts (M) hotels insist on half-board in high season; hotel rates in general here are real bargains. Rimini makes a good base for excursions into the historic hinterland.

You will certainly eat well for less here than you will pay in most of Italy. Even the top category of restaurants offer really excellent value for your lira. Wander out into the remoter areas if you are interested in wine, as there you will find all sorts of interesting local brews.

Regional Food and Drink. The cuisine of this region, everything considered, is the finest and most famous in Italy. The most famous dish is *tagliatelle alla bolognese* or *al ragù,* thin slices of *pasta* made with eggs and served with a succulent ragout, which only the Bolognesi make properly. *Tortellini,* which resemble tiny hats, are stuffed with a mixture of pork, eggs, cheese and spices, and are served either with a ragout or in soup. *Lasagne al forno* are broad thick slices of *macaroni*—with cheese, tomato sauce and meat added—cooked in the oven. *Agnolotti* are squares of *pasta* stuffed with meat, white *ravioli* are filled with *ricotta* (a kind of cottage cheese) and/or such vegetables as spinach or squash.

The cooks of the region also do wonders with meat and fish dishes, *zampone* is a pig's forefoot which has been stuffed with highly seasoned pork. This is boiled for four hours, sliced in one-inch thicknesses and eaten with a *salsa verde* (green sauce) or mustard. *Cotoletta alla bolognese* is a veal cutlet dipped in egg, with a slice of ham and melted cheese topping it. In the Adriatic resorts you will find *brodetto,* a marvelous soup, with quantities of fish and slices of bread floating in it, usually flavored with saffron. Try *piada,* the local bread.

The wines of the region are headed by the red sparkling *Lambrusco*, which comes both sweet and dry. The dry variety is ideal with pasta and meat in general. The amber-colored *Albana* goes very well with fish, and *Sangiovese* is particularly indicated for roasts. A less well-known wine is the *Vino del Bosco*, found around Ferrara. Though red and sparkling, it is good with fish.

Bologna Bologna (051). *Baglioni* (L), Via Indipendenza (225.445). An historic hotel, reopened and refurbished in the grand manner, exuding luxury from its pastel-toned walls hung with old masters. AE, DC, MC, V. *Corona d'Oro* (M), Via Oberdan 12 (236.456). Charming small hotel, centrally located. AE, DC, MC, V. *Royal Carlton* (L), Via Montebello 8 (249.361). Central, ultra-modern elegance. 240 airconditioned rooms; car park. AE, DC, MC, V.

Elite (E), Via Saffi 36 (437.417). Big, modern, on outskirts; sleek, functional airconditioned rooms, suites; piano bar; excellent cuisine in Cordon Bleu restaurant. AE, DC, MC, V. *Garden* (E), Via Lame 109 (522.222). Converted monastery; central but quiet; smallish rooms and baths; cloister. AE, DC, V. *Internazionale* (E), Via Indipendenza 60 (245.544). Central, attractive and efficient. AE, DC, MC, V. *Milano-Excelsior* (E), Via Pietramellara 51 (246.178). Near the railway station; modern, airconditioned; reader-recommended for friendly atmosphere, thoughtful service. AE, DC, MC, V.

Alexander (M), Via Pietramellara 45 (247.118). First class comforts. AE, DC, MC, V. *Dei Commercianti* (M), Via Pignattari 11 (233.052). Newly renovated; close to the cathedral. Rooms with terraces and scenic-view windows. *Nettuno* (M), Via Galliera 65 (247.508). Central and comfortable. AE, DC, MC, V. *Palace*, Via Montegrappa 9/2 (278.954). Breakfast only. AE, DC, V. *Roma* (M), Via D'Azeglio 9 (274.400). Very central; airconditioned. Wholly satisfactory. AE, MC, V. *San Donato* (M), Via Zamboni 16 (235.397). With restaurant. AE

Lembo (I), Via Santa Croce 26 (418.845). 38 rooms, all with bath. *Orologio* (I), Via IV Novembre 10 (231.253). Very central; small, friendly atmosphere. AE, DC, MC, V. *San Felice* (I), Via Riva Reno 2 (557.457). 33 rooms, all with bath or shower. AE, V. *San Giorgio* (I), Via Moline 17 (238.435). 30 rooms with shower. *Tre Vecchi* (I), Via Indipendenza 47 (231.991). Large, comfortable, airconditioned rooms many with bath or shower; good restaurant. AE, V.

Restaurants. This is the top gastronomic city in Italy, yet prices are not high in comparison with Paris or London. *Battibecco* (E), Via Battibecco 4 (275.845). Closed Sat., Sun., 1–25 Aug., 24–31 Dec. Reserve. Behind Palazzo Accursio. Small, serving exquisite food. AE, DC, MC, V. *Cordon Bleu* (E), Via Saffi 38 (423.466). Closed Sun. and Mon. noon. In *Hotel Elite;* excellent, known for inventive cuisine. Reserve. AE, DC, MC, V. *Dante* (E), Via Belvedere 2 bis (224.464). Closed Mon., Tues. noon and 1–19 Aug. Outstanding for atmosphere, service and fine food. AE, DC, MC, V. *Rossi* (E), Via delle Donzelle 1 (279.959). Closed Sun. and July. Near Piazza Maggiore; an excellent spot for exceptional food and wine. Reserve. AE, DC, MC, V. *Grassilli* (E), Via Del Luzzo 3 (222.961). Closed Wed., July, and 24 Dec. to 1 Jan. Classic cuisine carried off to perfection. Reserve. AE, DC, MC, V. *Notai* (E), Via Pignattari 1 (228.094). Closed Sun. Elegant and excellent. AE, DC, MC, V. *Pappagallo* (E), Piazza Mercanzia 3 (232.807). Closed Mon. and 6–24 Aug. Stunningly decorated, fine cuisine, service, wines. AE, DC, V. *Tre Frecce* (E), Strada Maggiore 19 (231.200). Closed Sun. eve., Mon., mid-July to mid-Aug. Medieval surroundings, excellent *pastas*. AE, DC, MC, V.

Alla Grada (M), Via della Grada 6 (523.323). Offers table and counter service. Closed Mon. and Aug. *Antico Brunetti* (M), Via Caduti di Cefalonia 5 (234.441). AE. Closed Sun. eve. and Mon. AE, DC, MC, V. *Bacco* (M), Center-gross (862.451). Lunch only. Closed Sat., Sun., Aug. On outskirts at big commercial center. Caters for businessmen but is worth the trip for classic cuisine with creative touches. *Birreria Lamma* (M), Via de'Giudei 4 (236.537). Closed Wed. Central, popular beer hall where you can eat well. *Buca San Petronio* (M), Via de'Musei 4 (224.589). Closed Wed. eve. and Thurs. Central and quite good. *Da Bertino* (M), Via delle Lame 55 (522.230). Closed Sun. Local favorite for good food at modest prices. AE, DC, MC, V. *Duttòur Balanzon* (M), Via Fossalta 3 (232.098). Closed Sun. Central, also has *tavola calda*. AE, DC, V. *Guido* (M), Via Andrea Costa 34 (418.907).

Closed Mon. Offers table and counter service. AE, DC, V. *Imer* (M), Via San Giuseppe 3. Classic and comfortable. *La Cesoia da Pietro* (M), Via Massarenti 90 (342.854). Closed Sun. eve., Mon. Menu offers variations on culinary themes. AE, DC, V. *Leonida* (M), Vicolo Alemagna 2 (239.742). Closed Sun. Excellent truffles. *Luciano* (M), Via Nazario Sauro 19 (231.249). Closed Wed. Varied menus; good value. Meals carefully prepared and nicely served. *Osteria de'Poeti,* Via de'Poeti 1. Excellent wines and rustic food. *Palmirani* (M), Via Calcavinazzi 2. A must. *Silverio* (M), Via Nosadella 37/a (330.604). Closed Mon. Good atmosphere and creative cuisine, not the place for traditional Bolognese cooking. AE, DC, MC, V.

Bertino (I), Via delle Lame 55 (522.230). Closed Sun. Popular neighborhood trattoria. Simple meals, prepared with care. *Da Carlo* (I), Via Marchesana 6 (233.227). Closed Tues. Charming medieval surroundings; delicious game. AE, DC. *Da Cesari* (I), Via de'Carbonesi 8 (237.710). Spirited local clientele; imaginative specialties. AE, DC. *Ruggero* (I), Via degli Usberti 6 (236.056). Closed Sun., Aug. Popular for fine roasts and boiled meats; good fish on Fridays. *Trattoria di Re Enzo* (I), Via Riva di Reno 79 (234.803). Closed Sun. Cheerful spot with Neapolitan fare; wonderful seafood.

Osterias. *Delle Dame,* Via delle Dame. Warm atmosphere and live music. *Picci.* Fireplace and tasty *crostinos.*

Busseto Parma (0524). Verdi's home and hub of gourmet heaven. *Due Foscari* (M), piazza Carlo Rossi 15 (92.337). Tenor Carlo Bergonzi's family runs this fine hotel with restaurant. MC, V. *Ugo* (M), Via Mozart 3 (92.307). Closed Mon., Tues. Great local cuisine. AE, DC.

At **Roncole,** *Guareschi* (M), (92.495). Lunch only; open for dinner Sat. eve. Closed Fri., July and 20 Dec–31 Jan. Rustic and renowned. Reserve.

Cattolica Forli (0541). Beach resort; less smart than Rimini and Riccione. *Caravelle* (E), Via Padova 6 (962.416). Modern; beach cabanas and pool; 45 rooms with bath. AE, DC, MC, V. *Victoria Palace* (E), Viale Carducci 24 (962.921). All rooms with bath; beach facilities. AE, DC, MC, V. *Beau Rivage* (E), Via Carducci 82 (963.101). Beach facilities. AE, DC, V.

Diplomat (M), Viale del Turismo 9 (967.442). Good value; beach. AE, DC, MC, V. *Napoleon* (M), Viale Carducci 52 (963.439). Very comfortable. AE, DC. *Negresco* (M), Viale del Turismo 6 (963.281). Very comfortable. *Royal* (M), Viale Carducci 30 (961.133). Pool, beach facilities. *Maxim* (M), Via Facchini 7 (962.137). More basic. *Nettuno* (M), Via Rasi Spinelli. *Plaza* (M), Viale Oriani. *President* (M), Via Gran Bretagna. *Columbia* (I), Via Spinelli 36 (961.493). Most rooms with shower. *Nora* (I), Via Carducci 14 (961.120). Most rooms with bath.

Restaurants. *Lampara* (M), at port (963.296). Closed Nov. and Tues. off-season. Some fish dishes pricey. AE, DC, V. *Moro-Da Osvaldo* (M), Via Mazzini 91 (962.438). Closed Wed. Good seafood, reasonably priced. AE, DC, MC, V.

Cervia Ravenna (0544). Beach resort of which Milano Marittima is virtually a part, rather more elegant and cosmopolitan than Cervia proper.

At **Cervia,** *Beau Rivage* (M), Lungomare Grazia Deledda 116 (971.010). Open 29 May to 11 Sept. Facing sea. *Buenos Aires* (M), Lungomare Grazia Deledda 130 (973.174). Open April to 15 Oct. Modern. AE, DC, MC, V. *Excelsior* (M), Viale Roma 74. Private beach. *Nettuno* (M), Lungomare D'Annunzio 34 (971.156). Open May to Sept. Sea view, own beach, garden. AE, DC, V. *El Trocadero* (M), Lungomare D'Annunzio 32. All rooms with shower.

At **Milano Marittima,** *Aurelia* (E), Viale 2 Giugno 34 (992.082). Open May to Sept. Pool, beach, tennis. AE, DC, V. *Gallia* (E), Piazzale Torino 16 (994.471). Open May to 22 Sept. Pool, tennis. AE, DC. *Mare e Pineta* (E), Viale Dante 40 (992.262). Beach, tennis, riding in own pine grove. Open 14 May to 19 Sept. AE, DC, MC, V. *Le Palme* (E), VII Traversa 12 (994.562). Smart but informal; well-furnished; pretty garden with tennis; two steps to beach.

Deanna (M), Viale Matteotti 131 (991.365). Open May to Sept. Comfortable; pleasant rooms; tennis courts, garden, short walk to beach. AE, DC, MC, V. *Della Nazione* (M), Via Toti 13 (991.562). Excellent private beach.

Cesenatico Forli (0547). *Cristallo* (M), Via Carducci 98 (83.476). *Des Bains* (M), Via dei Mille 52 (81.119). Open 15 May to 20 Sept. Attractive terrace, short walk to beach. AE, DC, V. *Esplanade* (M), Viale Carducci 120 (82.405). Open 15 May to Sept. Attractively furnished and well-equipped; modern; overlooking shore boulevard and beach. MC, V. *Grande* (M), Piazza Costa 1 (80.012). Large, smart; on beach, tennis, dancing. *Internazionale* (M), Via Ferrara 7 (80.231). Open June to Sept. Right on beach; pool, tennis. *Torino* (M), Viale Carducci 55 (80.044). Open 15 May to Sept. On Beach. AE, DC, MC, V. *Villa Maria* (M), Via Carducci 96. On beach. 34 rooms, most with shower.

Restaurants. *Gallo-Da Giogio* (M), Via Baldini 21 (81.067). Closed Wed., Oct., Nov. Excellent seafood; check can mount up. AE, DC, MC, V. *Gambero Rosso* (M), molo Levante (81.260). Favorite for seafood; some dishes pricey. AE, DC, MC, V.

Ferrara Ferrara (0532). Art city. *Ripagrande* (M), Via Ripagrande 21 (34.733). Tops. AE, DC, MC, V. *Ferrara* (M), Piazza della Repubblica 4 (33.015). Central, modern. *Touring* (M), Viale Cavour 11 (26.096). 36 rooms, most with bath or shower. AE, DC, V. *De La Ville* (M), Piazzale Stazione 11 (53.101). Modern, airconditioned. On edge of town.

Restaurants. *Astra* (M), Viale Cavour 55 (26.234). In *Hotel Astra.* Good food, try *pappardelle.* AE, DC, MC, V. *Da Giovanni* (M), largo Castello 32 (35.775). Closed Tues. and 3–23 Aug. Very good. DC, V. *Europa* (M), Corso della Giovecca 49 (21.438). Good dining in whimsical 17th-century building at town's center. *Grotto Azzurra* (M), Piazza Sacrati 43 (37.320). Closed Sun., 2–10 Jan., 1–15 July. Also very good. *La Provvidenza* (M), Corso Ercole 1 d'Este 92 (21.937). Closed Mon. Excellent *cappelletti. Ristorantino* (M), Vicolo Agucchie 15 (25.922). Closed Sun., Mon. noon, 10 Aug. to 6 Sept. Somewhat sophisticated; try *capellacci di zucca* (squash ravioli). *Le Stanze* (M), Via Vignatagliata 61 (48.993). Closed Mon. Classic Ferrara cuisine; excellent homemade desserts. AE, DC, V. *Pizzeria Pulcinella* (I), Via Borgoleoni. Good *pizzas.*

Forli Forli (0543). *Della Città* (M), Via Fortis 8 (28.297). All rooms have bath or shower. AE, DC, MC, V. *Principe* (M), Via Bologna 153 (34.630). Just outside center, modern, good. AE, DC.

Restaurants. *Principe* (M), Via Bologna 153 (34.630). Closed midday, Thurs, Sun, Aug. Fine hotel restaurant. AE, DC. *Roma* (M), will serve you a more than adequate meal. *Vecchia Forlí* (M), Via Maroncelli 4 (26.104). Closed Mon. Central; good classic cooking. AE, DC, V. *Pinin* (I), Via Mameli 15. Good value.

Gabicce Mare Pesaro e Urbino (0541). Beach resort. High season 1 July to 31 Aug. *Capo Est* (E), Vallugola (953.333). Smart resort hotel in quiet location on hillside; pool, tennis. *Alexander* (M), Via Panoramica 35 (961.166). Bright, modern decor; 46 rooms with bath; pool, garden. DC, V.

Bahia (M), Via Panoramica 5 (961.377). Modern; pool. *Tre Ville* (M), Piazza Giardini (961.361). All rooms with shower, balcony and sea view; stairs down to sandy beach; some noise from adjacent piazza.

Restaurants. *Cambusa* (M), at port (962.784). Closed Wed. off-season and Nov. *Tic Tac* (M), Viale della Vittoria 77 (963.044). Closed Tues. Family-run, totally unpretentious; delicious food.

Imola Bologna (0542). **Restaurant.** About 32 km (20 miles) from Bologna, *San Domenico* (E), Via Sacchi 1 (29.000). One of Italy's best and most gracious dining places, with exquisite food and ambience, and impeccable service; all in all, well worth a detour. Closed Mon. 1–14 Jan., 25 July–17 Aug. AE, DC, V.

Lido delle Nazioni Ferrara (0533). Well-planned resort, with horse riding, nightclub and artificial lake for power-boat racing. Beaches here for sunning only, as water is heavily polluted. *Delle Nazioni* (M) (39.276). Best; with pool, tennis, beach; specializes in spacious family-size apartments which will take parents and up to 4 children easily; good children's recreation areas. *Club Spiaggia Romea* (I) (85.130). Tennis, beach, excellent value.

Marina di Ravenna Ravenna (0544). Resort, beach fine but water polluted. *Park* (E), Viale delle Nazioni 181 (431.743). Open 1 Apr.–31 Oct. Best; pool, tennis, access to beach through pinewoods. AE, DC, V.
At **Marina Romea,** *Corallo* (M), Via Italia 102 (446.107). Open June–Aug. Overlooking sea and pines; pool.
Restaurant. *Al Pescatore-Saporetti* (M), Via Natale Zen 13 (430.208). Closed Tues., Jan. Modest exterior hides elegant seafood restaurant. Prices at top of category. AE, DC.

Misano Adriatico Forlì (0541). Budget beach resort. *Gala* (M), Via Pascoli 8 (615.109). Small, pleasant rooms with showers. AE, DC, MC, V. *Savoia* (I), Via della Repubblica 1 (615.319). AE, V. Comfortable; on shore boulevard. *Villa Rosa* (I), Via Litoranea 4 (613.601). On the beach; sea view. Open May to Sept.

Modena Modena (059). *Canalgrande* (E), Corso Canalgrande 6 (217.160). Central; luxurious apartments; period decor in public rooms; modern airconditioned bedrooms with radio, TV. AE, DC, MC, V. *Fini* (E), Via Emilia Est 441 (238.091). Just outside center, modern decor, 93 airconditioned rooms. AE, DC, MC, V.
Donatello (M), Via Giardini 402 (351.331). Good. AE, DC, MC, V. *Estense* (M), Via Berengario 11 (242.057). Central, modest but comfortable. AE, DC, V. *Roma* (M), Via Farini 44 (222.218). Very central. AE, DC, MC, V. *San Geminiano* (I), Via Moreali 41 (210.303). Basic.
Restaurants. This city vies with Bologna for the top gastronomic position in this region. *Borso d'Este* (E), Piazza Roma 5 (214.114). Closed Sat. lunch, Sun. and Aug. Excellent dining. AE, DC, V. *Bianca* (M), Via Spaccini 24 (311.524). Closed Sat. noon, Sun. and Aug. Fine local dishes. AE, DC. *Fini* (M), Largo San Francesco (223.314). Closed Mon., Tues., Aug., 24–31 Dec. Ranks with the finest of Italy; try their *pasticcio di tortellini,* and if you're still hungry go on to the *cotoletta alla bolognese* or *zampone.* AE, DC, MC, V. *Osteria Toscana* (M), Via Gallucci 21 (211.312). Closed Thurs. and Aug. Northern Italian cuisine; varied menu. AE. *Vinicio* (M), Via Cantelli 3 (217.810). Closed Sun., Mon. noon and Aug. Brilliant new star on Modena's culinary horizon. DC.

Parma Parma (0521). Reserve early for fairs in May and Sept. *Palace Maria Luigia* (E), Viale Mentana 140 (281.032). Handsome modern furnishings. AE, DC, MC, V. *Park Stendhal* (E), Piazzetta Bodoni 3 (208.057). Overlooks Palazzo Pilotta; 45 airconditioned rooms, with bath. AE, DC, MC, V. *Park Toscanini* (E), Viale Toscanini 4 (289.141). Older, but comfortable; car park.
Button (M), Strada San Vitale 7 (208.039). Central; breakfast only. AE, DC, MC, v. *Torino* (M), Borgo Mazza 7 (281.047). Very central; comfortable; garage; breakfast only. AE, DC, MC, V.
Restaurants. Here's a third city fighting hard for top honors in the food line in this region - remember Parma ham? *Brozzi* (M), Via Trento 11 (771.157). Closed Sat. and July. Near the station. Unassuming decor, tasty specialties. *Canon d'Or* (M), Via Nazario Sauro 3 (285.234). Closed Sun. night, Mon. and 15–31 Aug. Good food and atmosphere. *La Filoma* (M), Via XX Marzo 15 (34.269). Elegant ambiance, comfortably palatial surroundings. Try the *filetto al mandarino.* AE, DC, V. *Dei Corrieri* (M), Strada Conservatori 1 (34.426). Closed Sun. Fine old trattoria. *Greppia* (M), Strada Garibaldi 39 (33.686). Closed Thurs., Fri., mid-June to mid-July. Central; highly thought of for local cuisine. AE, DC, MC, V. *Parizzi* (M), Strada Repubblica 71 (285.952). Closed Sun. eve., Mon., 21 July to 17 Aug. Outstanding even in honored company; everything is good. AE, DC, V. *Antica Osteria con cucina Parma Rotta* (I), Via Langhirano 158 (581.323). Closed Sun. from June to Sept; Mon. from Oct. to May. One of the oldest of the osterias; delicious lamb and kid on the spit. *Locanda del Quatiere* (I), Borgo Cocconi 59/a (35.653). Closed Mon. Casual, con-

vivial spot. Imaginative twists on classic dishes. AE, DC, MC, V. *Sant'Ambrogio* (I), Viale delle 5 Piaghe (24.482). Closed Mon. Rustic trattoria in town center.
At **Felino,** try *Hostaria Bianchini* (M). Excellent local specialties.

Piacenza Piacenza (0523). *Roma* (E), Via Cittadella 14 (23.201). Central, air-conditioned; restaurant overlooks city; garage. AE, DC, MC, V. *Cappello,* Via Mentana 6/8 (28.211). Good location; comfortable.
Restaurants. *Antica Osteria del Teatro* (E), Via Verdi 16 (23.777). Closed Sun., Aug. Gourmet specialties, exceptional quality. AE, DC. *Berté* (M), at Quarto (560.105). Rustic. Closed Mon. and 15 July to 15 Aug. *Peppino* (M), Via Roma 183 (29.279). Closed Mon., Aug. AE.

Ravenna Ravenna (0544). Important art city, famed for its mosaics. *Bisanzio* (E), Via Salara 30 (27.111). Near San Vitale; good, air conditioned; breakfast only. AE, DC, MC, V. *Jolly* (E), Piazza Mameli 1 (35.762). Near station and Sant'Apollinare; large, air conditioned, comfortable. AE, DC, MC, V.
Argentario (M), Via Di Roma 45 (22.555). Central for sightseeing; breakfast only. *Centrale Byron* (M), Via 4 Novembre 14 (22.225). Central; breakfast only. AE, DC, MC, V. *Trieste* (M), Via Trieste 11 (421.566). Short walk from center; comfortable.
On Via Romea, Strada Statale 16, 2.5 km (1½ miles) outside town, *Motel Romea* (M) (446.061). 36 rooms with shower. *Ponte Nuovo* restaurant. AE, DC, MC, V.
Restaurants. *Bella Venezia* (M), Via 4 Novembre 16 (22.746). Closed Sun. Probably the best. AE, DC, MC, V. *Tre Spade* (M), Via Rasponi 35 (32.382). Closed Mon., July 20–Aug. 25. Noteworthy, but can be expensive. AE, DC, MC, V. *Ca' de Ven* (I), Via Ricci 5 (30.163). Closed Mon. Vast wine cellar serving thick pancakes and delicious coldcuts.

Reggio Nell'Emilia Reggio Nell'Emilia (0522). *Astoria* (E), Viale Nobili 2 (35.245). Beside park, airconditioned, garage; good grillroom. AE, DC, MC, V.
Europa (M), Viale Olimpia 2 (49.190). A bit out of the way; unassuming, recent, airconditioned, garage. AE. *Posta* (M), Piazza Cesare Battisti 4 (32.944). Closed Aug. No restaurant. Garage. AE, DC, MC, V. *Villa al Poggio* (M), Via Boccaccio. Pleasant, good value.
Restaurants. *La Casseruola* (E), Via San Carlo. Tops, host Ivano helps you choose. *Girrarosto* (E), Viale Nobili 2 (35.245). In Hotel Astoria. Fine. AE, DC, MC, V.
Campana (M), Via Simonazzi 14/b (39.673). Good regional dishes. *Ermete* (M), Via Emilia San Pietro 16. In quiet courtyard, family-run, recommended. *Maiorca* (M), Viale dei Mille 44/d (35.203). Traditional specialties. AE, DC, MC, V. *Tamurè* (M), Via Caggiati 8/b (30.722). Has delicate and delicious cuisine. AE, DC. *Zucca* (M), Piazza Fontanesi 1 (485.718). Wine-red walls, *art nouveau* decor; try *tortelli di zucca.* Closed June and July 20–Aug. 20. AE, DC.

Riccione Forli (0541). Noted beach resort; lavishly supplied with excellent accommodations. *Abner's* (E), Lungomare della Repubblica 7 (600.601). Modern, by sea, heated pool, beach. AE. *Atlantic* (E), Lungomare della Libertà 15 (601.155). Posh, modern, on shore boulevard; heated pool. AE, DC, MC, V. *Promenade* (E), Viale Milano 67 (600.852). Richly appointed; beach front, attractive garden. AE, DC, MC, V. *Savioli Spiaggia* (E), Viale D'Annunzio 2/6 (43.252). Overlooking marina, reputation for comfort and service. Heated pool, solarium, terraces, launches for excursions. AE, DC, MC, V.
Des Bains (M), Via Gramsci 56 (601.650). A few steps from beach; pleasant dining terrace. *Club* (M), Viale d'Annunzio 58 (42.105). On main avenue at heart of resort activity. Good, medium-sized hotel. *Dory* (M), Viale Puccini 4 (642.896). Central but on quiet street near beach; terrace bar. MC, V. *Daniel's* (M), Lungomare della Costituzione (43.227). Across shore boulevard from beach. All rooms with balcony, sea view. *Lungomare* (M), Viale Milano 7 (41.601). Facing beach. Open 20 May to 20 Sept. AE, DC, MC, V. *Vienna e Touring* (M), Viale Milano 78 (601.700). Well-run hotel near beach at center of resort. Heated pool, tennis. AE.

Restaurants. *Pavone Azzurro* (M), Viale D'Annunzio 72. Large and lively; open late. *Pescatore* (M), Via Ippolito Nievo 11 (42.526). Closed Tues. off-season, Nov. Bright decor, excellent seafood; can be a bit pricey but worth it. v. *Punta de l'Est* (M), Viale Emilia 73 (42.448). Closed Mon., Nov. Good. AE, DC, MC, V.

Rimini Forli (0541). Cosmopolitan and usually crowded beach resort. This list is not exclusive—there are many other excellent establishments. *Grand* (L), Piazzale Indipendenza 2 (56.000). Truly deluxe; beautifully appointed; with private beach and pool, lovely garden, terraces, tennis, piano bar. AE, DC, MC, V. *Ambasciatori* (E), Viale Vespucci 22 (55.561). Overlooking sea; heated pool. AE, DC, MC, V. *Imperiale* (E), Viale Vespucci 16 (52.255). Open all year. Elegant; quiet rooms, sea views; heated pool. AE, DC, MC, V. *Waldorf* (E), Viale Vespucci 28 (54.725). Open all year. On shore boulevard, but quiet; attractive public rooms; rooftop pool. AE, DC, MC, V.

Admiral (M), Via Pascoli 145 (381.771). Near beach, well-run and functional. AE, DC, MC, V. *Brown* (M), Via Pola 29 (55.495). Open all year. Central but away from crowds. Terraces; parking. *Biancamano* (M), Via Cappellini 1 (55.491). Just behind *Grand*, a few steps from beach; comfortable, well-furnished, small pool in garden. *Apogeo* (I), Via Oriani 11 (84.552). Open all year. Central, fairly quiet location. Pool.

Restaurants. *Belvedere* (E), Molo Levante (50.178). Open 20 March to 20 Sept. Closed Mon. Seafood. AE, DC, MC, V. *Nello al Mare* (E), Lungomare V. Emanuele 12. Facing the sea. Closed in winter. *Elio* (E), Via Vespucci 35. Top quality food. *Bicocca* (M), Via Santa Chiara 105. Popular with locals. *Dallo Zio* (M), Via Santa Chiara 16 (52.325). Closed Wed., July. Near Arch of Augustus, an informal seafood restaurant. *Tonino* (M), Via Ortaggi 7. Across bridge of Tiberius from center. Seafood.

Salsomaggiore Terme Parma (0524). *Grand Hotel e Milano* (L), Via Dante 1 (770.141). Big, smart, elegant; quiet location in park with heated pool, spa treatments. AE, DC, MC, V. *Centrale Bagni* (E), Largo Roma 4 (771.142). Large, well-furnished. *Porro* (E), Viale Porro 10 (78.221). In tranquil hillside park; indoor pool, solarium, spa treatments. AE, DC, MC, V.

Daniel (M), Via Massimo D'Azeglio 8 (770.241). Pleasant, modern; quiet location. AE, DC. *Valentini* (M), Viale Porro 10 (78.251). Large, with all spa facilities. AE, DC, MC, V. *Suisse* (I), Viale Porro 5 (79.077). Small.

Restaurants. *Alle Querce* (M), Via Parma 85 (771.184). At Campore; cordial host, fine food. AE, DC, V. *Il Guscio* (M), Borgo Castellazzo 3 (70.290). Closed Tues. Good, some dishes pricey. v.

At **Castell'Arquato** nearby, *La Rocca* (M) (803.154). Well worth the trip. Reserve. Closed Wed. and July. Also *Faccini,* at Sant'Antonio (896.340). Closed Wed. and July. Outstanding family run trattoria.

San Leo Pesaro an Urbino (0541). Medieval town and fortress. In Marches region but near Rimini (bus service) and San Marino.
Restaurants. *Castello* (M) (916.214). Closed Fri. and Nov. On main square; unpretentious but good. v. *La Rocca* (M), on road to fortress (916.241). Closed Mon. and Oct. Rustic, local dishes.

San Marino Repubblica di San Marino (0541). Southwest of Rimini, independent republic.
Restaurants. *Righi La Taverna* (M), Piazza della Libertà (991.196). Closed Wed. off-season and 15 Dec. to 1 Feb. Good country cooking, rustic decor. Snack bar on street level, restaurant upstairs. AE, DC, MC, V. *Quercia Antica* (M), Via Capannaccia (991.257). Country style. Other good restaurants, all (M), along the Rimini–San Marino highway: *Da Ettore, La Nonna, Da Mario.*

Secchia Modena (059). *Motel AGIP* (M), on Autostrada del Sole (A1) (518.221). Pride of the chain; big, well-furnished. AE, DC, MC, V.

Sestola Modena (0536). Summer and winter sports resort. *San Marco* (E) (62.330). Open 20 Dec.–15 Mar.; 20 June–10 Sept. Tennis; in quiet pine woods, relaxing atmosphere in a converted Renaissance villa, complete with Italian garden. Low rates for category. AE, DC, MC.

GETTING THERE AND AROUND. By air. Bologna airport (Borgo Panigale) is the region's central entry point by air. It is 4 miles out of town and the downtown air terminal is at the rail station, with a bus service available. There is an airport also at Rimini (Miramare), quite close to town (4 miles), with the terminal in the Piazza Tripoli.

By train. Bologna is the focal point of train travel in this area, as well as being a major crossing point of the traffic from east to west in the upper part of the peninsula. Main line services from Milan, Venice, Florence and Rome pass through, as does the service up the east coast from the Brindisi, Ancona and other major ferry ports.

There are excellent services to major points in the region, Modena, Parma, Ferrara, for example—with a fast train to Ravenna.

By car. There could hardly be an easier region for getting from one point of interest to another. SS9, the ancient Via Emilia, technically starts north of Milan, but it is advisable to use the autostrada ring road to by-pass the city and get onto the Roman road just short of the junction with the autostrada del Sole, which travels with it past Piacenza, Parma, Reggio Emilia, Modena and Bologna to end, for our purposes, at Rimini.

If you want an exploring base, try either Bologna or Parma.

LIGURIA

The Two Rivieras and Genoa

The region of Liguria is contained in a narrow strip of coastline stretching 349 km., 217 twisting miles, from the French border to Tuscany and never more than 40 km. (25 miles) wide. The sea that beats upon these shores has given them their character and their history. What every schoolboy knows is that Genoa, set in the heart of this rocky coast, is the birthplace of Christopher Columbus. And America's discoverer was only one, and not the first nor the last, in a long line of seafaring men whose activity centered in the ports of the two Rivieras of Italy.

Liguria is favored by year-round mild climate; this and the ease with which it can be reached from the rest of western Europe, has helped to make it one of the most popular regions in Italy for visitors. An impressive number of foreigners—British, American, French—have permanent residences here. For centuries, its charm has inspired poets and artists, many of whom came for a brief visit and stayed on. Italians from inland cities flock to its beaches in summer or maintain their villas along its length. The flavor of the area is cosmopolitan, a mellow blend of rustic with sophisticated, provincial with smart set, primitive and old-fashioned with luxurious and up-to-date. The eye is caught, the attention is held by the contours of the coastline, curving serpentinely in an east-west arc from Ventimiglia to La Spezia; by the Ligurian Alps, plunging in sheer cliffs or sloping gradually to the sea; by the glamor and color of the resorts, the busy ports, the stately yachts against the skyline and the grandiose view across the Gulf of Genoa from a hairpin curve on the highway.

Exploring Liguria

Liguria takes its name from the Liguri, the tribe that peopled the area 700 years before Christ. Centuries before the Liguri, prehistoric man lived in caves and left his traces in graffiti, rock paintings and bone implements in the Grimaldi caves of Ventimiglia, at the western end of Liguria, and on the island of Palmaria, off La Spezia.

By the 3rd century B.C., when the Romans conquered Liguria, Genoa was already an important trading station. The Via Aurelia was built to link Rome and what is now France. The Middle Ages and the Renaissance saw the rise of Genoa as a great seaport, and the history of the city— jumping-off place for the Crusades, commercial center of tremendous wealth and prestige, strategic bone of international contentions—was of key importance to Europe.

Thereafter, Genoa declined in rank as a seapower. Napoleon reduced all of Liguria to an ineffective "family estate of the Bonapartes," as Tolstoy speaks of it in *War and Peace*. When the Emperor was finally defeated at Waterloo, the region became part of Piedmont and reacquired its separate identity only after the unification of Italy.

In modern times, Liguria has enjoyed enormous popularity as a region, rather than for isolated cities. In fact there are parts of it that are now swamped with holiday-makers turning what were once attractive small seaside towns into Italian versions of Coney Island or Blackpool. Some parts of, for example, the Ponente Riviera have become especially popular with German and other European package tour operators for their family trade. However, large sections are still fairly unspoilt—and here, as in many other areas, the watchword is "head for the hills."

The Western (Ponente) Riviera

Approaching Liguria by car or train from France, you've barely crossed the border into the Riviera di Ponente before you come upon prehistoric and contemporary landmarks. The first structure you see on the left of the ancient Roman Aurelia highway is the Voronoff Castle, where the Russian scientist raised monkeys to use in his famous glandular experiments in rejuvenation. A little farther, on the right, a left takes you to the Grimaldi Caves, home of prehistoric man.

Just before the border town of Ventimiglia are the Hanbury Gardens at Mortola, filled with the living flora of 5 continents; the entire western coastline from Ventimiglia to Genoa is known also as the Riviera of Flowers, because flower cultivation is a major industry here. The climate here is the mildest of the two Ligurian coasts. The high Maritime Alps, sloping to the sea, break the winds from the north, and the resort towns that follow—Bordighera, Ospedaletti, San Remo, Taggia, Imperia, Diano Marina—are temperate the year round.

A word about Ventimiglia: ancient *Albintimilium* was a pre-Roman settlement and contains important archeological remains in the largest museum of its kind in Liguria. In the town proper are vestiges of a Roman theater; a provincial road swings up the Nervia River valley to the lovely-sounding medieval town of Dolceaqua (Sweetwater), with a ruined castle, and Pigna, also of Roman times.

Bordighera, first town in Europe to grow date palms, has a magnificent mile-long promenade with marvelous views up and down the Italian and

French coasts. It's one of the Riviera's most attractive resorts, with lovely old—but well-kept—buildings in lush gardens. There's an atmosphere of calm elegance that's favored by English-speaking tourists.

An interesting small place to visit is Coldirodi, near Ospedaletti, once the headquarters of the Knights of Rhodes, whose picture gallery contains paintings by such masters as Guido Reni, Veronese and Velazquez.

San Remo is the largest center in this half of Liguria and the most popular. The town's only business is tourism and there are a hundred hotels and pensions of every category, facilities for yachts of all tonnages, miles and miles of beach, lavish public gardens, an attractive Old Town, a 13th-century cathedral, swimming pools, and a funicular railway that takes you up to the Mount Bignone skiing resort 1,287 meters (4,221 ft.) in 45 minutes.

An unusual half-day excursion from San Remo leads to Bussana Vecchia, a picturesque ghost town that was partially destroyed by an earthquake in 1887. The inhabitants packed up and left en masse after the quake. Now once-lively houses are empty shells, overgrown by wild flowers and guarded by the bell tower of Bussana's church.

Imperia, the provincial capital, is really two towns: Oneglia, the lower, center of Italian olive oil production, and Porto Maurizio, above it, with a broad avenue named after Theodore Roosevelt, who stayed here. 8 km. (5 miles) inland, at Pontedassio, is the Spaghetti Historical Museum, which is not an elaborate practical joke but a quite serious enterprise and interesting to all lovers of *pasta*. A 1279 document mentions a basket of "macaronis", thus disproving the Chinese connection, as Marco Polo returned only 16 years later from the Far East. Further north are the ski runs at Monesi and nearby areas, with gradual slopes for beginners and speedier ones for practiced skiers. In August, the natives of Imperia stage a spectacular local custom: a sort of sea battle called the *Palio del Mare*.

Diano Marina, today a beach resort, is a very old town, dating back to Roman times. The fortified part has a walled castle (*castello*) that beetles over the lower city. The Knights of Malta still meet in the castle. This is one of the coastal spots that has suffered from the explosion in the package tour trade.

The province of Savona begins just beyond Imperia. It contains many of Liguria's well-known coastal resorts, like Laigueglia, Alassio, Loano, Pietra Ligure, Finale Ligure, Spotorno, and others better-known to Italian than to international tourists. This is a region which caters to English-speaking as well as French visitors. You will certainly have no difficulty here over language, and you will probably be able to find comfortable hotels without great difficulty. But do not expect peace and quiet.

Savona is industrial. Unless you're terribly interested in one of the largest European collections of cable cars for unloading coal, it will hold no great attraction, most of the year. At Easter time, on Good Friday, there is a procession of artistically carved wooden coffers depicting episodes of the Passion. The carvings, by celebrated artists of the Genoese school, are of great value.

Pegli, on the western outskirts of Genoa, has summer homes of the old patrician Genoese families—Villa Durazzo Pallavicini, Villa Doria—that are worth seeing, set in ample parks and gardens. Villa Doria houses a Naval Museum, while Villa Pallavicini has an Ethnographic Museum; for the average tourist, the collections serve only as an excuse for having a look at these princely residences.

Genoa

The natives of this city have nothing to be ashamed of, really, in the old Latin saying: *"Genuensis, ergo mercator"* —Genoese, therefore merchant. Out of their maritime and commercial enterprises, they made themselves wealthy and lavished that wealth on beautifying their city. Because of its commercial reputation, Genoa is too frequently overlooked as a city of beauty rivaling that of many a recognized artistic center. But discerning writers have spoken of Genoa the Proud and of the majesty of her buildings, set in a great semi-circle around the port.

The port area, like port areas all around the world, is what tourist guides usually define as picturesque and what a sociologist will flatly call slums. Ships and installations stretch for miles on either side of the Maritime Station. From Cape Faro, on the left, to the mouth of the Polcevera, there are 20 km. (13 miles) of port area: docks, freight elevators, plants, warehouses, railroad tracks and public services.

Immediately behind the docks, the lower city begins. On the Piazza Caricamento, the Gothic Palazzo San Giorgio, once seat of a powerful bank and money lender to European sovereigns, stands aloof from the porticos of Sottoripa, where steamy little trattorias and nautical supply storerooms abound. The historic quarter behind Sottoripa is one of Genoa's oldest and most characteristic sections, a maze of alleys known as *carugi,* many flanked by old palaces seven or eight stories high that keep these little lanes in perpetual shadow. It's a fascinating part of the city—quiet, for no cars can pass through these byways, yet animated with the business of everyday life and commerce. On the aristocratic Via Lucoli, a bit wider than the other carugi, elegant ladies shop and promenade in the late afternoon. On the Piazza San Matteo at the heart of the quarter is a group of houses dating from the 12th century and belonging to the Doria family, one of the most important in Genoa's history. Many of the Dorias, including the illustrious Andrea, are buried in the crypt of the little medieval church of San Matteo.

Quite close by, the cathedral of San Lorenzo was begun in 1118; the marvelous chiaroscuro effects of its Gothic portals and the black and white stone bands of the facade are typical of the Genoese architecture. The bell tower, cupola and ceiling were added in the 16th century, and its chapels and treasury are full of works of art. The treasury especially is an excitingly modern museum, combining medieval richness in an imaginative setting. Just behind the cathedral, the Palazzo Ducale is a much-rebuilt edifice that was once residence of Genoa's doges, or dukes.

Across the large modern Piazza de Ferrari, the handsome Via Venti Settembre opens its procession of fantastically decorative palaces in the Art Nouveau style, and the Via Dante leads to picturesque Porta Soprana, with its medieval towers and adjacent garden, where there is a small medieval house that is supposed to be Christopher Colombus' birthplace.

From the Piazza de Ferrari you can walk up the Via Venticinque Aprile to the Piazza Fontana Marose, where the modern center of Genoa begins. Turn into the Via Garibaldi, named for the Ligurian-born national hero; it's a relatively short street, compact with princely mansions and lovely villas, where you can catch glimpses of lush gardens. The Renaissance Palazzo Tursi is Genoa's city hall, where some relics of Columbus and Paganini's violin are preserved. Step inside the portal to take a peek at the lovely courtyard and loggia. The Palazzo Bianco (White Palace) and Palazzo Rosso (Red Palace) are stunning old buildings that have been beautifully adapted to house important painting collections.

The Via Cairoli and Via Bensa will lead you to the enormously rich church of the Annunziata, with a severe neoclassic facade that by no means prepares you for the splendidly frescoed vaults and domes of the Baroque interior, some of which was irreparably damaged by World War II bombs.

Just outside the church, to the right, is the beginning of the Via Balbi, another of Genoa's typically aristocratic (and traffic-noisy) main streets. You should visit the colorful Palazzo Reale, with its beautifully furnished picture gallery, splendid Mirror Gallery and garden terrace commanding a fine view of the port.

Beyond the Principe Station is the huge Palazzo Doria, built by Genoa's admiral Andrea Doria in the 1500s. A richly decorated residence with lovely formal gardens, it has all the flavor of Genoa's mighty days of empire, when her fleets sailed to all points of the known world and beyond, across uncharted seas on historic missions of exploration.

Before you leave the center of Genoa to explore its more modern quarters and panoramic hilltops, you may want to visit the National Gallery at Palazzo Spinola in the Piazza Pellicceria; here are antique furnishings and decorations and some very good paintings, including Antonello da Messina's *Ecce Homo*. There are three interesting churches in the old part of town above the Porta Soprana, where some striking modern edifices tower over centuries-old streets and dwellings. The delicate octagonal bell tower of Romanesque San Donato and the unusual majolica-studded steeple of Sant'Agostino stand out above the rooftops. The majestic Romanesque basilica of Santa Maria di Castello is worth a visit. Have a look at Sant'Agostino's handsome new art museum and at the Chiossone Museum's oriental collections.

You can get a good overview of the city from the top of the Granarolo funicular, actually a cog railway that climbs to one of the fortified gates, Porta Granarolo, in the 17th-century city walls. You start from Piazza Principe, behind the Principe Station on Piazza Acquaverde, and in 15 minutes you are almost 1,000 feet up, with a fine view. To get the even better view from Righi, you will have to take a bus or taxi; the Righi funicular from Largo Zecca will remain closed for a complete overhaul through 1989 and perhaps even longer.

The Eastern (Levante) Riviera

The landscape changes; the hills begin to drop sharply to the sea, the curves in the road wind tighter around sparkling little bays and inlets and the general impression is less of sedateness, more of ruggedness.

Quarto dei Mille, in the suburbs of Genoa to the east, is of historical interest as the starting point of Garibaldi's thousand-man expedition, which liberated Sicily and led to the unification of Italy. Nervi is the oldest winter resort on the eastern Riviera. A two-mile cliff walk, chiseled out of the solid rock, is its greatest pride, and here, too, you can take hot sea baths, if that's your cup of tea. Nervi is famous for its parks, which combine luxuriant vegetation, historic palaces and gorgeous sea views. The towns of Bogliasco, Pieve Ligure, Sori and Recco are lively and colorful, if less exploited. Camogli is an attractive spot, noted, amongst other things, for the celebration of the *Festival of San Fortunato,* in May, when there is a wonderful fry-up of freshly caught fish in two huge frying pans, each 12 feet in diameter.

Portofino and Rapallo

At Camogli, the main road (S1) leaves the coast and goes overland to Rapallo branching down to Portofino by way of Santa Margherita and Paraggi. Of all these resorts, Portofino is without doubt the smartest place on the entire Ligurian coast. It had long been a favorite with artists, yachtsmen and some of the more discerning members of high society, and when the Lido of Venice started to slide down the slippery social slope, the knowledgeable took to Portofino instead. Here they were not likely to be crowded out again, except by day trippers, who come in their hundreds, for it is a small place and it has no beach. But it has beauty—the narrow inlet where the yachts lie, the brilliant blue of the water, and clouds of flowers shrouding the buildings that climb the heights on either side. At night it is a little paradise.

Before the foreigners arrived, Portofino was a little fishing village and its cove was filled with highly-colored fishing boats, not with yachts. They are there still, side by side with the luxurious craft of the newcomers. Above, a castle broods, and in the Chapel of St. George lie bones of that saint. On his feast day, April 23, the reliquary is carried through the streets, bands bray and drums pound, and the local inhabitants have a grand time. This region is also headquarters for the literary set, until 1956 headed by the witty critic Sir Max Beerbohm, who lived for many years at Rapallo.

There are side trips you won't want to miss while you're in this region. Tradition can take you back to nearly legendary times when Richard the Lionheart passed by here and stayed at Portofino "on his way to Syria," as in the song.

But first, it's the scenery you will relish. We recommend a stroll to the lighthouse at sunset. It's a pleasant walk, up the little stairway that climbs from the port toward San Giorgio. The view from this point will make you want to go farther. Walk along the lighthouse path, to the right of the church. From the lighthouse itself you will see the whole coast stretched out before you all the way to La Spezia.

San Fruttuoso is wedged right at the foot of Mount Portofino. A boat from Rapallo, Portofino or Santa Margherita will take you there, though you could follow a footpath from Portofino. But it's a good walk—from four to five hours roundtrip depending on your pace. Walking has its rewards. You'll see the fine lines of boats in the port and the Abbey built by the Benedictines of Monte Cassino. In the cloister there is the Dorias' tomb, a work that shows the transitional period between the Romanesque and Gothic styles. A little farther on you will look down and see right through the transparent waters to the bronze statue of the *Christ of the Depths,* lying sunken in the sea before the village.

Down the coast from Rapallo, Chiavari is a low-key resort, center of the orchid-raising industry. Ligurian sailors brought the art of weaving macramé towels, with long, hand-knotted fringes from Arabia. They still make them here, as well as craftsmanlike chairs and furniture. From Chiavari, a provincial road goes north by way of Borgonovo and Borzonasca to the skiing resort of Santo Stefano d'Aveto at 1,004 m. (3,295 ft.).

Sestri Levante has a beach with soft, fine sand, and a wooded promontory joined to the mainland by a narrow strip of land. The promontory is the private park of a local hotel; there are other excellent hotels and boarding houses in the town itself.

From Sestri, the Via Aurelia climbs steeply through the Bracco Pass 613 m. (2,011 ft.), offering a broad panorama of the Gulf of Genoa before the road slides down again to La Spezia, at the southeastern tip of Liguria. Another highway, the N370, branches off just outside Sestri Levante and hugs the coast all the way to La Spezia. Well engineered, it gives you the chance of visiting all the little spots, especially those in the Cinque Terre.

The Cinque Terre

Boats take you up the coast from Portovenere to the towns of the Cinque Terre—the Five Lands—Riomaggiore, Manarola, Corniglia, Vernazza and Monterosso, most developed of the five, with its 20 hotels and pensions and good beaches. The towns are also linked by train from Genoa—about an hour's ride away. The trip by rail through the Cinque Terre is in tunnels all the way, with the train popping out briefly at each little port.

This 10-km. (6-mile) stretch of coast below densely wooded hills is still relatively unspoilt, though possessed of picturesque fishing harbors nestling among the steep rocks, old churches, secluded coves, grapevines on terraced hillsides. You can visit all the towns by car on the N370, although you may find that one or two will need the last little spurt on foot. They are all full of character and worth seeing. Monterosso is the largest, with its twisty streets, attractive views and huge giant, like a piece of statuary left over from a de Mille epic. You can walk along the cliffs to the next town, Vernazza, though the going is a bit rough in places. In fact, if you have the legs for it, you can visit all five towns this way.

The Cinque Terre is an area we highly recommend for anyone who wants to relax in fairly simple surroundings. The isolation of centuries is now firmly broken and troops of visitors pour in—but on the right day one can still enjoy the delights of local food, glorious scenery, friendly people and a gentler pace. Make sure that you go well equipped with stout shoes!

La Spezia next along the coast, is an important naval base with charms of its own that appeal to poets. Illustrious authors—Dante, Petrarch, Shelley, Byron, D'Annunzio, D.H. Lawrence—have lingered here or have written about Spezia's Gulf of Poets, although, of course, that was before La Spezia became the big, busy town it is now.

Portovenere, at the tip of the peninsula closing the Gulf of La Spezia's western side, is a picturesque fishing village with a castle and some delightful medieval houses. You can reach it by road along a highway winding across the tops of the cliffs overlooking the naval installations on this side of the gulf. It is already, however, a favorite excursion spot at weekends. Boat excursions can be made from here to three off-shore islands—Palmaria, Tino and Tinetto—all with ancient remains.

Lerici

On the eastern shore of Spezia Gulf is Lerici, with more than a touch of Tuscany about it. This was an old Pisan village, and its castle is a rare example of Italian medieval military architecture, with shining strips of alternating black and white stone. It was from Lerici's Villa Magni that Shelley set out on the tragic sailing trip in which he drowned.

The last stretch of road from La Spezia leads southeast to the ancient episcopal town of Sarzana and the Etruscan/Roman ruins of Luni, on the very edge of Tuscany. Sarzana has a number of historic churches, filled with art and relics, including that of the blood of the Savior. At Luni, the remains of an amphitheater, a basilica and baths testify that this was once a prosperous Roman settlement. In 1955, an ancient altar apparently dedicated to the worship of the moon was discovered here, but the epoch is uncertain.

The Hinterland

The hill towns and resorts are frequently disregarded by the guide books and tourist agencies. Yet a case can be made for the hinterland. For one thing, you'll meet an entirely different type of Italian, locals who are less commercially minded, and vacationers who've done the more obvious beach resorts and show a friendly sense of adventure that takes them to new and unexploited places. There is contemplative peace in the wooded hills of Liguria that is lacking along the coast. And there are other activities than swimming or lolling in the sun: fishing, for instance, in gurgling mountain streams, mountain climbing and walks along rambling paths that lead unexpectedly to a dim, cool grotto in the woods, or a rustic sanctuary or chapel, or to a breathtaking view for miles over a valley rolling leisurely to the sea. In summer, the air is cooler and you sleep better at night.

There are good roads from the seaside towns: Ventimiglia, Bordighera, San Remo, Taggia, Imperia. They wind their way amidst scenery resembling a miniature Switzerland, leading in an hour to altitudes of 900 to 1,200 meters (2,000 to 4,000 ft.) above sea level, to woods of chestnut and beech trees and stately pines. Perinaldo, Baiardo and Colle di Nava are three such places in the province of Imperia; San Romolo, above San Remo, is in a pine wood at an altitude of 786 m. (2,579 ft.).

Sassello, due north from Savona, is 385 m. (1,263 ft.) up in a fertile hollow, surrounded by wooded mountains. From here there are a number of walks and excursions to Madonna di Bei Baià, Mount Beigua, Mount Reixa and Bric Berton, localities which were sacred to tribal gods in a past so distant that Romans were a novelty in these parts. Other places where there are hotels are Calizzano, Bardineto, Dego, Millesimo, Stella and Urbe, all within driving distance of Savona.

The Levante Riviera is connected by several roads through mountains and forests to Piacenza, Parma and the Milan-Bologna motorway.

PRACTICAL INFORMATION FOR LIGURIA

WHEN TO GO. Liguria is an all-year-round tourist area. A strip of coastland swinging in an arc about Genoa at its center, protected by the mountains beyond from the cool breezes of the north, it enjoys a climate allegedly milder than that of other regions in the same latitude. It is thus a region where you may take refuge from the cold in winter, but also where the presence of the sea prevents the summer from being intolerably hot. The bathing beaches throughout the region are extremely crowded in July and August; in winter, too, quite a number of visitors frequent the resorts of the Riviera di Ponente, westward from Genoa.

TOURIST OFFICES. Alassio: AAST, Via Gibb 26 (40.346) and at rail station on Piazza Savona (43.043). **Bordighera:** AAST, Palazzo del Parco (162.322). **Camogli:** AAST, Via Venti Settembre 33 (770.235). **Chiavari:** AAST, Corso Assarotti 1 (310.241). **Diano Marina:** AAST, Giardini Ardissone (496.956). **Finale Ligure:** AAST, Via San Pietro 14 (692.581).

Genoa: AAST, Via Porta degli Archi 10/5 (541.541); also at Brignole rail station (562.056) and at Principe rail station (262.633).

Imperia: AAST, Via Matteotti 22 (60.730). **Lerici:** AAST, Via Roma 47 (967.346). **Nervi:** AAST, Piazza Pittalunga 4 (321.504). **Ospedaletti:** AAST, Viale Regina Margherita (59.085). **Portofino:** AAST, Via Roma 35 (69.024). **Rapallo:** AAST, Via Diaz 9 (51.282). **San Remo:** AAST, Largo Nuvoloni 1 (85.615). **Santa Margherita Ligure:** AAST, Via Venticinque Aprile 2/b (287.485). **Sestri Levante:** AAST, Via Venti Settembre 33 (41.422). **La Spezia:** EPT, Viale Mazzini 47 (36.000). **Spotorno:** AAST, Via Aurelia 43 (745.128). **Varazze:** AAST, Viale Nazioni Unite (97.298). **Ventimiglia:** AAST, Via Cavour 61 (351.183) and rail station (358.197).

SEASONAL EVENTS. Camogli: the May Fish Fair sees shoals of fish fried in a huge pan in the main piazza.

Genoa: the prestigious Euroflora flower and garden show is held here every four years, (next in 1989); while Oct. is the month of the internationally renowned Boat Show.

Nervi: the International Ballet Festival is held in the beautiful parks here in Jul.
San Remo: as elsewhere, Feb. is the time for a colorful carnival.
Savona: carnival in Feb.
La Spezia: the Palio del Golfo, a famous rowing contest, is held in Aug.

TELEPHONE CODES. You will find the telephone area code for each town against its name in the Hotel and Restaurant listings (after the province name). If there is a different area code from the majority of the establishments—say when a hotel or restaurant is in an outlying place—then the code is given in front of the telephone number.

HOTELS AND RESTAURANTS. The coastal area, with its popular tourist resorts, is comparatively expensive and hotels will often insist on half-pension in the high season. The interior is a fascinating area with few hotels—but the ones there are are reasonable, both in cost and comfort. There's plenty of good eating in small, fairly cheap, trattorias.

Regional Food and Drink. The Ligurian regional cuisine is one of the most appetizing in Italy—not too heavy, and, in keeping with the character of a coastal area, plentiful in fish. Throughout Italy you will find many fish dishes which declare their origin by the label *alla Genovese.*

One dish which can only be made by the Genoese (they say so themselves) is *pesto,* a sauce made of fresh basil and garlic, mixed by pestle and mortar with pine nuts and sharp cheese, and a fine local olive oil - with variations, some very fishy (anchovies, that is). It is excellent with *lasagnette,* or *trenette,* more widely known as *linguine. Cima alla Genovese* is breast of veal stuffed with eggs, cheese and vegetables.

Mushrooms grow in abundance in the Ligurian hills and a variety of dishes are made with them. Try also the *Torta Pasqualina,* of artichokes and eggs.

Liguria does not produce much wine, nor that of the best of the Italian vintages, but it has a few which might be noted. Its best wine region is that of the Cinque Terre, near La Spezia, which produces a dry white wine that is almost golden in color. The area around Savona produces the white *Pigato* and the pleasantly light *Rossese,* a dry red. In most restaurants you'll find the very dry white *Vermentino Ligure.*

Alassio Savona (0182). Beach resort. *Diana* (E), Via Garibaldi 110 (42.701). Open 1 April to 20 Oct. Pricey front rooms have fine sea view; back rooms get bad rail noise. Indoor pool, beach facilities. AE, DC, MC, V. *Mediterraneo* (E), Via Roma 63 (42.564). Open 1 April to 15 Oct. On sea; garden terraces, beach facilities; some road noise. AE, MC, V. *Spiaggia* (E), Via Roma 78 (43.403). Open 20 Dec. to 15 Oct. Overlooking sea; beach facilities; some road noise. AE, MC, V. *Puerta del Sol* (E), Via Boni 87 (42.618). Smallish, very comfortable; pool.

Beau Sejour (M), Via Garibaldi 102 (40.303). Overlooking beach; comfortable rooms, delightful terrace. *Ideale* (M), Corso Dante 45 (40.376). In town, near beach. Open 1 May to 15 Oct. *Majestic* (M), Corso Leonardo da Vinci 300 (42.721). Open 20 April to 16 Oct. Large, comfortable; beach facilities.

Eden (I), Passeggiata Cadorna 20 (40.281). Open 1 Feb. to 31 Oct. On beachfront, smallish; pleasant dining terrace; beach facilities. AE, MC. *Torino* (I), Via Torino 25 (40.616). Reader-recommended; beach facilities.

Restaurants. *La Palma* (E), Via Cavour 5 (40.314). Closed Tues. Open 23 Dec. to Nov. 7. Small, reserve; caters to smart clientele with excellent food and service. AE, DC. *La Capanna* (M), Via Genova 29 (44.088). Closed Wed. off-season. Open 1 March to 15 Dec. Small, reserve; local cuisine. AE, V. *La Liggia* (M), Via Aleramo 3 (469.076). Closed Mon. Open 11 March to 6 Jan. Attractive terrace. MC, V. *Al Mare* (M), Porticciolo Ferrari (44.186). Closed Mon. Fine seafood restaurant of yacht club.

Ameglia La Spezia (0187). 24 km. (15 miles) from La Spezia, *Locanda dell'Angelo* (E), Viale Venticinque Aprile, between Sarzana and Marinella (64.391). One of Italy's best; excellent cuisine and carefully selected wines. About 90,000 lire per person. AE, DC, MC, V. Now has 37-room hotel (M) in handsome modern villa.

Bordighera Imperia (0184). Elegant resort of the Riviera di Ponente. *Cap Ampelio* (E), Via Vergilio 5 (264.333). Open 16 Dec. to 14 Oct. On hillside overlooking town and sea; smart, modern decor, attractive grounds, heated pool. AE, V. *Del Mare* (E), at Capo Migliarese (262.201). Open 23 Dec. to 31 Oct. Large, handsome modern hotel in elevated position overlooking sea; gardens, sea-water pool, beach club, elegant panoramic restaurant. AE, V.

Astoria (M), Via Tasso 2 (262.906). Small, pleasant, on hillside; quiet, well-furnished; garden. Open 21 Dec. to 31 Oct. AE. *Britannique et Jolie* (M), Via Regina Margherita 35 (261.464). Open 20 Dec. to 25 Sept. Comfortable, traditional, with garden. MC. *Excelsior* (M), Via Biamonti 30 (262.970). Open 20 Dec. to 15 Sept. Quiet and attractive.

Aurora (I), Via Pelloux 30 (261.312). Open 20 Dec. to 15 Sept. Central; attractive, garden. AE, MC. *Villa Elisa* (I), Via Romana 70 (261.313). Open 20 Dec. to 20 Oct. Lovely villa above town in quiet garden; well appointed rooms with bath. AE, MC, V. *Jean Pierre* (I), Via Bellavista 4 (260.668). Small, clean; reader-recommended.

Restaurants. *Le Chaudron* (E), Piazza Bengasi 2 (263.592). Closed Mon. Reserve. Delightful atmosphere, delicious food. AE, MC, V. *La Reserve* (E), Via Arziglia 20 (261.322). Closed Sun. evening and Mon. Open 20 Dec. to 1 Nov. Seaside view and setting; innovative and classic dishes. AE, DC, MC, V.

Chez Louis (M), Corso Italia 30 (261.602). Closed Tues. On pretty boulevard; good for light lunches. DC, V. *Romano* (M), Piazza del Popolo 15 (261.682). Closed Wed. Good trattoria. *Piemontese* (M), Via Roseto 8 (261.651). Closed Tues. Open 18 Dec. to 5 Nov. AE, DC, V.

Camogli Genova (0185). Picturesque port. *Cenobio dei Dogi* (E) (770.041). Open 1 March to 6 Jan. Outstanding for quiet location overlooking gulf; elegant appointments, beautiful park and seaside terraces; pool, tennis. AE.

At **Ruta,** above Camogli, *Portofino Vetta* (E) Via Gaggini 8 (772.281). Open 1 March to 31 Oct. Well-furnished, 12-room haven; good restaurant.

Restaurants. *Gai* (E), Piazzetta Colombo (770.242). Closed Thurs. and Jan. Reserve. Small; seafood only. AE, DC, MC, V. *Rosa* (E), Largo Casabona 11 (771.088).

Closed Tues. Open 15 Dec. to 30 Sept. On sea, with beautiful view; good food. AE.
Vento Ariel (E), Calata Porto (771.080). Closed Wed. and Feb. Reserve. Tiny place
serving the day's catch of fish. AE, DC, MC, V.
Camogliese (M), Via Garibaldi 78 (771.086). Closed Wed. off-season and Nov.
Seaside veranda. *Tony* (M), Salita San Fortunato (770.110). Closed Wed. and Oct.

Chiavari Genova (0185). Harbor and resort. *Giardini* (M), Via Vinelli 9
(313.951). Little atmosphere but comfortable. AE, DC, MC, V. *Monterosa* (I), Via Mari-
netti 6 (300.321). Large, modest; pleasant atmosphere.
Restaurants. *Copetin* (E), Piazza Gagliardo 15 (309.064). Closed Tues. evening,
and Wed. and mid-Jan. to Feb. Seafood only; best in town. AE, MC. *Gargantua* (M),
Piazza Roma 48 (306.167). Closed Wed. Local cuisine. AE. *Rosetta* (M), Via Nino
Bixio 5 (306.533). Closed Sun. evening, Mon., Feb. and March. Good.
At **Leivi**, 7 km. (4 miles) north, *Ca Peo* (E) (319.090). By reservation only. Closed
Mon., Tues. noon and 11–30 Nov. Atmosphere of gracious country house; excellent
cuisine; one of region's best. V.

Cinque Terre La Spezia (0187). Five picturesque towns on sea.
At **Monterosso**, largest town, *Porto Roca* (E) (817.502). Open 1 March to 7 Nov.
Lovely situation on headland. AE, MC, V.
Restaurants. Most close during the winter. *Il Gigante* (M) (817.401). Open 15
March to 15 Oct. AE, DC, V. At **Manarola**, *Da Aristide* (M) (920.000). *Marina Piccola*
(M) (920.103). AE, DC. At **Vernazza**, *Gambero Rosso* (M) (812.265). *Taverna del
Capitano* (M) (812.201).

Diano Marina Imperia (0183). Beach resort. *Diana Majestic* (E), Via Oleandri
15 (495.445). Open 1 April to 31 Oct. Modern, balconies, on private beach; bright
smallish bedrooms, gardens and pool.
Bellevue Méditerranée (M), Via Ardoino 2 (495.089). Open 19 Dec. to 5 Nov.
On beach; pleasant rooms; pool, garden. MC. *Golfo e Palme* (M), Via Torino 12
(495.096). Open 1 May to 31 Oct. On beach; quiet, attractive. AE, DC, MC, V. *Sasso*
(M), Via Biancheri 7 (494.319). Pleasant, quiet, short walk to beach. AE, MC, V.
Astra (I), Via Filzi 30 (497.011). Open 20 Dec. to 15 Oct. Simple, pool. *Gabriella*
(I), Via dei Gerani 9 (403.131). Open 1 May to 10 Oct. Quiet, nice garden, beach
facilities.
Restaurants. *Pesce d'Oro* (E), Corso Garibaldi 7 (496.516). Closed Mon. off-
season. Seafood specialties. AE, DC, MC, V. *Il Caminetto* (M), Via Olanda 1 (494.700).
Closed Mon. Good atmosphere. AE, DC, MC, V. *Candidollo* (I), Diano Borello
(494.700). Closed Mon. lunch, Tues. A few kilometers inland, a good value spot
with wonderful views.

Finale Ligure Savona (019). **Restaurants.** *Ai Torchi* (E), Via Annunziata 12,
at Finale Borgo (690.531). Closed Tues. and Feb. Delightful old setting, fine food.
V. *Osteria del Castel Gavone* (M), at Perti Alto (692.277). Closed Tues. and Jan. Terrace, with beautiful view. MC.

Genoa/Genova Genova (010). Most hotels are on noisy streets; ask for a quiet
room. *Bristol Palace* (E), Via Venti Settembre 35 (592.541). In heart of city, rather
traditional elegance. AE, DC, MC, V. *Savoia Majestic* (E), Via Arsenale di Terra 5
(261.641). Facing Principe station; elegant appointments; spacious rooms, best in
category. AE, DC, MC, V.
City (M), Via San Sebastiano 6 (592.595). Very central, but quiet; modern and
comfortable. AE, DC, MC, V. *Viale Sauli* (M), Viale Sauli 5 (561.397). Near Brignole
station; comfortable and pleasant. No restaurant. AE, DC, MC, V. *Vittoria-Orlandini*
(M), Via Balbi 45 (261.923). Near Principe station, in slightly elevated position with
a view. AE, DC, MC, V.
Rio (I), Via Ponte Calvi 5 (290.551). Central, in old part of city; basic comforts.
AE, DC, MC, V.

Restaurants. *Aladino* (E), Via Ettore Vernazza (566.788). Closed Sun. Central. Good classic cooking. AE, DC, V. *Cardinali* (E), Via Assarotti 60 (870.380). Closed Sun. and Aug. Reserve. Known for quality meats, fine cuisine. AE, DC, MC, V. *Gran Gotto* (E), Via Fiume 11 (564.344). Closed Sun. and Aug. Classic choice for regional dishes. AE, MC, V. *La Santa* (E), Vico Indoratori (293.613). Closed Sun. and Aug. Reserve. Small, intimate, good atmosphere; fine seafood. DC, V. *Zeffirino* (E), Via Venti Settembre 20 (591.990). Closed Wed. Attractive place, cordial service. AE, DC, MC, V.

Da Franco (M), Archivolto Mongiardino 2 (203.614). Closed Sun. and Aug. Colorful, typical. *Da Genio* (M), Salita San Leonardo 61 (546.463). Closed Sun. and Aug. Good trattoria; regional cuisine. *Da Mario* (M), Via Conservatori del Mare 35 (297.788). Closed Sat. and Aug. In old *caruggi* district; popular for seafood. AE, MC, V. *Il Cucciolo* (M), Viale Sauli 33 (546.470). Closed Mon. and Aug. Near Brignole station; some Truscan specialites. AE. *Lino* (M), Via San Martino 11 (311.052). Closed Sun. and 15 Aug. to 15 Sept. Classic, unpretentious trattoria. *Osteria Pacetti* (M), Borgo Incrociati 22 (892.848). Closed Mon. and Aug. Just behind Brignole station; local specialties, atmosphere. AE, DC. *Primo Piano* (M), Via Venti Settembre 36 (540.284). Closed Sun. and Aug. Central, attractive, favored by businessmen. AE, DC, V.

On the sea at **Boccadasse,** *Gheise* (E), Via Boccadasse 29 (319.097). Closed Mon. and 25 July to 25 Aug. Popular; fine grilled specialties. *Da Vittorio* (E), Belvedere Firpo 1 (312.872). Closed Mon. Seaside dining. AE, DC.

Imperia Imperia (0183). **Restaurants.** *Lanterna Blu* (E), at Porto Maurizio, Via Scarincio 32 (63.859). Closed Wed. off-season and Sept. On little port, *simpatico,* fine for fish. AE, DC, MC, V. *Nannina* (E), Corso Matteotti 56 (20.208). Closed Sun. eve. and Mon. Well-prepared seafood. AE, DC, V.

At **Oneglia,** *Albatross* (E), Piazza Nino Bixio 1 (24.611). Closed Mon. Creative fish dishes. AE, DC, MC. *Salvo Cacciatori,* Via Viessieux 14 (23.763). Closed Mon. and 1–15 Oct. Fine seafood. AE.

La Spezia La Spezia (0187). Large town and naval base. *Jolly* (E), Via Venti Settembre 2 (27.200). Modern and comfortable; good views of bay. AE, DC, MC, V. *Astoria* (M), Via Roma 139 (35.122). Adequate. AE, DC, MC, V.

Restaurants. *Carlino* (M), Piazza Battisti 39 (32.291). Closed Sun. evening, Mon. and 15–31 Aug. Good choice of local specialties. AE, DC, V. *Dino* (M), Via Da Passano 19 (21.360). Closed Sun. evening, Mon. and 20 June to 10 July. Central, good. AE. *La Posta* (M), Via Don Minzoni 24 (34.419). Closed Sat., Sun. and Aug. One of the best in town. AE, DC, MC, V.

Lerici La Spezia (0187). Picturesque resort on bay of La Spezia. *Shelley* (M), Lungomare Biaggini 5 (968.204). Comfortable, good views; some noise from road. AE, DC, MC, V. *Italia* (M), Piazza Garibaldi (966.566). Attractive old building; good central location on port; no elevator. AE, DC.

Restaurants. *Conchiglia* (M), Piazza del Molo (967.334). Closed Wed. and Dec. Reserve. Small place on port, excellent for seafood. AE, DC, MC, V. *Due Corone* (M), Via Mazzini 14 (967.417). Closed Thurs. and Jan. On port. AE, DC, MC. *Da Paolino* (M), Via San Francesco (967.801). Closed Mon. and Sept. Very attractive place; good atmosphere; seafood specialties, some pricey. AE, MC.

Nervi Genova (010). Elegant seaside resort, suburb of Genoa. *Astor* (E), Via delle Palme 16 (328.325). Smart, very comfortable; lovely garden. AE, DC, MC, V. *Esperia* (M), Via Val Cismon 1 (321.777). Closed Nov. Modern, all rooms with terrace; solarium, gardens.

Giardino-Riviera (M), Via Ancona 2 (328.581). Small, very attractive setting. *Villa Bonera* (I), Via Sarfatti 8 (326.164). Comfortable rooms in lovely 17th-century villa.

Restaurants. *Harry's Bar* (E), Via Somma 13 (326.074). Closed Tues. and Sept. Reserve. Small, smart; international cuisine. AE, MC. *Patan* (E), Via Oberdan 157 (328.162). Closed Wed. and Aug. Typical trattoria, good local dishes.

Marinella (M), Passeggiata Anita Garibaldi 18 (321.429). Closed Fri. and Tues. evening. On seaside promenade, good seafood. AE, DC, MC, V.

Ospedaletti Imperia (0184). Seaside resort. *Rocce del Capo* (E), Via Colombo 102 (59.733). Small, very comfortable; indoor/outdoor pools, beach facilities. DC, MC, V. *Petit Royal* (M), Corso Regina Margherita 86 (59.026). Open 20 Dec. to 21 Sept. Pleasant, small, a bit old-fashioned. AE, MC.

Portofino Genova (0185). Very fashionable resort; no beach. All hotels must be booked way ahead. *Splendido* (L) (269.551). Very attractive location above village in luxuriant park; beautifully decorated; very smart clientele. Open 15 March to 28 Oct. AE, DC, MC, V. An alternative is *Portofino Vetta* (E), at Ruta (*see* Camogli). *Piccolo Hotel* (E) (69.015). A relaxed and friendly hotel which attracts young people. AE, DC, MC, V.
San Giorgio (M) (69.261). Open 1 March to 31 Dec. Small, quiet. AE, DC, MC, V.
Restaurants. *Batti* (E), Vico Nuova (69.379). Closed Fri. and Dec. to Jan. Picturesque and expensive *osteria*. *Navicello* (E), Salita della Chiesa (69.471). Closed Tues. and Nov. Just off main piazza. Reserve for both. *Il Pitosforo* (E) (69.020). Closed Jan., Feb., Tues. Waterfront restaurant serving fish only.
At **Paraggi,** *Carillon* (F.) (86.721). Evenings only, open 1 Jan. to 30 Sept. *The* place for very chic, very expensive suppers.

Portovenere La Spezia (0187). Very picturesque port; interesting old castle. *Royal Sporting* (E) (900.326). Open 15 April to 30 Sept. Modern, good views, all resort amenities. AE, DC, MC, V. *San Pietro* (M) (900.616). At old castle, interesting *art nouveau* decor; old-fashioned; wonderful views. AE, MC.
Restaurants. *Iseo* (M), on port (900.610). Closed Wed. and 1 Jan. to 28 Feb. AE, DC, MC. *Da Mario* (M), on port (900.215). Closed Mon. evening, Tues. and Nov. Seafood specialties. *Taverna Corsaro* (M), on port (900.622). Closed Thurs. AE, DC, MC, V.

Rapallo Genova (0185). Favorite seaside resort, sandy beach. *Bristol* (L), Via Aurelia 369 (273.313). Palatial and posh; pool, park. Open 21 Dec. to 31 Oct. AE, DC, MC.
Astoria (M), Via Gramsci 4 (273.533). Central, smallish. AE, DC, MC, V. *Moderno* (M), Via Gramsci 6 (50.601). Lovely old villa with terraces; modern rooms. DC, MC, V. *Riviera* (M), Piazza Quattro Novembre (50.248). Open 21 Dec. to 1 Nov. Central, best in category. AE.
Giulio Cesare (I), Corso Colombo 52 (50.685). Open 20 Dec. to 31 Oct. Smallish, pleasant; some highway noise.
Restaurants. *Cuoco d'Oro* (M), Via della Vittoria 5 (50.745). Closed Mon. and Nov. Good atmosphere. *Hostaria del Nostromo* (M), Via San Pietro 19 (56.761). Closed Mon., Tues. and Wed. evenings. *Simpatico* host, Genoese cuisine. *Romina* (M), Via Savagna 3 (64.289). Closed Wed. Peaceful place, good local dishes. *Savoia* (I) Piazza IV Novembre 3 (274.021). Closed Sun. Bright modern restaurant which specializes in delicious pizza.
At **Santa Maria del Campo,** *Pepita* (E), one of the best in area.
At **San Pietro di Novella,** *Ardito* (M), Via Canale 9, (51.551). Closed Tues.
At **San Massimo,** above Rapallo, *U Giancu* (M) (56.189). Closed Wed.

San Fruttuoso Genova (0185). Pretty little bay, with old abbey of the Doria family, near Camogli. *Da Giovanni* (M) (770.047). Closed Wed., Jan. and Feb. Reserve. Small, good restaurant.

San Remo Imperia (0184). Number One resort of the Riviera di Ponente. *Royal* (L), Corso Imperatrice 80 (79.991). Open 20 Dec. to 15 Oct. In lovely grounds near casino, overlooking sea; traditional and modern furnishings, saltwater pool, tennis, dancing terrace; outdoor grill serves up *al fresco* lunches. AE, DC, MC, V.

Astoria (E), Corso Matuzia 8 (70.791). Open 20 Dec. to 30 Sept. In gardens above main road; old-world comfort and service in neoclassic palace; pool. AE, DC, MC, V. *Grand Hotel Londra* (E), Corso Matuzia 2 (79.961). Open 21 Dec. to 30 Sept. Imposing, elegant; pool in handsomely landscaped grounds. AE, DC, MC, V. *Méditerranée* (E), Corso Cavalotti 76 (75.601). Very comfortable, well-furnished rooms, many overlooking seaside park; pool. AE, MC, V.

Montecarlo (M), 2 miles (3.5 km) east (889.255). Many rooms with terrace; family-managed; swimming pool. AE, DC, V. *Nazionale* (M), Via Matteotti 5 (77.577). Next to Casino; good. AE. *Paradiso* (M), Via Roccasterone 10 (85.112). Open 17 Dec. to 31 Oct. Attractive, quiet place in this noisy town; nice garden. AE, DC, MC, V.

Restaurants. *Caravella* (E), Giardini Vittorio Veneto 1 (80.902). Closed Mon., Tues. evening. Top restaurant, known for seafood specialties. AE, MC, V. *Ristorante Casino* (E), Corso Inglesi (79.901). Closed Sun. Very elegant restaurant serving traditional Italian food, many fish dishes. AE, DC, MC, V. *Gambero Rosso* (E), Via Matteotti 71 (83.037). Closed Tues. and Feb. Very elegant and expensive. AE, DC, MC, V. *Da Giannino* (E), Corso Trento Trieste 22 (70.843). Closed Sun., Mon. noon. One of best in town. DC, MC, V. *Pesce d'Oro* (E), Corso Cavallotti 272 (66.332). Closed Mon. and June. Best choice for seafood. AE. *Rendez-Vous* (E), Via Matteotti 126 (85.609). Closed Sun. evening and Mon. Very elegant, with interesting menu; some choices quite reasonable for category. AE.

Grottino (M), Via Gaudio 47 (83.178). Closed Tues. off-season. Simple seafood specialties. *La Lanterna* (M), Via Molo di Ponente 16 (86.055). Closed Thurs. AE, DC. *Nostromu* (M), Piazza Sardi (80.767). Closed Wed. and May. AE, DC, V.

Santa Margherita Ligure Genova (0185). Select seaside resort. *Imperial Palace* (L), Via Pagana 19 (288.991). In elevated position overlooking sea; amidst exotic vegetation in extensive grounds; smart and elegant; pool. AE, DC, MC, V. *Continental* (E), Via Pagana 8 (286.512). Open 21 Dec. to 31 Oct. In pretty garden setting; attractive salons and bedrooms with sea views. AE, DC, MC, V. *Miramare* (E), Lungomare Milite Ignoto 30 (280.713). On shore drive overlooking bay; palace type, lovely grounds, modern comforts, pool. AE, V.

Mediterraneo (M), Via della Vittoria 18/a (286.881). In center of town; attractive old-world villa; pleasant garden and patio. DC. *Metropole* (M), Via Pagana 2 (286.134). Open 16 Dec. to 31 Oct. Just outside town; pretty bedrooms and gardens; a touch of elegance; beach. AE, DC, MC, V. *La Vela* (M), Via Nicolo Cuneo 21 (286.039). Large, Renaissance-style villa in elevated position with view of sea. 16 well-furnished rooms; good atmosphere; terraces, gardens. MC, V.

Conte Verde (I), Via Zara 1 (287.139). Open 23 Dec. to 31 Oct. Central, simple, good. AE, MC, V. *Fiorina* (I), Piazza Mazzini 26 (287.517). Open 22 Dec. to 31 Oct. Central. MC.

Restaurants. *All'Ancora* (E), Via Maragliano 7 (280.559). Closed Mon. Open 1 March to 19 Dec. Very good seafood specialties. *Cambusa* (E), Via Bottaro 1 (287.410). Closed Thurs., Jan. and Feb. Another fine seafood place; nice terrace. *Cesarina* (E), Via Mameli 2/c (286.059). Closed Wed. and 15 Feb. to 15 March. Cheerful, *simpatico* and good. V.

Basilico (M), Via Montecarlo 7 (288.812). Closed Mon. Known for peach *flambée*. *Faro* (M), Via Maragliano 24/a (286.867). Closed Tues. Spartan decor, absolutely fresh fish from family's boats. *La Bassa Prora* (M), Via Garibaldi 7 (286.586). Closed Mon. evenings, Tues. Pleasant. Modern seafood restaurant on waterfront. AE, V. *Trattoria dei Pescatori* (M), Via Bottaro 44 (286.059). Closed Wed. One of the best in area for seafood.

Sestri Levante Genova (0185). Beach resort. *Castelli* (E), Via alla Penisola 26 (41.004). Open 15 May to 30 Sept. Borders on deluxe, in splendid isolated position overlooking bay and coast; medieval-style buildings with modern comforts; terrace dining, natural rock pool and lift to rocky terraces on sea. AE, DC, MC, V. *Villa Balbi* (E), Via Rimembranza 1 (42.941). Open 1 April to 30 Sept. In town, overlooking sea; richly furnished salons; garden and pool. AE, DC, MC, V.

Mimosa (M), Via Lombardia 31 (41.449). Quietly situated outside town; small, pleasant, pool. AE, DC, MC, V. *Miramare Europa* (M), Via Cappellini 9 (41.055). Open 1 May to 15 Oct. Small, terraces overlooking bay.

Helvetia (I), Via Cappuccine 43 (41.175). Open 15 March to 30 Sept. Small, pretty location on little bay; beach facilities.

Restaurants. *Angiolina* (E), Via della Rimembranza 49 (41.198). Closed Tues. Superlative *zuppa di pesce* and wine of the Cinque Terre. AE, V. *Sant'Anna* (E), Lungomare de Scalzo 60 (41.004). Closed Thurs. Attractive ambiance; excellent Ligurian cuisine. AE, DC, MC, V. *Schooner San Marco* (E), at the port (41.459). Closed Wed. Open 1 April to 20 Dec. Lovely seaside restaurant; exquisite seafood. AE, DC, MC, V.

Mira (M), Viale Rimembranze 15 (41.576). Closed Wed. and Nov. Fish specialties. *Portobello* (M), Via Portobello 16 (41.566). Closed Mon. Specialties of neighboring Emilia region.

Spotorno Savona (019). Seaside resort. *Royal* (E), Lungomare Kennedy 125 (745.074). Open 1 May to 15 Oct. Large, modern, overlooking sea; terraces, beach facilities. AE, MC, V. *La Pineta* (M), Via Serra 22 (745.412). Open 20 May to 30 Sept. Attractive, small; quiet hillside location in pinewoods at edge of town. V.

Restaurants. *Pino* (M), Via Berninzoni 164 (745.890). Closed Mon. Seafood. *A Sigogna* (M), Via Garibaldi 13 (745.016). Closed Tues.

At picturesque **Noli**, neighboring town, *Elena* (M), Via Musso 4 (748.922). *Ines* (M), Via Vignolo 1 (748.086). Closed Mon. V. *La Torre* (M), Via Sartorio 1 (748.765). Closed Wed. off-season. Reasonable pizzeria.

Varazze Savona (019). Near Genoa. **Restaurants.** *Cavetto* (M), Via Santa Caterina 7 (97311). Closed Thurs. and Nov. Old favorite with Genoese for fish dishes, somewhat pricey. AE, DC, MC. *Conchiglia d'Oro* (M), Via Aurelia 133 (698.015). Closed Wed. in summer, and Tues. off-season. Closed Nov. and Dec. Small; reserve. Excellent family-run seafood restaurant.

Ventimiglia Imperia (0184). Near French border. Avoid town on Friday, chaotic market day. *La Riserva* (M), at Castel d'Appio (39.533). Open 1 April to 30 Sept., 15 Dec. to 6 Jan. and on weekends in other months. Delightful inn; pool, wonderful view. AE, DC, MC, V.

Restaurants. *La Capannina* (M), Via Marconi (351.726). Closed Mon. On sea. *Il Corsaro* (M), Passeggiata Cavallotti 13/b (351.874). Closed Tues. and 15 Nov. to 31 Dec. On beach. *La Mortola* (M), Mortola Inferiore (39.432). Closed Nov. Mon. evening, Tues. Worth the few kilometer journey for the excellent food and friendly atmosphere.

At **San Lodovico** frontier, *Balzi Rossi* (E), Piazzale De Gasperi (38.132). Closed Sun. eve. and Mon. Elegant place with marvelous view; refined cuisine. AE.

GETTING THERE AND AROUND. By air. The region's airport is at Genoa, called—unsurprisingly—Cristoforo Colombo. It has direct flights from London/Gatwick, on British Airways and Alitalia. The terminal is in Piazza Acquaverde with a bus service (approx 30 mins.).

By train. The main rail line follows the coast, with spurs inland from Vezzano near La Spezia to Parma, from Genoa to Turin and Milan, and from Savona to Turin. Local service along the main line is frequent, making it easy to visit the smaller resorts, such as Portofino, from Genoa or from other resorts. You can also hop along the Cinque Terre, nipping in and out of the tunnels to see the small fishing villages.

There are two main stations in Genoa—Principe and Brignole—trains usually stop at both.

By car. All the main points of interest in Liguria lie along the coast, threaded on the old, wiggly Route 1 from the French border, all the way through Genoa and La Spezia to Leghorn just south of Pisa. Countryside enthusiasts should not, however, miss the little mountain roads leading north from the coast where the views are magnificent. Boxed in by four autostrade, it is something of a forgotten land—and none the worse for that. Autostrada A12 has relieved much of the pressure on the coast road, but even now it is sometimes necessary to queue to enter such favorite spots as Portofino—usually on weekends. Apart from reaching Liguria by the obvious French entry at Ventimiglia, there are the direct A6 motorway from Turin and the A7 from Milan.

By bus and boat. Local bus services complete the transportation network along the coast and provide access to the mountainous hinterland. There are a number of boat excursions along the coast, notably those touching on Portofino and San Fruttuoso and on the Cinque Terre.

GENOA MUSEUMS. A town with as rich a history as Genoa would naturally be well supplied with palaces and works of art. Several of the palaces are now museums, with frescos, loggias, coffered ceilings and all the appurtenances of by-gone wealth. Look at our entry under *Museums* in the *Facts at Your Fingertips* section for general points.

Musei d'Arte Orientale Chiossone, Villetta Dinegro, Via Piaggio. Wide-ranging collection of Japanese, Chinese and Siamese art and artefacts in a very attractive park setting. Tues. to Sat., 9.30–11.45, 2–5.15, closed Sun. and Mon.

Museo di Sant'Agostino, Piazza Sarzana. Sculptures, paintings, frescos from Genoa's churches and palaces, in handsomely adapted monastery of Sant'Agostino.

Museo del Tesoro di San Lorenzo, at the Cathedral of San Lorenzo. This really is a treasure in every sense. Fabulous works of religious art in a truly imaginative modern setting. Outstanding. Tues. to Sat., 9.30–11.30, 3–5.45, closed Sun. and Mon.

Palazzo Bianco, Via Garibaldi. Large and fine art collection, especially strong in Flemish and Dutch artists, though with plenty of Genoese works. Tues. to Sat., 9–1.15, 3–6, Sun. 9.15–12.45, closed Mon.

Palazzo Reale, Via Balbi 10. Free entry. Large, echoing palace. Some good works, including those by Castiglione, sculptures by Parodi, and others. Open daily 9–1.30.

Palazzo Rosso, Via Garibaldi 18. Another palace in the palatial quarter. This one recreates what the Genoese wealthy families were able to amass. Bursting with lovely things. Rubens, Veronese, van Dyck and many more. Tues. to Sat., 9–1.15, 3–6, Sun. 9.15–12.45, closed Mon.

Palazzo Spinola, Piazza Pellicceria 1. Having passed through the hands of two of Genoa's greatest families, the Grimaldis and the Spinolas, this palace now houses some excellent art in faded splendor. Tues. to Sat., May to Sept. 9–7, Tues. to Sat., Oct. to Apr. 9–5, Sun. 9–1, closed Mon. Entry free.

PIEDMONT

Italy's Window on France

Piedmont—the region of Turin and the magnificent Valle d'Aosta in the northwest corner of Italy—is one of the delightful surprises in a land of spectacular natural beauty and regional individuality. Bordering on France and Switzerland, the region has some of the characteristics of those countries blended with its basic Italian heritage—and an ever-growing number of foreign visitors are including Piedmont in their itinerary.

Geographically it combines the lure of the highest peaks of the Alps in ranges that circle fanwise along the south, west and north boundaries and the broad flat lands of the plain. Turin, its capital city, lies at the base of the mountainous circle in a level area that marks the beginning of the fertile Valley of the Po, which expands into broad plains to Milan and beyond. Its mountains and valleys provide Piedmont with some of the most beautiful scenery in Europe. In summer the peaceful towns and villages of the Alpine valleys attract many tourists in search of cool, restful holidays, where the most strenuous exertion need not be greater than a walk in the woods. For the more ambitious there is mountain-climbing. This may include the tallest in Europe, Mont Blanc, Monte Rosa, the Cervino (Matterhorn), the Gran Paradiso, and also many lesser peaks.

As for winter sports, Piedmont's mountain valleys provide the scene for some of the finest skiing in the world. For shorter stays, Piedmont offers great attractions in its heritage of historical and architectural landmarks dating from early Roman times down through medieval and Baroque periods. Some of the 14th- and 15th-century castles hidden away in rugged mountain retreats were able to escape destruction through the years and remain tangible witness to more turbulent times.

The region represents the latest word in modern development, with Turin containing some of Italy's finest mass production industries. It is also the home of Borsalino hats and of vermouth. And to top it off, Piedmont offers the gourmet a treat in combining the best of French with Italian cuisine.

A Bit of History

Piedmont originally was inhabited by Celtic tribes who, when they could not beat off the encroaching invaders from Rome, ended up by joining them. As allies of the Romans, the Celts fought off Hannibal when he came down through the Alpine passes with his elephants, but finally lost, and their capital Taurasia—the present Turin—was destroyed. The Romans rebuilt the city, giving its streets the grid pattern which has persisted until now and which makes travelers think of an American city. Today ruins of Roman buildings are to be found in various parts of the region and particularly in the town of Aosta.

With the downfall of the Roman empire, Piedmont suffered the fate of the rest of Italy and was successively occupied and ravaged by barbarians who came from the east and the north. By the 10th and 11th centuries the area was a battleground for feuding lords. Turin was strong enough to withstand predatory knights and during the 12th and 13th centuries governed itself as a Commune—a sort of independent republic. In the 11th century a French feudal family, the Savoys, managed to rule Turin for a brief time and then came back at the end of the 13th century. With the exception of a short period of about 20 years from 1536 when François I of France annexed the area for his own country, the region was governed by counts and dukes from the Savoy family right up to 1798, when the French Republican armies came down to Italy. When Napoleon's empire fell, the Savoys returned to Piedmont.

After 1848 Piedmont was one of the main centers of the Risorgimento—the revival of the spirit of Italian unity. Victor Emmanuel II became king in 1848 and under the leadership of Cavour, Garibaldi and Mazzini the movement for Italian unity and the efforts to forge an Italian nation proceeded with great patriotic fervor. In 1861 the Chamber of Deputies in Turin proclaimed the Kingdom of Italy and moved the capital to Florence until Rome could become the nation's capital.

This move marked the end of Piedmont's importance in the political sphere, but the architecture of Turin, with the regal splendor of its buildings and the stateliness of its parks, bears witness to its period as a capital city. Turin then turned to industrial and commercial pursuits and the development of arts and sciences as befitted a progressive industrial city. Today the region is the center of Italy's automobile, metal-working, chemical and candy industries. The importance of Turin is further enhanced by the fact that its industries are highly diversified. Clothing, paper and liquor manufacture also contribute widely to its commercial activities. Piedmont's industrial importance entered the political picture again during World War II when its workers opposed the Fascist and Nazi war efforts as resistance fighters both in the hills and in the city.

Piedmont offers excellent holiday facilities both in its capital city of Turin and in the many towns and villages of its Alpine valleys. Turin itself is more appealing in spring and autumn. The mountain valley towns and hamlets are best in summer, when their altitude and the breezes from glacier-topped mountain peaks provide a cool respite from summer heat. Most of the holiday resorts in Piedmont are open in winter because the terrain and abundant snow lend themselves to ideal skiing conditions.

Turin

Although Turin, the capital of Piedmont, is a genuinely Italian city, its proximity to France and its century-old ties to the neighboring country give it a constantly recurring French accent. In fact, the peculiar Piedmontese accent you overhear in the streets will make you think it's some kind of French dialect.

Situated on the left bank of the Po, facing a hill, the city is in the middle of the plain that marks the beginning of the Po Valley. In the distance to the south, west and north are the Alps, giving a feeling of protected encirclement. From the hill across the river, Turin seems almost completely level, with the exception of the tower building called the Mole Antonelliana.

Turin is characterized by its wide streets, crossing at right angles, its many beautiful squares, its fine buildings and its modern spirit. Coming into Turin by train, the traveler gets his first contact with the city on entering the Piazza Carlo Felice, a beautifully landscaped park with a fountain in the center. Going out of the square to the north, the visitor enters the porticoed Via Roma, one of the most modern streets of the city. It connects the Piazza Carlo Felice with the Piazza San Carlo and farther along with the Piazza Castello. First opened in 1615, this street was largely rebuilt in 1931 and 1936 with shops opening onto porticos. At the entrance to the Piazza San Carlo there are the two churches of Santa Cristina and San Carlo, which give the same effect as the two churches beside each other in the Piazza del Popolo in Rome. This square is considered by some the second best in Italy, after St. Mark's in Venice. In the center is a statue of Duke Emanuele Filiberto of Savoy, victor of the 1557 battle of St. Quentin, sheathing his sword. Continuing north on Via Roma you come to the Piazza Castello, which gets its name from the imposing structure in the center. Originally the location of the city gate in Roman days, the castle is an imposing combination of brick, stone and marble work.

Juvara designed the castle's splendid Baroque façade and, inside it, he built a tremendous marble staircase which leads up to the royal apartments. The large assembly hall was the scene of the first Italian Senate meetings. Although it still retains the name of Palazzo Madama, for Queen Maria Cristina who made it her home in the 17th century, the building now houses the civic museum of ancient art. North of the castle is the Royal Armory, one of Europe's most important collections of armor. Nearby is the impressive new Teatro Regio.

Adjoining the castle, on Piazza San Giovanni, is the cathedral, with a façade of white marble, which was built in the 15th century. From the interior two monumental staircases of black marble lead to the shadowy Chapel of the Holy Shroud; enclosed in a heavy coffer above the altar is the piece of linen believed to be the shroud in which Jesus Christ was wound when taken from the cross and which retains the marks of His head and body. Three-dimensional NASA photographs have proved these to be the prints of a man who had undergone flagellation. The weaving technique dates the shroud in the time of Christ, while pollen in the textile indubitably belongs to flowers of Palestine. Controversy rages about the authenticity of this relic but, argument apart, it is a mysterious and fascinating object.

South of the castle is the Via Accademia delle Scienze, which leads to the Piazza Carignano. On the right side of the latter square the visitor will see the Carignano Theater, built in 1752, and on the left is the Palazzo Carignano, which is a masterpiece of Baroque architecture. It was the birthplace of Vittorio Emanuele II in 1820 and the Italian Parliament met here from 1860 to 1865. Across the piazza is the Egyptian Museum with a superb collection, and the beautifully arranged Sabauda Gallery on the second floor, with a magnificent display of art, especially rich in Dutch and Flemish paintings.

From the Piazza Carignano you go on to the Piazza Carlo Alberto and to the Via Po, where in the courtyard of the university there is a plaque dedicated to Erasmus of Rotterdam, who earned his doctor's degree there in 1506. Farther along and to the left is the Via Montebello, where the Mole Antonelliana is located. This unusual structure, built in 1863, was originally intended to be a Jewish synagogue. It became a bizarre oddity, however, when the tall, thin spire was added. A terrace atop the dome offers a wonderful view of the city, the plain surrounding it and the semi-circle of Alps beyond.

Continuing down the Via Po toward the river you come to the vast Piazza Vittorio Veneto, which leads to the city's oldest stone bridge. Across the bridge is the Church of the Great Mother of God, built on the pattern of the Pantheon in Rome. To the right, along the Corso Moncalieri is Monte dei Cappuccini, whose church, Santa Maria del Monte, and convent date from 1583.

Along the left bank of the River Po is the Parco del Valentino, which formed part of the *Italia 61* exposition held to commemorate the centennial of Italy as a united nation. Remaining from this exposition are several decaying structures such as Nervi's Palazzo del Lavoro, once famed for their striking modern design. The better-maintained Exposition Hall houses trade fairs and a biennial automobile show. An outstanding building in this area is the Castello del Valentino, erected in the 17th century after the pattern of French châteaux. The interior is particularly elaborate, with frescoed walls and rich decorations.

Farther along, close to the river's edge, are the medieval village and castle. Built in connection with the Turin Exposition of 1884, this collection of buildings is one of the most picturesque places in Turin. A visit to the village is a startling experience, for it gives the effect of going back to the Middle Ages. Here are houses, churches, stores, and craftsmen's shops similar to those found throughout Piedmont. But here there are no modern buildings next door. And up the hill nearby there is the castle. This does not represent any particular castle but is a composite of the features of castles extant in various parts of Piedmont.

Turin's Automobile Museum on Corso Unita d'Italia is well worth a visit; evocative of old films and past luxuries, ranks of antique autos stand with brass and chrome fittings brightly gleaming. Some models date back to 1893; others bear such names as Bugatti, Rolls Royce and Isotta Franchini.

The suburbs of Turin consist of two distinct areas. First, there is the *collina torinese* (the hill of Turin) on the right side of the Po River, a wooded section easily accessible by auto, bus and trolley. Beyond the hill, Turin's suburbs include an interesting variety of villages, abbeys and castles that have striking historical and artistic interest.

The Rest of the Province

16 km. (10 miles) from the center of Turin is the Basilica of Superga, an imposing structure marking the breaking of the French siege of 1706. The site provides a breathtaking view of the panoramic semi-circle of the Alps which rise around the Turin plain. A memorial park with a boulevard a mile and a half long lined with 10,000 trees commemorating Turin's World War I dead, leads to the *Victory Statue,* topped by a beacon light. This gigantic female figure, nearly 60 feet tall, is the largest cast bronze statue in the world.

Going southeast along the hill you come to Chieri, with its vast cathedral, erected around the year 1400. Nearby are the villages of Santena, with the tomb of Camillo Cavour, one of modern Italy's founders, and the village of Castelnuovo Don Bosco, birthplace of Saint John Bosco (1815–88) known for his work for youth. At the southern end of the hill is Moncalieri, with a 15th-century castle. West of Turin are Rivoli, its castle, now a modern art museum, and medieval town of Avigliana.

In this area there are three interesting abbeys. The Abbey of San Michele—near the attractive old town of Avigliana—was built on the peak of Mount Pirchiriano in the 11th century but later, when the monks enlarged it, they had to build part of the building on supports over 90 feet high. It is a popular trip from Turin, and worth seeing for the architecture, sculptures and the Savoy tombs. Also architecturally noteworthy are the abbeys of St. Anthony of Ranverso and that of Vezzolano, said to have been started by Charlemagne. The latter lies east from Turin, just north of Castelnuovo Don Bosco, and should be seen by all who like Romanesque building and sculpture.

Of all the castles built by the Savoy dynasty around Turin, the most elaborate is that of Stupinigi. Built in 1729 as a hunting lodge, it is more a royal villa, with many wings, landscaped gardens and forests. Its interior is sumptuously decorated and today houses the Museum of Art and Furniture.

Lesser-known attractions of the Piedmont region include a castle at Aglié containing Etruscan and Pompeian relics, as well as fine frescos and statues. Bosco Marengo is an old town still retaining vestiges of its walls and castle, whose Santa Croce Church contains works by Vasari and other Renaissance artists. At Villar San Costanzo there are fascinating rock formations. Orta San Giulio boasts its Sacred Mountain, a 16th-century sanctuary where there are 20 chapels, several oratories and a church. At Pessione, 19 km. (12 miles) east of Turin, is the fascinating Martini-Rossi Wine Museum.

Aosta and Asti

For the tourist or vacationist who wishes to get away from the city, the incomparable beauty of Piedmont's Alpine valleys has much to offer both in winter and summer. In scores of mountain valleys literally hundreds of villages offer a complete range of tourist facilities. Alpine crests, many with a permanent expanse of glaciers, hilltop castles, clear mountain lakes and streams, chestnut groves, pine forests and green meadows, all provide a spectacular combination of scenic beauty.

Most striking is the area called Valle d'Aosta. In 1947 this section acquired political autonomy and became a region in its own right, but from a tourist point of view it can well be considered part of the Piedmont area. Here are Europe's highest mountains, Mont Blanc, Monte Rosa, and Gran Paradiso and the Cervino, and on them or around them are the vast extensions of glaciers covering more than 200 square miles. Valle d'Aosta includes not only the valley of the Dora Baltea, but also scores of other smaller tributary valleys. The principal city—Aosta—bears witness to its Roman origin in its regular streets and many well-preserved ruins. Its picturesque aspect is heightened by numerous churches, towers and buildings of the Middle Ages. Nearby there are many well preserved 14th- and 15th-century buildings, but the castles at Fenis and Issogne are the most interesting. The climate of Valle d'Aosta is particularly pleasant and healthy and has given rise to the establishment of several spas.

Other areas of Piedmont can be divided roughly into four groups of valleys which include the valleys of tributaries and mountain streams which in turn feed into them. These are Pinerolo Valley, Susa Valley, Lanzo Valley and Canavese Valley. All provide fascinating scenery, pleasant climate and scores of holiday resorts with accommodation of all types for both winter and summer visitors.

Asti, the famous wine center known for its *Asti Spumante,* and excellent red wines (*Barbera, Freisa* and *Grignolino*), and Alessandria, where the world-famous Borsalino hats are made, have interesting medieval buildings next door to new bustling industries. Valenza, noted for its gold and silver work, Casale Monferrato, an important cement center, Vercelli, known for its rice market, Biella, for its wool industry, and Ivrea, as the headquarters of the international Olivetti firm, are other towns filled with striking architectural monuments of feudal times.

Mountain Sports Centers

Piedmont and Valle d'Aosta excel in facilities for winter sports. The highest mountains in Europe provide a background for skiing on their sloping approaches. Many towns and villages are equipped with hotels, cableways and chair lifts. Here are a few of the most important resorts.

Sestriere. Characterized by its "tower" hotels where every room has an outward view. This is the most famous and best equipped ski center in Piedmont. At 2,033 meters (6,670 ft.) this center has lots of sun, 74 ski runs, four cableways, 21 ski lifts, two chair lifts, skating rink, and good snow from November to May. Like all of the resorts, it offers special "ski-week" rates, all-inclusive of hotel, meals, ski lessons and lifts.

Courmayeur. Against the background of the highest mountain in Europe, Mont Blanc, Courmayeur, because of its position at 1,228 meters (4,029 ft.) among thick pine groves, is as much a favorite in summer as in winter. It has the world's largest funicular railway. By linking the various ski areas, it helps create a total of 80 km. of ski runs. Placed as it is just beyond the Italian end of the Mont Blanc tunnel, Courmayeur is popular and easy to get to.

Claviere. This French-Italian border center was among the first of the many Italian ski resorts to be developed. Claviere has excellent ski slopes that overlap with those of the French resort of Mongenèvre, connecting with the so-called "Milky Way." Snow conditions are particularly favorable well into spring. Slate roofs, narrow streets and architectural unity make it easy on the eye, too.

Breuil-Cervinia. Situated at the foot of Mount Cervino (Matterhorn), this center boasts of year-round skiing since its pasture slopes border the limits of the Cervino glacier. At 2,050 meters (6,726 ft.) it is high enough to make nearby peaks more accessible, and its eight cablecars rise to some stupendous lookout points. Slightly below Breuil, in the valley of the Matterhorn, is **Valtournanche,** popular with both summer and winter vacationers.

Gressoney. This is a double-barreled resort, with two settlements, Gressoney St. Jean and Gressoney La Trinité, the second (and more fashionable) 244 meters (800 ft.) higher than the first. Like Breuil-Cervinia in the famed Valle d'Aosta section, the Gressoneys provide access to the Monte Rosa group of peaks.

Bardonecchia. Not far from the French-Italian border, this small town is on the Modane-Turin rail line. Besides skiing, it offers hockey and skating facilities.

Limone-Piemonte. This is the biggest winter sports resort of southern Piedmont. Less famous internationally than the northern places, it is popular with Italians rather than with foreigners—and for that reason is less expensive than the better-known places. Halfway between Nice and Turin, almost on the French frontier, it has the advantage also of providing a major ski center within easy reach of both the French and Italian Rivieras, a great convenience for those who want to split winter vacations between the mountains and the sea.

Sauze D'Oulx-Sportinia. 81 km. (50 miles) from Turin, this vacation resort has suffered a construction boom that has left it overbuilt and anonymous. It gets plenty of sun and snow, and its ski facilities offer various grades of difficulty. It's especially popular with British skiers.

But not all of the resorts are designed for ski enthusiasts. There are good spas at Acqui and Bognanco, and a famous one at St. Vincent. This spa, on the Turin-Aosta line, also attracts visitors who come to visit the gambling casino or to enjoy a quiet vacation.

PRACTICAL INFORMATION FOR PIEDMONT

WHEN TO GO. Piedmont is a two-season region, visited in winter for skiing and other sports and in summer for lake or mountain vacations. The period from Christmas through the first week of January is the big one for winter sports, after which resorts are quieter for about a month, before entering another lively period from February 10 to March 10. During January and February the weather is less reliable.

The peak summer season runs from around the middle of July to the middle of August for mountain resorts like those in the Valle d'Aosta. Busy Turin, the capital, is best visited between the end of April and the middle of June, or the end of September and the middle of October. During cooler months, Po Valley fog combines with heavily polluted air to cast a gray pall over the province's flatlands, including the capital.

TOURIST OFFICES. Alessandria: EPT, Via Savona 26 (51.021). **Aosta:** Regional Tourist Board, Piazza Chanoux 8 (35.655). **Asti:** EPT, Piazza Alfieri 34 (50.357).

Ayas-Champoluc: AAST, Piazza Centrale (307.113). Bardonecchia: AAST, Viale Vittoria 47 (99.032). Cogne: AAST, Piazza Chanoux 38 (74.040). Courmayeur: AAST, Piazzale Monte Bianco (842.061). Cuneo: EPT, Corso Nizza 17 (3258). Gressoney: AAST, Palazzo Communale, in St. Jean (355.185). Ivrea: AAST, Corso Vercelli 1 (424.005). Limone Piemonte: AAST, Via Roma 38 (92.101). Macugnaga: AAST, Piazza Municipio (65.119). Novara: EPT, Corso Cavour 2 (23.398). Orta San Giulio: AAST, Piazza Motta (90.355). Saint Vincent: AAST, Via Roma 52 (22.39). Sauze d'Oulx: AAST, Piazza Assietta (85.009). Sestriere: AAST, Piazza Agnelli 11 (76.045). Turin: EPT, Via Roma 222 (535.181) and at Porta Nuova rail station (531.327).

SEASONAL EVENTS. Jan. and Feb.: sports competitions are held in the winter resorts.

Aosta: Jul. and Aug. see an organ festival.

Asti: the Palio, a horse race and pageant in medieval costume, takes place on the third Sun. of Sept.

Cuneo: Feb. is enlivened with a carnival, complete with snow clowns flocking.

Ivrea: also with a Feb. carnival—this one the best of them all—lasting several days and including costumed parades and floats.

Limone Piemonte: Feb. carnival.

Turin: carnival time in Feb.; in Apr., there's an automobile show; Jun. 24 sees celebrations for patron saint John; and, in Dec., Turin's Teatro Regio opens its opera season.

TELEPHONE CODES. You will find the telephone area code for each town against its name in the Hotel and Restaurant listings (after the province name). If there is a different area code from the majority of the establishments—say when a hotel or restaurant is in an outlying place—then the code is given in front of the telephone number.

HOTELS AND RESTAURANTS. Although the main cities in the region are expensive, exactly the opposite is true of the country areas, where you will find good accommodation at budget prices. Restaurants, too, in the country towns and villages are fairly inexpensive and you'll find lots of local food at surprisingly low rates. And, on the subject of local specialties, you might want to try one of the wine itineraries that the EPT or the local wine consortia organize, tasting as you go.

Regional Food and Drink. Piedmont cooking echoes the geography of the region which produced it—the basic Italian dishes are treated with French finesse, modified by a touch of the rustic quality of mountain cooking. The favorite form of pasta is *agnolotti,* similar to *ravioli,* small squares of dough filled with meat, spinach or cheese. *Fonduta*—melted cheese, eggs and sometimes grated truffles—is another regional specialty. The truffles are not black, but white, a specialty of Piedmont, and the cheese that goes into the dish is *fontina,* from the Valle d'Aosta. Perhaps the oddest Piedmontese dish is *cardi in bagna cauda.* This is made of edible thistles, chopped raw, and then dipped in a hot sauce made of butter, oil, anchovies, cream and shredded garlic. Italian restaurants the world over put breadsticks on the table. They originated in Turin, where they are called *grissini.*

In many restaurants, you'll find a seemingly endless assortment of delicate *antipastos,* a typical feature of regional cuisine. Turin is famed also for its delicate pastries and fine chocolates, especially for hazelnut-flavored chocolates known as *gianduiotti.*

Piedmont produces many excellent wines. The reds are full-bodied and rich; among them are *Barolo, Nebiolo, Freisa, Barbera* and *Barbaresco.* Best known of the whites is *Asti Spumante,* a sweet sparkling wine that also exists in a brut version that is quite close to champagne. Piedmont is also the inventor of vermouth, which was developed by A. B. Carpano in 1786 and now appears under a number of brand names—*Martini, Cora, Cinzano,* etc.

Alessandria Alessandria (0131). Important city. *Alli Due Buoi Rossi* (E), Via Cavour 32 (445.252). Very central; comfortable and efficient. AE, DC, MC, V. *Lux* (M), Via Piacenza 72 (51.661). Centrally situated, functional. No restaurant. AE, DC, V.

Restaurants. *Alli Due Buoi Rossi* (M), Via Cavour 32 (445.252). Closed Sat. and Aug. Hotel restaurant serving regional dishes. AE, V. *Al Forchettone* (M), Spalto Rovereto 59 (60.179). Closed Sat. and Aug. Varied menu; reasonable. *Grappolo* (M), Via Casale 28 (53.217). Closed Mon. eve. and Tues. Aug. 1–21. Nicely decorated; classic dishes. AE.

Aosta Aosta (0615). Center of the beautiful valley. High season Easter, 1 July to 30 Sept., and Christmas.

Ambassador (M), Via Duca degli Abruzzi (42.230). On outskirts; good. DC, MC, V. *Europe* (M), Piazza Narbonne 8 (40.566). Central, traditional older hotel. AE, DC, MC, V. *Rayon du Soleil* (I), at Seraillon, above town (362.247). Closed mid Oct.–Mar. 1. Pleasant small hotel with garden, views. *Valle d'Aosta* (M), Corso Ivrea 146 (41.845). On outskirts; handsomely decorated; fine mountain views. AE, DC, MC, V.

Restaurants. *Cavallo Bianco* (E), Via Aubert 15 (362.214). Closed Sun. evening, Mon., mid-June to mid July. One of Italy's best; beautiful locale, excellent seasonal specialties. Reserve. AE, DC, V.

La Croisée (M), Viale Gran San Bernardo 7 (362.441). Closed Mon. Nov 1–15. Local dishes. AE, DC, MC, V. *Piemonte* (M), Via Porte Pretoriane 13 (40.111). Closed Sun., Jan. and June. Small, no frills, but good. *Vecchio Ristoro* (M), Via Tourneuve 4 (33.238). Closed Sun., July, and Feb. Old mill, local specialties.

Asti Asti (0141). Home of Asti Spumante. *Salera* (E), Via Marello 19 (211.815). Just outside center, comfortable. AE, DC, MC, V. *Rainero* (I), Via Cavour 85 (353.866). Central, smallish. No restaurant. AE, DC, MC, V.

Restaurants. *Gener Neuv* (E), Lungo Tanaro 4 (57.270). Closed Sun. evening, Mon., Aug. and Jan 1–10. Reserve for evening. Fine food and excellent wines. *Il Vicoletto* (E), Vicolo Anfossi 6, at Via Garibaldi (52.114). Closed Mon. and Aug. Limited choice; good atmosphere. *Falcon Vecchio* (M), Vicolo San Secondo 8 (53.106). Closed Sun. evening, Mon., Aug. Near main piazza, simple and good. *La Vigna* (M), Via Guttuari 4 (51.668). Closed Sun.

Ayas-Champoluc Aosta (0125). Quiet resort in Valle d'Aosta. High season 1 Feb. to 15 March, 1 July to 31 Aug. and Christmas. *Anna Maria* (M) (307.128). Small, very good; simple, hearty cuisine; garden. *Monte Rosa* (M), at Periasc (305.735). Open 1 July to 15 Sept. and 20 Dec. to 20 Jan. Very pleasant, good views.

Bardonecchia Torino (0122). Important year-round resort; good skiing. High season Feb., Easter, 15 July to 31 Aug. and Christmas. *Des Geneys-Splendid* (M), Viale Einaudi 21 (99.001). Open Dec. 16–Apr. 14; June 26–Sept. 14. Lovely location in pinewoods; good. AE, V. *Riki* (M) (93.53). Open Dec. 16–March; July–Aug. Central position; ultra-modern decor and comforts; pool, mini-golf, nightclub. AE, DC, V. *Asplenia* (M), Viale della Vittoria 31 (98.70). Open 1 July to 31 Aug., 1 Dec. to 30 April. Nice, small hotel. MC, V.

Restaurants. *Nuovo Trau* (M), Via Medail 58 (99.892). Closed Mon. Regional specialties. *Medail* (M), Via Stazione 2 (98.44). Closed Mon. DC, MC, V.

Breuil-Cervinia Aosta (0166). Valle d'Aosta resort. High season 5 Feb. to 25 April, 26 July to 23 Aug. and Christmas. *Cristallo* (E), (948.121). Open 1 Dec. to 2 May, 1 July to 31 Aug. High above town; elegantly modern; pool, tennis. AE, DC, MC, V. *Breuil* (M) (949.537). In village; comfortable wood-paneled rooms. *Hermitage* (M) (948.998). Closed May–early July. Smallish, best of (M) hotels, near lifts. AE, V. *Planet* (M) (949.426). Open 1 Nov. to 30 April and 1 July to 15 Sept. Attractive. *Bucaneve* (I) (949.119). Open July 1–Sept. 30; Dec. 1–mid-May. Nice, small hotel. AE, V. *Neiges d'Antan* (I) (948.775). Open 3 Dec. to 3 May, 5 July to 13 Sept. Small, delightful inn. AE.

Restaurants. *Neiges d'Antan* (M), at Perrères (948.775). Closed Mon. May, June; mid-Sept–Dec. 1. Inn (see above). Rustic, chic; all-in price includes wine and transport. AE, V. *Pavia* (M) (949.010). Open 1 Dec. to 5 May and 15 July to 5 Sept. Lively restaurant with fine views.

Cogne Aosta (0165). Winter and summer resort in Valle d'Aosta. High season 20 Dec. to 6 Jan., 1 July to 31 Aug. *Bellevue* (M) (74.825). Comfortable; lovely views. *Petit* (I) (74.010). Only 18 rooms, good atmosphere. *Miramonti* (M) (74.030). Small, attractive.

Restaurants. *Lou Ressignon* (M), Via Bourgeois 81 (74.034). Closed Mon. evenings and Tues. off-season. Cozy chalet serving local dishes. AE, DC, V. *Notre Maison* (M), at Cretaz (74.104). Closed Mon., Oct, and Nov. Typical Alpine decor and cuisine. DC.

Courmayeur Aosta (0165). Most important winter sports and summer resort of the Valle d'Aosta. High season 22 Dec. to 5 Jan., 5 Feb. to 21 March, 11 July to 30 Aug. *Palace Bron* (E), at Plan Gorret (842.545). Open 4 Dec. to 30 April, 1 July to 18 Sept. In quiet location above town; posh, comfortable, ideal for relaxing. AE, DC, V. *Pavillon* (E), Strada Regionale 60 (842.420). Open 1 Dec. to 30 April and 1 June to 31 Oct. Near cableways; smallish, modern version of a chalet; attracts lively crowd. AE, DC, MC, V. *Royal* (E), Via Roma 83 (843.621). Open 15 Dec. to 30 April and July 1 to 15 Sept. Central position; informal but elegant, modern attractive rooms. AE, DC, MC, V.

Bouton d'Or (M) (842.380). In town; small, beautifully furnished. No restaurant. AE, DC, MC, V. *Cresta et Duc* (M), Via Circonvallazione 7 (842.585). Open 22 Dec. to 14 April and 27 June to 15 Sept. Well appointed; 38 pleasant rooms. AE, DC, MC, V. *Croux* (M), Via Circonvallazione 94 (842.437). Open Dec. 21–Apr. 30; July–Sept. Central; bright, comfortable. AE, MC, V. *Panei* (M), Viale Monte Bianco 60 (842.358). In town, tiny. AE, V.

Restaurants. *Al Camin* (E), Via dei Bagni (841.497). Closed Wed. Open 1 Dec. to 15 May and 20 June to 20 Oct. Smart. AE, MC, V. *K2* (E), at Villair (82.475). Closed Mon. Quality and atmosphere. Aperitifs at quiet *Glarey* or chic *Posta*. *Pierre Alexis* (M), Via Marconi 54 (843.517). Closed Mon. Central.

At **Entreves,** *Brenva* (M). Closed Mon. Simple but good. V. *Maison de Filippo* (M). Closed Tues., June, and Nov. Attractive inn, popular for local country cooking. AE, MC, V. *Pilier d'Angle* (89.129). Closed Mon., May and Oct. Pleasant dining with nice view. V.

Cuneo Cuneo (0171). Important commercial city.

Restaurants. *Le Plat d'Etain* (E), Corso Giolitti 18 (61.918). Closed Sun., June 23–July 14. Small, reserve; exceedingly good French cuisine. AE, DC, MC, V. *Tre Citroni* (M), Via Bonelli 2 (62.048). Closed Wed. and 15–30 June; 15–30 Sept. Very pleasant, family run place for well-prepared seasonal specialties. AE, DC, MC, V.

At **Boves,** 10 km (6 miles) from Cuneo, *Rododendro* (E), at San Giacomo (680.372). Closed Sun. eve., Mon. and Tues. noon. Reserve. Exquisite food with a French accent. Worth the detour. About 90,000 lire per person. AE, DC, MC, V.

Gressoney Aosta (0125). Important winter sports and summer resort, with more fashionable Gressoney La Trinité about 244 meters (800 ft.) higher than Gressoney St. Jean. High season 23 Dec. to 8 Jan., 10 Feb. to 10 March and 10 July to 31 Aug.

At **La Trinité,** *Busca-Thedy* (M) (366.136). Quiet, pleasant. *Residence* (M), at Edelboden (366.148). Open 1 Dec. to 30 April, 1 July to 30 Sept. Alpine modern decor, fine views. AE, DC, MC, V.

At **St. Jean,** *Gran Baita* (I) (355.241). Open 1 Dec. to 10 May and 20 June to 20 Sept. Small, homely place. *Stadel* (I), (355.264), at Bielciuken. Small, lots of atmosphere and comfort.

Ivrea Torino (0125). Known for medieval monuments and its carnival. *La Serra* (E), Corso Botta 30 (44.341). Centrally located; modern, very comfortable; terrace, indoor pool, sauna; convention center. AE, DC, MC, V. *Sirio* (M), at Lake Sirio (424.247). Quiet and pleasant, noted for fine restaurant. AE, V.

Restaurants. *Moro* (M), Corso Massimo d'Azeglio 41 (422.136). Closed Sun. Fine local cuisine. AE, DC, MC, V. *Leon d'Oro* (M), Via Arduino 23 (46.341). Closed Fri., 15–30 July. Central, good. AE, DC, MC.

Limone Piemonte Cuneo (0171). Principal winter sports and summer resort of southern Piedmont. *Principe* (M) (92.389). Smallish, in quiet panoramic position. Open 15 Dec. to 15 April and 1 July to 1 Aug. MC, V.

Restaurants. *Mac Miche* (M) (92.449). Reserve. Closed Mon. evening, Tues. and 15 June to 10 July. Atmosphere. AE, DC, MC, V. *Mignon* (M) (92.363). Closed Wed. Pleasant inn.

Macugnaga Novara (0324). Picturesque resort and mountain-climbing center. High season Easter, 15 July to 31 Aug. and Christmas. *Nuovo Pecetto* (I), at Pecetto (65.025). Open 1 Dec. to 12 Sept. Charming atmosphere, good views. *Zumstein* (I), at Staffa (65.118). Open 18 Dec. to 25 April and 15 June to 20 Sept. Pretty place with garden. MC.

Restaurant. *Chez Felice* (M) (65.229). Closed Thurs. By reservation only. Typical local cuisine.

Novara Novara (0321). Industrial center, important buildings. *Italia* (E), Via Solaroli 8 (399.316). Central, modern, comfortable. AE, DC, MC, V.

Restaurants. *Da Giorgio* (E), Via delle Grazie 2 (27.647). Closed Mon. and Tues. noon. Fairly central; seafood specialties. AE. *Caglieri* (M), Via Tadini 12 (456.373). Closed Fri. Good food, garden terrace. *Teatro Coccia* (M), Piazza Martiri della Libertà (24.055). At the castle, fine traditional cuisine.

Orta San Giulio Novara (0322). Lake resort. High season Easter and 1 July to 15 Sept. *San Rocco* (E) (90.222). Lovely, quiet, converted 17th-century convent; lakeside garden. AE, DC, MC, V. *La Bussola* (I) (90.198). Overlooking lake, tiny; small pool in attractive garden. AE, MC, V.

Restaurants. *San Rocco* (E), Via Gippini 11 (90.222). Good restaurant of attractive hotel (see above). *Antico Agnello* (M), Piazzetta Regazzoni (90.259). Closed Tues. off-season. Very attractive little inn in town; good simple food; crowded on Sun.

Santa Vittoria D'Alba Cuneo (0172). Wine producing town, subject of novel and film. **Restaurants.** *Al Castello* (M), Via Cogne 4 (47.147). Closed Tues. evening, Wed., Jan. and first week in Aug. In atmospheric old castle, very good local cuisine and, naturally, exceptional wines.

At **Cinzano,** *Muscatel* (M) (47.039). Closed Tues, Aug. 15–31. Same type. AE, DC, MC, V.

Saint Vincent Aosta (0166). Chic spa resort, casino. High season 15 June to 30 Sept and Christmas. *Billia* (L), Viale Piemonte 18 (34.46). Elegance and all creature comforts; lovely rooms with view; indoor pool, large park. AE, DC, MC, V. *Elena* (M), Piazza Zerbion 2 (21.40). Closed Nov. Central, quite comfortable. No restaurant. AE, MC, V.

Restaurants. *Batezar-Da Renato* (E), Via Marconi 1 (31.64). Closed Wed. and Thurs. noon, July 1–15. Smart clientele; seasonal specialties. AE, DC, MC, V. *Le Grenier* (E), Piazza Zerbion 1 (22.24). Closed Mon. noon and Tues. Atmosphere, good food. AE, DC, V. *Tre Porcellini* (M), Via Roma (34.07). Closed Thurs. and Nov. AE, V.

Sauze D'Oulx Torino (0122). Low-key winter resort. High season 1 Feb. to 15 March, July to Aug. and Christmas. *Capricorno* (M), at Le Clotes (85.273). Open 28 Nov. to 18 Apr.; 13 June to 12 Sept. Tiny, quiet, in pinewoods; 5 minutes by chairlift from center; favored by British skiers. *Gran Baita* (I) (85.183). Open 1 Dec. to 20 April, 1 July to 31 Aug. Pleasant place with garden.

Sestriere Torino (0122). Top winter sports and summer resort. High season 1 Feb. to 15 March, Easter and Christmas. *Cristallo* (E), Via Pinerolo 5 (77.234). Open 1 Dec. to 25 April. Smart, attractive. AE, DC, V. *Grand Sestriere* (E), Via Assietta 1 (76.476). Open 21 Dec. to 4 April. Large, elegant, very comfortable. AE, DC, MC, V. *Duchi d'Aosta* (M) (77.123). Reservations through Club Méditerranée. Striking cylindrical building. Open 20 Dec. to 18 April. *Miramonti* (I), Via Cesana 3 (77.048). Open 1 Nov. to 1 May and 29 June to 9 Sept. Smallish, pleasant.

Restaurant. *La Baita* (M), Via Louset 4/a (77.496). Closed Tues. and May. Rustic decor, very good *polenta* and other local specialties.

Torino/Turin Torino (011). Regional capital, industrial and trade center, art city. *City* (E), Via Juvarra 25 (540.546). Fairly central, elegant modern decor. No restaurant. AE, DC, V. *Jolly Ligure* (E), Piazza Carlo Felice 85 (55.641). Central, totally renovated, very attractive and comfortable. AE, DC, MC, V. *Principi di Piemonte* (E), Via Gobetti 15 (519.693). A *Jolly* hotel. Very central, elegantly furnished rooms and suites; best in town. AE, DC, MC, V. *Turin Palace* (E), Via Sacchi 8 (515.511). Central; quiet, spacious and well-furnished rooms; good service and atmosphere. AE, DC, MC, V.

Genio (M), Corso Vittorio Emanuele 47B (650.5771). Central, smart contemporary decor. AE, DC, MC, V. *Venezia* (M), Via Venti Settembre 70 (513.384). Central, reliable. AE, DC, MC, V. *Victoria* (M), Via Nino Costa 4 (553.710). Central, attractive modern ambience, good atmosphere. AE, DC, MC, V.

Restaurants. *Villa Sassi* (L), Strada Traforo del Pino 47 (890.556). Closed Sun. A 17th-century villa, one of the Toulà chain of luxurious restaurants. Exquisite food and wines in exceptional setting just outside city center. Also has 12 rooms. AE, DC, MC, V.

Cambio (E), Piazza Carignano 2 (546.690). Closed Sun. and Aug. Gilt and mirrors, 19th-century decor in historic locale; excellent classic cuisine. AE, DC, MC, V. *Due Lampioni* (E), Via Carlo Alberto 45 (546.721). Closed Sun. and Aug. Longtime favorite; wide range of fine choices. AE, V. *Gatto Nero* (E), Corso Turati 14 (590.414). Closed Sun., and Aug. Tuscan ambience and cuisine. AE, DC. *Monte Carlo* (E), Via San Francesco da Paolo 37 (541.234). Closed Sat. noon, Sun. and Aug. Folksy place, prices just above (M). AE, DC, MC, V. *Rendezvous* (E), Corso Vittorio Emanuele 38 (539.990). Closed Sat. evening, Sun. and Aug. One of Turin's most elegant and classic. *La Smarrita* (E), Corso Unione Sovietica 244 (390.657). Closed Mon. and Aug. Reservations a must in this sophisticated spot, excellent dining, fixed menu. AE, DC, MC, V. *Tiffany* (E), Piazza Solferino 16 (540.538). Closed Sat. lunch, Sun. and Aug. Very posh, frequented by Turin society; top-level cuisine. AE. *Vecchia Lanterna* (E), Corso Umberto 21 (537.047). Closed Sat. noon, Sun. and Aug. Sumptuous decor and cuisine; very up-market. DC, MC, V.

Bue Rosso (M), Corso Casale 10 (830.753). Closed Mon., Sat. noon and Aug. Leader at (M) level. AE, DC, V. *Bridge* (M), Via Giacosa 2/b (687.609). Very good. AE, V. *Capannina* (M), Via Donati 1 (545.405). Closed Sun. and Aug. Regional dishes. *Il Ciacolon* (M), Viale Venticinque Aprile 11 (661.0911). Evenings only, closed Sun., Mon. and Aug. Venetian cuisine. *Al Ghibellin Fuggiasco* (M), Via Tunisi 50 (390.750). Closed Sat., Sun. evening and Aug. Attractive decor; Tuscan specialties. AE, DC, MC, V. *Ostu Bacu* (M), Corso Vercelli 226 (264.579). Closed Sun. and Aug. Typical locale; regional dishes. *Taverna Della Rose* (M), Via Massena 24 (545.275). Closed Sat. noon, Sun. and Aug. Near Porto Nuova station; very good. AE, MC, V.

Antica Trattoria Parigi (I), Corso Rosselli 83. *Cesare* (I), Via Carlo Alberto 3. *Da Mauro* (I), Via Maria Vittoria 21 (839.7811). Closed Mon., July. Lively family-run. *Da Osvaldo* (I), Via Mercanti 16. Central, unpretentious. *Da Roberto* (I), Via Lagrange 22. Hearty dishes. *Spada Reale* (I), Via Principe Amedeo 53 (832.835).

Cafés. Turin's cafés are redolent of old-world atmosphere. Don't miss *Baratti & Milano*, Piazza Castello 29. Nearby *Mulassano*, Piazza Castello 9. *San Carlo*, Piazza San Carlo 156. *Torino*, Piazza San Carlo 204.

GETTING AROUND. By air. Turin's Caselle airport is about 11 km. (7 miles) outside the city; it's often fogged in during the winter months, and flights are then rerouted to Genoa. There is a bus service approx. every 45 mins into Turin from Caselle, taking about 30 mins. The terminal is at Corso Siccardi 6.

By train. Turin is the transportation hub of the region. The main rail line from Genoa and Alessandria passes through Asti and Turin, continuing on into France at Modane. Another main line links Turin with Milan, and there are secondary lines to Piedmont's other cities.

By car. Superhighways connect Turin with Aosta, Alessandria and Milan, and drivers wishing to discover Piedmont would do well to make Turin their center, pausing, perhaps, on the way down the Valle d'Aosta from the Mt. Blanc or Grand St. Bernard tunnel. This historic valley has an autostrada sweeping down from Aosta to Turin, which besides providing for fast travel, means that the old road, meandering along between the castled villages, is largely traffic-free—and from it run several lesser valley roads that reward investigation. Chief among the latter are the Gressoney, with Monte Rosa at its head; Valle del Cervino, reaching toward the Matterhorn; and Val de Cogne, which leads to the Gran Paradiso mountains. At the northern end, beyond Aosta, there is the Grand St. Bernard road up to the monastery; and beyond Courmayeur the much more enchanting Little St. Bernard pass, which is so lightly used now that it has the charm of a small country road strung with mountain villages.

Some ingenuity with a map, preferably large scale, will produce various round trips in the area. For example: Turin to Courmayeur, over the Little St. Bernard into France, down the Val-d'Isère, return to Italy over the Col du Mt. Cenis, and back to Turin; about 370 km. (230 miles) turning left all the time through breathtaking scenery. But except for the motorway section it is slow going all the way. On the other hand, in a southern sweep round Turin outlined by Vercelli, Cuneo and Mantua, there are such places as Limone, Acqui, Asti, Alba and Sestriere, all worth seeing.

TURIN MUSEUMS. Turin is a city with one major and several almost as important galleries. Among the latter is the Egyptian Museum, which surprises by the size of its collection. We give further general points about museums and galleries under *Museums* in the *Facts at Your Fingertips* section.

Armeria Reale, Piazza Castello. Adjoining the Royal Palace, the Royal Armory contains an impressive array of historical pieces, many of them works of art.

Galleria Sabauda, Via Accademia delle Scienze 6. A fine collection of art in a Baroque palace. Works by Botticelli, Bernardo Daddi, Gentileschi and strong in Flemish and Dutch masters. Tues. to Sat., 9–2, closed Mon.

Museo Civico di Arte Antica, Palazzo Madama, Piazza Castello. Gothic, Renaissance and Rococo material, with a wide selection of decorative art. Tues. to Sat., 9–7, Sun. 10–1, 2–7, closed Mon.

Museo Egizio, same building as Galleria Sabauda. Big display of ancient Egyptian artefacts, well-displayed and very interesting to Egyptophiles. Daily 9–2, 3–7, closed Mon.

Palazzo Reale, Piazza Castello. Marvelous interiors, mostly Rococo—tapestries, gilded ceilings and lovely frescos. Tues. to Sat., 9–2, Sun. 9–1, closed Mon.

LOMBARDY, MILAN AND THE LAKES

The Scenic North

The Lombardy area of Italy stretches gently south from the fringes of the Alps to the river Po. It is a land of industry, of pastoral tranquility, of breathtaking beauty and of a history of 2,000 years of strife.

Bergamo, Brescia, Como, Cremona, Mantua, Milan and Pavia are its chief cities and all of them have antecedents almost as ancient as those of Rome itself. Their cathedrals, their ancient and gorgeously decorated palaces, their old battle towers, their museums and the magnificent works of art which they include, comprise a wealth of incomparable magnificence.

The lake region—Como, Garda, Maggiore and Lugano—is at the foot of the Alps, which drop, seemingly almost perpendicularly, for more than 1,800 meters (6,000 ft.) to the shimmering surface of the blue lakes beneath. There are good reasons for Lombardy's popularity with honeymooners!

Although some of the lake resorts fall administratively within the Piedmont area, they are included here as making for better tourist orientation.

From the Etruscans to Mussolini

More than 3,000 years ago—the date and the details are lost in the mysteries of Etruscan inscriptions—explorers from the highly civilized Etruscan kingdom of Tuscany, wandered northward beyond the River Po. The Etruscans extended their dominance into this region for some hundreds of years but left little of their culture. They were succeeded by the Cenomanic Gauls who, in turn, were conquered by the legions of Rome in the latter days of the Republic.

The region became known as Cisalpine Gaul and under the rule of Augustus it became a Roman province. Its warlike, independent people became citizens of Rome. Virgil, Catullus and both the Plinys were born in this region during this relatively tranquil era.

The decline of the Roman Empire was followed by the invasions of the Huns and the Goths, who finally brought about the destruction of the grandeur which was Rome. Attila and Theodoric in turn gave way to the Lombards, who ceded their iron crown to Charlemagne as the emblem of his vast but unstable empire.

Even before the fragile bonds which held this empire together had begun to snap, the cities of Lombardy were erecting walls in defense against the Hungarians, still on the warpath, and also against each other. These communes did, however, form the Lombard League, which in the 12th century finally defeated Frederick Barbarossa.

Once the invaders had been definitely defeated, new and even more bloody strife began. In each city the Guelphs—bourgeois supporters of the popes—and the Ghibellines—noble adherents to the so-called Emperors—clashed with each other. The communes declined and each fell under the yoke of neighboring or local powerful rulers. The Republic of Venice dominated Brescia and Bergamo. Mantua was ruled by the Gonzaga, and the Visconti and Sforza families took over Como, Cremona, Milan and Pavia.

The Battle of Pavia in 1525 brought on the 200 years of Spanish occupation, when the generals of Charles V defeated the French and gave Francis I the chance to coin the famous phrase: "All is lost save honor." The Spaniards were on the whole less cruel than the local tyrants and were hardly resisted by the Lombardians.

The War of the Spanish Succession, in the early years of the 18th century, threw out the Spaniards and brought in, instead, the Austrians, whose dominion was "neither liked nor loathed" during the nearly 100 years of its existence.

Napoleon and his generals routed the Austrians. The Treaty of Campoformio resulted in the proclamation of the Cisalpine Republic, which quickly became the Republic of Italy and, just as rapidly, the Kingdom of Italy, which lasted only until Napoleon's defeat brought back the Austrians. But Milan, as the capital of Napoleon's republic and of the Kingdom of Italy, had had a taste of glory, and the inherently independent character of its citizens, with those of the other Lombardian cities, was not slow to resent and combat the loss of its "national" pride.

From 1820 on, the Lombards joined with the Piedmontese and the House of Savoy in a perpetual struggle against the Habsburgs and, in 1859, finally defeated Austria and brought about the creation of the Kingdom of Italy two years later.

Milan and other cities of Lombardy have not lost their independence and their hatred of domination. Nowhere in Italy was the partisan insurrection against Mussolini—to whom they first gave power—and the German regime better organized or more successful. Milan itself was liberated from the Germans by its own partisan organization before the entrance of Allied troops; escaping Allied prisoners could find sanctuary there when fighting was still going on far to the south.

Lombardians are a forthright people. They are as much inclined to taciturnity as any Italian is ever apt to be and when they do talk they mean exactly what they say. When they quote a price there is little use haggling about it. Where your Milanese is inclined to be very, very money-minded, his compatriot on the rice farm or in the mountains, although interested in dollars and pounds, is really much more interested in you as an individual.

Milan

Milan is the industrial, banking and commercial capital of Italy, regardless of Church and State. Its art collections compare favorably with those of Rome and Florence. Its theater rivals that of Rome. Those of its historic buildings which have survived centuries of strife and destruction are carefully preserved masterpieces. Its people are proud, determined and businesslike (a very pleasant change from some other parts of Italy). They know they've wrought miracles in the past, and they are still busy performing miracles in the present—especially in the field of modern architecture, as the newer sections of the city show.

Milan is a sprawling city, a veritable nightmare to the tourist seeking to drive either in or out of its maze of inner and outer districts. But once in, with the car safely parked in a central hotel garage—where it is advisable to leave it most of the time—the visitor finds that Milanese life, art and beauty revolve around, and can be found in, a remarkably small area.

In almost the exact center of the heart of Milan is the truly great Cathedral, third largest church in the world, and the largest Gothic building in Italy. Don't be misled by its facade, one of its least attractive and most modern sections, although impressive enough. Consider that the building was started in 1386, consecrated in 1577 and not wholly completed until 1897. Walk completely around the cathedral, noting especially its 135 marble spires, the beautiful *Madonnina* surmounting them all. Note especially the lines of the apse and its three vast and intricate windows, built in 1389 and generally attributed to Nicolas de Bonaventura, the only one of the master builders who designed and constructed this cathedral to leave his name to posterity. Note, too, but don't try to count, the 2,245 marble statues of all periods which decorate the exterior of the edifice.

The majesty and grandeur of the Cathedral's interior, with its five great aisles and enormous pillars, are best appreciated in the half-light always found there. The stained-glass windows are from the 15th and 16th centuries, and the light piercing them and reflecting down onto the choir gives a superb study in the mystical effect of shadow properly used.

You will want to see the tomb of Giacomo Medici, by Leoni, in the right transept, and the choir in the presbytery, with its great bronze *ciborium* done by Pellegrini. In the crypt of this presbytery is the body of St. Carlo Borromeo, once Archbishop of Milan.

Either walk or take the elevator to the terraces of the cathedral. There, through a startling and amazing array of spires and statues, you can see all of Milan, all of the Lombardy plains and the Alps beyond—provided it is a clear day.

The great square in front of the cathedral, with its vari-colored tile pavement, is the Piazza del Duomo. On two sides of it are the *portici* where

Milanese love to congregate. Here begins the Galleria Vittorio Emanuele, traditional gathering place with its cafés, bars, restaurants, outdoor yet sheltered tables, bookshops and, of course, souvenir shops. Stroll through it slowly and come out into the Piazza della Scala, home of the Teatro della Scala, where Verdi's fame was established, completely renovated after its World War II destruction by Allied bombs in 1943. It was reopened at a performance led by the great Arturo Toscanini himself, in 1946.

Go along the Via Verdi, then the Via Brera to the Palazzo di Brera, home of the Pinacoteca di Brera, one of Italy's greatest collections of art. The 15th–18th centuries period, notable in Italian art, is especially well represented here. Luini, Bramantino and Foppa are outstanding examples of the Lombard school. The *Dead Christ* by Mantegna is a remarkable work of the Venetian school, as is Tintoretto's *Discovery of the Body of St. Mark*. Other Venetians displayed are Veronese, Giovanni Bellini, Canaletto and Titian. In addition, there are fine works from other Italian schools, including Raphael and Caravaggio, and many outstanding foreign paintings. Modern art and temporary shows are two doors down in Palazzo Citterio.

From the Castello Sforzesco to The Last Supper

Stroll back now to the Piazza del Duomo and from it along the Via Mercanti, past the ancient Palazzo della Ragione and a small medieval square and along the Via Dante to the Castello Sforzesco (or alternatively turn right out of the Brera to reach Via Pontaccio, left along it, which will bring you out at the side of the Castello). This fortress was used by the famed Sforza family of despots, dukes of Milan, founded by a peasant boy, who, on whim, legend says, became a soldier, a captain, a leader. *Sforza* he was nicknamed by his young comrades in arms because of his strength and his prowess at arms, and he handed down the name to his family, which grew, and remained, "the strong."

Leonardo da Vinci, Bramante and Filarete started this fierce-looking castle for Ludovico Sforza. The restoration was carried out in the early 1900s by Beltrami. The three pyramidal stages, the heavy facade and its two towers give a true impression of strength and vigor. In the Corte Ducale you will find a magnificent collection of sculpture, including Michelangelo's last work, the *Rondanini Pietà*, interior furnishings, paintings and archeological masterpieces. The 15th-century to 18th-century paintings on the first floor are second only to those which you may have seen previously in the Pinacoteca. In this collection also are priceless examples of Japanese and Chinese art dating from 300 B.C.

Later you should definitely visit the Palazzo dell'Ambrosiana, built in the early 17th century, which now houses the Ambrosiana Gallery, again with Italian paintings of the 15th–18th centuries, and a marvelous library. Notable here, in addition to Botticellis, Titians, Raphaels, etc., are 1,750 drawings by Leonardo da Vinci.

In the Via Torino, not far from the Piazza del Duomo, you will find one of the most beautiful Renaissance churches in all Italy. It is San Satiro, built by Bramante in 1480, with magnificent optical illusion used in its interior to suggest a vast spaciousness where, in fact, there is none. Actually it is a relatively small church for one of this type in Italy.

Quite nearby is San Lorenzo Maggiore, oldest of Milan's Christian churches. Rare 4th-century mosaics are set in the niches of its Chapel of

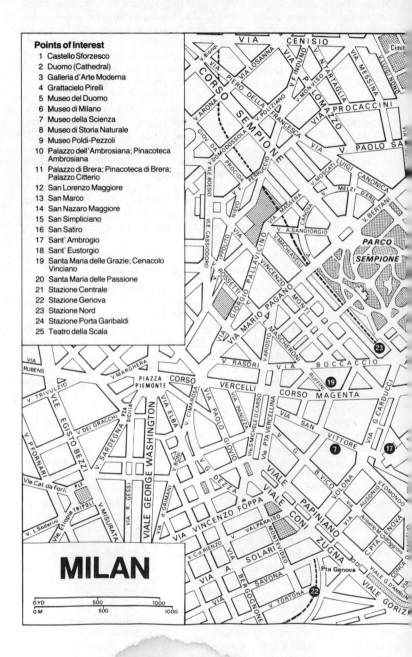

Points of Interest

1. Castello Sforzesco
2. Duomo (Cathedral)
3. Galleria d'Arte Moderna
4. Grattacielo Pirelli
5. Museo del Duomo
6. Museo di Milano
7. Museo della Scienza
8. Museo di Storia Naturale
9. Museo Poldi-Pezzoli
10. Palazzo dell'Ambrosiana; Pinacoteca Ambrosiana
11. Palazzo di Brera; Pinacoteca di Brera; Palazzo Citterio
12. San Lorenzo Maggiore
13. San Marco
14. San Nazaro Maggiore
15. San Simpliciano
16. San Satiro
17. Sant' Ambrogio
18. Sant' Eustorgio
19. Santa Maria delle Grazie; Cenacolo Vinciano
20. Santa Maria delle Passione
21. Stazione Centrale
22. Stazione Genova
23. Stazione Nord
24. Stazione Porta Garibaldi
25. Teatro della Scala

MILAN

0 YD 500 1000
0 M 500 1000

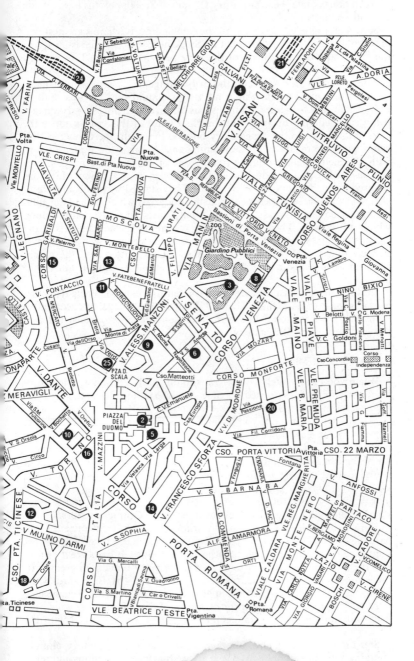

St. Aquilinus, while the 4th-century Chapel of St. Hippolytus has two fine
Roman columns.

Sant Ambrogio, in the Piazza of the same name, is Milan's greatest medieval monument. It was founded by St. Ambrose in 386 (he is buried in
the crypt) and is a handbook of the very best in 11th- and 12th-century
architecture.

Santa Maria delle Grazie, on the Corso Magenta, is another of Milan's
great church monuments which no visitor should miss. It was built in
1466, and in 1492—while Columbus was discovering America—Bramante
enlarged it, adding the apse. But the chief point of this visit is not to the
church itself, but to the dependency outside to its left, the Cenacolo Vinciano, once the refectory of the Dominicans. An artist decorated its wall
with a scene proper to a dining room—one of the most famous paintings
ever created, Leonardo da Vinci's *Last Supper*. It is a fresco which has
suffered more than its share of disasters. They started with Leonardo himself, who was a great experimenter, using materials which he had not sufficiently tested—in this case tempera, totally unsuited to the damp wall on
which it was used. Then, too, it had to withstand the concussions of the
wartime bombardment of Milan. The incredibly delicate work of restoration continues, inch by inch, but it has to be admitted that the much-
restored work is just a dim shadow of the vibrant painting it must once
have been.

Sant' Eustorgio, just outside the 14th-century gates of Porta Ticinese,
contains the Portinari Chapel, behind the apse. This chapel has been called
"a perfect jewel in stone" and is the work of Michelozzo, constructed in
the middle of the 15th century.

Environs of Milan

When you have visited Milan, you should think a bit about the rest of
Lombardy. If you are pressed for time skip everything else in the province
for at least a brief tour of the lakes region.

If you have a car—of if you haven't, lots of buses are available—make
a quick trip at least down to one of the world's greatest and best-known
monasteries, the Certosa di Pavia, a complete masterpiece of Renaissance
art of the Lombardian motif. It was finished only in the 16th century, but
it was started in 1396 by the Visconti; who are well represented in the
works of art to be seen. The sculpture of the facade, with its multi-colored
marble and its lacy structure, is extremely beautiful, as are the richly decorated ceilings and magnificent choir stalls of its Gothic interiors.

Only 8 km.(5 miles) from the Charterhouse is Pavia itself, ancient Lombard capital, called Ticinum by the Romans and once a rival of Milan for
domination of Lombardy, when both were free cities. It has a great history
and the monumental structures of its days of glory remain, in great part,
unchanged today. The cathedral was begun in 1488 by Bramante, while
Leonardo da Vinci designed the majestic dome and a true Renaissance
interior. See, too, the 12th-century Church of San Michele, in which the
medieval emperors (Charlemagne among them) were crowned with the
iron crown.

San Pietro in Ciel d'Oro, another Romanesque 12th-century church,
contains both the sarcophagus of the great philosopher Boethius and relics
of St. Augustine. There are medieval towers—it used to be called the city
of a hundred towers—a mighty Visconti castle and the delightful university, founded in 1361.

Cremona and Mantua

Down the Po from Milan and Pavia, in the center of the plains of Lombardy, is Cremona, whose name has been revered by musicians and all lovers of music for many generations. For it was in this medieval city that the Stradivari, Guarneri and Amati families produced the finest violins in the world. The Stradivarian Museum, in part of the Municipal Museum, is rich in relics of these and of the composer Monteverdi. The Piazza del Comune is one of the most impressive of Italy's squares, with its beautiful 12th-century Duomo. In this cathedral are a wonderful set of frescos telling stories from the New Testament. Beside the Duomo are the huge Gothic Torrazzo—known as the tallest bell tower in Italy—octagonal Baptistery, and Loggia dei Militi.

Continuing eastward you will come to Mantua, on the banks of the Mincio River. Near this old town the poet Virgil was born; Mantegna's tomb is in its Basilica of Sant'Andrea, while Mantua's host of medieval monuments date back chiefly to the days of the princely Gonzaga family.

Its main Piazza Sordello has two interesting 12th- and 13th-century palaces and the 18th-century facade of the cathedral which itself is early 16th. The towering mass of the Castel di San Giorgio, which was a part of the Gonzaga residence, is just behind. The battlemented walls of this castle jut out over the lakes which the Mincio forms around Mantua. Its famous 15th-century Camera degli Sposi, or Bridegroom's Chamber, is decorated with frescos of the Gonzaga family by Mantegna. Also housed here is a rare collection of Roman coins although the archeological museum has been moved to the Monastero Maggiore in Corso Magenta.

Adjoining San Giorgio, but facing on the square, is the Palazzo Ducale, once center of a brilliant court ruled by witty Isabella d'Este. Decorating its walls are Romano's rosy nudes, tapestries and paintings by Rubens, Tintoretto, and other great masters. Other spots to visit are Mantegna's home (housing a museum), the arcaded Piazza dell Erbe, a favorite for evening promenades, and the 16th-century Palazzo del Te on the edge of town, with fantastically inventive frescos.

Brescia and Lake Garda

66 km. (41 miles) along S236 lies Brescia. The ruins of a Capitoline Temple, built by the Emperor Vespasian in A.D. 73 testify to Brescia's Roman origin. Outstanding among the sculptures in the adjoining Roman Museum is the famed 1st-century bronze *Winged Victory*. More relics of the early days of the area are in the Museum of Christian Art (also in the Via dei Musei) with a remarkable collection of early medieval ivory diptychs and triptychs, crosses, jewels and statues. The Pinoteca Tosio-Martinengo, in the Piazza Moretto, accommodates—beside the works of the Brescia School—pictures by Raphael, Tintoretto, Tiepolo and Clouet.

Palladio and Sansovino contributed to the splendid marble Loggia, the great Lombard-Venetian palace overlooking the Piazza della Loggia. Another Palazzo, called just that, is topped by the 16th-century Torre dell'Orologio (Clock Tower). An imposing Torre del Popolo rises above the medieval Broletto, the Tribunal, and on the Piazza del Duomo the 17th-century Baroque cathedral is flanked by the 12th-century Rotonda. Among the churches worth visiting is the Madonna del Carmine, behind which a flight of stairs climbs to the ramparts of the Venetian castle, high enough to give a panoramic view over the town and across the plain to the distant Alps.

Lake Garda is a mere 19 km. (12 miles) northeast on N45bis, which follows closely the western shore from Saló to Riva on the way to Trento. The narrower of the two Gardesane Strade, N249, keeps equally close to the eastern shore on the return south to Peschiera; N572 completes the circuit to Salo. This drive round the two basins into which the lake is divided—the lower wide and framed by gentle hills, the upper long and narrow amidst steep cliffs and mountains—should be complemented by a leisurely cruise on the lake by steamer.

Italy's largest lake—52 km. (32 miles) long and 16 km. (10 miles) wide—extends over three provinces, Brescia, Trento and Verona, with their varied art treasures and no less varied natural beauties within easy reach. This explains the great popularity of the lake resorts, especially with German tourists. The greatest attraction is the narrow southern peninsula of Sirmione, where the Roman poet Catullus was born, supposedly in the large villa which is said to have belonged to his family. Though its ruins are still imposing, the outstanding site here is the medieval Scaligeri Castle built into the lake, all the more attractive when viewed from a *trattoria* serving the excellent local Lugana wine.

At Solferino, a few miles south, Napoleon III defeated Franz Joseph in 1859, both Emperors risking their lives in this battle, which was so bloody that it led to the foundation of the Red Cross, beside heralding the collapse of the Austrian domination of Italy seven years later.

The history of Desenzano del Garda extends back into pre-history, but Salò further north has preserved more of its medieval palaces, as well as a 15th-century cathedral with a Renaissance portal. At Gardone Riviera, now a very popular resort, the poet Gabriele D'Annunzio (1863–1938) built the Vittoriale, a villa complex set in lovely gardens. Often condemned as a monument to kitsch, especially his tomb, it is infinitely less offensive than the more recent architecture round the lake. Moreover, it blends perfectly with the olive and orange groves, which after Toscolano and Gargnano give way to the Trentino Alpine setting. As the lake narrows the water assumes a darker blue between the rugged mountains. The road pops in and out of tunnels and over innumerable bridges on its scenic way.

Riva, at the northernmost tip of the lake, flourished from the 12th to the 14th centuries, when most of the churches, towers and palaces were built. Riva has the one museum on the lake that shouldn't be missed, as well as an avenue of magnolias that are quite magnificent when in bloom. Two miles southeast, Torbole attracted Goethe by its excellent climate—the town is still a health resort—which is shared by the Riviera degli Olivi extending 48 km. (30 miles) south. The highest concentration of Roman ruins, medieval castles and churches, stately Renaissance villas and modern hotels can be found at: Malcesine, which is also close to the ski centers on Monte Baldo, 1,748 m. (5,735 ft.); Torri del Benace, behind medieval ramparts and below a Scaligeri castle; Garda, where a particularly picturesque castle dominates a particularly picturesque bay; Lazise, with a Romanesque church in the old quarter surrounded by walls; and finally Peschiera, where medieval and Renaissance palaces vie for attention.

Bergamo, Lake Iseo and Lake Como

From Brescia it is only 23 km. (14 miles) northwest to Iseo, the pleasant little town that gave Lombardy's fourth-largest lake its name. Completely surrounded by mountains, the main attraction is the densely wooded Mt. Isola guarded by two rugged cliffs in the center of the blue water.

The old city of Bergamo lies at the foot of the Bergamese Alps. Actually Bergamo is two cities—Lower Bergamo and Upper Bergamo. High up on the hillside, walled in by the ruins of ancient Venetian fortifications, surmounted by an ancient fortress, is Bergamo Alta. The principal monuments here—the 12th-century Palazzo della Ragione, the massive Torre del Comune, the Duomo of Bergamo, the Church of Santa Maria Maggiore, the Colleoni Chapel and the Baptistery—are in or near the Piazza Vecchia. The dome and the sanctuary of the Colleoni Chapel are decorated by Tiepolo's frescos of the life of St. John the Baptist.

Slightly lower, in Bergamo Bassa, in the Accademia Carrara, you will find one of Italy's greatest and most important art collections. Many of the Venetian masters are represented—Mantegna, Carpaccio, Tiepolo, Guardi, Canaletto—and there are some magnificent Bellinis and Botticellis. The citizens of Bergamo are fiercely proud that Donizetti was born there. Nor is this their only claim to musical fame, for the town is also the birthplace of the famous peasant dance, the *bergamasque*.

Unless wedded to autostradas or the railway, by far the quickest and loveliest road to the next lake is from Bergamo directly to Lecco on the southeastern base of Lake Como. Lecco possesses a fair share of the lake towns' assorted medieval churches and towers, Renaissance palaces and neo-Classical villas, yet northern Lombardy's prominence on the tourist map is due to the breathtaking beauty of the scenery. A good sample of the usually snowcapped Alps is included in the panoramic view from Piani d'Erna, easily accessible by funicular up Mt. Resegone (1,875 meters, 6,152 ft.). And as with all lakes, the road circuit should be complemented by boat trips; best here are the leisurely paddle steamers, though there are also hydrofoils and ferries.

Besides a respectable Museum of Antiquities, Como features a 14th-century cathedral, the 13th-century Broletto Palace, and a medieval tower. On the lakeside is the lovely Villa Olmo, but most of all there is the view to the north over the lake, which is bordered by a profusion of gardens. Cernobbio on the west shore is the most elegant lake resort. On an eastern promontory is Torno, close by the still extant spring which Pliny the Younger—both Plinys were born in the Como region, which is inordinately proud of them—described so carefully in a well-known letter to a friend. The nearby Villa Pliniana has only a very remote connection with the famous Romans, as you may imagine, since it dates from the 16th century.

The steamers pass the only island, picturesque Comacina, where early-medieval Christopolis is now being excavated next to the villas the Brera Academy puts at the disposal of painters. Tremezzo is the center of the Tremezzina Riviera, blessed by a particularly mild climate that favors luxuriant vegetation. From Cadenabbia a ferry crosses to Bellagio, where the three sections of the lake meet. Here is the Villa Serbelloni, while equally pretty Varenna, halfway up the western shore, is graced by the Villa Monastero, seat of the Nobel Prize Association and with lovely gardens. Farther north are Bellano and Dongo, where Mussolini was captured in April 1945 and executed two days later by Italian partisans.

Lake Lugano and Lake Maggiore

Lake Lugano, north of Varese, is a good bit more than half Swiss. Only that part of the shoreline between Porto Ceresio and Ponte Tresa, and the Campione region, are Italian. Lugano is Swiss. But Campione d'Italia, a kind of Italian island in Swiss territory, is an ideal little place. Further, it has an excellent casino where you have your choice of three rooms to do your gambling, depending on the limit you care to play for. Though the town belongs to Italy, Swiss money and stamps are used. There are no frontier formalities.

At Ponte Tresa the lake steamer enters the straits of Lavena. Here the Tresa River cuts the village in half and forms the exact frontier between Italy and Switzerland.

From Santa Margherita, on the south shore, take the cable railway up to Belvedere Station and go on from there a little less than a mile to Lanzo d'Intelvi, high on a plateau and affording a view of the entire Lugano lake section, a rugged and wild region, whose ancient olive trees at the base of the mountains half shield its ultramodern hotels and aging villas.

Lake Maggiore is perhaps, next to Como, the best known of the Italian lakes, chiefly because of its west bank (Piedmontese) resorts such as Stresa, an old-established health and tourist resort lately endowed with a large Congress Building. Stresa is a recommended center for exploring the region.

Lake Maggiore is a gem. With the towering masses of Switzerland's Alps to the north, the famed Borromean Islands more or less in the center, the summer resort section of Stresa on the west, world-famed Locarno (Swiss) to the north, Laveno to the east and Arona to the south, Maggiore is a two-mile-wide ribbon of beauty connecting the plains of Lombardy with the Alps of Switzerland. Its scenery for the 64 km. (40 miles) of its length is so varied that it easily takes its place among the natural wonders of the world. Nowhere are the views more majestic than at Belgirate, a charming holiday spot with 11th-century castle ruins, 16th-century church containing works by Bernardino Luini, and a villa once inhabited by Napoleon's Josephine.

Take the steamer from Stresa, if you are stopping here, or from Laveno, on the Lombardian side of the lake. There are several trips available. Take them all, if you have the time, because each touches an attractive part of this lovely region. Go up to Locarno by way of Griffa, Porto Valtravaglia, and Cannero Riviera. You'll touch, too, at the village of Cannobio before you enter Switzerland's waters, then at Brisago and Ascona, and finally at Locarno.

Perhaps the loveliest of these cruises though, is that from Laveno to Stresa and Arona, or, as the case may be, from Stresa to Arona and Laveno. You will see the charming Punta Castagnola and the so-called "Gulf of Pallanza." The Borromean Islands are directly before you, with the Alps constituting the backdrop for their picturesque splendor. If you are interested in the picturesque, by the way, you should get off the boat for a while at Verbania Pallanza, whose 17th-century Palazzo Dugnani has a splendid collection of peasant costumes. The Villa Taranto here has magnificent botanical gardens, with somewhere around 20,000 species, and something exciting for the gardening enthusiast most of the year. It was created by a Scots enthusiast, Captain Neil McEachern, and ranks with Europe's finest. Open to the public daily from morning to evening.

Thence you will go by Baveno and its gardens to the "Fishermen's Island"—named Isola dei Pescatori or Isola Superiore—whose quaintness has made it a favorite haunt of artists and writers.

Then on to the second of the Borromeans—Isola Bella, short for "Isle of Isabella." Its gardens, its walks and its ten terraces, stretching down from the uppermost reaches of the Island's banks to the lake itself, form a sumptuous setting for the 17th-century Palazzo Borromeo, which blends into the landscape without in the least dominating it. All about you there is a profusion of exotic plants, Renaissance statuary and sparkling fountains. Isola Madre, smallest of the three islands, consists mainly of a beautiful sub-tropical garden.

PRACTICAL INFORMATION FOR MILAN

WHEN TO GO. Spring and fall are Milan's best seasons. Winter is cold and foggy, while summer is hot and smoggy. And most definitely do *not* plan a vacation between April 14 and 23, for then the city's hotels and restaurants are packed with the annual Trade Fair crowds.

USEFUL ADDRESSES. EPT Information Office, Via Marconi 1, at Piazza Duomo (809.662); Central Rail Station (669.0532); Linate Airport (744.065); City Information Office, Galleria Vittorio Emanuele (870.545).

U.S. Consulate, Piazza della Repubblica 32 (652.841); British Consulate, Via San Paolo 7 (869.3442).

SEASONAL EVENTS. Apr.: the city celebrates its commercial rites at the Trade Fair, from the 14th–23rd. **Dec.:** on the 7th, the Milanese celebrate the feast day of the city's patron, Sant'Ambrogio (St. Ambrose) with the grand opening of La Scala's opera season and with the traditional fair of "Oh! Bei, Oh! Bei" (named for the exclamations of visitors); during the fair, stalls around the Basilica of Sant'Ambrogio sell a profusion of goods.

TELEPHONE CODE. The telephone code for Milan is 02.

HOTELS. It is good practice to make reservations well in advance, as the city is always filled with visitors. During the Trade Fair, 14–23 April, tourists are often forced to seek accommodations in fairly distant cities. Should you arrive without reservations there is a booking service at the central railroad station and at the EPT office on the Via Marconi. Room rates for Milan hotels average about 15% above general guidelines. Some hotels close during August.

Deluxe

Duca di Milano, Piazza della Repubblica 13 (62.84). CIGA. Smallest of luxury hotels; 60 beautifully furnished rooms; intimate atmosphere. AE, DC, MC, V.

Duomo, Via San Raffaele 1 (88.33). In historic building facing cathedral; fine duplex suites, efficient service. MC, V.

Galileo, Corso Europa 9 (77.43). Central; well furnished, good atmosphere. AE, DC, MC, V.

Pierre, Via De Amicis 32 (805.6220). Milan's newest luxury hotel, cutting edge elegance. No restaurant. AE, DC, MC, V.

Expensive

Ascot, Via Lentasio 3 (862.946). Closed Aug. Fairly central, on quiet street; smallish, very comfortable. No restaurant. AE, DC, MC, V.

Carlton Senato, Via Senato 5 (798.583). Closed Aug. Central, in smart shopping district. Bright, modern. Ask for room on Via Spiga. AE, MC, V.

Cavalieri, Piazza Missori 1 (88.57). Centrally situated near Duomo; modernized rooms with good views. No restaurant. AE, DC, MC, V.

Diana Majestic, Viale Piave 42 (202.122). CIGA. Semi-central; 100 rooms in handsome hotel decorated in *art nouveau* style. AE, DC, MC, V.

De la Ville, Via Hoepli 6 (867.061). Very central; elegant period furnishings. No restaurant. AE, V.

Excelsior Gallia, Piazza Duca D'Aosta 9 (62.77). Luminous salons, spacious rooms, furnished for maximum comfort. AE, DC, MC, V.

Grand Hotel et de Milan, Via Manzoni 29 (870.757). Milan's most elegant and atmospheric hotel; Old World luxury. No restaurant. AE, DC, MC, V.

Jolly President, Largo Augusto 10 (77.46). Near Duomo, large, comfortable and efficient. AE, DC, MC, V.

Marino all Scala, Piazza della Scala 5 (867.803). Conveniently located in center; tasteful decor. No restaurant. AE, DC, MC, V.

Plaza, Piazza Diaz 3 (805.8452). Very central; attractively decorated rooms in contemporary style. No restaurant. AE, DC, MC.

Moderate

Ariosto, Via Ariosto 22 (490.995). Near Sempione Park at Conciliazione Metro stop. Attractive; no restaurant. AE, DC, MC, V.

Ariston, Largo Carrobbio 2 (805.7286). Friendly service; standard comfort. No restaurant. AE, MC, V.

Canada, Via Lentasio 15 (805.2527). Fairly central; small, quiet and comfortable. AE, DC, MC, V.

Casa Svizzera, Via S. Raffale 3 (869.2246). Closed 28 July–24 Aug. Very central, modern, quiet; good value. No restaurant. AE, DC, MC, V.

Centro, Via Broletto 46 (875.232). Large clientele from business and fashion worlds. Decor circa 1960. No restaurant.

Gran Duca di York, Via Moneta 1/a (874.863). Very central; fine, small, good atmosphere. No restaurant. AE.

Gritti, Piazza Santa Maria Beltrade (801.056). Bright, clean, cheerful. AE, DC, MC, V.

King, Corso Magenta 19 (874.432). Roomy, recently restored in pseudo-antique style. No restaurant. AE, MC, V.

Lancaster, Via Sangiorgio 16 (315.602). Closed July and Aug. At far side of Sempione park; pleasant, small. No restaurant. AE, MC, V.

Madison, Via Gasparotto 8 (608.5991). At main station, handy to Metro for center; modern, good. No restaurant, but good breakfast. AE, MC, V.

Manzoni, Via Santo Spirito 20 (705.700). Central near smart shopping streets; quiet, unpretentious, reasonable. No restaurant.

Zurigo, Corso Italia 11a (808.909). Modern and clean. No restaurant. AE, MC.

Inexpensive

Adler, Via Ricordi 10 (221.441). Near Piazzale Loreto, handy to Metro and bus, good, small.

Antica Locanda Solferino, Via Castelfidardo 2 (657.0129). Excellent value; modern comfort, quaint decor in 19th century building. No restaurant.

Bolzano, Via Boscovich 21 (669.1451). Near central station and Metro; friendly, basic comforts. AE, DC, MC, V.

Brera, Via Pontaccio 9 (873.509). Mildly eccentric. Rooms combine faded grandiose with 1970s tacky. No restaurant.

Città Studi, Via Saldini 24 (744.666). Near university, outside center; pleasant. AE, V.

London, Via Rovello 3 (872.988). Very central; simple but comfortable.

Pensione Rovello, Via Rovello 18a (873.956). Sparkling clean rooms in this tiny hotel, a favorite with young travellers and models. No restaurant.

Vecchia Milano, Via Borromei 4 (875.042). Pleasant hotel in 17th-century building. TV room, bar. No restaurant.

RESTAURANTS. It is always wise to reserve your table. Prices are 20% above guidelines and almost all those listed are closed in August.

Milanese Specialties. Although Milan does not have a great number of local specialties, it is one of the best cities for food in Italy. The liberal use of butter in preparing food of excellent quality adds a distinctive flavor to the Milanese cuisine. Among the most favored specialties is *osso buco alla milanese,* veal knuckle served with *risotto,* rice which has been cooked until almost all the liquid has evaporated and a creamy sauce remains. *Risotto alla milanese* has saffron added, which colors the dish a rich yellow. *Costoletta alla milanese* is a breaded veal cutlet. The favorite cheese of Milan is *Gorgonzola.* Other well known cheeses are *Bel Paese* and *Taleggio,* both mild, and *Mascarpone,* very much like cream cheese.

Milan's pastry specialty is *panettone,* a raised fluffy cake, flecked with dried raisins and a variety of candied fruit.

The regional wines are *Freccia Rossa, Grumello, Inferno, Lugana, Sassella* and *Valgella.*

Expensive

Alfio, Via Senato 31 (780.731). Closed Sat, Sun. noon and Aug. Popular with VIPs who pay top prices for fine cuisine. AE, DC, MC, V.

Biffi Scala, Piazza della Scala (876.332). Closed Sun., Aug. Afternoon tea and supper only. Very smart. AE, DC, MC, V.

Giannino, Via Sciesa 8 (545.2948). Closed Sun., Aug. One of Milan's most famous. Attractive garden decor; excellent seafood. AE, DC, MC, V.

Gran San Bernardo, Via Borgese 14 (331.9000). Closed Sun. Reserve; Milanese cuisine. AE, DC, V.

Marchesi, Via Bonsevin de la Riva 9 (741.246). Closed Sun. and Mon. noon, Aug. One of Italy's best. Host Gualtiero offers "nouvelle cuisine" *all 'italiana* with exquisite results. Average check runs 100,000 lire. AE, DC, MC, V.

Rigoletto, Via Monti 33 (498.8687). Closed Sun. Tasteful decor, fine cuisine. AE, DC, V.

Savini, Galleria Vittorio Emanuele (805.8343). Closed Mon., 3 weeks in Aug. A Milan tradition for elegant dining. AE, DC, MC, V.

Scaletta, Piazzale Stazione Porta Genova (835.0290). Closed Sun., Mon., Easter, Christmas. Reserve far ahead. Vies with *Marchesi* for top quality, superb food and wines in delightful setting.

El Toulà, Piazza Ferrari 6 (870.302). Closed Sun. Very smart link in a famous restaurant chain. AE, DC, MC, V.

Moderately Expensive

Bella Pisana, Via Pasquale Sottocorno 17 (708.376). Closed Sun. and Mon. noon, Aug., Christmas–5 Jan. Summer garden, very good food. AE, MC, V.

Boeucc, Piazza Belgioioso 2 (790.224). Closed Sat., Sun midday, Aug. Summer terrace; classic cuisine. AE, DC, MC, V.

Calajunco, Via Stoppani 5 (204.6003). Closed Sun., Aug. Fine seafood. AE.

Don Lisander, Via Manzoni 12/a (790.130). Closed Sat eve., Sun, 2 weeks in Aug, 2 weeks at Christmas. Refined atmosphere and cuisine. AE, DC, MC, V.

La Nôs, Via Amedei 2 (805.8759). Closed Sun. and Mon. noon. Lots of atmosphere; Milanese cuisine. AE, DC, MC, V.

Al Porto, Piazzale Generale Cantore (832.1481). Closed Sun. and Mon. noon. Tops for seafood. Reserve well ahead. AE, DC.

Quattro Mori, Via San Giovanni sul Muro 2 (870.617). Summer garden; excellent choice. AE, MC, V.

Moderate

Briciola, Via Solferino, corner of Via Marsala (655.1012). Closed Sun., Mon., Aug. Trendy place attracting youthful crowd. Creative decor; specialty *carpaccio.* AE, DC, V.

Brasera Meneghina, Via Circo 10 (808.108). Closed Mon., Aug. Typical old Milanese trattoria.

Al Buon Convento, Corso Italia 26 (805.0623). Closed Sun., Aug. Old fashioned, family run. Delicious home-made cooking. Try duck casserole with maize pudding. V.

Cantina Piemontese, Via Laghetto 11 (784.618). Closed Sun. Near Duomo. Rustic; good pastas and sparkling house wine. AE, DC, V.

Ciovassino, Via Ciovassino 5 (805.3868). Closed Sat. noon, Sun. and Aug. In the Brera district. AE, DC.

Charleston, Piazza del Liberty 8 (798.631). Closed Sat. noon and Mon. Good food and pizza; fast, efficient service.

Franco il Contadino, Via Fiori Chiari 20 (808.153). Closed Tues. and July. Near the Brera; good pasta. AE, DC, MC, V.

La Libera, Via Palermo 21, (805.3603). Closed Sat., Sun. midday, Aug. Young crowd comes for excellent food, jazz, and draught beer. Imaginative cooking, like veal kidneys with broccoli and juniper berries.

Opera Prima, Via Rovello 3, (865.235). Closed Sun. Classic, stylish surroundings, good food, and efficient service. AE, MC, DC, V.

Osteria dei Binari, Via Tortona 1 (839.0753). Closed Sun. Evenings only. Old world atmosphere, somewhat pricey.

La Pantera, Via Festa del Perdono 12 (805.7374). Closed Tues., Aug. *Classico-moderno* decor, good traditional Tuscan dishes. AE, DC, MC, V.

Quattro Toscani, Via Plinio 33 (208.130). Closed Sat. Near Loreto Metro stop.

Il Rigolo, Via Solferino 11 (805.9768). *Corriere della Sera* journalist hangout. Busy, business-like, with delicious seafood specialties. AE, V, MC.

Solferino, Via Castelfidardo 2, (659.9886). Closed Sat. midday, Sun. Plain, old-fashioned establishment with Milanese specialties.

Tencitt, Via Laghetto 2 (795.560). Closed Sat. midday, Sun., Aug. Ultra-1980's decor, nouvelle cuisine specialties. Try rice with pumpkin and scampi. AE, MC, DC, V.

Inexpensive

Al Cantinone, Via Agnello 19 (807.666). Closed Sat. midday, Sun. On onetime spot of the stables of La Scala. Basic decor, lively atmosphere, reliable food. Near Duomo. AE, MC, V.

La Bruschetta, Piazza Beccaria 12 (802.494). Closed Mon. Tiny, busy, first-class pizzeria.

La Piazzetta, Piazza Solferino 25 (659.1076). Closed Sun., Aug. Small dining room; appetizing fare.

La Ranarita, Via Fatebenefratelli 2. Closed Sun. Small, modern-style pizzeria. Delicious desserts.

Summertime, Via Vincenzo Monti 33 (498.8747). Spacious, Art Nouveau surroundings. Excellent value; small garden.

Torre di Pisa, Via Fiori Chiari 21 (874.877). Closed Sat. midday, Sun., Aug. Excellent Milanese and Tuscan cuisine; lively clientele. AE.

Takeaway Bar Solferino, Via San Marco 33 (659.377). Convenient self-service system; foreign clientele. Closed Sat. midday, Sun.

13 Giugno, Via Gioulio Uberti 5, off Corso Indipendenza (719.654). Closed Sat. midday, Sun., Aug. Ex-pop star proprietor serves imaginative food in charming Art Deco interior; garden in summer. AE, MC, V.

SNACKS AND PIZZAS. For gourmet snacks and gastronomic delights, don't fail to visit the Peck shops on Via Victor Hugo and Via Cantu, near the Piazza del Duomo. There are several good trattorias ranging from (M) to (I) along Corso

Garibaldi. Good pizzerias—**L'Altra Calafuria,** Via Solferino 12; **Calafuria,** Via Radegonda 14 and **Pizza Pazza,** Piazza Santo Stefano 10.

GETTING THERE AND AROUND. By air. Linate airport, 11 km. (7 miles) outside town, is used mainly by national and European flights, while Malpensa, 50 km. (30 miles) from Milan, handles intercontinental flights (including those from New York via Alitalia), which may be rerouted to Malpensa, Turin or Genoa airports in case of fog. Buses connect the airports with the central station and with Porta Garibaldi station. Taxis charge about 16,000 lire from Linate, 90,000 lire from Malpensa.

By train. Milan's main railway terminal is the Central Station in Piazzale Duca d'Aosta, a monument to Mussolini's architectural dominance. A number of smaller stations handle commuter trains from outlying areas and from Turin. Milan is at the center of north Italy's spider's web of rail lines—with Venice, Genoa, Bologna, Florence, Pisa and the south all on excellent services. From the north France and Switzerland are on express routes.

By car. Farther south all roads may lead to Rome, but here in the north they all lead to Milan. Entering Italy from France or Switzerland, coming across northern Italy from Yugoslavia—or down to the first-ever autostrada, A4, from the north—you are almost sure to find yourself heading for Milan. However, it is advisable to venture no closer than the motorway-type outer circle, from which it is easy to get onto one of the spokes raying in all directions. For although the hub of Lombardy's road system, Milan itself is definitely *not* the place for a motor-touring holiday, being one of the least pleasant cities in Europe in which to drive, and almost impossible to find your way into and out of.

By bus and subway. Getting around the city is easy enough. The network of *Metropolitana,* bus and tram lines covers the city very well. There's an ATM (transport authority) information office on the mezzanine of the Duomo station of the Metro. The Metro runs from 6.20 A.M. to midnight.

Tickets are on sale at newsstands, tobacconists, bars and Metro stations and are valid for 75 minutes of surface lines or for one Metro ride. Tourist tickets are on sale at EPT offices on Via Marconi and at the Central Station, or at the ATM office at Via Ricasoli 2.

By taxi. Taxis wait at stands or can be called at 117 or 67.67, 85.85 or 83.88.

MUSEUMS. Although world-famous as an industrial center and renowned for its elegant shopping, Milan also has a surprisingly large number of excellent museums, among them a couple of Europe's greatest. Be sure to double-check the opening times which are liable to change. We also give some general points under *Museums* in the *Facts at Your Fingertips* section.

Musei del Castello Sforzesca, Piazza Castello. The great fortress in itself is worth seeing, but it also houses several collections—archeological, sculptural, decorative arts and armor. Tues. to Sun., 9.30–12, 2.30–5.30. Closed Mon.

Museo del Duomo, Piazza del Duomo. The history of the cathedral, with quite a bit of associated art. Tues.–Sun. 9.30–12.30, 3–6. Closed Mon.

Museo Poldi-Pezzoli, Via Manzoni 12. Picture gallery with works by Botticelli, Tiepolo and many others; plus 15th–18th-century glass, Persian carpets, etc. Tues.–Sat. 9.30–12.30, 2.30–5.30; Sun 9.30–12.30; Thurs. 9 P.M.–11 P.M.

Palazzo Citterio, Via Brera 12. a few doors down from the Pinacoteca Brera. Houses the modern art sections of the Pinacoteca collections, along with temporary exhibits. Check locally for hours.

Pinacoteca Ambrosiana, Piazza Pio XI. Notable collection includes works by Jan Brueghel, Titian and Leonardo. Daily 9.30–5, closed Sat.

Pinacoteca di Brera, Via Brera 28. A really massive gallery with everything that it takes—Mantegna, Raphael, Bronzino, El Greco, Piero della Francesca etc., Tues.–Thurs 9–6; Fri., Sat. 9–2; Sun. 9–1. Closed Mon.

Sant'Eustorgio, Portinari Chapel, Corso di Porta Ticinese. Frescos of the Life of St. Peter the Martyr by Foppa. Daily 9–12, 3.30–6.30. Closed Wed.

Santa Maria delle Grazie, Corso Magenta. In the Cenacolo Vinciano is the *Last Supper* by Leonardo da Vinci, one of the main reasons for many people visiting Milan. Long lines because only 15 people can enter at once. Mon. to Sat., 9–1.30, 2–6.30, Sun. 9–3.

Teatro alla Scala, Piazza della Scala. The world's most prestigious opera house. The museum is a shrine for all opera buffs, full of material and mementoes of the lyric art. Mon. to Sat., 9–12, 2–6, (2–4 on Sat.), closed Sun.

NIGHTLIFE. Good spot—but expensive—is the roof garden of the **Palace Hotel** with a beautiful view of the city. The **Champagneria,** Via Clerici 1, is classy and costly. Elegant, for dancing, **Charlie Max,** Via Marconi 2.

The **Astoria Club,** Piazza Santa Maria Beltrade—with a good floorshow—is one of the best in town. **William's,** Foro Buonaparte 71, is another.

Bounty, Via Larga 16, and **Nepentha,** Piazza Diaz, are both popular. Other favorites are the noisy and lively **Porta d'Oro** in the Plaza Hotel; and **Patuscino** and **Ragno,** both on Via Madonnina, both for drinks, no floorshow.

MUSIC. The most famous spectacle in Milan is the **La Scala Opera,** whose productions are among the world's most impressive. Either orchestra or chorus goes on strike occasionally, but the show goes on. The opera season runs from December to May, the concert season from October to December. The house is invariably sold out well in advance, but ask your concierge to find tickets for you; you'll have to pay for this service, but it's worth it to avoid the complicated business of getting seats. You can reserve for non-subscription performances through CIT offices abroad, but reservations can be made no more than 10 days prior to the performance.

You can also visit concerts at the **Angelicum** and the **Conservatorio.**

SHOPPING. Milan's status as Italy's leading industrial and financial center is reflected in the chic of its elegant shopping streets, the Via Montenapoleone, Via Manzoni and Via delle Spiga. The Duomo area also is heart of a smart shopping district, where quality and prices are at top levels. Silk is a good buy here, along with fine leather goods; boutique fashions are ultrasmart and expensive.

There's good shopping at more accessible prices along Corso Buenos Aires, Corso XXII Marzo, and Corso Porta Romana. For fun, go to the flea market held every Saturday in the Via Calatafimi from early morning to evening.

Shops are closed Monday morning.

PRACTICAL INFORMATION FOR
LOMBARDY AND THE LAKES

WHEN TO GO. The region's typically Continental climate—with cold, foggy winters and hot summers—makes spring and fall the best seasons for a visit. The lake resorts are fine in summer, but may be crowded; however, their temperate climate makes them an attractive proposition in April and May, September and October.

TOURIST OFFICES. Bellagio: Lungolago Manzoni 1 (950.294). **Bergamo:** AAST, Via Tasso 2 (210.204); EPT, Viale Vittorio Emanuele 4 (242.226). **Bormio:** AAST, Via allo Stelvio 10 (903.300). **Brescia:** EPT, Corso Zanardelli 34 (43.418). **Cadenabbia-Griante:** AAST, Via Regina 1 (40.393). **Cernobbio:** AAST, Via Regina 33/b (510.198). **Como:** AAST, Piazza Cavour 33 (265.592); EPT, Piazza Cavour 17 (262.091). **Cremona:** EPT, Galleria del Corso 2 (23.233). **Desenzano del Garda:** AAST, Piazza Matteotti 27 (914.1510). **Gardone Riviera:** AAST, Viale Roma 8

(20.347). **Mantua/Mantova:** EPT, Piazza Mantegna 6 (350.681). **Menaggio:** AAST, Piazza Garibaldi 8 (32.334). **Pavia:** EPT, Corso Garibaldi 1 (22.156). **Sirmione:** AAST, Viale Marconi 8 (916.114). **Stresa:** AAST, Piazzale Europa 1 (30.150). **Tremezzo:** AAST, Via Regina 1 (40.493). **Varese:** AAST, Via Sacco 6 (284.624); EPT, Piazza Monte Grappa 5 (283.604).

SEASONAL EVENTS. Bergamo and Brescia: the opera season gets underway in Jan.; in Feb., there are carnival celebrations at Bagolino, in the province of Brescia; in May–June Bergamo and Brescia host a piano festival. Bergamo's Donizetti festival is in Aug.–Sept.

Comacina: Jun. 23 is the eve of the Feast of St. John, the occasion for a torchlight procession by boat to this little island.

Como: the Musical Autumn covers Sept. and Oct.

Gardone Riviera: the summer season of concerts and theater at the Vittoriale's outdoor theater begins in Jul., continuing into Aug.

Mantua: on Aug. 15, the "madonnari"—street artists whose specialty is recreating famous paintings on the city's sidewalks—gather for a contest.

Stresa: Musical Weeks are held in Aug. and Sept. with international artists taking part.

Varese: a flower festival in Jul.

TELEPHONE CODES. You will find the telephone area code for each town against its name in the Hotel and Restaurant listings (after the province name). If there is a different area code from the majority of the establishments—say when a hotel or restaurant is in an outlying place—then the code is given in front of the telephone number.

HOTELS AND RESTAURANTS: Hotels are fairly expensive in the cities in this region, though the country areas can provide good, reasonable accommodations. Food goes much the same way, pricey in the cities but plentiful and budget-priced in the country, with lots of atmospheric trattorias to enjoy. Lake resort hotels usually close in winter.

Regional Food and Drink. Along with *risotto,* a creamy rice dish popular throughout the region, a favorite first course consists of *polenta,* a kind of corn meal mush. In Bergamo, it's served with roasted game birds, or with cheese or mushrooms. Large *ravioli,* called *casonsei* in Brescia or *Marubini* in Cremona, have a variety of stuffings. Mantua's *tortelli di zucca* are exquisite *ravioli* stuffed with squash and are rather sweet. *Minestrone,* a thick vegetable soup, is famous, while *pizzoccheri,* dark, whole-grain noodles, that are the specialty of the Sondrio area, are less well-known. For Pavia's *zuppa pavese,* hot broth is poured over a raw egg on toast.

Cremona is known for its *torrone,* a refined version of nougat, and for *mostarda,* candied fruits in mustard syrup, much like chutney. Mantua's *torta sbrisolona* is a delicious, crumbly almond and butter cake. Local cheeses include the soft *taleggio* of Bergamo, creamy *stracchino* and *crescenza,* and heady *gorgonzola.* While the lake area specializes in fish, Pavia serves frogs in a number of dishes.

Lombardy is not wine country to the same extent as are many other regions. The Valtellina area produces robust reds, such as Sassella, Grumello, Inferno and Valgella. The Oltrepo Pavese is known for such reds as *Barbera, Bonarda* and *Barbacarlo* and also for its whites, among them *Riesling, Pinot* and *Cortese.* This area produces some fine dry *spumante,* using the *champenois* method. The area of the Franciacorta produces both whites and reds; the Lake Garda region's *Chiaretto* is a popular rosé.

Belgirate Novara (0322). Lake Maggiore resort. High season Easter, 1 July to 15 Sept. *Villa Carlotta* (M), on Stresa road (76.461). Large traditional, older hotel; pool, tennis, beach on lake. AE, DC, MC, V. *Milano* (M) (76.525). Unpretentious, comfortable; lake view. AE, DC, MC, V.

Bellagio Como (031). Lake Como resort. *Grand Hotel Villa Serbelloni* (L) (950.216). Open 15 April–15 Oct. Spacious rooms in lovely 16th-century villa on lakefront; large park, pool, beach, tennis. Courteous service, charming ambience. AE, DC, MC, V.

Belvedere (M) (950.410). Open 1 April to 10 Oct. Good; dining terrace, pool, wonderful view. AE, V. *Du Lac* (M) (950.320). Open 15 April to 15 Oct. Opposite landing stage, terraced garden, lake views. AE, DC, MC, V. *Metropole* (M) (950.409). Open 1 Feb. to 15 Nov. Fine location on lake; good rooms and restaurants; reasonable.

Restaurants. *Bilacus* (M), Salita Serbelloni 32 (950.480). Closed Mon. Open 15 March to 31 Oct. Pleasant dining terrace. *La Pergola* (M), at Pescallo (950.263). Closed Tues. Open 1 March to 30 Nov. Quiet, lakeside. AE, DC, MC, V. *Il Perlo* (M), on Civenna road (950.229). Closed Thurs. off-season. Open 1 March to 30 Nov. Pretty place with view. AE, DC, MC, V.

Bergamo Bergamo (035). *Cristallo Palace* (E), Via Ambiveri 35 (311.211). Outside center. Smart and modern. AE, DC, MC, V. *Excelsior San Marco* (E), Piazzale Repubblica 6 (232.132). Very central; comfortable and well-furnished. AE, DC, V.

Arli (M), Largo Porta Nuova 12 (222.014). Central. No restaurant. AE. *Capello d'Oro* (M), Viale Papa Giovanni 12 (242.606). Central, straightforward and unpretentious. AE, DC, MC, V. *Agnello d'Oro* (I), Via Gombito 22 (249.883). In Bergamo Alta, 17th-century inn, good atmosphere. AE, DC, V.

Restaurants. *Dell'Angelo* (E), Via Borgo Santa Caterina 55 (237.103). Closed Mon. Good atmosphere and cuisine. AE, DC, MC, V. *Dei Colleoni* (E), Piazza Vecchia 7 (232.596). Closed Mon. and Aug. In Bergamo Alta, historic surroundings, fine food. AE, DC, MC, V. *La Pergola* (E), Borgo Canale 62 (256.335). Closed Sun., Mon. noon and Aug. Just outside Bergamo Alta, excellent and panoramic. AE, DC, MC, V. *Trattoria del Teatro* (M) Piazza Mascheroni 3 (238.862). Closed Mon. and 15 to 30 July. In the Città Alta; traditional dishes. *Trattoria del Sommelier* (E), Via Fara 17 (221.141). Closed Sun. and Mon. noon. Attractive locale; refined cuisine. AE, DC, MC, V. *Da Vittorio* (E), Viale Papa Giovanni 21 (218.060). Closed Wed. and 2 weeks in Aug. Near station, specializing in fish. AE, DC, V.

La Fontana (M), Piazza Vecchi in Bergamo Alta (220.648). Closed Wed. Traditional fare, original touches. AE, V. *Gourmet* (M), Via San Vigilio 1 (256.110). Closed Tues. Panoramic location, delicious food. AE, MC, V. *Del Sole* (M), Via Colleoni 1 (218.238). Closed Tues. In Bergamo Alta, good. DC.

Bormio Sondrio (0342). Summer and ski resort. *Palace* (E) (903.131). Closed Nov. Modern, attractive and very comfortable. AE, DC.

Baita dei Pini (M) (904.346). Open 1 Dec. to 20 April and 15 June to 20 Sept. Comfortable rooms; good atmosphere. AE, V. *Larice Bianco* (M) (904.693). Open 1 Dec. to 30 April and 1 June to 30 Sept. Near ski school and cablecar; good. *San Lorenzo* (M) (904.604). Closed Nov. In town, many rooms with balconies; garden. AE.

Everest (I) (901.291). Open 20 Dec. to 30 April and 20 June to 30 Sept. Pleasant, small, with garden.

Restaurants. *Baita da Mario* (E), at Ciuk terminal of cablecar (901.424). Open 1 Dec. to 25 April and 1 July to 20 Sept. Delightful spot with views. *Kuerc* (M), Piazza Cavour 8 (904.738). Closed Wed., May, and Oct.–Nov. Regional specialties.

Brescia Brescia (030). *Vittoria* (E) Via delle 10 Giornate 20 (280.061). Venetian style hotel, recently restored, in central location. AE, DC, MC, V. *Ambasciatori* (M), Via Crocifissa di Rosa 92 (308.461). On outskirts, adequate. AE, DC, V. *Continental* (M), Via Martiri Libertà 267 at Roncadelle (278.2721). Closed Aug. 8–28. On outskirts, no restaurant. AE, DC, MC, V. *Master* (M), Via Apollonio 72 (294.191). Fairly central, nicely furnished. AE, DC, MC, V. *Motel AGIP* (I), Viale Bornata 42 (25.123). Just outside town; modern comforts. AE, DC, V. *Ai Ronchi* (I) Viale Bornata 22 (362.061). Motel on outskirts, in the direction of Verona. AE, DC, V.

Restaurants. *Palazzo Caprioli* (E), Via Capriolo 46/a (296.847). Closed Mon. and Aug. Elegant. AE, V. *Augustus* (M), Via Laura Cereto 8 (292.130). Closed Mon. evening, Tues. and Aug. Little atmosphere; good food, especially truffled *polenta*. *Cuccagnina* (M), Via Tresanda del Sale 8 (47.122). Closed Sun. Tiny, reserve. Local cuisine. *La Sosta* (M), Via San Martino della Battaglia 20 (295.603). Closed Mon., and 3 weeks in Aug. Exceptional ambiance in historic building; very good food. AE, DC, V.

Cadenabbia. Como (0344). Lake Como resort. *Bellevue* (E) (40.418). Open 1 April to 31 Oct. Large, old-fashioned, comfortable, on lake. DC, V. *Britannia Excelsior* (M) (40.413). Open 1 April to 30 Oct. Comfortable, old, with garden and view of lake. AE, DC, MC, V.

Cannobio Novara (0323). Lake Maggiore resort. High season, Easter and 1 July to 15 Sept. *Villa Belvedere* (M) (70.159). Open 20 March to 10 Oct. Quiet, tiny, with pool.
Restaurants. *Del Lago* (M), at Carmine Inferiore (70.595). Closed Tues. Open 1 March to 31 Oct. Lakeside. AE, DC, MC, V. *Molinett* (M) (70.151). On Intra road. Closed Wed. Open 22 Feb. to 18 Dec. On the lake.

Cassinetta di Lugagnano Milano (02). About 20 km. (13 miles) outside Milan. **Restaurant.** *Antica Osteria del Ponte* (E) (942.0034). Closed Sun., Mon., Jan. 1–15, and Aug. One of the best in Italy, well worth a detour for picturesque ambiance, superlative cuisine; about 90,000 lire per person. Reservations essential. AE, DC.

Cernobbio Como (031). Lake Como resort. *Villa d'Este* (L) (511.471). Open early April to 31 Oct. One of Italy's most luxurious hotels, in a lovely Renaissance villa on lake, in lush gardens; exceptionally well-furnished; business conventions known to disturb tranquillity. Pool, beach, golf, nightclub. AE, DC, MC, V.
Restaurants. Aside from the dining facilities of *Villa D'Este* (E), *Terzo Crotto* (M), Via Volta (512.304). Closed Mon, 10 Jan.–10 Feb. AE, DC, MC, V. *Vino Giusto* (M) (512.710). Closed Wed. Next to Regina Olga Hotel. AE, DC, V.

Chiesa in Valmalenco Sondrio (0342). Summer and winter sports resort. *Chalet Rezia* (M) (451.271). Open 20 Dec. to 15 April and 20 June to 15 Sept. Small, pretty chalet in quiet location, indoor pool.

Comacina Como (0344). Pretty island in Lake Como, off Sala and Lenno. **Restaurant.** *Locanda del Isola* (E) (55.083). Closed Tues. off-season. Open 1 March to 31 Oct. Delightful, must reserve.

Como Como (031). Lake resort. *Barchetta Excelsior* (E), Piazza Cavour 1 (266.531). On pretty lakeside piazza; comfortable. AE, DC, MC, V. *Metropole Suisse* (E), Piazza Cavour 19 (269.444). Closed 18 Dec.–14 Jan. Lakeside; good views. No restaurant. AE, DC, MC, V. *Villa Fiori* (E), on Cernobbio road (557.642). Closed mid-Dec. to mid-Jan. Attractive, gardens; views of lake, no restaurant. AE, DC, MC, V.
Como (M), Via Mentana 28 (266.173). Near station; cheerful, modern; heated pool. No restaurant. AE, DC, V. *Park* (M), Viale Rosselli 20 (556.782). Open 1 April to 31 Oct. Comfortable, smallish, near lake. No restaurant. AE, DC, V. *Tre Re* (M), Via Boldoni 20 (265.374). Central, with popular restaurant. Closed 10 Dec. to 9 Jan.
Restaurants. *Gesumin* (E), Via Cinque Giornate 44 (266.030). Closed Sun. and Aug. Attractive and excellent. AE, V. *Sant'Anna* (E), Via Turati 1 (505.266). Closed Fri, Sat. noon and Aug. Elegant. AE, DC, MC, V.
Celestino (M), Lungo Lario Trento 3 (263.470). Closed Wed. and Aug. A few steps from main piazza, pleasant and good. *Da Angela* (M), Via Foscolo 16 (263.460). Closed Mon. and Aug. Piedmontese cuisine, truffles, fine wines. Reserve.

AE, DC. *Faro* (M), Via Bernardino Luini 44 (269.596). Closed Wed. and Aug. AE, DC, V. *Forchetta d'Oro,* Via Borsieri 24 (275.341). Closed Mon. *Il Perlasca* (M), Piazza de Gasperi 8 (260.142). Closed Mon. Lakeview terrace, excellent food. Reserve. AE, DC, V.

At **Camnago,** *Navedano* (M), Via Pannilani 4 (261.080). Closed Tues. and Aug. Good food, summer terrace. AE, DC, MC.

Cremona Cremona (0372). *Continental* (M), Piazzale Libertà 26 (434.141). Fairly central; best in town. AE, DC, MC, V. *Astoria* (M), Via Bordigallo 19 (30.260). Central; fully modernized behind antique façade. AE, DC, V. *Motel AGIP* (M), near autostrada A21 (434.101). AE, DC, MC, V.

Restaurants. *Ceresole-Da Fulvio* (E), Via Ceresole 4 (23.322). Closed Sun. evening, Mon. and Aug. Central; smart, popular; reserve. AE, DC, MC, V. *Cerri* (M), Piazza Papa Giovanni 3 (22.796). Closed Tues., Wed., July and Aug. Central, family-run, quality trattoria. *Il Cigno* (M), Via del Cigno 7 (21.361). Closed Sun. Near Duomo. AE.

Desenzano del Garda Brescia (030). Lake Garda resort. High season Easter, 1 July to 15 Sept. *Park* (M), Lungolago Battisti 19 (914.3494). On lakeside drive; well-appointed. AE, DC, MC, V. *Tripoli* (M), Piazza Matteotti 18 (914.1305). Facing landing stage; small, comfortable. No restaurant. AE, DC, MC, V. *Villa Rosa* (M), Lungolago Battisti 89 (914.1974). Good atmosphere; garden. AE, DC, MC, V. *La Vela* (I), Viale dal Molin 20 (914.1318). Open Mar.–Oct. Lakeside; simple but good, small. AE, DC, V.

Restaurants. *Esplanade* (E), Via Lario 10 (914.3361). Closed Wed. Classic cuisine and service. *Molino* (E), Piazza Matteotti 16 (914.1340). Closed Mon. and 15 Dec.–15 Jan. Known for *zabaglione.*

La Vela (M), Viale dal Molin 25 (914.1318). Closed Wed. Open 1 March to 31 Oct. Lakeside dining; good food. AE, MC, V. *Matarel* (M), at Rivoltella (911.0304). Closed Fri. and 15 Jan. to 15 Feb. Unpretentious.

Gardone Riviera Brescia (0365). Lake Garda resort. *Grand* (E) (21.051). Open 15 April to 10 Oct. Large, on lakeside; garden terraces, heated pool; all comforts and good atmosphere. AE, DC, MC, V. *Villa Fiordaliso* (M) Gardone Riviera (20.158). Closed Sun. night, Mon., Jan.–Feb. Fine cuisine served in ancient villa or on terrace near the lake.

At **Fasano,** *Fasano* (E) (21.051). Open 1 May to 30 Sept. Fine hotel on lake, very comfortable; pool, beach. *Villa del Sogno* (M) (20.228). Open 1 April to 15 Oct. Small; park with pool; lake views. AE, DC, MC, V.

Restaurants. *La Stalla* (E), on road to Vittoriale (21.038). Closed Tues. and Jan. Rustic atmosphere, good food. AE, DC, V. *Emiliano* (M), Corso Repubblica 55 (21.517). Closed Wed. *Casinò* (M), at the casino (20.387). Closed Mon. and Jan. Dining on lakeside terrace. V.

Garda Verona (045). Lakeside resort. *Eurotel* (E), Via Marconi 18 (624.107). Open 1 April to 31 Oct. Large, modern, very comfortable; pool, park. DC, MC, V. *Regina Adelaide* (M), Via Venti Settembre (725.5013). Pleasant, well-furnished. AE, MC, V.

Gargnano del Garda Brescia (0365). Old town on Garda. **Restaurant.** *Tortuga* (E), at Porticciolo (71.251). Closed Mon. evening off season, Tues., Jan. and Feb. Small, elegant; worth a stop on your way around the lake. AE, V.

Limone sul Garda Brescia (0365). Atmospheric lakeside town on Lake Garda, a favorite with artists. High season Easter and 1 July to 15 Sept. *Capo Reamol* (M) (954.040). On lake; pool, terraces. No restaurant. Open April to Oct. *Leonardo da Vinci* (M) (954.242). Open 15 March to 30 Nov. Large, lakeside, pool.

Lodi Milano (0371). Interesting market town. **Restaurants.** *Isola Caprera* (M), Via Isola Caprera 14 (63.316). Closed Tues. and 27 July to 13 Aug. At Borgo Adda;

huge fireplace, lots of paintings; fine food. *La Quinta* (M), Piazza della Vittoria 20 (64.232). Closed Mon. and Aug. On main piazza; pleasant place serving local cuisine. AE, DC, MC, V.

Malcesine Verona (045). Important Lake Garda resort. *Du Lac* (M) (740.0156). Open 1 April to 10 Oct. Modern, overlooks lakeside promenade at southern end of town. *Excelsior Bay* (M) (740.0380). Open 1 April to 31 Oct. Lakeside, few minutes from town center; comfortable bedrooms with balcony; pool, garden. MC. *Malcesine* (M) (740.0173). Attractive villa-type; swimming off lakeside terrace; garden. MC. *Vega* (M) (740.0151). Open 1 April to 31 Oct. Central, on lakeside with bathing area; fine view; very good. AE, DC, MC, V.

Maleo Milano (0377). Near Cremona and Piacenza. **Restaurant.** *Sole* (E), Via Trabattoni 22 (58.142). Closed Sun. evening, Mon., Jan. and Aug. Simple, informal, tranquil inn; considered one of Italy's best for authentic cuisine. Reserve. About 60,000 lire per person. AE.

Mantova Mantova (0376). *San Lorenzo* (E), Piazza Concordia 14 (327.153). Very central; attractively furnished; modern comforts in old building. No restaurant. AE, DC, MC, V. *Apollo* (M), Piazza Don Leoni 1 (350.522). Facing station; smallish. No restaurant. AE, DC, MC, V. *Dante* (M), Via Corrado 54 (326.425). Central. No restaurant. AE, DC, MC, V. *Mantegna* (M), Via Fabio Filzi 10/b (350.315). Near sights; small, comfortable. No restaurant. AE, DC, MC, V.

Restaurants. *Il Cigno* (E), Piazza d'Arco 1 (327.101). Closed Mon., Tues., and 1 to 15 Aug. Not to be missed; one of region's finest; frescos, antiques and genuine Mantovan cuisine. AE, DC, MC, V. Prices not much above (M) range.

L'Aquila Nigra (M) Vicolo Bonacolsi 4 (350.651). Closed Sun. evening and Mon. Near the Palazzo Ducale; very popular. AE, MC. *Cento Rampini* (M), Piazza Erbe 11 (366.349). Closed Mon. In heart of town; simple, reasonable, good. AE. *Al Ducale* (M), Piazza Sordello 13 (324.447). Closed Sun. evening, Mon. and Aug. Facing Palazzo Ducale; reserve; intimate, good atmosphere and food. *Garibaldini* (M), Via San Longino 7 (329.237). Closed Thurs. evening and Fri. Longtime favorite in heart of town. AE, DC, V.

Just outside town, *Da Baffo* (M), Borgo Virgiliana (370.313). Closed Mon. and Aug. *Simpatico;* rustic. *Campana* (M), Via Santa Maria Nuova at Citadella (325.679). Closed Fri. and Aug. In country house, family-style cooking. *Rigoletto* (M), Strada Cipata 10 at Lunetta (371.167). Closed Mon. and 1–20 Aug. Beautiful view, interesting menu. AE.

Menaggio Como (0344). Lake Como resort. *Victoria* (E), Via Castelli 11 (32.003). Open 1 April to 30 Sept. Quiet location on lake; pleasant small garden, pool. AE, DC, MC, V. *Bellavista* (M), Via Quattro Novembre 21 (32.136). On lake, very modern, terraces, beach. AE, DC, MC, V.

Restaurants. *Lugano* (M), Via Battisti 7 (32.335). Closed Tues. and Feb. V. *Vapore* (M), Lungolago (32.229). Closed Wed.

Pavia Pavia (0382). *Ariston* (M), Via Scopoli 10 (34.334). Central, simple but comfortable. AE, DC, MC, V.

Restaurants. *Bixio* (M), Piazza Castello 1 (25.343). Closed Sun. evening, Mon. and Aug. Very central; attractive turn-of-century decor; very good food. AE, DC, V. *Giulio* (M), Via Guffanti 19 (26.304). Closed Tues. and Aug. Known for *risotto* and *involtini*. *Vecchia Pavia* (M), Via Cardinal Riboldi 2 (304.132). Closed Mon. and Aug. Central, good atmosphere, unusual dishes. AE, DC, V.

At **Certosa**, *Chalet* (M), Piazzale Certosa (925.615). Closed Mon.

Ponte di Legno Brescia (0364). Winter and summer resort. High season 1 Feb. to 31 March, Easter, 15 July to 31 Aug. and Christmas. *Mirella* (M) (91.661). Open 1 Dec. to 30 April and 1 June to 30 Sept. Modern, very comfortable; indoor pool; tennis, gardens. AE, DC.

Restaurants. *Grolla* (M) (91.775). Closed Tues. and June. Atmosphere. *Da Franco* (M) (91.402). Closed Mon., May and Oct. Food with a view. *Al Maniero* (M) (91.093). Closed Mon., 2 weeks in Jan., 24 Nov.–4 Dec. Nice place; regional dishes. AE, DC, MC.

San Pellegrino Terme Bergamo (0345). Most fashionable spa in Lombardy. High season 1 July to 31 Aug. *Terme* (M) (21.125). Open 16 June to 15 Sept. Comfortable, in quiet park. AE, DC.
Restaurant. *La Ruspinella* (M) (21.333). Closed Wed. and 2 weeks in Sept. AE, DC, MC, V.

Sabbioneta Mantova (0375). Walled Renaissance art town. **Restaurants.** *Ca' d'Amici* (M) (52.318). Closed Tues. and Jan. Good food and service. *Parco Cappuccini* (M), at Vigoreto (52.005). Closed Mon., Wed. evening and Christmas–Jan. Garden. AE.

Sirmione Brescia (030). Lake Garda spa resort. High season Easter and 1 July to 30 Sept. *Grand Terme* (E), Viale Marconi 1 (916.261). Open 10 April to 26 Oct. In quiet lakeside garden; very comfortable; heated pool. AE, DC, MC, V. *Sirmione* (E), Piazza Castello (916.331). Open 2 April to Oct. On the lake; spacious rooms in handsome villa; pool; spa facilities. AE, DC, MC, V. *Villa Cortine* (E), Via Grotte 12 (916.021). Open 1 April to 25 Oct. Secluded, in huge park on lake; tops for luxurious surroundings, furnishings and service; pool, beach and tennis. AE, DC, MC, V.
Continental (M), Punta Staffalo 7 (916.031). Open 1 March to 30 Nov. Very good; lakeside terraces; heated pool. AE, MC. *Olivi* (M), Via San Pietro 5 (916.110). Closed Jan. In quiet location with good views of lake; attractive, very comfortable; pool. AE.
Restaurants. *Mario* (E), Vicolo Strentelle 5 (916.326). Closed Thurs. and Jan. In center of town. AE. *Piccolo Castello* (M), Via Dante (916.138). Closed Tues. Terrace dining, good food. AE, DC, V. *L'Antica Taverna del Marinaio* (M) Closed Mon., early Nov.–late Feb. Fish specialties served on fine terrace by the lake. AE, DC, V.
At **Lugana Vecchia,** *Vecchia Lugana* (E) (919.012). Closed Mon. evening, Tues. and 1–7 Nov., Jan. In lakeside villa, exceptional cuisine.

Stresa Novara (0323). Principal summer resort on Lake Maggiore. High season Easter and 1 July to 15 Sept. *Des Iles Borromées* (L), Lungolago Umberto 67 (30.431). CIGA. Large and princely, in lovely park overlooking lake; beautifully furnished; beach, pool, tennis. AE, DC, MC, V.
Regina Palace (E), Lungolago Umberto 27 (30.171). Open 1 April to 31 Oct. In large park on lakeshore drive; palatial; ample, well-furnished rooms; heated pool, beach, tennis. AE, DC, MC, V. *Villaminta* (E), on Sempione road (32.444). Open 1 March to 15 Nov. Solid comfort, good service; marvelous views; pool, park and beach on lake. AE, DC, MC, V.
Astoria (M), Lungolago Umberto 31 (32.566). Open 20 March to 25 Oct. In garden overlooking lake; very comfortable rooms with good views; pool. AE, DC, MC, V. *Milan du Lac* (M), Piazza Imbarcadero (31.190). Open 19 March to 22 Oct. On busy square facing lake; good atmosphere. AE, DC, MC, V. *Speranza du Lac* (M), Piazza Imbarcadero (31.178). Open 19 March to 22 Oct. Facing lake and landing stage; comfortable. AE, MC, V.
Moderno (I), Via Cavour 33 (30.468). Open 1 March to 31 Oct. A few steps from landing stage.
On **Isola dei Pescatori,** *Verbano* (M) (30.408). Open 15 March to 31 Oct. Romantic, small, oasis of peace and quiet; lakeside terrace. AE, DC, V.
Restaurants. *Il Borromeo* (E), of Hotel Iles Borromées (30.431). One of CIGA chain's best restaurants; superlative service. AE, DC, MC, V. *Emiliano* (E), Corso Italia 48 (31.396). Closed Tues. and 20 Nov. to 20 Dec. Inventive dishes along with classic cuisine. AE, DC, MC, V.
La Barchetta (M), Via Garibaldi 10 (30.205). Closed Wed. AE. *Le Chandelle* (M), Via Sempione 23 (30.097). Closed Mon. and Jan. Rustic atmosphere. French-Italian

cuisine. AE, V. *Luina* (M), Via Garibaldi 21 (30.285). Open 19 March to 31 Oct. AE, DC, V.

Tremezzo Como (0344). Lake Como resort. *Grand Hotel Tremezzo* (E) (40.446). Open 1 April to 31 Oct. Large, pleasant hotel with pool in extensive grounds. AE.*Bazzoni* (M) (40.403). Open 1 April to 31 Oct. On lake; large; good in category. AE, DC, MC, V.

Restaurants. *Al Velü* (E), at Rogaro (40.510). Closed Tues. and from Dec. 25 to 7 Feb. Good food with fine views. *La Darsena* (M) (40.423). Closed Thurs. and 15 Oct. to 15 Nov. On lakeshore.

Varese Varese (0332). Prosperous city of gardens and villas. *Palace* (E), Via Manari 11 (312.600). Open 1 March to 30 Nov. On Campigli hill outside town; large, well-furnished resort hotel. AE, DC, V. *City* (M), Via Medaglie d'Oro 35 (281.304). Near station; fine medium-sized hotel. No restaurant. AE, MC, V.

Restaurants. *Lago Maggiore* (E), Via Carrobbio 19 (231.183). Closed Sun., 1–15 July. Central; elegant; for classic or local cuisine and fine wines. AE, DC, MC, V.

Brigantini (M), Via Medaglie d'Oro 33 (235.594). Closed Mon. and 20 July–8 Aug. Near station; hearty specialties. AE, DC, V. *Al Vecchio Convento* (M), Via Borri 348 (261.005). Closed Tues. evening and Wed. Attractive, rustic decor; classic dishes. *Da Vittorio* (M), Piazza Beccaria 1 (234.312). Closed Fri. Good central spot. AE, DC.

At **Ranco,** 24 km. (15 miles) away, well worth the trip is *Sole* (E), Piazza Venezia 5 (969.507). Closed Mon. evening, Tues. and Jan. Tasteful decor, superb food, courteous service; lakeside veranda. About 75,000 lire. AE, DC, V.

Verbania-Pallanza Novara (0323). Lake Maggiore resort. High season Easter, 1 July to 15 Sept. *Majestic* (E), Via Vittorio Veneto 32 (504.305). Open 20 April to 10 Oct. Fine old hotel on lake; indoor pool; all comforts. AE, DC, MC, V. *Belvedere* (M), Piazza Imbarcadero (503.202). Open 25 March to 10 Oct. At landing stage; comfortable.

Restaurants. *Le Beola* (E), Via Vittorio Veneto 28 (504.202). Closed Wed. Open 1 April to 31 Oct. Fine restaurant of Majestic Hotel; view of lake. AE, DC, V. *Milano* (E), Corso Zanitello (42.206). Closed Tues. and Jan. Lakeside terrace. AE, MC. *Il Torchio* (E), Via Manzoni 20 (503.352). Closed Mon. and 1–20 June. In town. AE, DC, MC, V.

GETTING THERE AND AROUND. By air. Milan's airports of Linate and Malpensa handle national, international and intercontinental flights, while Bergamo's airport at Orio sul Serio has some national flights.

By train and bus. Rail lines duplicate the road system, with the network radiating out from Milan, unquestionably the region's focal point. From the north the area is reached from Paris, Bern and Basel. There is a fairly complete coverage of bus lines to provide local transportation, though it tends to be slow.

By car. Major highways and autostrade crisscross Lombardy, most of them touching Milan's Tangenziale, which enables you to pick up one or another without entering the city. Fast superhighways link all major cities in the region, and put the lakes within easy driving distance.

By boat. Steamers and hydrofoils provide a fairly good system of connections between most of the resorts and all the major towns on the Lakes.

VENICE, THE VENETIAN ARC AND TRIESTE

Empire and Decay

By the 14th century, Venice had become the most powerful of Italy's numerous little republics. It dominated the Adriatic Sea, controlled all major trade routes to the East, then opened the 16th century by reaching inland to rule over all of what is now the Venetia region, a part of Lombardy, several towns in Apulia, the city of Ravenna. The Istrian Peninsula, between present-day Italy and Yugoslavia, fell under Venetian rule, bringing her control over Trieste. Dalmatia, too, succumbed. The fabulous city, swelled to the bursting point with power and riches, extended its power even farther—into the untold wealth of the Near East.

The Byzantine trend in the Venetian arts—especially well represented by mosaic designs still evident throughout the city today—began in the early centuries, when trade with the East drew Venice into close relations with that part of the world. Later, from the 11th to the 13th century, with a growing influence of Lombard-Romanesque architecture making itself felt, there came into being the characteristic type of palace that has since made Venice famous the world over. Gothic styles during the 14th and 15th centuries helped create a new kind of Venetian-Gothic architecture and sculpture.

Only in the last half of the 15th century, however, did the real masters of Venetian painting appear upon the introduction of Renaissance art by Solari, Mantegna, Antonello da Messina, and Sansovino, the artist-sculptor. It was then that the really great school of Venetian painters soared to an all-time high through Carpaccio and the Bellinis to figures such as Titian, Tintoretto, Veronese, Giorgione da Castelfranco.

The decline of Venice came slowly, after the 16th century. For 400 years, the powerful maritime city-republic had stood firm against the Turks as a bastion of Christianity, an insurmountable rival in the battle for control of seaborne commerce. Now the tide changed. Turkey's Ottoman Empire grew steadily in the eastern Mediterranean area; a changing pattern of world affairs opened new trade routes in the Atlantic and left those of the Mediterranean far behind. Like her steadily dwindling fortunes, the art and culture of Venice also slipped away. Only her monuments to a notable past remained.

True, there was a brief 18th-century revival of art sparked by such painters as Tiepolo, Ricci, Piazzetta, Canaletto, Guardi and Longhi; but, politically and financially, the city that once represented an empire now lay weak and wasted. She had no other recourse than to bow under the pressure of a conquering Napoleon, who, in 1797, by the Treaty of Campoformio, turned Venice over to Austria. Sixty-nine years later, in 1866, the city and region finally became a part of the united Kingdom of Italy.

Exploring Venice

The City of Canals, built on a lagoon five km. (three miles) off the coast, supports 100,000 residents rabbit-warrened into an utterly impossible maze of alleys, palaces, tiny squares, bridges, old churches, hovels, marketplaces and dark waterways so much alike that you won't recognize one from another. It's not a place to hurry through.

Though protected by a seawall against the Adriatic, the high tides continue their inexorable winter invasions of the city, flooding the Piazza San Marco ever more often. After examining a host of extravagant plans for a decade and a half—including a rubber barrage cutting the lagoon in half but permitting ships to enter through the three openings at the Lido, at Malamocco and Chioggia—yet another commission has been appointed to study the ecological impact of preventing the tides from sweeping the canals clean. Venice may sink as much under the weight of committee reports as under the weight of water.

We think that you can do the round of sightseeing that we cover in the following pages in three days—it'll be packed and keep you on the hop all the time, but it could be done. It would be much better to spread it over a week, so as to be able to savor things more. If you find the pace is likely to be too hot, concentrate first on Piazza San Marco, the Grand Canal tour and lagoon islands, picking up the other quarters later. If the crowds get you down, just get away from San Marco where they congregate.

The Grand Canal

Up bright and early on your first morning, head for the center of the city at Piazza San Marco, picking up a city map that includes an illustrated guide to the Grand Canal. Postpone a gondola ride on the Canal until the quieter evening hours (and remember to be firm about the price and length of ride). Instead, take a leisurely cruise along the length of the Grand Canal on the *vaporetto* (Line 1) and pick out the points of interest with the help of the map. Try to sit in the prow for a clear view.

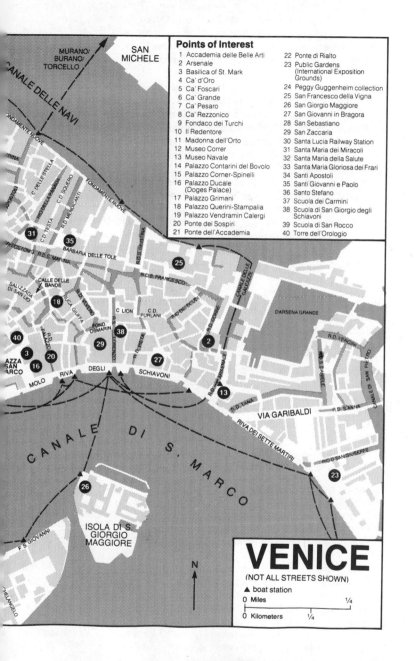

Points of Interest

1 Accademia delle Belle Arti
2 Arsenale
3 Basilica of St. Mark
4 Ca' d'Oro
5 Ca' Foscari
6 Ca' Grande
7 Ca' Pesaro
8 Ca' Rezzonico
9 Fondaco dei Turchi
10 Il Redentore
11 Madonna dell'Orto
12 Museo Correr
13 Museo Navale
14 Palazzo Contarini del Bovolo
15 Palazzo Corner-Spinelli
16 Palazzo Ducale
   (Doges Palace)
17 Palazzo Grimani
18 Palazzo Querini-Stampalia
19 Palazzo Vendramin Calergi
20 Ponte dei Sospiri
21 Ponte dell'Accademia

22 Ponte di Rialto
23 Public Gardens
   (International Exposition
   Grounds)
24 Peggy Guggenheim collection
25 San Francesco della Vigna
26 San Giorgio Maggiore
27 San Giovanni in Bragora
28 San Sebastiano
29 San Zaccaria
30 Santa Lucia Railway Station
31 Santa Maria dei Miracoli
32 Santa Maria della Salute
33 Santa Maria Gloriosa dei Frari
34 Santi Apostoli
35 Santi Giovanni e Paolo
36 Santo Stefano
37 Scuola dei Carmini
38 Scuola di San Giorgio degli
   Schiavoni
39 Scuola di San Rocco
40 Torre dell'Orologio

VENICE
(NOT ALL STREETS SHOWN)

▲ boat station

0 Miles   ¼

0 Kilometers   ¼

This main street of the city, more than 3 km. (2 miles) long and measuring up to 230 feet across, winds like an inverted letter "S" through the whole of Venice, passing under three bridges and among 200-odd 14th–18th-century Gothic-Renaissance palaces. Never more than 17 feet deep, the Grand Canal flows from San Marco Station with interest all the way.

With the help of your guide (live or printed), and starting out from San Marco, look for Santa Maria della Salute to your left, domed masterpiece of 17th-century baroque architecture by Longhena, and on the right, Corner Palace, known as Ca' Grande, by Sansovino (1537), now Venice's Prefecture. To the left again, you'll see the never-completed Venier dei Leoni Palace, which houses the late Peggy Guggenheim's wide-ranging collection of modern art.

First of the bridges you'll pass under is the contemporary wooden Ponte dell'Accademia, which takes its name from the Accademia delle Belle Arti, on your left, treasurehouse of Venetian painting. On the left, a bit farther on, the Ca' Rezzonico begun in 1660 by Longhena, houses the Museum of 18th-century Venice. Next to it, in one of the two Gothic Giustiniani palaces, Wagner composed *Tristan and Isolde.* Next, on the same side of the canal, is Ca' Foscari, 15th-century Gothic, seat of Venice's university.

After the Sant' Angelo boat station on your right, you'll see the 15th-century Palazzo Corner-Spinelli and the Palazzo Grimani, 16th-century masterpiece by Sanmicheli. After the Ponte di Rialto, built in 1592 by Antonio da Ponte, leaving the vegetable and fish markets on your left, you'll come upon the magnificent Ca' d'Oro, on the right. The most beautiful palace on the canal, it's in Venetian Gothic style and was built in the 15th century. To the left is Ca' Pesaro, built at the end of the 17th century by Longhena. It houses the Gallery of Modern Art. In the imposing early 16th-century Palazzo Vendramin Calergi, on your right, Richard Wagner died in 1883; it's now the sumptuous winter home of the gambling casino. The Fondaco dei Turchi, on your left, is a century-old reconstruction of a 13th-century palace in Venetian-Byzantine style.

St. Mark's and the Doges' Palace

The Piazza San Marco is the heart and soul of Venice, an immense, regal square of story and legend, bordered on three sides by palatial arcades in two tiers and faced on the other by the Basilica of St. Mark, one of the world's most magnificent churches. The piazza is an ideal place to sit over morning coffee and drink in Venice and the feel of the buildings surrounding you.

The mortal remains of the saint, martyred in Alexandria, were brought here by two Venetian merchants. St. Mark's was originally built as a shrine for these relics in 838, and reconstructed a century later on a Latin cross ground-plan. In the 11th century it was completely redone in the Byzantine manner, on a Greek-cross plan, probably inspired by the Church of the Twelve Apostles in Constantinople. The wealthy Venetians had reached the point where they could afford a church matching the splendor of those they had seen in the East.

The result was essentially what you see today: five arched and columned portals, echoed above by an arcaded story surmounting a gallery, and, finally, the five Oriental domes. The little turrets are a Gothic addition.

Inside, the incredible richness of St. Mark's is something you won't forget easily. The whole interior is faced with rare marble below and mosaics on a glittering gold background above. Hollows of the five domes alternate with barrel-like vaults to roof over the inner shape of a Greek cross that characterizes the basilica. Four great arms are divided into aisles by marble colonnades supporting galleries and a museum on the second floor. And wherever you turn, panels, colored mosaics, chapels, a golden altar, entire ceilings of masterpieces build one upon the other for supremacy in beauty and skill. To name only a few of the works, their authors, and precisely where to find them would fill a chapter in any book; English-speaking guides (names from EPT Tourist Office) offer their services at reasonable fees and know their subject well. Among others, don't fail to see the 12th-century mosaics in the central dome and nave, and the Pala d'Oro, a 10th-century altarpiece studded with precious gems, old gold and lustrous enamel.

Stepping outside the basilica into the vestibule, look for the stairway that leads up past second-floor galleries (excellent view of the church's upper interior here) and a museum to the outer terrace. Here, in the center, are replicas of the four horses of gilded bronze, a Greek work dating from the 3rd century B.C. which once adorned the Hippodrome of Constantinople; conquering Venetians brought them home in 1207 as a symbol of their triumph and the march of Venice towards its imperial destiny. The originals are inside. Of the five great arches you see, four are 17th-century mosaics and the one in the center is framed by Lamberti's 15th-century sculptures.

Walk downstairs now, outside the basilica, and stand before its arched central doorway with your back to it, facing Piazza San Marco. On your left is a bell tower reproduced on the same spot where its original tipped over and collapsed one day in July 1902; inside, an elevator takes you to the top for a bird's-eye view of Venice and the lagoon area. Over there on your right, the Torre dell'Orologio (Clock Tower), built in 1496, bears a huge gilded, enameled timepiece and two great Moorish figures who strike the hours. The Fabbrica Nuova (New Building) leads into the Correr Museum, where, arranged over two floors, the entire history of Venice—from its days as a republic until World War I—unfolds. The best things here are the Bellini and Carpaccio paintings in the picture gallery.

Turn left from your position in front of St. Mark's facing the square, and advance into the Piazzetta (Little Square) San Marco, with the Libreria Vecchia (Old Library) on your right, the Palazzo Ducale (Palace of the Doges) on your left, and St. Mark's Basin ahead.

Next to St. Mark's Basilica, Palazzo Ducale is perhaps the purest expression of Venetian prosperity and power in the 15th-century period when the Most Serene Republic reached its peak. Built like a horseshoe in three great wings, with its fourth side blocked off by a part of the basilica, this Gothic-Renaissance fantasia of pink-and-white marble, huge windows, balconies and enormous rooms and halls—former residence of the Doges (Dukes) of Venice—is entered through Porta della Carta, a Gothic gateway between the basilica and the palace, which opens into an immense courtyard hemmed in on all sides by the palace wings. Cross the courtyard, decorated with a wealth of arches and statuary, to the Scala dei Giganti (Stairway of the Giants), which was completed in 1501 after 17 years' labor.

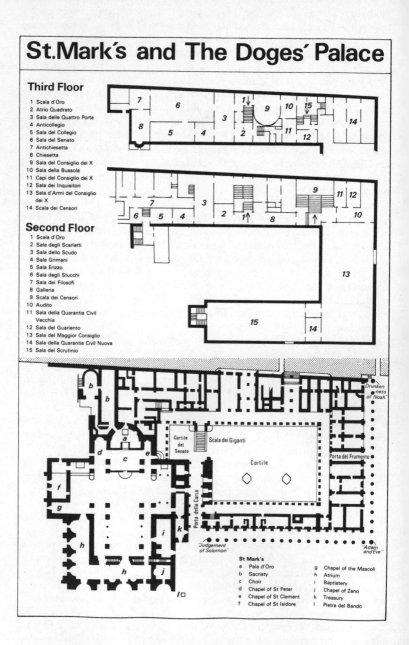

St.Mark's and The Doges' Palace

Third Floor

1 Scala d'Oro
2 Atrio Quadrato
3 Sala delle Quattro Porte
4 Anticollegio
5 Sala del Collegio
6 Sala del Senato
7 Antichiesetta
8 Chiesetta
9 Sala del Consiglio dei X
10 Sala della Bussola
11 Capi del Consiglio dei X
12 Sala dei Inquisitori
13 Sala d'Armi del Consiglio dei X
14 Scala dei Censori

Second Floor

1 Scala d'Oro
2 Sala degli Scarlatti
3 Sala dello Scudo
4 Sala Grimani
5 Sala Erizzo
6 Sala degli Stucchi
7 Sala dei Filosofi
8 Galleria
9 Scala dei Censori
10 Audito
11 Sala della Quarantia Civil Vecchia
12 Sala del Guariento
13 Sala del Maggior Consiglio
14 Sala della Quarantia Civil Nuova
15 Sala del Scrutinio

"Drunkenness of Noah"

Porta del Frumento

Cortile del Senato   Scala dei Giganti

Cortile

Porta della Carta

"Judgement of Solomon"

"Adam and Eve"

St Mark's

a Pala d'Oro
b Sacristy
c Choir
d Chapel of St Peter
e Chapel of St Clement
f Chapel of St Isidore
g Chapel of the Mascoli
h Atrium
i Baptistery
j Chapel of Zeno
k Treasury
l Pietra del Bando

Any tour through the palace is exhausting if you intend to absorb it all with a lingering eye—and, by the way, talking about eyes, you should try to choose a bright day for the exploration, as this is not the best lit building in the world. Like St. Mark's Basilica, this place has become a treasury of art works; here they are not mosaics but paintings. Best approach is a leisurely room-to-room visit, with either a guide or an English-language listing of the contents of each room.

Among the highlights to look for: *The Rape of Europa* by Veronese; a series of Tintoretto paintings on mythological subjects (*Mercury and The Graces* is just one); the same artist's greatest work, *Paradise,* in the Great Council Hall, and his *Apotheosis of Venice* on the ceiling of the Senate Chamber; another *Apotheosis* is in the Great Council Hall, this time by Veronese.

From the east wing of the Palace of the Doges, behind St. Mark's Basilica, the slender, covered Bridge of Sighs (Ponte dei Sospiri) arches over a narrow canal to the cramped, gloomy cell blocks that once held Italian patriots who rebelled against Austrian occupation of Venice in the late 18th century. The bridge is so named because the prisoners passed over it on the way to face their inquisitors in the Doges' Palace. There's an interesting tour of the palace's Secret Itineraries, including the torture chamber and Piombi prison, from which Casanova escaped.

Eastern District

Then, passing under the Clock Tower off Piazza San Marco, head into the Merceria, one of Venice's busiest streets, a favorite shopping quarter, which opens the way into the city's eastern district. Continue along the Merceria to the Church of San Giuliano, then branch off into Calle delle Bande as far as the Church of Santa Maria Formosa, built in 1492 by Coducci. Walk around this church into the Campiello Querini-Stampalia, where a 16th-century palace of the same name has an art gallery open to the public; dusty and rather dull, it could be skipped to leave more time for the rest of the itinerary.

Return to the Church of Santa Maria Formosa now, following Calle di Borgolocco to Campo Santa Marina, where you turn right, cross Ponte di Cristo (Bridge of Christ) and take the Fondamenta Sanudo and Calle Castelli to the Church of Santa Maria dei Miracoli, a 15th-century Venetian Renaissance masterpiece by both the Lombardos that is even more beautiful inside. See the choir of this church in particular; the marble carvings and reliefs are exquisite throughout.

Outside again, use Calle Gallina to reach Campo dei Santi Giovanni e Paolo, in the center of which stands a tremendous statue of Colleoni on horseback, executed mainly by Verrocchio; it portrays the great Venetian warrior in his fiercest mood; note the eyes and drawn mouth. On the same square is the vast 15th-century Gothic Church of Santi Giovanni e Paolo, which became the burial place of the Doges.

Take Barbaria delle Tole out of the square, continuing along it into Campo Santa Giustina, and behind the church-like edifice there, turn left into Calle Te Deum, then right to the Church of San Francesco della Vigna, by Sansovino in 1534, with a pretty cloister. From this point, directions—never easy in Venice—become rather difficult. Follow Salizzada di San Francesco and later Salizzada delle Gatte, swerving right from Campo Ugo Foscolo into Calle dei Furlani, where the 16th-century Scuola di San

Giorgio degli Schiavoni houses a collection of Carpaccio's most celebrated paintings. Up Calle Lion, across the canal called Rio di San Lorenzo, turn left as far as Ponte dei Greci (Bridge of the Greeks), then right into Fondamenta dell'Osmarin, up the street through Campo San Provolo and finally into Campo San Zaccaria, where Gambello's 15th-century Church of San Zaccaria and 13th-century Romanesque belfry constitute one of the finest churches in Venice. Take time here to look through the chapels and altars for priceless works by Bellini (especially his *Madonna*), Tintoretto and Titian.

Near the church, Sottoportico San Zaccaria leads into Riva degli Schiavoni. Take this avenue to the left, past the little Church of the Pietà), making a left turn after the next bridge into Calle del Doge, which brings you to the magnificent Church of San Giovanni in Bragora, a Gothic 15th-century structure featuring art works inside by Cima and Vivarini.

On Campo dell'Arsenale, the Arsenal, founded in 1104 as an immense dockyard from which the old Republic of Venice fleets put out to sea, still stands within the original walls that defended it. Four carved lions from ancient Greece guard the great Renaissance gateway leading inside the area, where the old *squeri* (docks) used to build Venice's war galleys remain almost intact. On nearby Campo San Biagio is a fascinating Naval Museum, well worth a visit.

Walk down Via Garibaldi, a filled-in canal, to the island and church of San Pietro, a charming backwater with a leaning belltower on a grassy *campo*.

Venetian Lagoon and the Islands

For an excursion to the Lagoon and the Islands, head for Fondamenta Nuova, along the north–central banks of Venice, where Line 12 *vaporetti* leave for the lagoon islands of Murano, Burano and Torcello. Make certain to check departure schedules, posted at the landing, in order to know when to catch the next boat out. Reckon on 4–5 hours for the round trip. There are two ways of doing the circuit—to state the obvious—one is to go to the farthest island, Torcello, and then work your way back; the other is to start with the nearest and so on. It is probably easier to go to Torcello first, as you can then cut your trip short more easily if you want to. Don't take guided excursions.

From the Fondamenta Nuova it's a 10-minute run to the first—and smallest—of the islands at San Michele, occupied by Venice's unique cemetery and the Church of San Michele in Isola, built in 1478 by Coducci. Make a landing here if you want to visit either cemetery or church; otherwise, the general view of both en route is satisfactory enough. Interestingly, funeral cortèges in Venice take the form of long lines of polished gondolas draped in black velvet and heaped with flowers.

Island No. 2 requires a little time ashore. This is Murano, actually sprawled over five small islands, where the sole major industry—glassblowing—has been handed down from father to son for generations, making it the source of an art for which Venice has achieved a worldwide fame. Depending upon time available, see the Museo Vetrario (Museum of Works in Glass), a historical collection of glassware in the 17th-century Palazzo Giustiniani; visit any of the glass-blowing establishments that extend a hearty welcome to visitors (just walk right in), along Fondamenta dei Vetrai, the main street; and the 12th-century Church of Santa Maria e Donato, a gem.

Next stop, at Burano, less than an hour on the direct run by *vaporetto* from Venice, you find a small island fishing village that for centuries has been the heart of Venice's lace industry. Here, women sit outside their brightly painted houses, gossiping and making lace. You'll see plenty of lace displayed at the shops on the main piazza and, at slightly higher prices, in the shops around Piazza San Marco. Don't be fooled though; a lot of the lace on sale comes from China. You can see authentic antique pieces at the Scuola dei Merletti.

Another mile by water ends the trip at Torcello, an island on which the early Venetians first landed in their flight from barbarian hordes many centuries ago. Reportedly, it became the first colony in the Venetian Lagoon area. Torcello's cathedral was built in the 7th century, rebuilt in the 11th, when its majestic bell tower was added. It is worth a visit for its 12th- and 13th-century mosaics.

Western and Northern Districts

If churches, art and sculpture, and further ramblings through the back streets and along the old canals of Venice continue to interest you, enter the western and northern district of the city, with a side trip to the island suburb of Giudecca. Head out of Piazza San Marco by way of the Merceria, crossing Rialto Bridge into Venice's western district. You will spot five churches along the way, and should visit these:

Santa Maria Gloriosa dei Frari, near the Rio Terra dei Saoneri, a Gothic structure built between 1338 and 1443 for the Franciscan Order, is one of the city's most beautiful churches. Built like a crucifix, it contains Bellini's magnificent *Madonna and Four Saints,* the Titian masterpiece entitled *Assumption,* and the evocative tomb of Canova, one of Italy's artistic greats. Here, too, is the Church of San Rocco and, to its left, the Scuola di San Rocco; in the latter are 56 individual paintings by Tintoretto, depicting subjects from both the Old and New Testaments, that are considered some of the greatest works of his long career. Among the highlights: a *Crucifixion* (which *he* thought was best) and an *Annunciation.* An American-based fund has financed their restoration.

Return to Piazza San Marco, then leave for a visit to the southwestern district, passing under the arcades of the Fabbrica Nuova at the far end of the square. Head for Campo Morosini, with its 14th-century Church of Santo Stefano, and cross the Grand Canal on Ponte dell'Accademia. The Accademia, on the other side, houses a magnificent collection of Venetian paintings from the Gothic era to the 18th century; the Bellini *Madonnas* and Veronese's vast *Feast in the House of Levi* are outstanding. Not far from the Accademia, at one end of the Campo Santa Margherita, is the Gothic Church of Santa Maria dei Carmini and the Scuola Grande dei Carmini, a school in which there are ceiling paintings by Tiepolo and others by Piazzetta.

From here, follow the Fondamenta del Soccorso, turn left along the Fondamenta San Sebastiano, and arrive shortly at the 16th-century Church of San Sebastiano, well-known among Venetians for its paintings by Veronese, who was buried there in 1588.

Later, perhaps after lunch, you should leave Piazza San Marco again through the narrow, winding Merceria, past Rialto Bridge (without crossing it this time), into Venice's northern district. Of eight churches en route, center your attention on these:

Church of the Santi Apostoli, on Calle Dolfin; Church of the Madonna dell'Orto, a 15th-century Gothic beauty, where Tintoretto is buried. Restored with British funds, it's at the end of Calle Larga dei Mori.

Incidentally, a passage through the northern district will also bring you to Ponte delle Guglie (Bridge of the Spires), which crosses the Cannaregio, second largest canal in Venice. Turning right just before this bridge, follow the narrow Calle del Ghetto, through the old Jewish Ghetto, where you can visit the old synagogues and a fascinating little museum.

To visit San Giorgio Maggiore on its own little island you will have to take the boat from the Riva degli Schiavoni. The work mainly of Palladio, this beautifully proportioned church dominates the Venice skyline, floating opposite St. Mark's Square. The interior is cool and magnificent, with two fine Tintorettos and a lovely cloister. Take the boat on to the next stop in order to wander along the island of La Giudecca. There is only one notable spot to visit, the Franciscan church of Il Redentore (Redeemer), one of Palladio's masterpieces, commemorating the 1579 visitation of the plague. Next, take the boat across the Giudecca Canal to the Zattere in the Dorsoduro section. Being away from the maelstrom of central Venice it has preserved its atmosphere and is worth wandering through.

The Lido

From the International Exhibition gardens, *vaporetti* leave every 10 minutes for the 15-minute trip across the Venetian Lagoon to the Lido. This is one of the most fashionable stretches of sand in Italy, one of the world's best-known seaside playgrounds, and has been so for many decades. It is a swank, chic resort which draws wealth and its hangers-on, season after season. Unless you are a guest at one of the top hotels, you are likely to find the Lido expensive, dull and very disappointing.

Once there, walk (or take a bus, if you prefer) straight down Viale Santa Maria Elisabetta, the Lido's main street, which runs past dozens of tastefully decorated hotels, restaurants, villas, outdoor cafés and pensions across the island to end at the wide stretch of sand beyond. As you would expect, there is a casino here, summer only, to add that inevitable international touch of gambling to the scene.

Exploring the Venetian Arc and Trieste

On the southern Venetian plain, a green carpet spotted with low, rolling hills, crops grow luxuriantly. North and south of the plain, a semicircle of gradually ascending plateaus and high meadows rises to the snow-tipped Italian Alps around Cadore and Cordevole. Rivers like the Adige begin up there, flowing down through Venetia to the sea, where ports handle shipborne commerce and fisheries dot the coastline.

But, like the Lazio region and ancient Rome, all of Venetia falls under the historical and spiritual influence of its capital at Venice. Take any city in the sprawling Venetia area—Verona, Vicenza, Padua, Treviso, Belluno, even Rovigo to the south. All repeat in one way or another the grace and refinement of Venice. No lagoons, perhaps, but the architecture, paintings and way of life stem from old Venice and the power she once held over this region.

Venetia, as a region, takes its name from the city of Venice, which, in turn, came into being when the Veneti people fled their mountains and plains for sheltered coastal lagoons to escape the northern barbarian invaders many centuries ago. In time, these ex-farmers and shepherds driven to the sea formed a community on canals, consolidated it, adopted seafaring ways, and created a city that ultimately became a dominant power and an arbiter of culture and the arts.

The important centers of the Venetia region reflect the rise and fall of Venice, following much the same collective pattern as the region as a whole, but with small differences which account to some extent for their individual historical charm.

Verona, for example, was once an ancient Etruscan village. It grew under the Gauls, became a Roman colony in 89 B.C., then rose to power and prosperity within the Roman Empire. The city continued to flourish through the guidance of leaders like Theodoric, Alboin, Pepin and Berenger I, reaching its artistic and cultural peak in the 13th and 14th centuries under the Della Scala family. In 1404, however, Verona sought security by placing itself under the control of Venice, remaining there until 1797, when Napoleon delivered the entire Venetian region to Austria.

Padua has a similar past. Originally called Patavium by the Romans, it enjoyed its heyday under the rule of the Carraresi family between 1319 and 1405, with the entrance of Tuscan Renaissance artists such as Giotto, Filippo Lippi and Donatello, whose works may still be seen in Padua today. In 1405, following Verona's example, Padua, too, sought the protection of Venice. Vicenza (Roman Vicetia) followed much the same course.

Padua and Vicenza

The first obligatory trip out of Venice should include the chain of art cities lying westward. You leave via a 4-km. (2½-mile) bridge over the lagoon to reach the industrial suburb of Mestre, then continue for another 29 km. (18 miles) across both the Brenta and Mirano Canals into Padua, with its works of art by Giotto, Donatello and Mantegna.

Padua (Padova) is worth a one-day stopover if you have the time. Concentrate on the area around Piazza del Santo. Donatello's famed statue of *Gattamelata*—the Venetian general Erasmo da Narni on horseback, 1453—can be seen in this square. More of his works are to be found in the nearby Basilica of Sant' Antonio, built between 1232 and 1307 over the tomb of St. Antony of Padua, whose death is still commemorated each June 13 by pilgrims visiting here from all parts of Italy and many foreign countries.

The town's pride, however, is its university, founded in 1222, on Via 8 Febbraio. Additionally, try not to miss the 650-year-old Scrovegni Chapel (frescos by Giotto), on Corso Garibaldi. It is also called the Madonna dell'Arena, and these frescos are among the most beautiful anywhere in Italy, with all the calm magnificence the master was heir to. The 13th-century Church of the Eremitani contains some fragments of Mantegna frescos, while the Municipal Museum on the Piazza del Santo has an interesting collection for a provincial gallery.

Another 31 km. (19 miles) out of Padua brings you to the town of Vicenza. Tour the Piazza dei Signori, dominated by Palladio's first major work, the Basilica Palladiana. Visit the 14th-century Church of San Lorenzo, with frescos by Montagna and Buonconsiglio, on Corso Fogazzaro. Walk the length of Corso Palladio, named for the artist who built so many of Vicenza's beautiful buildings; 15th-century palaces line the street.

The Teatro Olimpico, Palladio's last work, is Vicenza's outstanding art treasure and represents an important step both in theater and scenic design, based as it is on classical models and yet using false perspective in the permanent scenery. If you get the chance to see a performance there you should certainly do so in spite of any language difficulties, especially if you are a theater buff.

A 20-minute walk to Monte Bèrico brings you to a Baroque church dominating an 18th-century esplanade and bearing art works by Montagna and Veronese. A few minutes away by car lies the Villa Valmarana with its Tiepolo frescos. Not far off stands Palladio's Villa Rotonda, whose symmetrical perfection has inspired architects for centuries. For movie and opera buffs it was made memorable by being used as the location for Joseph Losey's version of *Don Giovanni*.

If you plan to settle in Vicenza for a few days you might want to run up to Asiago, at 1,000 m. (3,300 ft.), a summer-winter sports area.

Verona and Treviso

Verona is perhaps second only to Venice for its classic buildings and medieval monuments. You could spend three or four days here; but if your time is limited, try to see the Arena, Piazza delle Erbe, Tombs of the Scaligeri, the Roman Theater, the cathedral, and the Churches of Sant'Anastasia, San Fermo Maggiore and San Zeno.

The 1st-century Arena, one of the world's largest and best-preserved Roman amphitheaters, borders Piazza Brà, off which Verona's main street, Via Mazzini, leads to Piazza delle Erbe. Openair opera performances and concerts take place there during the summer months. It comfortably seats 25,000 spectators and is so acoustically perfect that even those in the last row hear clearly. Naturally, the program changes from year to year, but among the favorites that keep coming back are *Aida* and *Turandot*—whose spectacular staging makes them ideal operas for this vast stage. There's also the Horse and Agricultural Fair, Italy's oldest, from March 12–20, when farmers from one end of the peninsula to the other crowd into the city for the nearest thing to an old-time American fair.

The tombs of the Scaligeri honor Verona's one-time ruling Della Scala family. Located just off Piazza dei Signori, with these beautifully-sculptured 14th-century burial places you find the monument to Dante who, when Florence exiled him, was given refuge here by Bartolomeo Della Scala. In the vicinity of Piazza dei Signori, too, is the Church of Sant'Anastasia, built in Gothic style between 1290 and 1481, wherein art works by Pisanello, Montagna and Di Bartolo have been collected.

Farther off, through Via Massalongo and Via Duomo, you reach the city's cathedral, a Romanesque church started in 1139, holding art by Sansovino, Sanmicheli and Titian. However, for a study of Veronese painting, it's best to visit Verona's rich Museum of Art, housed in the medieval Castelvecchio, along Corso Cavour. The Biblioteca Capitolare, near the cathedral, is one of the oldest in the world.

Romeo and Juliet? Go to the Via del Pontiere, where you'll be charged a small sum to see what is alleged to be the tomb of Juliet. Or find Via

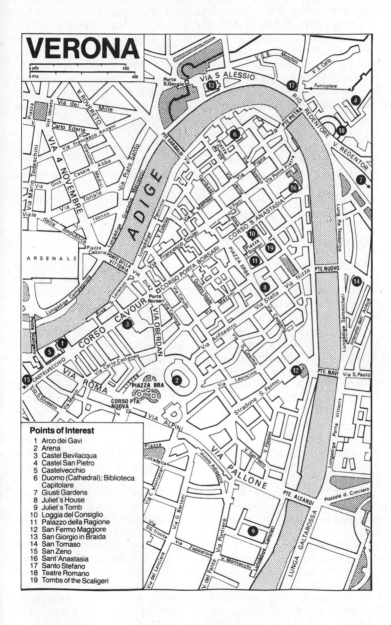

VERONA

0 yds   400
0 ms   400

Points of Interest

1 Arco dei Gavi
2 Arena
3 Castel Bevilacqua
4 Castel San Pietro
5 Castelvecchio
6 Duomo (Cathedral); Biblioteca
   Capitolare
7 Giusti Gardens
8 Juliet's House
9 Juliet's Tomb
10 Loggia del Consiglio
11 Palazzo della Ragione
12 San Fermo Maggiore
13 San Giorgio in Braida
14 San Tomaso
15 San Zeno
16 Sant'Anastasia
17 Santo Stefano
18 Teatre Romano
19 Tombs of the Scaligeri

Cappello 17–25, a 13th-century building in which the lovely Juliet Capulet lived. Of Romeo, alas, the landmarks are vaguer.

Approximately 31 km. (19 miles) north of Venice is Treviso, a small town badly damaged by World War II air raids, but well rebuilt. It is a delightful place to wander in, the streets, especially those still containing the old, overhanging houses, having much character. The surrounding ramparts give a fine view of the Alps to the north. See the area around Piazza dei Signori, with its two ancient palaces and tower; the cathedral, housing works by Titian, Bordone, Lombardo; and the Church of San Niccolo, 14th-century Gothic, and adjacent chapter house, which contains about 40 striking portraits by Tommaso da Modena dated 1352.

From Treviso, across the Piave River, where Italian resistance after the October retreat in 1917 brought eventual victory in June of the next year, the road winds into Conegliano, a village Venetians know well for its excellent wines. A railroad branch runs 13 km. (8 miles) out of Conegliano up to Vittorio Veneto, site of the Italian World War I victory over Austro-Hungarian troops; so well remembered is that battle by Italians that at least one street in most Italian cities today carries the name.

Venetian Villas

The Venetia region is rich in Palladian villas, the country houses of Venetians who vacationed here while administering their vast estates. Vicenza, Padua, or Treviso are recommended bases for a thorough study of Andrea Palladio's architectural gems, although you might prefer the smaller hamlets—Bassano di Grappa, Asolo, or Marostica.

Many of the villas are privately owned, while some can be visited on only one or two days a week. And you may even have to peer at a number through closed gates or over hedges. Check with EPT offices for details.

The northern group of Palladian villas includes Villa Godi-Porto, Villa Piovene at Lonedo, approached by a steep stairway affording a splendid view over the valley, and Villa Caldogno, with its Veronese frescos. At Bagnolo there's the colossal Villa Pisani, its endless apartments decorated with 18th-century frescos by Tiepolo and Francesco Simonini. One of the most interesting villas in this region is Villa Malcontenta, built in the shape of a cross and topped by a dome. Reminiscent of Villa Rotonda in Vicenza, it was one of Palladio's earliest works. Villa Pisani at Stra has some splendid Tiepolo frescos.

Nearer Treviso, in the eastern group of Palladian villas, is Villa Barbaro at Maser. A beautiful Renaissance creation, it has Veronese frescos and magnificent grounds. Villa Emo at Fanzolo stands on a wide plain, its broad portico and arcades blending with its surroundings.

Visit the nearby village of Castelfranco—27 km. (17 miles) west of Treviso—girdled by crenelated walls and by water, with a superb Giorgione (one of the many masterpieces stolen and recovered in Italy in recent years) in its Duomo. Delightful Cittadella, 11 km. (7 miles) further on, is encompassed by medieval fortifications. On the road from Bassano del Grappa to Schio is Marostica, another fortified town, with a lively main piazza.

Among other fascinating but less-wellknown localities within easy reach of Padua are:

Asolo, about 11 km. (7 miles) west of Bassano del Grappa, whose beauty made it a favorite of Robert Browning and the great Italian actress Duse;

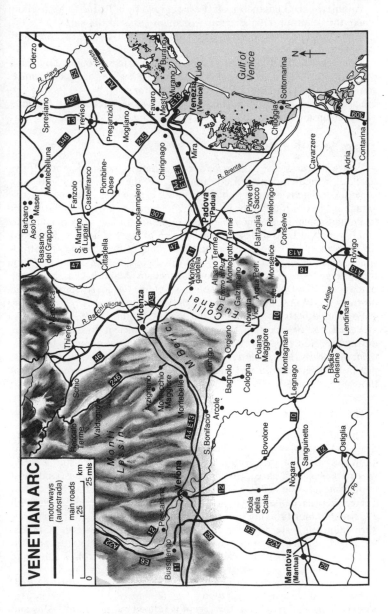

Adria, 49 km. (30 miles) from Padua to the southeast, which was once an Etruscan city and contains relics of those times;

Valsanzibio di Galzignano, off the main road from Padua to Monselice, where the beautiful Villa Pizzoni-Ardemani basks in the sun;

Monselice, fast road south from Padua, which boasts fine specimens of architecture plus views;

Montagnana, 25 km. (16 miles) west through Este, surrounded by a fine wall with 24 towers and a number of fortified gates, and with a Veronese painting of the Transfiguration in the cathedral;

Lastly, for lovers of wine, the town of Soave lies tucked into the hills off the main motorway, halfway between Verona and Vicenza.

Sun, Sand and Mud

Venice's Lido is one of Europe's most famous sand strips, though the sea itself is mud-colored and unattractive. Yet the snob value of the very expensive *cabanas* is such that they are as hard to get as a place in the garage at Mestre. If it is sun and not hobnobbing you are after, take a ferry to Punta Sabbioni and enjoy the miles and miles of fine sand reaching to and beyond the Lido di Jesolo. This stretch of coast is heavily developed for mass tourism, though again both the state of the sea and the atmosphere leave much to be desired. Lido di Jesolo itself is a popular spot for package tours. To the south, on flat reclaimed land backed by sparse pinewoods, less sophisticated establishments line the coast from Chioggia down to Ravenna. The sea unfortuntately remains the steady mud-color.

For a mud bath by choice, Abano Terme, 13 km. (8 miles) southwest of Padua, can't be beaten. Frequented by the ancient Romans, popular during the Middle Ages, 150 hot springs provide the mud used in the treatment of arthritic and rheumatic diseases. Nearby Montegrotto Terme dispenses therapeutic mud and water from the same hydrothermal basin of the Euganean hills.

The Trieste Area

The off-the-beaten-track provinces of Italy's easternmost crescent are those of Udine, Gorizia, and Trieste—although the district as a whole is known as Friuli-Venezia Giulia. To introduce this region in a simpler way, we call it the Trieste area, thus focusing attention on its largest and most important city. The region enjoys a special autonomous status with its own elected diet (parliament) primarily because of its mixed population, with a German minority living along its northern border and a Slovenian minority along its eastern border, including the cities of Trieste and Gorizia. Also the Friulians, who represent the majority of the inhabitants, are ethnically not real Italians but have their own language, which is similar to the Rhaeto-Romanic of Switzerland and Ladin of South Tryol.

In the north, along the borders of Carinthia (the southern Austrian Federal state) and in the northeast along the frontier with Slovenia (the northwestern Yugoslav republic), the region is framed by the Carnic Alps and the West Julian Alps which descend slowly along the eastern border to the Karstic plateau between Monfalcone and Trieste. The heart of the region is formed by the rich and fertile Friulian plain reaching to the sea.

This varied area is worth exploring for its historic towns of Udine, Cividale and Aquileia, for the romantic, abruptly cut coast between Monfalcone and Trieste, for the beautifully situated city and port of Trieste, and for the splendid beaches of Grado, Caorle, Lignano and Bibione.

Exploring the Trieste Area—The Inland Route

Assuming that you are traveling to Friuli in a northeastern direction from Venice, passing Treviso and Conegliano, your first stop is likely to be Sacile, with a centuries-old bird fair. After the trading is over, there is a contest to see who can give the most perfectly whistled imitation of bird songs.

Next you come to Pordenone, whose arcaded main street, the Corso Vittorio Emanuele, is lined with Venetian-style patrician houses ending on a little square where stands the 13th-century town hall in Venetian-Gothic style, with a very interesting clock tower and a gallery of paintings. Next to it soars the 15th-century cathedral, with an older, Romanesque tower powerfully standing apart from it.

Udine, 127 km. (79 miles) from Venice, stands on a mound supposedly erected by Attila the Hun so that he might watch the burning of Aquileia, an important Roman center to the south. The Patriarch Elia later made it into a trading center. You can visit its art gallery in the massive Renaissance castle, the 13th-century Romanesque cathedral and Archbishop's Palace, all with fine paintings by Tiepolo. Piazza della Libertà, with loggia and porticos, is one of the loveliest in Italy. Notice the clock tower with its lion of St. Mark, and the two figures on the top who strike the hours on the great bell. If you have time to spare, Udine reveals all sorts of pleasant little corners, especially where the Roggia River laps against the walls of the houses in scenes reminiscent of Venice.

It's 17 km. (10 miles) from Udine to Cividale, historically perhaps the most interesting town of the entire region. It was probably founded by Julius Caesar when he served as commander of the Roman legions at Aquileia, and for this reason the first name of the town was forum Julii. However, Cividale acquired its present name and fame when it was the capital of the Duchy of the Germanic Longobards and after 774 of Frankish Margraves; it was then called Civitas Austriae, abbreviated to Civitas and then dialectically into the present name. The most interesting historic remains of the Longobard period are found in the so-called Longobard Little Temple and in the Archeological and the Cathedral Museums. An impressive event in Cividale is the Sword Mass, celebrated every year at Epiphany. It recalls the investiture ceremony of the Patriarchs of Aquileia, who were confirmed by the Holy Roman Emperor of the German Nation, whose vassals they were. The priest wears a helmet while celebrating Mass, and presents the sword three times as a symbol of secular power.

If you're heading for Tarvisio, turn north here at Udine for the 89-km. (55-mile) trip up through the mountains to the Austrian border where this summer and winter resort, together with several villages around it, is becoming increasingly popular. On the way to Tarvisio, you'll see rebuilt Gemona and Venzone, where the 1976 earthquake destroyed interesting old churches and town fortifications. At Carnia, a side road branches off from the road to Tarvisio, taking you to the unpretentious Carnic winter and summer mountain resorts of Ravascletto, Forni Avoltri, Forni di Sotto and Forni di Sopra.

The Coast Route

An almost continuous sand fringe sloping gently to the sea extends from Punta Sabbioni just outside Venice all the way to Grado, dotted with resorts accessible by branch roads from A4.

Inland, at the southern end of A28, lies Portogruaro, a small town consisting of two sinuous streets between which Lemene River flows. Features of interest: colorful porticos, a cathedral with noteworthy frescos, a leaning tower, a town hall of the 14th century in pointed arch and Renaissance style, three ancient city gates, and a museum containing a notable archeological collection.

Farther east, you can make a side trip to the beach resort of Lignano, one section of which is called Sabbiadoro (Golden Sands), by turning right after Latisana.

Next comes Cervignano in rich farm country. Turn right here to the former Roman capital at Aquileia, and the beach and lagoon at Grado.

Aquileia was founded around 200 B.C. Named after an eagle seen flying overhead while envoys of the Senate were planning Augustus' campaign against the Germans, it boasts an impressive basilica built in 1021, and a museum with towers, statues, tombstones, mosaics, and other relics of Roman times. A Roman forum has been discovered and partially restored. When Attila the Hun swept down on the area, the inhabitants of the town fled before him and founded Grado on an island off the coast. Its port on the lagoon commands a group of islands scattered about the estuary, and there is an attractive beach. Quays and canals run right into the center of town; the houses look out over the water. It is full of boats, fishermen, and pleasure craft, in sharp contrast to the magnificent Byzantine cathedral.

Returning 19 km. (12 miles) from Grado to Cervignano you turn east for Monfalcone, famous for its shipyards. Shortly after, you come to Duino. This is a village populated by fishermen, small farmers and innkeepers. The remains of its old fort, standing on a cliff above the sea, originate probably from the 6th or 7th century; next to it there is the majestic "new castle", constructed in the 15th-16th century and still in the possession of the Princes of Thurn and Taxis. A little farther is the Gulf of Sistiana with fine swimming facilities and a yacht harbor.

Just before Trieste, in a beautiful location on a small promontory on the coast is the white castle of Miramare. A visit here is a must; from June to September a Sound and Light spectacle recreates the history of Archduke Maximilian of Habsburg, who for a brief period became the Emperor of Mexico and who, prior to departing for Mexico, built Miramare as his home. On view the year round are its rich collection of mementos and art objects and a large park with many trees, beautiful flower beds and romantic vistas of the sea. Before you reach Trieste itself, side roads take you down to the little bays sheltering the lovely small beach resorts of Sistiana and Grignano.

Trieste

Modern Trieste has relics dating back to Roman times, a 2nd-century theater and an Augustan arch, but the whole city can be seen in one day. Be sure to include the 17th-century castle and the Cathedral of San Giusto on their hillside esplanade, as well as the impressive Piazza Unità by the sea.

Surrounded by beautiful countryside with a rugged coastline, Trieste was until 1918 the chief port of the Austrian Empire, which built it to its present size from a small fishing town, as well as one of the leading ports of all Europe. It was awarded to Italy by the Versailles Peace Conference and has since experienced continuous decline. Its economy was revived somewhat by U.S. assistance between 1945 and 1953 when it was part of the Free Territory of Trieste, occupied by U.S. and British forces, before reverting to Italy.

The best view of Trieste and the bay is from Opicina on the Karstic plateau above the city, which can be reached by cog-wheel streetcar or by a road offering beautiful vistas at every curve.

PRACTICAL INFORMATION FOR VENICE

WHEN TO GO. The best times to visit Venice are May, and between the first week of September and the first two weeks of October. It is reasonably cool then, with less chance of rain and a greater possibility that the annual swarm of tourists won't crowd you out. You *can* go in mid-summer, too—but don't complain when heat waves begin rippling across the canals and a bathing suit appears to be the only necessary item in your wardrobe.

If you like seeing familiar sights in a new light, you might visit Venice in February or March. It is a time of mists, of possible floods, of chill winds from the sea; but it is also the month when the city becomes a living entity, devoid of tourists, pursuing its own affairs and, when bathed in cold, brilliant sunshine, totally captivating.

TOURIST OFFICES. AAST, Calle Ascensione 71c, under portico off Piazza San Marco (522.6356). American Express, San Moise 1474 (520.0844). CIT, Piazza San Marco 4850 (528.5480). City of Venice Tourist Board, Ca' Giustinian, off San Marco. Santa Lucia rail station (715.016); and, summer only, Piazzale Roma 540D (522.7402).

British Consulate, Campo Santa Maria della Carità 1051, Dorsoduro (522.7207).

SEASONAL EVENTS. Appreciative of the peculiarities of its climate, Venice schedules its outstanding arts and cultural events for the beginning and end of the more usual tourist season—that is to say, for May, and for September/October—thus avoiding the hottest months. However, the International Biennial Committee now operates year-round, sponsoring shows and events in all the arts in the city's innumerable piazzas and palazzi.

February: carnival month in Venice, with uniquely colorful celebrations.

July: the third Sun. sees the Feast of the Redeemer, recalling the time in 1576 when Venetians suffered a particularly devastating plague. Those that survived built the Church of the Redeemer, which stands on Fondamenta San Giacomo, in the suburb of Giudecca. Venetians and visitors alike flock to the church for a day of worship, feasting and carnival that invariably ends with a regatta in which all the boatmen appear in local costume, the scene illuminated by a vivid firework display.

July–August: In even-numbered years, the International Biennial Art Exhibition is held in pavilions in the public gardens.

September: the month opens with an historical regatta on the Canal.

November: the Feast of the Madonna della Salute, on the 21st, is the occasion of solemn religious rites within the Church of Santa Maria della Salute, built in 1631 as a token of gratitude from the Venetian Republic's Senate and people for the end of a plague a year earlier.

December to May: the traditional season at the 159-year-old La Fenice Theater, where *Rigoletto* and *Traviata* were first performed.

TELEPHONE CODE. The telephone code for Venice is 041.

HOTELS. A city which sometimes seems to contain no buildings other than palaces, Venice has converted many of them into hotels. Room rates here run about 20% above guidelines. Low season rates are as much as 30% less in all categories. High season is April 1 to October 31 and December 31 to January 2.

Reserve in advance, months ahead for summer, especially if you have your heart set on a particular hotel. If stuck, the AVA Hotel Association booths at the rail station, airport and Piazzale Roma municipal garage can almost always find you a room in any category, even in high season. They are open daily from 9 to 9, and the 20,000 lire deposit they require is rebated on your hotel bill. At Carnival, the two week period before Lent, Venice is booked solid. Lido hotels are, with few exceptions, open only from April or May through September or October. High season runs from July through mid-September.

Deluxe

Bauer Grünwald, Campo San Moise (520.7702). Near San Marco, large, in a lovely old palace on the Grand Canal, with a modern wing facing San Moise. Terrace restaurant and roof garden for summer dancing; rooms are spacious and well-furnished; service is swift and courteous. AE, DC, MC, V.

Cipriani, Giudecca 10, on Giudecca Island (520.7744). Open end-Feb. to mid-Nov. Five minutes from San Marco by launch. Location a little inconvenient, but Venice's most spacious hotel. Gardens, huge pool, terrace restaurants surrounding a handsome old villa with stunningly furnished rooms. Smartest and most expensive in Venice. AE, DC, MC, V.

Danieli, Riva degli Schiavoni (522.6480). CIGA. A favorite among Anglo-Saxon tourists, with good reason. Superb location next to the Doges' Palace looking across to San Giorgio Maggiore. The older part is a gorgeously decorated Renaissance palace; there are modern wings. Ask for the better rooms; some are cramped. The rooftop terrace restaurant is famed for food and view. AE, DC, MC, V.

Excelsior Palace, Lungomare Marconi 41 (526.0201). The Lido's only deluxe hotel, stands on the beach itself. 257 rooms, most with bath, airconditioned. Open 1 May to 30 Sept. Outstanding hotel that has made the Lido world-famous, with its spacious, fashionable, private beach. Modern decor in rooms and suites, nightclub with disco, pool, tennis. CIGA. AE, DC, MC, V.

Gritti Palace, Campo Santa Maria del Giglio (794.611). CIGA. On Grand Canal, a few minutes from San Marco. A place of distinction, preferred by Hemingway; a favorite of those who like quiet elegance. Beautifully appointed, many suites; terrace restaurant on Grand Canal. AE, DC, MC, V.

Expensive

Cavaletto e Doge Orseolo, Calle del Cavaletto (520.0955). On side canal next to Piazza San Marco; comfortable and attractive. One of best in category. AE, V.

Europa e Regina, Calle Larga Ventidue Marzo (520.0477). CIGA. Twin hotels offering ample, well-furnished rooms with view of Grand Canal; dining terrace on canal; caters to groups. AE, DC, MC, V.

Grand Hotel des Bains e Palazzo al Mare, Lungomare Marconi 17 (765.921). 303 large, well-furnished rooms, most with bath, airconditioned. Ideally situated on the Lido between the sea and its own park, directly connected with its private beach by an under-passage, pool. CIGA. Own Pagoda restaurant on shore. AE, DC, MC, V.

Londra Palace, Riva degli Schiavoni (520.0533). Historic palace; modern comforts in attractively decorated rooms, many with view of lagoon. Handsome lounges, bar, terrace restaurant. AE, DC, MC, V.

Metropole, Riva degli Schiavoni (520.5044). Overlooking St. Mark's basin, with the distinctive air of a small, exclusive hotel. Rooms overlooking the garden are especially inviting. Decorated throughout with exquisite taste, and run with careful attention to detail. AE, DC, MC, V.

Monaco e Grand Canal, Calle Vallaresso (520.0211). Wonderful location on Grand Canal; chic clientele and warm, intimate ambiance. Beautifully furnished rooms and salons. Dining terrace on canal. Good atmosphere. AE, V.

Saturnia Internazionale, Calle Larga Ventidue Marzo (520.8377). Near San Moise and San Marco, a handsome Renaissance palace with quiet bedrooms, though some rooms are small. Good atmosphere, service. Excellent restaurant (see list). AE, DC, MC, V.

Moderate

Accademia, Fondamenta Bollani (521.0188). Small, quiet pension in attractive villa with garden just off Grand Canal near the Accademia. Tops for atmosphere. AE, DC, MC, V.

Bel Sito, Campo Santa Maria del Giglio (522.3365). Central; ask for new rooms or others on courtyard. AE, DC.

Bisanzio, Calle della Pietà (520.3100). Quiet location off Riva degli Schiavoni; small, rather elegant. No restaurant. AE, DC, MC, V.

Concordia, Calle Larga San Marco (520.6866). Just behind San Marco; rooms furnished in Venetian style. No restaurant. AE, V.

Do Pozzi, Calle Larga Ventidue Marzo (520.7855). Short walk to San Marco; small, quiet, just off mainstream. AE, MC, V.

La Fenice, Campiello la Fenice 1936 (523.2333). At famous theater, near San Marco, charming place with attractive rooms, pretty garden court. A top choice in category.

Flora, Calle Bergamaschi, off Calle Larga XXII Marzo (520.5844). Open 10 Feb. to 10 Nov. Small, very well-furnished, in quiet location near San Marco. No elevator but very good atmosphere, pretty patio. No restaurant. Top choice. AE, DC, MC, V.

Pausania, Fondamenta Gheradini on Rio San Barnaba (522.2083). Near the Ca' Rezzonico landing stage, in medieval palazzo with courtyard and garden. AE, MC, V.

San Cassiano, Calle della Rosa (522.3051). On Grand Canal, near Rialto. Interesting location; avoid noisier, more expensive rooms on Grand Canal. AE, DC.

Scandinavia, Campo Santa Maria Formosa (522.3507). A somewhat overpowering decor—glass chandeliers and dizzying combinations of Venetian damask—confirms you're in the heart of Venice, closeby St. Mark's. AE, V.

Torino, Calle delle Ostreghe (520.5222). Tiny, but occupying a fine location near Santa Maria del Giglio; an excellent base for sightseeing. AE, DC, MC, V.

Inexpensive

Alboretti, Rio Terra Sant'Agnese (523.0058). Compact good-value hotel, with a little garden courtyard and upstairs sitting room. No restaurant. AE, MC, V.

Pagnelli, Riva degli Schiavoni (522.4324). Near San Marco. Several types of rooms; spacious twins 9 and 5 are best.

La Residenza, Campo Bandiera e Moro (528.5315). Open 16 Feb. to 16 Nov. and 8 Dec. to 7 Jan. In beautiful old palazzo on charming piazza; lots of atmosphere, adequate comforts. No restaurant. AE, DC, MC.

San Stefano, Campo San Stefano (520.0166). Central. A 12-room gem; well-furnished rooms. No restaurant.

On **Giudecca,** slightly inconvenient because *vaporetto* essential for getting about, **Casa Frollo** (5222.723). Near Zitelle *vaporetto* landing. Highly recommended for private villa atmosphere. Book way ahead. Sadly, threatened with eviction and may have to close.

RESTAURANTS. Except in top hotels and some restaurants (our list isn't exhaustive) it is practically impossible to eat well in Venice, where most of the places in the tourist mainstream serve prefabricated, insipid and uninspired food to the undiscerning masses, often at inflated prices. In all cases, you'll spend 20% more to eat here than our guidelines indicate.

Venetian Specialties. Venetian cooking means fish. Generally speaking, it hasn't the variety of the professional culinary art as practiced in cities like Rome, Florence or Bologna. But the way Venetians prepare fish is something else again. Try *granseole veneziane* (a tasty kind of local crab), prepared Venetian style, or nearby Comacchio Valley eels served roasted or with sauce. Also delicious here are shrimps *(scampi).* Meat specialties are *fegato alla veneziana* (fried liver and onions), and game birds, served with excellent salads of bitter red *radicchio* from Treviso. Sample, too, the *risi e bisi* (a traditional Venetian soup served with rice and peas). Also traditional is the hearty *pasta e fagioli,* a thick and tasty soup. The local *prosciutto di San Daniele* is a variety of the famous Italian dried ham. For dessert, try *tiramesù,* a luscious concoction of creamy cheese, coffee, and chocolate with pound cake.

The cooking of the entire Veneto region follows closely the example of its capital city. We might add *gnocchi* and *polenta* as favorites of Venetia in general, especially the hill and mountain sections, where this sort of hearty rib-filling nourishment is more appropriate to the climate than it is to that of humid sea-level Venice. Lake Garda is famous for its trout, along with several other fish specialties. The countryside produces particularly fine grapes, cherries, chestnuts and applies.

For a dry red wine *Bardolino* or *Valpolicella* (the latter has the higher alcohol content of the two); while *Merlot* and *Cabernet* are dry reds from the Friuli region. Dry whites include *Soave Bianco* and *Tocai. Prosecco,* a sparkling white, nudges over towards the sweet side. In addition these regional products are worth trying: *Garganera di Gambellara,* a very white wine of moderate alcoholic content, good for warm-weather drinking; *Recioto,* a sweetish red wine, a trifle heavy, which comes from the neighborhood of Verona; *Valpentena,* a very dry red wine; *Vini dei Colli Trevigiani,* white and very dry; *Vini dei Colli Euganei,* white and sweet. Try *grappa,* the local aquavit.

Expensive

Antico Martini, Campo San Fantin (522.4121). Closed Tues. and Wed. noon. Open 1 March to 30 Nov. Excellent and elegant; also has a piano bar from 10 P.M. In summer you dine outdoors on the Fenice theater square. AE, DC, MC, V.

Cipriani, at Cipriani hotel on the Giudecca (520.7744). Open mid-Feb. to mid-Nov. Terrace; poolside buffet; classic dining room with banquettes, chandeliers. All very smart. Hotel launch from San Marco. AE, DC, MC, V.

Caravella, Calle Larga Ventidue Marzo, in Saturnia International hotel (708.901). Closed Wed. from Nov. to Apr. Reserve. Small, intimate atmosphere; old sailing-ship decor. Assiduous service; superlative cuisine. AE, DC, MC, V.

Cortile, Calle Larga Ventidue Marzo (708.901). Outdoor restaurant of Saturnia International. Indoors in winter. Attractive patio setting; fine food; good atmosphere and service. AE, DC, MC, V.

La Colomba, Piscina Frezzeria (522.1175). Closed Tues. and Nov. Mainly seafood in several dining rooms decorated with contemporary art. Has become increasingly touristy. AE, DC, MC, V.

Danieli Terrace, Riva degli Schiavoni (522.6480). The epitome of elegant dining in Venice; excellent cuisine, unforgettable view, pricey minimum. AE, DC, MC, V.

La Fenice, Campiello Marinonio (522.3856). Closed Sun., Mon. lunch, and mid-Jan. to mid-Feb. Beside theater. Attractive, elegant place for Venetian cuisine. AE, DC, MC, V.

Graspo de Ua, Calle dei Bombasieri (522.3647). Closed Mon., Tues. and Dec. Traditional Venetian inn, cordial, very good. Let host suggest menu. AE, DC, MC, V.

Harry's Bar, Valle Valleresso 1323 (523.6797). Closed Mon. and 8–21 Jan. At San Marco *vaporetto* landing, Venice's most famous bar, nostalgic favorite with Americans; Italian reputation for good food; inventor of Bellini and Titian cocktails. Same ownership as Locanda Cipriani, offers motorlaunch excursions for lunch or supper at Locanda. AE, DC, MC, V.

Moderate

Antica Besseta, Calle Salvio (721.687). Closed Tues, Wed., Jan. and 15 July to 15 Aug. Fine, authentic, family-run. Near San Giacomo dell'Orio.

Da Arturo, Calle dei Assassini (528.6974). Closed Sat. and Sun. Near Campo Sant'Angelo. Small, welcoming trattoria.

Ai Coristi, Calle della Chiesa (522.6677). Closed Wed. Near La Fenice. Pleasant and reasonable.

Ai Padovani, Fondamenta Gheradini (523.8660). On Rio San Barnaba, with Venice's only floating vegetable market moored in front. Cordial service. Make reservations. Closed Sun. during July, Aug., and Sept. AE, DC, V.

Conte Pescaor, Piscina San Zulian (522.1483). Intimate, with lots of old-fashioned Venetian atmosphere. Good seafood specialties. Closed Sun., Mon. lunch, two weeks in Aug., and Jan. 7 to early Feb. AE, DC, MC, V.

Corte Sconta, Calle del Pestrin (522.7024). Closed Sun., Mon., mid-June to mid-July and 10 Jan. to 10 Feb. Reserve. Near San Giovanni Bragora. Very popular for seafood; informal Venetian atmosphere. AE, DC, V.

Il Cortile, Calle Larga XXII Marzo (520.8938). Dine by candlelight at this open-air garden court restaurant. In winter it moves indoors to wood-paneled salons. Crepes and flambées a specialty. Closed Wed. AE, DC, MC, V.

Fiaschetteria Toscana, Campo San Giovanni Crisostomo (528.5281). Closed Tues. and July. Attractive, a favorite with Venetians for excellent cuisine; courteous service. DC, MC, V.

Fiore (M), Calle Scaleter (721.308). Closed Sun. and Mon. In San Polo district.

Da Ignazio, Calle dei Saoneri (523.4852). Handy for Rialto, with classic Venetian cuisine. Closed Sat.

Da Ivo, Calle Fuseri (528.5004). Closed Sun. and Jan. Reserve. Both fish and meat specialties in small place with delightful atmosphere. AE, MC, V.

Locanda Montin, Fondamenta Eremite (522.7151). Closed Tues. evening and Wed. Near San Trovaso, an atmospheric old trattoria.

Noemi, Calle dei Fabbri (522.5238). Near St. Mark's, so at upper end of price range. Try the veal chop *alla zingara,* with olives and capers. Closed Sun. AE, DC, MC, V.

Poste Vecie, Pescheria (721.822). Closed Mon. evening, Tues. and 10 Nov. to 20 Dec. At Rialto fish market; colorful and classic seafood trattoria. AE, DC, V.

Inexpensive

Antica Adelaide, Calle Racchetta in Cannaregio district (520.3451). Closed Sun. Friendly, informal, worth searching for.

Ai Cugnai, Calle San Vio (528.9238). Popular neighborhood tavern with vine-shaded courtyard. Closed Mon. and Jan.

Crecola, next to S. Giacomo dell'Orio (89.481). Closed Tues. Pizzeria.

Gazebo, Rio Terrà San Leonardo (716.380). Friendly trattoria near the station and Ghetto. Pizza on menu. Closed Thurs. AE, DC, MC, V.

Vino Vino, Campo San Fantin (522.4121). Informal wine bar next-door to and under same management as Antico Martini (see above). AE, DC, MC, V.

Zucca, Ponte del Megio at San Giacomo dell'Orio (522.0861). Closed Mon. Attractive, good food.

CAFES. Florian, on Piazza San Marco, is Venice's most historic and famous café. It's an institution, with nostalgic gilt and plush decor and delicately painted mirrors. There's much more atmosphere inside than at the sea of tables on the piazza, and it costs less besides (even though it's still staggeringly expensive—how about $10 for a pot of, albeit delicious, hot chocolate?).

GETTING TO AND AROUND VENICE. By air. Venice's airport (Marco Polo-Tessera) is on the mainland, 10 km. (6 miles) away. It takes direct flights from London/Heathrow, though not from New York. Take an airport bus (about 4,000 lire) to Piazzale Roma (the train station) or the Cooperativa San Marco motorboat service (about 11,000 lire per person) to San Marco. A taxi from the airport to Piazzale Roma costs about 40,000 lire.

By Train. Venice train station looks like any other and it's quite a shock for the first-time visitor to step out of a bustling train-filled station and instead of the customary street traffic of a city square to find himself in danger of walking straight down the station steps into the Grand Canal, at whose west end the station is located. You take a *motoscafo* (motorboat) or a *vaporetto* (waterbus) to the landing nearest your hotel. If you are staying at one of the leading hotels, you can arrange to be met at the airport or station and, of course, you will pay for the service. If you are going to take public transport, get specific directions on how to get to your hotel, either before you get to Venice or when you arrive at the station or airport. A luggage cart is a lifesaver. Porters can be found at some of the main *vaporetto* landings (look for the men in blue).

By car. Reaching the region of Venetia by road from almost anywhere is the easiest thing in the world, including coming from England exclusively by motorway via Belgium, Germany and Austria, to come to Lake Garda over the Brenner Pass. Once arrived in Venice itself, the only thing to do with your automobile is to park it in the garages at Piazzale Roma or on the Tronchetto parking island (reasonable; bus 75 connects it with Piazzale Roma and *vaporetto* 34 links it with Piazza San Marco). or at the parking areas of San Giuliano, Fusina or Mestre, on mainland (closed winters). Or you could leave your car in Padua and take the train into Venice.

You cannot drive in Venice. Most of the streets are water, and those that aren't are always running up and down steps over the city's hump-backed bridges. You can take your car to the Lido, however, on the car ferry that leaves from the Tronchetto landing stage.

Porters' charges are fixed according to a rather involved schedule, depending on the distance, number of bags, etc. For example, between any two points within the center of town (bounded by the railway station and Piazzale Roma), you pay 8,000 lire for one or two bags, 2,000 for each additional one. Surcharge for night service. Desk at airport will book one for you, or take a luggage cart.

Gondolas are extremely expensive; inquire at your hotel or at local tourist office for current rates, and come to terms with the gondolier *before you set out.* You can figure on at least 50,000 lire for a 50-minute ride for up to 5 people (though they will often try to charge much more for much less), 60,000 after 9 P.M.

Water taxis also are expensive, have complicated fare systems; often overcharge.

Vaporetto fare is 1,500 lire up. You can buy a tourist ticket for about 8,000 lire, valid for 24 hours and useful on a busy sightseeing day. If you are staying a few days, the *Carta Venezia* is a good buy (issued at the ACTV office at Sant'Angelo landing on Line 1; passport-type photo needed).

Grand Canal Ferries *(Traghetti).* Not many tourists know about the two-man gondolas that ferry people across the Grand Canal. The fare is 300 lire, which you give to one of the gondoliers as you get on; every few minutes the boat leaves its little dock and makes the brief crossing to the other side. These ferries can save an enormous amount of walking. They cross between:

Santa Maria del Giglio and San Gregorio
San Barnaba and San Samuele
Sant'Angelo and San Tomà
Riva del Carbon and Riva del Vin
Santa Sofia and Pescheria (Market)
San Marcuola and Fontego dei Turchi
Ferrovia (at the rail station) and San Simeon Piccolo.

Tours. CIT offers 2-hour tours of Venice, one on foot and one by gondola; a 3-hour excursion to Murano by motorlaunch.

MUSEUMS. Though in some ways the entire city of Venice is one big wonderful museum, you will not want to miss the following outstanding collections of art. The hours are subject to change, so check locally before setting out. There are some general points on the subject of museums in the relevant section of *Facts at Your Fingertips*

Accademia delle Belle Arti, Campo dell Carità, in the Convent and Church of Santa Maria della Carità on the Grand Canal. A stunning collection of most of the greatest Venetian painters. Tues.–Sat. 9–2, Sun. 9–1, closed Mon. Entrance fee normally, but free on 1st and 3rd Sat. plus 2nd and last Sun.

Ca' d'Oro, Grand Canal, Cannaregio. Recently reopened after major redecoration inside and out. Houses the Franchetti collection of pictures and sculptures, mainly Renaissance. Tues. to Sat. 9–2, Sun. 9–1, closed Mon.

Ca' Pesaro, left bank of the Grand Canal at Santa Croce. Museum of Modern Art. Almost more interesting as a building than as a gallery. Closed indefinitely.

Ca' Rezzonico, left bank of Grand Canal at Dorsodoro. Decorative arts, works by Guardi, Longhi and Tiepolo. Mon. to Thurs., Sat., 10–4, Sun. 9–12.30, closed Fri.

Museo Correr, Piazza San Marco; entrance under Portico dell'Ascensione on west side of piazza. Historical collections and many famous Venetian works by Bellini, Carpaccio, etc. Mon., Wed. to Sat 10–4, Sun. 9–12.30. Closed Tues. Shorter hours in winter.

Palazzo Ducale, Piazzetta San Marco. The Doges' Palace, heart and center of Venetian history, packed with interest. Daily 8.30–7.

Palazzo Querini-Stampalia, Campiello Querini, near Church of Santa Maria Formosa. Art gallery and library; works by Schiavone, Bellini, Palma Vecchio, etc. Daily 10–3, closed Mon.

Raccolta Peggy Guggenheim, Palazzo Venier dei Leoni, left of the Salute. Magnificent home of the Peggy Guggenheim collection of modern art; highly recommended. Open Wed. to Fri., Sun. and Mon. 12–6, Sat. 12–9 (no admission Sat. 6–9). Closed Tues. and Nov. through Mar.

Scuola dei Carmini, Campo Carmini, opposite church of the same name. Works by Tiepolo—especially a superb ceiling. Mon. to Sat., 9–12, 3–6. Closed Sun.

Scuola di San Giorgio degli Schiavoni, Calle Furlani, far off in the eastern section, not far from the Naval Museum. Carpaccio is the star here with a series of works in a Renaissance oratory. Tues. to Sat. 10–12.30, 3.30–6, Sun. 10.30–12.30. Closed Mon.

Scuola di San Rocco, Campo San Rocco, opposite Santa Maria Gloriosa dei Frari. 56 works by Tintoretto in a beautiful 16th-century building. The Great Hall is a masterpiece. Daily 10–1, 3.30–6.30.

In Murano you will find the **Museo Vetrario,** a famed glass museum, reopened after extensive restoration; glass objects from Roman times onward. Daily 10–4, Sun. 9–12.30, closed Wed.

SHOPPING. Venetian glassware is as famous as the city's gondolas, and from your first stroll around St. Mark's Square you will be engulfed with displays of it. Venice does make beautiful glass, but there is also a good deal of cheap glass on hand, so you will do well to orient yourself before buying. Don't be discouraged by the mediocre examples you may see in window displays, or touted around with "no obligation to buy."

The trip to the glass-blowing center of **Murano** is classic, and you might want to take it, using the regular steamer services, and have a look at the goods in the factory showrooms; prices are generally the same as in Venice. Whether you buy at Murano or Venice, we recommend that you carry your purchases away with you. Having them shipped may create untold problems.

Venetian lace is exquisite—and also very expensive—but whether you are in the mood to buy or merely want to look at lace and linens visit *Jesurum & Co.,* established in an old former convent just behind St. Mark's cathedral at Ponte Canonica 4310, or take another island visit—to **Burano,** famed for its needlepoint. Almost no lace is made in Venice any more, a lot of what you see is imported from Korea, Formosa and China. Burano's museum displays gorgeous antique lace, and you can visit the island's lace school on Piazza Galuppi. Open daily from 9–6, closed Tues.

You'll find attractive and practical gift items, including stationery, in handprinted paper at the Piazzesi shop at Santa Maria del Giglio.

PRACTICAL INFORMATION FOR
THE VENETIAN ARC AND TRIESTE

WHEN TO GO. The seaside resorts of the region are at their busiest from the beginning of July through August. For the hill towns of the region, you would do well to avoid the really hot months and stick to May, June or September. The spas, such as Abano, Montegrotto and Recoaro, are at their liveliest in August, and continue to be well-frequented until mid-October. The Lake Garda resorts are popular from mid-June to September, while the best time to visit the art cities of Verona, Padua, Vicenza and Treviso, is spring or fall.

The summer resorts located in the hill and mountain areas of the Trieste region are at their busiest from late June through August. The seaside resorts are filled up from mid-June through August, and the winter sports season peaks December through February. Generally, though, if contemplating driving through the Trieste region, late spring and early fall are the best times to choose.

TOURIST OFFICES. Abano Terme: AAST, Via Pietro d'Abano 18 (669.455). **Asiago:** AAST, Palazzo Municipale (62.221). **Bassano del Grappa:** AAST, Viale delle Fosse 9 (24.351). **Garda:** AAST, Lungolago Regina Adelaide (725.5194). **Gorízia:** AAST, Corso Verdi 100/E (83.870); EPT, Via Mazzini, Condominio Caselgrandi (83.127). **Grado:** AAST, Viale Dante Alighieri 68 (460.502). **Lignano Sabbiadoro:** AAST, Via Latisana 42 (71.821). **Malcesine:** AAST, Via Capitanato (740.0044). **Montegrotto Terme:** AAST, Viale della Stazione 37 (793.384). **Padua:** AAST, Piazzetta Pedrocchi 18 (44.711); EPT, Riviera Mugnai 8 (650.124) and at rail station (27.767). **Pordenone:** AAST, Piazza della Motta 13 (21.912); EPT, Via Mazzini 12/B (27.977). **Treviso:** EPT, Via Toniolo 41 (547.632). **Trieste City:** AAST, Piazza della Cattedrale 3 (795.863) and Piazza Unita d'Italia 4 (750.297); EPT, Via San Francesco 37 (73.55). **Udine:** AAST, Piazza Patriarcato angolo via dei Missionari (295.972); EPT, Via Morpurgo 4 (23.707). **Verona:** AAST, Via Dietro Anfiteatro 8 (592.828); EPT, Via Valverde 34 (30.086). **Vicenza:** EPT, Piazza Duomo 5 (44.805) and Palazzo Chiericati, Piazza Matteotti (528.944).

SEASONAL EVENTS. Marostica: Sept. sees a legendary chess game played with living figures in medieval costume (every two years).

Treviso: the city celebrates its patron saint from Oct. 16–24.

Trieste: in Jun. there is an important International Trade Fair; at Grado, on the first Sun. in Jul., there is a boat-borne procession to the shrine of Barbana; also in Jul., the city presents an openair operetta festival, and the International Science-Fiction Film Festival.

Verona: Mar. brings musical events and the oldest and largest agricultural fair in Italy; the openair opera in the Roman Arena begins Jul.; while Shakespeare is presented in the Roman amphitheater Jul. and Aug.; for details of festivals, contact Ente Autonoma Spettacoli Lirici Arena di Verona, Piazza Bra 28, 37100 Verona (23520/22265).

Vicenza: Jan. sees goldwork and jewelry shows in this, the center of Italian goldworking; Apr. through Feb. the city celebrates spring with drama productions, exhibitions, concerts etc.; also in Jun., there are more goldwork/jewelry shows; and in Sept., the Teatro Olimpico presents classical drama—a must for all theater buffs.

TELEPHONE CODES. You will find the telephone area code for each town against its name in the Hotel and Restaurant listings (after the province name).

If there is a different area code from the majority of the establishments—say when a hotel or restaurant is in an outlying place—then the code is given in front of the telephone number.

HOTELS AND RESTAURANTS. Both hotels and restaurants tend to be pricey in the Veneto. The coastal strip boasts innumerable hotel complexes that cater for package tours, and so can be enjoyed at moderate cost. But beware the prices if you are eating away from the home base. Trieste itself has a good range of prices in its hotels, but there is not all that much available in the surrounding area. But the restaurants in the Trieste region are another kettle of fish, as there is quite a fair selection of quite inexpensive trattorias to choose from.

Regional Food and Drink. Cooking in the Trieste area is quite varied because of the multinational background of the region, because of the different kinds of ingredients offered by the mountains, plains and sea, and because for centuries it belonged to the Austrian Empire. For seafood Trieste and Grado are among the best places in the Mediterranean; fish is prepared with olive oil in the Istrian and Dalmatian manner, grilled, fried, baked or boiled. San Daniele in Friuli is famous for its raw, dried and smoked hams and Friuli also specializes in *polenta,* hares, pheasants and other small game, as well as many excellent vegetables served cooked or in salads, notably *radicchio rosso* (a special type of red salad) during the winter months. *Risotto* and *spaghetti* acquire a distinct local flavor, and the *minestra di fagioli* (bean soup) is delicious.

Veal, pork and beef are usually prepared in the Austrian style (in Trieste you can get anything from *Wiener Schnitzel* to *Tafelspitz* and *Goulash*), while chicken, sausages and other smoked pork are mostly of Slovenian origin. Practically all the cakes and pastries are also an Austrian and Slovenian contribution, ranging from *Apfelstrudel, Krapfen* (jelly doughnuts) and Viennese-type cakes in Trieste to *gubana* (a rolled sweet bread filled with nuts and raisins, etc.) in Cividale.

The best local white wines are *Riesling, Pinot* and *Tocai,* while *Merlot, Cabernet* and *Pinot nero* are fine reds. The wine producing areas are the Collio, Colli Orientali, Grave, Isonzo and Latisana. One of the best-known and rarest wines of the area is the Sauterne-like *Picolit,* produced in very limited quantities. *Grappa,* an aquavit, is produced for export and is distilled in various and precious versions for local connoisseurs.

Abano Terme Padova (049). Leading spa. *Royal Orologio* (L), Viale delle Terme 66 (669.111). Open mid-Mar. to mid-Nov. Large, elegant; ample, well-furnished rooms; spa treatments available; indoor pool; 9-hole golf course in park. AE, DC, MC, V. *Bristol Buja* (E), Via Montirone 2 (669.390). Open 20 Dec. to 18 Nov. Large, centrally located; well-appointed rooms with balcony. Thermal pools, tennis. AE, DC, MC, V. *La Residence* (E), Via Monte Ceva 8 (668.333). Closed Dec. through Feb. Modern, central; soundproofed rooms with all amenities including stereo and terrace; roof garden, thermal pools. AE, DC, MC, V.

Ariston Molino (M), Via Augure 5 (669.061). Open 3 March to 30 Nov. Comfortable; thermal pool, garden, tennis. AE, DC, MC, V. *Ritz* (M), Via Monteortone 19 (669.990). Pleasant; thermal pools, park, tennis. AE, DC, MC, V. *Terme Astoria* (M), Piazza Colombo 1 (669.030). Open 18 Feb. to 25 Nov. In park; thermal pools, tennis. AE, DC, MC, V.

All'Alba (I), Via Valerio Flacco 32 (669.244). Large, central; spa treatments. AE, DC, MC, V.

Asiago Vicenza (0424). Summer and winter resort. *Linta Park* (E), on Bassano road (62.753). Outside center with fine view; bright, modern decor, indoor pool. V. *Bellevue* (M), at Kaberlaba (63.367). Closed 20 April to 20 May. Small, isolated and peaceful; comfortable rooms; tennis. *Croce Bianca* (M), Via Quattro Novembre 30 (62.642). Open 15 Dec. to 15 April and 15 June to 15 Oct. Traditional older hotel on main street, basic rooms; cosy bar. V.

Restaurant. *Casa Rossa* (M), at Kaberlaba (62.017). Closed Thurs. Rustic, fine local cuisine.

Asolo Treviso (0423). Lovely town. *Villa Cipriani* (E), Via Canova 298 (55.444). CIGA. Elegant, romantic villa; beautifully furnished rooms with view; garden; famed restaurant. AE, DC, MC, V.

Restaurants. *Ca' Derton* (M), Piazza D'Annunzio 11 (52.730). Closed Mon. evening, Tues. and 12–31 Aug. Old-world atmosphere and good local cuisine. Reasonable. AE. *Charly's One* (M), Via Roma 55 (52.201). Closed Mon. Attractive English pub decor; Venetian and regional dishes. Can be pricey. MC, V.

Bassano del Grappa Vicenza (0424). Picturesque town, famous ceramic center. *Belvedere* (M), Piazzale Generale Giardino 14 (29.845). On busy main road; short walk to all sights; clean and comfortable; ask for quiet room. AE, DC, MC, V.

Restaurants. *Ca'Sette* (E), Via Cunizza da Romano 4 (25.005). Closed Sun. evening, Mon. and 1–15 Nov. Just outside town, handsome 18th-century villa serving fine seasonal specialties. Summer dining in garden. AE, DC, V. *Belvedere* (M), Viale delle Fosse 1 (26.602). Closed Sun. Rather elegant setting, classical cuisine. AE, DC, MC, V. *Al Ponte* (M), Via Volpato 60 (25.269). Closed Mon. evening and Tues. Overlooking famous bridge, some fish specialties pricey. *Al Sole* (M), Via Vittorelli 41–43 (23.206). Closed Mon., and July. Old-world atmosphere; regional cuisine; Bassano's famous asparagus in springtime. AE, DC, MC, V.

Bibione Venezia (0431). Popular beach resort. High season 15 June to 31 Aug. *Principe* (E), Via Ariete 41 (43.256). Open 15 May to 15 Sept. Fairly large, well-equipped resort hotel. AE, DC, MC, V. *Bembo* (M), Corso Europa 29 (43.418). Open 15 May to 15 Sept. Modern beach hotel. *Palace* (M), Via del Leone 44 (43.135). Open 20 May to 10 Sept. Modern; pool and beach.

Caorle Venezia (0421). Interesting old town with adjoining, well laid-out beach area. High season 15 June to 31 Aug. *Airone* (M), Via Pola 1 (81.570). Open 20 May to 20 Sept. Good, comfortable beach hotel; pool, sea view. DC, V. *Metropole* (M), Via Emilia 1 (82.091). Open 20 May to 23 Sept. Modern, pleasant; pool, garden, beach facilities. AE, V.

At **Santa Margherita**, 15 km. (10 miles) by bus or ferry, *San Giorgio* (E) (82.351). Open 13 May to 25 Sept. Large, modern resort hotel on beach. AE, MC, V.

Restaurants. *Da Duilio* (E), Strada Nuova 13 (81.087). Closed Mon. and Tues. noon off-season, and Jan. Noteworthy quality in seafood and other specialties. AE, DC, MC, V.

At **Santa Margherita**, *La Tortuga* (M), Via Amalfi 1 (81.888). Closed Tues. and 15 Nov. to 15 Dec. At port, very good food. V.

Chioggia Venezia (041). Picturesque island fishing town. **Restaurants.** *El Gato* (M), Campo Sant' Andrea 653 (401.806). Closed Mon. Cordial service, good food. AE, DC, MC, V. *La Piazzetta* (M), Piazzetta Venti Settembre (403.541). Closed Mon. off-season. *Simpatico* atmosphere.

Conegliano Treviso (0438). Art town. **Restaurants.** *Tre Panoce* (E), Via Vecchia Trevigiana 50 (60.071). Closed Mon. and Aug. Just outside town. Lovely country setting, creative cuisine and classic favorites. AE, DC, V. *Cima* (M), Via Ventiquattro Maggio 61 (22.648). Closed Tues. and 15 July to 15 Aug. Outstanding chef. *Canon d'Oro* (M), Via Venti Settembre 129 (22.171). Closed Sat. Town's oldest inn, very good. AE, DC, V. *Al Salisà* (M), Via Venti Settembre 2 (24.288). Closed Mon. and Aug. Historic surroundings, elegant decor, refined cuisine. AE, DC, MC, V.

Duino (040) Trieste. Fishing port. *Motel AGIP* (M), at autostrada A4 (208.273). Good, modern accommodations; fine restaurant. AE, DC, MC, V.

At **Sistiana**, pretty little beach near Duino, *Europa* (E) (200.230). Fine resort hotel with beach facilities and gardens. *Posta* (M) (299.103). Small, pleasant. No restaurant. AE, V.

Giavera del Montello Treviso (0422). **Restaurants.** *Agnoletti* (M), Via della Vittoria 131 (876.009). Closed Mon., Tues., 1–20 Jan. and 1–15 July. A gem, an inn since 18th-century; mushrooms in infinite variety and other specialties. If it's closed, try *Bazzichet* (M), Via Bongiovanni 4 (876.018). Closed Mon. and Fri. Simple, reasonable and good.

Gorizia Gorizia (0481). Border town. *Internazionale* (M), Via Trieste 173 (20.334). Automobile Club's hotel for motorists in transit; quite good. DC, V. *Palace* (M), Corso Italia 63 (82.166). Fairly large; comfortable modern hotel. AE, MC, V.
Restaurants. *Bella Capri* (M), Via Morelli (85.758). Closed Mon. Good; pizzas, too. *Al Fogolar* (M), Stradone della Maivizza 256 (390.107). Closed Mon. and July. Good southern Italian cuisine. *Lanterna d'Oro* (M), Borgo Castello 20 (85.565). Closed Sun. and Mon. Good atmosphere and cuisine in old castle. AE, DC, V.

Grado Gorizia (0431). Important spa and beach resort. High season 1 July to 31 Aug. *Antica Villa Bernt* (E), Via Colombo 5 (82.516). Open 20 May to 30 Sept. Small, villa hotel; attractive and comfortable. DC, MC, V. *Savoy* (M), Via Carducci 33 (81.171). Open 1 April to 31 Oct. Central, well-furnished; thermal pool. DC. *Tiziano Palace* (M), Riva Slataper 8 (80.884). Open 1 May to 30 Sept. Large, central; good views. AE, DC, MC, V.
At **La Rotta,** *Al Bosco* (M) (80.485). Open 1 May to 30 Sept. Quiet, smallish hotel on beach.
Restaurants. *Da Nico* (E), Via Marina 10 (80.470). Closed Thurs. Typical seafood trattoria. *Adriatico* (M), Campiello della Torre 3 (80.002). Closed Wed. Good local cuisine, emphasizing fish. *Colussi* (M), Piazza Carpaccio 1 (80.471). Closed Mon. and 20 Nov. to 20 Dec. Both meat and fish dishes; summer garden.

Grignano Trieste (040). Yachting port, near Miramare and Trieste. High season 15 June to 15 Sept. *Adriatico Palace* (L) (224.241). Open 1 April to 15 Oct. Spacious, well-furnished rooms, most with balcony and sea view; own beach club; smart atmosphere. AE, DC, MC, V.

Lido di Jesolo Venezia (0421). Popular beach resort, especially with package tours. All hotels open May to Sept. High season 15 June to 31 Aug. *Las Vegas* (E), Via Mascagni 2 (971.515). Large, modern, right on beach; functional bedrooms, all with balcony and sea view; terraces, pool. AE, DC, MC, V. *Bellevue* (E), Via Oriente 100 (961.233). At **Jesolo Pineta,** in attractive surroundings, on beach; pool, tennis. *Atlantico* (M), Via Bafile 11 (91.273). Good medium-sized hotel with sea views; beach. AE. *Byron Bellavista* (M), Via Padova 83 (971.023). On beach, modern; pool. AE, DC, MC, V. *Galassia* (M), Via Treviso 7 (972.271). Right on beach; very comfortable; pool, garden.
Restaurants. *Da Alfredo* (M), Via Baffile at Largo Tempini 13 (91.227). Closed Oct. Elegant, smart. DC. *Alla Darsena* (M), Via Oriente 166, at Jesolo Pineta (980.081). Closed Thurs. and 15 Nov. to 10 Dec. Informal atmosphere; seafood specialties. AE, DC, MC, V.

Lignano Sabbiadoro Udine (0431). Beach resort with three nuclei. High season 1 July to 31 Aug.
At **Lignano Pineta,** prettiest section with gardens and pinewoods, *Grief* (E), Arco del Grecale 23 (422.261). Open 15 May to 20 Sept. Fairly large resort hotel with pool; beach facilities. AE, DC, MC, V. *Bella Venezia Mare* (M), Arco del Grecale 18/a (422.184). Open 15 May to 25 Sept. Attractive medium-sized hotel in garden; beach facilities. AE, DC, MC, V. *Medusa Splendid* (M), Raggio Scirocco 33 (422.211). Open 15 May to 15 Sept. Good, with pool, beach facilities. AE, DC, MC, V.
At **Lignano Riviera,** smart section, *Eurotel* (E), Calle Mendelssohn (428.992). Open 14 April to 20 Sept. In lovely park; comfortable; heated pool. AE, DC, MC, V. *President* (E), Calle Rembrandt 2 (428.777). Open 10 May to 10 Sept. Very good, in quiet park; beach facilities. AE, DC, MC, V.
At **Sabbiadoro,** most built-up section, with scores of hotels, *Atlantic* (M), Lungomare Trieste 160 (71.101). Open 1 May to 30 Sept. Fine location in pinewoods fac-

ing beach; modern, well furnished rooms. AE, DC, MC, V. *Columbus* (M), Lungomare Trieste 22 (71.516). On shore boulevard, facing beach. AE, DC.

Restaurants. *Siesta* (E), Corso delle Nazioni 50 (428.673). Open 1 May to 30 Sept. Attractive, elegant place for classic cuisine. AE, DC, MC, V. *Bidin* (M), Viale Europa 1 (71.988). Closed Wed. Small, family-run, very good. Reserve. AE, DC, MC, V. *Al Cason* (M), Corso Continenti 167 (428.527). Open daily Easter to 1 Oct. Pleasant rustic atmosphere, good seafood.

Maser Treviso (0423). Site of beautiful Villa Barbaro, frescoed by Veronese. **Restaurant.** *Da Bastian* (M), at Muliparte on Cornuda road (565.400). Closed Wed. dinner, Thurs. and Aug. Attractive, modern; fine seasonal specialties from surrounding countryside.

Monfalcone Gorizia (0481). Shipbuilding center. **Restaurants.** *Hannibal* (E), Via Bagni (790.112). Closed Mon. At marina, caters to yachtsmen. AE. *Da Bruno* (M), Via Cosulich 7 (481.803). Closed Sat. noon and Sun. Elegant, mainly seafood, can be pricey. AE, DC, MC, V.

Montegrotto Terme Padova (049). Spa. High season 1 April to 31 May and 1 Aug. to 31 Oct. *Bertha International* (E), Largo Traiano 1 (793.100). Open 1 March to 7 Jan. Large, smart; very comfortable rooms; thermal pools, tennis, garden. AE, DC, MC, V. *Esplanade Tergesteo* (E), Via Roma 54 (793.444). Open 1 March to 30 Nov. Large, elegantly modern; well-furnished rooms, posh salons; all spa amenities, thermal pools. AE, DC, V.

Caesar (M), Via Aureliana (793.655). Open 1 March to 30 Nov. Comfortable, well appointed, all spa amenities. AE, DC, MC, V. *Terme Neroniane* (M), Via Neroniana 21 (793.466). Open 1 Mar.–5 Jan. Handsome, comfortable hotel with lush park, pools, spa facilities. AE.

Paderno di Ponzano Veneto Treviso (0422). *Relais El Toulà* (L), Via Postumia 37 (969.191). In stately Venetian villa, just 12 beautiful rooms; exclusive, patrician atmosphere; huge pool and all creature comforts; near Treviso. Superb restaurant. AE, DC, MC, V.

Padova Padova (049). *Padovanelle* (E), at Ponte di Brenta (625.622). Smart, modern, low building in park of racetrack outside town; pool, tennis; quiet and comfortable. AE, DC, MC, V. *Plaza* (E), Corso Milano 40 (656.822). Central, large; undistinguished rooms. AE, DC, MC, V.

Donatello (M), Via del Santo (875.0634). Closed 15 Dec. to 15 Jan. Opposite basilica; smallish, nice atmosphere. AE, DC, MC, V. *Europa* (M), Largo Europa 9 (661.200). Central, modern; good restaurant. AE, DC, MC, V. *Majestic* (M), Piazzetta dell'Arco 2 (663.244). Central, comfortable, small. AE, DC, V.

Restaurants. *Isola di Caprera* (E), Via Marsilio di Padova 11 (39.385). Closed Mon. evening and Tues. Very central; longtime favorite. AE, DC, MC, V. *El Toulà* (E), Via Belle Parti 11 (26.649). Closed Sun., Mon. noon and Aug. Reserve. Small, beautifully decorated, in historic palace in center of town. AE, DC, MC, V.

Cavalca (M), Via Daniele Manin 8 (39.244). Closed Tues. lunch and Wed. Central, family-run; local cuisine. AE, DC, MC, V. *Al Fagiano* (M), Via Locatelli 45 (652.913). Closed Mon. and July. Near basilica, busy, quite good and reasonable. *Giovanni* (M), Via Maroncelli 22 (772.620). Closed Sun. and Aug. On outskirts, lively and popular place; good food.

Pizzeria (I), directly across from basilica.

Café. *Pedrocchi,* historic old meeting place at center of town. A must for aperitifs.

Soave Verona (045). Home of famous wine, a picturesque medieval town. **Restaurants.** *Al Gambero* (M), Corso Vittorio Emanuele 5 (768.0010). Closed Tues. Old-world atmosphere; local dishes and wine. AE, DC. *El Grio* (M), at Costeggiola (767.5184). Closed Mon. evening, Tues. and 16 Aug. to 6 Sept.

Solighetto Treviso (0438). About 32 km. (20 miles) north of Treviso. **Restaurant.** *Da Lino Alla Posta* (M), Via Brandolini 1 (82.150). Closed Mon., July and Christmas. One of the best in region; a pretty inn; excellent and inventive cuisine. AE, DC, MC, V.

Tarvisio Udine (0428). Summer and winter sports resort on the Austrian border. High season 1 July to 31 Aug., 20 Dec. to 10 Jan. *Nevada* (M) Via Kugj 4 (23.32). Attractively furnished. AE, DC, MC, V. *Friuli* (I), Via Vittorio Veneto 104 (20.16). Smallish, homely atmosphere.

Treviso Treviso (0422). *Continental* (M), Via Roma 16 (57.216). Near station. Comfortable, modern. No restaurant. AE, DC, MC, V. *Al Fogher* (M), Viale della Repubblica 10 (20.686). Outside town, on road to Vicenza; good. AE, DC, V. *Campeol* (M), Piazza Ancillotto (540.871). In center of town; small, pleasant, reasonable. AE, DC, MC, V.

Restaurants. *El Toulà* (E), Via Collalto 26 (540.275). Closed Mon. and 10–25 Aug. *Art nouveau* decor, varied and superb cuisine. AE, DC, MC, V.

Beccherie (M), Piazza Ancillotto 10 (540.871). Closed Thurs. evening, Fri., July. In old center of town, atmosphere and local cuisine. DC, MC. *Al Bersagliere* (M), Via Barberia 21 (541.988). Closed Sun., Mon. noon and Aug. Beautiful old locale, refined specialties. AE, DC, MC, V. *Carletto* (M), Via Bibano 46 (62.955). Closed Mon. and Aug. Cordial, *simpatico,* very good food. Just outside town; hotel next-door. AE. *L'Incontro* (M), Largo di Porta Altinia 13 (547.717). Closed Wed., Thurs. noon and Aug. Near station, elegant, modern; courteous service. *Harry's Dolci* (M), Piazza Signori 6 (579.888). Branch of Venetian Harry's. AE.

Trieste Trieste (040). Important port, cultural crossroads. *Duchi d'Aosta* (E), Piazza Unità d'Italia 2 (62.081). CIGA. On beautiful piazza overlooking sea; fairly small with lots of atmosphere; spacious, nicely-decorated rooms; cheerful grill room. AE, DC, MC, V. *Savoia Palace* (E), Riva del Mandracchio 4 (76.90). Central, on port; large, very comfortable, good views. AE, DC, MC, V. *Colombia* (M), Via della Geppa 18 (69.434). Central, near station; well-furnished. No restaurant. AE, DC, MC, V. *Continentale* (M), Via San Nicolò 25 (65.444). Very central, good medium-sized hotel. No restaurant. AE, DC, MC, V.

At **Opicina,** on the Karstic plateau above Trieste, about 12 km. (7 miles) away, *Park Obelisco* (E), Via Nazionale 1 (212.666). Open 1 March to 31 Dec. 30 well-appointed rooms in smart, modern resort hotel; pool, tennis in lovely park. DC.

Restaurants. *Harry's Grill* (E), Piazza Unità d'Italia 2 (62.081). In Duchi d'Aosta Hotel, elegant old-world decor, excellent and pricey cuisine. AE, DC, MC, V. *Nastro Azzurro* (E), Riva Sauro 10 (755.985). Closed Sat. evening and Sun. Attractive, the city's best seafood restaurant. Not all choices expensive. AE.

Adriatico-Da Camillo (M), Via San Lazzaro 7 (34.122). Closed Mon. and Aug. Small, cordial; seasonal specialties. AE, DC. *Birreria Dreher* (M), Via Giulia 75 (566.286). Closed Wed. Austrian cuisine in typical beer cellar. *Bottega del Vino* (M), Castello di San Giusto (795.959). Closed Tues. and Jan. Unique setting in medieval castle; good food and atmosphere. AE. *Suban* (M), Via Comici 2 (54.368). Closed Mon., Tues. and Aug. Historic old trattoria serving very good Middle-European fare, with imaginative variations. AE, DC, MC, V.

At **Opicina,** *Daneu* (M), Via Nazionale 194 (211.241). Closed Thurs. and Oct. Simple, very good Slovenian inn. AE, DC, V.

Udine Udine (0432). *Astoria* (E), Piazza Venti Settembre 24 (505.091). Central, comfortable. AE, DC, V. *Continental* (M), Viale Tricesimo 73 (46.969) Just outside town; good. *President* (M), Via Duino 8 (292.905). Modern, functional rooms. No restaurant. AE, DC, MC, V. *Motel AGIP* (M), Viale Ledra 24 (34.351). Fairly central. Large, standard comforts. DC, V.

Restaurants. *Buona Vite* (M), Via Treppo 10 (21.053). Closed Sun. evening, Mon. and Aug. Attractive, specializing in seafood; Venetian cuisine. AE, DC, V.

Antica Maddalena (M), Via Pelliccerie 4 (25.111). Closed Sun. evening, Mon. and Aug. Small trattoria with lots of atmosphere; good food. AE, DC, MC, V. *Alla Lepre* (M), Via Poscolle 27 (295.798). Closed Sun. and Aug. Picturesque wine shop serving regional dishes. AE, DC, V. *Alla Vedova* (M), Via Tavagnacco 9 (470.291). Closed Sun. evening, Mon. and Aug. Typical atmosphere and decor; traditional local cuisine; summer garden. *Vitello d'Oro* (M), Via Valvason 4 (291.982). Closed Tues. evening, Wed. and July. Attractive locale; varied menu, mainly seafood. AE, DC, MC, V.

At **Cividale,** 15 km. (11 miles) away, *Al Castello* (M), Via del Castello 18 (733.242). Closed Wed. and July. Picturesque inn. *Alla Frasca* (M), Via De Rubeis 10 (731.270). Closed Sun. evening and Mon. Lovely old place, very good and varied menu. AE, DC, MC, V. *Al Fortino* (M), Via Carlo Alberto 46 (731.217). Closed Mon. evening, Tues. and June. In old castle, vaulted ceilings, huge hearth; fine local dishes. V.

At **Tricesimo,** 12 km. (8 miles) away, *Boschetti* (E), Piazza Mazzini 10 (851.230). Closed Sun. evening and Mon. One of the best in region for ambiance and excellent cuisine. AE, DC, V.

Verona Verona (045). *Due Torri* (L), Piazza Sant'Anastasia 4 (595.044). Outstanding; on site of 19th-century inn, near cathedral and Adige river; all rooms individually decorated with period pieces; excellent service and cuisine. AE, DC, MC, V. *Accademia* (E), Via Scala 12 (596.222). Central; pleasant, large, contemporary furnishings. No restaurant. AE, DC, MC, V. *Colomba d'Oro* (E), Via Cattaneo 10 (595.300). Near the arena; attractive old building; clubby salons, traditional bedrooms. No restaurant. AE, DC, MC, V. *Victoria* (E), Via Adua 6 (590.566). Central, modern comforts, very good. AE, DC, V.

Giulietta e Romeo (M), Vicolo Tre Marchetti 3 (23.554). In old part of town behind arena; small, simple, good atmosphere. No restaurant. *Torcolo* (M), Vicolo Listone 3 (800.7512). Very central; plain facade but well decorated bedrooms; reasonable. No restaurant.

Restaurants. *Arche* (E), Via Arche Scaligere 6 (800.7415). Closed Sun. evening, Mon. and 1–22 July. Central, tiny, elegant and exceptional seafood. Reserve. *Il Desco* (E), Via San Sebastiano 7 (595.358). Closed Sun. Central, handsome, for exquisite and creative cuisine. AE, DC, MC, V. *Dodici Apostoli* (E), Corticella San Marco 3 (596.999). Closed Sun. evening, Mon. and mid-June to 10 July. Historic surroundings, Renaissance decor; once one of Italy's best, still very good; tops for atmosphere. AE, DC. *Al Vecio Mulin* (E), Via Sottoriva 42 (28.270). Closed Sun. evening and Mon. On banks of Adige, small, very good seafood. V.

La Greppia (M), Vicolo Samaritana 3 (800.4577). Closed Mon. and 1–15 Oct. Fine local cuisine. Very central, handy to sights. *Marconi* (M), Via Fogge 4 (595.295). Closed Sun., Tues. evening and Aug. Central, classic cuisine, courteously served. AE, DC, MC, V. *Re Teodorico* (M), Piazzale Castel San Pietro (49.990). Closed Fri. and Nov. Delightful setting, fine view of city; good food. AE, DC, V. *Torcoloti* (M), Via Zambelli 24 (26.777). Closed Sun., Mon. evening. Central. AE, DC, MC, V. *Mondo d'Oro,* off Via Mazzini, light meals.

Vicenza Vicenza (0444). *Campo Marzio* (E), Viale Roma 21 (547.700). Smallish, comfortable. AE, DC, MC, V. *Europa* (E), Viale San Lazzaro (564.111). On outskirts, good for motorists. AE, DC, V. *Basilica* (I), Piazza Erbe 9 (21.204). Small, homey and atmospheric, right at center of town. AE, V.

At **Arcugnano,** 7 km. (4 miles) outside town, *Michelangelo* (M), Via Sacco 4 (550.300). Country villa of 16th-century, lovely rooms; sports facilities.

Restaurants. *Due Mori* (M), Via Due Ruote 24. Closed Wed. Good for both pizza and local dishes. V. *Gran Caffè Garibaldi* (M), Piazza dei Signori 5 (544.147). Closed Tues. evening and Wed. Very good food, vast menu, at center of town. AE, DC, MC, V. *Al Pozzo* (M), Via Sant'Antonio 1 (221.411). Closed Tues. and Sun. in July and Aug. Pleasant and central for snacks, fine *antipasto,* full meals. AE, DC, MC. *Da Remo* (M), Via Ca'Impenta 14 (911.007). Closed Sun. evening, Mon. and Aug. Best in town; on outskirts near autostrada exit, in attractive country house; local cuisine. AE.

Scudo di Francia (M), Contrà Piancoli 4 (233.368). Closed Sun. evening and Mon. Handsome Gothic setting; very good food and service. AE, DC, V.

GETTING THERE AND AROUND. By air. The airports for the Venetian Arc are at Venice itself (for international traffic) and at Verona. For Trieste the most important airport is that of Ronchi dei Legionari, about 32 km. (20 miles) outside Trieste. There is a bus service into town.

By train. For the Venetian Arc: the main rail lines from Milan (via Verona and Vicenza) and from Rome (via Florence and Bologna) meet at Padua, where cars for Venice are detached if the train is to continue on to Treviso and Gorizia or to Trieste. For Trieste: main rail lines connect all the chief towns of the Trieste area with Venice and Padua. The Udine line continues north into Austria, while the Trieste line crosses into Yugoslavia.

By car. The main highway in the region is the A4, which connects Padua and Venice with Trieste. If you take the A4 northward from Milan, you will find autostrade peeling off to Treviso and Vittorio Veneto (A27), Prodenone (A28), and Udine (A23). The area can be reached from Austria over the Plucken Pass or, more simply, via Villach and Tarvisio; or else by the Coccau Pass and Monte Croce Carnico. Traffic to Yugoslavia goes through various border stations in the province of Trieste and through the Stupizza Station in the province of Udine.

By bus. Buslines provide fair local services between the smaller centers of the region.

Tours. CIT has a full-day tour of the Venetian villas by motor coach, and a delightful full-day *Burchiello* motorlaunch cruise up the Brenta River to Padua (summer only). Apply at CIT offices in Venice or Padua.

THE DOLOMITES

A Panoramic Playground

The superbly rugged mountain scenery of this area has attracted knowledgeable visitors from neighboring regions for centuries, but the Dolomites were catapulted on to the international wintersports scene only with
the Olympics of 1956 in Cortina d'Ampezzo. These Eastern Alps (Alpi
Orientali) rise majestically from the Passo dello Stelvio below the 3,905-
meter (12,812-ft.) Ortler overlooking Switzerland the whole length of the
Austrian border eastwards to the 2,234-meter (7,329-ft.) Monte Cavallo.
Hardly less spectacular is the gradual descent to Tarvisio, where an equally dramatic chain, the Karavankes, take over into Yugoslavia.

Increasingly popular for skiing, sleighing and skating, the valleys and
meadows, crystal-clear lakes and stupendous cliffs provide also an ideal
setting for some of Europe's best climbing and most pleasurable walking,
beside the usual sports of summer resorts—and all in an unusually crisp,
dry air. The dividing line between all these activities can be grandly ignored, as an important international slalom competition is held at Solda
in July, while heated indoor pools remain open year round.

The facilities and natural attractions of the region are almost uncount-
able. Accommodations range from deluxe hotels all the way down to
rooms in spotlessly clean and welcoming village houses; the sports infra-
structure—funiculars, chair-lifts and ski-lifts giving access to some 600
miles of ski-runs, breathtaking ski-jumps and toboggan chutes, and hoist-
ing the more leisurely mountaineers in summer; waterfalls and torrents
abounding in trout, lakes scattered over high meadows (300 in Trentino
alone) many with golden perch and pike; and above all the variations of

an unspoilt landscape, with toy villages and fairy castles set against a backdrop of delicately-hued cliffs and awe-inspiring glaciers.

In their hundreds are the sports schools for ski, tobogganing and mountaineering; and the village orchestras, each dressed in the distinctive local costumes, worn by the country people on the numerous feast days. Though there are only six *High Routes of the Dolomites,* even the most demanding walker will be satisfied by the profusion of scenic beauty. The routes meander without excessive difficulties through lush meadows, bright with wild flowers, the dominating brilliant blue of gentians and the pink of dwarf rhododendrons shading into every color nature has conceived. In the many National Parks, including Italy's largest round Stelvio, rare flora is matched by fauna extinct or in danger of extinction elsewhere, like the brown bear and the ibex. Blueberries might not make a satisfactory meal, but milk and cheese from huge cartwheels do, so that hunger is no pressing problem, with friendly farms never far out of sight.

And all this in better weather than might be expected at such heights, as the southern slopes of the Alps are open to the sun and protected from the cold winds, while fog is rare. Alycanthus flowers in winter, almond blossoms follow in March, the lower valleys are verdant with a subtropical vegetation, the orchards a riot of colors.

A Minimum of History

There is no lack of history in this region—it is just that there is not quite the surfeit prevalent in the rest of the country. In the Miocene Age, millions of years ago, the stupendous arc of the Dolomites confined the sea that covered the plain of Venetia. The fertile foothills of the Trentino–Alto Adige (South Tirol) were inhabited as far back as the sixth millenium B.C., as proved by stone weapons and utensils found in tombs. Pre-history left mysterious rock carvings and the remains of a lake dwellers' village perched on stilts in Lake Ledro. In the second century B.C. the local Celtic tribes were subjugated by the Romans, whose greatest gift to the region was the grape, now as then producing excellent wine. Curiously enough, it was collected from the beginning in barrels and not in clay amphorae or leather sacks as further south.

More durable than the East Goths and Lombards of the 5th century A.D. were the Bavarians who made it the southern bastion of their duchy till this entrance into Italy was granted by the Emperor Conrad II to the Bishops of Brixen and Trent. These ecclesiastical princes in their turn enfeoffed the Counts of Tirol, who doubled as Dukes of Carinthia. The heiress of these fiefs left them to the Habsburgs in 1363, and they remained with the House of Austria until their incorporation into Italy in 1918.

The mainly German-speaking inhabitants of this autonomous region live in the Province of Bolzano (Bozen) and are represented by their own party, the Volkspartei, in the Italian parliament. The bilingual status becomes immediately apparent by the German and Italian wording on the signposts.

The Cynosure of Europe

From 1545 to 1563 the eyes of the world were on Trento, the small town on the Adige, where the structure of the Catholic Church was revised in the famous Council of Trent, the starting point of the Counter Reformation which brought half of Europe back to Catholicism. Surprisingly, the Council was not held in the moated residence of the prince-bishops, the Castello di Buonconsiglio, the Castle of Good Counsel, an unusual blend of medieval and Renaissance features, but in the Cathedral, and in the Renaissance Church of Santa Maria Maggiore.

The graceful fusion of Austrian and Venetian architecture is at its finest in the Via Belenzani, with its 16th-century Palazzo del Municipio, the splendid painted facade of the Palazzo Geremia, the Palazzo Alberto-Colico and the Baroque Church dell'Annunziata. On the corner of the Piazza del Duomo the frescoed Palazzo Cazuffi faces the severe Romanesque Cathedral and the 13th-century Palazzo Pretorio with its impressive tower. In the center of the square is the Neptune Fountain. The arcaded medieval palaces and towers of the Via Cavour complete the tour of the old town.

Dante's statue is placed in a public garden, surrounded by the Palaces of the Regional and the Provincial Government, the railway station and the tourist office. Next to the Ponte San Lorenzo across the Adige is the funicular station for the Sardagna, with its panoramic view over the town, but, for a glorious sweep over the Alps, Mount Paganella 14 km (9 miles) north is the place, easily accessible despite its height—2,125 meters (6,972 ft.). The double circle round Trento, the first of gentle hills, the second of imposing mountains, is broken by several lakes in attractive valleys and on high plateaux. Lying in the heart of its province, Trento is the obvious center for exploring its scenic beauty.

The Mountains and Valleys of Trentino

On the 24 km. (15 miles) south on A22 to Rovereto, take the exit Rovereto Nord to the Plateau of Folgaria and Lavarone which, with almost 100 hotels and inns, is rightly a favorite for all-year-round tourism. Several roads cross the lush meadows at 1,000 meters (3,300 ft.), past the imposing Austrian fortifications of the First World War, through numerous villages with funiculars up the ski slopes of Monte Cornetto.

The 15th-century castle of Rovereto rises on a bluff between the Adige, endless vineyards and the numerous palaces of the old town. Isera, across the river, is worth a stop which can be made all the more attractive by sampling the local Marzemino wine. After Mori N240 leads past Lake Loppio to the cypresses and palm trees of Torbole on Lake Garda.

For the return to Trento, N45bis along the Sarca is more than just an alternative, especially as it allows an excursion to the Alpine Botanical Garden on Mount Bondone, with over 2,000 species of plants.

But once on Lake Garda, it would be hard and, moreover, wrong to resist the temptation to continue westward round the head of the Lake, via Riva and always on N240, past Lake Ledra to the valleys of the Giudicarie, connected by the Chiese river. N237 follows the river north till its source in Lakes Malga Boazzo and Malga Bissina, nourished from the glaciers of Monte Fumo 3,418 meters (11,214 ft.) to name but the highest of those mighty peaks. The long corridor from the Lombard plain abandons the Chiese for the upper course of the Sarca, below the Brenta, the most eerie chain of the Dolomites. 2,300 meters (7,550 ft.) is the average of these fantastic pinnacles, among which the enormous Campanile Rosso fully justifies its name of bell tower.

A short walk through the pine woods at Pinzolo leads to the Church of San Vigilio, remarkable for the long fresco of the *Dance of Death* painted on the outside in the 16th century. The Sarca turns west (left) into the Genova Valley, a wonderland of waterfalls, while N239 enters the Rendena Valley to Madonna di Campiglio, at 1522 meters (4,994 ft.) the main summer and winter resort in the Brenta Dolomites, with several lovely small lakes in the vicinity. Over the Campo Carlo Magno Pass, 1,682 meters (5,519 ft.), where Charlemagne supposedly stopped on his way to Rome to be crowned emperor, to the junction with N4 from Como—a highly recommended drive—at Dimaro. The Sole, Peio and Rabbi Valleys below the Gruppo del Cevedale, 3,764 meters (12,350 ft.), offer a tantalizing choice of mountain resorts.

Rather than follow N42 westward along the northshore of the huge artificial Lake Santa Giustina, branch south (right) on N43 into the delightful Non Valley to its capital Cles. However attractive this valley, with its apple orchards on the banks of the Noce, numerous castles and the picturesque Hermitage of San Romedio high up on a cliff, if there is time for only one side trip, then it should be to Lake Tovel, 1,178 meters (3,865 ft.), surrounded by fir forests, even if the measures against pollution—alas, even in the heart of the mountains—have not yet succeeded in reviving the algae that once turned the water an alarming blood-red.

After skirting most of Lake Santa Giustina, N43 rejoins N42 before the Mendel Pass, 1,363 meters (4,472 ft.), open all year. The descent zig-zags through dense woods and past several castles to the Adige Valley, with Bolzano (Bozen) on the further bank.

Bolzano (Bozen), Meeting Place of Two Nations

Needless to say, A22 from Trento to Bolzano (Bozen), 60 km. (37 miles) following the Adige north, likewise offers rewarding sidetrips, especially into the Cembra Valley northeast (right) from Lavis. The Trentino Folkloric Museum is housed in the former Augustine Monastery of San Michele. The best Grappa is produced here, while once South Tirol (Alto Adige) is entered near Salurn, the villages bear the names of famous wines, like Tramin and Caldaro (Kaltern). And, of course, the Adige becomes the Etsch, because language is a delicate matter in these parts.

Protected by mountains in the north and east, on the main traffic artery between the German North and the Latin South over the Brenner Pass, and at the convergence of several valleys, Bolzano has been destined by nature to be the province's capital. Its central position in the bus network makes Bolzano an excellent base from which to explore—even by the tiniest mountain roads. The mild, sunny climate at 272 m. (892 ft.) favors the luxuriant orchards and vineyards, which are watered by three rivers. It is disputed over which the Romans built a bridge, but the medieval town rose on the triangle formed by the juncture of the Isarco (Eisack) and the Talvera (Talfer) and extended only later to the confluent with the Adige.

The architecture of the old town is typically Tirolean, that means Austrian with some Lombard-Venetian features. High-gabled houses in narrow arcaded streets—the famous *Lauben* are an outstanding example—wrought-iron signs indicating artisan shops next to stairs leading down to centuries-old cellars where locals and tourists alike enjoy the excellent native wines.

The center of the town is the Piazza Walther and the Gothic Duomo with its elegant, lacy spire. In the Via Portici, the main arcaded street, is the Palazzo Mercantile, a beautiful Baroque building which has been the center of trade for 200 years. The fruit and vegetable market, (Piazza delle Erbe), a riot of color from the delicious produce of the region, takes up a considerable space at the junction with Via Museo, which not unexpectedly leads past the Museum—interesting paintings and especially good Tirolean woodcarvings—to the bridge over the Talvera. Across the river are the old Parish Church of Gries with its famous 15th-century altar by Michael Pacher, as well as the Benedictine Abbey with a fine Baroque church.

Recross the river to follow the Lungotalvera promenade upstream to the 13th-century Castel Mareccio (Schloss Maretsch) with five squat towers, a convention center with a good restaurant and whose restored frescos can be visited. It also has a Wine Tasting Center. Worth visiting, too, is the medieval Franciscan Church, with a magnificent altar carved in wood by Hans Klocker in about 1500, frescos and a vaulted cloister. Closer to the Duomo is the former Dominican Monastery, with outstanding 15th-century frescos in the church, the chapels and the cloister.

Three funiculars connect the town with the plateaux of San Genesio (Jenesien), 1,080 meters (3,543 ft.), Colle (Kohlern), 1,100 meters (3,609 ft.), and Soprabolzano, 1,221 meters (4,006 ft.), not only affording splendid panoramas over the Dolomites, but also lovely, easy walks through forests and meadows, past villages and castles. Perhaps the finest of these medieval fortresses is within walking distance of the town, higher up the Talvera. Castel Roncolo (Schloss Runkelstein) was built in 1237 on a high rock, enlarged and decorated with murals depicting knightly prowess in the 14th century.

Shades of the Romans

In two valleys to the east, the Val Gardena and the Val Badia, live the Ladini, descendants of soldiers sent by Emperor Tiberius to conquer this area and wipe out its Celtic inhabitants. They did so, sent for their wives and families, were forgotten, and here their descendants still remain in the long narrow *cul-de-sacs* that form the Dolomite valleys. Here survive some of the Rhaeto-Romanic dialects known as Ladin or Romansch, derived from Latin and peculiar to parts of Switzerland and the Tirol.

The Val Gardena (Grödner Tal) branches east from A22 at Ponte Gardena (Waidbruck) and is connected by several passes, the Sella Pass, 2,214 meters (7,264 ft.), the Campolongo Pass, 1,875 meters (6,152 ft.) and the Valparola Pass, 2,192 meters (7,192 ft.) with N48, the main lateral through the Dolomites. It is impossible to decide which of these drives is the most scenic. The only satisfactory solution is to try all three, best combined with a visit to the Val Badia (Thurner Tal), that likewise branches from A22 to the same passes. The two valleys contain several of the most popular winter sport centers, especially Santa Cristina, 1,248 meters (4,095 ft.) and Ortisei (St. Ulrich), 1,236 meters (4,055 ft.) in the Val Gardena. Woodcarving is an important industry, from the sublime to the ridiculous. Ortisei's main church is a large Byzantine building whose huge front door has a bronze knocker in the shape of a coiled snake. Gilded lamps inside are supported by carved figures of angels and saints.

Two roads cross the Alpe di Siusi (Seiser Alm) from Val Gardena via Siusi (Seis am Schlern) to Prato (Blumau) on A22, at the Bolzano Nord exit. Besides offering wonderful skiing, the 40 square miles of highlands afford stupendous views of the Val Gardena and Dolomite peaks. You can see about 50 miles in each direction. In spring it has the appearance of an immense flower carpet spread around the feet of rocky peaks over 2,500 meters (8,200 ft.) high, with the flora of the snow region, flowers not seen at lower altitudes.

Merano's Grape Cure

N38 follows the Adige 27 km. (17 miles) north via Terlano (Terlan), producer of another famous wine, to Merano (Meran), one of the few winter sports resorts that offer a combination of skiing and sun bathing in generally mild winter temperatures. Merano is popular with the not-so-young for its amenities as well as for its health-giving qualities.

Its sheltered position gives it a superb climate, never over 80 degrees in summer, rarely below freezing in winter. Each winter the 9 championship tennis courts are converted into a skating rink. Skiing is within easy reach via the funicular railways that rise to the high Alpine slopes of Avelengo and San Vigilio. The first climbs from 1,037 to 2,195 meters (3,600 ft. to 7,200 ft.), reaching the plateau of Avelengo in only 20 minutes.

Spring waters in Merano are recommended for digestive and circulatory diseases and have a powerful curative action on the skin. The rich sweetness of the famous Merano grapes is attributed to the radioactive soil. As a result there's a rush by health addicts to sample the district's wines: *Termeno,* extremely aromatic; *Terlano,* almost like a Rhine Wine; and a strong muscat called *Rametz.* Indeed, this "grape cure" is Merano's big attraction. In the 2nd-century-B.C. Romans were mending their digestions this way, and to take the two-week cure in the fall is still considered one of the best tone-ups possible.

The old part of the city lies at the foot of Mount Benedetto. Along the narrow but sun-filled streets are houses with huge wooden doors, capped with little towers, and a 14th-century Gothic cathedral with a curious crenelated facade. The Via dei Portici is lined with arcades. The Castle of the Princes of Tirol (Castello Principesco), built in the 15th century, and the nearby museum are worth a visit.

The Adige River—fed by 150 glaciers—is one of many streams that gurgle through the town. The Passirio (Passeier) River tumbles along at a terrific pace; canoe races here are as exciting as any in the world. On both sides of the river hotels and pensions, parks, gardens, and wide avenues decorated with flowers and trees jostle each other for space.

Although the accent is on cures rather than sports, there are all kinds of possibilities for the energetic: tennis, polo, swimming at the Lido—a huge establishment with three pools, a beach and lawns—trout fishing in the Passirio, mountain climbing, and all sorts of excursions to nearby castles, lakes, and mountain passes with some of the most spectacular views to be seen in Europe. To the west near Bormio is the tortuous Stelvio Pass. Next to the Stelvio is the Solda where you can ski in July.

Plenty of spectator sport is available, too, with national and international horse races during the summer and autumn at the race track. The Grand Prix of Merano is linked up with Italy's national lottery, making it one of the most highly staked races in Europe.

Route N38 continues along the Adige west, skirting the Stelvio National Park, joins N40 that crosses the Park from the Stelvio Pass and then turns north following the Adige to its source in Lake Resia (Reschen), to enter Austria over the Resia Pass, 1,504 meters (4,935 ft.). A lovely exit by the backdoor, pleasantly uncrowded even in the summer months. And though South Tirol's two main towns have been visited, an infinity of scenic beauty still remains to be explored.

N44 leads to the main exit, the Brenner, following the Passirio northeast. The first branch west (left) mounts a moraine to Tirolo, a village where the local counts built a castle in the 12th century that eventually gave its name to the entire province. The view over the Meran Valley makes this historical site unforgettable. Just below is the 13th-century Brunnenburg, where a room is dedicated to the American poet Ezra Pound who lived here in 1955. The rest of the castle is an Agricultural Museum.

N44 passes through Rifiano (Riffian) with a charming Baroque church and skirts the Texel National Park to San Leonardo, where 44bis follows the Passirio northwest and enters Austria over the Timmelsjoch, 2,483 meters (8,147 ft.), the highest pass in the Eastern Alps. N44 stays not far below, winding northeast up the Monte Giovo Pass (Jaufen), 2,094 meters (6,870 ft.), to join A22 at Vipiteno (Sterzing), a late-medieval town with a fine town hall, the Church of the Holy Spirit and the Mutscher Museum which contains four altar pictures by that 15th-century painter and a Mithras stone. Reifenstein Castle has been guarding the valley since 1100 and has been enlarged several times in the Gothic style.

It is only 14 km. (9 miles) north to the Brenner Pass. Southward A22 keeps close to the Eisack, crosses the artificial Franzensfeste Lake and leaves Novacella (Neustift) to the left. This 12th-century Augustine Abbey certainly deserves the short detour, for its splendid Baroque church, the Romanesque chapel, the Gothic cloister and a glass of Sylvaner wine in the cellar.

Bressanone (Brixen) has been the see of the Bishops of South Tirol for a thousand years and a fashionable resort for some fifty. Two arcaded streets lead to the Baroque Duomo, whose 14th-century cloister is decorated with a cycle of medieval frescos. The Diocesan Museum is in the 13th century castle. Connected by road and funicular to its own mountain, the Plose, which is large enough to qualify as a highland, gently rising to 2,574 meters (8,445 ft.), Bressanone, like Bolzano and Merano, is the hub of several highly popular valleys.

Chiusa (Klausen) served as background for Albrecht Dürer's famous painting *The Great Fortune*. The winding medieval streets below the Benedictine Monastery of Sabiona (Säben), built as a castle in the 10th century, seem unchanged since the days of the great German painter. After Ponte Gardena (Waidbruck) below the impressive 12th-century Trostburg, the Isarco Valley narrows in the Porphyr Gorge shortly before Bolzano.

The High Road of the Dolomites

Before we begin the description of these routes, we should say that a lot of them are impassable for most of the winter, and that the attractive trips are mainly for June through September (e.g., The Great Dolomites Road excursion).

Route N49 follows the Rienza (Rienz) through the lovely valley of the Pusteria (Puster) to San Lorenzo, at the entrance to the Gadera Valley, and Brunico (Bruneck), complete with medieval quarter below the castle of the Bishops, at the entrance to the equally attractive Tures (Tauferer) Valley. The valley of the Pusteria rises gently via Monguelfo (Welsberg), with its castle and Baroque church, to Dobbiaco (Toblach), one of the oldest of the Dolomite resorts. N49 continues east via San Candido (Innichen) with a Romanesque Benedictine monastery to the Austrian border, while N51 turns sharp south through the wildly romantic Landro (Höhlenstein) Valley past Lakes Toblach and Misurina to Cortina d'Ampezzo.

However grandiose this trip may be, superlatives must be reserved for the Great Dolomites Road (Strada delle Dolomiti) approach, 110 km. (68 miles) of unsurpassed mountain scenery starting at Cardaro (Kardaun), two miles east of Bolzano on A22. Karneid Castle stands at the entrance to the narrow Ega Valley, which is followed past the popular resort of Nova Levante (Welschnofen) to the superb Lake Carezza (Karer), 1,530 meters (5,020 ft.), between the towers of the Latemar and the peaks of the Catinaccio (Rosengarten), famed in German legend.

Just before the Carezza Pass, 1,753 meters (5,752 ft.), another scenic road returns along the foot of this fabled massif, which owes its name to the rose colors at sunset, through the Tierser Valley to A22.

The impact of the Dolomites, jagged, broken and splintered into incredible needles, spires and towers is never stronger than on reentering Trentino and joining N48 at Vigo di Fassa. These coral rocks rose from the sea millions of years ago and the hard dolomite became engrained with softer calcite, twisted into fantastic shapes by rain and wind, but most of all by the Ice Age. Erosion denuded the peaks, isolated the pinnacles and sculptured the rock walls.

The Fassa Valley is followed to Canazei, renowned for its dry climate and persistent sunshine, in summer thirteen hours or more a day. N48 climbs to the Pordoi Pass, 2,239 meters (7,346 ft), second highest in the Eastern Alps, close to strangely shaped towers, like La Salsiccia (The Sausage), used for training climbers. To the left rises the Sella, 3,151 meters (10,338 ft.), to the right the Marmolada Group, 3,342 meters (10,965 ft.), highest and most beautiful. Every turn along the steep slopes of the Col di Lana, scene of heavy fighting in World War I, reveals a different facet, like Andraz Castle and the Sasso di Stria (Witches' Rock) before the tunnel leading to the Falzarego Pass, 2,105 meters (6,907 ft.). Having by now run out of superlatives, a "stop and admire" must suffice.

The descent is even more awe-inspiring. Ahead are the Five Towers peaks, the almost vertical Tofana di Rozes, and in the east, the higher peaks of the Cortina mountains. Starting down, the road goes past Pecol, a resort town, into the Boito Valley. At the Crepa tunnel you'll get your first—and striking—view of Cortina and the cross-shaped Ampezzo Valley. Passing under the ropes of the cable to Belvedere Rock, a war memorial, you wind downhill past pleasant houses and broad meadows.

Cortina d'Ampezzo, Jewel of the Dolomites

An incongruously lush meadow at 1,224 meters (4,016 ft.), edged with dense forests and ringed with magnificent mountain ranges. All around the town are peaks; Sorapis' long subsidiary ridges are formed like tongues; Cristallo's suggest a cathedral; the curious Cinque Torri seem like five towers with crenelated ramparts; the Pelmo and the Civetta stand like guards, while the "King of Cadore," the Antelao, is distinguished by its large buttresses and its glacier. At the end of the valley are the low crags of the Montagne del Bosco Nero, the Black Forest Mountains, and pointed Becco di Mezzodi. Lack of space prevents a more detailed description, which each fully deserves. As Cortina is synonymous with mountaineering and skiing, suffice to say that the great wall of the Civetta, 1,200 meters (3,937 ft.) of sheer verticality, is classified in the top category of difficulty for climbers, while numerous funiculars and lifts lead to skiruns satisfying champions and beginners.

But jewels come expensive and that is what Cortina has been, ever since its elevation to one of Europe's foremost winter sport resorts by the Olympic Games of 1956. The nightlife is no less intensive and varied than the day sports, with dancing continuing almost until it is time to put the skis on again. Some hardy types manage both, at least for a time; most pick and choose. Even some sightseeing might be thrown in: the walls and floor of the parish church are of light green marble, the ruby onyx font is decorated like a Greek urn and a skeleton kept rings on its fingers.

As Cortina is an important crossroads, there is a choice of excursions second to none in the Dolomites. Top priority goes to Lake Misurina, a deep-blue sapphire embedded in the emerald of firs and pines. Though only 16 km. (10 miles) northeast of Cortina, Misurina is a well-equipped resort in its own right, with ice skating as an added attraction, reached on N48 over the Tre Croci Pass, 1,808 meters (5,932 ft.), then turning north to round the massif of Monte Cristallo. From Misurina a road winds up to 2,300 meters (7,546 ft.) just below the Tre Cime di Lavaredo (Three Turrets) as well as the highland of Monte Piano, 2,325 meters (7,628 ft.) with splendid meadows in summer that double as no less splendid snowfields in winter. For the return, take N48bis through the Popena Bassa Valley north to the junction with N51 near Lake Durren and turn west on the Alemagna, so called because it was the main road to Germany for a thousand years, for a complete tour round Cristallo, with the even higher peak of Le Tofane, 3,243 meters (10,640 ft), thrown in for good measure on the approach to Cortina.

An alternative, and because it is longer it offers even more, is N48 east from Misurina for 21 km. (13 miles) to Auronzo on artificial Lake Santa Catarina in a gently sloping basin surrounded by magnificent spruce forests. Next tantalizing choice at Cima Gogna: either follow N48 east through the Sole Valley to Sappada, an up-and-coming ski resort near the source of the Piave, in the heart of the Cadore; with the possibility of turning northwest at San Stefano on N52 over the Kreuzberg Pass, 1,636 meters (5,368 ft.), to San Candido and Dobbiaco, to return to Cortina on N51.

South to Belluno

Or you could follow the Piave south via the railway junction at Calalzo past artificial Lake Cadore to Pieve di Cadore, a mere 31 km. (19 miles) from Cortina, unbelievably close considering all the scenic beauty the route takes in. The house where Titian was born around 1483 may be visited and his *Madonna and Saints* can be seen in the church near the fine 16th-century Palazzo della Comunità.

N51 follows the Piave south through the area devastated in 1963 when a giant landslide from Mt. Toc into artificial Lake Vaiont caused a tidal wave to spill over the top of the dam, killing some 2,000 people. The Alemagna, the German Road, is no less attractive in the gentler lower Piave Valley to the junction of this river with the Arde at Belluno, a Roman foundation but marked by centuries of Venetian domination. The Roman remains are confined to the Municipal Museum, the days of the medieval commune evoked in the squares and streets of the old town, but the main street, Via Mezzaterra, and Piazza del Mercato are distinguished by Renaissance palaces the Venetians built after they took over in the early 15th century. The heart of the city is the Piazza del Duomo with the cathedral and the splendid Palazzo dei Rettori Veneziani and a medieval tower. The Venetian School is honorably represented in the Picture Gallery.

A Last Round-Up

The main towns and resorts of the Dolomites have been described, but barely half of the valleys and mountains. These sins of omission can only be justified by lack of space, partly expiated by briefly mentioning some of the grandest scenery—

The drive from Pieve di Cadore up the lower Piave Valley then east on N52 along the Tagliamento to Tolmezzo. Then between the majestic arc sweeping from the Cansiglio Plateau, through the Carnian and parts of the Julian Alps to the Carso in the north, with the Canin Massif, including the Sella Nevea at 1,189 meters (3,901 ft.), to the south. This route will lead to Tarvisio near the Austrian border. Nearby are Fusine Laghi and Monte Santo di Lussari, both beauty spots. All-year-round Ravascletto is linked to the Zonclan Plateau.

The mountainside valleys of the Pusteria Valley. The Plan di Corones (Kronplatz), a wide flat top, 2,272 meters (7,454 ft.), south of Brunico (Bruneck), but also accessible from Valdaora (Olang) and San Vigilio. The Aurina (Ahrn), Anterselva (Antholz), and Gsies Valleys, all close to Brunico. The Alta Badia (Upper Badia Valley), reached from San Lorenzo di Sebato, spreading out fanlike between the Sella, Gardenazza, Lavarella and Fanes mountain groups, which provide an unlimited number of ski runs.

The Ortles (Ortler) area in the Stelvio National Park is ideal for ski-alpinists. Prato allo Stelvio (Prad am Stilfser Joch), where the Solda (Sulden) Valley cuts into the Venosta (Vinschgau) Valley, provides easy practice slopes, while the advanced can choose between Solda, Trafoi (named after three holy springs), Watles and San Valentino-Resia ski areas. The glaciers round the Stelvio Pass, 2,700 meters (8,800 ft.) to 3,400 meters (11,150 ft.), near the Dolomites' highest peak, the Ortles, are *the* summer skiing centers and provide the high note needed to end this chapter.

PRACTICAL INFORMATION FOR
THE DOLOMITES

WHEN TO GO. The Dolomites are year-round vacation territory. They provide refreshingly cool-altitude resorts during the hot weather and tingling air and sparkling snow as a background for skiing and skating in winter. In these mountains August is the most popular summer month, with the winter sports season at its height over the Christmas-New Year holidays, and then resuming towards the end of January until the middle of February.

TOURIST INFORMATION. Aurunzo: AAST, Viale Roma 22 (94.26). **Belluno:** AAST, Piazza dei Martiri 27E (25.163). **Bolzano:** AAST, Piazza Walter 28

(25.656); EPT, Piazza Parrocchia 11–12 (993.808) **Bressanone:** AAST, Viale della Stazione 9 (22.401). **Canazei:** AAST, Via Roma 24 (61.113). **Cortina d'Ampezzo:** AAST, Piazzetta S. Francesco 8 (32.31 or 27.11). **Dobbiaco:** AAST, Via Roma (72.132). **Levico Terme:** AAST, Viale Dante Alighieri 6 (706.101). **Madonna di Campiglio:** AAST, (42.000) **Merano:** AAST, Corso Libertà 45 (35.223). **Nova Levante:** AAST, Via Carezza 5 (613.126). **Ortisei:** AAST, Piazza Stetteneck (76.328). **Pieve di Cadore:** AAST, Via XX Settembre 18 (22.34). **San Vito di Cadore:** AAST, Via Nazionale 9 (94.05 or 91.19). **Trento:** AAST, Via Alfieri 4 (983.880); Assessorato Turismo, Corso 3 Novembre 132 (895.111).

SEASONAL EVENTS. Bolzano: South Tirol wine fair in the second half of Mar.; 1st May sees the Flower Market; early May, the Gastronomic Week; May Festival comes in late May; late Aug. the International Busoni Piano Competition; mid-Sept. International Fair.

Cortina d'Ampezzo: Jan. through Feb., Wintersports Competition.

Corvara: early Aug., feast with local costumes.

Caldaro (Gröden Valley): Jan., long-distance ski races; late July, festival with local costumes.

Merano: Mar., Ice-Skating Competition; Easter Mon., Peasant Gallop; Grand Prix horse racing in late Sept.; early Oct., Grape Festival and Procession.

Puster Valley: Jan. Ski Marathon, Innichen to Antholz; Mar., Kronplatz Slalom.

Resia: Ski yachting to Stelvio Pass.

Ritten: mid-July to mid-Aug. Summer Festival, theater and concerts.

Termeno: May, tasting of Gewürztraminer; Wine Festival, late Sept.

Tirolo: early Sept., Folkloric Feast and Procession.

Trento: 20–26 June, Vigilian Festival, folklore.

TELEPHONE CODES. You will find the telephone area code for each town against its name in the Hotel and Restaurant listings (after the province name). If there is a different area code from the majority of the establishments—say when a hotel or restaurant is in an outlying place—then the code is given in front of the telephone number.

HOTELS AND RESTAURANTS. This is an area with seasonal closing for hotels and restaurants. It is wise to check in advance as to exact dates of opening and closing as these change regularly. Because of the mild climate hereabouts, airconditioning is exceptional. Hotel rates are generally low.

As this is a bilingual region, we have organized the towns under their Italian names, with the German version following. You may find that the local usage is the reverse.

Food and Drink. The cooking of the Dolomites region is, like everything else, Italian and Austrian with the accent on the latter. Some of the more popular dishes are: *Selchcarrée mit Kraut* (smoked pork with sauerkraut), *saure Suppe* (tripe soup), and *Knödl* (dumplings). *Fastenknödl* are filled with breadcrumbs, vegetables, and eggs. *Leberknödl* contain chopped liver and appeal to many visitors. A wide variety of sausages fill delicatessen windows. *Speck* is smoked raw ham, the local version of prosciutto.

There are some excellent wines in the Trentino and Alto Adige: the wines from the Val d'Isarco, *Teroldeto* from Mezzalombardo, *Riesling, Missiano, Traminer* and *Lagrein,* either red or rosé.

Appiano/Eppan Bolzano (0471). *Schloss Korb* (E), 3 miles outside this famous wine town at **Missiano** (633.222). 56 rooms in a castle; pool; park. Open Easter–31 Oct.

Angerburg (M), at **San Michele** (52.107). Attractive grounds. Open Apr.–early Nov.

Auronzo di Cadore Belluno (0435). *Vienna* (M), (93.94). Small. Open mid-June–mid-Sept. AE, DC, MC, V.

Belluno (0437). *Astor* (M), Piazza dei Martiri 26 (24.922). Good value rooms, but no restaurant. *Europa* (M), Via Vittorio Veneto 158 (24.705). Most rooms with showers; on outskirts. AE. *Dolomiti* (M), Via Carrera 46 (27.077). Fairly recent; no restaurant. V.

Restaurants. Apart from the hotel restaurants (Europa closed Sun.), try *Al Borgo* (M), Via Anconetta 8 (24.006). A bit out of town, but excellent value. AE, MC.

Bolzano/Bozen (0471). *Grifone* (E), Piazza Walther 7 (977.056). Very central, offers modern comforts, traditional hospitality. AE, DC, MC, V. *Park Hotel Laurin* (E), Via Laurino 4 (980.500). CIGA. Spacious, well-furnished rooms, all comforts, in attractive turn-of-century building with gardens, park, pool. Its *Belle Epoque* restaurant is closed Sat., and lunch Sun. AE, DC, MC, V.

Alpi (M), Via Alto Adige 35 (971.981). Central, near station. Large, modern and comfortable. AE, DC, MC, V. *Luna/Mondschein* (M), Via Piave 15 (975.642). Comfortable, attractive rooms; friendly service (in the same family for 200 years); pleasant restaurant with open-air terrace; lovely garden; garage. AE, DC, MC.

Restaurants. *Abramo* (M), Piazza Gries 16 (280.141). Closed Sun. Attractive place with summer terrace, excellent cuisine. Best in town, though located in a suburb. AE, V. *Chez Frederic* (M), Via Diaz 12 (271.011). Closed Mon. evening, Tues., three weeks in July. Intimate place, food with a French accent. AE, DC.

Butzenhausl (I) Via Andreas Hofer 30 (976.183). Closed Mon. Crowded, lively smokey. Popular hangout for the local intellectual set. *Cavallino Bianco/Weisses Roessl* (I), Via dei Bottai 6 (973.267). Closed Sat. evening and Sun. Typical Tyrolean spot in the center of town. *Grifone/Greif* (I) Hotel Grifone/Greif, Piazza Walther (977.056). Closed Sun. Pleasant dining outside at tables on Piazza Walther. Local specialties. AE, DC, MC, V.

Bressanone/Brixen Bolzano (0472). *Dominik* (E), Via Terzo di Sotto 13 (30.144). Indoor pool. Open mid-Mar.–mid-Nov. AE, MC, V. *Elefante* (E), Via Rio Bianco 4 (22.288). Pool; garden; and Elefante Villa Marzari (E), 14 rooms in 16th-century building. Closed mid-Nov. to Christmas; Jan 10–Feb. *Gasser* (E), Via Giardini 19 (22.105). At the fork of the river. Open mid-April–mid-Oct. AE, DC, MC.

Albero Verde-Grüner Baum (M), Via Stufles 11 (21.333). Pools and garden. Closed mid-Nov.–mid-Dec. AE, DC, MC, V. *Temlhof* (M), Via Elvas 76 (22.658). Good views. Open Easter–mid-Nov. AE, DC, MC.

Corona d'Oro (I), Via Fienili 4 (24.154). Smallish, with restaurant (closed on Tues.). AE. *Jarolim* (I), Piazza Stazione (22.230). Pool, garden, across from the station. Restaurant closed Tues. AE, DC, V.

Restaurants. *L'Elefante* (M), see above. Fine food in centuries-old inn, one of the region's best. Closed Mon; mid-Nov. to Christmas, 10 Jan–Feb.

Fink (M), Via Portici Minori 4 (23.883). Rustic specialties. Closed Thurs; June.

Brunico/Bruneck Bolzano (0474). *Royal* (E), 2 miles out at Riscone (Reischach) (21.221). Pool and garden. Open mid-Dec.–Mar., June–Sept. AE, MC, V. *Rudolf* (M), also out at Riscone (21.223). Pool and garden, too. Closed mid-May–June, plus Nov. DC, MC.

Andreas Hofer (M), Via Campo Tures 1 (85.469). Garden and famous restaurant (closed Sun.). Hotel closed late April–early May; late Nov.–early Dec. *Majestic* (M), out at Riscone (84.887). Pool. Open mid-Dec.–end-April, June–mid-Oct. DC. *Post*, (I), Via Bastioni 9 (85.127). Homey, traditional. Restaurant, cafe; pastry shop. Closed Nov.

Caldaro/Kaltern Bolzano (0471). *Kartheinerhof* (M), (963.240). Pool and garden. *Europa* (I), (963.370). Garden.

At the lake, 5 km. (3 miles)—*Seegarten* (M), (963.260). Openair dining in summer. Open April–Oct. *Seehof* (M), (963.389). Attractive garden; best on the lake. Open April–Nov. *Seeleiten* (M), (962.300). Indoor pool. Closed mid-Nov.–mid-Dec. AE, DC.

Canazei Trento (0462). *Alla Rosa* (M), (61.107). AE, DC, MC, V. *Bellevue* (M), (61.104). Comfortable hotel with fine views. MC. *Caminetto* (M), (61.230). Seasonal and attractive. MC. *Dolomiti* (M), (61.106). Fairly large, complete with garden. MC. *Al Sole* (I), (61.157). *Bernard* (I), MC.
Restaurant. *El Garber* (M), (61.395). Good local cuisine. Open mid-Dec.–mid-April, mid-June–Sept. Closed Tues.

Castelrotto/Kastelruth Bolzano (0471). *Cavallino D'Oro/Goldenes Rössel* (M), (71.337). Smallish, with restaurant (closed Tues.). Closed Nov. V. *Madonna* (M), (71.194). Pool and garden.

Chiusa/Klausen Bolzano (0472). *Rierhof* (M), (47.454). *Sylvanerhof* (M), just out of town going north (47.557). Pretty garden and pool. Restaurant (closed Tues.). Hotel closed mid-Jan.–mid-Feb.

Cles Trento (0463). *Punto Verde* (M), (21.275). Pool and garden.

Cortina D'Ampezzo Belluno (0436). *Miramonti-Majestic* (L), Localita Pezzie 103 (42.01). A luxurious hotel, magnificently located; way up-market with a touch of old-world formality; swimming pool, tennis, golf course in attractive surroundings. Closed Easter–30 June; Sept–Christmas. AE, DC, MC, V.
Cristallo (E), Via R. Menardi 42 (42.81). Large, well-kept, with lots of wood paneling, good-sized comfortable rooms, many with balconies and fine views. Pool, mini-golf and tennis. A CIGA hotel. Open 1 July–10 Sept., 20 Dec.–25 Mar. AE, DC, MC, V. *De la Poste* (E), Piazza Roma 62 (42.71). On main piazza, with terrace as local launch pad. Lovely rooms, good atmosphere and service. Closed 20 Oct.–19 Dec. AE. *Europa* (E), Corso Italia 207 (32.21). Small rooms but comfortable. Good mountain views. Closed Easter–June; Sept–Christmas. AE, DC, MC, V. *Victoria* (E), Corso Italia 1 (32.46). On main street; attractive local decor, pleasant rooms. Mid-Dec.–Mar., 1 July–30 Sept. AE, DC, MC, V.
Concordia e Parco (M), Corso Italia 28 (42.51). Pretty setting. 22 Dec.–18 Mar., 10 July–Aug. AE, DC, V. *Corona* (M), Via Cesare Battisti 15 (32.51). 10 minutes from center, quiet attractive place; furnished with modern art; handy to ski lift. 20 Dec.–Mar., July.–mid-Sept. DC, MC. *Cortina* (M), Corso Italia 94 (42.21). Central and modern. Mid-Dec.–mid.-April, mid-June–mid-Sept. AE, DC, MC, V.
Fanes (I), Via Roma 136; (34.27). Open mid-Dec.–5 April, late-June–late-Oct. AE, DC, MC, V.
Restaurants. The grillrooms of the Cristallo and de la Poste are elegant and quite good (E). *El Toula* (E), Via Ronco 123 (33.39). Attractive and elegant. Must book. Open mid-Dec.–Easter and mid-July to mid-Sept. Closed Mon. AE, DC, V.
Bellavista-il Meloncino (M), Localita Gillardon (61.043). Out of town a bit, but with lovely summer al fresco eating. Must book. Closed Tues., June and Nov. *Fanes* (M) hotel restaurant (see above), good for homey food. *Franco* (M), Piazzetta San Francesco (46.81). Good pizza.

Dobbiaco/Toblach Bolzano (0474). *Cristallo* (M), (72.138). Panoramic locale, indoor pool. Open mid-Dec.–Mar., June–Sept. AE. *Union* (M), (72.146). Near station, indoor pool. Open June–mid-Oct; mid-Dec.–Easter. *Villa Santer* (M), (72.142). Modern hotel furnished in traditional Tyrolean style. Pool and garden. *Dolomiten* (I), (72.136). Fair value.
On **Monte Rota/Radsberg**—*Alpino Monte Rota-Alpen Radsberg* (M), (72.213). Lovely views and indoor pool, at 1,650 meters (5,414 ft.) up by cablecar. Open mid-May to Nov; Dec. to Easter.

Levico Terme Trento (0461). *Grand* (E), (706.104). The spa treatment, with thermal pool, cure rooms, and also an attractive park. Open mid-June–mid-Sept. AE.
Ambassador (M), (707 101). *Bellavista* (M), (706.136). Attractive grounds, thermal pool. Open Easter–Sept., Xmas–mid-Jan. AE.

Madonna di Campiglio Trento (0465). *Savoia Palace* (E), (41.004). Central, fairly elegant and comfortable. Open early-Dec.–mid-April, July–Sept. AE, DC.
Campiglio Ferrari (M), (42.022). *Grifone* (M), (42.002). 40 pleasant rooms. Open Dec.–mid-April, mid-July–mid-Sept. AE, MC. *Oberosler* (M), (41.136). Well appointed; near lifts.
Bellavista (I), (41.034). *San Raphael* (I), (41.570).
At **Campo Carlo Magno**—*Golf* (E), (41.003). 124 rooms; 9-hole golf course at 1,680 meters (5,512 ft.). Attractive views. Open Dec.–Mar., July and Aug. AE, MC, v. *Carlo Magno Zeledria* (M), (41.010). In park. Open late-Dec.–April, late-June–Sept. Full board only. DC, MC.

Marlengo/Marling Bolzano (0473). Near Merano and good for the grape cure. *Jagdhof* (M), (47.177). *Marlena* (M), Via Tramontana 6 (47.166). Pools, indoor and out. Closed Jan. MC. *Nörder* (M), (47.000). *Oberwirt* (M), (47.111). Pool, openair dining in summer. Open mid-Mar.–mid-Nov. *Paradies* (M), (45.202). Garden, pool, tennis.
Marlingerhof (I), (47.157). Restaurant (closed Mon.). Closed Feb. AE, DC, v.

Merano/Meran Bolzano (0473). *Palace* (L), Via Cavour 2 (34.734). Central, but in quiet garden, pools in and out. Excellent restaurant, evenings only, Mon.–Sat. Closed Nov.–mid-Dec; Jan. 6–mid-March. AE, DC, MC, v. *Bristol* (E), Via Ottone Huber 14 (49.500). Central, great views. Open early-April–early-Nov. AE, DC, MC, v. *Schloss Rundegg* (E), Via Scena 2 (34.364). 30 rooms in a converted castle; pool and garden. Beauty, fitness treatments. AE, DC, MC, v. *Minerva,* (M), Via Cavour 95 (36.712). Turn of the century hotel, furnished in period style. Pension rates are very economical. Closed Nov–mid-Mar. AE, DC.
At **Freiberg**, 7 km. (4½ miles) out—*Castel Freiberg* (L), (44.196). Period furnishing in old castle; fine views; pools. Open early-April–early-Nov. AE, DC, MC, v.
Meranerhof (E), Via Manzoni 1 (30.230). Pool and lovely garden. AE, DC, MC, v. *Villa Mozart* (E), Via San Marco 26 (30.630). Beautiful villa, superb comforts and cuisine, gourmet cooking courses. Reserve well ahead. Closed Nov.–Easter. AE. *Riz Stefanie* (E), Via Cavour 8 (37.745). Pool in garden. Open Mar.–Oct. AE, DC, v.
Adria (M), Via Gilm 2 (36.610). Open Mar.–Nov. *Anatol* (M), Kastanienweg 3 (25.511). *Bavaria* (M), Kirchsteig 15 (22.275). *Burgl* (M), Haslerweg 11 (30.034). *König Laurin* (M), Laurin Str. 24 (46.086).
Bayrischer Hof (I), Via Mainardo 37 (49.655). *Maria Christine* (M), Via Dante 51 (24.453). Pool.
Restaurants. *Andrea* (E), Via Galileo 44 (37.400). Closed Mon., Jan. and Feb. Gourmet dining, exquisite ambiance and service. Reserve. DC, MC, v. *Villa Mozart* (E), hotel restaurant (see above). Owner of *Andrea* serves hotel guests and parties of 6 or more with exceptional cuisine and wines in *art nouveau* ambiance. About 120,000 lire per person. *Flora* (E), Via Portici 75 (31.484). Closed Sun.; mid-Jan.–mid-Feb. AE, DC, MC, v. *Tiffany Grill-Schloss Maur,* (E), Hotel Palace, Via Cavour 2/4 (034.734). Warm Tiffany decor. Emphasis on Italian and international cuisine. Closed during hotel closure. AE, DC, MC.
Terlano Putz (M), Via Portici 231 (35.571). Closed Wed; Jan 15–Feb 15. At other end of price scale, serves good food.

Naturno/Naturns Bolzano (0473). *Aquila/Adler,* (E), Via Rezia 7 (76.203). Family run since 1810; Tyrolean character. One of the best in the valley. Restaurant; bar. Closed Easter–mid-June; mid-Oct.–mid-Dec. AE, DC, MC, v. *Feldhof* (E), Via Municipio 4 (87.264). Pool, thermal establishment, garden. Open mid-Mar.–Nov. 5.
Lindenhof (M), (87.208). Pool and garden. Open April–early-Nov. *Sunnwies* (M), (87.157). Pool and garden. Open April–early-Nov.

Nova Levante/Welschnofen Bolzano (0471). *Cavallino Bianco* (E), (613.113). Attractive resort-type hotel, well-furnished rooms; indoor and outdoor pools; tennis. Open mid-Dec.–end-April, mid-May–mid-Oct. AE, DC, MC, v.

Ortisei/St. Ulrich Bolzano (0471). *Aquila-Adler* (E), (76.203). Most of the 85 rooms with bath; indoor pool and large, attractive garden. Open mid-Dec.–mid-Mar., mid-May–early-Oct. AE, DC, MC, V.

Angelo-Engel (M), Via Petlin 35 (76.336). With restaurant (closed Tues.). AE, DC, MC, V. *Gardena-Grödnerhof* (M), (76.315). Open mid-Dec.–Easter, June–Oct. *Mondschein* (M), (76.214).

Maria (I), (77.047). *Planlim* (I), (77.150).

At **Roncadizza/Runggaditsch,** just out of town—*La Perla* (M), (76.421). Pool and garden. AE. *La Rodes* (M), (76.108). Pool and garden.

Pieve di Cadore Belluno (0435). *Giardino* (M), (33.141). Small and reasonable; restaurant closed Sun. and in June. DC.

At **Tai di Cadore,** just outside Pieve—*Canada* (M), (22.82). Best around, with pretty garden. Closed mid-Sept–mid-Oct. Restaurant closed Fri. AE.

Prato Allo Stelvio/Prad Am Stilfserjoch Bolzano (0473). *Prato allo Stelvio* (M), (75.006). Pool. Open June through Aug. *Stern* (M), (75.123). *Zentral* (M), (75.008).

Resia/Reschen Bolzano (0473). *Al Moro–Zum Mohren* (M), (83.120). Pool. Open all year except last half April and Nov. to mid-Dec. AE, V.

Rovereto Trento (0464). *Leon d'Oro* (M), Via Tacchi 2, (37.333). No restaurant. AE, DC, MC, V. *Rovereto* (M), Corso Rosmini 82 (35.222). Restaurant closed Fri. and Sun. evenings. AE, DC, MC, V.

Sant'Ilario (I), (411.605). Terrace. Good view from restaurant.

San Candido/Innichen Bolzano (0474). *Cavallino Bianco-Weisses Rössl* (M), (73.135). Pool and garden. Open mid-Dec.–Mar, mid-May–mid-Oct. *Park Hotel Sole Paradiso–Sonnenparadies* (M), (73.120). Indoor pool and attractive grounds. Open mid-Dec.–late-Mar., mid-May–early-Oct. AE, DC. *Posta* (M), (73.133). Open mid-Dec.–late-April, end-May–Sept. AE, DC. *San Candido-Innichen* (M), (73.102). Open mid-Dec.–mid-April, mid-May–mid-Oct.

Lindenhof (I), (73.422). Garden.

San Leonardo in Passiria/St. Leonhard in Passeier Bolzano (0473). *Bergland* (M), (85.287). Pool and garden. *Stroblhof* (M), (85.128). Pool (indoors and out), garden. Open mid-July–Oct., and over Xmas/New Year. Full pension only. MC.

San Lorenzo in Banale Trento (0465). *Mühlgarten* (M), (84.782). Small; pool and garden. *Sonnenburg* (M), (86.399). Pool and garden.

San Martino di Castrozza Trento (0439). *Excelsior Cimone* (E), (68.261). Informal yet smart; handy for the lifts. *Majestic Dolomiti* (E), (68.033). Most of the 124 rooms with bath; pool. MC.

Colfosco (M), (68.224). Open mid-Dec.–mid-April, mid-June–mid-Sept. MC, V. *Orsingher* (M), (68.544). Open mid-Dec.–end April, July–mid-Sept. AE, DC, MC, V. *Regina* (M), 68.017. Good views. Open mid-Dec.–mid-April, mid-June–mid-Sept. AE, MC, V. *Savoia* (M), (68.094). Great views. Open mid-Dec.–mid-April, July–mid-Sept. AE, DC, MC, V.

Europa (I), (68.575). *Miramonti* (I), (68.069).

Santa Cristina Val Gardena/St. Christina in Groden Bolzano (0471). *Interski* (M), (76.660). Pool and garden. Open mid-Dec.–mid-April, late-June–Sept. Half-pension only. *L'Diamant* (M), (76.780). Pool (indoor) and garden, fine views. Open early-Dec.–Easter, mid-June–early-Oct. Full pension only.

Uridl (I), (73.215).

At **Monte Pana**—*Sport Hotel Monte Pana* (E), (76.128). A couple of miles out; great views, indoor pool; full pension only. Open mid-Dec.–early-April, July–mid-Sept. AE, DC.

San Vigilio di Marebbe/St. Vigil in Enneberg Bolzano (0474). *Almhof* (M), (51.043). Open Dec.–mid-April, June–mid-Oct. Full pension only. DC, MC, V. *Condor* (M), (51.017). Open Dec.–April, June–Sept. AE, V. *Floralp* (M), (51.115). Open mid-Dec.–mid-April, June–Sept. DC.

Sappada Belluno (0435). *Corona Ferrea* (M), Borgata Kratten (69.103). Open mid-Dec.–Mar., July–Sept. AE, V.
At **Cima Sappada**—*Bellavista* (M), (69.175).

Siusi/Seis Am Schlern Bolzano (0471). *Stella-Alpine / Edelweiss* (M), (71.130). Excellent views, pools. Open mid-Dec.–mid-April, mid-May–mid-Oct. *Dolomiti / Dolomitenhof* (M), (71.128). Pool and views. Open mid-Dec.–end-April, June–Sept. *Genziana / Enzian* (M), (71.150). Indoor pool, full pension only. Open mid-Dec.–end-April, June–mid-Oct.
Europa (I), (71.174).
At **Razzes / Ratzes**—*Razzes / Ratzes* (M), (71.131). Magnificent views, pool. Open mid-Dec.–end April, mid-May–Sept.
At **Alpe di Siusi / Seiser Alm**—*Eurotel Sciliar* (E), (72.938). Fine views, half pension only. Open Xmas-mid-April, mid-June–mid-Sept. AE, DC.

Solda/Sulden Bolzano (0473). *Sulden* (E), (75.481). Pool, fine views. Open end-Oct.–April, July–mid-Sept. AE, DC.
Alpina (M), (75.422). Pool. DC. *Cristallo* (M), (75.436). Pool. DC. *Marlet* (M), (75.475). Ortles views, pool. Open end-Nov.–early May, July–Sept. *Zebru* (M), (75.425). Views and pool. Open end-Dec.–early-May, end-June–mid-Sept. DC.
Robert (I), (75.433).

Stelvio, Passo dello/Stilfser Joch Bolzano (0342). *Passo dello Stelvio* (M), (903.162). On the summit of the pass. Full pension only. Also has a reasonable restaurant with good food and service.

Termeno/Tramin Bolzano (0471). *Traminerhof* (M), (86.384). Pool and garden. Open April–mid-Nov. Restaurant closed Tues. V.

Tirolo/Dorf Tirol Bolzano (0473). *Castel* (E), (93 693). Pools. *Gartner* (E), (93 414). Lovely gardens plus pools. Full pension only. Open April–Oct. DC.
Erika (M), (93 338). Garden and pools. Open Mar.–Nov. Half-pension only. AE, DC, MC, V. *Küglerhof* (M), (93 428). In a quiet location, garden and pools. Open end-Mar.–early-Nov.
Kronsbühel (I), (24 818). Garden and pool.

Trento (0461). *Grand Hotel Trento,* (E), Via Alfieri 1 (981.010). Traditional, comfortable. Restaurant; bar; garden. AE, DC, V.
Accademia, (M), Vicolo Colico 4/6 (981.010). Close to Piazza del Duomo; ancient house with modern, comfortable rooms. Restaurant; lovely courtyard. AE, DC, MC, V.
Everest (M), Corso Alpini 14 (986.605). *Motel Agip* (M), Via Brennero 168 (981.117). AE, DC, V.
Restaurants. *Accademia* (M), Vicolo Colica 6 (981.580). Closed Mon. Very pleasant ambiance, innovative cuisine. AE, DC, V. *Alla Mora,* (M), Via Roggia Grande 8 (984.657). Attractive restaurant with pleasant courtyard. Local specialties, salad plates, and seafood featured. Closed Mon. *Chiesa* (M), Via San Marco 64 (985.577). Close to the castle. Furnished with antiques; interesting cuisine. Closed Sun. AE, MC, V.

At **Calavino,** 19 km. (12 miles) west—*Castel Toblino* (M), (44.036). Fine food in romantic castle setting. Also has 4 rooms.

At **Pergine Valsugana,** 16 km. (10 miles) east—*Al Castello* (M), (531.158). Another attractive conversion, 23 rooms, 14 showers and good food.

Valdaora/Olang Bolzano (0474). *Mirabell* (M), (86.191). At **Valdaora di Mezzo.** Indoor pool, garden. Open mid-Dec.–mid-April, mid-May–mid-Oct. DC, MC.

Post (M), at **Valdaora di Sopra** (86.127). Pool. Open early-Dec.–late-April, mid-May–mid-Oct.

Bergfall (I), (86.484). *Keil* (I), (86.151).

Vipiteno/Sterzing Bolzano (0472). *Agnello-Lamm* (M), (765.127). *Aquila Nera-Schwarzer Adler* (M), (764.064). Indoor pool. Closed part of June and mid-Nov.–mid-Dec. AE, DC. *Fugger* (M), (765.329). Pool.

Mondschein (I), (765.309).

GETTING AROUND. By air. Bolzano has a tiny airport for small planes, but the main ports of entry by air are to the south of the region—Venice, Trieste and Verona. These then link up into the Dolomites by train or motorway.

By train. This is not an especially good region for getting around by rail, as one would expect in such a mountainous part of the country. However, all the main towns are linked, and lines come in from Munich and Vienna on the west and east. From the south the lines radiate up from Trieste, Venice and Verona, with Conegliano and Udine as exchange points.

By car. To reach Cortina d'Ampezzo from Venice by car takes only 3 hours on the direct route through Treviso and Belluno. From the west take the A4 autostrada from Milan and change to A22 at Verona. At Ora-Auer take SS48.

The A22 is the Brenner Pass into Austria, the most obvious route when coming from Britain via Germany. Alternatively, drive across Switzerland coming out over the Ofen Pass to Bolzano—a slow route, but a delight all the way. The high passes are open only from June through mid- or end-September.

By bus. There is a weekend service from Venice to Madonna di Campiglio or Canazei, and a daily one in season from Venice–Cortina, about 3 ½ hours. Local buses from Trento, Bolzano and Merano railway stations provide connections with resorts.

SIGHTSEEING NOTE. It should be noted that virtually all of the many castles in this region are closed at least half the year—mainly from October to Easter—and many are open only from June through September, or even just July and August. Be sure to check before a visit, to avoid disappointment.

THE MARCHES

Ambitious Dukes and the Holy House

It's quite possible that the majority of travelers to Italy will not know where to look for the Marches on the map. If you trace the Apennine backbone southwards to a point roughly opposite Florence, then look towards the Adriatic coast at the same approximate level, you will find Pesaro on that coast. From the eastern watershed of the Apennines, skirting independent San Marino, to a point just north of Pesaro, is the northern boundary of the Marches; and so, for about 180 km. (110 miles) going south, Apennines and Adriatic coast enclose a rectangle of land as far as the Trento River which forms the southern boundary.

It is a region of high mountains; heavy masses of them to the west— Catria, Nerone, Montefeltro—throwing across the area spurs which do not reach the sea save at one point, Conero, just below Ancona, where on that account the only good natural port is to be found. Hence the rivers are in full spate during the rainy season and when the snows melt; while some of them are dry chasms during summer. The silt of these torrents has formed small fertile plains along their course. A region, then, of smallholders, of somewhat isolated little towns in those alluvial plains; a hard country, where the coast is of little service to man, where every inch of land has to be exploited, where vine and olive are persuaded to grow up to incredible heights; and hence, a tough population, decisive in religion and politics.

Ascoli Piceno recalls the *Picas,* the woodpecker that figured on the banners of the early tribes, chiefly Sabines, whose name, too, is rife. Metauro is the river on which the Carthaginian defeat took place and the death

of Hasdrubal. Remains of Roman roads and viaducts, and Trajan's arch
at Ancona (a Greek name by the way), remind one that this was a province
of Augustus' Italy. The name *Marche* is of German origin; it was a frontier
province, a "Mark" of the Empire of Charlemagne, who redonated it to
the Church. It was already deeply imbued with Christianity, often grafted
on to its pagan rites.

Until 1860 the Marches were Papal dominions, and archbishops and
legates were its rulers. For centuries the Church had to fight, often with
fire and sword, to maintain its supremacy against imperial ambitions,
against the lordlings and local squires—the Sforzas, Malatestas, Monte-
feltros, Della Roveres. Sometimes the Church made the best of a bad job
by appointing successful lords her "vicars." The exploits of these, the fiery
passage of oppressing cardinals, the fearsome scourge of Cesare Borgia—
all this the country still remembers; the fact that most sizable towns were
rebellious independence-seeking communes, with their own rulers, courts
and civilization has given them an indefinable character which still remains; you can "feel" the personality of Urbino, Tolentino, Ascoli Piceno
and Osimo.

Religious and pagan usages are mingled; sheaves and baskets of grain
are carried in procession with the Virgin; at Easter, a man with face and
chest covered with hair, saddled, and with firecrackers exploding behind
him, chases the crowd; while the "woodpecker chase" at Monterubbiano
has probably survived from Sabine days. For St. Emidio, bunches of basil,
blessed by the priest, are worn; in certain parts they tattoo themselves with
the signs of the Passion; pilgrims carry stones up to the Mount of St. Poli-
sia, and, heaving them into the chasm, listen for the clang of the saint's
golden spinning wheel. And the wine carts, like the sails of fishing-boats,
are sometimes painted with Christian and pagan symbols intertwined.

Exploring the Marches

It is a good idea to set up headquarters on the coast. From Ancona you
can reach a string of pleasant seaside resorts; Gabicce Mare, Pesaro, Fano,
Senigallia, Falconara to the north, and Porto Recanati, San Giorgio and
San Benedetto, to the south. These days, all of the Adriatic beaches are
crowded in summer, and hotels have been built at every spot where bathing is possible. Even the mountainous background of the Monte Conero
Riviera guarantees little peace—and you will certainly need a car to reach
such spots as Scoglio del Trave and Portonovo.

Ancona's cathedral, dedicated to San Ciriaco, is beautifully situated
with an excellent view of this interesting town and its colorful harbor. The
lovely white-and-rose stone door with its St. Markish lions welcomes you;
the cathedral, one of the finest of Romanesque, is solid and dignified, its
interior spacious. The marble Arch of Trajan, a little way off, is perhaps
the finest Roman arch in Italy. Between cathedral and port, the old town
is worth wandering in: stone ramps under Gothic arches, tiny piazzas, and
giddy stairways.

Closeby is the National Museum of the Marches, providing a complete
historical and archeological background (but check, as it has been closed
indefinitely). A little farther into town is the art gallery, Pinacoteca Comunale Francesco Podesti, with a good local collection including works by
Titian, Crivelli, Lorenzo Lotto and others.

Southwards, all within easy walking, are: Palazzo del Senato, San
Francesco delle Scale and its magnificent Gothic portal, Santa Maria della

Piazza, with its beautiful cozy 13th-century facade, its little arches and majolica, like a toy church; and the exquisite twisting columns and traceried arches of the Loggia dei Mercanti. Palazzo della Prefettura is a fine, severe building that shares Piazza del Plebiscito with the Church of San Domenico.

Both Senigallia (29 km., 18 miles) and Fano (65 km., 40 miles) are popular family beach resorts. The latter is also of interest for its Portico di San Francesco, Palazzo del Ragione, Cathedral and Arch of Augustus, as well as a starting point for the pleasant journey along the valley of the Metauro to Urbino.

Urbino

This is a dream of a city, in a broad setting of rolling hills, punctuated by cypresses in a patchwork of vineyards and tilled fields. A living monument to the Renaissance, it has three great names to its credit: Duke Frederico da Montefeltro who reigned from 1444 to 1482, a broad-minded, artistic prince; Raphael, and Bramante. Perched on a rock, the Ducal Palace is Urbino's sun and center. Its library with illuminated manuscripts, picture gallery with works by Uccello, Piero della Francesca, Signorelli, and Titian, objets d'art, wood inlays, the finest of their kind, in Frederico's study, its courtyards and staircases, will tell you more of the bursting wealth and artistic energy of the Renaissance in Italy than all the history books can. There are interesting buildings galore in Urbino, among them Raphael's birthplace, restored in appropriate 16th-century style.

Urbino also has its share of landmarks and more of those very old and fascinating houses you have seen in other parts of the country. There's a special feeling to Urbino; you'll get to feel familiar with it as you wander about the city. We encourage you to discover its look-out points as well. From the little Church of San Giovanni you get an unusual prospect of the Ducal Palace. Go to the Monte Titano, from the Piazza Roma, and from there follow the panoramic way all along the small road which leads around to the hill facing it. You'll have a memorable view of the city and its ramparts.

Pesaro, a short distance north of Fano, is a watering-place, and an interesting old town. Its Palazzo Ducale is the chief building, and the 14th century San Francesco the most interesting church; Sant' Agostino is also worth seeing. The town boasts many art galleries—and Rossini, who was born there in 1792. The art gallery in the Municipal Museum is worth a visit, if only to see Bellini's huge and complex altarpiece, the *Pala di Pesaro*. You may be interested in the fine ceramic section as well.

Loreto

Loreto lives entirely on the sanctuary built around the Holy House, reputedly the home of the Virgin at the time of the Annunciation and later transported here by angels in the 13th century, when the Holy Land was overrun by Mohammedans. The church was the work of several of Italy's finest architects—Giuliano da Maiano, da Sangallo, Bramante and Vanvitelli among them. It is a veritable museum, with superb bronze doors and many frescos, including some especially fine ones by Signorelli. Special trains for sick pilgrims are run from all over Italy to Loreto. The special pilgrimage days are March 25th, August 15th, September 8th, December 8th and 10th. On the last date, *Festival of the Transference of the Holy House,* bonfires are lit all over the region.

From Loreto to Macerata is only a few miles by road, or an hour's run by a very scenic railroad from Ancona. Macerata is a pretty town; it is worth looking in at the local library and gallery and the ancient university, but there is little else except its scenery and the 6,000-seat Arena Sferisterio, built in the 1820s. In July and August it becomes the scene of an opera festival with international stars.

As you are passing by way of Recanati, stop to visit the art gallery that contains many paintings by Lorenzo Lotto. It will have dawned on you by now that he was especially busy around this area, in fact he finally moved into the monastery attached to the Holy House in Loretto in 1552, and became a lay brother there in 1554.

Cingoli is a little town nearly lost in the heart of the countryside—the Romans called it *Cingolum*—but its altitude offers an exciting view of the entire region all the way to the sea.

Tolentino, along the same line and road, has much more personality. It is the town where Napoleon signed the famous treaty with the Pope. Treaty-towns are almost always pleasant—Rapallo, Stresa and so on; it must have been part of the PR exercise which signing treaties involved to make sure that the locale was an attractive one. The cathedral is interesting; but the chief monument is the Church of Santa Nicola, where the Chapel of the Saint is admirably frescoed.

Still along the same route is Camerino, at 600 meters (2,000 ft.) above sea-level—a magnificent sight. Ruled by the Varanis, a ducal family, for 300 years, it saw more than its share of fratricide, stranglings, and murders in church. San Venanzio (13th century) is the most interesting of its churches; the art gallery is unusually attractive.

Fabriano is one of those impressive cities, wearing the aura of past majesty like an emperor in exile. In the Middle Ages, its power and wealth were immense; and it was a center of art and learning. Moreover it was, as early as the 12th century, one of the greatest paper-making towns in the world; it invented water-marks, and its paper-mills are still worth a visit. The art gallery is a revelation to those who do not know the naive and graceful work of the Marches school of painting. The Palazzo del Podestà is a noble building, the cathedral harmonious, the Church of San Benedetto is worth a visit, and the oratory of Gonfalone with its carved wooden ceiling delightful; the 13th-century Sant' Agostino has a remarkable doorway.

If the jewel of the northern Marches is Urbino, that of the southern extremity is Ascoli Piceno. If you want a seaside base from which to explore the southern part of the region, San Benedetto is to be recommended. Ascoli Piceno, on a plain at the confluence of two swift rivers—the Castellano and the Tronto—is severe from a distance, built of monumental travertine stone. But its picturesque alleys, its towers, its nobly simple buildings, its bridges are highlighted by the octagonal 12th-century baptistery, the massive dignity of the cathedral, the picture gallery in the Palazzo Comunale—which should all be seen. But above all, do not miss the Piazza del Popolo, with the austere Palazzo del Popolo, whose Renaissance gate is surmounted by a statue of Pope Paul III; San Francesco, with its ascetic 13th-century interior and two hexagonal towers; and next door, the graceful 16th-century Merchants' Loggia.

Ascoli Piceno is the scene of one of Italy's most colorful events, the *Tournament of the Quintana,* in early August. Townspeople in 15th-century costume take part in torchlight parades, pageants and jousts, bringing the Middle Ages to life in the perfect setting of Ascoli's piazzas.

PRACTICAL INFORMATION FOR THE MARCHES

WHEN TO GO. The Marches is best in spring and fall, and year-round along the coast, where the winters are mild. Early spring is a lovely period throughout the region. From July until late August, the heat drives everyone to the coast, which in turn becomes too crowded for comfort. However, by September—when the main body of vacationers has begun to depart—it is possible to enjoy some of the more pleasant coastal resorts, before they shut up shop for the winter.

TOURIST OFFICES. Ancona: AAST, Via Thaon de Revel 4 (33.249), and in summer also at Numana, Piazza Santuario (936.142), and at Sirolo, Piazza Vittorio Veneto (936.141); EPT, Via Marcello Marini 14 (28.313) and at rail station (43.221). **Ascoli Piceno:** AAST, Via Malta 1 (53.045); EPT, Corso Mazzini 229 (51.115). **Fano:** AAST, Viale Battisti 10 (82.534). **Loreto:** AAST, Via Solari 3 (977.139). **Macerata:** EPT, Piazza Libertà 12 (45.807). **Pesaro:** AAST, Via Trieste 164 (69.341) and Via Rossini 41 (63.690). **Porto San Giorgio:** AAST, Via Oberdan 8 (378.461). **San Benedetto del Tronto:** AAST, Viale delle Tamerici (22.37). **Senigallia:** AAST, Piazzale Morandi 2 (62.150). **Urbino:** AAST, Via Puccinotti 35 (24.41).

SEASONAL EVENTS. Ascoli Piceno: Feb. is carnival time, with colorful celebrations from Sun. before Ash Wed. until Shrove Tues.; the first Sun. in Aug., there is the Giostra della Quintana (Tournament of the Quintana), which among other things includes a chess game using live players dressed in 15th-century costume, and held in the handsome main piazza.

Fano: Feb. is carnival time here, too.

Loreto: the birth of the Virgin Mary and the Transference of the Holy House are celebrated with religious feasts on, respectively, Sept. 8 and Dec. 10.

Macerata: mid-July–mid-Aug. opera festival in the 6,000-seat, 1820s Arena Sferisterio.

San Benedetto del Tronto: carnival time in Feb.

TELEPHONE CODES. You will find the telephone area code for each town against its name in the Hotel and Restaurant listing (after the province name). If there is a different area code from the majority of the establishments—say when a hotel or restaurant is in an outlying place—then the code is given in front of the telephone number.

HOTELS AND RESTAURANTS. In general, hotel and restaurant prices are lower by 15–20% than our guidelines for the various categories would indicate. Beach resorts in this region are heavily favored by Italian families and German and Scandinavian tourists.

Regional Food and Drink. A specialty of the coastal towns is *brodetto,* a noble edifice of fish (at least thirteen varieties, they say), on a firm foundation of toast, frescoed with carrot, celery, tomato, laurel tips and white wine. Then there's *calcioni,* an oven-baked dish which you will recognize, after you have penetrated its brown carapace, as a ravioli in a slightly different guise. The typical and most elaborate pasta dish of the Marches is *vincisgrassi,* sometimes called *pasticciata,* a very rich layering of sheets of egg pasta, meat sauce and mozzarella. Its name supposedly is an Italian corruption of the name of an Austrian prince, Windisch Graetz, whose cook invented the dish while his master was in Italy fighting Napoleon. Ascoli's best-known specialty is *olive all'Ascolano,* large local olives that are pitted and then stuffed with a meat mixture whose recipe is a jealously-conserved secret; they're then breaded and fried—a most unusual dish.

Verdicchio is the typical wine of the region; it's tart and greenish-white. *Rosso Piceno, Rosso Conero* and *Falerio dei Colli Ascolani* are all worth trying.

Ancona Ancona (071). Chief city, major port, art town, seaside resort. High season 1 July to 15 Sept. *Grand Palace* (E), Lungomare Vanvitelli 24; (201.813). Central, overlooking port; smallish, comfortable; roof garden. AE, DC, MC, V. *Jolly Miramare* (E), Rupi Via Ventinove Settembre 14 (201.171). Large modern hotel, good views. AE, DC, MC, V. *Fortuna* (M), Piazza Fratelli Rosselli 15 (42.662). On railway station square. AE, DC, MC, V. *Roma e Pace* (I), Via Leopardi 1 (202.007). Very central, handy for important sights. AE, DC, MC, V.

Restaurants. *Miscia* (E), Molo Sud 44 (201.376). Closed Sun. evening. Near the fish market; proprietress dictates all-fish menu (no choice), very good; slow but courteous service. *Giardino* (M), Via Fabio Filzi 2 (51.660). Closed Fri. Large central, with summer dining in garden. AE. *La Moretta* (M), Piazza Plebiscito 52 (202.317). Closed Sun. Very central, good. AE, DC, MC, V. *Passetto* (M), Piazza Quattro Novembre (33.214). Closed Wed. Best in town. Both fish and meat specialties, seasonal menu. AE, DC, V.

Ascoli Piceno Ascoli Piceno (0736). Medieval town. *Marche* (M), Viale Kennedy 34 (45.475). Smallish, unassuming, inexpensive for standard. AE, DC.

Restaurants. *Da Mario al Pennile* (M), Pennile di Sopra (42.504). Closed Weds. Just outside town; rustic; exquisite pastas. V. *Gallo d'Oro* (M), Corso V. Emanuele 13 (53.520). Closed Sun. evening and Mon. Near Cathedral, good local specialties, mushrooms in season. AE, DC, MC, V. *Tornasacco* (M), Via Tornasacco 27 (54.151). Closed Fri. Central; regional specialties, fine wines. AE, DC, V. *Vittoria* (M), Via Bonaccorsi 7 (50.535). Closed Fri.

Fabriano Ancona (0732). Medieval buildings. *Janus* (E), Piazza Matteotti 45 (41.91). Large, comfortable. AE, DC, MC, V.

Restaurants. *Il Pollo* (M), Via Corridoni 22 (24.584). Closed Tues. and Aug. Luscious *lasagne.* AE. *Taverna Da Ivo* (M), Via Vittorio Veneto 16 (54.97). Closed Sat. V. *Tre Archi* (M), Via Ramelli 34 (41.70). Closed Mon. DC, V.

Fano Pesaro e Urbino (0721). Beach resort, important monuments. High season 1 July to 31 Aug. *Elisabeth* (E), Viale Carducci 12 (878.241). Best; smallish, attractive; short walk to beach AE, DC, MC, V. *Beaurivage* (M), Viale Adriatico 124 (84.682). On beach promenade, pleasant though anonymously furnished rooms. *Continental* (M), Viale Adriatico 148 (84.670). Open 20 May to 20 Sept. On shore drive, overlooking beach, comfortable. *Astoria* (I), Viale Cairoli 86 (82.474). Open 1 May to 30 Sept. Fine in category. On beach.

Restaurants. *Alceo* (E), Via Panoramica 101 (603.171). Closed Mon. and Jan. Outside town; seaside terrace, very good seafood. *Dal Capitano* (M), Via Roma 1 (82.173). Closed Mon. Near Arch of Augustus; tasty and inexpensive for category. *Long Beach* (M), Via de Gasperi 9 (82.613). Closed Mon. off-season, and in Nov. Busy, efficient, seaside restaurant with varied menu. *Tutta Frusaglia* (M), Viale Buozzi 75 (82.006). Closed Wed. Try *risotto alla Rossini.* V.

Frontone Pesaro e Urbino (0721). A small hilltop village, near Pergola. **Restaurants.** *Amabile* (M), at Belvedere (786.147). Closed Tues. Homemade pasta, other homey delights, very reasonable. *Taverna della Rocca* (M), Via Leopardi (786.109). Closed Wed. off season and 10–20 Oct. Atmospheric hostelry in cellars of Malatesta castle; good pastas and grilled meats.

Gabbicce Mare Pesaro e Urbino (0541). Beach resort. High season 1 July to 31 Aug. *Capo Est* (E), Gabicce Monte, at Vallugola (963.333). Open 1 May to 30

Sept. Overlooking little port, quiet, attractive, resort hotel; lift to beach; pool, terraces. *Alexander* (M), Via Panoramica 35 (961.166). Open 1 May to 30 Sept. Bright, modern decor; pool, garden. DC, V. *Majestic* (M), Via Balneare 10 (961.274). Open 10 May to 30 Sept. Comfortable, pool. DC.

Restaurants. *Bayon* (E), Via del Porto 20 (962.822). Open evenings only, except Sat. and Sun. when open for lunch also. Closed in winter. Smart and attractive; seafood menu. V. *La Cambusa* (M), Via del Porto 38 (962.784). Closed Wed. off season, and in Nov. Pleasant place, best off season for local specialties and pizza. V.

At **Gabicce Monte.** *Grottino* (M), on Piazzetta (962.595). Closed Wed. and Jan. Not a grotto at all, but lovely terrace; fine seafood. DC.

Jesi Ancona (0731). Medieval walled town. **Restaurants.** *Galeazzi* (M), Via Mura Occidentali 5 (57.944). Closed Mon. and Aug. Very good local cuisine and famous Verdicchio wine; reasonable. *Italia* (M), Viale Trieste 28 (48.44). Closed Sat.

Loreto Ancona (071). Pilgrimage center. High season Easter and 15 July to 15 Sept., 7–12 Dec. *Giardinetto* (M), Corso Boccalini 10 (977.135). AE, DC, V.

Restaurants. *Centrale-Al Girrarosto* (M), Via Soleri 7 (97.173). Closed Tues. In town, simple but good. V. *Da Orlando Barabani* (M), Via Villa Constantina at Loreto Archi (977.696). Closed Wed. and July. Outside town, lovely view, good food. DC.

Macerata Macerata (0733). Scenic hilltop resort, Renaissance buildings. High season 10 July to 13 Sept. *Centrale* (M), Via Armaroli 98 (47.276). Near main piazza, modest. *Motel AGIP* (M), Via Roma 149 (34.248). Just outside town; no frills, but adequate comfort. AE, DC, MC, V.

At **Montecassiano,** 4 miles (6.5 km) north, *Villa Quiete* (M), at Vallecascia (599.559). Pretty location, quiet, with gardens. AE, DC, MC, V.

Restaurants. *Motel AGIP* (M), Via Roma 149/b (34.248). Closed Sat. Local cuisine. AE, DC, MC, V. *Piccolo Mondo* (M), Corso Repubblica 7 (47.383). Closed Fri. and Aug. Central; try *vincisgrassi*. V. *Secondo* (M), Via Pescheria Vecchia 28 (44.912). Closed Mon. Best in town; delicious vegetarian *fritto misto,* pastas and roasts. DC, V.

Numana Ancona (071). At southern end of Monte Conero Riviera. High season 25 June to 8 Sept. *Numana Palace* (E) at Marcelli (930.155). Open 1 May to 30 Sept. Overlooking beach; with pool, gardens. MC, V. *La Scogliera* (M), at port (936.152). Open 1 May to 30 Sept. Smallish; nice views; pool, beach with facilities. V.

Restaurants. *Mariolino* (E), at Marcelli (930.135). Closed Mon. off season. Seafood only. DC. *Teresa a Mare* (M), Via del Golfo 26 (936.153). Open Easter to Oct. Best off season; both fish and meat specialties.

Pesaro Pesaro e Urbino (0721). Art city, seaside resort. High season 1 July to 31 Aug. *Vittoria* (E), Piazzale Liberta 2 (34.343). Attractive turn-of-century building near beach; period decor in salons; rooms remodeled with all comforts. AE, DC, MC, V. *Caravelle* (M), Viale Trieste 269 (64.078). Open 10 May to 20 Sept. Central, modern beach hotel with pool. AE, DC, V. *Mamiani* (M), Via Mamiani 24 (35.541). In town center, handy for sightseeing; comfortable; no restaurant. AE, DC. *Spiaggia* (M), Viale Trieste 76 (32.516). Open 1 May to 30 Sept. Directly on beach; pool.

Restaurants. *Da Carlo al Mare* (E), Viale Trieste 265 (31.453). Open 1 May to 30 Sept. Excellent soups, seafood. AE, DC, V. *Nuovo Carlo* (E), Viale Zara (68.984). Closed Tues. from Nov. to March. Small and good. AE, DC, V. *Lo Scudiero* (E), Via Baldassini 2 (64.107). Closed Thurs. and July. In center of town, a fine restaurant, varied menu. AE, DC, MC, V. *Il Castiglione,* Viale Trento 148 (64.934). Closed Mon. Regional specialties. *Da Teresa* (M), Viale Trieste 180 (30.222). Closed Mon. and Nov. Pleasant seaside veranda for seafood.

At **Gradara,** Francesca da Rimini's castle, *La Casaccia* (M), Via Giurbiano 14 (964.031). Closed Tues. off season and Nov. Simple and satisfying. *La Gradarina* (M), Via Gaggera 9 (964.132). Closed Mon. and Oct. Try *strozzapreti* pasta. Avoid both at peak tourist season and weekends.

Portonovo Ancona (071). Secluded small resort on Monte Conero Riviera near Ancona. *Emilia* (M) (801.117). Open 1 March to 31 Oct. Small, quiet hotel on hillside, attractively furnished; pool, gardens. *Fortino Napoleonico* (M) (801.124). Built around an old fortress; comfortable, on sea. AE, V.
Restaurants. *Emilia* (E), in hillside hotel (801.117). Closed Mon. and for lunch June to Aug., 1 Oct. to 31 March. Exquisite seafood in lovely surroundings. AE, V. *Da Malvina* (M), on beach (801.183). Open Easter to 31 Oct. Fish specialties.

Porto San Giorgio Ascoli Piceno (0734). Beach resort. High season 1 July to 31 Aug. *Gabbiano* (M), Via Oberdan 4 (378.306). Comfortable medium-sized hotel with good beach. DC, V. *Garden* (M), Via Battisti 6 (379.414). Nicely furnished, close to beach in garden setting. DC, V.
Restaurants. *Davide* (M), Via Mazzini 102 (677.700). Closed Mon. Pleasant, near station. AE, DC, MC, V. *Faro* (M), Via Giovanni XXIII (47.33). Closed Mon. and Sept. Seafood, some pricey. V. *Miramare* (M), Lungomare Sud (45.24). Closed Mon. off season. Tasty regional specialties, *simpatico* atmosphere. V.

San Benedetto del Tronto Ascoli Piceno (0735). Important beach resort. High season 1 July to 31 Aug. *Roxy* (E), Via Buozzi 6 (44.41). Modern resort hotel with pool. AE, DC, V. *Calabresi* (M), Viale Colombo 1 (60.548). Located at hub of resort activity; near beach. AE, MC, V. *Sabbiadoro* (M), Lungomare Marconi 46 (81.911). Open 25 May to 15 Sept. Sea views; beach. DC, V.
At **Porto d'Ascoli,** *Ambassador* (M), Via Cimarosa 5 (659.443). Open 1 May to 30 Sept. Fine resort hotel; pool, tennis. AE, DC, MC, V. *Excelsior* (M), Viale Rinascimento 137 (650.945). Open 1 May to 30 Sept. Large, comfortable beach hotel. V. *International* (M), Viale Rinascimento 45 (650.243). Good, all comforts. V.
Restaurants. *Albula* (M), Via Fileni 3, (26.76). Closed Tues. Modest ambience, excellent seafood. *Angelici* (M), Via Mazzocci 34 (84.674). Closed Mon. Garden terrace. *La Stalla* (M), Via Marinuccia 35, on road to Grottamare (49.33). Closed Mon. Rustic specialties.
At **Porto d'Ascoli,** *Mattia* (M), Via Gobetti 8 (659.597). Closed Mon. and Nov. Seafood. DC.

Senigallia Ancona (071). Beach resort. High season 25 June to 8 Sept. *Excelsior* (E), Lungomare Dante 142 (61.491). Open 1 May to 30 Sept. On beach promenade, bright and spacious salons; many rooms with balcony, sea view. AE, DC, MC, V. *City* (M), Lungomare Dante 12 (63.464). Ultra-modern, overlooking beach; rooftop restaurant. AE, DC, MC, V. *Massi* (M), Giardini Morandi 11 (62.934). Open 1 May to 30 Sept. Attractive small hotel; balconies, flowered terraces; beach facilities. DC, V.
Restaurants. *Albatros* (E), Via Rieti 69 (64.762). Closed Mon. off season. Inviting place with interesting, varied menu, mostly fish. AE, DC, V. *Villa Sorriso* (E), Via Gramsci 10 (62.428). Closed Mon. Elegant; local and Piedmontese dishes; good house wine. *Bice* (M), Via Leopardi 105. Good country-style food. *Boschetto* (M), at Filetto, 6 miles (9.5 km) south west (66.404). Closed Mon. and Nov. Pretty location outside town; pleasing menu; reasonable.

Sirolo Ancona (071). On Monte Conero, above Numana. High season 25 June to 8 Sept. *Monte Conero* (M), at Badia San Pietro (936.122). High above coast, a peaceful haven; pool, tennis. V.
Restaurants. *Della Rosa* (E), Corso Italia 39 (936.219). Closed Mon. and Dec. to Jan. In old part of Sirolo, small, veranda with view of sea; fish specialties. V. *Monte Conero* (M) (936.122). Fine restaurant of hotel (see above). V. *Sara,* Corso Italia 9 (936.246). Closed Wed. off season and Nov. Modest appearance, excellent

seafood. v. *Taverna del Trave* (M), Via Varano 2 (808.014). Closed Tues. In attractive villa, simple but succulent dishes.

Urbino Pesaro e Urbino (0722). Important Renaissance art city. *Montefeltro* (M), Via Piansevero 2 (38.324). On outskirts; adequate but anonymous. DC. v. *San Giovanni* (M), Via Barocci 13 (28.27). Central, in renovated medieval palazzo; basic rooms; good atmosphere. v.

Restaurants. *Il Cortegiana* (M), Via Puccinotti 13 (45.39). Closed Mon. Near Palazzo Ducale. v. *Nuovo Coppiere* (M), Via Porta Maia 20 (320.092). Closed Wed. *Simpatico* and good. AE, DC, MC, v. *Nuova Fornarina* (M), Via Viti 12 (45.14). Closed Mon. v. *San Giovanni* (M), Via Barocci 3 (34.86). Closed Thurs. Atmospheric cellar restaurant of hotel (see above). v.

GETTING AROUND. By air and sea. The region's airport is just outside Ancona at Falconara. Ancona itself is an important port of embarkation for Yugoslavia and Greece.

By train. The main rail line from Milan and Bologna to Lecce follows the coast of the Marches, while the Rome—Falconara (Ancona) line passes through Fabriano and Iesi. There are secondary lines from Fano to Urbino, from Civitanova to Macerata and from Porto d'Ascoli to Ascoli.

By bus. Local buses connect the smaller towns.

By car. Although it is easy enough to get to the Marches and to travel along the coast without an automobile, the many interesting though not-too-well known places inland which you might wish to visit are fairly inaccessible by other forms of transport. The Autostrada Adriatica 14 parallels the old coastal road from Rimini to Pescara, bypassing Ancona. From points on either road, you can visit the interior towns of Urbino, Loreto, Macerata and Ascoli Piceno. On the west side of the region there is one main road which, so to speak, boxes it in, while in the center there are nothing but small, winding roads, slow to drive on.

ABRUZZI-MOLISE

Remote and Rugged Grandeur

Although the Abruzzi is better known than the Molise section of the region, both are distinctive for their natural beauty, the preservation of their old traditions, and the fact that they have been less explored than many other parts of Italy. The Abruzzi and Molise on the Adriatic side are bounded by the Marches in the north and by Apulia in the south, but in the west they are separated from the Tyrrhenian Sea by Lazio (Rome) and Campania (Naples). The region is composed almost entirely of hills and mountains belonging to the Central Apennines (the Abruzzi), and a small part to the southern Apennines (Molise), with watersheds flowing into the Adriatic Sea.

Abruzzi-Molise economy is basically agricultural and pastoral. In addition to wheat fields where the earth will allow it, potatoes and vegetables are cultivated, the latter especially in the coastal regions. Vineyards, olive and fruit trees flourish near the coast. Sheep-raising is a traditional occupation.

Centuries ago, the tribes in this region resisted, but finally fell under Roman domination. The Lombards later added Molise to the Duchy of Benevento, and the Abruzzi to that of Spoleto. In 843, the internal central region became an autonomous country called Marsia. In the 12th century, Pope Adrian IV gave the region to Norman King William I of Sicily, but Norman domination remained only in Molise. Abruzzi lined itself up with the Swabians, and took part in the struggle between Frederick II and the Church. The rest of the history of the area revolved around individual towns, local lords and warlike bishops, and in continual insurrections against Spanish, Austrian and Bourbon regimes until 1860, when it was united with Italy.

The shepherd is the symbol of Abruzzi. Jacketed and gaitered with goat-skin, carrying a weirdly-carved club, he moves with his huge flocks on the upland pastures in summer; he has stone pens for his sheep, and a hut of stone where he practices playing bagpipes and the *pifferi,* a rustic oboe. When winter approaches, he comes down to the plains, along broad pri-mordial grassy tracks; you often see his migrating flock mixed up with cursing motorists in busy lowland towns. Sometimes he makes one of a city-strolling two-man bagpipe-and-*pifferi* band; their wailing is a presage of Christmas in Rome, as "waits" are elsewhere.

Exploring the Abruzzi

L'Aquila is a handsome hilly town; 600 meters (2,000 ft.) up, it is cool in the baking Abruzzi summer, and its cold winters are brightened by live-ly cultural events. At one of the highest points in town, the Piazza del Duomo is a breezy open space that serves as marketplace each morning, when foodstuffs and local handicrafts are spread out in the shadow of the cathedral of San Massimo, where you should see architectural illusions created by Andrea del Pozzo (of Rome's Sant'Ignazio) in the dome frescos. It's a short walk from here to San Bernardino, whose fine facade shows that the force of Renaissance innovations thrust deeply into these then remote valleys. The church also has a lovely Andrea della Robbia altar-piece in the second chapel on the right and the richly worked marble tomb of San Bernardino; the elaborate carved gilt ceiling is worth your attention, too.

Continuing on toward the massive 16th-century fortress built by the Spanish, make a brief detour to see the fine Romanesque church of Santa Maria Paganica. The mighty fortress, or Castello, stands out against the distant backdrop of the Gran Sasso massif; now a national museum, the Castello contains a mixed bag of archeological exhibits, some good Gothic and Renaissance art by Abruzzese masters, and a collection of antique ce-ramic ware from the picturesque little pottery-producing town of Castelli, not far away on the slopes of the Gran Sasso. The tourist showpiece at L'Aquila is the Fountain of the Ninety-Nine Spouts (each of which is a different mask) near the station.

For a closer look at the majestic mass of the Gran Sasso, which stretches for 36 km. (22 miles) and rises to a height of 2,941 meters (9,650 ft.) at Corno Grande, highest peak in the Apennines, take the funicular at Fonte Cerreto, just beyond Assergi. In 15 minutes you ascend to Campo Impera-tore, at 1,800 meters (6,000 ft.), where you can get a marvelous view of the entire massif from the Duca degli Abruzzi refuge.

Just outside L'Aquila's walls, set apart on a green hillside, Santa Maria di Collemaggio is of great artistic interest. Its Romanesque facade is a har-mony of pink and white stone arranged in geometric patterns that are nice-ly broken by sculptured portals and rose windows. Most of the interior has been restored to its original simplicity; there are some very old frescos and the Renaissance tomb of Celestine V, the hermit pope who abdicated the papal throne after only five months, earning Dante's literary contempt in *The Inferno.*

Between Aquila and Sulmona, stop off at Popoli for a look at the curious Taverna Ducale, a centuries-old inn whose history is written in the myriad inscriptions and coats of arms embedded in its facade. Also make the detour to San Clemente in Casauria, a Cistercian abbey founded in the 9th century. The church was built in the 12th century along Romanesque lines, with some Gothic elements; it's one of the finest of Abruzzo's many abbey churches and it contains a magnificent pulpit and beautiful ciborium. On the opposite side of Popoli there's another lovely old church, San Pelino, at Corfinio.

Sulmona

At the somewhat depressing entrance to the town of Sulmona, its cathedral has often been rebuilt and has lost most of its character. It must be remembered that Abruzzi is highly subject to earthquake shocks (a score of serious ones in the last 500 years, with the most recent in 1984), hence the frequent use of the word "rebuilt" in descriptions of buildings. Sulmona's main street is named after Ovid, who was born here; in local lore the famous Roman is regarded as a sorcerer rather than as a poet. The Palace and Church of the Annunziata, on Corso Ovidio, are really lovely buildings, with graceful doors and traceried windows. At the center of town, the Corso widens into the Piazza del Carmine, where there's a handsome Gothic portal (all that remains of a very old church) and a pretty Renaissance fountain fed by an ancient aqueduct.

Sulmona is famous for the production of *confetti*, varicolored sugared almonds that are distributed as favors at Italian weddings and christenings. Here at the center of town are any number of *confetti* shops, their windows bright with fanciful arrangements of the candies.

Southwest of Sulmona, Scanno is a tumble of rooftops on a hillside overlooking a pretty lake. The women of Scanno, who still wear their severe but elegant local costumes on Sundays and holidays, are known for their fine embroidery work.

If you have the time, you can take a chairlift up to Colle Rotondo, 1,650 meters (5,413 ft.) for an overall view of the mountains, where there's good skiing during the winter. Just west of Sulmona is Cocullo, where the villagers celebrate their patron San Domenico by decorating his statue with live snakes (non-poisonous, of course) and carrying it in procession through the streets. If you happen to be in the area on the first Thursday in May, don't miss this unusual sight.

The towns of Pescasseroli and Civitella Alfedena are good starting-points for excursions in the Abruzzi National Park; they have visitors' centers and small natural history museums, and can provide information and itineraries. Among the most beautiful spots in the park are the Camosciara near Villetta Barrea, where there's a lovely lake, the Val Fondillo and the Diavolo Pass on the road to Avezzano.

Avezzano is an untidy town rebuilt after the total destruction of the 1915 earthquake. Nearby are the important telecommunications center of Fucino, with its huge saucer-shaped antennae; the interesting excavations of Alba Fucens, a pre-Roman settlement; and the attractive medieval town of Tagliacozzo. There's another entrance to the National Park at Pescina.

Pescara is the largest of the beach resorts strung along the coast; all provide adequate, but not particularly attractive, bathing. In the vicinity are Penne, an all-of-a-piece old village that's built entirely of rosy brick, and Atri, well worth a visit for its cathedral, one of the region's most impressive. At Loreto Aprutino, the church of Santa Maria in Piano has some delightfully *naïf* frescoes, notably that of the *Last Judgment* on the inside of the facade, in which the elect manage to walk a tightrope-like span into paradise, while the damned plunge into a torrent below.

Just inland from Pescara, the hilltop town of Chieti has a major attraction in the Museo Nazionale's important collection of archeological finds that includes the *Warrior of Capestrano,* a larger-than-life-sized statue out of a still-dim past. And if you're still interested in Romanesque churches, there's another exceptional abbey church, Santa Maria Arabona, at Manoppello.

Lanciano has an interesting old central nucleus that dates to the Middle Ages, when the town was one of the chief trading centers of the Mediterranean area. Merchants came from all over Europe, from the Middle East and Africa to buy its cloth at an annual fair that lasted two to three months. Be sure to see 13th-century Santa Maria Maggiore, with its varied columns and sculptured Gothic portal.

On the Adriatic watershed of the Gran Sasso, Teramo is known for its cathedral, at the center of the older, lower part of town. Its squared-off facade has an extraordinary Gothic portal, lively with mosaics and statues and guarded by a pride of Romanesque lions. Inside, the frontal of the main altar is a magnificent example of 15th-century silverwork.

Exploring Molise

Molise offers a particular vision of rural traditions and ancient remains in a beautiful natural setting. It's an area very much off the beaten track, except for the fishing port of Termoli, where you can catch an excursion boat to the Termiti islands, and where there's a sandy beach that attracts vacationing Italians. The 12th-century cathedral is Termoli's architectural pride.

Campobasso, the capital, lies in the center of a plateau from which there is an excellent view of the area. The western part is mostly mountainous, the highest points being near Capracotta (highest town in the Apennines), in the Matese mountains and in the chain of the Mainarde mountains. From here flow the larger Molise rivers—the Biferno, the Volturno and the Trigno—which irrigate many parts of the section. Campobasso is a picturesque city with narrow, winding streets. At its highest point is the severe Monforte Castle, built in 1549, beneath which are the two interesting churches of San Giorgio and San Bartolomeo. The modern part of the town lies below.

To the south are the remains of Sepino, the ancient Roman city of Saepinum, which has been preserved thanks to the remarkable symbiosis with the modest stone dwellings of the medieval village of Altilia. Set in green farm country, this archeological site offers a rewarding view of an entire ruined city of the imperial age, complete with temples, theater and baths, as it was later adapted by a colony of poor peasants and shepherds to their minimal needs. Now many of the Roman edifices have been cleared of the accretions of time, while the medieval buildings have been restored to house a small museum of antiquities.

In the lush countryside of meadowland and beech forests near Isernia, there's another site of great interest at Pietrabbondante. Here, the remains of a pre-Roman city, one of the most important civil and religious centers of the Samnite peoples that inhabited this area, are well worth your attention. The graceful semicircle of stone tiers that forms the ancient theater nestles into the hillside, the high backs of its seats obviously designed for the comfort of the spectators.

At Isernia, a hilltop town with fine views, you might wish to stop to see the lovely lace and rustic pottery that's produced here. Not far from Isernia, the Benedictine Abbey of San Vincenzo al Volturno was founded in the 8th century, razed by the Saracens and later rebuilt. You can visit the small but fascinating underground crypt that survived intact to see the precious 9th-century frescos covering its walls and ceiling. Throughout the Molise region you'll find any number of rock-perched villages, of no great artistic importance but nonetheless interesting for the feeling of time-lessness which pervades their weathered stones and is reflected in the ruddy, wrinkled faces of the elders who sit outside on a fine day, hands busy at some equally timeless task.

PRACTICAL INFORMATION FOR ABRUZZI-MOLISE

WHEN TO GO. The best times for a visit to Abruzzi-Molise are early fall and late spring, when the snows—though they may linger on the mountains—have de-parted the roads that wind up through the hills. The region can be visited year-round, however, for the coast enjoys a mild climate which makes it tolerable in winter, while sea breezes temper the heat of summer.

As for the mountain resorts, many are high enough to be comfortable in summer. In winter, they offer skiing and other sports—though they cannot compare in this respect with the great Alpine centers. The coastal resorts are crowded out in July and August by Italian families on vacation.

TOURIST OFFICES. L'Aquila: AAST, Via Venti Settembre 8 (22.306); EPT, Piazza Santa Maria di Paganica 5 (25.149). **Campobasso:** EPT, Piazza della Vittoria 14 (95.662). **Chieti:** EPT, Via Spaventa 29 (65.231). **Francavilla a Mare:** AAST, Piazzale Sirena (817.169). **Isernia:** EPT, Via Farinacci 9 (39.92). **Pescara:** AAST, Corso Umberto 44 (22.593); EPT, Via Nicola Fabrizi 173 (23.939). **Pescasseroli:** AAST, Viale Principe de Napoli 32 (91.461). **Roccaraso:** AAST, Viale Roma 60 (62.210). **Scanno:** AAST, Piazza Santa Maria della Valle (91.317). **Sulmona:** Via Roma 21 (53.276). **Tagliacozzo:** AAST, Piazza Argoli 16 (63.18). **Teramo:** EPT, Via del Castello 10 (51.222). **Termoli:** AAST, Piazza Stazione 21 (27.54).

SEASONAL EVENTS. Festivals in this region are usually a part of the celebra-tion of local patron saints.

Cocullo: on May 6, this little town attracts throngs of spectators to view the ex-traordinary procession of townsfolk, who drape both the statue of their patron saint—Dominic—and themselves with live snakes, to recall the banishment of all poisonous serpents from the district by the saint.

Isernia: traditional events accompanied by the wearing of medieval costume take place here in Sept.

Rivisondoli: one of the most picturesque events in Abruzzo-Molise is presented here on Jan. 6 in the shape of a Christmas tableau.

Scanno: in Aug., this pretty town becomes the setting for a festival that includes outdoor theater, a costumed pageant, and folk dancing; New Year's Eve sees a torchlight procession.

TELEPHONE CODES. You will find the telephone area code for each town against its name in the Hotel and Restaurant listings (after the province name). If there is a different area code from the majority of the establishments—say when a hotel or restaurant is in an outlying place—then the code is given in front of the telephone number.

HOTELS AND RESTAURANTS. Prices in the region are generally 15–20% lower than our guidelines. You should also note that the coastal resorts are totally occupied by vacationing Italian families during July and August. The two facts are not entirely unconnected!

Regional Food and Drink. The favorite *pasta* here is known as *maccheroni alla chitarra* because the *pasta* is cut into thin strips on the strings of a guitar-shaped utensil. *Pincisgrassi* is baked *pasta,* alternated with layers of cheese and sauce. Suckling pig is another favorite dish. Desserts include *parrozzo,* a rich chocolate cake; *zeppole, pasta* again, but this time sweet, and a candyish confection made of dried figs, honey, almonds and nuts.

In the Molise area, roast lamb and kid are favorites, and lamb also appears in various stewed versions. Isernia is famous for its beans, grown locally and served in soups and stews.

The region produces both red and white wines. Among the reds, *Cerasuolo di Abruzzo* is sweet, *Montepulciano* is dry. The best dry white wine is *Trebbiano.* This district is the home of a sweetish liqueur known as *Cent'Erbe.*

Campobasso Campobasso (0874). Provincial capital. *Roxy* (M), Piazza Savoia 7 (91.741). Enlarged and modernized in 1983. AE, DC, V. *Skanderberg* (M), Via Novelli (93.341). Attractive, well-appointed with good views. AE, MC, V.

Restaurants. *Abruzzese* (M), Piazza Battisti 12 (65.392). Closed Sun. Very central, good local dishes. DC. *La Griglia* (M), Via Novelli at Hotel Skanderberg (93.341). Closes Sat. and Sun. MC, V.

At **Ferrazzano,** 5 km. (3 miles) southeast, *Da Emilio* (M), (978.376). In picturesque hamlet, very good country cooking. Closed Tues. and Jul. V.

Campo Imperatore L'Aquila (0862). Summer and winter resort at 6,900 feet (2,100 m), on south slope of Corno Grande mountain.

Restaurants. *Campo Imperatore* (M), at upper terminal of cablecar, big hotel refuge. *La Villetta* (M), at **Fonte Cerreto,** lower terminal of cablecar (606.134). Open 15 June to 15 Sept. Pleasant spot. AE.

Chieti Chieti (0871). Provincial capital.

Restaurants. *Bellavista* (M), Corso Marrucino 78 (65.637). Closed Mon. and Aug. Roof garden restaurant with wonderful view. AE. *Nino* (M), Via Principessa di Piemonte 7 (65.396). Closed Fri. and Aug. Converted wine cellar, hearty fare. *Regine* (M), Via Solferino 20 (63.249). Inventive cuisine in restaurant of Hotel Angiò. AE, DC. *Venturini* (M), Via Cesare de Lollis 10 (65.863). Closed Tues. and July. Local specialties in tranquil old palazzo courtyard. AE, DC, MC, V.

Francavilla a Mare Chieti (085). Family resort with broad, sandy beach.

Restaurants. *Casa Mia* (E), Via Alcione 115 (817.147). Closed Mon. and Jan. Excellent seafood. AE, DC. *La Nave* (E), Piazzale Sirena (817.115). Closed Wed. and 3–18 Sept. Unusual seafood specialties. AE, DC, MC, V.

Giulianova Teramo (085). Fishing port, beach resort. *Don Juan* (E), Lungomare Zara 97 (867.341). Open 18 May to 20 Sept. Attractive, Mediterranean-style, on beach; 150 rooms, most with balcony, pool, gardens. AE, DC, MC, V. *Riviera* (M), Lungomare Zara 47 (862.020). Open 20 May to 20 Sept. On beach; contemporary decor; pool, gardens. AE, DC, MC, V.

Restaurants. *Da Beccaceci* (E), Via Zola 18 (862.550). Closed Tues. and 15–31 Dec. Finest fish restaurant around; quality slumps when crowded. AE, DC, MC, V. *Del Torrione* (E), Piazza Buozzi 63, in **Giulianuova Alta** (863.895). Closed Mon. and Jan. In old town; smart, very good food and fine view. DC.

Isernia Isernia (0865). Beautifully situated town. *Tequila* (M), Via San Lazzaro (265.174). In quiet location outside center of town. AE, DC, MC.

Restaurants. *La Molisana* (M), Via Don Sturzo 14 (21.05). Closed Fri. Simple, good regional dishes. AE, DC. *Taverna Maresca* (M), Via Marcelli 86 (39.76). Closed Sun. and Aug. Typical place for authentic local cuisine.

Lanciano Chieti (0872). Medieval city. *Excelsior* (M), Viale della Rimembranza 19 (23.113). Modest but satisfactory overnight. AE, DC, V.

Restaurant. *Taverna Ranieri* (M), Via De Crecchio 42 (32.102). Closed Mon. Exceptional cuisine, both local and international, at top level. AE, DC, V.

L'Aquila L'Aquila (0862). Art city, mountain scenery. *La Cannelle* (M), Via Santa Maria del Ponte (69.81). Just below town, near railway station; large; bright, contemporary comforts, indoor/outdoor pools. AE, DC, MC, V. *Castello* (M), Piazza Battaglione Alpini (29.147). Facing castle; elegant small hotel, good service. No restaurant. *Duca degli Abruzzi* (M), Viale Giovanni XXIII 10 (28.341). In the center of town; solid comfort. AE.

Restaurants. *Tre Marie* (E), Via Tre Marie 3 (20.191). Closed Sun. evening and Mon. Turn-of-century frescos and wood paneling create old-world atmosphere; cuisine consists of local specialties.

Aquila-Da Remo (M), Via San Flaviano 9 (22.010). Closed Sun. Pleasant and unpretentious. *Tetto* (M), rooftop restaurant of Hotel Duca degli Abruzzi (28.341). Elegant setting, breathtaking views.

At **Coppito**, outside town (hourly bus), *Salette Aquilane* (M) (639.145). Rustic, cordial atmosphere, tasty local dishes. Closed Sun. evening, Mon. and July.

Pescara Pescara (085). Provincial capital and beach resort; rated one of Italy's noisiest cities. High season 1 July to 31 Aug. *Carlton* (E), Viale Riviera 35 (373.125). Facing sea; comfortable rooms, beach facilities. AE, DC, MC, V. *Esplanade* (E), Piazza Primo Magio 46 (292.141). On shore boulevard; large, well-equipped; beach, roof garden. AE, DC, MC, V.

Restaurants. *Duilio* (M), Via Regina Margherita 11 (378.278). Closed Sun. eve., Mon., Aug. Fine seafood. Check can mount up. *Guerino* (M), Viale Riviera 4 (23.065). Closed Mon. off-season. Tops for seafood and good service. AE, DC, MC, V.

Cantina di Jozz (M), Via delle Caserme 61 (690.383). Closed Sun. evening and Mon. off-season. Small. Book for pleasant meal. DC. *Leon d'Oro* (M), Via Roma 29 (373.137). Closed Mon. Near station; excellent fare, can be pricey.

Pescasseroli L'Aquila (0863). Mountain resort in Abruzzo National Park. *Grand del Parco* (E) (91.356). Open 15 June to 30 Sept. and 18 Dec. to 31 March. Magnificently situated; large, comfortable; heated pool. AE, V.

Restaurants. *Il Caminetto* (M) (91.615). Closed Mon. and June. Nice atmosphere. AE, DC, MC, V. *Girrarosto* (M), Via Principe di Napoli (91.465). Closed Wed. Simple but satisfying. *Alle Vecchie Arcate* (M), Via delle Chiesa (91.381). Closed Tues. Pleasant, good food. V.

Roccaraso L'Aquila (0864). Smart summer and winter sports resort favored by Romans. *Excelsior* (M), Via Roma 24 (62.479). Open 24 June to 4 Sept. and 18 Dec. to 15 April. V. *Motel AGIP* (M), on Highway 17 (62.443). Has good restaurant. AE, DC, MC, V.

Scanno L'Aquila (0864). Picturesque mountain town overlooking lake. *Mille Pini* (M), at chairlift terminal (74.387). Small, quiet. *Del Lago* (M), on lake (74.343). Best, lovely location; gardens. AE, DC, MC, V.

Restaurant. *Gli Archetti* (M), Via Silla, in old town (74.645). Closed Tues. Homemade pasta, roast lamb.

Sulmona L'Aquila (0864). Important mountain town. *Europa Park* (M), on Highway 17 north (34.641). Outside town; large, comfortable. MC, V.

Restaurants. *Cesidio* (M), Piazza Solimo 25 (52.724). Closed Fri. Simple, good, very reasonable. AE, DC. *Costanza* (M), at Europa Park Hotel (34.641). Traditional dishes; freshwater fish caught locally. *Italia-Da Nicola* (M), Piazza Venti Settembre (33.070). Closed Mon. *The* place for homemade pasta, *alla chitarra* and otherwise. AE, DC, MC. V.

Tagliacozzo L'Aquila (0863). Mountain town, Gothic buildings; skiing nearby. *Miramonti* (M), Via Giorgina (65.81). Closed Oct. Pleasant little place. v.

Teramo Teramo (0861). Provincial capital. Fine cathedral. *Sporting* (M), Via De Gasperi (414.723). Just outside town; modern hotel with pool. MC, V.
Restaurants. *Duomo* (M), Via Stazio 9 (321.274). Closed Mon. and 7–21 Nov. Exceptionally good; local cuisine and delicious novelties. AE, DC, MC, V. *Tre Galli* (M), at **Bivio Nepezzano** (558.174). Closed Mon. On main highway; reasonable, popular and crowded.

Termoli Campobasso (0875). Medieval town on promontory; fishing port. **Restaurants.** *Belami* (M), Piazzale Stazione (25.57). Closed Sun. evening and Mon. Classic spot. *Captain Blood* (M), Via Giudicato Vecchio (71.295). Closed Mon. off-season and Oct. Atmospheric cellar restaurant in old town; good food. AE, DC. *Il Drago* (M), Corso V. Emanuele 58 (71.139). Closed Tues. Both fish and meat specialties. AE, V. *Torre Saracena* (M), 5 km. (3 miles) outside town on Adriatica highway (33.18). Closed Mon. Interesting locale in old watchtower on beach; delicious seafood, some pricey.

GETTING AROUND. By air. Alitalia flies into Pescara, the region's only major airport—mostly internal flights.

By rail and bus. The main rail line across Abruzzo links Rome with Pescara. L'Aquila is on a secondary line that connects with the main line at Terni or at Sulmona. In any case, the mountainous nature of the region makes train and local bus travel very slow going.

By car. To reach Abruzzi, you will be coming either from the north by the Autostrada Adriatica, starting at Bologna, or—more interestingly—from Rome by the scenic autostrada to L'Aquila. The last, L'Aquila, is the best center from which to visit the region. From it, two autostrade make their separate ways to the Adriatic coast and tie up at some point with even the most minor roads.

The Molise region can be reached by driving down through the Abruzzi National Park to Isernia, or by leaving the A2 south of Rome at the Cassino exit and coming to Isernia through Venafro. Thereafter, a trip through Boiano, Campobasso and Casaclenda to Termoli on the coast, over approximately 80 extremely tortuous miles, provides a splendid overall experience of the area.

UMBRIA

The Mystic Province

The subtle influence of Umbria, known as the Green Heart of Italy, is difficult to recreate in words. Even among the hills, the country is undramatic, but the strange, bluish haze which diffuses the landscape and has caused so many writers to characterize Umbria as mystic and ethereal, lends the area a special charm. The colors, mostly soft tones of grays and greens, create a sense of peace. Hills covered with olive groves, or in the less cultivated parts, with pines, rise with deceptive gentleness from the flatness of the broad plain. It is only from directly below, or from one of the many towns built on them, that you realize how steep the hills really are. On the terraced lower slopes and on the plain are the famous Umbrian grape vines, carefully trained to grow over dwarf elms. Slim poplars divide the fields and shade the dusty white roads. Everything seems as motionless as if the scenery were painted—and, indeed, it is a landscape that you will often recognize in the paintings of local artists, even when they were decorating churches far from their native soil.

Exploring Umbria

Even in Italy, where regions rich with artistic inheritance are the rule, Umbria remains outstanding. Almost every small town contains treasures from the past. There might be a lovely Della Robbia plaque, some outstanding fresco or painting, or fine piece of sculpture. Perhaps a particularly well proportioned square, civic building, or a church is the source of local pride.

Minor arts, such as embroidery, lace-making, ceramics, and iron working, still flourish in Umbria, but in general, the current products are not to be compared with the old. Don't fail to notice the vestments in the cathedral museums. Glance up at the delicate wrought iron balconies, at the torch holders, and at the majolica plaques decorating the house-fronts.

Even the briefest crossing of Umbria will show well-preserved examples of architecture recording the passing of the Etruscans, Romans, their medieval successors and Renaissance descendants down to the present day.

Most of the surviving buildings left by those mysterious people, the Etruscans, are centered in Umbria. Several of the walled cities have portions of original Etruscan masonry incorporated into later defenses. A few gates and arches still stand. Foundations of various temples remain, some as they were laid, others with later buildings superimposed on them. The best preserved models of their skill are their family tombs.

The Romans are represented by their usual quota of temples, fora, amphitheaters and bridges, many of them adapted by citizens of later ages for their own use. Medieval castles, standing grim and alone or with walled towns clustered around them, testify to the turbulence of the history which gave them birth. Handsome palaces, marvelously decorated churches and, in contrast, narrow, twisting streets, darkened by overhanging houses, represent the Renaissance and baroque periods.

Since the majority of the Umbrian cities and towns are either placed some distance up the slope or actually crown the top of a hill, there are invariably magnificent views. You can often find restaurants at vantage points overlooking spectacular scenery. The local wines definitely add to the appreciation of the vast panorama spread below.

In addition to its natural beauty, art, history and wine, Umbria offers its share of traditional festivals. The most interesting of these is the *Feast of the Candles,* at Gubbio, while the most important religious events naturally take place in Assisi. For the music lover, operas and concerts are given in Perugia's Morlacchi Theater, and yearly, in September, there is an excellent musical festival. The Spoleto Festival (June–July) is world famous. Orvieto celebrates Corpus Domini in June with a magnificently costumed procession.

Perugia

Two points indicate Perugia as the logical center for short trips off the beaten path. It is the largest and richest, both materially and artistically, of the cities of Umbria, and its size and central location ensure the best regional transportation.

In the distance, Perugia displays a lovely silhouette against the sky. Built on a hill-top high above the plain, the city's skyline is set off to its fullest advantage. However, as one approaches, little more than its location proclaims it to be of anything but recent construction. In spite of all the beauty it contains, Perugia has sacrificed much of its charm to progress. A few of its once-numerous spires still rise, but the usual fortress is absent, and the walls are largely invisible, the city's expansion having concealed the medieval nucleus behind modern buildings.

Long before the Romans showed the first signs of civilization by assaulting the Sabines, Perugia was the site of a flourishing city, and before the first of its many recorded falls, had become one of the centers of Etruscan culture. This civilization, in conjunction with that of Greece, was to have the greatest influence in the formation of the Romans. Little is known of these people, but in three fields they left a distinct mark: they were fine architects and taught much to their conquerors. They were also notable sculptors. But perhaps their most important legacy was their religious influence, and many have felt it a logical step to conclude that the intensity and mysticism of the Umbrian stems from this source.

One of the finest collections of Etruscan relics in existence is to be seen in Perugia's Museum of Etruscan and Roman Antiquities. There is an Etruscan gate (Porta Marzia) in good condition, and incidentally, about 200 feet to the right of it, one of the few stretches of the city's medieval wall still stands, unhidden by later construction.

Of the Roman period—highlighted by Octavian's sack of Perugia in 40 BC, four years after the fatal Ides of March which saw the murder of his uncle, Julius Caesar—there are few traces. Over one Etruscan gate is the inscription *Augusta Perusia,* probably dating from the rebuilding of the city at the order of its destroyer, who became Rome's first emperor, Caesar Augustus. In 1962 a 1st-century Roman reservoir was discovered under the Piazza IV Novembre.

The bulk of the old part of the city dates from the late Middle Ages and Renaissance and is concentrated around the top and upper slopes of Perugia's hill. The oldest portion is naturally nearest the top, and as the city grew, a second level developed which is known as the Lower City.

Along the highest ridge runs the city's main street, the Corso Vannucci, an odd mixture of old and new. At one extreme is the lovely square with its magnificent 13th-century fountain flanked by the cathedral and Municipal Palace. At the other end are the *Hotel Brufani-Palace,* Perugia's biggest, and a block of 19th-century buildings which can take a lion's share of the guilt for ruining the city approach. From the same street run a series of arched tunnels and narrow alleys. These lead steeply down through the medieval town.

Two names have lent Perugia widespread familiarity. Perugina chocolate is well-known for its delicious flavor. Perugino is the nickname of the 15th-century painter Pietro Vannucci, the most distinguished figure of the Umbrian School. Some of his best work is in the Stock Exchange, one of the sightseeing musts of Perugia.

In addition to being a fine 13th-century building, the Municipal Palace contains four rooms of artistic importance, a library, and the National Gallery (Pinacoteca). On the ground floor are the rooms of the Merchants' Guild, and the Exchange with its adjoining chapel. The first is magnificently decorated with wooden panels, carved and inlaid with rare delicacy. The Exchange, also in a remarkable state of preservation, is enriched by the brush of Perugino. Its chapel is the work of his pupils. On the right side of the altar is a charming *Madonna* by Perugino's most famous pupil, Raphael. The Notary's Room, on the third floor, contains some good painting, while the Pinacoteca, on the fourth, should not be missed by anyone interested in art.

The most powerful medieval pope, Innocent III, whom King John of England recognized as sovereign, had written a treatise *De Contemptu Mundi* (On the Contempt of the World), but death paraphrased this to *Sic Transit Gloria Mundi* (Thus passes the Glory of the World). Keeping lonely vigil on the night of July 16, 1216, the Pope suffered an embolism and his body was found, naked and robbed of the tiara and precious vestments, in the cathedral the following morning.

The Gothic cathedral is now entered by an ornate Baroque doorway. The wedding ring of the Virgin Mary, a circle of white onyx about an inch in diameter, is kept in a reliquary on a splendid silver altar in the first chapel on the left. In the Chapterhouse Museum are some finely illuminated books and a *Madonna* by Signorelli among a few paintings.

Three of Perugia's medieval streets should be mentioned as particularly interesting. The Maestà della Volte, a favorite photographic subject; the Via dei Priori, which leads to the Oratory of San Bernardino, decorated with the reliefs of Agostino di Duccio, and the Via Baglioni. The Via Baglioni is an architectural curiosity almost completely covered over by later buildings, now incorporated into an escalator system connecting upper and lower city.

Perugia's University for Foreigners in the Gallenga Palace, the choir stalls of the Churches of San Pietro and Sant' Agostino, the curious 13th-century church of San Ercolano, and the 6th-century Sant' Angelo are all of interest if time permits.

Assisi, Home of St. Francis

On a clear day, from Perugia's upper city, Assisi can be seen to the south, compact and gray against the mass of Mt. Subasio. Assisi has such charm that other towns might seem drab by comparison. This is high praise when you consider the enormous volume of tourists and pilgrims who visit the tiny city and its important shrines.

Although Assisi lived through a history very similar to that of its neighbor and bitter enemy, Perugia (in 1492 a Perugian army led by a Baglioni sacked Assisi), it is today completely associated with the cult of St. Francis. This saint and founder of the monastic order which bears his name was born in 1182, the son of a well-to-do cloth merchant. His young manhood gave no indication of the future development of his character, for he led the life of a 12th-century rake. The great change followed a serious illness which he contracted on his return from a spell in a Perugian jail, where he was held after capture in one of the frequent clashes between the two cities.

Francis became convinced that the root of all evil lay in the desire for possessions and in 1207 adopted a life of austere poverty. Believing that God's command to repair his church referred to the crumbling San Damiano outside the city walls, he sold his father's stock of cloth, but the priest refused to accept the proceeds. Francis returned the money when he realized that the command was a symbolic one and that the Church as a whole was meant. He started preaching and immediately attracted large numbers of followers into his fraternity of Minor Brothers. In 1212 he allowed a 17-year-old girl of noble family, the future St. Clare, to organize a convent of Poor Ladies at San Damiano.

Beloved and venerated throughout Italy, he accompanied the Fifth Crusade to Egypt in 1219, was received by the Sultan and given special permission to visit Jerusalem. On his return he resigned the leadership of his fraternity, but reserved himself the right to elaborate the rules of the order into which the universal brotherhood of love had to be transformed on the insistence of Pope Honorius III. St. Francis was extremely lucky to have been born at the time he was, had he come on the scene a few decades later he would certainly have been condemned as a heretic. As it was, the Franciscan movement was the last major revisionary philosophy to be received into the bosom of the Church. The simple tenets of the Franciscan Order of Mendicant Friars were those he had adopted for himself—poverty and asceticism combined with the duties of preaching and assisting the needy, in his time mainly the numerous lepers. The movement spread throughout Christendom and is today organized as Franciscans, Capuchins, Observants, Conventuals for men, and as Poor Clares for women.

Almost everything of importance to be seen in Assisi is in some way associated with the memory of the saint. The huge Basilica was started to honor him in the two years between his death in 1226 and his canonization. Originally, the land on which the church stands had served as the execution ground for condemned criminals and bore the suggestive title of Infernal Hill. St. Francis, in his humility, had asked to be buried there. His wish was granted, and by order of the Pope the name of the spot was changed to Hill of Paradise. Funds flowed in. The saint's great popularity brought many to work on his memorial without pay and the lower church was completed in the record time of 22 months. About 10 years later, the upper church and huge, double arched cloisters were added.

To prevent the saint's remains from being stolen, Francis' indefatigable successor, Brother Elias, who organized the building of the lower church, had the body removed to a secret vault cut in the living rock under the church. This tomb defied all attempts to locate it until 1818. Two flights below the floor of the lower church the visitor can see the coffin containing the body of the saint. The crypt is severely handsome, and its four corners hold the bodies of Francis' four closest followers.

Both the upper and lower churches, which together make up the big, two-level Basilica, are artistic treasurehouses. The lower level, dim and crypt-like on the brightest of days, is marvelously frescoed by master artists of several periods. The oldest of these paintings are classified as primitives and are attributed to a mid-13th-century artist, known only as the Master of St. Francis. Afterwards, at different times, Cimabue, Giottino (pupil of Giotto), Simone Martini, and Pietro Lorenzetti were commissioned to add to the glory of the building. Lorenzetti's fresco of the Virgin, Child Jesus, and St. Francis, to the left of the altar, is particularly sensitive and is considered to be one of the finest pieces produced by the Sienese School of that period (1330). To get the most pleasure from this visit a flashlight is invaluable.

To the left of the altar, in the sacristy, are preserved a number of relics of the saint. Among them are his patched, gray cassock, the cruel cord, made of camel hair and needles, which belted his waist, and the crude sandals which he wore when he received the Stigmata in 1224. The Stigmata, according to Roman Catholic belief, are the five wounds which Christ suffered at his crucifixion, and which can supernaturally appear on the body of an intense believer.

The top portion of the walls of the upper church are decorated with a number of frescos by unidentified artists, probably of the Roman school. More important are the 28 scenes from the life of St. Francis with which Giotto enriched the lower half of the walls of the nave. Beside the Basilica is a lovely cloister enclosing a small cemetery.

Assisi is well worth the stiff walk up Via San Francesco to the central Piazza del Comune, flanked by 13th-century palaces and the Roman Temple of Minerva, still used as a church. In the porphyry font of the Romanesque 12th-century Cathedral of St. Rufino, the draper's son was baptized

John, but was always called Francis according to the whim of his franco-phile father. Thirteen years later the most brilliant emperor of the century was held over the same font as its greatest saint. Frederick II had been born in a hastily erected tent at nearby Jesi.

The 13th-century basilica of St. Clare is most impressive in its simplicity. The saint's body, quite blackened by time, lies open to view in the crypt, while the closed cloisters of her followers adjoin the church. In a side chapel can be seen one of the most famous and best-loved crucifixes in the world. Before this cross St. Francis prayed and first recognized his mission, and later was to have his visions of Christ and the Virgin.

In contrast, just below the town the tiny Monastery of San Damiano is full of sunshine. Originally, the cross mentioned above hung in the chapel here. The Franciscan monk acting as guide will show you the little court where St. Francis wrote, the table where St. Clare performed a miracle, and the choir with its legends. It is an exquisite spot with a glorious view.

A road climbs Mount Subasio, offering magnificent panoramas above St. Francis' favorite retreat, the Eremo delle Carceri, located in a dense forest three miles behind the town. The formidable Papal stronghold built by Cardinal Albornoz in the 14th century also is worth a visit.

Below the town is the ostentatious, frescoed Santa Maria degli Angeli, built over the cell with its adjoining chapel, the Portiuncola, where St. Francis died. Nearby is the garden where, ever since the saint rolled among the roses while wrestling with temptation, the bushes have been thornless.

Leaving Assisi we turn first south via Foligno to Spoleto and Orvieto, then visit some other outstanding Umbrian cities.

Spoleto

Some 100 km. (62 miles) from Rome on the Via Flaminia, at the foot of Monteluco, Spoleto rises on the Sant' Elia hill, surrounded by a pleasant landscape which, in addition to its panoramic view, offers many opportunities for mountain and hillside excursions. Spoleto is a very old city, rich in evidence of the civilizations which succeeded one another there—from Umbrian through Roman, medieval, Renaissance to modern. Time has fused together the different periods within the town's ancient walls in an enchanting way. St. Francis, gazing at this area, said he had never seen anything as pleasing as the Spoleto valley (one of the most important autographs of the saint can be seen in the cathedral). Michelangelo stated that he found "true peace" among the oaks of Monteluco.

Among the most important and characteristic monuments in Spoleto are the fortress and the Ponte delle Torri, San Salvatore Basilica, the cathedral with Filippo Lippi frescos in the apse as well as the painter's funeral memorial, the Sant' Eufemia and San Pietro churches, the Roman theater and the Arch of Druso.

Spoleto has gained an added measure of fame with its Festival of Two Worlds, organized by Gian-Carlo Menotti. The festival presents the latest creative trends in art (music, theater, painting and sculpture) in the ancient setting of the town. Classical opera and concerts in the Piazza del Duomo are highlights of the festival. An exhibition of modern sculpture set up for the 1962 festival in Spoleto's streets and piazzas has remained as a permanent gift to the town.

If you are thinking of small tours in the area, we encourage you to go to Monteluco and to the Church of San Pietro. The Monteluco road passes right by San Pietro, whose foundations date back to the 5th century. Its 12th-century facade is adorned with remarkable Romanesque reliefs. At the top of thickly wooded Monteluco you'll find a tiny monastery founded by St. Francis with an enchanting view of the valley.

Orvieto

Of all the hill cities, Orvieto has the most spectacular situation. Whether you arrive by rail or road, the city breaks into view with astonishing impact and suddenness. As you roll up the valley or wind down the steep hills, before you, in the middle of the flat plain, stands the island of volcanic rock above whose brown cliffs the defense-minded Etruscans who founded Orvieto raised its walls. Like the *mesas* of the southwestern United States, the cliffs of this natural fortress rise sheer from the floor of the valley. Built of the same porous stone, Orvieto is now crumbling and slowly sinking into the rock on which it stands. Special metal braces shore up the cliff and it is planned to revive a cable railway from the railroad station to the town center.

On the hill top Orvieto is rather flat, so that the narrow, twisting streets and old houses lack the thrill of changing levels, so characteristic of the other cities. There are a number of first-rate attractions which make Orvieto worth a visit, but it has less of the power of transporting the visitor into the past than some other Umbrian towns.

Like Perugia, Orvieto has given its name to its most famous product, one of the best wines which Italy produces. Don't fail to try a glass of Orvieto at one of the wine shops in the cathedral square. Some of these wineshops have long, tunnel-like cellars, stretching under the square right up to the cathedral.

The cathedral itself, a magnificent 13th-century building of alternating stripes of black and white marble, is the pride of the city. It was designed by the Sienese architect Maitani (note the similarity with his other great work, the Cathedral of Siena) to commemorate the miracle at Bolsena. This event befell a priest who doubted the Doctrine of Transubstantiation while he was saying mass. The Host bled, proving that it really was part of Christ's body. Contrasting with the severe horizontal stripes of the sides, the facade is elaborately adorned with delicate sculpture and strikingly-colored mosaics of biblical scenes. To appreciate the full effect of its brilliant colors, the front should be seen in bright sunlight. The most important of these decorations are the bas-relief plaques which flank the cathedral's three doors. They are probably the work of Maitani and his pupils. Note the marvelous rose window over the door. The cathedral's modern bronze portals designed by Emilio Greco were hung in 1970 amid a raging controversy as to their artistic merit and appropriateness. The viewer can judge for himself whether or not they harmonize with the magnificent facade.

Inside there are some very interesting frescos. There is a *Virgin and Child* in the north aisle by Gentile da Fabriano (1426), a bit the worse for wear. The Corporal Chapel which lies off the north transept is dedicated to the miracle described above and is richly decorated, with a wonderful medieval reliquary containing the linen cloth of the Bolsena miracle, shown only at Easter and the Feast of Corpus Christi.

On the other side of the cathedral, through a great wrought-iron screen, lies the Chapel of San Brizio or the New Chapel. The frescos here were started by Fra Angelico and Benozzo Gozzoli and superbly finished by Signorelli. There are not that many works by Signorelli around and these are striking in the extreme. The subjects themselves catered to his sense of the dramatic—*The Preaching of the Antichrist,* with the portrait figures of himself and Fra Angelico down in one corner, *The End of the World,* and a *Resurrection of the Body,* with the corpses heaving themselves out of the ground. This work was supposed to have had a considerable effect on Michelangelo and to have provided him with inspiration for his Sistine wall, but it is a work of considerable imagination in its own right.

To the right of the Duomo stands the handsome Palace of the Popes, for Orvieto's impregnable position provided refuge for 32 pontiff sovereigns. It is now used as a museum and houses an oddly assorted collection of relics and pottery, church vestments, painting, woodwork, and sculpture. A small but interesting Etruscan Museum is right opposite the cathedral.

The city abounds in interesting monuments. The 11th-century Palazzo Vescovile, oldest papal residence, the 12th-century Palazzo del Capitano del Popolo, the churches of San Domenico, San Francesco, Sant' Andrea, with its impressive 12-sided bell tower, and the Church of San Giovenale are all among the best of the city's buildings. Near the ruins of the fortress, another of the chain of Papal strongholds set up by the castle-building Cardinal Albornoz, is the Well of St. Patrizio (St. Patrick). This remarkable engineering feat was commissioned by Pope Clement VII to ensure Orvieto's water supply in case of siege, and was finished in 1537 by Antonio Sangallo, who was busy as the architect of Rome's Palazzo Farnese at the same period.

The Smaller Cities

You will find that these lesser-known cities are close enough to one another to be conveniently visited without taking too much of your scheduled time.

A trip to Città di Castello, north of Perugia, is well worthwhile. During the city's three artistically rich centuries, the Cathedral, the churches of San Domenico and San Francesco, and the Vitelli Palace with works by Raphael and Signorelli, were built. Lovers of modern art shouldn't miss the recently opened Burri Museum.

We have already mentioned Gubbio, also to the north, in connection with the city's annual *Feast of the Candles.* This festival takes place on May 15, beginning with a picturesque procession through the streets from the town to the Abbey of Sant Ubaldo a mile away. The local people all wear period costume, giving it a charm rather like the Sienese *palio.* The festival itself centers around a race by three teams carrying huge candle-shaped wooden pillars, through the town and up a hill to the monastery. If you miss Festival time, there are plenty of reasons for visiting Gubbio anyway. The old part of the town, the Città Vecchia, is fascinating. There's a fast flowing river, the Camignano, to wander beside and, above, a splendid Gothic Consular Palace with a museum and art gallery. The 15th-century Ducal Palace was built of red brick and grey stone for Federigo da Montefeltro, Duke of Urbino—subject of a famous portrait by Mantegna—and has a very fine doorway, frescos and chimney pieces. From the Roman theater, going back to Augustus' time, you have a particularly fine view of the city.

To the south of Perugia, before you reach Foligno, make a stop at Spello to visit the ruins of Roman ramparts built under Augustus and to see Pinturicchio's paintings in Santa Maria Maggiore. They tell of the life of the Virgin in a delightfully fresh and lively way. There is another painting partly by him in Sant'Andrea.

You won't want to pass through Foligno without taking a look at the Piazza della Repubblica, or without having seen the Cathedral, the Communal Palace and the Palazzo Trinci, most of which houses an art gallery. Everything is conveniently located in the center.

Right next to Foligno is Montefalco, a city with an appropriate name (Falcon's Mount)—it really is the Balcony of Umbria. In the Church of San Francesco, and again in San Fortunato 1 km. out of town in the direction of Spoleto, you'll find frescos by Benozzo Gozzoli and work by other Umbrian painters. Beautifully situated, Montefalco is delightful not just for itself, but for the views of the surrounding countryside that it provides.

Narni is another ancient town high on a hill, from which its massive 14th-century fortress, commissioned by the ubiquitous Cardinal Albornoz, commands a thickly forested pass and the plain below. Narni's Romanesque cathedral and handsome medieval palace are a perfect backdrop for the gorgeously costumed pageant enacted each May, when horsemen representing the town's rival quarters joust for a coveted prize. Just below Narni are the ruins of the Roman bridge of Augustus which once spanned the River Nera.

There is much more to see in Umbria. Try to visit Todi and its Piazza de Popolo, truly an extraordinary grouping of excellent examples of the Gothic style. The cathedral (12th to 14th century) is Romanesque-Gothic, and it stands on the still older site of a former Roman temple.

Near Terni are the 500-foot waterfalls of Marmore which have drained the waters of the Velino into the Nera since 272 BC, but now flow only on Sundays and holidays, spectacularly illuminated at night. They may be closed temporarily because they are dangerously eroding the rocky masses along their course.

Citta della Pieve (the birthplace of Perugino), Gualdo Tadino, and Norcia are all worth seeing for the medieval splendor of their churches and palaces. At every turn in the road you will see imposing castles crowning green hills, and readily agree that no itinerary of Italy is complete without a visit to this lovely area.

PRACTICAL INFORMATION FOR UMBRIA

WHEN TO GO. As far as climate alone is concerned, it would be as well to avoid Umbria—a centrally located district with no cooling coast—during the main tourist season of July and August, for it can get very hot then, and stick to April, May or September. However, some of the main events of Umbria's chief tourist attraction, Assisi, occur in the middle of August, so if you want to take them in you have to endure the heat. But since all three of the principal tourist centers—Orvieto and Perugia, as well as Assisi—are well above 1,000 feet, the altitude does do something to help.

TOURIST OFFICES. Assisi: AAST, Piazza del Comune 27 (812.534). **Città di Castello:** AAST, Via Di Cesare 2b (855.4817). **Foligno:** AAST, Porta Romana

(60.459). **Gubbio:** AAST, Piazza Oderisi 6 (927.3693). **Orvieto:** AAST, Piazza Duomo 24 (41.772). **Perugia:** AAST, Via Mazzini 21 (25.431) and Corso Vannucci 94a (23.327). **Spoleto:** AAST, Piazza della Libertà 7 (28.111). **Terni:** AAST, Via Battisti 7 (43.047). **Todi:** AAST, Piazza del Popolo 38 (883.062).

SEASONAL EVENTS. Assisi: solemn processions mark Holy Week in Apr.; Apr. 30–May 1 sees the Calendimaggio Festival of medieval costume, music and flowers; Corpus Christi is observed in mid-Jun.; Jul. sees the Fest Musica Pro, a mainly modern music festival with international artists; on Aug. 1–2, the religious observance of the Feast of the Pardon; on Aug. 12, the Feast of St. Clare; finally, St. Francis is honored on his feast days of Oct. 3–4.

Citta di Castello: Aug. and Sept. see a chamber music festival.

Foligno: on the second Sun. in Sept. is the Quintana Tournament, with the wearing of special costume by the participants.

Gubbio: the Festa dei Ceri here takes place on May 15, and is a breakneck race of bearers carrying towering "candles"; the last Sun. of May is the occasion of a crossbow tournament, the Palio dei Balestrieri.

Narni: at end Apr./start May comes the Corsa all'Anello—the Ring Tournament—the culmination of ten days' special events and costumed pageantry.

Orvieto: mid-Jun. sees an impressive pageant in medieval costume.

Perugia: there is usually a jazz festival sometime in Jul.; and in Sept., the Sagra Musicale Umbra, a festival of sacred music, is held.

Spoleto: Mid-June to mid-Jul. sees the Festival of Two Worlds, the brainchild of Gian Carlo Menotti; while in Sept. there is an experimental lyric season.

Todi: Apr. is the occasion of a prestigious antiques fair.

TELEPHONE CODES. You will find the telephone area code for each town against its name in the Hotel and Restaurant listings (after the province name). If there is a different area code from the majority of the establishments—say when a hotel or restaurant is in an outlying place—then the code is given in front of the telephone number.

HOTELS AND RESTAURANTS. As one would expect with an area so popular with visitors, Umbria is well-equipped with hotels. Interestingly, many still consider it a bargain region, especially for restaurants, but it can fill up at a tremendous rate when such wing-dings as the Spoleto Festival are afoot. So if you are intending to visit when hotel space is likely to be at a premium, be sure to make your plans well in advance.

Regional Food and Drink. The most famous food specialty of Umbria is the truffle, best of which are found in the area around Norcia. Many regional dishes are given a touch of truffle before they're served. Local pasta, rather thick, homemade spaghetti, is called *ciriole* or *strengozzi.* Try it *al tartufo,* with a dressing of the excellent local olive oil and truffles. Umbrian pork products—all manner of *prosciutto, salame* and sausages—are known throughout Italy for their quality; naturally they are the mainstay of the regional cuisine. You'll find such dishes as *faraona alla leccarda,* roast guinea hen with a thick sauce of olives and herbs, and the renowned lentils of Castelluccio, unbelievably small.

Umbria's best know wine is the dry white *Orvieto. Torgiano* and *Rubesco* are fine local reds. Among the many as yet undiscovered wines of the region, those of *Sagrantino, Colli del Trasimeno* and *Assisi* are pleasant, as, indeed, are most of the unpretentious house wines produced by local growers for the region's restaurants.

Assisi Perugia (075). Birthplace and shrine of St. Francis. *Subasio* (E), Via Frate Elia 2 (812.206). Near Basilica; traditional; spacious; flowered terrace restaurant. AE, DC, MC, V. *Fontebella* (M), Via Fontebella 25 (812.883). 37 rooms, comfortable; excellent Frantoio Restaurant. AE, DC, MC, V. *Giotto* (M), Via Fontebella 41 (812.209). Open 15 March to 15 Nov. Overlooking valley, near Basilica; terrace restaurant. AE, DC, MC, V. *Dei Priori* (M), Via Mazzini 15 (812.237). Open 1 March to 10 Nov. Just off main piazza; small and pleasant. AE, DC, MC, V. *San Francesco* (M), Via San

Francesco 48 (812.281). Well-furnished, medium-sized hotel near Basilica. No restaurant. AE, DC, MC, V. *Umbra* (M), Vicolo degli Archi 6 (812.240). Open 15 Dec. to 14 Nov. Off main Piazza; quiet, comfortable. AE, DC, MC, V. *Minerva* (I), 28 rooms (812.416). *Roma* (I), Piazza Santa Chiara (812.390). 29 rooms. Both central.

At **S. Maria degli Angeli,** *Antonelli* (I), 105 rooms (819.572).

Restaurants. *Buca di San Francesco* (M), Via Brizi 1 (812.204). Closed Mon. and July. Atmospheric cellar restaurant; *spaghetti alla buca.* AE, DC, MC, V. *De Cecco* (M), Piazza San Pietro (812.437). Closed Tues. and 11 Dec. to 1 March. AE, DC, V. Good *trattoria. La Fontana-Da Carletto* (M), Via San Francesco 8 (812.933). Closed Tues. and Feb. Seasonal dishes, good house wine. DC, V. *La Fortezza* (M), Via della Fortezza (812.418). Closed Thurs. and Feb. Off Piazza Comune. Very good food. V. *Il Frantoio* (M), Via Fontebella 25 (812.977). Closed Fri. from Nov. to Mar. Various *pastas* and *risottos.* AE, DC, V. *Medioevo* (M), Via Arco dei Priori 4 (813.068). Closed Wed. Jan. to Feb; 20 June–10 July. Beautiful medieval setting, good food. *La Stalla* (M), Via Eremo della Carceri 8 (812.317). Closed Mon. Rustic setting with terrace. Try the local cheeses. *Taverna dell'Arco,* (M), Via San Gregorio 8 (812.383). Closed Tues. and Jan. Medieval surroundings; local dishes. AE, DC. *Umbra* (M), Via degli Archi 6 (812.240). Closed Tues. and 15 Nov. to 15 Dec. Tranquil spot, excellent dining. AE, DC, MC, V.

Citta di Castello Perugia (075). Fine buildings. *Tiferno* (M), Piazza Sanzio 13 (855.0331). Central, comfortable. Has excellent restaurant (M). Closed Sun. evenings and Mon. AE, DC, MC, V.

Foligno Perugia (0742). Interesting churches. **Restaurants.** *Da Giovanni* (M), Via Oberdan 1 (50.526). Closed Sun. Fine restaurant of *Hotel Posta;* game in season. AE, DC, V. *Da Remo* (M), Via Cesare Battista 49 (50.079). Closed Mon. Inventive variations on local cuisine.

Gubbio Perugia (075). Medieval art city, folklore center. *Cappuccini* (E), Via Cappuccini (922.241). Below town in secluded location, converted convent; attractively furnished rooms. AE, DC, MC, V. *Bosone* (M), Via Venti Settembre 22 (927.2008). Closed Feb. Near sights; meals at *Traverna del Lupo.*

At **Monteluiano,** 3 km. (2 miles) outside town on Via Buozzi, *Montegranelli* (M), (927.3372). Quiet country villa, lovely surroundings. MC, DC.

Restaurants. *Alla Balestra* (M), Via Repubblica 41 (927.3810). Closed Tues. and Feb. on central street; nice summer terrace. AE, DC, V. *Dei Consoli* (M), Via dei Consoli 59 (927.3335). Closed Wed. and Feb. Good choice. AE, DC, V. *Fornace di Mastro Giorgio* (M), Via Mastro Giorgio 2 (927.5740). Closed Mon. and Feb. Beautiful medieval setting; very good food, atmosphere. AE, DC, V. *Grotta dell' Angelo* (M), Via Gioia 47 (927.1747). Closed Tues. and Jan. 10 to Feb. 1. Friendly place, rustic specialties; reasonable. MC. *Porta di Tessenaca* (M), Via Baldassini 266 (927.2765). Closed Wed. Former stables of the Dukes of Urbino. Try the mixed grilled meats. AE, V. *Taverna del Lupo* (M), Via Ansidei 21 (927.4368). Closed Mon. and Jan. Handsome medieval locale, excellent *pastas,* grilled meat.

Norcia Perugia (0743). Medieval town. **Restaurants.** *Grotta Azzurra* (M), Via Alfieri 12 (816.513). Closed Tues. Original dishes, created by host; delicious truffled specialties are pricey. AE, DC, MC, V. *Posta* (M), Via Battisti 10 (816.274). Open every day. Hearty local cuisine; try *lenticchie* (lentils). AE, DC, MC, V.

Orvieto Terni (0763). Magnificent cathedral. *Aquila Bianca* (E), Via Garibaldi 13 (41.246). Central, traditional, well kept. No restaurant. AE, DC. *Maitani* (E), Via Maitani 5 (42.011). Opposite cathedral, solid comfort and service. AE, DC, MC, V. *Virgilio* (M), Piazza del Duomo 5 (41.882). On cathedral square, tiny and comfortable. AE, V.

At **La Badia,** below town, *La Badia* (E), (90.359). Exceptional ambiance in converted medieval monastery, beautifully furnished, many antiques; pool, tennis. AE, MC, V.

Restaurants. *Morino* (E), Via Garibaldi 37 (41.952). Closed Wed. and Jan. Best in town; excellent menu and selection of regional wines. AE, DC, MC, V. *Dell'Arcora* (M), Via di Piazza del Popolo 7 (42.766). Closed Thurs. and Jan. Central, good. AE, DC, MC, V. *Del Cocco* (M), Via Garibaldi 4 (42.319). Closed Fri. AE, DC, MC, V. *Maurizio* (M), Via del Duomo 78 (41.114). Closed Tues. Handy for cathedral. DC, MC, V. *San Giovenale* (M), Piazza San Giovenale (40.642). Closed Tues. Fine *trattoria.* AE, DC, MC, V. *Le Grotte del Funaro* (I), Via Ripa Serancia 41 (43.276). Closed Mon. Located deep in volcanic caves below the town; good traditional cooking. AE. *Wine cellar* (I), on Piazza del Duomo, right of Via del Duomo, for hearty sandwiches, cold *vino.*

Perugia Perugia (075). Art city. *Brufani Palace* (E), Piazza Italia 12 (62.541). Small, elegant, centrally located with fine views. AE, DC, MC, V. *Perugia Plaza* (E), Via Palermo 88 (34.643). Comfortable, well-equipped modern hotel in lower city. Good restaurant. Closed Mon. AE, DC, V. *La Rosetta* (M), Piazza Italia 19 (20.841). Central; old and new wings. Attractive restaurant. AE, DC, MC, V. *Il Grifone* (M), Via Silvio Pellico 1 (32.049). At heavily trafficed intersection on outskirts. Bright, modern. AE, DC, MC, V. *Palace Hotel Bellavista* (M), Piazza d'Italia 12 (20741). Shares palazzo address with Brufani; good range of prices. AE, DC, MC, V.

At **Corciano,** 12 km. (8 miles) outside Perugia, *Colle della Trinità* (M), at Fontana (79.548). Lovely surroundings.

Restaurants. *M.R.* (E), Via dei Priori 78 (21.889). Closed Sun. and Aug. Innovative menu changes with seasons. AE, DC, MC, V. *Ricciotto* (E), Piazza Dante (21.956). Closed Sun. and 15–30 July. Tasteful decor, refined menu. AE, DC, MC, V. *Bocca Mia* (M), Via Rocchi 36 (23.873). Closed Sun. *Falchetto* (M), Via Bartolo 20 (61.875). Closed Mon. Very good; try *falchetti,* spinach-*ricotta* dumplings. AE, DC, MC, V. *La Lanterna* (M), Via Rocchi 6 (66.064). Closed Sun. and 26 July to 20 Aug. Delicious local cuisine. AE, DC. *La Taverna* (M), Via delle Streghe 8 (61.028). Closed Mon. and 15–31 July. Long time favorite for homemade *pastas.* AE, DC, MC, V.

Spoleto Perugia (0743). Art and festival town. It is almost impossible to find hotel space during Festival in June–July. Book way ahead; try **Terni** hotels. *Gattapone* (E), Via del Ponte (36.147). Intimate. Suites with view. Book way ahead at all times. DC, MC, V. *Dei Duchi* (M), Viale Matteotti 4 (44.541). Attractive modern hotel, comfortable rooms with view. AE, DC, MC, V. *Manni* (I), Piazza Collicola 10 (38.135). Closed 10 Jan. to 15 Feb. Pleasant small hotel, near all sights. No restaurant. AE, DC, MC, V. *Nuovo Clitunno* (I), Piazza Sordini 8 (38.240). Central, attractive. DC, V.

On **Via Flaminia,** outside town, *Motel AGIP* (I), (49.340). **Restaurants.** *Dei Duchi* (E), Viale Matteotti 4 (44.541). Delightful hotel-restaurant; maintains high standards. AE, DC, MC, V. *Tartufo* (E), Piazza Garibaldi (40.236). Closed Wed. and 15 July to 5 Aug. Excellent fare, not all dishes expensive. AE, DC, MC, V. *La Barcaccia* (M), Piazza Fratelli Bandiera 3 (21.171). Closed Tues. and 6 to 25 Jan. In heart of old town; outdoor tables. AE, DC, MC. *Del Festival* (M), Via Brignone 8 (32.198). Closed Thurs. and Feb. Central, friendly; good local dishes at reasonable prices. *Panciolle* (M), Largo Muzio Clemente 4 (45.598). Closed Mon. Romantic setting in medieval quarter. AE, V. *Sabatini* (M), Corso Mazzini 52 (37.233). Closed Mon. and Jan. Attractive, good. *Pantagramma* (I), Via Martemi 4 (37.241). Closed Mon. No-frills restaurant with good pizza. AE, DC, V.

Terni Terni (0744). Administrative and industrial center. *Valentino* (E), Via Plinio 3 (55.246). Large modern hotel in center of town; comfortable rooms. AE, DC, MC, V. *De Paris* (M), Viale delle Stazione 52 (58.047). Central; no atmosphere but satisfactory comforts. No restaurant. AE, DC, MC, V. *Garden* (M), Viale Bramante 4 (43.846). On edge of town; attractive modern building, terraces, garden; good for motorists. AE, DC, MC, V.

Restaurants. *Alfio* (M), Via Galilei (420.120). Closed Sat. and Aug. Near Piazza Tacito, classic. *La Fontanella* (M), Via Plinio 3 (55.246). Closed Mon. Fine restaurant of *Valentino Hotel;* varied menu. DC, MC, V. *Tre Colonne* (M), Via del Plebiscito 13 (54.511). Closed Mon. and Aug. Warm atmosphere, offers local specialties. DC.

Todi Perugia (075). Picturesque medieval town. *Bramante* (M), Via Orvietana (884.8382). Closed Jan. Outside town, handsome old building, modern comforts. AE, DC.

Restaurants. *Umbria* (E), Via San Bonaventura 13 (882.737). Closed Tues. and Dec.–Jan. Under arches just off main piazza, small and excellent; terrace with marvelous view. *Jacopone-da Peppino* (M), Piazza Jacopone 5 (882.366). Closed Mon. and July. Rustic, good local dishes.

Torgiano Perugia (075). 10 miles (15 km) outside Perugia. *Le Tre Vaselle* (E), (982.447). A *Relais* hotel; comfortable rooms and courteous service in country villa. Outstanding restaurant, one of Italy's best for original interpretations of Italian cuisine. Recommended when not crowded with business meetings and banquets. AE, DC, MC, V.

Trevi Perugia (0742). Hill town. **Restaurants.** *Cochetto* (M), Via Dogali 13 (78.229). Closed Tues. Popular place in town; veranda with view; good local specialties, especially truffles; crowded on Sun. and holidays. AE, DC, MC. *L'Ulivo* (M), (78.969). Closed Mon., Tues., except in summer. Just outside town; rustic. AE, DC.

GETTING AROUND. By air. There is no airport in the region. The nearest is at Rome.

By train. Train travel is complicated by the necessity to change trains in order to reach Perugia. The main line runs from Rome to Orte (coming from Florence you have to change trains at Orte), proceeding on to Terni and then eastward to Spoleto, Foligno and on to Ancona. For Assisi and Perugia you must change trains at Foligno. There's another, secondary line to Perugia from Terni via Todi. Orvieto, on the main Rome—Florence line is served by frequent trains. Umbrian stations are usually some distance from the towns they serve. Where this is the case, a regular bus service takes you into town. Bus tickets are often available at the station bar.

By bus. There is a good local bus service between towns, with terminals in all the main centers.

By car. The average tourist takes in Umbria only on his way between Rome and Florence, which allows for seeing Assisi and Perugia on one route and Orvieto on another. Traveling by automobile, it is possible—by being slightly more than an average map-reader and making some zigzags—to include all three, plus Viterbo, in one trip from Rome to Florence. This would add around 80 miles to the journey, compared with the direct routes, but provide some 250 miles of superb scenic and cultural value. It would be a shame to do the trip too quickly.

CAMPANIA

Naples, Pompeii and the Romantic Isles

Campania is a region of names to conjure with—Capri, Sorrento, Pompeii, Paestum—names evoking visions of cliff-shaded coves and sun-dappled waters, of mighty ruins, golden in the sunset. And Naples, a tumultuous, animated city, the very heart of Campania, stands guard over these treasures.

Campania stretches south in flat coastal plains and low mountains from Baia Domizia, Capua and Caserta to Naples and Pompeii on the magnificent bay, past Capri and Ischia down along the rocky coast to Sorrento, Amalfi and Salerno, and farther still past the Cilento promontory to Sapri and the Calabria border. Inland lie the bleak fringes of the Apennines and the rolling countryside around Benevento.

On either side of Naples, the earth fumes and grumbles, reminding natives and visitors alike that all this beauty was born of cataclysm. Toward Sorrento, Vesuvius smolders sleepily over the ruins of Herculaneum and Pompeii, while north of Naples, beyond Posillipo, the craters of the Solfatara spew steaming gases. And nearby are the dark, deep waters of Lake Averno, legendary entrance to Hades.

With these reminders of death and destruction so close at hand, it's no wonder that the southerner in general, and the Neapolitan in particular, chooses to take no chances, plunging enthusiastically into the task of living each moment to its fullest.

Here in the Campania you will find a way of life which will seem at first to be nothing more than *dolce far niente* but which is actually not that at all. It is rather the inextinguishable belief that the art of living lies

323

in enjoying what surrounds you, not passively, but with enthusiasm—the sun, a glass of wine, a conversation, a traffic jam.

Conquerors and Sybarites

Campania was probably settled by the ancient Phoenicians, Cretans and Greeks. Traces of their presence here date back to approximately 1,000 B.C., some 300 years before the legendary founding of Rome.

Herculaneum is said to have been established by the great Hercules himself and, as excavation of this once great city—Greek, and later Roman—progresses, further light will be thrown on the history of the whole Campania region.

The origin of Naples, once called Parthenope and later Neapolis, presumably can be traced to what are now the ruins of Cumae nearby, which legend tells us was already in existence in 800 B.C.

Greek civilization flourished for hundreds of years all along this coastline, but there was nothing in the way of centralized government until centuries later when the Roman Empire, uniting all of Italy for the first time, surged southward and absorbed the Greek colonies with little opposition.

The Romans were quick to appreciate the sybaritic possibilities of such a lovely land and it was in this region that the wealthy of the Empire built their palatial country residences. Generally the peace of the Campania was undisturbed during these centuries of Roman rule.

Naples and the Campania, with the rest of Italy, decayed with the Roman Empire and collapsed into the abyss of the Middle Ages. Naples itself regained some importance again under the rule of the Angevins in the latter part of the 13th century, and continued its progress later—in the 1440s—under Aragon rule.

The nobles who served under the Spanish viceroys in the 16th and 17th centuries, when their harsh rule made all Italy quail, enjoyed their pleasures, and the more luxurious points in the Campania began to look up. Taverns and gaming houses thrived. Business boomed, in spite of the tyranny of Spain—which, it must be added, milked the area with its taxes.

After a short-lived Austrian occupation, Naples became the capital of the Kingdom of the Two Sicilies, which the Bourbon kings established in 1738. Their rule was generally benevolent as far as Campania was concerned, and their support of the Papal authority in Rome was an important factor in the historical development of the rest of Italy. Their rule was important artistically, for not only did it contribute greatly to the architectural beauties of the region but it attracted scores of great musicians, artists and writers, who were only too willing to enjoy the easy life of court in such magnificent natural surroundings.

Finally Garibaldi launched his famous expedition, and in 1860 Naples was united with the rest of Italy.

Times were relatively tranquil through the years which followed—with tourists of one nation or another thronging to Capri, to Sorrento, to Amalfi and of course to Naples—until World War II. Allied bombings did considerable damage in Naples and the bay area. At the fall of the Fascist government, the sorely-tried Neapolitans rose up against Nazi occupation troops and in four days of street fighting drove them out of the city. A monument to the *Scugnizzo*—the typical Neapolitan street urchin—celebrates the youngsters who participated in the battle.

The war ended. Artists, tourists, writers and ordinary lovers of beauty began to flow again into that Campania region which one ancient writer called "most blest by the Gods, most beloved by man." As the years have gone by, some parts have gained increased attention from the smart visitors, some have lost the cachet that they had. The balance is maintained, with a steady trend to more and more tourist development. The main tourist centers—the islands and the Sorrento and Amalfi coasts—were practically untouched by the 1980 earthquake, which shook Naples' already precarious housing situation into a desperate state. Elsewhere in the region there was terrible devastation which can still be seen.

Naples, the Heart of Campania

The best view of Naples is that from the sea, and since you'll surely take the steamer to Capri or Ischia sometime during your stay, you'll have a chance to absorb that breathtaking coastline, dominated by the lowering slopes of ever-threatening Vesuvius.

For a different perspective on the city and its surroundings, take a bus, taxi or funicular up to the Vomero, Naples' modern residential district on a hillside to the west, where the Certosa di San Martino, described below, is an excellent vantage point. Down to the left is Naples, with its gently curving shoreline, docks and palm-lined, sea-side avenues. Far below is the Castel Nuovo (1282) of Charles I of Anjou, its severe and primitive shape contrasting sharply with the Hohenstaufen's Castel dell'Ovo (1154), nearby, and with the far more modern buildings near it. Look along the bay. There is the busy port and, on the shore beyond, the industrial zone. There is the beginning of the autostrada to Pompeii and Salerno, flanked by heavily built-up and tacky suburbs that hide the ruins of Herculaneum. Beyond is Pompeii and Vesuvius itself, a thin wisp of smoke curling over its momentarily tranquil peak.

Back along the shore, there is Castellamare, where the coast road breaks off to the right to climb to the Plain of Sorrento. You can't see the road as it winds around those hillsides in the dim distance but you can see the vague outlines of little towns, and if your eyes are very, very keen you can see Sorrento itself, perched high up on the cliff-side almost opposite you.

To your left the coast vanishes in a sharp point quite close to a mountainous little islet which seems to spring from the sea itself. That is Capri. In the dim distance is the Mediterranean—center of the earth to the pagan world. Ischia is probably a little out of sight to your right, as are Pozzuoli and Cumae.

Exploring Naples

To visit Naples you need patience, stamina and caution. Short-lived city administrations have been ineffectual in the face of acute unemployment and housing problems; the result is delinquency and urban decay. Still, two of Naples' chief attractions remain unchanged: its people and its beautiful views.

To see people you don't need to go anywhere in particular. Just wander through the streets, down along Via Toledo, through the Umberto Gallery, or down the Riviera di Chiaia and along the lovely waterfront drive, or even up or down any of the little side streets which wander off in all directions. Keep your sense of humor, keep a tight grip on anything you may be carrying, watch your pocketbook, remember that if you get lost

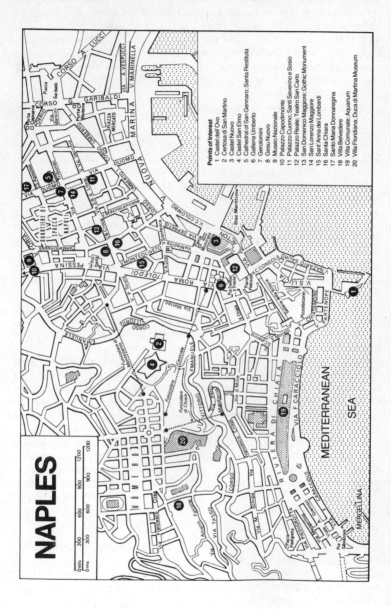

NAPLES

0 yds 300 600 900 1200
0 ms 300 600 900 1200

Points of Interest

1 Castel dell'Ovo
2 Certosa di San Martino
3 Castel Nuovo
4 Castel San Elmo
5 Cathedral of San Gennaro; Santa Restituta
6 Galleria Umberto
7 Gerolomini
8 Gesù Nuovo
9 Museo Nazionale
10 Palazzo Capodimonte
11 Palazzo Cuomo; Santi Severino e Sosio
12 Palazzo Reale; Teatro San Carlo
13 San Domenico Maggiore; Gothic Monument
14 San Lorenzo Maggiore
15 Sant'Anna dei Lombardi
16 Santa Chiara
17 Santo Maria Donnaregina
18 Villa Belvedere
19 Villa Comunale; Aquarium
20 Villa Floridiana; Duca di Martina Museum

MEDITERRANEAN

SEA

you can always get back to the waterfront by going in the general direction of Vesuvius, and then enjoy yourself. A lot of that enjoyment will come from just watching the Neapolitans, who are among the most spontaneous, volatile people on earth.

For a fine view of the city and bay go to the Certosa di San Martino. It's the Carthusian monastery up on the slopes of the Vómero, perhaps the finest example of the typically Neapolitan Baroque, which now contains the Museum of San Martino. In addition to being known for its priceless works of art and for its relics of the Kingdom of Naples, it is noted for having the balcony which affords that incomparable view of the city and bay. On your way out this time take a good look at the typically Neapolitan *presepi* (cribs), which are to all Italian, but particularly Neapolitan, children what the Christmas tree is to ours. There's even more here we enthusiastically recommend. The Monk's Choir is a joyous Baroque work you must see. Go through the audit-room to reach it. And from the Floridiana Villa, on the rim of Vómero, you have the whole panorama before you, as well as the villa's gardens with their camellias, and indoors the Duca di Martina Museum of porcelain, ivory and enamels.

You will want to return to the Castel Nuovo, on the Piazza del Municipio, facing the harbor. Its massive bulk dominates the scene and is, for all, a focal point of interest. It was built in 1282 for Charles I of Anjou and has been restored to its original form although it was reconstructed in 1452 for Aragon's Alfonso I. Note especially the Arco di Trionfo, on the west side, between two of the three towers. It dates from 1467 and is generally considered one of the best pieces of the Italian Renaissance. It is richly ornamented with bas-reliefs and is credited to Francesco Laurana.

The sprawling Palazzo Reale on the Piazza del Plebiscito dates from the 17th century. Sumptuously furnished, it houses in addition to many extremely rare tapestries and paintings, the National Library, with its treasures of incunabula. The Piazza Plebiscito itself dates from the brief reign of Napoleon's puppet king, Murat. Canova carved the statues Ferdinand and Charles III of Bourbon you see in the center of the square.

No tour of Naples would be complete without a visit to the National Archeological Museum, on Piazza del Museo. Notable are the many sculptures, paintings, bronzes and both decorative and utilitarian pieces from Herculaneum and Pompeii. In addition, Greek and Roman sculpture at their finest are found there—note especially the *Aphrodite* attributed to Praxiteles, the *Farnese Bull,* the *Drunken Satyr,* from the House of the Faun in Pompeii, the *Drunken Silenus* and the *Narcissus,* from a Praxiteles original. Recent renovations and increased attention from the authorities have made the museum much pleasanter than it used to be.

The Capodimonte Gallery specializes in the Italian school from the 14th through the 16th centuries. Titian, Botticelli, Raphael, Giovanni Bellini and Mantegna are wonderfully represented as are some of the most outstanding of the Flemish school, such as Breughel and Joos van Cleve. El Greco and Velazquez, of the Spanish school, are also included in the tremendous scope of this museum's masterpieces. The museum itself is a marvel of display techniques, perfectly lighted and well arranged, with all works clearly labeled. Its collections of porcelain and armor are worth a visit. Don't miss the view from the roof-terrace.

Naples's San Carlo Theater is of course one of the most famous opera houses in the world, as indeed well it might be in view of its location in a region renowned for *bel canto*. From its stage have come many of the most famous of the world's singers and its productions of the great Italian operas can be favorably compared with those of the Metropolitan, La Scala and Covent Garden.

Naturally the city has its share of Gothic, Renaissance and Baroque churches on antique foundations. The Cathedral of San Gennaro was erected in 1300 over the ruins of an earlier church dating back to the 5th century, which in turn was built over a Temple of Caesar. Attached to the left nave is Santa Restituta, which preserves under its Baroque decorations the fourth-century basilica plan. Santa Chiara, once favored by the court and the aristocracy, has been restored to its original Gothic-Provencal style. Visit the pretty cloister, decorated with lovely tiles (due to be restored) and cross to see the Baroque Church of Gesù Nuovo, opposite.

Santi Severino e Sosio, with a 16th-century wooden choir; the Church of the Gerolimini, with its frescos and paintings of the 17th and 18th-century Neapolitan school; Santa Maria Donnaregina, with the tomb of Queen Mary of Hungary, dating from 1326; and San Domenico Maggiore, with Gothic arches from the 14th century, are probably the best of the Neapolitan churches. Others have paintings, frescos or architecture well worth a visit—but only if you have sufficient leisure.

You can't leave Naples without going into the very heart of the old city, crowded bustling Spacca. Especially since you will be able to see more fine old works as you rub elbows with the Neapolitans. Take a look at the crumbling palaces on the Via San Biagio ai Librai; then turn into Via San Gregorio Armeno and wander along Via dei Tribunali, past the Baroque Church of San Pietro a Maiella, continuing on to Port'Alba and Via Roma.

Exploring Campania

Once you have discovered Naples you must begin wandering afield. Take a car if you can afford it or if you happen to have one of your own. If you have no car, no matter. Trains, trams and buses abound. Because of its traffic and delinquency problems and dearth of adequate hotels we cannot recommend Naples as a base for visiting the region; use the coastal resorts instead.

The SITA company runs half-day bus tours of this area. CIT offers a half-day tour to Pompeii or a full-day tour that also takes in Amalfi and Sorrento. There are full-day CIT tours to Capri or Ischia.

Before starting to explore the coastal region, there is one town inland that should not be missed, especially if you like the more impressive Roman monuments. Benevento is 68 km. (42 miles) east and has a magnificent Arch of Trajan, built around 114 A.D., well-preserved and with its carved details much easier to scan than those of similar remains that have been eroded by metropolitan pollution. There are other interesting things in town, too. A huge Roman theater, the work of Hadrian and Caracalla, and the delicious liqueur, known throughout Italy and beyond—*Strega*.

An exploration of the coast to the west of Naples could start at Posillipo, the long promontory separating the Bay of Pozzuoli from the Bay of Naples. Go out by the Via Acton, through the Santa Lucia quarter, past the Castel dell'Ovo, along Via Partenope and the Via Caracciolo to Mergellina. By bus or car, climb to the belvedere in the small park atop Posillipo, fashionable residential section.

On the other side of Posillipo are the smoky desolation of Bagnoli's steel mills, and Pozzuoli. This whole region is of volcanic origin and even in ancient days the spas of Agnano Terme and Bagnoli were well known. Solfatara still emits sulphur-charged steam jets from various apertures in the earth's crust, and sounds ominously underground. The Temple of Serapis at Pozzuoli proper also shows signs of volcanic activity. On the three columns that remain standing you can see the ancient highwater mark; the earth's crust is still rising in the Pozzuoli area. Other Roman ruins abound in the region.

An ancient doorway to Hell is just 4 km. (2½ miles) from Pozzuoli. The Lago d'Averno, a huge crater, was believed to be the direct entrance to Hades. In fact, the whole region is fraught with legend. Not far away is the Mare Morto of ancient Romans, who identified it as the Stygian Lake of the Dead, where Charon ferried souls across to the underworld. Near Lake Averno, too, is a spring which was thought to flow directly from the Styx, and it was there that Aeneas descended into Hades with the guidance of the Cumaean Sibyl. The original Styx, of course, is a river in southern Greece.

This Sibyl lived not far from Averno, just around the shores of the lake and past the oyster beds, famed among ancient gourmets. Cumae was among the first Greek colonies in the Neapolitan region, and there is no doubt whatever that the Cave of the Cumaean Sibyl existed. It still does. It is an enormous gallery, some 107 meters (350 ft.) long, opening into a chamber where the Sibyl uttered her prophecies.

The Cumaean Acropolis is on a lava hill near the sea overlooking the lower part of the city. It's famous not only for the Sibyl but for remains of a temple to Apollo on a lower walk-way, for Jupiter's temple above it, a Greek cistern, an octagonal fountain-basin, ruins of a Christian basilica, and another glorious view of the Cape of Miseno and the Gulf of Gaeta. An unanswered question is whether Cumae was the original Naples in the 8th century B.C. or if even older Greek colonies hadn't already preceded it. Before you leave the area, stop at Arco Felice, erected under the Emperor Domitian. The 20-meter-high (65-ft.) brick archway is on the road between Cumae and Averno.

Herculaneum

Parts of Herculaneum and Pompeii are closed to visitors for restoration or further excavation. Note that all archeological sites are closed on Mondays and some Sundays; we give some useful details about entry in the *Practical Information* section at the end of the chapter as at presstime, but we advise you to check with the EPT for any updating.

Hercules himself is said to have founded Herculaneum, which became a famous watering resort for the Roman elite after passing through periods of Greek and Samnite domination. It was damaged by an earthquake in 63 A.D. Then, 16 years later, the gigantic eruption of Vesuvius in the year 79 buried it completely under a tide of mud and lava. Casual excavation was begun early in the 18th century, but nothing was done properly until Mussolini ordered systematic excavation in 1927.

Then it was found that the sea of mud and lava that was roughly 35 feet deep had so seeped into the crevices and niches of every building as to shut out the air and preserve their contents even better than those of Pompeii, much of which were broken or burned by the hot cinders which rained onto that city.

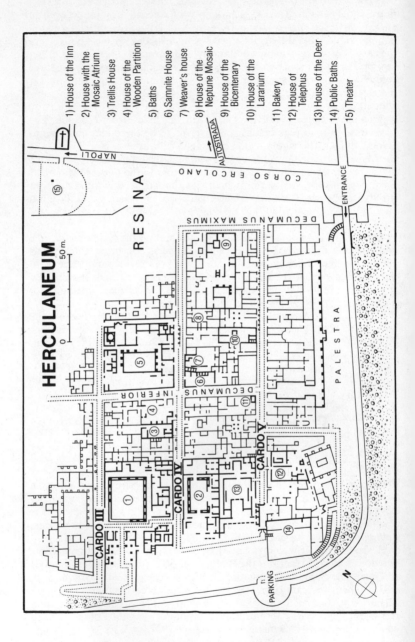

HERCULANEUM

0　　　　　50 m.

1) House of the Inn
2) House with the Mosaic Atrium
3) Trellis House
4) House of the Wooden Partition
5) Baths
6) Samnite House
7) Weaver's house
8) House of the Neptune Mosaic
9) House of the Bicentenary
10) House of the Lararium
11) Bakery
12) House of Telephus
13) House of the Deer
14) Public Baths
15) Theater

RESINA

NAPOLI

CORSO ERCOLANO

AUTOSTRADA

ENTRANCE

DECUMANUS MAXIMUS

DECUMANUS INFERIOR

CARDO III

CARDO IV

CARDO V

PALESTRA

PARKING

N

Naturally, most of the magnificent relics of Herculaneum and of Pompeii are now ensconced in museums throughout the world, but more than enough remains to fascinate any visitor endowed with even the smallest amount of imagination. Here, sealed and preserved for us for close on 2,000 years, are the traces of a glorious and distinctly carefree past.

There were stoves and pots to cook in; styled walls and porticos and mural paintings, tapestries and brocades and hangings and clothes; gold, silver, bronze and brass ornaments and decorations. Metal-workers must have abounded. So did sculptors and painters and housebuilders, and wine-shops and baths and prostitutes and even thieves. There is the tale, perhaps apocryphal, of a discovery made in 1932, when excavators found two perfectly preserved bodies. One, apparently a wealthy patrician, lay on his face. Beside him lay the second, his hand in the patrician's money bag. Death caught him red-handed.

Experts say that when Herculaneum is finally completely excavated it will shed much more light on Roman life during imperial times than any other remains unearthed so far. Here there is more of a sense of a living community than Pompeii is able to convey. If your time is short, you will likely get more out of a visit here than to Pompeii.

Pompeii

Pompeii was much larger than Herculaneum, 20,000 inhabitants as against an estimated 5,000, and excavations have progressed to a much greater extent. It seems to have been to some extent a pleasure resort, judging from the number of hotels, restaurants and bars.

Particularly to be noted in Pompeii are the decorative mural designs of four periods, including some of the finest and oldest thus far discovered. After close to 2,000 years their colors, even in the open-air *atria,* inner courtyards, retain their brilliance, the shade known as "Pompeian red."

You can reach the excavations at Pompeii easily by the Circumvesuviana, and you can have a pleasant lunch at the restaurant-cafeteria near the Forum, and make a rewarding short detour to see the exceptional frescos at the Villa dei Misteri. Buy a detailed guidebook before you set out, complete with a map of the excavations. You'll get a good idea of how a provincial Roman city really lived. This one was generously endowed with an extensive forum, lavish temples and baths, patrician villas, and a thriving commercial district whose walls still carry political advertisements and notices.

Guide or no guide, you will be confronted with endless locked gates. Only a very few of these conceal Pompeian pornography, which appears quite innocent in these days of hard porno movies. Italy's chronic carelessness about its great archeological heritage is evident at Pompeii; the ruins are overgrown with weeds, and much is closed off. Streets and individual monuments are fairly well marked; guards on duty at the most important villas will unlock their gates for you, insisting on explaining their sights and, naturally, expecting a tip for this often unrequested service (have a supply of 100 and 500 lire coins on hand for this purpose). Until the administrators of the Pompeian excavations show some imagination in assisting tourists and policing the guards, much of the fascination and interest of Pompeii will be lost in exasperation. When you hire a guide, agree on the fee (for 2 hours) in advance, then write down the time you start, showing the time to him. He will try to slow you down if you want only a 2-hour

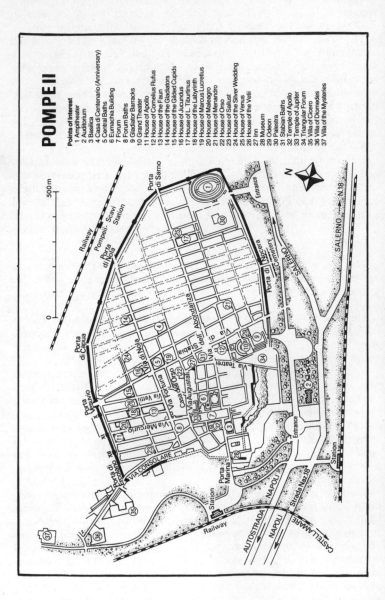

POMPEII

Points of Interest

1 Amphitheater
2 Auditorium
3 Basilica
4 Casa di Centenario (Anniversary)
5 Central Baths
6 Eumachia Building
7 Forum
8 Forum Baths
9 Gladiator Barracks
10 Grand Theater
11 House of Apollo
12 House of Cornelius Rufus
13 House of the Faun
14 House of the Gladiators
15 House of the Gilded Cupids
16 House of Jucundus
17 House of L. Tiburtinus
18 House of the Labyrinth
19 House of Marcus Lucretius
20 House of Maleagro
21 House of Menandro
22 House of Orso
23 House of Sallust
24 House of the Silver Wedding
25 House of Venus
26 House of the Vetii
27 Inn
28 Museum
29 Odeon
30 Palestra
31 Stabian Baths
32 Temple of Apollo
33 Temple of Jupiter
34 Triangular Forum
35 Villa of Cicero
36 Villa of Diomedes
37 Villa of the Mysteries

tour, then charge you for an extra 2 hours the moment the first 2 hours has elapsed. But he will do this always with a smile.

One of the most recent and interesting finds was at Oplontis, just outside Pompeii. This sidetrip is worth making, if only to see the frescos and protective methods that are being adopted for their preservation.

Vesuvius

You may want to see Vesuvius itself, the cause of all this ruin and, as a concomitant, of all this preservation. It looms stark and black above Herculaneum and Pompeii and the populous modern towns that send risky propagations straggling up its lower slopes, where vineyards and orchards grow on fertile volcanic soil. Higher up its aspect is dramatically desolate. Actually, Vesuvius has two peaks, Mt. Somma (1,132 meters, 3,713 ft.) and Vesuvius proper (1,277 meters, 4,189 ft.). The chair lift (Seggiovia) that used to go up to the top has been closed indefinitely. Excursions on foot start from the Seggiovia station, which you reach by car from the Ercolano exit on the Naples–Salerno highway or by Circumvesuviana railway and bus (take a local train to the Ercolano stop; from here scheduled buses, infrequent in off-season, take you up to the Seggiovia station). Hawkers and souvenir vendors here are particularly bothersome. The main route up the west side involves a 20-minute walk by the slippery lava. The other approach from the south side by car involves a toll road and a steep climb on foot. Wear sturdy, closed shoes.

However you arrive at the crater, you must pay about 2,000 lire for a compulsory guide, who warns you of the sheer drop from the edge, not the place if you suffer from vertigo. On a clear day you will have an unparalleled view of the Bay of Naples and the Campania countryside.

Caserta and Capua

Caserta and Capua, about 32 km. (20 miles) north of Naples, are worth looking at if you happen to be proceeding either north or south by car, if you are a student of history, a garden fan, or if you are particularly interested in seeing the headquarters of the Allied High Command during World War II. These headquarters were established in the Royal Palace at Caserta late in 1943 and remained there until 1947.

The palace was built by Vanvitelli in 1752 for the Bourbon kings of Naples and Sicily and was intended to be more grandiose and beautiful than Versailles. It is not. Its gardens and fountains, though, are lovely, as are the somewhat tacky palace itself, the theater, the chapel and the so-called royal apartments. The town of Caserta is a dead loss.

Capua is only a few miles west of Caserta and is now just a little market village, with the ruins of its ancient wall and amphitheater which date to pre-Roman times. To the student of history this sleepy little town is fascinating. Here the Samnites made their most determined stand against the Roman legions moving southward. Here, a little later, those same Samnites, with Carthaginian and Greek aid, rebelled against Roman rule during the Carthaginian wars. Here Hannibal camped for one entire year while he waited for aid from home and while Rome mustered the strength to defeat him.

Still later, Rome established here a great school for gladiators, the school which produced the famous slave gladiator Spartacus, who led a revolt of slaves and gladiators and made Capua his fortress for two years, defying all of Rome.

Nothing remains of all of this except a museum with interesting archeological relics, including the impressive series "The Mothers", 200 votive statues, and a Temple of Mithras where Spartacus prayed for aid against the Roman Senate.

But go back south—rapidly—avoiding as much as possible the sights and scents between either Capua or Caserta and Naples. Roads from either town pass through the sordid slum fringes of Naples.

Along the Bay of Naples

From Naples you can get a fast train to Sorrento, and as the coast from Naples to Torre del Greco is depressingly industrialized, you may be wise to do so. There are some lovely views of the bay from the Naples–Pompeii superhighway, though, and you may want to take a look at Castellammare di Stabia, now a grubby, overbuilt port.

Castellammare—known then as Stabia—existed, perhaps, before Pompeii. Pliny the Elder had his villa there. Like Pompeii, it was destroyed by the eruption of Vesuvius in 79 A.D., but unlike Pompeii, it was rebuilt almost immediately because of its magnificent setting as a country residence for the wealthy. Incidentally, its volcanic spring water was noted even then for its health-giving qualities.

To Sorrento

From Castellammare to Sorrento your drive curves precipitously through tiny towns, masses of flowering trees and bushes, orange and olive groves, down onto the Sorrento plain, a vast perfumed garden on a natural terrace high above the Bay of Naples. Here, certainly, you will want to linger for a time. Emperors and kings, popes, the greatest musicians, writers and artists, have made Sorrento their preferred abode for more than 2,500 years. And one look at the view will tell you why, although the town has become over-touristy.

Once again be sure to get a room overlooking the bay. Far down the sheer cliff on which you are perched is the crystal-clear blue water. Directly opposite and far across is Naples at its best, gleaming distantly in the brilliant sun. Off to the left, seeming only a stone's throw from the headland, is Capri, and Vesuvius lowers in the background at the base of the bay far down to the right.

At the foot of the cliff there is a little harbor, Piccolo Sant' Angelo, where the boats dock and where fishermen mend their nets. Nearby, there is a small beach from which bathers swim in water that is so high in salt content that it is next to impossible to sink.

At Punta del Capo are the ruins of Villa Pollius, beautifully situated on the shoals. The tiny islets are the Isles of the Mermaids, famed in mythology, and all of the grottos which abound along the cliffside are called the Grottos of the Mermaids, since from time immemorial these waters have been the true habitat of those fabled beings.

The Amalfi Drive

From Sorrento, when you resume your trip, you'll continue along the Amalfi Drive, around the Campanella Point—so close to Capri—and along the Gulf of Salerno. If you are going to be driving your own car, we should warn you that this is a tortuous road, writhing its way along the coast, past caverns, little inlets, cliffs and gardens, curving sharply every 20 feet, and you will miss some stunning views.

Positano, a delightful fishing village now dedicated exclusively to tourism, slopes picturesquely down to the sea and its pebbly beach. Once hailed as the "the poor man's Capri," because it had become the haunt of writers, artists, sculptors and other impoverished appreciators of beauty, it has shared the fate of other discoveries of the artistic and is overrun by wealthier visitors, who have taken over what the artists found. It's known for its colorful fashion boutiques.

A little farther along is Praiano, a rocky little village, the Conca di Marini and, just a short distance more, Amalfi, first of the sea republics and for centuries one of the great cities of Italy. Today it is a small though noted residential resort, but in the Middle Ages its population was close to 100,000. In the 11th and 12th centuries it was a sturdy rival of Genoa and Pisa for control of the Mediterranean.

Tidal waves account in great part for Amalfi's decline, if it can be called decline. The sea there is by no means always so calm as it appears. The town straggles up the Lattari slope, but much of it once was down along the sea. In 1073 a tidal wave washed most of it away, destroying every ship in the bay. The palace of the archbishop, moderately high up the slope, vanished. Again in 1343, Petrarch tells us, the sea devoured the town, and in comparatively recent times, in 1924, it was damaged again.

The same sea which brought repeated disasters to Amalfi also carved out a beautiful grotto, known as the Grotta dello Smeraldo for the emerald light which filters through the seawater to play upon strangely shaped stalactites and stalagmites. It can be reached by elevator from the Positano–Amalfi road, but a trip to it by boat along the coast from Amalfi offers marvelous views of towering mountains and lush villas.

One fabulous remnant of Amalfi's past remains; the cathedral, towering at the top of a long stairway, its height above the sea having often been its salvation. Here in this one edifice are united Moorish, Greek, Lombard, Norman and early Gothic architectural styles in a harmonious whole. It was built in 1203, remodeled in the 18th century and contains the body of Sant'Andrea (St. Andrew), the brother of St. Peter, brought from Constantinople early in the 13th century to rest in the crypt. On 30 November, his feast day, a miracle is said to occur occasionally, when the *Manna di Sant'Andrea,* an oily liquid, oozes from his tomb.

The Cloister of Paradise in the cathedral and the cloisters in the Hotel Luna and the Hotel Cappuccini, both former monasteries, are of Moorish origin, too, and date likewise from the 13th century.

The Church of Atrani, a bit farther along the road, has bronze doors as beautiful as those of the cathedral in Amalfi. Atrani is famous as the birthplace of Masaniello, the young fisherman who led a revolt against the Viceroy of Naples in 1647. There is yet another lovely view from the site.

Ravello and Salerno

Ravello, situated in the folds of Monte Lattari, is one of the most picturesque spots along the Gulf of Salerno. It prospered during Amalfi's days of glory. Its bright luxuriant gardens, flowering with almost tropical vegetation, still make it one of the glories of Italy. Visit, briefly, the Duomo di San Pantaleone, which dates from the 11th century, whose pulpit, resting on mosaic columns and sculptured wild beasts (1272), is one of the best examples of the Cosmatesque style so common in southern Italy.

Quite nearby is the Palazzo Rufolo, built by the Rufoli family, during the 11th and 12th centuries. Don't be misled by the disreputable walls. Within is a scene from the earliest days of the Crusades. Norman and Arab mingle in profusion in a welter of color-filled gardens. The complex of the palace was briefly home to some famous early figures, the only English pope, Adrian IV, Robert the Wise and Charles of Anjou. The luxuriant gardens, it is said, gave Wagner the idea of Parsifal's Garden of the Flower Maidens. From Ravello's piazza, take the 20-minute walk to Villa Cimbrone, perched like an eagle's nest on the cliffs; its garden terrace offers a truly magnificent panorama of the whole bay of Salerno.

Back on the coast road, drive on past Minori and Maiori, two towns once pretty, now overbuilt, but pause briefly at Minori to see the ruins of an imperial Roman villa. The scenic road then winds past the Capo d'Orso, where the galleons of Charles V were defeated, past Cetara, where first the Arab Saracens landed in Italy, past the twin rocks of Vietri, home of the gnomes in legend and now a major ceramics center, then go on to Salerno.

Salerno was the scene of the Allied landing in Italy in World War II. In medieval times it was the world capital of medicine. The monastery of the Benedictine monks, who probably founded its medical school, offered the best instruction then available. From here came the legendary Four Masters—one Latin, one Hebrew, one Greek and one Arab—who gave the world of that day its greatest science. One of the best known of all medieval medical texts was the *Code of Health,* the *Regimen Sanitatis Salerni,* written at Salerno in doggerel Latin verse and translated into almost every European language.

Many times destroyed by invasion and pillage, Salerno has always been speedily rebuilt, and even today there are few traces of the ravages of those September days in 1943 when the Germans almost pushed the American forces back into the sea.

The cathedral boasts the remains of the evangelist St. Matthew, brought back from the Holy Land by pilgrims in the 10th century. The cathedral dates from 1080 and is an exceptional building, with a medieval courtyard and fabulous gold and silver reliquaries in its treasury. Descend to the crypt, a kaleidoscope of bright frescos and multicolored marble.

Eboli and Paestum

Southeast from Salerno are Battipaglia and Eboli, undistinguished rural centers. Dusky water buffalo graze in the fields, and each roadside stand proclaims that its *mozzarella* is the freshest. Southward the plains stretch on along the coast to Sapri. All the towns in this region have ancient Greco-Arab origins but all today are modest little country villages. Great improvements have been made since Carlo Levi's best-selling book, *Christ Stopped at Eboli,* in which he gives an interesting account of the customs, traditions and superstitions of Lucania, where the people still believe in black magic and witchcraft as well as in the legends of ghostly bandits who once commanded the area. There is nothing to detain you in Eboli.

Southward from Eboli lies Battipaglia and 23 km. (14 miles) further on towards the sea is Paestum, with some of the best preserved of Greek

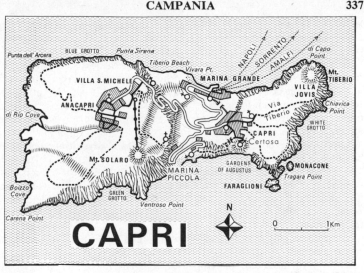

CAPRI

architectural monuments, not excepting even Greece itself. Once it was a thriving Greek colony called Poseidonia, founded by settlers from Sybaris more than 600 years before Christ. Only in 273 B.C. did it become Roman and acquire its present name. Today it is a group of ruins in the lonely, tranquil plains of the Sele River.

Go to the Temple of Poseidon (or Neptune), a perfect example of Doric architecture, through the Porta Aurea. Note its 36 fluted columns and the extraordinarily well-preserved entablature. The Basilica nearby is one of the oldest of Paestum's monuments, dating from very early in the 6th century B.C. The name is an 18th-century misnomer, it was a temple sacred to the wife of Zeus, Hera, and is about the earliest building on the site. Behind it an ancient road leads to the Forum of the Roman era, near which is a single column of the Temple of Peace. A little to the north are the ruins of a Roman amphitheater and the museum, which contains important Greek frescos found in ancient tombs nearby. Off to the side is the Temple of Ceres. Try to see the temples at sunset, when the light enhances the deep gold of the stone and the air is sharp with the cries of the crows that nest high on the temples.

If you still have a day or so, push on along the coast toward Agropoli and Santa Maria di Castellabate on the rugged Cilento promontory. A little further on, Acciaroli is a delightful small fishing town, with miles of sandy beach to one side of it. Beyond the recent excavations of the ancient city of Velia, Palinuro is a beautiful spot, "discovered" some years ago by the Club Méditerranée and more recently by Italy's well-off powerboat set. Finally, on the Calabria border, Sapri is a gentle, old-fashioned watering place on the main railway line from Naples.

Capri

Another route that you can take from Naples is by boat to Sorrento and Capri. Take the big, comfortable boat that chugs across the bay, past the ruins of Herculaneum, past Torre Annunziata, beneath Vesuvius' menace, past Castellammare and Vico Equense, on to Sorrento. There, if you have the time, if you like the place, and above all if it is evening, we would advise breaking the trip, if only to look once again at the night scene of lighted Naples across the bay. From Sorrento you can get another boat or a hydrofoil to Capri in the morning.

So you come to Capri, the ancients' island of the goats, so-called, perhaps, because only goats, human or otherwise, dared its precipitous cliffs and slopes. But Capri has been called many things. It is truly "all things to all men," but each finds there what he seeks. The legend of Tiberius' orgies, largely discounted now, persists, as in fact do the orgies themselves among a certain element of the jet set.

Capri itself never seems to change. Today, as always, it is a pint-sized paradise. It is almost 6 km. (4 miles) long and almost 3 km. (2 miles) wide and in spots more than 300 meters (1,000 ft.) high. Unlike the other islands of the Bay of Naples, Capri is not of volcanic origin. Geologists say that it is an integral part of the limestone chain of the Apennines, left above water when some subterranean cataclysm sank its connecting link with the mainland.

The Phoenicians were its earliest settlers and to them is attributed the construction of the stairway of 159 steps which links Marina Grande where you will disembark to "Upper Capri"—Anacapri. The Greeks came in the 4th century B.C. and after them the Romans made it a favorite playground.

Augustus had a villa there and he built baths, aqueducts and conduits. Tiberius made it his favorite resort and spent the later years of his life there, in one or another of the 12 villas he scattered over the island, refusing to return to Rome even when he was dying. Fantastic grottos, soaring conical peaks, caverns great and small, plus unknown ruins and thousands of legends combine with the tales of Suetonius to give Capri a flavor of whispered and mysterious evil—a beauteous evil found nowhere else—and an intoxicating quality as heady as its rare and delicious wines.

Capri was one of the strongholds of the Barbary pirate Barbarossa, who first sacked it and then made a fortress of it. Moors and Greeks previously used its heights as strongholds and, through generation after generation, pirates from all corners of what was then the world made periodic depredations. The British, in 1806, wanted to make of it a small Gibraltar and built fortifications with that in mind. The French took it away from them in 1808 before they could complete their plans.

But the Roman influence was the strongest. It was not the warlike touch. Rather it was the Sybaritic influence, acquired by the Roman patricians from the earlier Greek colonists over on the mainland. Capri became, and has remained, a pleasure island.

You will land from your boat at Marina Grande and then go up to your hotel at the town of Capri itself, unless you are like the Swede Axel Munthe, who, addicted by choice to Anacapri, could never forget the age-long quarrel between those two villages and never passed a night in the lower town. You may have to wait in line for the funicular.

Capri, the town, is highly commercial, deliberately sets out to be a tourist center, and delights in the offbeat. When it is not too crowded, it can be pleasant and relaxing. When it is packed (on holiday weekends, especially), it is pure purgatory, with far too many people in too small a place. Happily, the beauties of Capri, the island, are more than enough to compensate for the deficiencies of a relatively small percentage of its visitors, or the noisiness of the day trippers, brought by the shipload at the height of the season.

In Capri you will find the magnificent Gardens of Augustus, from which you can look down on Marina Piccola's bathing establishments. The Church of Santa Costanza, of 11th-century Byzantine construction, and the Certosa of San Giacomo, 14th-century Carthusian monastery, are among the few survivals of medieval Capri. The ruins of the Castle of Castiglione, high up on the heights of San Michele, and the fabulous Castello di Barbarossa—800 steps up—are superbly sited.

You should see, of course, the impressive ruins of the Villa of Tiberius, one of the 12, and you will see the cliff from which he is falsely reported to have had his ex-favorites flung. You will see, too, the Villa Jovis, also Tiberian in origin, and, from the sanctuary above it, look out across the Bay of Naples for a truly magnificent vista. Tiberius was 69 when he came to live on Capri. He passed the final decade of his life on the island, ruling the empire from its luxurious seclusion, mainly from this very villa.

But Capri's natural wonders are far more entrancing. The famed Blue Grotto is but one of many such caverns and some connoisseurs think it not the most beautiful. There is the Green Grotto, the Yellow Grotto and the Pink and the White. Their colors, in each case, result from the refraction of light from the walls and the waters through the varying-sized entrances. All these grottoes have been known from the earliest days of antiquity, and were used in the days of the Greeks and the Romans, notably the Grotto dell'Arsenale. In 1964, two Greek statues were hauled up from the depths. If your time is limited, skip this expensive, potentially disappointing jaunt. Go to Anacapri instead. It's an interesting little place; see the Church of San Michele and Villa San Michele.

Ischia

The charms of Capri have long been established, and the island therefore suffers the fate of many places that become too famous—it is overrun with visitors; so those who discovered Capri in the first place, before it became crowded, have moved off to a new discovery which is rapidly going the same way. The trail blazers simply crossed the Bay of Naples to the island of Ischia and a host of luxurious new hotels and villas were put up to accommodate the newcomers, with the result that Ischia, too, has problems with overcrowding in the summer months.

More than twice the size of Capri, Ischia is of volcanic origin, and the volcano, Mount Epomeo, shoots up to a height of 788 meters (2,585 ft.). But don't be alarmed—it hasn't erupted for 6½ centuries. In fact, you can hike up to the summit. Porto d'Ischia is the island's chief settlement and a spa. Besides the superb landscape, with lush vegetation, olive groves and pinewoods, the island has thermal springs.

Porto d'Ischia, where the biggest luxury hotels are found, is the usual port of debarkation. For this reason, many visitors stop here. Distances are so short that it doesn't really matter much where you put up; all parts of the island are accessible from whatever base you prefer. And Porto d'Ischia isn't one of those workaday ports of entry from which the visitor immediately takes off for more interesting parts. It's an enchanting resort whose flat-roofed oriental houses climb steeply up the hillside above the water, whose narrow streets frequently turn into flights of steps, and whose villas and gardens are topped and backed by beautiful growths of pine. If you elect to stay here, you can expect excellent bathing from the half-mile beach whose eastern end, of fine sand, is the most attractive. The slope is relatively gentle. The chief man-made features of the town are the 15th-century Castle of Ischia and a small museum.

Many visitors prefer to go on a couple of miles to Casamicciola Terme, a popular bathing resort with a fine sandy beach next to the pier where steamers come in, and smaller beaches on either side of the town. There are mineral springs here also, some of them reaching temperatures near boiling. Just 2 km. (a little over a mile) along the coast is Lacco Ameno, with more thermal amenities as well as some archeological interest.

If you want to avoid the crowds, you might try Forio (although this town has become very popular with foreign residents), or Sant'Angelo, on the southern coast. It has a lovely beach at Lido dei Maronti.

The chief attractions of the island, besides its beaches, are the opportunities afforded for skin diving, its magnificent scenery, an unbeatable climate pleasant all year around, and perhaps not least the *Epomeo* white wine produced on the slopes of the extinct volcano.

Procida

The island of Procida owes its existence to not one, but four volcanic craters, with a fifth crater off the shore forming the tiny island of Vivara. It's a wild and rugged place full of sweeping views. The small population of fishermen and vineyard workers lives in little domed houses. It has few hotels and pensions, but if you are looking for genuine atmosphere you could do a lot worse. Sadly, this cannot be true very much longer.

PRACTICAL INFORMATION FOR NAPLES

WHEN TO GO. Mild all year round, Naples' climate is ideal in spring and fall. Winter months may have some rainy periods, but it's rarely cold enough for more than a light coat. The summer months of July and August are usually very hot; most restaurants and many shops close during August.

USEFUL ADDRESSES. Tourist Information. EPT, Via Partenope 10/A (406.289), with booths at Central and Mergellina stations, airport and autostrada service areas (San Nicola, Tre Ponti Ovest, La Pineta); AAST, Palazzo Reale at Piazza Plebiscito (418.744), with booths at Piazza del Gesu (552.3328), Piazza Garibaldi, at Borgo Marinaro near Castel dell'Ovo, and at hydrofoil pier at Mergellina.

General Post Office: Piazza Matteotti (312.069). Long distance phones: Via Depretis 48, Via Torrione San Martino, corner Via Bernini. Galleria Umberto, Central Station, Pier and Airport.

SEASONAL EVENTS. Religious feasts in Naples are colorful and intense, especially those of San Gennaro in **May** and **September,** when the cathedral fills with the faithful who beseech their patron saint for a sign of heavenly favor—the liquefaction of his dried blood. In **May,** International Music Weeks, with opera and concerts.

The feast of the Madonna del Carmine, **July** 16, is an occasion for processions, street fairs and fireworks.

Summer brings outdoor theater and music festivals, mainly at Castel Nuovo and Capodimonte Palace.

In **December** the opera season opens at San Carlo. At Christmas there are special shows of elaborate Neapolitan *presepi,* or Christmas cribs.

TELEPHONE CODE. The telephone area code for Naples is 081.

HOTELS. Good accommodations in Naples are scarce, so reserve well in advance. Deluxe standards are a notch or two below those of luxury hotels elsewhere in Italy. High season 1 April to 31 October.

Deluxe

Excelsior, Via Partenope 48 (417.111). CIGA. Excellent position on shore drive with view of bay. Elegant period furnishings in salons and most bedrooms. Fine Casanova restaurant. AE, DC, MC, V.

Expensive

Britannique, Corso Vittorio Emanuele 133 (660.933). Elevated position with good view. Friendly, efficient service and clean, well-kept rooms. AE, DC, MC, V.

Majestic, Largo Vasto a Chiaia 68 (416.500). A few blocks from shore drive. Large, comfortable. Panoramic restaurant. AE, DC, MC, V.

Mediterraneo, Via Nuova Ponte di Tappia 25 (551.2240). Central location just off Piazza Municipio. Solid, traditional comforts. Roof garden. AE, DC, MC.

Jolly Ambassador's, Via Medina 70 (416.000). A 30-storey tower. Very central, with great views and rooftop restaurant. Comfortable rooms and efficient staff. Reassuringly reliable. AE, DC, MC, V.

Paradiso, Via Catullo 11 (660.233). In elevated position with good views, quiet and comfortable. Rates are in the lower levels of this category. Garage. DC, MC, V.

Moderate

Cavour, Piazza Garibaldi 32 (283.122). Near Stazione Centrale. Clean and comfortable rooms. Elegant restaurant and piano bar. AE, DC, MC, V.

Palace, Piazza Garibaldi 8 (264.575). On central station square, large, older hotel. AE, DC, V.

Inexpensive

Belvedere, Via Tito Angelini 51 (364.540).On Vomero hill, near San Martino and funicular. Small and satisfactory. Helpful staff, good restaurant.

Rex, Via Palepoli 12 (416.388). Fairly quiet location near Santa Lucia waterfront. Eclectic decor. AE, DC, MC, V.

RESTAURANTS. The Santa Lucia waterfront restaurants are popular with tourists. For food with a view, go to the establishments on Posillipo or to Marechiaro.

Neapolitan Specialties. In Naples you'll find the simple but tasty cuisine of the Campania region, along with a few specialties that you should try here, at source. There's *pizza,* of course, and *maccheroni al ragù,* in a meat sauce that requires hours of blending and simmering. *Minestra maritata,* a poor-man's soup of pork, no longer appears on many menus; it is a typical Neapolitan one-dish meal. Pastry specialties are cream-filled, sculptural *sfogliatelle* and *pastiera,* traditionally an Easter cake, made of *ricotta,* sweet corn and essence of orange blossom, usually available all year round.

Expensive

Le Arcate, Via Falcone 249 (683.380). Closed Tues. Terrace dining with memorable view. DC, MC, V.

La Cantinella, Via Nazario Sauro 23 (404.884). Closed Sun. At Santa Lucia. The emphasis is on seafood, but everything is good. AE, DC, MC, V.

Casanova Grill, Hotel Excelsior, Via Partenope 48 (417.111). Art deco-look restaurant with buffet. AE, DC, MC, V.

Ciro, at Santa Lucia (415.686). Closed Wed. Classic cuisine *alla marinara.* AE, DC, MC, V.

La Fazenda, Via Marechiaro 58 (769.7420). Closed Sun. and two weeks in Aug. Rustic specialties, charcoal-grilled fish. V.

Il Galeone, Via Posillipo 16/a (684.581). Closed Tues. Elegant and excellent dining in a very attractive spot with view. AE, MC, V.

Giuseppone a Mare, Via Russo (769.6002). Closed Sun. On the sea at Posillipo, one of Naples most famous seafood restaurants. AE, DC, MC, V.

Moderate

Al 53, Piazza Dante 53 (341.124). Closed Sat. Longstanding favorite for classic Neapolitan food.

D'Angelo, Via Falcone 203 (365.363). Closed Tues. Halfway up Vomero hill, with a view to relish. DC, V.

Bergantino, Via San Felice 16 (310.369). Closed Sat. and Aug. Bustling favorite of businessmen and families, with an extensive choice. Open for lunch only.

Bersagliera, Borgo Marinaro 10 (415.692). Closed Tues. on Santa Lucia waterfront. Serves uncomplicated classics in touristy but fun atmosphere.

Ciro, Via Santa Brigida 71 (324.072). Closed Sun., Aug. Known for traditional Neapolitan cuisine.

Dal Delicato, Largo Sermoneta 34 (667.047). Closed Sun. Book for evening. Very popular, exquisite pastas and pizzas. AE, DC.

Da Mimi all Ferrovia, Via Alfonso d'Aragona 21 (338.525). Closed Sun. Just off Piazza Garibaldi, a family-run place with fine local dishes. V.

Dante e Beatrice, Piazza Dante 44 (349.905). Closed Wed. Unpretentious and economical.

Da Peppino, Via Palepoli 8 (415.182). Closed Sun. Near Santa Lucia, known for *linguine con scampi* and other delicious dishes.

Don Salvatore, Via Mergellina 5 (681.817). Closed Wed. Known for luscious pizzas and *linguine cosa nostra.* AE, DC, MC, V.

Rugantino, Via dei Fiorentini 45 (325.491). Closed Sun. Central, just off Via Diaz. Attractive place with a touch of class. DC, MC, V.

La Sacrestia, Via Orazio 116 (664.186). Closed Wed.; and Sun. in July and Aug. One of Naples' best, serving a variety of tempting specialties. AE, DC, V.

Starita, Borgo Marinaro (404.349). Closed Mon. One of the atmospheric places on the Santa Lucia waterfront. DC, V.

Umberto, Via Alabardieri 30 (418.555). Closed Wed. Near Piazza dei Martiri; lively, neon-lit, serving Neapolitan fare. AE, DC, MC, V.

Inexpensive

Bellini, Via Santa Maria di Costantinopoli 80 (459.774). Closed Wed. Pizzeria.

Gennarino, Piazza Garibaldi 126 (283.448). Closed Sun. Pizzeria.

Lombardi, Via Benedetto Croce 59 (206.496). Closed Mon. Pizzeria.

Luciano, Piazza San Francesco. Down-to-earth prices for seafood.

Port'Alba, Via Port'Alba 18 (459.713). Closed Tues. Pizzeria.

La Quercia, Vico Quercia 5 (323.329). Closed Mon. Trattoria.

Cafés: Caflish, Via Toledo 253 and Via Chiaia 143; **Gambrinus,** Piazza Trieste e Trento; **Verdi,** Via Verdi 23.

GETTING THERE AND AROUND. By air. There's a bus service (14, red) from Capodichino airport to Piazza Garibaldi which takes approximately 25 minutes. The terminal in town is by the central rail station. Service leaves at roughly 20 minute intervals from 7 A.M. to 9.30 P.M. Taxis standing at the airport charge double the meter amount for their return.

By train. The Metropolitana, really an urban railway, connects Piazza Garibaldi, Piazza Cavour, Montesanto, Piazza Amedeo and Mergellina, continuing on to Pozzuoli.

Funiculars help with the hills: the Funicolare Centrale (Via Toledo–Piazza Fuga), Funicolare de Chiaia (Via del Parco Margherita–Via Cimarosa) and Funicolare Montesanto (Piazza Montesanto–Via Morghen) all serve the Vomero, and another at Mergellina (Via Mergellina–Via Manzoni) climbs to Posillipo.

By car. Traffic in Naples is chaotic, parking is scarce and thefts are common, so don't bring your car. If you must, then park it in a garage for the duration of your stay (and agree on terms beforehand).

By bus. There are plenty of buses, but avoid rush hours . . . which on some lines seem to last all day. The fare for bus, subway, and funicular fare is 600 lire.

By taxi. In the city, taxis start at about 2,000 lire; there are supplements for luggage, night service, holidays—but be firm if you think you are being overcharged. Radiotaxi numbers: 364.444 or 364.340.

EXCURSIONS. The Circumvesuviana suburban railway runs from Corso Garibaldi, near the central station, to Pompeii and Sorrento, while the Cumana railway runs in the other direction toward Baia and Cuma.

To Vesuvio, take Line 1 of the Circumvesuviana (Napoli—Torre Annunziata) from Corso Garibaldi to the Ercolano stop. It's a 40-minutes bus ride from there to the terminal of the chairlift (Seggiovia). It's a steep, dusty climb to the crater, and at the top, guide service is compulsory.

To get there by car, you take the Naples–Salerno highway to the Ercolano exit and then follow the signs to the Seggiovia terminal. Hawkers and souvenir vendors are particularly bothersome here. You can take the Circumvesuviana to Ercolano and to Pompeii (Pompeii Scavi stop).

Boats for Capri and Ischia leave from the Molo Beverello, near Castel Nuovo. Hydrofoils for the islands leave from Molo Beverello and from Via Caracciolo.

For a view of Naples from the sea take the sightseeing boat that leaves from the Luise dock at Mergellina, in front of the Chalet delle Rose; cost—about 3,000 lire. It runs from June through Sept. in the late afternoon hours.

PRACTICAL INFORMATION FOR CAMPANIA

WHEN TO GO. Along the coast of Campania, spring and fall are the best seasons for touring; winters are mild, with some heavy rain, while summers are hot, and coastal roads and resorts are crowded. During Easter week and August, Capri, Sorrento and the Amalfi coast overflow with visitors. Beach resorts generally are at their leisurely best in June and September. The mountainous inland areas around Avellino and Benevento have a cooler climate.

TOURIST OFFICES. Amalfi: AAST, Corso Roma 19 (871.107). **Avellino:** EPT, Piazza Libertà 50 (35.175). **Benevento:** EPT Via Giustiniani 34 (21.960) **Capri:** AAST Via Umberto I 19 (837.0686). **Caserta:** EPT, Corso Trieste 39 (321.137). **Cava dei Tirreni:** AAST, Corso Umberto 208 (841.148). **Ischia:** Corso Vittoria Colonna 16 (991.464). **Maiori:** AAST, Viale Capone (877.452). **Paestum:** AAST, Via Magna Grecia 151 (811.016). **Pompeii:** AAST, Via Sacra 1 (863.1041). **Positano:** AAST, Via Saracino 2 (875.067). **Ravello:** AAST, Piazza Vescovado 13 (857.096). **Salerno:** AAST, Piazza Amendola 8 (224.744); EPT, Piazza Ferrovia (231.432). **Sorrento:** AAST, Via De Maio 35 (878.2104). **Vico Equense:** AAST, Corso Umberto (879.8343).

MUSEUMS. There are some excellent museums in Naples and we list some of them below. More details, with especially up-to-date opening times, are available from Naples EPT office. Some earthquake-damaged museums will be open on a limited basis only until restorations have been completed. See the *Museums* section in *Facts at Your Fingertips* for extra, general, points.

Castel Nuovo, Piazza Municipio. Copied after the Château of Angers, the castle has interesting interiors as well as the Triumphal Arch of Alfonso I. Entry free.

Certosa di San Martino, Charterhouse of St. Martin, Via Torrione di San Martino, Vómero. Convent dispensary, refectory, museum; 18th-century Neapolitan paintings; famous *presepi*. Tues. to Sat., 9–2, Sun. 9–1, closed Mon.

Cappella Sansevero, Via de Sanctis 19, by Piazza San Domenico Maggiore. Masterpieces of 18th-century sculpture, a Baroque experience. Mon. to Sat. 10.30–1.30, 5–7. Sun. 11–1.30.

Museo Archeologico Nazionale, Piazza Museo. With Pompeii and Herculaneum almost on Naples' doorstep, you would expect this to be a really important collection of Greek and Roman antiquities, and you would not be disappointed. As with many Italian galleries, this one is going through a massive facelift and quite a lot of the rooms may be closed. Mon. to Sat. 9–2, Sun 9–1.

Museo e Gallerie Nazionali di Capodimonte, Tondo di Capodimonte. Rich collection of paintings of Neapolitan and Roman schools among much other art; porcelain, armor as well. Tues. to Sat., 9–2, Sun. 9–1, closed Mon.

Museo Nazionale della Ceramica Duca di Martina, Villa Floridiana, Via Cimarosa 77, Vómero. A national ceramics collection, with the Duca di Martino porcelains, majolica, ivories and enamels. Tues. to Sat., 9–2, Sun. 9–1, closed Mon.

Museo di Palazzo Reale, Piazza del Plebiscito. Royal apartments, with furnishings and decorations. Mon. to Sat. 9–2, Sun 9–1.

Museo Pignatelli, Riviera di Chiaia 200. Neo-classical villa. Tues. to Sat. 9–2, Sun. 9–1.

Teatro San Carlo, Piazza Trieste e Trento. A great opera house with magnificent 18th-century interior decoration. Daily 9–12, closed Mon.

SEASONAL EVENTS. Amalfi: on Jun. 27 a statue of patron saint, Andrea, is carried up the steep cathedral steps on the shoulders of strong-winded bearers; a costumed pageant and fireworks complete the festivities.

Capri: the year begins with a bang amid New Year's Day celebrations; fireworks, band music and general merrymaking mark the occasion.

Caserta: during Sept., the arts festival, Settembre a Borgo, is held.

Cava dei Tirreni: the last Sat. and Sun. of Jun., this hill resort near Salerno is the scene of a "historical reenactment" in the form of the Disfida dei Trombonieri, a pageant in medieval costume.

Nola: on either Jun. 22 or the following Sun., the Festa dei Gigli, a colorful procession of towering "lilies" borne by the town's strongest men, takes place; Nola is situated inland from Naples.

Pompeii: the Roman Theater here is the setting for classical drama during Jul. and for a festival of music and dance in Aug.

Ravello: at the end of Jun. there is a festival of Wagnerian music to celebrate the composer's sojourn here.

Sorrento: patron saint, Antonino, is honored on Feb. 14 with a typical festa.

The entire region erupts with festas and fireworks during the summer months, when many of the local patron saints have their feast days.

TELEPHONE CODES. You will find the telephone area code for each town against its name in the Hotel and Restaurant listings (after the province name). If there is a different area code from the majority of the establishments—say when a hotel or restaurant is in an outlying place—then the code is given in front of the telephone number.

HOTELS AND RESTAURANTS. High season rates apply at all coastal resorts in July and August and extend from April/May through September at Sorrento and Amalfi coast resorts, where Christmas and Easter also draw crowds and command top rates. Cilento resorts close up tight from fall to spring, while at least some hotels and restaurants are open in Sorrento and on the Amalfi coast year round. It's always a good idea to book ahead and is imperative in the high season.

Hotels and restaurant prices in Capri are 20–30% higher than in the rest of Campania and are at the top of our guidelines. Restaurants in resort towns are open every day during the week in the high season, but may close for long periods in winter.

Regional Food and Drink. Campania's cuisine is quite simple and relies heavily on the bounty of its fertile farmland. Its tomatoes are exported all over the world, but to try them here is a new experience. Even during the winter you can find tomato sauce made with fresh tomatoes plucked from the jewel-like strands you see hanging outdoors on kitchen balconies.

Campania is the homeland of pasta—usually cooked *al dente*—and pizza. The best variations of these are the simplest, either *spaghetti al filetto di pomodoro* or *pizza al pomodoro* or *alla marinara,* both garnished with fresh basil, important ingredient of many local dishes. *Spaghetti alle vongole* is simplicity itself: pasta, clams, olive oil and garlic.

Meat may be served *alla pizzaiola,* which has nothing to do with pizza, but is simply a tomato sauce with garlic. Fish is a staple, though some types are pricey on restaurant menus. Fried *calamari* or *totani* (cuttlefish) appear on most menus. Mozzarella is fresh and delicious throughout the region, and an *insalata caprese* (slices of red tomato and white mozzarella with a garnish of green basil) is one of the most gratifying dishes you can choose on a hot summer's day.

Among the region's wines, *Gragnano, Falerno, Lacrima Christi* and *Greco di Tufo* are fine. *Falerno* was known to the ancient Romans, though it may not have resembled its modern descendant which is dry and white. Ischia and Ravello also produce good wines.

Amalfi Salerno (089). Historic seaside town. High season 1 June to 30 Sept., Christmas and Easter. *Luna* (E), on main road (871.002). Central, remodeled convent complete with cloisters, good restaurant, 42 rooms, many with view. Swimming pool and disco in Saracen tower on the sea. AE, DC, MC, V. *Santa Caterina* (E), on main road, about 1.5 km. (1 mile) from center (871.012). The best; beautiful villa; 54 rooms, most with balcony, sea views. Flowered terraces, lift to private swimming area and saltwater pool. Small 9-room villa annex in garden. AE, DC, MC, V.

La Bussola (M), Lungomare Cavalieri (871.131). Overlooking small port; clean and comfortable. Terraces and sun deck on sea. AE, MC, V. *Dei Cavalieri* (M), Via M. Comite 26, 1 km. (½ mile) from center (871.333). Bright, modern decor, some antiques. Garden terraces and stairs to private swimming area. No restaurant; meal options at various restaurants. AE, DC, MC, V. *Miramalfi* (M), Via Quasimodo 3, 0.5 km. (¼ mile) from center (871.588). Splendid position, 44 good-sized rooms with balcony; lift to pool, sea. AE, DC, MC, V. *Marina Riviera* (I), on main road, in town (871.104). Small, well-furnished, with good views. *Santa Caterina* (E), Strade Amalfitana (871.012). Large and lovely mansion. One of the best hotels on the entire coast.

Restaurants. *Caravella* (M) Via M. Camera 12 (871.029). AE, MC, V. Family-run, classic local dishes. *Gemma* (M), Via Cavalieri di Malta (871.345). One of the best for regional cuisine; summer terrace overlooking main street. *Il Tarì* (M), Via Capuano (871.832). On main street, small, good. AE, V. *Taverna del Doge* (M), Via Supportico (870.323). On main street, atmosphere, fine food. AE, DC, MC, V. *Cantina del Nostromo-Zaccaria* (M), Via Colombo (main road entering Atrani) (871.345). Locals claim it's the best; all fish menu. *Lemon Garden* (I), Valle dei Mulini. Open June to Sept. only; a long walk up hill past ancient paper mills, but worth it for view, food and quiet.

Avellino Avellino (0825). *Jolly* (E), Via Tuoro Cappuccini 97/A (321.91). Modern comforts in large hotel. AE, DC, MC, V.
Restaurants. *La Caveia* (M), Via Tuoro Cappuccini 48 (382.77). Closed Mon. Very good food. AE, V. *Da Tonino* (M), Via Chiesa Conservatorio (311.17). Closed Sun. evenings and Mon. In center of town. *Soldatiello* (M), Piazza Garibaldi 26 (370.27). Closed Tues. Central, unpretentious.

Benevento Benevento (0824). *President* (E), Via Perasso 1 (210.00). Central, adequate, sole choice for an overnight stay. V.
Restaurants. *Pascalucci* (M), at Piano Cappelle (245.48). Open every day. Excellent and varied antipasto table. *Pedecini* (M), Piazza Bissolati 12 (21.731). (257.31). Closed Mon. In town, modest.

Capri Napoli (081). Fabled island in the Bay of Naples, near Sorrento. High season Easter, June to Sept.

Anacapri. Upper town on island. *Europa Palace* (E), Via Capodimonte 2/b (837.0955). Outstanding; suites with private pool. Open April to Oct. AE, DC, MC, v. *San Michele* (M), Via Orlandi (837.1427). Villa hotel, 36 rooms, splendid view. Open Mar. 25–Oct. MC, v. *Bellavista* (I), Via Orlandi (837.1463). Nicely furnished rooms, view. DC, v. *Villa Patrizia* (I), Via Pagliaro (837.1014). Open April to Oct. Smallish and comfortable. No restaurant. AE, v.

Restaurants. *Do Riccio* (M), Via Gradola 11 (837.1380). Closed in winter. On cliff above Blue Grotto, seafood specialties. AE. *Rondinella* (M), Via Orlandi 145 (837.1223). Closed Thurs. off-season. Simple. AE, DC, MC, v.

Capri. Main town. *Quisiana* (L), Via Camerelle 2 (837.0788). Open 1 April to 1 Nov. Capri's poshest, most expensive hostelry. Central but quiet, spacious rooms, beautifully furnished, pool. AE, DC, MC, v. *Luna* (E), Via Matteotti (837.0433). Open April to Oct. Splendid location; terraces, gardens, pool. AE, MC, v. *La Palma* (E), Via V. Emanuele (837.0133). Open April to Oct. Large, attractive, off main piazza. No restaurant. AE, MC, v. *Pazziella* (E), Via Fuorlovado (837.0044). Open 1 April to 10 Oct. Only 15 rooms in tastefully furnished villa. No restaurant. *Regina Cristina* (E), Via Serena (837.0303). Modern, balconied rooms, pool. AE, v. *Scalinatella* (E), Via Tragara 8 (837.0633). Open 15 March to 31 Oct. Very well-equipped; lovely rooms with terraces, wonderful view. No restaurant.

Flora (M), Via Serena 26 (837.0211). Open 15 March to 20 Oct. A 15-room villa hotel. No restaurant. AE, DC, MC, v. *La Floridiana* (M), Via Campo di Teste (837.0101). Delightful spot, terraces overlooking sea. MC, v. *Gatto Bianco* (M), Via V. Emanuele (837.0203). Open 1 April to 31 Oct. Attractive hotel, central but away from the madding crowd. AE, DC, MC, v. *La Pineta* (M), Via Tragara (837.0644). Comfortable rooms with terrace, pool. MC, v. *Villa Sanfelice* (M), Via Li Campi (837.6122). Open 1 April to 31 Oct. At center of town, garden, pool. No restaurant. v. *Villa Pina* (I), Via Tuoro (837.7517). Open 15 April to 30 Sept. Pretty, with pool; climb stairs to entrance. v. *Villa Krupp* (I), Via Matteotti 12 (837.0362). Quiet. Lenin and Gorky stayed here. No lift, no restaurant. *Belsito* (I), Via Matermania (837.0969). Small, pleasant pension. v.

Restaurants. *La Brunella* (E), Via Tragara 24 (837.0279). Open 20 March to 5 Nov. Excellent local cooking in pretty little hotel dining room. AE, DC, v. *Canzone del Mare* (E), at Marina Piccola (837.0104). Open Easter to 30 Sept. Smart spot for poolside lunches; delicious pastas and seafood. AE, MC, v. *Capannina* (E), Via delle Botteghe 14 (837.0732). Closed Wed., except for in Aug. Chic and romantic. AE, v. *Faraglioni* (E), Via Camerelle 75 (837.0320). Open 1 April to 30 Sept. Closed Wed. off-season. Elegant, private-club atmosphere. AE, v. *Glauco* (E), Bohemian air, lovely terrace. *Luigi* (E), on sea at Faraglioni (837.0591). Open Easter to 30 Sept. Very good, lunch only (boat from Marina Piccola). AE. *La Pigna* (E), Via Roma 8 (837.0280). Open 1 April to 31 Oct. Closed Tues. Panoramic, one of Capri's best. AE, DC, MC, v.

Aurora (M), Via Fuorlovado 18 (837.0181). Open 1 April to 31 Oct. Excellent. AE, MC, v. *Geranio* (M), Via Matteotti 8 (837.0616). Open 20 March to 15 Oct. Closed Thurs. Beautiful site; good food. AE, v. *Grottino* (M), Via Longano 27 (837.0584). Closed Tues. and Nov. 3–Mar. 20. Just off the *piazzetta*. *O Saraceno* (M), Via Gradini, Sottomonte. Nice *trattoria* for pizza or prawns flambé. v. *La Sceriffa* (M), Via Acquaviva 29 (837.7953). Closed Tues. Open Easter to 31 Oct. Delicious dining with a view.

Caserta Caserta (0823). *Jolly* (E), Viale Vittorio Veneto 9 (325.222). Handy for station and palace; large, modern, fully air conditioned; pool. DC, MC, v. *Reggia Palace* (M), Viale Carlo III (458.500). At Autostrada del Sole, big commercial hotel, good overnight stop for drivers. AE, DC, v.

Restaurants. *La Tegola* (M), Viale Carlo III (442.689). Closed Wed. and Sun. evenings. At railway station. *La Massa* (I), Via Mazzini 55 (321.268). Closed Mon. and Aug. 5–20. Unpretentious place near palace. AE, DC, v.

At **Caserta Vecchia**, on hillside 8 km. (5 miles) away, *La Castellana* (M), Via Torre 4 (371.230). Closed Thurs. Atmosphere, regional specialties.

Castellabate Salerno (0974). Seaside resort area on Cilento coast. High season 1 July to 31 Aug. *Castelsandra* (E), At San Marco di Castellabate (966.021). Open 20 April to 31 Sept. Very pretty resort hotel, all comforts; good value. AE, DC, V. *Punta Licosa* (M), at Ogliastro Marina (963.024). Open 1 June to 30 Sept. Air conditioned beach hotel. *Santa Maria* (M), at Santa Maria (961.001). Open 1 April to 15 Sept. Comfortable hotel on beach.

Cava dei Tirreni Salerno (089). Hill resort above Amalfi coast. High season 1 June to 30 Sept, Christmas and Easter. *Due Torri* (M), Via Maddalena a Rotolo (843.830). Attractive, pool, tennis. AE, DC, V. *Scapolatiello* (M), at Corpo di Cava (463.838). Terraces, pool. A charming spot with good restaurant. AE, DC, MC, V.

Conca dei Marini Salerno (089). Near Amalfi. High season same as Amalfi. *Belvedere* (E), on main road (871.266). Open 1 May to 30 Sept. Beautiful position on sea, large airy rooms, salt water pool. *Saraceno* (M), on main road (872.601). Disneyland exterior, Orientalesque decor, splendid views, terraces, swimming. DC, V.

Restaurant. *Ciccio* (M), on main road (871.030). Closed Tues. and Feb. Good dining; *spaghetti al cartoccio.*

Ischia Napoli (081). Large island, good beaches. Most hotels and restaurants are seasonal. High season 1 July to 30 Sept.

Barano. Quiet town above thermal springs and beautiful Maronti Beach. *Parco Smeraldo* (M), on Maronti Beach (990.127). Resort hotel with spa treatments. V.

Casamicciola. Spa and summer resort. *Cristallo Palace* (E), Via Eddomade (994.362). Open 1 April to 31 Oct. Just off shore drive; large, balconies, pool. MC, V. *Manzi* (E), Piazza Bagni (994.722). Open 1 April to 31 Oct. On hillside, attractive, pool, gardens. AE, DC, V. *Elma* (M), Corso V. Emanuele (994.122). Open 1 April to 31 Oct. Comfortable, balconied rooms, pool. AE, DC, MC, V.

Forio. Promontory town above beautiful beaches, thermal springs. *Parco Regine* (M), on Citara Beach (907.366). Spa treatments, pool. V.

Restaurants. *La Meridiana* (M), on San Francesco Beach. Very good. V. *Negombo* (E), on San Montano beach (986.152). Open 19 April to 19 Oct. Beach club with fine restaurant, evenings by reservation only. *La Romantica* (M), Via Marina 46 (997.345). Closed Nov. Seafood, good service. AE, DC.

Ischia. Town composed of Ischia Porto, where steamers dock, and Ischia Ponte, beach resort and spa. *Aragona Palace* (E), Via Porto 12 (981.383). Open end April to 15 Oct. Balconied rooms, pool. AE, DC, MC. *Excelsior Belvedere* (E), Via E. Gianturco 3 (991.020). Open 24 April to 10 Oct. Best; quiet, comfortable, with pool, gardens, beach. AE, DC, MC, V. *Parco Aurora* (E), Via D'Avalos (982.022). Open 1 April to 31 Oct. Terraces, pool, on sea front; low rates in category. MC, V. *Punta Molino* (E), Lungomare Telese (991.544). Open 25 Apr. to 31 Oct. Vies with *Excelsior* for top honors. Set apart on sea with pool, beach, gardens. AE, DC.

Alexander (M), Lungomare Telese (993.124). Open 23 April to 23 Oct. Large, attractive modern building, pool, garden. Pricey in category. *Ambasciatori* (M), Via R. Gianturco 20 (992.933). Open 1 April to 31 Oct. Comfortable, airy rooms, many with balcony. *Nuovo Lido* (M), Via R. Gianturco 31 (991.550). Open 1 April to 15 Oct. Close to beach; pleasant rooms with balconies. AE, DC, MC, V. *Regina Palace* (M), Via Cortese 18 (991.344). Open 16 Mar. to 15 Nov. and 20 Dec. to 10 Jan. In pine grove; terraces and pool. AE, V.

Villa Diana (I), Corso V. Colonna 212 (991.785). Open 1 April to 31 Oct. Attractive, good-sized pension, near beach. *Villa Paradiso* (I), (991.501). Open 1 April to 31 Oct. Fine family-run villa hotel near beach. *Villarosa* (M), (991.316). Open 25 March to 31 Oct. Pretty rooms, attentive service in gracious villa.

Restaurants. *Giardini Eden-Da Ugo* (E), Via Nuova Cartaromana 40 (993.909). Open May to Sept. Lunch only. On the shoals at Ischia Ponte for swimming, sunbathing and/or delicious seafood. *Porticciullo* (E), on the port. Closed Nov. Familyrun; very good. AE. *Da Alberto* (M), Bagno Lido (981.259). Open Easter to mid-Oct. Simple, good, beach restaurant. *Gennaro* (M), Via Porto 66 (992.917). Open 1 April to 31 Oct. A favorite for seafood. AE, DC, MC, V. *Massa* (M), Via Seminario 35 (991.402). Closed Tues. Open 16 Feb. to 14 Nov. At Ischia Ponte. *Zi Nannina* (M), Lungomare Telese (991.350). Open 1 April to 30 Sept. Dining with a sea view.

Lacco Ameno. Spa and beach resort. *Regina Isabella* (L), Piazza Umberto (994.322). Open 1 Apr. to 15 Oct. CIGA, best on island; sumptuous, smart; 130 beautifully furnished rooms, pool, beach, tennis, spa treatments. AE, DC, MC, V. *La Reginella* (E), Piazza Santa Restituta (994.304). Open 12 March to 31 Oct. Attractive, Mediterranean-style; pool, beach. AE, DC, V. *San Montano* (E), Monte Vico (994.033). Open 1 Mar. to 31 Oct. Splendid position atop seaside promontory. Comforts include pool, spa treatments. Pricey in category. AE, DC, MC, V.

Restaurant. *Padrone del Mare* (M), Corso Rizzoli 6 (996.159). Closed Tues. from Oct. to March. Classic seafood spot.

Sant'Angelo. Picturesque fishing village near good beaches. *San Michele* (M), located above town (999.276). Open 1 March to 31 Oct. Good views, pool, spa treatments. *Vulcano* (M), above beach (999.322). Smallish, comfortable; pool, spa. *Casa Rosa* (I), Via Fondolillo 7 (999.328). Above beach, pleasant hotel with terraces, pool.

Restaurant. *Dal Pescatore* (M), Piazza Troia (999.206). Open 16 March to 31 Oct. Delicious vegetable *antipastos,* good fish and local wine. MC, V.

Maiori Salerno (089). Overbuilt beach resort on Amalfi coast, best off-season. High season same as Amalfi. *Pietra di Luna* (M), Lungomare (877.500). Open 1 April to 21 Oct. Large, overlooking beach across road; 90 rooms with view of coast or hills. AE, DC, MC, V.

Restaurant. *Mammato* (M), Lungomare (877.036). Closed Tues. Good local cuisine.

Marina di Camerota Salerno (0974). Pretty village-resort on Cilento coast. High season 1 July to 31 Aug. *Baia delle Sirene* (M), (932.236). Open 1 June to 30 Sept. Modern resort hotel on sea; pool, tennis.

Restaurants. *Pusigno* (M), on Palinuro road (932.150). Open 15 June to 15 Sept. Good dining with a view. AE, DC, MC, V. *Valentone* (M), Piazza della Chiesa (932.004). Closed Sun. off-season and Feb. Home-style food.

Paestum Salerno (0828). Greek temples and broad beaches. High season 18 June to 18 Sept. and Easter. *Martini* (M), at Porta Giustizia entrance to temples (811.020). Only 13 rooms in bungalows in pine grove. AE. *Villa Rita* (I), near Porta Giustizia (811.081). Simple but adequate overnight. DC.

At **Laura,** 5 km. (3 miles) north, *Le Palme* (M), (851.025). Open 1 March to 31 Oct. Large, comfortable resort hotel. AE, DC, MC, V. **Restaurants.** *Nettuno* (M), Porta Giustizia (811.028). Closed Mon. off-season. Garden with view of temples. AE, DC, MC, V. *Sea Garden* (M), Porta Giustizia (811.020). AE. *Museo* (M), at temples (811.135). Closed Mon. off-season. Good and reasonable lunch stop.

Palinuro Salerno (0974). Beach resort on Cilento coast. High season 1 July to 31 Aug. *Saline* (E), on road to Agropoli (931.112). Open 1 April to 31 Oct. Modern resort hotel on beach; pool, tennis. AE, DC, V. *King's Residence* (M), on promontory (931.324). Open 1 April to 31 Oct. Quiet location with good views; pool. AE, DC, V. *San Paolo* (M), on hill above town (931.214). Good value; pool, tennis. *La Torre* (M), on port (931.264). Open 15 May to 15 Oct. Good outdoor restaurant. AE, DC.

Pompeii Napoli (081). *Bristol* (M), Piazza Vittorio Veneto 863.1625. Satisfactory overnight. AE, DC, V. *Rosario* (M), Via Roma (863.1002). Large traditional old hotel.

Restaurants. There is a restaurant/cafeteria (M) and picnic area within the excavations. *Anfiteatro* (M), Via Roma 125 (863.1245). Closed Mon. Simple, pleasant. *Zi'Caterina* (M), Via Roma 18 (863.1263). Closed Tues. At center of town, some distance from excavations.

Positano Salerno (089). Smart, colorful resort with stairways for streets. High season same as Amalfi. *San Pietro* (L), 2.5 km. (1½ miles) outside town on Amalfi road (875.455). Closed Nov. to Mar. An extraordinary hotel, set apart on flowered terraces high above the sea with spectacular views. Lift to private beach and tennis; hotel boat; minibus service into town. AE, DC, MC, V. *Le Sireneuse* (L), Via Colombo 30 (875.066). Smart, in town, tastefully furnished, comfortable rooms, most with view; pool. AE, DC, MC, V.

Ancora (M), Via Colombo (875.318). Open 1 April to 15 Oct. Lovely villa-type; terraces. DC, V. *Casa Albertina* (M), Via Tavolozza 4 (875.143). Short climb up from road. Small, attractively decorated, good views. AE, DC, MC, V. *Covo dei Sarceni* (M), at Marina (875.059). Open 1 April to 31 Oct. Only hotel directly on beach; good-sized rooms, terrace restaurant, pool. AE, DC, V. *Palazzo Murat* (M), Via dei Mulini (875.177). Open 1 April to 15 Oct. Handsome old villa in heart of town but in quiet garden. Modern annex. No restaurant. *Poseidon* (M), Viale Pasitea (875.014). Open 18 April to 14 Oct. Uphill from beach, beautifully furnished salons, garden terrace with pool; all rooms with balcony. AE.

Restaurants. *Buca di Bacco* (M), on beach Via Rampa Teglia 8 (875.699). Open 1 Apr. to 5 Nov. Very good; veranda overlooking beach. AE, DC, V. *Capurale* (M), Via Marina (875.374). Best food and lowest prices on the beach. *Covo dei Saraceni* (M), Via Marina (875.059). Open 1 April to 31 Oct. Fine local cuisine served on terrace with view. AE, DC, V. *Da Vincenzo* (M), near Bar De Martino (no phone). Fun, good value.

Praiano Salerno (089). On Amalfi coast. High season same as Amalfi. *Tritone* (M), on coast road (874.333). Open 15 April to 5 Oct. Cliffside hotel with spectacular views, large pool, lift to beach. Minibus service into Praiano. AE, V.

Restaurants. *La Brace* (M), at Vettica (874.226). Closed Wed. off-season. AE, DC, V. *San Gennaro* (I), at Vettica; no phone. Simple, good. Beautiful view.

Procida Napoli (081). Volcanic island in Bay of Naples. High season 15 May to 15 Oct. *Le Arcate* (I), at Chiaia (896.7120). Open 15 March to 15 Oct. Good views, beach. AE, V. *L'Oasi* (I), at Ciraccio (896.7499). Small villa with garden.

Ravello Salerno (089). High season as Amalfi. *Palumbo* (L) Palazzo Confalone (857.244). Tiny, excellent; old-world atmosphere, marvelous views. *Caruso Belvedere* Caruso (M) Via Toro 52 (857.111). Rambling old palace, large rooms, old-fashioned but comfortable, wonderful views, garden. AE. *Rufolo* (M) (857.133). Atmosphere, pool, views. AE, DC, MC, V. *Parsifal* (I), (857 144). Delightful old building, modern comforts; good value. AE, DC, MC, V. *Villa Maria* (I) Via Santa Chiara (857.170). Family-run pension set in a garden. Simple but homey and restful. Restaurant and bar. AE, DC, MC.

Restaurants. *Caruso Belvedere* (M) (857.111). Closed Tues. Open 1 May to 31 Oct. Good food, famed house wine, nostalgic ambiance. AE, V. *Compà Cosimo* (I), Via Roma 44 (957.156). Closed Mon. off-season. Good local cooking in this popular *trattoria*. V. *Garden* (M), Via Chiunzi (857.227). Closed Fri. Behind Villa Rufolo. Good house wine. *Palumbo* (M), Via Toro (857.244). Closed Wed. off-season. Local and French cuisine, fine wines. Edges into pricey category. AE, DC, MC, V.

Salerno Salerno (089). Port city. *Jolly* (E), Lungomare Trieste (770.050). Big, modern hotel, all comforts. AE, DC, MC, V. *Plaza* (M), Piazza Ferrovia (224.477). At railway station and SITA bus terminal; clean, modern comfortable. No restaurant. AE, DC, V.

Restaurants. *Antica Pizzeria* (M), Vicolo della Neve 24 (225.705). Closed Wed. Hearty local dishes, delicious pizza. *La Brace* (M), Viale Trieste 13 (225.159). Closed Sun. Small; excellent fish and pizza. *Il Gambero* (M), Via Cuomo 9 (225.031). Closed Sun. Fine seafood. *Nocola dei Pricipati* (M), Corso Garibaldi 201 (225.435). Closed Sat. and Sun. evenings. Longtime favorite for fish specialties. AE, DC, V.

Sant'Agnello Napoli (081). Near Sorrento. High season 1 April to 30 Sept.
Restaurant. *Il Capanno* (M), Rione Cappuccini 58 (878.2453). Open 1 May to 30 Sept. Closed Mon. Rustic and unpretentious.

Sorrento Napoli (081). Important resort. High season 1 April to 30 Sept. *Cocumella* (E), Via Cocumella 7 (878.2933). Historic old villa with tasteful blend of antique and contemporary decor. Restaurant, bar, pool, tennis. AE, DC, MC. *Europa Place* (E), Via Correale 34 (878.1501). Large palace-type hotel overlooking sea; terraces, garden, old-world atmosphere. *Excelsior Vittoria* (E), Piazza Tasso 34 (878.1900). Fine old hotel, excellent service and accommodations; pool, gardens. AE, DC, MC, V. *Imperial Tramontano* (E), Via Vittorio Veneto (878.1940). Open 1 March to 31 Oct. Handsome, traditional hotel on cliff overlooking sea; pool, gardens, elevator to swimming area. AE, DC, V. Also see Sant'Agnello.

Bellevue Syrene (M), Piazza della Vittoria 5 (878.1024). Spacious rooms in stately villa with gardens, views, lift to sea. Very good value. AE, DC, MC, V. *Eden* (M), Via Correale 25 (878.1909). Open 1 Mar. to 31 Oct. Central, friendly, bright rooms, garden. *Minerva* (M), Via Capo 30 (878.1011). Open 1 April to 31 Oct. Outside town, high above sea, good views; private-villa atmosphere; pool. V.

Villa di Sorrento (I), Via Fuorimura 4 (878.1068). Central, small hotel. No restaurant. AE, DC, MC, V.

Restaurants. *Cavallino Bianco* (M), Via Correale 11/a (878.5809). Closed Tues. Dining terrace, pizza. *Beppe* (M), Via S. Antonino 12 (878.4176). Closed Mon. Central, very good. *Cattedrale* (M), Via Sersale 4 (877.2584). Closed Tues. Attractive; seafood. AE. *La Lanterna* (M), Via San Cesareo 23 (878.1355). AE, V. *Parrucchiano* (M), Corso Italia 71 (878.216). Closed Wed. off-season. Classic place for good food. One of the best in the Sorrento area with wide choice of local dishes. AE, V. *Antica Trattoria,* Via Padre Reginaldo Giuliani 33. Centrally located in old town, good ambience and food. *Zi'Ntonio* (M), Via De Maio 11 (878.1623). Closed Thurs. and Feb. Pleasant courtyard. AE, DC, MC, V.

Vico Equense Napoli (081). Picturesque town on Sorrento peninsula. High season 1 July to 30 Sept. *Le Axidie* (E), at Marina Equa (879.8181). Open 1 April to 30 Sept. Modern wing on old monastery, antiques; balconied rooms, pool, tennis, beach. MC. *Capo La Gala* (E), at Scraio (879.8278). Open 1 April to 30 Sept. For lovers of sun and sea, 18 rooms directly on private beach; smart, informal. AE, V.
Restaurant. *Pizza a Metro-Da Gigino* (M), Via Nicotera 10 (879.8426). Closed Wed. Famous for pizza assembly line and good food. AE, MC, V.

GETTING AROUND. By air. The region's airport is at Naples—at Capodichino—with regular national and international flights. There is a 25-min. bus service into Naples, to the main rail station, running roughly every 20 minutes from 7 A.M. to 9.30 P.M.

By boat. Hydrofoils, steamers and car ferries connect Capri, Ischia and Procida with Naples and/or Pozzuoli. There's a summer service between Salerno, Amalfi, Positano and Capri and year-round service between Sorrento and Capri. During the summer only residents of the islands may embark their cars.

By train. The main north–south rail line from Rome to Naples has two branches: one passes along the coast via Gaeta and Formia, the other runs inland via Cassino and Caserta. Benevento is on a main line from Naples to Foggia, while Avellino is on a secondary line. From Naples, the principal line to the south passes through Salerno and forks at Battipaglia, with the coastal branch passing through Paestum and the base of the Cilento.

The Circumvesuviana and Cumana suburban railways out of Naples are useful for getting to places like Pompeii and Sorrento.

By bus. There is a regular bus service between Naples and Caserta, Avellino, Salerno and Benevento. Local buses connect smaller towns. The SITA line serves the Amalfi coast, connecting with the Circumvesuviana at Sorrento and with the main rail line at Salerno. Summer coach service Rome–Sorrento–Amalfi. Inquire at CIT, Rome.

By car. The Autostrada del Sole runs through Campania, touching Caserta, Naples and Salerno and connecting with the A17 autostrada to Bari that passes Avellino. For the Sorrento peninsula, take the Naples–Pompeii–Salerno highway and exit at Castellamare, just after Pompeii. Roads on the Sorrento peninsula are narrow and tortuous, requiring capable driving skills and strong nerves.

PLACES OF INTEREST. Scavi di Ercolano (The Herculaneum Excavations). A smaller site than Pompeii. Opens at 9 and closes an hour before sunset, daily. Admission 4,000 lire. Closed Mon.

Scavi di Pompeii (The Pompeii Excavations). One of the great archeological sites of the world, as much for its romantic story as for its historical importance. As with Herculaneum, all the best finds have been moved to the Archeological Museum in Naples, but there's still a lot to see on the ground. Open 9 to an hour before sunset (naturally, that's early in winter, around 3). Entrance fee 5,000 lire. Closed Mon.

Paestum. Once a prosperous Greek colony, Poseidonia. Its massive temples are a remarkable sight, especially the Temple of Neptune, one of the best preserved Greek Doric temples anywhere in the world, including Greece itself. Open 9 to an hour before sunset. Closed Mon.

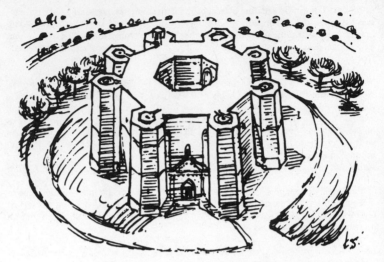

THE DEEP SOUTH

Gargano, Apulia, Lucania and Calabria

Many tourists believe that with a visit to Naples, a drive round the Amalfi coast to Salerno, and possibly as far afield as Paestum, they have seen Italy's south; yet they have barely passed through the gate, however spectacular what they have seen may be. Over 650 km. (400 miles) of driving are needed to reach the southernmost tip of Calabria, Italy's "toe", some 32 km. (20 miles) beyond Reggio Calabria. On the Adriatic shore the little-known "Deep South" begins farther north at Termoli. Here old main road and new *superstrada* alike cut inland to avoid the rugged contours of the Gargano Peninsula, Italy's "spur". From Termoli, too, there's 650 km. (400 miles) to be done at the wheel if you follow the coast road all the way to Santa Maria di Leuca at the tip of Italy's "heel."

Italy's far south is composed of the ancient provinces of Apulia (called Puglia in modern Italy), Lucania (known also as the Basilicata), and Calabria. Apulia forms Italy's "heel", Lucania constitutes the "instep" and "arch" and the territory between, and Calabria provides the "toe." The Gargano Peninsula, the "spur", is a part of Apulia; despite recent package-tour development it is still relatively unspoilt. It should be seen before it becomes too popular. It is a wild region, yet idyllic, where olive trees stretch for mile after mile, where towns are rare and where a huge, cool forest adds a surprisingly northern touch.

But most of Apulia consists of hills and plains covered with olive groves and dotted with imposing castles, interesting towns, the *trulli*—simple circular dwellings, unchanged since Stone Age days (until very recently)— and some fine harbors.

Considerable improvements have been made in what has long been Italy's poorest region. The first great step was the introduction of DDT at the end of the Second World War. The entire coast of this area was so malaria-infested that only a few hardy souls could live here. Today the land is mostly fertile and well-tilled, with sugar-beet a vital, and very profitable, main crop in certain parts. New roads have both opened the area to commerce and have allowed tourists to travel throughout the region in ever-increasing numbers. This increase in tourism has stimulated the need for labor-intensive operations, such as hotels, restaurants, garages and service stations, bringing both work and money at the same time.

The coast resorts on the fine sandy beaches are in full development. Many have been ruined by overbuilding with big beach hotels and forlorn ranks of bungalows which remain empty for ten months of the year. Italian vacationers crowd the coasts in July and August, when it is very hot here.

Exploring the Deep South

The Gargano Peninsula is one of the surprises of southern Italy; it has breath-taking scenery, well-equipped resorts and a friendly refreshing atmosphere. Along its northern coast over 64 km. (40 miles) of sandy beach and dunes enclose two large lagoons, with flat fertile plains extending inland from them to the base of the limestone mountains. In summer the plains are golden with grain crops and olives cover the lower mountain slopes. By car, your jumping-off point for this region is Poggio Imperiale, south of Termoli. From San Severo, Gargano's only railway line reaches the north coast at picturesque Rodi Garganico after a *very* laborious mountain journey. 16 km. (10 miles) further on, it peters out at Peschici.

Rodi Garganico and Peschici are lovely white towns shut in between mountains and sea. Vieste, however, which lies on a small peninsula, is the main commercial center of this region. A coastal road runs to Porto di Mattinata, in the plain on the Gargano limestone massif's southern side, passing one cliff headland after another, uphill and downhill through the miles of olive groves that give the region much of its special character. It is not long since mules were almost the only means of transport in these parts, but today, when work in the fields is done, the local population returns home on tractors. Fishing is an important industry. Trawlers sail out of Manfredonia, smaller fishing boats out of Peschici, the most picturesque and charming town on the Gargano.

Vieste, with a magnificent, long sandy beach south of the town, is crowded with tourists during the hot summer months. The coast road from Vieste gives you tantalizing glimpses of crystal-clear water in enchanting rocky inlets. Finally, a left turn off the main road leads you to Testa del Gargano, where the Pugnochiuso promontory hosts two hotels in an internationally known holiday complex with a fine white sand beach. All along the Gargano coast the contrast of turquoise waters and white limestone cliffs topped with deep green scrub pines is breathtaking.

Smack in the middle of the Gargano peninsula stands the majestic Foresta Umbra, literally, the shady forest. The odd thing about this wood, 2,600 feet above sea level, is its density and coolness, and the fact it grows exactly the same trees—especially beeches—as you find in the English counties close to London. Emerging from its coolness into the sudden, oven-like temperature of a blazing August day is an extraordinary experience.

The only highway through the Foresta Umbra is S 528, winding and tiring. It leads from the northern coast west of Peschici to Monte Sant' Angelo, Gargano's capital, a fantastic white town, built right on top of the limestone's southernmost ridge. It is an important place of pilgrimage, for in 491 St. Michael appeared to some country shepherds in a cave here and left his red cloak behind. In the 8th century, an abbey was built on the spot, and thousands of crusaders paid homage to the angel here before embarking from the once-busy port of Manfredonia, 16 km. (10 miles) to the south, on the edge of the plain called the *Tavoliere* (chessboard) of Apulia.

Inland Apulia

Inland, Foggia is the plain's commercial center. It boasts a Romanesque cathedral (1179), but little else of note. San Severo, to the north, is a wine-producing center. Westwards, Lucera's chief feature is the great castle and towers built by Frederick II in the 1270s to protect the town. His successors transformed a Saracen mosque into a Gothic cathedral (about 1300). The ancient Roman arena can still be seen.

The autostrada (A14) and the old main road down Italy's east coast, turn inland after Termoli to dodge the Gargano Peninsula. After passing San Severo, Foggia and Cerignola they return to the coast at Barletta. Near San Severo, with its various baroque buildings, are the ruins of Castel Fiorentino, where Frederick died in 1250.

The autostrada exit at Canosa di Puglia leads northeast to the coast at Barletta, while a country lane meanders in the opposite direction to the great abode of Frederick, his favorite and most impressive castle, the Castel del Monte (built around 1240), rising in solitary splendor above the plain and commanding one of the finest views in southern Italy. The expertly restored octagonal construction with eight towers (see our chapter-head drawing) has been ranked in splendor and significance with the Colosseum. Nearby, under the medieval church of Ruvo di Puglia, a 4th-century B.C. cemetery was unearthed in 1979, providing valuable clues to life in ancient times.

The southern part of Bari's province offers other Norman monuments at Gravina and Gioia del Colle, the latter having a striking castle. Within easy driving distance of Bari is Castellana Grotte, with its recently discovered underground caverns noted for their interesting stalagmites and stalactites. There are two lengths of tours of the grottos, one taking about an hour, the other two. Altamura possesses remnants of prehistoric walls and a cathedral begun by Frederick II. Alberobello, the district capital, possesses a major tourist attraction in its trulli.

The trulli are considered peculiar to Apulia, but old buildings of the same style can be seen in Malta, and it is clear that something similar was used in many Mediterranean areas in bygone centuries. Basically, the trullo is a simple circular, stone-built one-roomed dwelling, roughly constructed without mortar or squaring-off of the stones. Their roofs vary. Those at Alberobello are today conical, but many old trulli in other parts of Apulia have outside stone staircases leading up to flat roofs incorporating grainstores—to keep the grain away from at least most of the rats and mice. Both types of ancient trulli have simple holes in the roof to let out the smoke of fires used for cooking.

Nowhere else is there such a large collection of these curious buildings as Alberobello, where they form almost a village on their own. This little collection is being carefully preserved. Out in the country, though, lots of old trulli are being abandoned in favor of modern variations. These latter are square, built of brick and stucco, and have proper windows and chimneys. Often, too, they are brightly colored. You see them not only in the countryside but also clustered in many coastal villages on both sides of the Salentine Peninsula, the official name of Italy's "heel." The pretty towns of Martina Franca and Oria present interesting mixtures of medieval and Baroque buildings, with a sprinkling of trulli nearby.

Further south is Lecce, a beautiful Baroque town bearing the stamp of successive Spanish governors. Greeks and Romans both held sway here, and it was an independent dukedom when the Normans captured it in the 11th century. The town center was largely built in the 16th and 17th centuries, the cathedral in 1670, bishop's palace in 1632, and seminary in 1709, all grouped together in the Piazza del Duomo (Cathedral Square), thus creating an unusually attractive and homogeneous architectural whole. There is a 16th-century castle and some extraordinary 17th-century buildings, the churches of Santa Croce and the Rosario and the Governor's Palace (1695), all in the decorative and sometimes bizarre local Baroque style. Santi Nicolò e Cataldo is an impressive admixture of eras and styles.

The Apulian Coast

Apulia's coast displays no less variety. Barletta is a naval base and port, with a Colossus, an enormous bronze statue, presumed to be of one of the Byzantine emperors. The city also features numerous medieval churches and a superb cathedral, which is a composite of styles; Gothic, Norman and Renaissance, topped off by a fine Romanesque campanile. Two baroque palaces are complemented by yet another of Frederick's large castles.

Trani, Bisceglia and Molfetta all stand out because of their fine stone buildings, recalling the Venetian towns on the Yugoslav Dalmatian coast. Trani's cathedral, with splendid bronze doors (1179), is one of the loveliest churches in Apulia. It was begun in 1094 and is more Pisan than Norman in inspiration. Bisceglie, too, boasts a fine cathedral.

Bari is by far the largest of the towns here. It consists of a tiny medieval old town on a peninsula and a vast 19th-century city built to a grid-pattern plan. Bari is a port, as well as an industrial center, with an unusual claim to fame. Here, in an 11th-century basilica with a later candy box painted ceiling, lie the bones of Santa Claus. The Father Christmas of modern times was in reality a Bishop of Myra (in present day Turkey), called Nicholas, who lived nearly 1,700 years ago. His kindness to children brought him great renown and he was canonized after raising a murdered boy from the dead. In the 11th century, allegedly, some Bari sailors obtained possession of his bones and brought them home, where the church you can see today was raised for them. It is dedicated of course to St. Nicholas (San Nicola). His transmutation into Santa Claus occurred in New York. The feast of St. Nicholas on December 6th is still fêted in Holland and many other countries; in Dutch, the baby-talk version of "Sint Niklaas" (St. Nicholas) is "Sinter Klaas". It was Dutch settlers' children in New York who first transferred the saint to Christmas Day and started leaving clogs—forerunners of our modern stockings—for the kindly old bishop to deposit his presents in. As well as the basilica with its bones of the saint, Bari has a Norman castle, rebuilt by Frederick II in 1233, and a fine cathedral. The Archeological Museum houses finds from all over Apulia (open 9–2, closed Mon.).

Brindisi, though smaller, is nevertheless more important as a port, a position it has held for well over 2,000 years. It's not recommended for anything more than a brief stop to see such churches as San Giovanni al Sepolcro and San Benedetto (both 11th-century), reminders of its medieval splendor. In those days, much wealth passed through the ports of southern Italy. From Brindisi, excellent sandy beaches stretch toward Bari, studded here and there with modern holiday villages. Nearby Ostuni is a pictur-esque town that spills over the hillside in an exotic jumble of whitewashed rooftops and arches.

Warning. Brindisi and Bari provide frequent and fast carferry crossings to Greece, but take extra precautions in both towns against car theft and broken windows when parked.

From just south of Bari to the farthermost tip of the Salentine Peninsula, the coast consists almost all the way of low sandstone cliffs, whose rocks in several places have been worn into fantastic shapes. Nowhere are these more striking than at Santa Cesarea Terme, an old-fashioned spa with a modern sea bathing area. Here you can swim and sunbathe in the middle of pillars and columns and arches that look like the ruins of an old town, but are in reality merely the result of interaction between sea and sand-stone.

In one or two other places, much higher cliffs of different geological composition breast the sea. Otranto, a little north of Santa Cesarea Terme, shelters in the lee of one such promontory. It is the easternmost port on the strait which gives it its name, but has lost much of its importance be-cause of its remoteness.

The Salentine Peninsula's western coast possesses many strikingly love-ly sections. The white town of Gallipoli, perched on an island reached by a causeway, is perhaps outstanding. But little Santa Caterina, with its viv-idly-colored box-like houses (mostly modern trulli), has a charm of a dif-ferent sort—one repeated to a lesser degree in several other villages on this stretch of coast. The shore itself is edged mostly by low volcanic rocks rising only a few feet above the water's level and interspersed with sandy coves.

Taranto, even more ancient than Brindisi in its origins, is today mainly a fine 19th-century town. Its position is magnificent. It occupies a peninsu-la on one side of a lovely bay overlooking a narrow entrance into a large landlocked bay called the "Mare Piccola" (Small Sea). The "Mare Gran-de" is Taranto's even finer deepwater anchorage in the bay, created by stretching breakwaters from offshore islands so as to leave only three en-trances. On the town's landward side, you have grand views towards the mountains, which once more begin to approach the coast. Taranto, the home of a Naval Academy, retains little from the past except the 14th-century Church of San Domenico. The local museum, however, has a fine collection of classical art objects and is well worth a visit to see the Helle-nistic gold ornaments.

Lucania (The Basilicata)

Westward from Taranto a fertile coastal plain, fringed with magnificent sand, extends for 80 km. (50 miles) with a number of new resorts, such as Castellaneta Marina and Marina di Ginosa. In the northwest of this plain, on the wide Gulf of Taranto, the temple ruins of ancient Metapontum are a reminder that all the best harbor sites, and many other spots as well, were settled by Greeks over 2,500 years ago. Pythagoras lived and worked at Metapontum.

Finally, at Rocca Imperiale, below one of Frederick II's great but ruined structures, road and coastal railway are hemmed in between steep mountainside and shore.

Inland Lucania is mountainous, impressive, still remote. Here, if you go a little way from the few main roads and penetrate into the hills, you can still see local folk threshing exactly as described by the great Roman poet Virgil in his *Georgics,* written 2,000 years ago. Life in the Basilicata is hard. Summers are scorchingly hot and winters bitterly cold, and the land is for the most part poor and stony.

Located in the instep of the boot, Lucania is probably the least known of Italy's areas, partly because of its remoteness from the more populous centers of the country, and partly because of the absence of nature or man, though it flourished briefly during the reign of Frederick II. The scenery is varied and extraordinary, unlike any other part of Italy. Great, sandy wastelands line much of the Ionian coast; inland there are areas of forests, inhabited by wolves and wild boar. The high, wild mountains are divided by deep, rocky gorges and contrasting broad valleys.

Inland, over tortuous roads, you reach Matera, picturesquely perched on a steep slope. Much-neglected Matera contains a 13th-century cathedral and other churches, of which the oldest dates from 718. It is noted primarily, however, for its numerous rock dwellings, houses, and even churches, hewn from the solid rock. Matera is a strange town, half deserted and entirely born of the mountains from which it has been fashioned.

Worth seeing is the panorama from the high-perched nearby village of Miglionico, a few miles southwest in whose medieval castle the feudal barons of the 15th century conspired together against Ferdinand I of Aragon.

Other points of interest are Venosa (the Roman Venusia), birthplace of the poet Horace; Melfi, containing churches from the 12th and 13th centuries; Acerenza, with its 12th-century cathedral; Lagopesole, another residence of Frederick—better preserved than Rocca Imperiale and Monte Vúlture—reached from Rionero in Vúlture—an extinct volcano whose cone dominates a huge area of the province.

The mountainous surroundings of Potenza, Lucania's capital, are more attractive than the town itself. Potenza was founded by the Romans, a vital staging post on the Via Appia from Rome to Brindisi, and from there to Rome's highly profitable eastern possessions. It was badly damaged in the 1980 earthquakes.

The Basilicata's western coast deserves a special mention, for it includes much of the lovely Gulf of Policastro. The beaches here are not much to write home about, but the scenery is superb. The humble village of Maratea is famed for its hilltop and monumental statue of Christ, halfway between the resorts of Porto di Maratea and Marina di Maratea. Porto di Maratea, on the coast, is a pretty little village, and the area boasts a few good seaside hotels. To see the full effect of the scenery, drive the road from Sapri to Praia a Mare, about 25 km. (15 odd miles).

Calabria

Calabria is a strange and beautiful land, even more ruggedly mountainous than the Basilicata. It consists of coastal shelves and small alluvial plains, with magnificent sweeps of mountain inland—from some viewpoints in the Piccola Sila Range that fills the southern parts of the "toe", you have stupendous views that are also first-rate lessons in geomorphology. You can see where silt brought down by springtime torrents in gullies dry the rest of the year, has pushed the land out into the sea. In places land has risen in relation to the sea to leave a narrow coastal shelf or plain. In the Capo Rizzuto region, you can even see a succession of these plains, looking like a giant's garden steps. No one thinks of Calabria as a region of art towns, and indeed it cannot hold a candle to the famous places farther north. But it has plenty of spots that are worth a visit and a surprising number of ancient churches and other historical remains.

Calabria might be defined as a peninsula at the end of a peninsula, the long, thin toe at the western end of Italy's boot. The region is made up of two strips of sea coast that sandwich between them a chain of mountains and wooded areas. Calabria's history is much the same as that of the rest of southern Italy: numerous invasions succeeded one another until the area reached a low point both materially and culturally. Now beach resorts are attracting tourists, while reforestation has created valuable woodland zones. But it is still essentially an agricultural region, with the Calabrians winning a difficult living from the terraced, intensively cultivated hillsides.

The region is divided into three parts, named after the three largest Calabrian cities: Cosenza, inland in the northern half of the region; Catanzaro, near the Ionian coast, farther south; and Reggio Calabria, at the tip of Italy, across the strait from Messina. In themselves these three cities are not particularly interesting for their architecture. Reggio is entirely modern, having been rebuilt after the earthquake of 1908, which devastated Messina also. However, the three cities command excellent views of the surrounding country and emphasize what is the most absorbing feature of Calabria: its striking countryside dotted with villages.

In the province of Cosenza, one of the stops on the Naples-Reggio railroad line is Paola, a picturesque coastal town famous as the birthplace of Saint Francis di Paola, to whom a sanctuary in late Renaissance style is dedicated. The ancient square of the village is also interesting.

The road from Paola to Cosenza is famous for its great vistas of mountains and sea. In the broadest part of the Calabrian peninsula lies the Sila, a famous forest and mountainous zone, now used also for pastureland in the areas where the trees have been cut.

Of Calabria's main towns, Castrovillari, Cosenza and Catanzaro lie high in the mountains, and are therefore cool in summer. All offer fine surroundings—in particular, the circular tour round Monte Gariglione makes a stupendous day's excursion from Catanzaro, though it's decidedly hard work for the driver. You make first for Taverna, and whichever way you do the circular drive, you pass through Villagio Mancuso, a mountain resort built in the 1930s (and looking it). Drive along Lake Ampollino, and enjoy the views from close to Petilia.

Tiriolo, near Catanzaro, on the narrowest part of the peninsula, commands a view including the Ionian Sea on one side, the Tyrrhenian on the other—and the famous volcano, Stromboli. Also nearby is the town of Squillace, on the gulf of the same name, a charming village with excellent beaches. In the vicinity is the ruined Church of Santa Maria della Roccella, a majestic Norman building of the 11th century.

Farther north, Lakes Arvo and Cecita, artificial basins, also offer striking scenery and a restful coolness in contrast to Calabria's hot, often treeless, coasts. This is the heart of the Sila Mountains, a region that is destined to become increasingly popular in both winter and summer. The roads are excellent, and there are a few good hotels in such strategic spots as Lorica, San Giovanni in Fiore, and Camigliatello. In the center of the Sila region, San Giovanni in Fiore is the site of the ancient Badia Fiorense. Lying in the area where the winter snows last longest (November–March), this town is also a good stopping place for winter sports enthusiasts.

Northeast of Cosenza, in the direction of Lucania, is the town of Rossano, an important center in the Byzantine period and therefore the town of Calabria richest in Byzantine remains, among them the beautiful Church of San Marco and (not far from the town) the Monastery of Santa Maria del Patire. The Diocesan Museum possesses the *Codex Purpureus,* one of the oldest Greek illuminated manuscripts in existence.

Other Norman and Byzantine buildings are to be seen at Santa Severina, Crotone, Vibo Valentia and Nicotera, all of them in the same general area. Farther from the coast, at Serra San Bruno, are the renowned Certosa of Saint Bruno and the Church of the Addolorata with its elegant Baroque facade, the work of an unknown local architect. Only a few miles away is the Ferdinandese, the restored summer residence of King Ferdinand II.

Traveling farther south and east towards the tip of the peninsula, you enter the province of Reggio Calabria, which is as formidably mountainous as the rest of Calabria, especially in the rugged Aspromonte section. At Gerace, safe on its high cliff, visit the sumptuous cathedral, the most extensive church of Calabria. At Stilo stop to see the equally famous little Church of La Cattolica, a gem of Byzantine construction, the sister-church of San Marco (Rossano).

Reggio Calabria, almost at sea level, is less attractive than Calabria's other towns, for the narrow coastal shelf here is filled with industry, and the views all along the coast north of Reggio, though fine, are spoilt for much of the way by factories and smoke. The Sicilian village of Scilla, in a very picturesque spot, recalls the ancients' tales of Scylla and Charybdis, the twin perils to navigators here—for if they avoided the whirlpool of Charybdis they were sure to smash onto the rocks of Scylla. The story is related in the *Odyssey* of Homer. One can well imagine the sailors' fear of having to navigate clumsy, almost keel-less vessels in these narrow, rocky waters. For us, however, the region's many cliffs provide magnificent scenery—provided industrial buildings don't clutter the foreground.

In Reggio's Archeological Museum you can see the famed *Warriors of Riace,* breathtaking 5th-century B.C. bronzes discovered off Calabria's coast in 1972, only a hint, experts say, of submerged artistic treasures. (Open Tues.–Sat. 9–1.30, 4–7, Sun. 9–12.30. Closed Mon.)

Don't overlook Calabria's coast resorts. You've probably never heard of them, and their names may mystify even Italian travel agents. But some are very nice indeed, though you'll have to be selective—overbuilding has ruined some of the region's loveliest beaches.

Some of the older towns along the coast have managed to reconcile tourism with history. Tropea, projecting from the Tyrrhenian (western) side of Italy's toe, is a town to make you dream dreams of bygone ages. Perched on the flat top of a sheer cliff, its cathedral dates from the 11th century. Its beachside hotels, however, are all moderately recent. And the ruined castle standing in the sea at Capo Rizzuto on the Ionian (eastern) coast, makes this another picturesque place for bathing.

PRACTICAL INFORMATION FOR
THE DEEP SOUTH

WHEN TO GO. The inland areas of these provinces suffer from extreme heat in summer coupled with bitter cold in winter. In the southern half of Apulia, however, these extremes are tempered in both seasons by breezes from the sea—not very strong, but enough to remove a little of the seasons' sting. In Calabria, in summer, the mountain towns and resorts provide welcome coolness. After a holiday on the sea, you might find it refreshing to round off your visit with a stay at a town such as Castrovillari, or in the mountains of the Sila, where you can manage without airconditioning even in mid-August.

In short, you can explore Italy's Deep South at any period of the year. In the heat of summer, it strikes you as extremely odd that the billboards advertising local hotels should all stress the provision of central heating: it's about the last thing you can envisage at this time of year. But it is definitely a must in winter, even along the more temperate coasts. Only in mainland Lucania does traveling in winter become a problem, and that is chiefly due to the shortage of good hotels and the difficult, tortuous, snow-covered roads.

As everywhere, the best time to visit is spring, when everything is green, and the beautiful wild flowers native to the Deep South are in full bloom. The last snows melt soon after mid-April, while the fall, too, is mild.

TOURIST OFFICES. Bari: AAST, Corso Vittorio Emanuele 68 (219.951); EPT, Via Melo 253 (225.327). **Barletta:** AAST, Piazza Aldo Moro (313.73). **Brindisi:** AAST, Via Rubini (210.91); EPT, Piazza Dionisi (21.944). **Catanzaro:** AAST, Piazza G. Rossi (45.530). **Cosenza:** AAST, Via Pasquale Rossi (39.095). **Foggia:** EPT, Via Emilio Perrone 17 (23.650). **Lecce:** AAST, Piazza S. Oronzo (24.443). **Matera:** EPT, Piazza Vittorio Veneto 19 (211.188). **Potenza:** EPT, Via Alianelli 4 (218.12). **Reggio Calabria:** AAST, Corso Garibaldi 329 (Teatro Comunale) (920.12) and at rail station (271.20); EPT, Via Demetrio Tripepi 72 (984.96). **Taranto:** EPT, Corso Umberto 113 (212.33).

SEASONAL EVENTS. The emotional, deeply held, religious sentiments of the Italian South are dramatically evident in the Holy Week processions that take place just before Easter, usually in April, in Bari, Brindisi, Reggio Calabria, and Taranto, where the procession of the Mysteries on Holy Thursday and Good Friday is quite spectacular.

Throughout the year, the smaller towns of southern Italy explode in enthusiastic observances in honor of local patron saints or some particular bounty of nature, as in the Mushroom Festival held at Camigliatello, in Sila, in October.

Bari: on May 7–8 the town honors its patron, San Nicola, with processions, fireworks, and general merrymaking; Jul. and Aug. there is an arts festival in Bari's castle.

Cosenza: in May, the numerous Calabrian towns in this province that were settled by Albanian refugees, stage a Spring Festival at which their original language, costume and folklore are the center of interest.

Lecce: Aug. sees the International Music Festival, as well as the Feast of Sant'Oronzo on Aug. 24–6, the latter an occasion for joyous celebration.

Nocera Tirinese: on Holy Sat. this small Calabrian mountain town in the province of Catanzaro is the scene of the highly unusual procession of the Vattienti, or Flagellants.

Potenza: on May 29 there's an elaborate pageant, the Parade of the Turks.

Reggio Calabria: Folklore Festival in Sept.

TELEPHONE CODES. You will find the telephone code for each town against its name in the Hotel and Restaurant listings (after the province name). If there is a different area code from the majority of the establishments—say when a hotel or restaurant is in an outlying place—then the code is given in front of the telephone number.

HOTELS AND RESTAURANTS. A variable region for price, and accommodations aren't always up to par. Some places—such as Bari during the September Trade Fair—will need advance planning. Quite a lot of establishments are seasonal, closing in the winter months, so check that as well. Summer airconditioning and winter heating are other points to keep an eye open for.

Regional Food and Drink. Southern cuisine is hearty and healthy (as dietary experts have discovered). Homemade pastas, fresh vegetables and pure local olive oil are staples.

In Calabria pasta takes on unusual forms and strange names, such as *fusilli, macarunni* and *scilatelli,* which is typical of Catanzaro. Sausages and local salami, including the fiery *soppressata,* are spiced with *peperoncino,* hot red pepper, used abundantly in Calabrian cuisine. You'll find pork, lamb and kid on menus inland, tuna and other fish on the coast, along with plenty of eggplant, tomatoes, the rosy onions of Tropea and rustic local cheeses, such as *caciocavallo* and *butirro.*

Apulia's pasta specialties are *orecchiette, troccoli* and *strascenate,* often served with a sauce of broccoli, oil and garlic. Fish stew here is known as *ciambotto.* The *tiella di cozze,* a casserole of rice, potatoes and mussels, is a classic of Spanish origin; you may find a *tiella* with fish or vegetables, or cheese—whatever is fresh and on hand.

Taranto is famous for its oysters, the Foggia area for its artichokes and pickled vegetables in oil. Apulia's fine grazing lands make lamb a good choice on local menus, where you'll probably also find *lampasciuni,* a kind of wild onion, quite bitter, served as an *antipasto* or *contorno.*

As for wines, Apulia offers the greatest variety. The reds are *Aleatico di Puglia,* sweet, and *Castel del Monte,* dry; white are *Locorotondo,* dry, and *Malvasia di Brindisi,* sweet. In Calabria, the dry reds and whites of Cirò are exceptional and heady; *Greco di Gerace,* dry, and *Moscato di Cosenza,* sweet, are both white. Luciana produces *Aglianico dei Vulture,* red, dry, and two white wines, both sweet; *Malvasia* and *Moscato.*

Alberobello Bari (080). Characteristic architecture. *Dei Trulli* (E), Via Cadore 35 (721.130). Variable winter closing. Only 19 rooms in *trullo*-style cottages in pinewoods; dining terrace, pool. AE, V.

Astoria (M), Viale Bari 11 (721.190). Many rooms with balcony or terrace; undistinguished but comfortable modern furnishings. AE, DC, MC, V.

Restaurants. Cucina dei Trulli (M), Piazza Ferdinando IV (721.179). Closed Tues. off-season. Rustic local dishes. AE, DC, V. *Poeta Contadino* (M), Via Independenza 21 (721.917). Closed Fri. Simple. AE, DC. *Trullo d'Oro* (M), Via Cavallotti 29 (721.820). Closed Mon. off-season. Ask for local cuisine, instead of tourist menu. AE, DC, MC, V. *Pugliese* (I), Via Gigante 4 (721.437). Closed Tues. Simple and homey, tables outside in summer. AE, DC, MC, V.

Bari Bari (080). Capital, important sea port. Advance booking mandatory for September, month of trade fair. *Jolly* (E), Via Petroni 15 (364.366). Near railway station; modern, comfortable. AE, DC, MC, V. *Palace* (E), Via Lombardi 13 (216.551). Central; large, caters for businessmen. AE, DC, MC, V.

Boston (M), Via Piccinni 155 (216.633). Central, functional. No restaurant. AE, DC, MC, V. *Grand Oriente* (M), Corso Cavour 32 (544.422). Large, quite central. No restaurant. AE, DC, V. *Leon d'Oro* (M), Piazza Moro 4 (235.040). Near railway station; modern, well-equipped. AE, V.

Restaurants. *La Pignata* (E), Via Melo 9 (232.481). Closed Wed. Best in region; exceptional local cuisine. AE, DC, MC, V.

La Buca (M), Via Cairoli 31 (213.976). Closed Mon. Good, reasonable. *Cesare* (M), Corso Cavour 215 (366.942). Closed Fri. Attractive, airconditioned. AE, DC, MC, V. *Damiano* (M), Via de Giosa 37 (544.516). Closed Sun. AE. *Due Ghiottoni* (M), Via Putignani 11 (232.240). Closed Sun. Good international cuisine. AE, DC, MC, V. *La Panca* (M), Piazza Massari 8 (216.096). Closed Wed. Rustic, intimate. AE, DC, MC, V. *Sorso Preferito* (M), Via De Nicolò (235.747). Closed Sun. *Simpatico* place; popular and crowded; reasonable. AE, DC, MC, V. *Vecchia Bari* (M), Via Dante 47 (216.496). Closed Fri. A classic; nicely decorated; excellent local specialties. AE, DC, V.

Barletta Bari (0883). Interesting architecture. *Artù* (M), Piazza Castello 67 (317.21). Central, commercial ticket. AE, DC, MC, V.

Restaurants. *Bacco* (M), Via Sipontina 10 (383.98). Closed Sun. evening and Mon. Inventive touches to local cuisine. *Il Brigantino* (M), Litoranea di Levante (33.345). Closed Wed. Just outside town; veranda on sea. Varied menu. MC. *La Casaccia* (M), Via Cavour 40 (337.19). Closed Fri. Central, simple, reasonable.

Brindisi Apulia (0831). Port. High season 15 July to 30 Sept. *Majestic* (E), Corso Umberto 151 (222.941) Best; on station square. AE, DC, MC, V. *Mediterraneo* (M), Viale Aldo Moro 70 (82.811) Modern, comfortable; semi-central. AE, DC, MC, V.

Restaurants. *La Botte* (M), Corso Garibaldi 72 (284.00). Closed Tues. and Nov. Attractive place, good food. AE, DC, MC, V. *Le Colonne* (M), Via Colonne 57 (28.059). Closed Tues. Near Roman columns at port, fine trattoria for seafood. AE, DC, V. *Giubilo* (M), Via del Mare at Hotel Approdo (29.668) Closed Tues. Pleasant and satisfying.

Castellana Grotte Bari (080). Interesting caves. *Vittoria* (M), Piazzale Grotte (735.008). Small, adequate overnight.

Restaurants. *Chiancafredda* (M), Via Chiancafredda 4 (736.710). Closed Tues. and Nov. Refined ambiance and cuisine, set apart from tourist haunts. DC. *Taverna degli Artisti* (M), at the caves (736.234). Closed Thurs. off-season and Nov.

Castellaneta Marina Taranto (099). Beach resort. *Riva dei Tessali* (E), at Orsanese (643.071). Open 1 April to 31 Oct. Well run, country-club atmosphere; attractive bungalows amid pines; large pool, sandy beach, 18-hole golf course. DC. *Villa Giusy* (M), at Bosco Pineto (643.036). Nice little resort hotel; pool. AE, V.

Castro Marina Lecce (0836). Near Santa Cesarea Terme. *Orsa Maggiore* (M), on shore road (97.029). On hill above beach. AE, DC, V. *Piccolo Mondo* (M), on shore road (97.035). Modest beach hotel. V.

Restaurant. *Zinzilusa* (M), Via Zinzilusa (97.326). Closed Fri. At famous grotto; good seafood, local wine; annexed pizzeria.

Castrovillari Cosenza (0981). Colorful town. *Motel ASTI* (M), Corso Calabria (21.720). V. *President* (M), Corso Saraceni (21.122).

Restaurant. *Alia* (M), at **Jetticelle**, on outskirts (46.370). Closed Sun. Well worth 10 minute detour from Autostrada del Sole; courteous service; variety of local specialties. AE, DC, V.

Catanzaro Catanzaro (0961). On fine mountain site. *Guglielmo* (E), Via Tedeschi 1 (26.532). Near railway station; smallish, comfortable. AE, DC, MC, V. *Grand* (M), Piazza Matteotti (25.605). Central. AE, DC, MC, V. *Motel AGIP* (M),

Trivio Fiumarella (51.791). Just outside town; dependable for standard comforts. AE, DC, MC, V.

At **Catanzaro Lido,** beach 12 km. (8 miles) south, *Palace* (M), Via Lungomare 212 (31.344).

Restaurants. *La Griglia* (M), Via Poerio 26 (26.883). Closed Sun. Small, very good local cuisine. *Motel AGIP* (M), Trivio Fiumarella (51.791). Closed Fri. Fine restaurant. AE, DC, MC, V. *Uno piu Uno* (M), Galleria Mancuso (23.184). Closed Mon., and Sun. in summer. V.

At **Catanzaro Lido,** *La Brace* (M), Via Melito Porto Salvo (32.852). Closed Thurs. Good food, nice view. AE, DC, V.

Cetraro Cosenza (0982). On sea. *San Michele* (E), at Bosco (91.012). Palatial, in park overlooking sea; isolated location; lift to private pebbly beach; pool, tennis. AE, DC, V.

Cirella Cosenza (0985). Good beach. *Guardacosta* (M) (86.012). Open 1 May to 30 Sept. Quiet location, good views, pool, beach.

Cosenza (0984). Medieval buildings. Best hotels are in Rende suburb. *Europa* (M), at Roges (465.064). Modern comforts; pool. AE, DC, MC, V. *San Francesco* (M), at Commenda (861.721). Large; pool. AE, DC, MC, V. In town: *Centrale* (M), Via Tigrai 3 (73.681). well-equipped; good parking. AE, DC, MC, V.

At **Castiglion Scalo,** *Motel AGIP* (M) (839.101). AE, DC, V.

Restaurants. *La Calavrisella* (M), Via De Rada 11/a (28.012). Closed Sat. and Sun. evenings. Rich antipasto, inventive pastas. AE, V. *Giocondo* (M), Via Piave 53 (29.810). Closed Sat. or Sun. Very small, reservations required. MC. *Villa Bernaudo* (I), Via Piave 55 (22.026). Closed Sun. Central, good local pastas, trout, meat, at reasonable prices.

Crotone Catanzaro (0962). Industrial city, port. **Restaurants.** *Bella Romagna* (E), Via Poggioreale 61 (21.943). Closed Sun. Excellent. MC. *Girarrosto* (M), Via Veneto 30 (22.043). Closed Sun. Unusual pastas; good grilled meat. DC, MC, V.

Foggia (0881). Modern commercial city. *Cicolella* (E), Viale Ventiquattro Maggio 60 (38.90). Victorian exterior, modern comforts; near railway station. AE, DC, MC, V. *President* (M), Via Ascoli 80 (79.648). On road to airport; modern, indoor pool. AE, DC, MC, V.

Restaurants. *Cicolella* (E), Via Ventiquattro Maggio 60 (38.90). Closed Fri. evening and Sun. In attractive ambiance, rustic local food. AE, DC, MC, V. *La Mangiatoia* (M), Viale Virgilio (34.457). Closed Mon. Try *troccoli,* local pasta. AE, DC, MC, V. *Nuova Bella Napoli* (M), Via Azzarita 26 (26.188). Closed Sun. In old part of town, seafood specialties. AE, DC, V.

Galatina Lecce (0836). Interesting church. **Restaurant.** *La Capanna* (M), Via Turati 25 (64.048). Closed Sun. and Aug. Fine lunch stop; try local dishes, authentic and unusual. V.

Gallico Marina Reggio Calabria (0965). **Restaurant.** *Fata Morgana* (M) (370.012). Closed Tues. Seafood specialties; seaside view. V.

Gallipoli Lecce (0833). Medieval citadel; good beaches nearby. *Costa Brada* (M), at Baia Verde beach (22.551). Closed Nov. Very good, modern beach hotel; spacious rooms with balcony. Minibus service into town. AE, DC, MC, V. *Le Sirenuse* (M), at Baia Verde beach (22.536). Open 1 April to 31 Oct. Large white hotel on beach; well-furnished, all doubles with balcony, sea view; ample pool, gardens. AE, DC, MC, V.

Restaurants. *Puglia Vera* (E), Baia Verde (22.551). Open summer only. Fine restaurant of Costa Brada Hotel. AE, DC, MC, V. *Marechiaro* (M), Lungomare Marconi (476.143). Closed Tues. off-season. Renowned *zuppa di pesce,* succulent shellfish.

AE, DC, V. *Zi Chè* (M), Piazza Dogana (476.706). Closed Mon. Modest but good; on port. V.

Gambarie D'Aspromonte Calabria (0965). Summer and winter sports resort. *Gambarie* (M) (743.012). Smallish, unpretentious.

Gioia del Colle Bari (080). Norman castle. **Restaurants.** *Corte dei Sannaci* (M), Via Circonvallazione (831.907). Closed Tues. and Nov. Outside town. Attractive rustic atmosphere, good food. V. *Gran Gala* (M), on Acquaviva road (833.432). Closed Fri. and Nov. AE, V. *Da Nico* (M), Via Di Vittorio 155 (830.622). Closed Sat. Just outside town, simple; traditional local dishes. V.

Isola di Capo Rizzuto Catanzaro (0962). Ionian coast resort. *Villagio Valtur* (M), at Meolo (791.121). Self-contained vacation village; all resort facilities.
At **Le Castella,** a few miles away, *Le Castella* (M) (795.054). Large cottage colony, chic, lively; up-market resort.
Restaurant. *Da Annibale* (M), Via Duomo at Le Castella (795.004). Hotel restaurant; rustic, very good local cooking.

Lecce Lecce (0832). Baroque architecture. *President* (E), Via Salandra 6 (51.881). Just outside center; large, modern, comfortable. AE, DC, MC, V. *Risorgimento* (M), Via A. Imperatore 19 (42.125). Very central, attractive; period furnishings, up to date comforts. AE, DC, MC, V. Both offer weekend discounts.
Restaurants. *Dolomiti* (M), Via Costa 6 (27.881). Closed Sun. Little atmosphere but good. DC. *Gino e Gianni* (M), Via Quattro Finite (45.888). Closed Mon. and Oct. Just outside town; seafood specialties. *Guido* (M), Via Venticinque Luglio 14 (25.868). Closed Wed. Pizzeria. *Patria Touring,* Piazzetta Riccardi 13 (29.431). Central, very good. *Plaza* (M), Via 140 Reggimento Fanteria 14 (25.083). Closed Sun. Classic ambiance, international and local dishes. *Tarocchi* (M), Via Idomeneo (29.925). Closed Tues. and Aug. Central, varied menu, seafood specialties. AE.

Leuca Apulia (0833). Land's end of Italy's heel. *L'Approdo* (M), Via Santuario (753.0156). Open 15 March to 15 Oct. Modest beach hotel. AE, DC, V.

Manfredonia Foggia (0884). Gargano port and resort. *Gargano* (M), Viale Beccarini (27.621). Closed Jan., Feb. Well-equipped, pool.
Restaurants. *Gambero* (M), Via Gargano 101 (23.255). Closed Fri. Fine seafood. *La Lanterna* (M), Piazza Marconi 2 (23.824). Closed Tues. Fish soups, local pastas. V.

Maratea Potenza (0973). Coast resort. *Santavenere* (L), Fiumicello (876.160). Open 1 June to 30 Sept. Lovely building amid gardens, on sea; attractive furnishings, some antiques, good service; beach, tennis. pool. AE, DC, V.
At **Acquafredda,** *Villa del Mare* (M), on coast road (878.007). Open 1 April to 31 Oct. Nicely furnished villa on cliff above sea; pool, gardens, lift to beach. AE, DC, MC, V.
Restaurants. *Za Mariuccia* (M), Via Grotte (876.163). Closed Thurs. and from Dec. to end Jan. On the port; fish dishes, good local wine. MC. *Taverna Rovita* (M), Via Rovita 13 (876.588). Open summer, Christmas, Easter. Tiny place; reserve for excellent local cuisine.

Matera Matera (0835). Rock-cut dwellings. *President* (M), Via Roma 13 (214.075). No restaurant. V. *De Nicola* (M), Via Nazionale 158 (214.821). Adequate overnight. *Italia* (I), Via Ridola (211.195). Unpretentious and friendly; good views.
Restaurants. *Al Bocconcino* (M), Vico Lombardo 52 (221.625). Closed Mon. Two sections, one for meat, country cooking, the other, closed Tues, for seafood. DC. V. *Da Mario* (M), Via Venti Settembre 14 (214.569). Closed Sun. *Sorangelo* (M), Via Lucana 48 (216.719). Closed Sun. Modest place, but with very good food. *Il Terraz-*

ino (I), Vico San Giuseppe 7 (222.016). Closed Tues. Restaurant cut into tufa rock; grills on an open fire. AE, DC, MC, V.

Mattinata Foggia (0884). On Gargano. *Alba* (M), (47.71). Simple, modern hotel. *Baia delle Zagare* (M), offshore road to Valle dei Mergoli (41.55). Open 1 June to 15 Sept. Secluded villa colony overlooking beautiful inlet; tennis, lift to beach.
Restaurants. *Papone* (M), highway 89 (47.49). Closed Mon. and Nov. In an old mill. AE, MC, V. *Del Portoghese* (M), Via Pellico 3 (43.21). Closed Fri. and in winter. Modest; very good seafood.

Ostuni Brindisi (0831). Picturesque town, near good beaches. *Rosamarina* (M), on beach (970.061). Open 1 June to 30 Sept. Part of huge vacation village, all resort facilities. DC, V. *Villaggio Valtur* (M), on beach (468.828). Open 1 June to 20 Sept. Large, self-contained bungalow colony; all sports. V.
Restaurants. *Chez Elio* (M), Via dei Colli Selva (972.030). Closed Mon. and Sept. Just outside town; good food and views. *Tre Torri* (M), Corso V. Emanuele 298 (971.104). Closed Tues. V. *Vecchia Ostuni* (M), Largo Lanza 9 (973.308). Closed Tues. Classic local pastas, grilled fish and meat.

Peschici Foggia (0884). Pretty old town on sea in Gargano area. *Solemar* (M), at San Nicola (94.186). Open 10 May to 30 Sept. In beautiful location; beach, pool. AE, DC, V. *Valle Clavia* (M), at Valle Clavia (94.209). Open 1 June to 15 Sept. Garden, tennis; no beach.
At **Manacore**, *Gusmay* (M), off main road (94.032). Open 1 May to 30 Sept. Isolated, modern; private beach. AE, DC, V.
Restaurants. *La Grotta* (M), at port (94.007). Open Easter to end Sept. In natural grotto; seafood, naturally. AE, DC, MC, V. *Da Peppino* (M), on the beach (94.012). Closed Tues.

Pizzo Catanzaro (0963). Fishing port. *Grillo* (M), Riviera Prangi (231.632). Open 1 April to 30 Sept. Attractive beach hotel. DC.
Restaurant. *Medusa* (M), Via Salomone (231.203). Closed Mon. Seaside terrace; *spaghetti alla Masaniello* and delicious ice cream. AE, DC, V.

Porto Cesareo Lecce (0833). Fishing port, summer resort. *Lo Scoglio* (M), Isola lo Scoglio (846.079). Open 1 May to 30 Sept. Set apart on rocky islet with causeway access; small; bathing area. AE.
Restaurants. *Grand'Italia* (M), Via Muratori 18 (845.094). Closed Tues. Big, bright, seafood restaurant. V. *Lo Scoglio* (M), Isola lo Scoglio (846.079). Closed Tues. and Nov. Very good restaurant of hotel (see above); open most of year. AE. *Il Veliero* (M), Via Muratori 18 (846.201). Closed Tues. and Nov. MC, V.

Potenza Potenza (0971). Regional capital, still shows damage of 1980 earthquake. **Restaurants.** *Fuori le Mura* (M), Via Quattro Novembre 34 (25.409). Closed Mon. Marvelous *antipasto* table. MC, V. *Da Peppe* (M), Largo San Michele (28.030). Closed Sun. Good food and excellent house wine. *Taverna Oraziana* (M), Via Orazio Flacco 2 (21.851). Closed Fri. Rustic atmosphere; local dishes only; try *capretto* (kid) in season. V.

Praia a Mare Cosenza (0985). Seaside resort. *Mondial* (M), Lungomare (72.214). Modest but comfortable beach hotel. AE, DC, MC, V. *Germania* (M), Via Roma 60 (72.016). On beach. DC, V.
Restaurants. *Normanni* (M), at Fiuzzi (72.263). Open 1 May to 31 Oct. Overlooking sea and Isle of Dino; seafood specialties. *Vecchio Frantoio* (M), Pian delle Vigne (72.626). Open Easter to 31 Oct. Rustic, panoramic; good local and international cuisine.

Pugnochiuso Apulia (0884). Resort area on Gargano. High season 1 July to 30 Sept. *Del Faro* (M) (79.011). Open 15 April to 3 Jan. Sea views, all resort activities. AE, DC, V. *Degli Ulivi* (M) (79.061). Open 15 March to 31 Oct. Same management, same amenities. AE, DC, V.

Reggio Calabria Reggio Calabria (0965). Port city. *Excelsior* (E), Via Vittorio Veneto 66 (25.801). Near National Museum and railway station. AE, DC, MC, V. *Palace Masoanri* (M), Via Vittorio Veneto 95 (26.433). Also central, comfortable. AE, DC, MC, V.
Restaurants. *Bonaccorso* (E), Via Battisti 8 (96.048). Closed Mon. and Aug. Excellent atmosphere and cuisine. AE, DC, MC, V. *Baylik* (M), Via Leone 1 (48.624). Closed Thurs. and July. A simple place for fish specialties. AE, DC, V. *Conti* (M), Via Giulia 2 (29.043). Closed Mon. off-season. Regional cuisine. AE, DC, MC, V. *La Pignata* (M), Via Tripepi 122 (27.841). Closed Wed. Cordial; economical and good. AE, DC, V.

Rodi Garganico Foggia (0884). Gargano town, beach resort. *Mizar* (M), at Lido del Sole (97.021). Open 16 May to 20 Sept. Comfortable beach hotel; very good restaurant; choose local dishes. AE, MC, V.

Santa Cesarea Terme Lecce (0836). Modest spa and fine bathing resort. *Le Macine* (M), Via Castro Marina (944.305). Open 1 April to 30 Sept. Pleasant small hotel; good restaurant.

Scalea Cosenza (0985). Beach resort. *De Rose* (E), off main highway (20.273). Attractive, quiet; beach, tennis, pool. AE, DC. *Santa Caterina* (M), off main highway (20.336). Good resort hotel; beach pool. V.

Scilla Calabria (0965). Mythical counterpart of Charybdis; colorful seaside town. **Restaurants.** *Il Gabbiano* (M), on San Gregoria beach; no phone. Open 1 June to 30 Sept. Rustic specialties, tasty swordfish. *La Pescatora* (M), Lungomare 32 (754.147). Closed Tues. Open 1 April to 15 Dec. Excellent seafood; overcrowded in July and Aug. V.

Sila (Catanzaro e Cosenza). Scenic mountain region; instep of Italy's boot. **Sila Grande** (0984). At San Giovanni in Fiore, *Dino's* (M), at Pirainella (992.090). Small, basic.
At **Lorica,** *Grand* (M) (997.039). Large, old-fashioned; good views. DC, V.
At **Camigliatello,** lively summer and winter resort, *Edelweiss* (M), Viale Stazione (978.044). Smallish, comfortable. DC, V. *Cristallo* (M), Via Roma (978.013). AE, DC, V.
At **Sila Piccola** (0961), at Taverna, *Faggio* (I), at Ciricilla (922.005). Attractive, chalet-type.

Soverato Catanzaro (0967). Beach resort. *Nettuno* (M), Via Magna Grecia (25.371). Open 1 June to 30 Sept. Unpretentious beach hotel. *Degli Ulivi* (M), Via Aldo Moro (21.487). Open 1 June to 30 Sept. Quiet, with beach, gardens. AE, DC, MC, V.
Restaurant. *Enzo* (I), Corso Umberto; no phone. Meals or snacks at all hours; simple local cuisine.

Taranto Taranto (099). Naval base, archeological museum. *Delfino* (E), Viale Virgilio 66 (32.05). Sea views, comfortable rooms; smallish pool on shoals. AE, DC, MC, V. *Mar Grande* (E), Viale Virgilio 90 (330.861). Well-furnished, spacious rooms; pool, gardens. AE, DC, MC, V.
Plaza (M), Via d'Aquino 46 (91.925). Large, very central. No restaurant. AE, DC, MC, V.
Restaurants. *Al Gambero* (E), Vico del Ponte 4 (411.190). Closed Mon. and Nov. Excellent seafood in attractive dining room on bay. AE, DC, V.
Assassino (M), Lungomare V. Emanuele 29 (92.041). Closed Sun. Good. AE, DC. *La Barcaccia* (M), Corso Due Mari 22 (26.461). Closed Mon. Some dishes pricey,

but all are good. AE, DC, V. *Marcaurelio* (M), Via Cavour 17. Closed Tues. Behind archeological museum; small, popular, good pizza. *Sirenetta* (M), Via Garibaldi (497.657). Closed Mon. Attractive nautical decor. Fine seafood.

Torre a Mare Bari (080). *Motel AGIP* (M), Adriatic highway (300.001). Large, standard comforts. AE, DC, V.

Restaurants. *Grotta della Regina* (E), Lungomare (300.041). Closed Wed. Terrace on beach; one of the best in area; fish specialties. MC, V. *Nicola* (M), Viale Principe Piemonte 3 (300.043). Closed Wed. *Spaghetti con scampi;* delectable seafood.

Trani Bari (0883). Noted cathedral. *Royal* (I), Via De Robertis 39 (41.306). Near station, adequate overnight. AE, DC, MC, V. *Albergo Lucy* (I), Piazza Plebiscito (41.022). Small, quiet hotel next to seaside gardens. *Trani* (I), Corso Imbriani 137 (588.009). Simple hotel near train station. AE, DC, V.

Restaurants. *Antica Cattedrale* (M), Piazza Archivio 2 (586.568). Closed Mon. off-season. Classy seafood restaurant by the cathedral. *Cristoforo Colombo* (M), Lungomare Colombo 21 (41.146). Closed Tues. and Nov. On sea in outskirts; shellfish and good local wines are the specialties. *Due Mori* (M), Lungomare Colombo 110 (401.051). Closed Wed. and Dec. Seafood. AE, V. *Duomo* (M), Piazza Archivio 2 (45.174). Closed Mon. Near cathedral, handsome ambiance, excellent menu.

Tremiti Islands Foggia (0882). Pretty islands off Termoli, overcrowded in summer. *Eden* (M) (663.211). Open 21 May to 24 Sept. Simple, pleasant. *Kyrie* (M), at San Domino (663.055). Open 21 May to 24 Sept. Best; small attractive resort hotel, bungalows, pool, rock bathing. Pricey. AE, DC, V.

Tropea Catanzaro (0963). Pretty old town above sandy beaches. *Pineta* (M), Via Marina (617.00). Open 1 April to 31 Oct. Pleasant little hotel in orange grove, near beach. V. *Le Roccette* (M), (62.362). Cottage colony on beach.

At **Parghelia,** *Baia Parahelios* (M), Località Fornaci (61.450). Open 15 May to 20 Sept. Set apart on sandy cove, cottage colony in olive grove by the sea; beach, tennis, pool.

At **Capo Vaticano,** *Park* (M), at Santa Maria (63.12). Open 20 April to 30 Sept. Quiet vacation haven, with beach, tennis.

Restaurant. *Pimm's* (M), Largo Migliarese (61.903). Open 1 April to 30 Sept. Closed Tues. AE, DC, MC, V.

Vibo Valentia Catanzaro (0963). Highland base for exploring coast and mountains. *501* (M), Via Madonnella (43.951). Pool, tennis. V.

Restaurants. At **Vibo Marina,** 9.5 km. (6 miles) below Vibo Valentia, on coast, *L'Approdo* (M) (240.640). Closed Fri. AE, DC, MC, V. *Maria Rosa* (M), on port (240.538). Closed Sun. *Il Fortino* (M) (240.591). Closed Mon. AE, DC, MC, V.

Vieste Foggia (0884). Lively Gargano resort. *Pizzomunno* (M), Litoranea road (78.741). Open 7 April to 8 Oct. Large, smart, resort hotel, all amenities; pool, tennis, sandy beach. Pricey. AE, DC, MC, V. *Mediterraneo* (M), Via Madonna della Libera (77.025). Open 1 April to 30 Sept. Comfortable; beach, gardens.

At **Portonuovo,** *Gargano* (M) (78.685). Open 1 April to 30 Sept. Modern building with good sea views. Choice of beach or rock swimming.

Restaurants. *Faro* (E) of Hotel Faro at Pugnochiuso (79.011). Open April–Sept. Good atmosphere, local specialties. AE, DC, V. *La Kambusa* (M), Viale 24 Maggio (77.162). Open 15 Mar.–31 Oct. Seafood. AE, V. *Rugantino* (M), Viale 24 Maggio. Closed Fri. Informal, good. AE, DC, V.

Villa San Giovanni Reggio di Calabria (0965). Commercial center and port with shortest crossing to Sicily. Hotels in town get constant truck traffic noise. Better accommodations at Alta Fiumara complex on highway at **Cannitello,** a few miles north, at *Castello* (M), (769.061). Quiet, distinctively furnished, splendid view of straits. Good restaurant and beach facilities.

Restaurant. *Piccolo* (M), Piazza Stazione (751.153). Open every day. A hotel restaurant convenient for a lunch stop before or after ferrying across the straits. AE, DC, MC, V.

GETTING AROUND. By air. Airports served by Alitalia are at Lamezia Terme and Reggio Calabria in Calabria, at Bari and Brindisi in Apulia—internal flights apart from the occasional charter.

By rail and bus. The main rail lines in this area trace the outline of the boot from Naples down to Reggio Calabria, then up the arch to Taranto, Brindisi, Bari and Foggia. Lecce is the rail terminal on the heel and is connected with Bari. A number of secondary lines provide local connections, as do the regional bus services.

By car. Italy's Deep South is fundamentally automobile country—after you have arrived by plane, ship or train at some such base as Bari, Brindisi or Taranto. The two main lines of approach by car are the Autostrada del Sole from Rome, passing Naples and Salerno, only occasionally in view of the sea on the way to Reggio Calabria; and, in the east, the Autostrada Adriatica (A14), which follows the coast from Rimini, to bypass the Gargano Peninsula on entering Apulia. After Barletta the road runs close to the coast until Bari, after which it turns away southward to Taranto. At Barletta, the A17 coming up from Naples joins the A14. After Naples, the Autostrada del Sole becomes the A3, and is toll-free as it sweeps through Calabria's magnificent mountain scenery.

However, the loveliest, if slowest, drive returning from Reggio Calabria is over the Aspromonte highland, descending to the Ionian coast from Locri to Monasterace, then striking inland again to the Serra San Bruno, and after Catanzaro, through the majestic forests of La Sila to Consenza and the autostrada. The absence of traffic makes this route a delight to drive. You should be warned that inland hotels and pensions are few and far between, and the ones along the coast are booked out in summer.

SICILY

Island at the World's Center

This fertile island lies in a strategic position in the Mediterranean which, at one and the same time, constitutes its importance, explains its history and accounts for its suffering through the millennia of foreign domination. An island, but not enough of an island, for it is visible, across a 2-mile-wide strait, to covetous eyes on the mainland of Italy; near, yet far enough away for the Romans (who were uneasy sailors) to use it mainly as a tactical base and as a granary owned by big landlords. It represents a modern social problem only partly solved by the regional government instituted in 1947, and recent industrialization around Catania and Gela. Moreover, the island's mountains are no bulwark against armed landings, for Sicily is rich in sweeping bays and inviting inlets, her coastal plains displaying their luxuriance like a shop-window to marauding seafarers.

There are lovely, bright wild flowers everywhere for those with a botanical bent, volcanos and great lava fields for the amateur vulcanologist, the sea for swimmers and underwater explorers, colorful, earnest fishing villages for those who love fishing villages, and there are vast sweeps of scenery on all sides. A 6,000-acre area between Punta Palermo and Torre San Teodoro, rich in wildlife and fauna, is to be reserved as a nature park.

There are about a dozen off-lying islands for islomaniacs, rare, ancient coins for numismatists, mountains and hills to climb, varied and various wines for the gourmet to sample, ceramist towns for shoppers, Neolithic, Stone Age and Bronze Age sites scattered among the many others. There are lively towns, mournful towns, Baroque towns, storybook settlements, and there are acres and acres of citrus groves and vineyards, where orange

369

trees and grapevines grow low, hugging the earth to stay out of the way of the withering blasts of the hot sirocco wind that occasionally blows from Africa. These and flowering shrubs are *everywhere* in Sicily.

A Tale of Two Cities

In a land where it is possible to ski on a snow-muffled volcano, walk among palms and orange-groves, and swim in the sea within sight of the almond-trees in flower—and all in the same day—why should the visitor to Sicily concern himself with Greeks and Carthaginians, Arabs and Normans, or the misrule of Bourbon and Aragon?

Awareness of a country's history is a very useful part of a traveler's equipment. In Sicily, such awareness is almost a necessity; only then will the visitor understand an island which is Italian, but quite unlike Italy; European, yet imbued with the color and subtlety of the East. The modern age seems to have been built on a Greek foundation, for here the heavy hand of Rome made little impression. Alertness can turn a visit to Sicily into a unique experience.

Sicily lies in one of the most strategic positions of any island on earth. In ancient times the Mediterranean was at the center of the known world, and Sicily was at the center of the Mediterranean. And since the world was, then as now, contended for by the opposing civilizations and ideologies of East and West, Sicily logically became their battleground. At the beginning it was a magnet for immigrants—the America of the ancient world—but Sicily has no metals, and since the settlers needed these, traders came to swap and remained to prey.

At Pantalica, near Syracuse, there is a mighty cliff-face pitted with square hewn-out caves. This was a burial-place for the Siculi, the earliest Sicilian inhabitants of importance. They had to fight for the island against the Greeks who began to build cities there 7 or 8 centuries before Christ, and against the Carthaginians, a Semitic people from North Africa, only 80 miles away. The Siculi were soon scattered, absorbed, or enslaved by the Greeks, and the issue became a straight struggle between Greek and "barbarian".

The recorded history of Sicily is a tale of two cities: of Syracuse for two millennia, of Palermo for the last thousand years, the one remembering above all the name of Dionysius, the other that of Frederick II.

By the 5th century B.C., Greek Sicily's history was that of Syracuse, of which most of the other cities were dependencies. One Syracusan tyrant (an absolute ruler), Dionysius, held the Carthaginians from the coast of North Africa to the south in check by building immense defensive works around his great city, which he made the most magnificent and powerful of his day, and himself the most potent of princes after the Persian king. The story of this period in Syracuse's fortunes is told in *The Mask of Apollo,* the historical novel by Mary Renault.

But even before this, Syracuse had prospered enough to sting Athens into sending a great fleet and army to destroy the city; instead, the army and fleet were themselves destroyed.

The Sicilian climate does not encourage long-sustained heroic efforts; as the Greeks grew languid, the Carthaginians resumed their aggressive tactics, and only Rome, looming large in the 3rd century, could stop them. Later, Rome took care of the Greeks also. So, by about 200 B.C., Syracuse and the island were Roman, at least in name.

Byzantium revived Syracuse into a pale ghost of its former grandeur, but the tale of the first city was ended and that of the second, Palermo, now began.

In the 9th century, the Arabs captured Sicily, and held it for two centuries. Their poets used it in their verse, their geographers described it, they built mosques and established an Emir in Palermo, which became the apple of their eye and to which they gave a soft languid Oriental air that has never left it.

But the climate had done its work again, and the self-indulgent Arabs were easily dislodged by a small force of determined Norman adventurers; and, for a century, Robert, Roger, and William tried in vain to maintain stern Nordic virtues while enthroned at Palermo in Oriental state.

Then a Swabian dynasty came to Sicily and brought one of the most surprising figures of history, Frederick II—Stupor Mundi, the Wonder of the World. His Palermo court swarmed with poets, scientists, and musicians, and the first school of Italian vernacular poetry flourished in an Orientalized city under a German prince.

The rule of the succeeding House of Anjou was cut short by the insurrection of the Sicilian Vespers (1282), a bloodbath which became a favorite subject with Romantic writers and the subject of an opera by Verdi. For the six following centuries the Sicilians, misruled by the House of Aragon and by corrupt Spanish viceroys, tossed from Savoy to Austria and back to Spain, plotted and rebelled, were repressed and crushed, and finally took to the hills to become outlaws and bandits, a policy which later developed into a national habit. In 1860, Garibaldi landed, and Sicily became part of Italy.

Exploring Sicily

For variety and contrast, and for a number of other reasons, it may probably be best to make the journey from Messina going west along the northern coast, around the blunted apex by Trapani, eastwards along the Africa-facing shore, and so northwards along the "Ionic" coastal plain; this route, with a few diversions inland, will give a fairly comprehensive picture of the island.

Our itinerary assumes that the traveler will land at Messina. The strait that Hercules swam across, clinging to his sacred bulls, is now traversed by modern travelers in a swift ferry. The classical-minded person, looking northeast from the steamer deck, can see the frowning rocks and the boiling waters of Ulysses' Scylla and Charybdis, guarding the straits. He remembers that he is making for a land saturated with mythology: where Proserpina and Pluto, Arethusa, Daedalus, Titans and Cyclops, escape from school text-books and pop up all over the place as the names of towns, hotels, and cafés. In fact, their deeds were long painted, together with the exploits of King Roger and the Saracens, by illiterate artisans on gaily-colored Sicilian carts.

From Messina to Cefalù

At five o'clock in the morning of December 28th, 1908, Messina was a flourishing city of 120,000 inhabitants. A few minutes later it was a heap of rubble, shaken to pieces by an earthquake which then gathered up the waters of the Straits and flung them, together with the bulk of ships, like mighty projectiles, against the wreckage in which 80,000 people lay dead or dying.

As you approach the magnificent sickle-shaped bay, there is little evidence of that disaster—save the curious flat look of the city; for anti-earthquake precautions once placed a restriction on the height of buildings. Messina is not a city of great interest, although the traveler might well learn here to appreciate the magnificent skill of the Italians as restorers. The cathedral, for example, has been entirely rebuilt as it was originally constructed by Roger in the 11th century. The Baroque fountain in front of it has been re-erected, and the splendidly decorated marble doorway of the church pieced together again. The fine clean interior is adorned with mosaics and works of art saved from the disaster. The other Norman church, the Annunziata, stood up to the seismic shock.

There are two interesting processions to be seen in Messina. For the *Vara,* on August 15th, monster carts loaded with figures of saints and angels move around the city; on the evening preceding this, the legendary Giants of Messina are pulled through the streets. These giant figures, in various versions, are found in many town processions on the island. They probably embody some vague folk memories of prehistoric inhabitants of gigantic stature. The Messina festival of the Madonna of the Letter takes place on June 3rd.

Two-thirds of Sicily lies above 274 meters (900 ft.), and the 240 km. (150 miles) or so of coastal road to Palermo skirt the most mountainous area. On your left as you journey are, successively, the Peloritani, the Nebrodi, and the Madonie ranges, averaging some 900 meters (3,000 ft.). The bare iron-grey peaks bear witness to the victimization of the forests for wood with which to build the galleons of millennia of seagoing peoples. The short torrential rivers, dry chasms in summer, plunge through Alpine-like uplands with poplar and ash, chestnut and almond, down to orange and lemon groves.

West of Messina, on the north coast, at a turning off to the right from the main highway, is Milazzo, a seaport town. It was founded by the Greeks, in 716 B.C., and has a rather impressive castle and a very attractive esplanade. But Milazzo's main interest to most travelers is that from here many people take a boat or *aliscafo* to the Aeolian (also called Lipari) Islands. On clear days you can glimpse these islands, lying to the north, all along the coast from near Milazzo to Cefalù.

Tindari and Cefalù

Tindari's sanctuary contains a Byzantine Black Madonna, reputedly miracle-working; pilgrims come from all over Sicily, especially on September 8th, to toil up the steep hill. The view, anyway, is heavenly. Tindari also has some Greco-Roman ruins of the old town; but unless you are an archeologist, it is better to reserve your enthusiasm for much higher-class ruins to come.

Farther along the coast there's Santo Stefano di Camastra, well known as a ceramics center. You may want to look about at a few of the shops and studios, and perhaps view one of the artisans at work. A short distance farther along the road is Castel di Tusa, where a right turning will bring you into this little, unspoiled seaside spot.

Cefalù, a photographer's paradise, is an enchanting little town on a spur jutting into the sea, at the foot of an immense rock, and away to the west is the sweeping bay of Imerese. One of the finest Norman cathedrals in Sicily dominates Cefalù. It was begun by King Roger in 1131, as a thank-offering for his happy landing from a storm at sea. The cathedral is as solid as the race that built it and the rock that soars above. But it has grace, too: the elegant three-arched façade, and the slim columns and tracery set off the imposing towers. And when you walk around it, you are struck by the subtlety which diversified those massive apses with fine blind arches. Entering its solemn three-naved interior, one is hardly prepared for being overpowered by the mighty 12th-century Byzantine mosaic of Christ, angels, and apostles which glimmers in the apse, and is perhaps more impressive than that at Monreale.

There's a small private museum down the street from the Cathedral; it can be recommended to coin collectors (who will not need to be told that Sicily minted the finest coins of antiquity) and to pottery lovers. It has a canvas by Antonello da Messina, the only painter of great stature produced by Sicily.

On past Termini Imerese, and just beyond the settlement of Fondachello, if you turn right at the small crossroads where a sign indicates Santa Flavia to the left, you can circle Cape Zafferano, with its Roman ruins at Solunto, its intriguing pastel town of Sant'Elia, and magnificent rock promontories as you round the cape. From Aspri, still on the cape, if you keep straight on, crossing Highway 113, you'll come directly into Bagheria, a dusty little town with a sense of humor and dim traceries of what must once have been elegance, for this used to be a summer outpost for the wealthy of Palermo (and still is for a few). It has a scattering of 17th- and 18th-century villas, some of which can be visited. Most intriguing is the Villa Palagonìa, its gardens full of grotesques, weird, half-animal, half-human statues, which may make you feel that you have entered a slightly distorted world. There are other villas to see but, unfortunately, most are in a sad state of disrepair, or downright neglect.

As you leave Bagheria you come to the Conca d'Oro (the Golden Shell), one of the loveliest bays, backed by mountains and once strewn with orchards and gardens, which are fast disappearing under the burgeoning city's unattractive suburbs.

Palermo

Palermo is one of those cities the traveler never forgets. Externally it is unmistakable, with the great rock of Pellegrino as its landmark. Internally it has a personality of its own—cynical, yet passionate, Oriental in its languor and in the shrewdness and subtlety of its jurists and politicians. It is a city of contrasts: smart shops and high-rise flats stand near mean street-level dwellings and garbage heaps.

Phoenician colony, Carthaginian town, the capital of an Arab Emirate, the commercial hub of Europe and Asia under the Normans, intellectual center under Frederick II—Palermo wears all these laurels gracefully. Its peculiarity is the happy marriage of Norman and Arab, when Mohammedan master craftsmen helped build and decorate Christian churches.

The most remarkable example of this is the Martorana church, so-called because it was donated to the nearby monastery founded by a patrician of that name, the cloister of whose adjoining house still survives. Its proper name is Santa Maria dell'Ammiraglio, referring to George of Antioch, Admiral of the Fleet. The bell-tower is a sermon in stone on tolerance: Nor-

man solidity and Arab fancy, strength and grace combined, have created
a masterpiece. The church of San Cataldo is next door and can only be
seen at the same time as the Martorana. If you want to get the flavor of
Palermo, wander among this group of buildings and ponder on what is
there—an Arab-Norman tower, San Cataldo's stern Norman interior
(with columns filched from Greek temples), red Oriental domes squatting
above, Martorana's Norman interior decorated in 17th-century baroque,
Greek inscriptions and a mosaic of Christ presenting the crown to Roger
II, first Norman king of Sicily, who wears Oriental robes. A palm in the
midst completes the picture, a commentary on all that Palermo stands for.

Two buildings dominate Palermo, the 19th-century Teatro Massimo,
closed indefinitely, and the 12th-century cathedral, whose fortress-like
dignity and strength are impressive, and even the Gothic towers add an
airiness not entirely irrelevant. But examined closely, it is apt to make architects blaspheme; for a "restorer" (and Palermitans hasten to tell you
that he was a Florentine) added an 18th-century dome and various other
monstrosities. The interior contains the royal tombs—among them that
of Frederick II. The cathedral was founded by the Archbishop of Palermo,
an English priest named Walter of the Mill, comically Sicilianized as Gualtiero Offamilio.

The traveler in a hurry who prefers a few deep rather than many superficial impressions, might make his way one morning along the Via Maque-
da, turning right up the Corso at the Quattro Canti (worthy of note) and,
passing the cathedral, left to Piazza della Vittoria. Stopping to admire the
Palazzo Sclafani on his left, he will see the Palazzo dei Normanni as he
rounds the Piazza. Here the Arabs built a palace for the Emirs; the Normans enlarged and beautified it (using Arab and Byzantine craftsmen),
and under Frederick II, it became a European center of art and culture.
Walking through its royal halls, the room of King Roger, the airy courtyards, admiring the Pisan tower, the traveler is unprepared for the sight
that meets his startled eyes as he enters the Cappella Palatina. A blaze
of gold, mosaics, and marble inlays glitter at him in the unreal play of
light and shadow. Here Norman, Arab, and Byzantine found that they
had one God in common, and glorified him. The traveler should then
climb up to the observatory tower and summarize it all—the cobalt sea,
the orchards, on the right the Arab castle of Favara and the buildings built
by Norman and Saracen, on the left the luxurious villas of wealthy Palermitans and, glittering where the mountains lie, Monreale, the greatest medieval cathedral of Italy.

Nearby, San Giovanni degli Eremiti is a happy adaptation of a mosque
to Christianity. In the delicate-arched shadowy cloister the visitor shares
what the monks saw as they sat on the marble benches to study the scrip-
tures 8 centuries ago: roses, palms, and above, a squat, mosque-like, small-
windowed building with four pink cupolas caught "in a noose of light".

There are many other things to see in the city which gave birth to that
fantastic adventurer Cagliostro: the gruesome catacombs of the Capuchin
convent with its thousands of fully-clothed mummified bodies, the Norman La Magione, San Francesco, the vast Pantheon-like San Domenico,
Santa Zita, and the archeological museum. The Zisa's splendid Arab-
Norman palace of William I (in the process of restoration), lies on the outskirts of the city, as do Santo Spirito, (where began the revolt of the Sicilian
Vespers), and the beautiful Santa Maria di Gesù. The Palazzo Abatellis
contains a rewarding art museum.

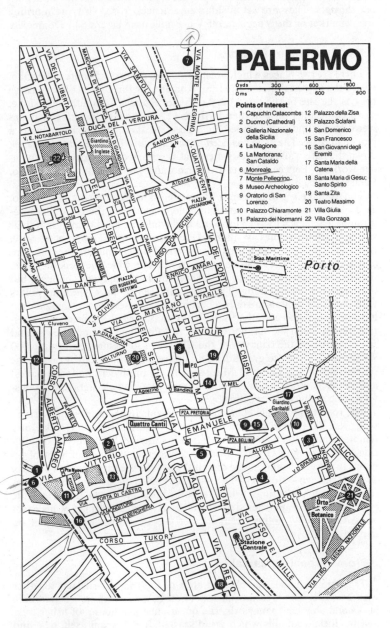

PALERMO

| 0 yds | 300 | 600 | 900 |
| 0 ms | 300 | 600 | 900 |

Points of Interest

1 Capuchin Catacombs
2 Duomo (Cathedral)
3 Galleria Nazionale della Sicilia
4 La Magione
5 La Martorana; San Cataldo
6 Monreale
7 Monte Pellegrino
8 Museo Archeologico
9 Oratorio di San Lorenzo
10 Palazzo Chiaramonte
11 Palazzo dei Normanni
12 Palazzo della Zisa
13 Palazzo Sclafani
14 San Domenico
15 San Francesco
16 San Giovanni degli Eremiti
17 Santa Maria della Catena
18 Santa Maria di Gesù; Santo Spirito
19 Santa Zita
20 Teatro Massimo
21 Villa Giulia
22 Villa Gonzaga

A last word about Palermo—try to see a performance at one of the puppet theaters. They are astonishing experiences. Also, visit the morning street market of the Vucciria, off Via Roma near Piazza San Domenico.

The Environs of Palermo

There are two places which must be visited: the first is Monte Pellegrino, where the Carthaginians defied the Romans for three years. The massive rock is the site of the Sanctuary of Santa Rosalia. Daughter of a duke, she became a hermit and died in the cave she chose to live in. Her bones were later found and, carried in procession through the city, caused a plague to cease. The cave has been most impressively turned into a chapel; down the bare walls trickles water that is gathered and regarded as wonder-working. Between Monte Pellegrino and Monte Gallo is Mondello, Palermo's beach resort.

The second place to be seen is Monreale, 8 km. (5 miles) out of Palermo. This glorious spot on the mountain side, once within the royal pleasure-grounds, explains why the Norman kings could not hope to maintain their strong northern virtues. William II, so the story goes, found a treasure, revealed to him in a dream by the Virgin, and with it built another treasure and another dream. The stone, color of Marsala wine, the striking apses, the well-proportioned towers of the cathedral are impressive enough, but the interior is breathtaking. The lofty, airy central nave, the slim pillars with their rich capitals are only a beginning, because a soaring imagination has attempted, successfully, to depict in mosaic what Michelangelo's Sistine frescos did in the suppler medium of paint: the Creation, the rise and fall of man, and the triumph of the Church. 130 pictures covering 6,000 square yards trace the events leading up to the Birth of Christ (along the central nave), His Life and Ministry (in the presbytery and side naves) and the Acts of the Apostles. The Moorish-looking cloisters and monastery are equally worth visiting.

The road to Monreale continues to Trapani. Just after passing Alcamo is Segesta. Don't be frightened by the word "ruins". Here is a Greek Doric temple almost intact; some have called it superior, for dignity and situation, to anything in Greece—which, considering the state of a lot of remains in Greece, would not be difficult! The hills are bare, the view superb. 25 centuries ago—around 430 B.C.—slaves hauled up these immense stones from the sulphur springs below to build the 35-foot columns. Here the tyrant Agathokles murdered all the citizens who complained of his exactions. Of the city, nothing remains but the admirable Greek theater on the heights above.

From Trapani to Marsala

Trapani commands the blunted apex of the triangular island together with Marsala. The area has an aspect all its own, with its isolated bare peaks and abundant vineyards, the queer cube-like houses of fisher folk, and the little windmills which grind sea-salt. Yet Trapani itself, neat and modern in its isthmus, seems but an appendix of Mount Erice, also called San Giuliano, the ancient Eryx (where Hercules challenged the king). The people, however, arouse interest; there are Arab, Phoenician, Norman types, and you will see peasants as Greek as any statue by Praxiteles. Pilgrims come to Trapani on March 25th to venerate the jewel-laden statue of the Madonna in the Church of the Annunziata. Most tourists, however, come in order to buy the pretty ornaments made by skilled craftsmen of Trapani from coral, and, more especially, to ascend Mount Erice, either by car or bus.

The ancient town of Erice seems to grow out of the fierce rock 760 meters (2,500 ft.) above Trapani. From its Cyclopean Phoenician walls the Egadi Islands can be seen, the coast of Africa is visible on a fine day, and the sunsets are fantastic almost every evening. Erice has to be visited to be believed; its isolation has developed a life and an architecture all its own. In the evening, dusk seems to creep slowly up the mountain from the coast.

Marsala is famous for its wine-making, of course, and for its memories of Garibaldi, who landed here. The English dominate the former and more profitable activity, while the Italians console themselves with their hero. The English also managed to smuggle in St. Thomas à Becket as patron saint. The Italians retorted by placing the Doric columns intended to be sent to England in the pleasant cathedral—still, however, dedicated to St. Thomas—which leaves the honors about even. You should see the nobly proportioned barrels in the old wine-making establishments, as well as the reconstruction and some original components of the Punic galley recovered off the coast.

Along the South Coast

The Africa-facing coast is a sadder one. The sea coast is picturesque enough with its olives, vines, and almonds; but beyond the grain fields of the lower hills, the rounded hillocks and the little valleys, lie the bleak plateaus with weaker vegetation around grey cottages.

The road passes through pleasant Mazara and Castelvetrano, earthquake-hit, and forks right to Selinunte (Selinus), an overwhelming sight. If you are interested in ancient things, just before Selinunte, at the town of Campobello, ask directions to the Cave di Cusa. This is where the stones and pillars for Selinunte were hewn from local rock, and you can see just how the Greeks, back in the 5th century B.C., went about their work. The history books say it was founded 6 centuries before Christ, and that a Carthaginian army under Hannibal destroyed it. This is historian's language. The attackers may have slaughtered 16,000 of its inhabitants, but no weapons of antiquity could have scattered these 50-foot long, 10-foot thick columns, only seismic shocks could have done that.

The heart of Selinunte was the Acropolis on the shore. At its seaward limit is the Tower of Pollux, an ancient lighthouse. The Acropolis was walled, traversed by two main thoroughfares, crossed by side-streets. Of its chief temple (to Demeter), the central Naos or holy of holies can be seen, with the adjoining chamber where the treasure was kept. The sacramental part of the building is astonishingly small; the Greek temple was one vast public promenade, the priests remaining apart in their still, small room.

Of the three temples near the station, the Temple of Apollo is one of the most colossal Greek structures in existence. The base blocks weigh 100 tons, yet were placed one on another, joined by a central key. The mathematically-minded visitor will note the careful town-planning that went into the making of this titanic city, where digging for archeological finds is still going on.

1. Municipal Museum
2. Temple of the Heavenly Twins
3. Temple of Jupiter
4. Temple of Hercules
5. Villa Aurea
6. Temple of Concord
7. Temple of Juno
8. Tomb of Tero
9. Temple of Esculapius
10. Sanctuary of Demeter
11. Archeological Museum

Sciacca, farther along the road, has been known for its thermal waters for 3,000 years. If you are driving through it, go to the Piazza Scandaliato, whence the view is magnificent, or along the road locally called Panoramica.

Farther east, about 11 km. (7 miles) beyond Ribera, if you have a genuine interest in ancient ruins, or "digs", take the right turning to Eraclea Minoa; that is, if you don't mind about 6 km. (4 miles) of road which is little more than a series of potholes held together rather loosely by 2- and 3-foot stretches of pavement. Some work has been done on excavations and preservation (and there is a good, small museum), but perhaps best is to imagine what a superb site this must have been in its "days of glory" perched here, high above the sea.

Agrigento and its Temples

Those interested in antiquity will now find fulfillment of their greatest expectations. After the lone temple of Segesta, the tremendous strewn columns of Selinunte, comes the revelation of Agrigento. Egypt has its Valley of the Kings, Agrigento its Valley of the Temples. Temples, buildings, monuments, and odd works of art number a hundred or more. They are in fair state of preservation, and their setting is magnificent, particularly in late winter and early spring, when the valley is smothered with flowers and the whole vast area is alight with almond blossom. Moreover, the modern city of Agrigento, built where the Acropolis of the ancient one stood, is close at hand.

The short drive up from Porto Empedocle is a revelation of riotous scent and blossom at any season save summer. The modern port recalls the encyclopedic genius Empedocles, the most illustrious son of Agrigentum (or Greek "Akragas"), who, they say, directed the excavation of the gap separating the modern town's site from the "Athenian rock" which travelers now climb for the view across the Valley of the Temples to the sea. The city of Phalaris, the tyrant who pleasantly shut up his enemies inside a monstrous red-hot bronze bull, was erected by Carthaginian prisoners. Pindar thought it the greatest metropolis in the world, and another Greek said that its inhabitants built their temples as if they never expected to die, but lived as if they expected to die tomorrow.

The ancient city had at least ten times as great a population as the modern one. On the northeast side of the Valley of Temples, the chief buildings are the temple and sanctuary of Demeter (or Ceres), and the ancient walls. To the south are the temples of Juno, Concord, and Hercules; to the west, the temple of Jove, the 8th wonder of the world; the sacrificial altars, and the temple of Castor and Pollux, the Heavenly Twins (Tempio dei Dioscuri).

The Temple of Concord, symbol of Agrigento, is the best preserved in the world after that of Theseus in Athens; the four columns of the Temple of Castor and Pollux are the most photographed—they will be familiar to most people, for they are often used as symbolic of Sicily. When the almond trees around this temple are in bloom, it makes an exquisite picture. In February, the temples and almond blossom form a magnificent backdrop for an important International Folklore Festival. The temple of Juno is interesting, for the naos is fairly intact.

Agrigento's modern religious festival of San Calogero, on the first Sunday of July, keeps something of the Greek festivals: a decorated mule carries sheaves of corn together with loaves shaped like the limbs or organs healed by intervention of the saint. Apart from the Convent of Santo Spirito and the interesting Church of San Nicola, modern Agrigento has no great artistic attractions. Its climate, however, is superb.

The Heart of Sicily

Time was when travelers continued on along the coast from Agrigento, but these days many dip inland, and upland, through lovely farm country, to Enna, by way of Caltanissetta on S610. The latter is a bustling, lively town with a castle of Frederick III of Aragon perched, seemingly precariously, on a lonely crag. Beyond lies Enna, a fortress city which, at over 900 meters (3,000 ft.), was justifiably considered impregnable. Because of its dominance over much of this region in olden days, it has often been called the "navel of Sicily". It's a small city with a friendly atmosphere, dozens of climbing, winding streets, and incredible panoramas, including Etna. It also has a castle, built by Frederick II, which once had 20 towers. Now, with only 6 remaining, it is still impressive. Here, too, are an early 14th-century cathedral, a Swabian lookout tower, and a delightful climate.

From Enna, the road south (S117bis) leads through a series of pine and eucalyptus woods and lovely farmland scenery to Piazza Armerina. Some 6 km. (4 miles) out from town are the remains of the Emperor Maxentius' 3rd-century villa, the Villa Romana del Casale, an exceptionally complete and well-preserved example of a sumptuous Roman country house, in this case used as a hunting lodge. The spacious halls, airy courtyards and architecturally-complex baths were paved with beautiful mosaics, probably by master artisans called in from North Africa. Throughout the villa, magnificent mosaic pavements representing hunting scenes and mythological subjects, most in an excellent state of conservation, are comfortably visible from walkways.

From Piazza Armerina continue south to Caltagirone, a small city which has been turning out majolica and terracotta since the 17th century. Surprising bits and pieces appear about the town, and in the public gardens, and there is a museum showing pieces from every century. There are some interesting churches here. From Caltagirone you can dip southwest (S117bis) to Gela, a town of greatest interest to the archeological-minded, if you can put up with the oil refinery, or go southeast (S124) to Siracusa (Syracuse), stopping on the way at Noto, a Baroque gem.

Syracuse

The east coast is placid and prosperous. The towns, drawing their livelihood from the wide fertile plain of Catania, are modern and comparatively energetic, though still conscious of their Greek past. The great earthquake of 1693 is responsible for the aspect of most of its cities, for they were rebuilt when Baroque was the prevailing fashion, and the local temperament often gave this style those extra flourishes that so easily turn Baroque into bad taste.

Historical imagination is needed to see Syracuse as anything more than a rather ordinary pleasantish city. It is hard to realize that here was the largest, wealthiest city of ancient Europe, bulwark of Greek civilization, where Archimedes lived and Plato taught. The modern city clusters round an island, the Ortigia; the ancient city occupied this and spread for miles over the surrounding country. Moreover, most of the ancient city has vanished. The great Temple of Minerva was turned into the present cathedral, and the piquant contrast between later Baroque and the stern simplicity of Doric columns makes it an interesting curiosity.

Walking along the fine promenade—the Marina—you may find it difficult to believe that in this modest port one of the great sea battles of antiquity was fought. Here the Athenian navy perished—largely because its commander was afraid to leave owing to an eclipse of the moon, when he might have got away. The rather brackish papyrus-fringed spring of Arethusa at the marina is the one sung by poets as that of the nymph Arethusa who was pursued by Alpheus and transformed into a fountain. Its loss may well have influenced the defeat of the thirsting Athenian army, and thus the history of the world. On this walk, the pretty Marine Gate and the fine Maniace Castle, built by Frederick II at the very tip of the island, are well worth noting.

It is interesting to walk about the mainland north of Syracuse where the ancient city lay. The Latomie, caves whence the city's stone was quarried, are planted as gardens; one of them, with an entrance shaped like a huge ear, is known as Dionysius' Ear, for the tyrant, it is said, when interrogated prisoners would not talk, threw them in the cave and here listened to their conversation, for the caves have remarkable echoes and acoustic properties. The fortress of Euryalus, built by Dionysius as a protection against the Carthaginians, was a stronghold in an astonishing defense system covering 15,000 square yards. One 5-km. (3-mile) stretch of wall was built in 20 days by 60,000 men.

The finest thing in Syracuse, however—and with the best view—is the graceful Greek Theater, well-preserved and huge (134 meters, 440 ft. at the widest part). Classical theater performances are held there in even years. The regional archeological museum in Villa Landolina park has well-organized displays of interesting remains from prehistoric times to Greek and Roman eras, with informative graphics to help visitors make sense of the ancient sites in the area.

Catania and Mount Etna

The chief wonder about Catania is the fact that it is there at all. Its successive populations were deported by one Greek tyrant, sold into slavery by another, driven out by Carthaginians. Every time the city really got going again, *Force majeure* took a hand. Plague decimated the inhabitants, a mile-wide stream of lava from erupting Etna swallowed most of it in 1663 and, 30 years later, the disastrous earthquake forced the Catanese to begin all over again.

However, 18th-century town planners could not foresee 20th-century traffic; much of Catania's moldering Baroque charm is dimmed by traffic noise and smog. To Etna it owes a superb backdrop, the fertility of its hinterland, its site (for it is built upon nine successive strata of lava), and many of its buildings, constructed from the lava as well. The city of Lava and Oranges, the Italians call it.

Catania's greatest son is Bellini the musician, but it bears the imprint of the architect Vaccarini, who rebuilt the cathedral and the town hall round the elephant fountain, symbol of Sicily. The numerous Baroque churches, the Ursino Castle, the Benedictine Convent, and the Roman and Greek remains are worth seeing, as also the fine squares and parks (Piazza Roma, Villa Bellini, Piazza Stesicoro, Piazza dell'Università).

Of the many excursions, the finest is the trip around Etna by car or bus. The scenery is extraordinarily varied and lovely. The route passes through the flowery vale of Paternò, a typical hill-town topped by a castle; the orange groves around Biancavilla; Adrano, once an important Greek city, now celebrated for its Easter Passion Play. The best scenery is perhaps on the climb up to Randazzo at 600 meters (2,000 ft.). At Bronte is the castle presented to Lord Nelson by the King of Naples, together with the title of Duke of Bronte. Here, too, on the slopes of Etna, are Linguaglossa, Trecastagni, Francavilla di Sicilia, and other towns, as well as the cooled lava fields.

As for Etna itself, it has erupted in all 8 times in the last three decades. It is certainly not a sleeping giant! The most spectacular were '71 and '83 when rivers of molten rock flowed down to destroy the two highest stations of the funicular. In spite of its volatile history, excursions may still be made, (subject to local authorization) up the slopes of the rambunctious volcano.

Taormina

This delightful spot is a fitting close to a tour of the island, though its natural beauty has been spoiled by overdevelopment. But the nucleus of the charming town itself has retained its distinction, the arches, columns, cupolas, dark red cliffs, Cape Sant' Andrea, the incredible rock of Sant' Alessio, Etna, which from Taormina even looks benevolent, though sometimes at night it shoots flames skyward. The town is excellent value for the camera buff, photogenic in a slightly theatrical way.

The beaches below the village, a couple of miles by steep winding road, are disappointing despite the lovely setting. There are frequent bus services to romantic Isola Bella and Spisone, while Mazzaro in the middle is quickly reached by cable car. But the pebbles are hard on the feet and the water far from crystal-clear, so that several beach hotels have swimming pools.

The Greek Theater is, next to that of Syracuse, the largest of the classical theaters in Sicily. Much of it remains intact. Most visitors are tempted to prove its extraordinary acoustic properties by wafting stage whispers to their friends a hundred yards away on its perimeter. The Film Festival in July is followed by the Music Festival in August, both with their respective devotees, but most impressive of all is the view.

The Palazzo Corvaia is an interesting 15th-century building with the black and white lava and pumice work characteristic of Taormina. It makes a pretty picture with its contemporary, the delightful Church of Santa Caterina, behind which are remains of an intimate Roman theater— Taormina toned down even that grandiosely-planning people.

Almost everything to be seen in Taormina lies about the Corso Umberto, which is itself full of many-colored mansions of the 15th and 16th centuries, crammed with interesting details, many of them Moorish. Half way along the Corso is the Largo 9 Aprile, a noble square, with its 16th-century churches of Sant' Agostino and San Giuseppe, and the arched clock tower. Still following the Corso, and casting an appreciative glance at the fine door of the Ciampoli mansion, you come to the 16th-century cathedral, sturdy, squat-towered, simple, and forthright. The queer little fountain carries the emblem of Taormina (a crowned centauress holding a globe). This piazza is well worth lingering in; it is backed by the hill on which the castle lies, the steps rising to the Church of the Carmine, and, to the right of the fountain, the alleys lead up to the graceful vestige of the old abbey. The 15th-century contemporary of the latter, the Palazzo Spuches, lies near, its fine windows and decorated frieze around the roof still exciting the admiration of the 20th century.

Taormina is a town for walkers and view-collectors, who satisfy both enthusiasms by making for the medieval castle, San Pancrazio, the Belvedere or the incredible little settlement of Castel Mola, perched high above Taormina, on its own rocky escarpment, which appears poised ready to soar off into space. If you are one of the latter, but not the former, buses will take you to these places. They will also transport you farther afield to the caves of Sant' Andrea, to Monte Venere, or Francavilla. And buses are really preferable to private cars, not only because of the steepness of the winding roads and alleys, but mostly because of the totally insufficient parking space on the narrow ledge.

Sicily's Islands

At the northeast of Sicily, reached by boat from Milazzo and Messina, and less frequently, but on regular schedule from Catania and Palermo, as well as once-weekly from mainland Naples, are the Aeolian Islands (Lipari). Their charms are beginning to be appreciated if only because they lend themselves so well to one of the newest water sports, underwater exploring and fishing. Of volcanic origin, these islands are honeycombed with grottos in which fish lurk, and the clear warm waters are ideal for the swimmer intent on stalking his prey in and about them.

One of the group has a name almost synonymous for the word "volcano"—Stromboli. The active volcano on this island is the most spectacular feature of the region. The view from the sea at night is awe-inspiring, with the never-ceasing stream of incandescent lava flowing down the flank of the mountain into the sea—the *sciara del fuoco,* the flow of fire, the inhabitants call it. In spite of the lava and the frequent explosions which toss stones and flaming projectiles into the air, there is no danger from Stromboli. It has been behaving like this since ancient times. Because the lava flows freely instead of building up pressure internally, Stromboli remains a spectacle rather than a threat. An excellent grape, Malvasia, thrives in the richly volcanic soil.

A small companion islet nearby, Strombolicchio, is astonishing for the way its cliffs rise sheer out of the sea. They look unscalable, but a staircase has been cut out of the rock, and you can climb to the top and enjoy the remarkable view over the other islands of the archipelago.

Of these the largest is Lipari, from whose red lava rocks rise a 16th-century castle and a 17th-century cathedral on a plateau, called the Acropolis by the Liparians. Here is an incredible collection of ruins, covering almost a dozen ages of man, beginning with the prehistoric, going on through Greek steles, Corinthian ceramics, Roman relics. There are Byzantine churches, Spanish churches, and, fortunately, an excellent museum, displaying what has been discovered at this "melting pot" spot. Everywhere the views from Lipari are impressive, and there are delightful fishing villages, such as Canneto, in addition to the somewhat *gamin* charms of the "capital city" of Lipari.

Vulcano, true to its name, vies with Stromboli; it has hot sulphur springs and a still-active volcano that has been dormant for about a century. You can ascend the crater on muleback for a magnificent view. Salina is also noted for its Malvasia wine.

Panarea has no volcanos, but does very well without them—besides hot springs, it has many crevices from which smoke escapes, and at times the temperature of the earth reaches 220° F. in certain spots. This does not prevent it from being a fertile producer of grapes, olives, and capers. But don't go to Panarea if you like sandy beaches and hot showers, for you'll find neither.

Filicudi, one of the smaller islands, is noted for its Sea Bull Grotto, with its exceptionally limpid water. Alicudi is even smaller.

The island of Ustica lies all by itself north of Palermo and is reached by *aliscafo.* It has impressive grottos, pretty farms, lovely flowers, and fine seafood. It has established itself firmly on the tourist map for its ideal bathing and underwater fishing.

The Egadi Islands lie just west of Trapani and Erice, and are plainly visible from mainland Sicily. Here are medieval castles, villages evocative of North Africa and mysterious grottos. Some say the island of Marettimo, in this group, is the Ithaka of the *Odyssey.* Pantelleria has a cone reaching up 2,742 feet, and is clothed in small forest areas and sweeps of farms. Swimming and skindiving are exceptional here.

All of Sicily's islands, especially the Aeolians, are attracting growing numbers of summer vacationers, so their much-touted tranquillity becomes strictly relative in July and August—in fact, at that time of year some of them can be impossibly crowded. You'll probably find them much more satisfying off-season.

PRACTICAL INFORMATION FOR SICILY

WHEN TO GO. For the seaside holidaymaker, Sicily is both a winter and a summer playground. But the traveler who wishes to know the island visits in early spring, when the mountains are still snow-covered, the meadows green, and wild flowers profuse. Summer scorches the land and brings the *sirocco*, a hot African wind that lays a three-day blanket of listlessness over the island. Popular Taormina's season is year-long, with a peak from December to April.

Because of its climate, Sicily is more apt to play host to tourists on New Year's Day than most places; it is a good time to be there, for Sicilian celebrations are very colorful.

TOURIST OFFICES. Acireale: AAST, Corso Umberto 177 (604.521). **Agrigento:** AAST, Viale della Vittoria 255 (26.922) and Piazzale Moro (20.454). **Catania:** Railway station (322.440). **Cefalù:** AAST, Corso Ruggeri 114 (21.050). **Enna:** AAST, Piazza Garibaldi 1 (21.184). **Erice:** AAST, Viale Conte Pepoli (869.388). **Messina:** AAST, Piazza Cairoli 45 (293.3541) and Railway station (777.0731). **Siracusa:** AAST, Via Maestranza 33 (66.932) and at Archeological zone (60.510). **Taormina:** AAST, Piazza Santa Caterina (23.243). **Trapani:** Piazza Saturno (29.000).

SEASONAL EVENTS. Agrigento: in Feb. the Almond Blossom Festival includes an international folklore festival.

Catania: from June. to Sept., opera, rock music and theater are presented at the Greco-Roman theater. On Aug. 13, the Palio dei Normanni, a costumed tournament, takes place at Piazza Armerina.

Messina: mid-Aug. sees a series of events, including the parade of the Giganti (huge figures from local folklore) on the 13th–14th; and on the 15th, the Vara procession, a religious observance with popular overtones.

Palermo: Jul. 11–15 sees the celebrations for patron saint, Rosalia, with fireworks, processions and street fairs; in Oct. and Nov. there's a Festival of Sacred Music.

Piana degli Albanesi (near Palermo): the Epiphany, Jan. 6, is celebrated with Byzantine rites and a procession of townsfolk in gorgeous local costume; the similarly Byzantine Easter rites are also not to be missed.

Siracusa: May and Jun. in even-numbered years (next 1990), there is classical drama in the magnificent Greek theater.

Taormina: at the end of May is a show of local costume and elaborately decorated Sicilian carts; the Greek theater here is the setting in Jul and Aug. for various types of musical and theatrical entertainments.

Apart from the above, **Holy Week**—usually in April—inspires dramatic processions throughout the island. The most interesting are at Messina, Enna, and at Trapani—the Good Friday procession of the Mysteries, 17th-century statue groups, here, is both impressive and emotional.

TELEPHONE CODES. You will find the telephone area code for each town against its name in the Hotel and Restaurant listings (after the province name). If there is a different area code from the majority of the establishments—say when a hotel or restaurant is in an outlying place—then the code is given in front of the telephone number.

HOTELS AND RESTAURANTS. There are not that many good hotels on Sicily outside the principal tourist resorts, for example in Palermo, Salerno and Agrigento. Generally speaking, too, the hotels tend to be on the pricey side, with some notable exceptions. The paucity of choice makes it very important to plan any touring itinerary so as to be sure to have a decent pillow to comfort you at the end of the day. *Jolly Hotels* are very good here.

Regional Food and Drink. Sicily has no typical meat dishes; its specialities run to vegetables, fish and cereals. Order *melanzane* (eggplant); the Sicilians know dozens of ways of cooking and stuffing it—*caponata* is a pleasant mixture of eggplant, tomatoes, capers, olives and various other ingredients. They also do wonderful things with a local variety of cauliflower, which they call *broccoli.* One of the most typical pastas is *pasta con le sarde,* with a sauce made of fresh sardines, olive oil, anchovies, raisins and pine nuts, redolent of the distinctive flavor of wild fennel. Another is *spaghetti alla Norma,* named for Bellini's heroine, with a sauce of tomatoes and fried eggplant.

The few meat dishes feature *involtini,* stuffed meat rolls, and *falsomagro,* much the same thing. Fish takes the honors on Sicilian menus, and there are endless variations on the *tonno* (tuna fish) theme. A favorite snack are *arancini,* rice croquettes with a surprise filling of meat and cheese. The Arab *cuscus* is served in a number of local versions, usually with fish.

The sweets of Sicily are famous; monasteries and convents still compete in the production of masterpieces; the *sfinge* of San Giuseppe, the *trionfo di gola,* and incredibly realistic marzipan fruits and sea creatures. Sicilian ice cream is delicious; there's the justly famous *cassata* and thirst-quenching *granita di limone,* a kind of lemon ice. Queen of Sicilian pastries are very, very sweet *cannoli.* You'll see Sicilians popping into bars in the morning not for a *cafè* but for a *maritozzo* (brioche), split down the middle and filled with ice cream.

Sicilian wines are suited to its hearty, colorful and highly flavored food, and they're not sufficiently distinguished to worry about vintage. The dark red *Faro* is from the slopes of the Peloritani mountains; *Corvo di Salaparuta* has excellent dry white and red wines and a good *spumante,* too. *Regaleali,* from the Palermo area, is a good white, little known outside Italy and perfect with fish. At Marsala you'll find wineries with names like *Ingham* and *Whitaker,* reminders that the local dessert wine has been a favorite with the English for centuries.

Acireale Catania (095). On rocky coast near Catania. *Aloha d'Oro* (M), Strada Panoramica (604.344). Open 23 Dec. to 30 Oct. Just outside town; simple rooms, good lounges, terraces; pool, minibus service to sea bathing. AE, DC, V. *Santa Tecla* (M), at Santa Tecla (604.933). North of town, on sea; large, very comfortable, a touch of elegance; pool, bathing area. AE, DC, MC, V.

Restaurants. *Aloha d'Oro* (M), Strada Panoramica (604.344). Closed 1 Nov. to 21 Dec. Fine hotel restaurant, delicious ice cream. AE, DC, V. *La Grotta* (M), at Santa Maria La Scala (894.414). Closed Tues. Tiny seafood restaurant in grotto on port. *Panoramico* (M), on Highway 114, north (885.291). Closed Fri. and Nov. Interesting menu, good food and wines. AE, DC, MC, V.

Aci Trezza Catania (095). Fishing port 10 km. (6½ miles) north of Catania. *Faraglioni* (M), Lungomare (631.286). View of sea and islets; cannot be recommended in July and August, noisy peak of season.

Restaurants. *Al Sarago* (M), Via Marina 63 (636.298). Closed Wed. and Oct. Very good seafood, somewhat pricey. *Il Pirata* (M), Via Provinciale 180 (636.347). Closed Fri. off-season. Dining with marvelous view.

Aeolian Islands Messina (090). These small volcanic islands, just north of Sicily, offer simple but well-organized accommodations, are very crowded from mid-July to the end of August.

Lipari, largest, best-equipped island. *Carasco* (M), at Porto delle Genti (981.1605). Open 1 April to 27 Sept. Large, well-equipped resort hotel; on sea, pool, rock bathing. *Filadelfia* (M), Via Tronco (981.2795) and *Villa Diana* (M), Località Diana (981.1403) are on the inexpensive side, very welcoming. *Melingunis* (M), Via Marte (981.2426). Open 1 Mar. to 31 Oct. Smallish, very comfortable, old patrician villa. AE, DC, MC, V.

Restaurants. *Melingunis* (E), Via Marte at Marina Corta (981.2426). Open 1 Mar. to 31 Oct. Lovely dining room and terrace of Hotel Melingunis; fish specialties. *Filippino* (M), Piazza Municipio (981.1002). Closed Mon. off-season and Nov.–26 Dec. Excellent seafood, *maccheroni alla Filippino*. AE, MC, V. *Pulera* (M), Via Diana 51 (981.1158). Open 1 June to 31 Oct. Dining on island specialties in shady garden. Evenings only. AE, DC, V. *Turmalin* (M), Piazza Municipio (981.1588). Closed in winter. Very good, economical, cafeteria-style.

Panarea. Here you do without hot water and often without electricity. *Lisca Bianca* (I), (983.004). Open 1 April to 15 Oct. Quiet, panoramic, meals at Cincotta tourist village. *Piazza* (I), at San Pietro (981.1190). Open 1 June to 30 Sept. Small; pool, rock bathing.

Stromboli. *La Sciara* (M), at Piscità (986.004). Open Apr.–15 Oct. Full-fledged resort complex with pool. AE, DC, V. *Sirenetta* (M), at Ficogrande (986.025). Open 1 April to 20 Oct. On good beach; quiet, basic comforts.

Vulcano. *Arcipelago* (M), at Vulcanello (985.2002). Open 1 May to 30 Sept. Ultramodern, well-equipped resort hotel on sea; pool, rock bathing. AE, V. *Eolian* (M), at Porto Ponente (985.2152). Open 1 May to 30 Sept. Large, hacienda-style; inland location. AE, DC, V. *Sables Noirs* (M), at Porto Ponente (985.2014). Open 1 April to 15 Oct. Pioneer hostelry on island; small, simple, on sea.

Restaurants. *Blue Moon* (M), at Porto Ponente (985.2142). Open 1 May to 31 Oct. Excellent food on panoramic terrace, impromptu entertainment, some dishes pricey. *Lanterna Bleu* (M), at Porto Ponente (985.2287). Closed mid-Dec. to mid-Jan. Local specialties.

Agrigento Agrigento (0922). Famous temples, scruffy town. *Jolly Dei Templi* (E), Villaggio Mose, parco Angeli (76.144). Fairly near temples, quiet, well-equipped; pool. AE, DC, MC, V. *Villa Athena* (E), Via dei Templi (23.833). Best; lovely, well-furnished villa with pool, at the temples. V.

Akrabello (M), Parco Angeli (76.277). Large and modern, with pool. *Della Valle* (M), Via dei Templi (76.144). Comfortable, good view of temples. AE, DC, V.

Restaurants. *Le Caprice* (E), Strada Panoramica dei Templi 51 (26.469). Closed Fri. off-season and July. Luscious pastas, *spiedino alla Caprice*. AE, DC, MC, V.

Milleluci (M), Villaggio Mosè (76.128). Closed Fri. Antipasto a specialty. *Il Vigneto* (M), Via Cavaleri Magazzeni 11 (44.319). Closed Tues. and 1–15 Nov. Simple, unassuming, good. AE, DC, MC, V. In town, *Uaddan* (M), Viale Vittoria 313 (23.187). Closed Mon.

Caltanissetta Caltanissetta (0934). Archaeological finds of various eras. **Restaurants.** *Al 124* (M), at San Cataldo exit on Autostrada (68.034). Closed Mon. and Aug. DC. *Cortese* (M), Viale Sicilia 166 (23.187). Closed Mon. and Aug. Ask for local specialties.

Catania Cantania (095). Important city in Etna's shadow. *Excelsior* (E), Piazza Verga (325.733). Large; comfortable rooms; roof garden. *Jolly Trinacria* (E), Piazza Trento 13 (316.933). Contemporary decor, well-equipped rooms, efficient service. AE, DC, MC, V.

Motel AGIP (M), Via Messina 626, at Ognina (494.003). Furnishings standardized, adequate; ask for room with sea view. AE, DC, MC, V. *Nettuno* (M), Via Ruggero di Lauria 121 (493.533). On shore road to Ognina. Satisfactory, no frills; pool in season. AE, DC, MC, V.

At **Cannizzaro,** 8 km. (5 miles) north, *Baia Verde* (E), Lungomare (491.522). Big seaside resort hotel, open all year, posh and pricey. AE, DC, V. *Sheraton (E), Via Antonello da Messina 41 (271.557). Big seaside hotel, pool, all comforts. AE, DC, MC, V.*

Restaurants. *Costa Azzurra* (E), Via de Cristoforo 4, at Ognina (494.920). Closed Mon. and Aug. Seaside veranda, seafood specialties. AE, DC, MC, V. *La Siciliana* (M), Viale Marco Polo 52 (370.003). Closed Sun. evening and Mon. Book ahead for this delightful family-run trattoria, exquisite food. AE, DC, MC, V.

Commercio (M), Via Francesco Riso 8 (447.289). Closed Sat. and Aug. Known for fine pasta; try *rigatoni alla Norma.* AE, V. *Pagano* (M), Via de Roberto 37 (322.720). Closed Sun. and Aug. At back of Hotel Excelsior; good local dishes. *Rinaldo* (M), Via Simili 59 (532.312). Closed Tues. and 10 Aug. to 10 Sept. *Rosso Azzurro* (M), Piazza Trento (447.652). Closed Mon. and Aug. *Savia,* Via Etnea, café facing entrance to Bellini gardens, is famous for tempting snacks, pastries and ice cream.

At **Cannizzaro,** *La Posada* (M), Lungomare (631.666). Closed Mon. Fine *zuppa* or *fritto di pesce. Selene* (M), Via Mollica 24 (494.444). Closed Tues. and from 4–27 Aug. Try *linguine al cartoccio,* with seafood sauce. AE, DC, V.

Cefalù Palermo (0921). Magnificent cathedral; vast sandy beaches. *Baia del Capitano* (M), at Mazzaforno (20.003). Open 15 Mar.–31 Oct. Handsome, local-style; in olive grove near beach. V. *Kalura* (M), at Caldura (21.354). Open 1 March to 31 Oct. Attractive resort hotel; on sea, with beach, pool, tennis. MC, V. *Le Calette* (M), at Caldura (24.144). Open 1 May to 31 Oct. Modern; gardens, pool, beach. DC, V.

At **Santa Lucia,** *Sabbie d'Oro* (21.565). Open 1 May to 31 Sept. Big bungalow colony on beach; good value. Club Mediterranée center.

Restaurants. *La Brace* (M), Via Venticinque Novembre 10 (23.570). Evenings only; closed Mon. and Dec. thru Jan. Near cathedral; some dishes pricey. AE, DC, MC, V. *Il Gabbiano* (M), Lungomare Giardina (21.495). Closed Wed. Good pizza and seafood overlooking beach. AE, DC, MC, V. *Da Nino* (M), Viale Lungomare (22.582). Closed Tues. and 15 Jan. to 15 Feb. Simple, friendly, good. DC, MC, V. *Osteria Magno* (M), Via Amendola 8 (23.679). Closed Tues. Central; also serves pizza. DC, V.

Egadi Islands (0923) Trapani. Favignana, Levanzo and Marettimo, off the west coast of Sicily. Still quite undiscovered and unspoilt.

Favignana. *Approdo di Ulisse* (M), at Calagrande (921.287). Open 22 May to 3 Oct. Bungalow colony on sea; pool, tennis. V. *Punta Fanfalo* (M) (921.332). Open 1 May to 30 Sept. Large vacation village, attractive architecture, exceptional sports facilities.

Restaurants. *Egadi* (E), Via Colombo (921.232). Open 1 May to 30 Sept.; closed at midday. Excellent *zuppa di pesce, spaghetti all'aragosta. Matteo* (M) (921.822). Closed Tues. and Jan. to Feb. V.

Enna Enna (0935). Fortress city at 942 meters, over 2,000 ft. Only two modest hotels: *Belvedere* (I), Piazza Crispi 2 (21.020), and *Grande Scilia* (I), Piazza Colaianni 7 (21.644). AE, DC, V.

Restaurants. *Centrale* (M), Via 6 Decembre 9 (21.025). Closed Sat. Small, very good. AE, DC, MC, V. *Fontana* (M), Via Vulturo 6 (25.465). Closed Sun. off-season. Traditional Sicilian cuisine; inexpensive in category.

Erice Trapani (0923). Medieval town on peak above Trapani. *Ermione* (M), Via Pinita Comunale 43 (869.138). Modest hotel in splendid surroundings. AE, DC, MC, V. *Moderno* (M), Via V. Emanuele 63 (869.300). Delightful small hotel in town. Good atmosphere, nicely furnished, very good restaurant. AE, DC, MC, V.

Restaurants. *Al Ciclope* (M), Viale Nasi 45 (869.183). Closed Tues., and 1 Oct. to 31 March. Seafood. DC, V. *Taverna di Re Aceste* (M), Viale Conte Pepoli (869.084). Closed Wed. and Nov. Best in town; local *cuscus* specialty; some dishes pricey. AE, DC, MC, V. *La Pentolaccia* (M), Via Fardella. 80 types of pasta!

Marsala Trapani (0923). Wine center. **Restaurants.** *Delfino* (M), Lungomare Mediterraneos (969.565). Closed Tues. from Oct. to Jan. Seafood. AE, DC, V. *Kalos* (M), Piazza della Vittoria (958.465). Closed Fri. Sicilian specialties on pleasant terrace. *Zio Ciccio* (M), Lungomare Mediterraneos (981.962). Closed Mon. Rustic dishes, including *cuscus,* overlooking sea. V.

Mazara del Vallo Trapani (0923). Fishing port near Marsala. *Hopps* (M), V. Hopps 29 (946.133). Large, attractive, modern resort hotel; beach, pool. AE, DC, V.

Restaurants. *La Bettola* (M), Corso Diaz 20 (946.203). Closed Sun. from Oct. to May. Cordial service, very good. AE, DC, V. *La Chela* (M), Via Mattarella 9 (946.329). Closed Fri. from Oct. to Mar. Modest and economical. *Da Nicola,* Via Sansone 21 (94.270). Closed Mon. Summer garden; seafood specialties and pizza.

Messina Messina (090). Important city. Ferry crossing. *Jolly dello Stretto* (E), Corso Garibaldi 126 (43.401). At port, 99 comfortable rooms, good views. AE, DC, MC, V. *Europa* (M), at Pistunina, entrance to Messina-Catania autostrada (271.1601). Good. AE, DC, MC, V. *Royal Palace* (M), Via Cannizzaro 224 (21.161). Near railway station; modern, fine, well-furnished. AE, DC, MC, V. *Venezia* (M), Piazza Cairoli 4 (718.076). Central, no restaurant. AE, DC, MC, V.

Restaurants. *Alberto* (E), Via Ghibellina 95 (710.711). Closed Sun. and 5 Aug. to 5 Sept. One of the best on island; seasonal specialties, swordfish *involtini.* AE, DC. *Pippo Nunnari* (E), Via Ugo Bassi 157 (293.8584). Closed Thurs. and 1–15 July. Atmosphere; exceptional Sicilian dishes. AE, V.

Antonio (M), Via Maddalena 156 (293.9853). Closed Sat. Good seafood restaurant. AE, DC, MC, V. *Donna Giovanna* (M), Via Risorgimento 16 (718.503). Closed Sun. Near port. *Galeone* (M), Viale della Libertà (57.101). Closed Mon. Fine panoramic restaurant of Grand Hotel Riviera, outside center on shore. DC, MC, V. *Piero* (M), Via Ghibellina 121 (718.365). Closed on Sun. and Aug. Central, specializing in seafood. AE, DC, MC, V.

Milazzo Messina (090). Port city where many embark for Aeolian Islands. *Eolian Inn* (M), Salita Cappuccini (928.6133). Open March to Oct. Large, well-equipped resort hotel; pool, good views. *Residenzial* (M), Piazza Nastasi (928.3292). Open 25 March to 20 Oct. Central, handy to boats for the island. Good overnight choice. AE, DC, MC, V. *Silvanetta Palace* (M), at Mangiavacca (928.1633). Modern hotel on sea outside town; pool, bathing area. AE, DC, MC, V.

Restaurants. *La Bussola* (M), Via Rizzo 4 (928.2955). Closed Tues. Right on port; simple, but good. *Covo del Pirata* (M), Via Marina Garibaldi (928.4437). Piazza della Repubblica (928.1382). Closed Tues. Very central, good restaurant of small hotel. V. *Gambero* (M), Via Rizzo (928.1783). On port, touristy, crowded in season; good pasta and ice cream. MC, V.

Monreale Palermo (091). Magnificent mosaics near Palermo. **Restaurants.** *La Botte* (M), highway 186 at Lenzitti (414.051). Closed Mon., Aug. and Sept. Delicious Sicilian dishes; try pasta *alla capricciosa* or *alla Fra Diavolo.* AE, DC. *Conca d'Oro* (M), Circonvallazione (640.2297). Closed Mon.

Palermo Palermo (091). *Villa Igiea* (L), Salita Belmonte 43 (543.744). Superb comfort in lush gardens on sea. Period furnishings, grill room, pool. AE, DC, MC, V. *Politeama Palace* (E), Piazza Ruggero Settimo 15 (322.777). Large, modern, well-equipped. AE, V. *Jolly* (E), Foro Italico 22 (616.5090). Comfortable rooms; garden, pool, sea views. AE, DC, MC, V.

Europa (M), Via Agrigento 3 (625.6323). Fairly quiet. No restaurant. AE, DC, MC, V. *Mediterraneo* (M), Via Rosolino Pilo 44 (581.133). Central, near archeological museum. No restaurant. AE, DC, MC, V. *Metropol* (M), Via Turrisi Colonna 4 (588.608). On fairly quiet street; smallish. AE, DC, MC, V. *Motel AGIP* (M), Viale della Regione 2620, at Via Notarbartolo (552.033). Large, reliable, AE, DC, MC, V.

Restaurants. *Chamade* (E), Via Torrearsa 22 (322.204). Closed Mon. Elegant. AE, DC, MC, V. *Charleston* (E), Piazzale Ungheria 30 (321.366). Closed Sun. From June to Sept. moves to Mondello. Exceptional ambiance and cuisine; Palermo's best. AE, DC, MC, V. *Gourmand's* (E), Via della Libertà 37 (323.431). Closed Sun. Another choice for top cuisine, but contemporary decor is cold. AE, DC, MC, V.

La Cuccagna (M), Via Principe Granatelli 21/a (587.267). Closed Mon. *Simpatica* trattoria, interesting menu. *Ficodindia* (M), Via Emerico Amari 65 (324.214). Closed Fri. Atmosphere, good food. V. *'Ngrasciata* (M), Via Tiro a Segno 12, at Sant'Erasmo (230.947). Closed Sun. Famous for seafood; unpretentious and popular. *La Scuderia* (M), Viale del Fante 9, at Parco Favorita (520.323). Closed Sun.

evening. Very good food, lovely summer garden. Elegant but somewhat pricey. AE, DC, MC, V. *Lo Scudiero* (M), Via Turati 7 (581.628). Closed Sun. and Aug. Central, tasty local dishes. AE, DC, V. *Sicilia in Bocca* (M), Via Ariosto 47/1 (261.137). Closed Sun. Near Notarbartolo Station; small, rustic and hearty. *Spanò* (M), Via Messina Marine 22 (470.025). Closed Mon. Typical shore restaurant for seafood. *Trittico* (M), Largo Montalto 7 (294.809). Closed Sun. In summer moves to Fossa del Gallo at Mondello. Elegant, good food and service. AE, DC, V.

Palermo-Mondello Palermo (091). Beach resort just west of the city. *Mondello Palace* (E), Viale Principe di Scalea (450.001). Spacious, airy salons, terraces and pool, private beach. AE, DC, V. *La Torre* (M), Via Piano del Gallo (450.222). Set apart on rocky promontory; large, modern, pool, all water sports. AE, DC, MC, V. *Esplanade* (I), Via Capo Gallo 22 (450.003). Open 1 Feb. to 30 Nov. Quiet, short walk to beach, many rooms with bath and balcony. AE, MC.

Restaurants. *Charleston* (E), see Palermo restaurants. *Gabbiano* (M), Via Piano Gallo (450.313). Closed Wed. *Gambero Rosso* (M), Via Piano Gallo 30 (454.685). Closed Mon. and 15–30 Nov. Very good. *Trittico* (M), see Palermo restaurants. *Sympathy* (M), Via Piano Gallo 18 (454.470). Closed Thurs. Fine trattoria for seafood.

Pantelleria Island Trapani (0923). Southwest of Sicily, still uncommercialized. *Cossyra* (M), at Mursia (911.154). Open 27 May to 5 Nov. Large seaside hotel, balconied rooms; pool, rock bathing. *Di Fresco* (M), at Mursia (911.217). Open 1 April to 31 Oct. On sea, simple but comfortable rooms with balcony; patios, pool, rock bathing. *Punta Tre Pietre* (M), at Scauri (916.026). Open 1 June to 30 Sept. Informal; all rooms with balcony, sea view; stairs to pool, rock bathing.

Restaurants. *La Lanterna* (E), at Campobello (911.634). Open 1 May to 30 Sept. Evenings only, candlelit suppers. *Bartolo* (M), Via Catania 4 (911.428). Open 1 March to 31 Oct. Simple food, good local wine. *Le Lampare* (M), at Mursia (911.217). Open 1 April to 31 Oct. Fine restaurant of Hotel Di Fresco.

Piazza Armerina Enna (0935). Interesting archeological center. *Selene* (M), Via Gaeta (80.254). Simple but adequate for overnight.

Restaurants. *Da Battiato* (M), Contrada Casale (82.453). Closed nights. *Papillon* (M), Via Monzoni (82.524). Closed Mon. *Al Ritrovo* (M), highway 117b (80.648). Closed Mon. Very simple and inexpensive. Good food. *Da Totò* (M), Via Mazzini 29 (81.153). Closed Mon. and Dec.

Ragusa Ragusa (0932). Baroque churches. *Montreal* (M), Via San Giuseppe 6 (21.133). Adequate overnight. V.

Restaurants. *Orfeo* (M), Via Sant'Anna 117 (21.035). Closed Sat. and 1–15 Aug. Near cathedral. *Saracinu* (M), Piazza del Duomo at Ibla (46.976). Closed Fri. in old part of town.

At **Kamarina,** on beach about 20 km. (15 miles) away, *Kamarina Palace* (M), 911.719. Open 1 June to 25 Oct. Large vacation village, bungalows, no frills but huge pool, own *piazza,* shops; sandy beach.

San Vito lo Capo Trapani (0923). Northwest tip of Sicily, good beaches. *Cala 'Mpiso* (M), at Calle dell'Impiso (972.286). Open 1 May to 31 Oct. Large vacation village; beach, pool, tennis.

Restaurants. *Antica Trattoria Cusenza* (M), Via Savoia 24 (972.228). Closed Mon. Try *cuscus* here.

At **Scopello,** *Torre Bennistra* (M), Via Diaz (56.003).

Sciacca Agrigento (0925). Spa, seaside resort. *Delle Terme* (M), Lungomare delle Terme (23.133). Traditional spa hotel in park, high on hilltop way above town and sea. AE, DC, MC, V.

At **Sciaccamare,** vast holiday complex on promontory, *Torre del Barone* (E), (92.354). Open 1 May to 27 Nov. Unusual architecture, very modern; all rooms with terrace, sea view. All sports, resort activities. Vacation village formula. MC. *Stromboli* (M), (92.354). Open 1 May to 27 Nov. Same complex. MC.

Selinunte Trapani (0924). Site of Greek ruins. At **Castelvetrano,** *Selinus* (M), Via Bonsignore 22 (41.638). AE, DC, MC, V. *Zeus* (M), Via Vittorio Veneto 6 (81.988). AE, DC, MC, V. Both comfortable overnights.
   Restaurant. At **Marinella,** near ruins, *Lido Azzurro* (M), (46.211). Fresh-caught fish on seaside terrace. AE, V.

Siracusa Siracusa (0931). Important city with famous Greek theater. *Jolly* (E), Corso Gelone 45 (64.744). Central location, all comforts, restaurant. AE, DC, MC, V. *Motel AGIP* (M), Viale Teracati 30 (66.944). On heavily-trafficked access road; functional. AE, DC, MC, V.
   Restaurants. *Arlecchino* (M), Via dei Tolomei 5 (66.386). Closed Mon. and Aug. Central, little atmosphere, but very good food. DC, V. *Fratelli Bandiera* (M), Via G. Perno 6 (65.021). Closed Mon. and Oct. On Ortygia, near post office; rustic, good. AE, DC, V. *Jonico-Rutta e Ciauli* (M), Riviera Dionisio il Grande 194 (65.540). Closed Tues. Seaside terrace, inventive cuisine, cordial service. Best in town. AE, DC, MC.

Taormina Messina (0942). Beautiful town overlooking Etna and sea. *San Domenico* (L), Piazza San Domenico 5 (23.701). A *Relais* hotel. Luxurious comfort superimposed on background of 15th-century monastery, complete with Renaissance cloister. Rooms in newer section are larger. Swimming pool in lush gardens. Outstanding, somewhat aloof. AE, DC, MC, V. *Bristol Park* (E), Via Bagnoli Croce 92 (23.006). Open 1 March to Oct. Quiet, modern; pool, terraces. AE, DC, MC, V. *Excelsior* (E), Via Toselli 8 (23.975). Beautiful location overlooking bay; pool. *Jolly Diodoro* (E), Via Bagnoli Croce 75 (23.312). Quiet; gorgeous views; very comfortable; pool and park. AE, DC, MC, V. *Mediterraneo* (E), Via Circonvallazione 61 (23.901). Open Apr.–Oct. Modern, just above town, spectacular views; terraces, pool.
   Continental (M), Via Dionisio 2/a (23.805). AE, DC, MC, V. *Bel Soggiorno* (M), Via Pirandello 60 (23.342). Small, pretty villa with views. AE, DC, V. *Villa Belvedere* (M), Via Bagnoli Croce 79 (23.791). Open 25 Mar.–Oct. Terrace with pool. No restaurant. MC, V. *Villa Fiorita* (M), Via Pirandello 39 (24.122). Smallish, very comfortable, garden, pool. No restaurant. AE. *Villa Paradiso* (M), Via Roma 2 (23.922). Lives up to its name. AE, DC, MC, V.
   Campanella (I), Via Circonvallazione 3 (23.381). Tiny, pleasant, atop steps. No restaurant. *Villa San Pancrazio* (I), Via Pirandello 22 (23.252). Open 1 April to 20 Oct. and 20 Dec. to 10 Jan. Good atmosphere.
   Restaurants. *Ciclope* (M), Corso Umberto (23.263). Closed Wed. and 10–31 Jan. Longtime favorite. Excellent seafood, courteous efficient service. AE, MC, V. *Luraleo* (M), Via Bagnoli Croce 31 (24.279). Closed Tues. Attractive place, very good food. AE, V. *Poco Pago* (M), Via Patricio (24.165). Closed Wed. Trattoria. At Castelmola, *Faro* (M), below town (24.802). Closed Wed. Simple, country cooking with views.

Taormina-Giardini Naxos Messina (0942). Beach resort. *Arathena Rocks* (M), at Naxos (51.349). Open 1 April to 31 Oct. Quiet, well-equipped resort hotel; on sea. *Holiday Inn* (M), Via Jannuzzo at Naxos (51.931). Closed Jan.–Feb. Very large, modern seaside hotel, all comforts. AE, DC, MC, V.
   Restaurants. *La Cambusa* (M), Via Schisò 3 (51.437). Closed Tues. off-season. Popular, seafood specialties. V. *Sileno* (M), at Recanati (51.302). Closed Tues. and Nov. Delicious antipasto. AE, DC, MC, V.

Taormina-Mazzaro Messina (0942). Beach resort. *Sea Palace* (L), (24.004). Open Apr.–Oct. Comfortable, elegant; pool, beach. AE, DC, MC, V. *Villa Sant'Andrea* (E), on beach (23.125). Open 15 March to 31 Oct. Lovely villa, exceptionally well furnished throughout; garden terraces directly on beach; friendly. AE, DC, MC, V.

At **Capo Taormina,** *Capo Taormina* (E), (24.000). Open 1 March to 30 Nov. On sea; posh, all resort facilities.

Restaurants. *Oliviero* (E), at Villa Sant'Andrea Hotel (23.125). Open June to Sept. Very good atmosphere. AE, DC, MC, V. *Delfino* (M), (23.004). Open 15 March to 31 Oct. On sea. AE, DC, MC, V. *Da Giovanni* (M), (23.531). Closed Mon. and 7 Jan.–7 Feb. AE, DC, MC, V.

Trapani Trapani (0923). Fishing port. *Astoria Park* (M), at San Cusumano, Lungomare Dante Alighieri (62.400). Comfortable, pool, beach. AE, DC, MC, V.

Restaurants. *Dell'Arco* (M), Via Nino Bixio 110 (27.796). Closed Fri. AE, DC, V. *P & G* (M), Via Spalti 1 (47.701). Closed Sun. and Aug. Elegant little spot, try *cuscus,* delicious pastas. AE, DC, V. *Trattoria del Porto* (M), Via Staiti 45 (47.822). Closed Mon. Typical seafood restaurant.

Ustica Palermo (091). Island off the coast of Sicily. *Grotta Azzurra* (M) (844.9048). Open 15 June to 15 Sept. Modern, resort hotel with terraces, pool, bathing area. *Punta Spalmatore* (M) (844.9122). Open 1 May to 30 Sept. Large, 100-cottage tourist village, resort facilities.

GETTING THERE AND AROUND. By air. Sicily's airports are at Palermo and Catania. The Rome—Palmero flight takes about 50 minutes. Palermo airport (Punta Raisi) is 32 km. (20 miles) out; Catania's, 7 km. (4½ miles). Airport bus into town center, about 3,000 lire.

By sea. In addition to the frequent car/passenger ferries that cross from Villa San Giovanni on the mainland to Messina in 30 minutes or so, there are also car ferries from Naples to Palermo, daily service, nine hours; from Naples to Catania, weekly, 15 hours; and from Naples to Milazzo with stops at the Aeolian Islands, bi-weekly, 18 hours.

Hydrofoils make the crossing from Messina to Reggio Calabria in 15 minutes and provide quick service to the Aeolians from Milazzo. Ferries and hydrofoils connect Ustica with Palermo, and Pantelleria with Trapani.

By train. There are direct express trains from Milan and Rome to Palermo or to Catania and Siracusa. The Rome—Palermo train journey takes at least 12 hours.

The main rail lines on the island connect Messina, Catania, Enna, Palermo and Trapani. Secondary lines are generally slow.

By bus. Local buses link the smaller towns. There are good tourist bus services between the main cities and to all the important sites.

By car. Sicily has a good road all round the coast, some of it classified as autostrada, and a mass of small, wiggly roads inland. A superhighway connects the northern port of Palermo—where car ferries from Tunis, Genoa and Naples dock—with Catania in the east, via Enna, also linking Catania with Messina. Another leg of the superhighway extends from Messina in the direction of Palermo but only as far as Patti, where you must follow the narrow old road to Cefalù to pick up the final stretch of the superhighway to Palermo. The old road is tortuous and dangerous driving, so it is worth making the Enna detour to be on the superhighway all the way.

The superhighway to Trapani passes Segesta, while the fast road to Mazara del Vallo puts you within hailing distance of Selinunte.

To see Sicily by automobile, you have several options: to drive down from Rome or Naples on the Autostrada del Sole, a very long trip (around 1,250 km., 775 miles, mostly tolled), worthwhile only if you have time to stop off to see some of Calabria; to put your car on the overnight ferry from Naples and sail down while you sleep; or to rent a car on the island, where the major rental agencies have airport and downtown locations at Palermo and Catania.

SARDINIA

Italy's Emerald Isle

Crumbling classical ruins, tall cypresses, vine-terraced hills, gorgeous basilicas and noble *palazzi* . . . these trademarks of tourist Italy are not seen, or not often seen, in Sardinia. The Mediterranean's second largest island (Sicily is the first), now less than an hour from mainland Italy by air or about seven hours by boat, was historically just a little too far from imperial and papal Rome to take on the color and character of the Italian peninsula. The island has little in common with Sicily either, apart from some similarities in dialect and some memories of Phoenician and Arab occupations of long ago.

Sardinia most closely resembles Corsica, the French island across its 10-mile-wide northern strait. A dense bush or *macchia* (in Corsica the *maquis*), barely penetrable in some districts, covers large areas. Such a terrain breeds legends of brigandage and vendetta and in the central regions of Sardinia, if you detour from the main roads, you may pass through mountain villages which have been quite recently in the news for some kidnapping or shotgun killing: a broken romance may still be cause for a never-ending family feud. The official line on touring these areas is that foreign travelers run no risks provided they do not meddle in what is not their business.

Arriving in Sardinia you feel you have dropped into a time-warp. This is Italy as it used to be, before the trains ran on time, before Mussolini re-created Roman grandeur with monolithic construction schemes, before the "economic miracle" of the 1960s brought industry and agriculture into the modern age. This is the land where every town, including the sprawling cities of Cagliari and Sassari, has a distinctly provincial air; where your hotel bedroom may be dimly lit, the TV and frigobar of vintage design, the bathroom towels like either tablecloths or napkins; where there are no *autostrade* and all roads are lightly trafficked and you park easily, without payment, in the principal piazza; where trains move at a gentle pace, and infrequently, and about half the railroad network consists of single-track, narrow-gauge lines, now being refurbished and supplied with old steam locomotives for tourist excursions.

There are hamlets where the population comes to its doors to watch the foreign visitor pass through. Each doorway falls silent as you approach, and a babble of conversation breaks out behind you.

All this gives the island the character of D.H. Lawrence's impatient and self-pitying *Sea and Sardinia,* written in 1921—but it is not all like that. Life, though simple, is clean and cheerful. Seafood, the glory of the Sardinian cuisine, is always beautifully fresh and carefully presented. The Sardinians themselves are a courteous, rather deferential people. The true Sardinian, squat and black-haired, but nimble and graceful and better-looking than most, is a country-dweller at heart, with the country-dweller's virtues. As you tour the hinterland you will glimpse enchanting cameos of shepherds leading flocks of lively sheep, a patriarchal scene which used to be commonplace all over the Mediterranean and is rare in most countries nowadays.

But what is the "true Sardinian"? On the northwest coast they will tell you: "You haven't met any Sardinians yet, we're all Spanish round here"—and an Aragonese tracery of ironwork round a balcony reinforces the statement. Move to the northeast and the inhabitants boast a Genoese or Pisan ancestry—and the wrecks of Malaspina fortresses decorate the headlands. Travel south around the coast and you will encounter in their turn the physiognomies, customs, dialects, place-names and holy buildings of the Turks, the Moors, the Phoenicians, the Austrians and the mainland Italians. It could be there are no pure Sards—or Sardinians—left. If there are, they will be found in the south-central mountains, south of Nuoro, under the 6,000-foot summits of the Gennargentu massif, in the rugged country which is still ironically called Barbagia, "Land of Strangers."

Those Mysterious Nuraghesi

The Roman soldiers, following on the heels of Carthaginian invaders, gave the central mountain regions of Sardinia the name, "Land of Strangers." No doubt the thick-set savages, clothed in bearskins, whose military tactics were limited to ambush and swift retreat seemed strange enough to the Romans. But it was, of course, the Romans who were the strangers. The mountain people they were up against were descendants of the island's aboriginal population—and we may never know where they came from.

The earliest inhabitants of Sardinia are one of prehistory's enigmas. They have left scarcely a clue to their origins. Ancient writers called them *nuraghesi.* Their only monuments are citadels of cyclopean stones of idiosyncratic design, tumbled down and here and there rebuilt, called *nuraghi*: a feature as unique to Sardinia, as the Sphinx is unique to Egypt.

Archeologists date the *nuraghi* to around 1,300–1,200 B.C., a time when the Israelites were establishing themselves in Canaan, when the ancient Greeks were besieging Troy, when the Minoan civilization collapsed in Crete, when the Rameses Pharaohs reigned in Egypt and when many migrations took place around Mediterranean shores. During the next 1,000 years, the nuraghic peoples gradually withdrew into highland fastnesses to avoid contact with more disciplined and better-armed invaders. (The only weapons they knew, say the chroniclers, were stones hurled by hand and boulders rolled down from hilltops.) For another 1,000 years it was more of the same. In those times the enemies were successively the Romans, the Goths and Vandals (the real "barbarians"), the naval forces of Byzantium and the Saracen hordes. During and after the Middle Ages, Pisa secured the eastern coasts of the island, Genoa the northern, Aragon the northwestern. The southern shores harbored nests of pirates from Algeria and Tunisia.

Cradle of Royalty

Yet this was the land which gave Italy her one royal dynasty, the House of Savoy. It stemmed from a family of freebooters in the Alpine valleys of the frontier between France and Italy. By virtue of backing the winning sides in the various European conflicts of the 17th and 18th centuries, the Dukes of Savoy extended their influence over Piedmont in northern Italy and after the Congress of Vienna (1815)—when the map of Europe was redrawn but Sardinia was totally ignored—the then Duke of Savoy, with Austrian approval, proclaimed himself King Victor Emmanuel of Sardinia. He had a palace at Cagliari but his principal seat was at Turin on the mainland.

The whole of Italy, except Sardinia, was at that time under foreign rule, mostly Austrian; and even Sardinia's king, married to a Habsburg princess, took his orders from Vienna. But an era of new hopes and impulses towards constitutional liberties was at hand. In 1848, the "year of revolutions," little Sardinia actually declared war on mighty Austria—at first the Pope approved, then withdrew his support, and the bid for freedom failed. Year by year, through the efforts of such patriots as Mazzini, Garibaldi and Cavour (the last-named the Sardinian king's prime minister), Italian unity and independence came nearer. Again, in 1859, Sardinia prepared to fight Austria and again the promised help, this time from the French emperor, was withdrawn and the small kingdom's interests were betrayed.

Eleven years later, when Italian unity was achieved, the King of Sardinia (Victor Emmanuel II) became King of Italy, and for a time the nation's capital was the House of Savoy's mainland capital, Turin.

When Italy's royal capital and seat of government was transferred to Florence and then finally to Rome, Sardinia reverted to the role which geography had assigned her: an offshore island, rather primitive, with a lot of fish but not much else in the way of natural resources. Throughout her history, no Mediterranean power had thought it worth while to colonize her. All her wars had been fought on foreign soil. Even in World War II she escaped invasion and occupation and was little more than a naval base for Italian warships and an airfield for German fighter-bombers.

Not until 1948 was the island accorded its own regional government. Not until the 1960s, when it qualified with Sicily and Calabria for special development status under the Cassa per il Mezzogiorno (the fund for the distressed South), did Sardinia begin to share in the nation's post-World-War II prosperity.

A Green and Pleasant Land

You visit Sardinia for landscapes rather than cathedrals or monuments; for easy-going excursions with plenty of side-trips rather than a highly-organized itinerary; for a naive low-key entertainment scene rather than brilliant expensive night-life. Talking of expense: for some reason hard to fathom, the cost of living in Sardinia is somewhat higher than on the mainland. On the other hand, if you want to live really cheaply, and can rough it, many humble lodgings and tavernas are at your disposal.

This is not a big island. On its quiet roads, at moderate speeds, you could travel comfortably from northern tip to southern in five or six hours; from east to west in three. A fairly comprehensive tour of the island, coastline and interior, could be accomplished within the week.

Most visitors arrive by air or sea at Cagliari in the south, Olbia in the northeast or Alghero in the northwest. A sensible way to see the best of Sardinia, within the framework of a tour of Italy, is to fly or sail to Alghero, travel by road or rail to the south and return from Cagliari to the mainland by air or sea.

Alghero, an old walled town with at least two excellent hotels and one outstanding seafood restaurant, is the center for fine cliff scenery and splendid stalactite caves, the Grottoes of Neptune (400 steps down—400 up again). A picturesque *corniche* road runs south, but the tourist should head north for Sassari, the island's second city, an important cultural center, and from there run along the coast via another walled sea-citadel, Castelsardo, to the island's northern tip at Santa Teresa. Try to time your arrival in Santa Teresa for sunset: over the Bonifacio Strait, on most days a strange and memorable phenomenon. From Santa Teresa, better from neighboring Palau, you may visit the islands of the strait, Caprera (tomb of Garibaldi, the "sleeping lion whose breathing makes the ocean swell") and La Maddalena, historic Italian naval base, now a hideout for American nuclear submarines.

The scrub country, mostly cistus and juniper, is decorated with pine and olive windbreaks and in places you drive through avenues of hibiscus and oleander. Game birds are occasionally seen—there is said to be a wingless partridge, exclusive to the island. Zoological freaks are emblematic of Sardinia, but in the wilds they must be almost extinct. To inspect the *mouflon,* the ringleted mountain goat (alleged to have had the original Golden Fleece), it is best to try a zoo or wildlife park.

Flowery Sardinia becomes spectacular after you have turned south for Olbia. Tiny resorts and yachting villages such as Porto Cervo and Baia Sardinia appear to be set in botanical gardens. The unusually limpid sea in the inlets reflects masses of glossy green foliage and sheets of bougainvillea. This is the famed Costa Smeralda, developed by the Aga Khan, who discovered its charms by accident when his yacht ran in for shelter from a storm. The Costa Smeralda is still dominated by his personality—still measuring its attractions, one might say, by the yardstick of his fabled riches. "Secret paradise" of tycoons and actresses for some years, the Costa is now an open, upmarket vacationland. Sardinia's most expensive hotels are here. Here, too, scions of the House of Savoy return annually in their yachts—the male heirs are permitted to approach no nearer than this to the Italy their ancestors reigned over.

Olbia is a good touring center and a seaport, not heavily industrialized, at the head of a long wide bay. At the bay's mouth, Golfo Aranci is a blossoming resort. There are game reserves in the surrounding *macchia*-clad hills and if you go walking (along the tempting narrow-gauge railroad which links Olbia with Golfo Aranci, for example), you can find yourself ankle-deep in tortoises.

A little farther south, on the so-called Costa Dorata, there is good walking and bathing, especially on the firm sands of an estuary near Siniscola.

Turning inland, you arrive at Nuoro, a shabby provincial capital locked in a gorge in the hot, harsh mountainland which culminates in Gennargentu, the island's highest massif (6,000 ft.). Continuing south, on a sensational and extremely tortuous road through the Barbagia, you negotiate Sardinia's most primitive districts. Life in some of the villages has not altered much since the Middle Ages, but the only survivals of the old elaborate regional costumes are those worn by folk-dance troupes on feast days or perhaps, for a gimmick, by a gas station attendant.

An alternative to that difficult route is the highway from Nuoro to Oristano and thence by the dunes, canals and pastures of the lowland road to Cagliari.

Prehistoric Tops

Whichever route you choose, you should detour to Barumini, a calm and spotlessly clean little township with the finest and most accessible *nuraghe* set right beside the main road. You could spend a whole afternoon clambering over that extraordinary structure of concentric rings of boulders, chambers, passages, wells and beehive tower. From the air it looks like an old-fashioned toy top.

The southern landscapes are dotted with isolated conical hills, with caverns and basalt plateaux among them. On the Giara plateau, near Tulli, you may be lucky enough to see the dwarf horses of Sardinia (guided tour only), another zoological rarity.

Off the southwest coast, two large islets, San Pietro and Sant' Antioco, are worth visiting if time permits. San Pietro is where discerning southern Sardinians go for their weekends and vacations.

Cagliari, the island's capital, has impressive Italianate architecture and churches in a variety of styles—it is clear that the Aragonese have been here as well as the Austrians and Italians. The city has several magnificent viewpoints too, notably the Terrazza Umberto which once formed part of the Spanish walls. On the huge landlocked harbor, where supertankers lie and big ferry boats pass in procession, some fine stretches of beach and a backdrop of hills have promoted the growth of resort villages and vacation complexes. Golfers should note the location of the superb Is Molas championship course near Pula. Its sporting character, as well as its elegant hotel and restaurant and panoramic outlook, have received the tributes of Tom Watson, Jack Nicklaus and others. The surrounding wildwood supports a dwindling population of deer, hares and other game and on the muddy shoreline between Pula and Cagliari airport flamingoes are a common sight.

PRACTICAL INFORMATION FOR SARDINIA

WHEN TO GO. The north of Sardinia is cold and rainy in winter, the south mild and generally sunny. In summer the interior is torrid, but breezes refresh the ribbons of sandy beach which virtually encircle the island. Sun-worshippers choose June to September, but the best touring months are May and October. February is the month of solemn Lenten parades and May is the month of two great explosions of costume and color in Sassari and Cagliari (see *Seasonal Events* below)— annual affirmations of a strong folkloristic tradition. Even in high summer, though hotels may be full, you will never have to drive far to find a quiet beach.

TOURIST OFFICES. *Sardinian Tourist Department* (postal inquiries only): **Cagliari,** Via Mameli 97 (668.522). *Regional Tourist Offices:* **Cagliari:** Piazza Deffenu 9 (663.207); **Nuoro:** Piazza Italia 19 (30.083); **Oristano:** Via Cagliari 276 (74.191); **Sassari:** Viale Caprera 36 (23.37.29). *Local Tourist Offices:* **Alghero:** Piazza Portaterra 9 (979.054); **Arzachena:** Via Risorgimento (82.624); **Cagliari:** Piazza Matteotti 9 (669.255); Aeroporto Elmas, (24.02.00); **Palau:** Via Nazionale 94 (709.570); **Muravera:** Via Europa 22 (993.760); **Olbia:** Via Catello Piro 5 (21.453); **Santa Teresa di Gallura:** Piazza Vittorio Emanuele 24 (754.127); **Sassari:** Via Brigata Sassari 19 (233.534).

SEASONAL EVENTS. Carnivals on the last Sunday and Tuesday before Lent, usually in February, open the yearly calendar of events.
Cagliari: on May 1–4, the Sagra di Sant'Elfsio brings thousands of pilgrims on foot and by horse and cart, to participate in one of the biggest and most colorful processions in the world; some of the regional costumery dates back to 1657.
Costa Smeralda: important sailing regattas are held in Aug. and Sept.
Mamoiada (near Nuoro): the Mamutones carnival preceding Lent is a most unusual procession of fearsomely masked figures representing devils.
Nuoro: at the end of Jul. there is a three-day summer festival, the Sagra di San Pantaleo; and on Aug. 29 there's the Feast of the Redeemer, another chance to see richly decorated costumery.
Oliena: Good Fri. sees a dramatic pageant, the Incontru (Encounter).
Oristano: most spectacular of the pre-Lenten carnivals is the Sartiglia, a costumed parade and tournament; Sept. 11–14 sees the Sagra di Santa Croce, which combines religious celebrations with a lively fair.
Sassari: the biennial (falling in 1989) Regional Exhibition of Sardinian Handicrafts takes place in May; mid-May, on Ascension Thurs., there's a parade of costumed riders, the Cavalcata Sarda; while on Aug. 14 comes the procession of the Candelieri.

TELEPHONE CODES. You will find the telephone area code for each town against its name in the Hotel and Restaurant listings (after the province name). If there is a different area code from the majority of the establishments—say when a hotel or restaurant is in an outlying place—then the code is given in front of the telephone number.

HOTELS AND RESTAURANTS. The sophisticated life of Sardinia, such as it is, revolves around its comparatively expensive hotels and restaurants, most of which are newly built. In the listings below, the name of the province follows the place-name. Each province (there are only four of them, Cagliari, Nuoro, Sassari and Oristano) covers a wide area. "OLBIA, Sassari" does not mean that Olbia is near Sassari—in fact it is 70 miles away.
Regional Food and Drink. The cuisine is basically Italian. Inland, meat dishes are mostly veal- or mutton-based. On the coast, fish is synonymous with food—

restaurants offer meals of eight or nine courses, all fish, starting with river oysters and crayfish and progressing towards the deep sea by way of mussels, cockles, prawns, sprats, lobsters, swordfish, and striped bass; everything, in fact, but the fish we associate with this island, which is the sardine. The delicacy and variety of the seafood ensure that one never tires of this high-protein diet. Foreign conquerors have left legacies of bouillabaisse, couscous, and paella and there are native specialties like *maloreddus* (a saffron-flavored pasta) and *porceddu* (roast suckling-pig); and numerous regional variations on the pasta theme.

Wines are many and various, the reds usually eminently drinkable, the whites tending to a light and delicate quality. The Sardinian wine best known abroad is the amber-colored, heady Vernaccia, ideal with seafood.

Alghero Sassari (079). High season 1 July to 15 Sept. Colorful town, good beaches nearby. *Villa Las Tronas* (E), Lungomare Valencia 1 (975.390). Mansion on promontory; 31 spacious rooms with fine views; pool, rock bathing. Furnishings recall days of grandeur when royal Savoyards stayed here. AE, DC.
Calabona (M), Località Calabona (975.728). Open 1 April to Oct. Outside town, on sea. Large, modern, with pool, rock bathing. AE, DC, MC, V. *Carlos Quinto* (M), Lungomare Valencia 24 (979.501). Old-fashioned in an appealing way, exceptionally attentive staff, quite inexpensive out of season. AE, DC, MC, V. *Continental* (M), Via Kennedy 66 (975.250). Open 1 May to 30 Sept. Smallish, very comfortable, fairly central. No restaurant. AE, DC, MC.
At **Fertilia,** on sandy beach, *Dei Pini* (M), Località Le Bombarde (930.157). Open 1 May to 31 Oct. Quiet, set in pinewoods. *Punta Negra* (M) (930.222). Open Oct. to Apr. Resort hotel, on beach; pool. DC.
Restaurants. *Corsaro* (M), Via Columbano 11 (978.431). Closed Mon. In old part of town, justly famous. DC, MC, V. *Simpatico* locale, good food. AE, V. *La Lepanto* (M), Via Carlo Alberto 135 (979.159). Closed Tues. Tops in town; attractive; fine local cuisine, especially seafood. AE, DC, MC, V. *Il Pavone* (M), Piazza Sulis 3 (979.584). Closed Wed. and Dec.–Jan. Fine seafood restaurant on shore boulevard. AE, DC, MC, V. *Da Pietro* (M), Via Machin 20 (979.645). Closed Wed. off-season. In old town; small, delicious pastas with seafood sauce. AE, DC, MC, V.

Baia Sardinia Sassari (0789). Beach resort. High season 20 June to 15 Sept. *Bisaccia* (E) (99.002). Open 20 March to 15 Oct. Quiet; pool, beach. DC. *Villaggio Forte Capellini* (M) (99.057). Cottage complex. Open May to Sept. Garden, swimming pool, charming layout; worthwhile but somewhat pricey restaurant.
Restaurant. *Le Tre Botti* (M), Provincial highway at Liscia di Vacca turnoff (99.150). Open Easter to Oct. Tasty, crusty pizzas.

Barumini Oristano (0783). The *nuraghi* metropolis. **Restaurant.** *Zia Annetta* (I), Via Tuveri 8 (986.8006). Quaint, cottage-and-courtyard trattoria; inspired home-cooking. Memorable local wines.

Cagliari Cagliari (070). Capital and largest city. *Mediterraneo* (E), Lungomare Colombo 46 (301.271). Best; on sea with good views; comfortable, well-furnished rooms. AE, DC, MC, V. *Moderno* (M), Via Roma 159 (653.971). Central, near station; unpretentious. No restaurant. AE, MC, V. *Panorama* (M), Viale Armando Diaz 231 (307.691). One mile from center. 1982-built, large rooms, stylish décor; splendid panoramic views from top-floor bar and breakfast room. AE, DC, MC, V.
Restaurants. *Dal Corsaro* (E), Viale Regina Margherita 28 (664.318). Closed Tues. Elegant and excellent; mainly seafood. AE, DC, V. *Al Golfo* (E), at Hotel Mediterraneo, Lungamara Colombo (301.271). Closed Mon. and Aug. Posh overtones; fine cuisine. AE, DC, MC. *Ottagono* (E), Viale Poetto (372.879). Closed Tues. and Dec. On Poetto beach, sophisticated; sumptuous *antipasto* table.
Buongustaio (M), Via Concezione 7 (668.124). Closed Tues. Book for this popular place; rustic and informal. MC. *Il Gatto* (M), Viale Trieste 15 (663.596). Closed Sun. Popular and central; seafood specialties. AE, DC. *Italia* (M), Via Sardegna 26 (657.987). Closed Sun. and Dec. 15–Jan. 15. Central and hospitable. DC, MC, V. *Ro-*

setta (M), Via Sardegna 44 (663.131). Closed Mon. Longtime favorite. AE, DC, MC, V.

At **Capoterra** turnoff, 7 miles (11 km) out, on highway to Pula, *Sa Cardiga e Su Schironi* (M) (71.652). Closed Mon. and early Nov. Very large, very good; splendid seafood. AE, DC, V.

Cala Gonone Nuoro (0784). Interesting grottos, 8 km. (5 miles) of hairpin curves below Dorgali. High season 1 July to 10 Sept. *Mastino* (I) (93.150). Open 1 April to 30 Sept. High above sea; simple. DC, V.

Castelsardo. Sassari (079). Picturesque town, basket-weaving center. **Restaurants.** *La Guardiola* (M), Piazza del Bastione (470.755). Closed Mon. off-season and Nov. Backstreet cellar. Modest young chef provides best fish and seafood cuisine on north coast. Book ahead. MC, V.

Costa Smeralda Sassari (0789). Once exclusive, still expensive, undergoing continuous development, this area between **Olbia** and **Arzachena** has over 80 km. (50 miles) of beachfront and an excellent port at **Porto Cervo**. High season 1 July to 31 Aug. *Cala di Volpe* (L), (96.083). Open 14 May to 30 Sept. Secluded, exclusive; attractive architecture and furnishings; creature comforts include pool, tennis, first-rate Pevero golf course. AE, DC, MC, V. *Pitrizza* (L), at Pitrizza (92.000). Open 12 May to 30 Sept. Very private; several villas with 2–3 suites, each with terrace, handsome clubhouse, heated rock-carved pool; all on secluded bay. AE, DC, MC, V.

Romazzino (L), at Romazzino (96.020). Open 14 May to 15 Oct. Large, informally elegant and comfortable with pool, beach, gardens. AE, DC, MC, V.

Balocco (E), at Liscia di Vacca (91.555). Smallish, pleasant; pool, tennis, good views. AE, DC, MC, V.

Le Ginestre (E), near Porto Cervo (92.030). Open 1 April to 30 Sept. Very comfortable, attractive; pool, tennis. AE, DC, MC, V.

Nibaru (M), at Cala di Volpe (96.038). Open 1 May to 15 Oct. Smallish, pretty bungalows with pool. AE, DC, V.

At **Porto Cervo**, *Cervo* (L), (92.003). At the center of things, with atmosphere of posh but informal club; pool. AE, DC, MC, V. *Cervo Tennis Club* (E) (92.244). Only 16 very comfortable rooms; pool, tennis is the name of the game here. *Luci di la Muntagna* (M) (92.051). Open Easter to 10 Oct. Large, Mediterranean-style, on hillside overlooking port; pool, minibus to beach. AE, DC, MC, V.

Restaurants. *Cala di Volpe* (L), (96.083). Hotel restaurant, great setting and smart atmosphere. AE, DC, MC, V.

Pevero Gulf Club (E), at Cala di Volpe (96.210). Open 22 May to 30 Sept. Elegant and informal; very smart clientele. AE, DC, MC, V.

Rosemary (E), at Liscia di Vacca (no phone). Rustic.

At **Porto Cervo**, *Il Pescatore* (E), Molo Vecchio (92.296). Open 10 May–15 Oct. Candlelit suppers, seafood specialties. MC. *Pomodoro* (M) (92.207). A few steps from *Piazzetta;* simple, reasonably priced food.

Fonni Nuoro (0784). Barbagia center, base for excursions to Gennargentu. *Sporting Club* (M), at Monte Spada (57.154). 69 rooms. Beautiful location above town, marvelous views; authentic Sardinian cuisine. AE, DC.

Golfo degli Aranci Sassari (0789). Good beaches. High season 20 June to 15 Sept. *Baia Caddinas* (M), (46.898). Open 15 May to 30 Sept. Nicely furnished bungalows; beach, pool. *Gabbiano Azzurro* (M), (46.929). Open 1 June to 30 Sept. Directly on beach, just outside town; comfortable rooms with balcony.

La Maddalena Sassari (0789). Island off north coast, with lovely beaches, fine sailing; 15 minute boat trip from Palau. High season 20 June to 15 Sept. *Cala Lunga* (E), at Porto Massimo (737.389). Vacation village. Very nice resort hotel on sea with pool, beach and little port. AE.

On **Santo Stefano Island,** *Valtur* (M) (737.061). Vacation village, all sports.

Restaurants. *La Grotta* (M), Via Principe di Napoli 3 (737.228). Closed Mon. off-season and 15 Oct–15 Nov. Oldest and best on island; seafood. *Mangana* (M), (738.477). Closed Wed. and Dec. DC. *Da Pino* (M), Via Amendola (737.011). Closed Tues. off-season. On port.

Macomer Nuoro (0785). Commercial town, intersection of main roads. Near important *nuraghi*. *Motel AGIP* (M), at Bosa exit of Carlo Felice highway (71.066). Large and comfortable; fine restaurant serving Sardinian cuisine. AE, DC, MC, V.

Nuoro Nuoro (0784). Important inland city, center for excursions in Barbagia area. *Grazia Deledda* (M), Via Lamarmora 175 (31.257). Solid, older hotel. AE, DC, MC, V. *Sandalia* (M), Via Einaudi 14 (38.353). Modern, well-equipped. Commanding site above town; most luxurious public rooms in Nuoro. Excellent and varied cuisine.

At **Mount Ortobene,** *Fratelli Sacchi* (I) (34.030). Closed Feb. Small, in lovely setting with fine views. AE, MC.

Restaurants. *Canne al Vento* (M), Viale Repubblica 66 (36.641). Closed Sun. Local specialties. *Da Giovanni* (M), Via Quattro Novembre 7 (30.562). Closed Sat. Upstairs locale, family-type service and cooking. *Del Grillo* (M), Via Monsignor Melas 14 (32.005). Typical Sardiinian cuisine. AE, DC, V.

At **Mount Ortobene,** *Fratelli Sacchi* (M), hotel restaurant (31.200). Closed Mon. and Feb. The place for local specialties, especially roast lamb and pig; beautiful location. AE, MC.

At **Oliena,** *Su Gologne* (E), on road from Nuoro (287.512). Closed Nov. Touristy, but worth the detour for typical Sardinian food. AE, DC, MC, V.

Olbia Sassari (0789). Ferry port, good beaches nearby. High season 20 June to 15 Sept. *Mediterraneo* (M), Via Montello 3 (24173). Modern and functional; easy walk to ferry port. AE, DC, MC, V. *President* (M), Via Principe Umberto 9 (21.551). Good overnight if you miss the ferry. *Royal* (M), V. Moro, on northern approach to town (50.253). Quiet, friendly, modern; swimming pool.

At **Marinella,** 14 km. (8 miles) northeast on shore, *Abi d'Oru* (32.001). Open 15 May to 2 Oct. Very attractive, on bay; beach. AE, DC, MC, V.

Restaurants. *Grazia Deledda* (E), on road to Baia Sardinia (9.116). Closed winters. Classic island food and wine. *Tana del Drago* (E), on road to Golfo degli Aranci (22.777). Closed Mon. off-season. Rustic. DC. *La Palma* (M). Behind Royal; lovely tropical decor, superb seafood cuisine.

Oristano Oristano (0783). Medieval administrative center, now fishing and farming town with monumental remains. *Cama* (I), Via Vittorio Veneto 119 (74374). Modest, central; convenient for drivers. AE, MC, V. *Mistral* (I), Via Martiridi Belfiore (212.505). Good comfort for the price; on the edge of town. AE, DC, V.

At **Arborea,** high season 1 July to 13 Sept., *Ala Birdi* (M) (800.512). Cottages amid pines; beach.

At **Torre Grande,** high season 1 July to 31 Aug., *Del Sole* (M) (22.000). Open 1 April to 31 Oct. Beach hotel. AE, DC, MC.

Restaurants. *Il Faro* (E), Via Bellini 25 (70.002). Closed Sun. Seasonal specialties of the island; very good; not all dishes pricey. *La Forchetta d'Oro* (M), Via Giovanni Ventitresimo (70.462). Closed Sun. Standout for local cuisine. *Da Giovanni* (M), at Torre Grande beach, Via Colombo 8 (22.051). Closed Mon. and Oct. Seafood. *Da Salvatore* (M), Vico Mariano 2 (71309). Closed Sun. Classic seafood from local tidal basins. *Stella Marina* (M), Via Tirso 6 (72.506). Closed Sun. Reasonable and good. AE, DC, V.

Palau Sassari (0789). Ferry port for La Maddalena. High season 1 July to 31 Aug. *La Roccia* (I), Via dei Mille (709.528). Above the port. No restaurant. AE, DC.

Restaurants. *Il* Cisto (E), Via Capo d'Orso 26 (709.319). Open 1 June to 30 Sept. Sardinian specialties, dining under pretty arbor. AE, DC, MC, V. *Da Franco* (E), Via

Capo d'Orso 1 (709.558). Closed Mon. off-season and Dec. Interesting and unusual menu; excellent food and wines. AE, DC, MC, V.

Porto Conte Sassari (079). Beautiful bay 16 km. (9 miles) from Alghero. *El Faro* (L) (942.010). Open 1 April to 31 Oct. Tastefully furnished resort hotel on promontory; pool, rock and beach bathing, terrace restaurant. AE, DC, MC, V. *Corte Rosada* (M) (942.083). Open 1 May to 30 Sept. Pretty cottage complex in pinewoods, all resort facilities. AE, DC, MC, V.

Porto Rotondo Sassari (0789). Smarter even than Costa Smeralda. High season 20 June to 15 Sept. *San Marco* (L), 3 miles from Olbia (34.110). Open 1 April to 31 Oct. Delightful shady villa off village piazzetta. 31 fine rooms with bath. Breakfast only, but atmospheric trattoria at hand. AE, DC, MC, V.

Porto San Paolo Sassari (0789). On Coasta Dorata, easy of Olbia. High season 1 July to 31 Aug. *Don Diego* (M), at Costa Dorata (40.007). Open 1 April to 5 Oct. Pretty bungalow colony on beach, with pool, tennis.

San Pietro Island Cagliari (0781). The main village, Carloforte, is very pretty. **Restaurant.** *Da Nicolò* (M), Via Dante (854.048). Closed Fri, from 15 Nov. to 16 Jan. Interesting cuisine reflects Tunisian-Ligurian influences.

Santa Margherita di Pula Cagliari (070). Beach resort 32 km. (20 miles) from Cagliari. High season 1 July to 13 Sept. *Castello* (L), hotel of Forte Village (921.531). Open 15 May to 24 Oct. Large, very comfortable; lively vacation village atmosphere; all sports. DC, MC, V. *Is Morus* (E), (921.281). Open May to Oct. Mediterranean-style, modern, on white sandy shore amid pinewoods. Two distinguished restaurants, native and international cuisine. You can eat at straw-thatched tables on beach. Handy for *Is Molas* sports center and championship golf course. 20 mins. from Cagliari airport. AE, DC, MC, V.
Abamar (M) (921.555). Open 15 May to Sept. Large, modern, on sandy beach; pool, park. DC, MC, V. *Flamingo* (M), right on beach (920.8361). Set amid pines; comfortable resort hotel with adjacent cottages; restaurant.
Restaurants. *Is Morus* (E), at Is Molas Golf Club (920.9062). Chic; fine food. V. *Is Morus* (E), at Hotel Is Morus (921.424). Open 1 April to 31 Oct. Excellent choice of international or Sardinian dishes. AE, DC, MC, V. *Urru* (M) (921.491). Closed Mon. Regional specialties, summer terrace.

Sant'Antioco Island Cagliari (0781). Off southwest coast of Sardinia. **Restaurant.** *Da Nicola* (M), Lungomare Vespucci at Sat'Antioco (83.286). Closed Tues. and Oct. Unpretentious seafood restaurant; good *zuppa di pesce*. *La Torre* (M), Via Marconi 1 at Calasetta (88.466). Closed Mon. off-season and in Oct. Interesting cuisine with Arab overtones; good atmosphere.

Santa Teresa Gallura Sassari (0789). Pretty harbor, near good beaches. High season 20 June to 15 Sept. AE.
Corallaro (M), at Rena Bianca (754.341). Open 1 Jan. to 31 Oct. Pleasant, small, high above beach; pool, tennis. AE, V. *Li Nibbari* (M), at La Testa (754.453). Open 1 June to 30 Sept. Small, comfortable; pool. *Shardana* (M), at Santa Reparata (754.031). Open 15 May to 25 Sept. Bungalows furnished in rustic style, on sandy beach; rock pool, garden bar. AE.
Restaurants. *Canne al Vento* (M), Via Nazionale 23 (754.219). Closed Sat. off-season and Oct. Typical local dishes. *Mistral* (M), on Capo Testa road (754.490). Open 15 May to 25 Sept. Closed Mon. Good; some items pricey. *Riva* (M), Via del Porto (754.392). Closed Wed., Nov. and Dec. Strictly seafood, some pricey.

Sassari Sassari (079). Second largest city. *Grazia Deledda* (E), Viale Dante 47 (271.235). Modern comforts; pool. AE, DC, MC, V. *Frank* (M), Via Diaz 20 (276.456).

Simple but adequate. No restaurant. *Motel AGIP* (M), at Serra Secca, outside town (271.440). AE, DC, MC, V.

Restaurants. *Gallo d'Oro* (E), Piazza d'Italia 3 (230.044). Closed Fri. Classic international cuisine. *Il Senato* (M), Via Mundula 2 (231.423). Closed Mon. Central, small but attractive with good food. *Tre Stelle* (M), Via Porcellana 6 (232.431). Closed Sun. and Aug. Very good, especially for seafood island-style.

At **Ottava**, 11 km. (7 miles) northwest, *Sa Posada* (M) (20.643). Attractive rustic place for Sardinian cuisine. DC.

Siniscola Nuoro (0784). **Restaurant.** *Sa Valetta* (M), on Siniscola–Santa Lucia state highway (819.073). Bright, airy, facing sea. First-class presentation of typical maritime cuisine. Family-run, and a kind, handsome, cheerful family it is.

Stintino Sassari (079). Northwest coastal area. High season 1 July to 31 Aug. *Cala Reale* (M), near Capo Falcone (523.127). Open 1 May to 30 Sept. Modern resort hotel with pool, beach. *Rocca Ruja* (M), at Capo Falcone (527.038). A notch above others for comfort, prices; very good resort facilities. DC, V.

Restaurants. *Capo Falcone* (E), at La Pelosa (527.039). Open 1 April to 30 Sept. The view is worth top prices. *Silvestrino* (M), Via Sassari (523.007). Open 1 Feb. to 30 Sept. Fine trattoria, delicious *zuppa di aragosta.*

Villasimius Cagliari (070). Southeast coastal resort, near Cagliari. High season 1 July to 13 Sept. *Capo Boi* (E) (663.950). Open 1 June to 2 Oct. Very smart beach hotel with pool; attractive wooded grounds.

GETTING THERE AND AROUND By air. Daily direct flights (Alitalia, Alisarda and ATI) connect mainland airports of Turin, Milan, Genoa, Venice, Bologna, Pisa, Rome and Palermo with Cagliari, Alghero and Olbia.

By boat: The gigantic modern ferries of Terrenia Lines and the FS (State Railroad) connect Genoa and Civitavecchia on the mainland with Porto Terres (12 hours), Olbia (12 hours or 7 hours) and Cagliari (20 hours or 10 hours). There are also services between Cagliari and Palermo/Trapani in Sicily (12 hours), between Olbia and Livorno (9 hours) and between Porto Torres and Toulon in France (19 hours); daily or alternate days, reservations essential in summer, automobiles carried.

By train. There are fairly good train connections between Olbia, which is the usual port of entry, and Cagliari, Oristano and Sassari. You can reach Nuoro via Macomer and Alghero via Sassari. Service on the few other local lines is sketchy and slow.

By bus. Tour buses connect the most important cities with the most interesting sights on the island; inquire at the tourist offices or travel agencies. Local buses link the smaller towns, but are exasperatingly slow.

By car. The best way to get around Sardinia is by automobile. A surprising number of the roads are in good condition, but keep in mind that such roadside conveniences as gas stations and refreshments halts, on some routes, can be few and far between. Cars and campers may be rented at port or airport of entry (with or without chauffeur). Advance reservations may be made at car rental agencies on the mainland, Avis and Hertz at Costa Smeralda and elsewhere.

Cars may be taken on board all boat services from the mainland to the island. Italian State Railways operate modern car-passenger ferries from Civitavecchia to Golfo degli Aranci, near Olbia. Fares are lower than on private lines, but as with other services to the island, round-trip passages should be booked well in advance.

ENGLISH-ITALIAN
VOCABULARY

In the following vocabulary we have avoided those fine-sounding polite introductory phrases which bring an answering storm of swift Italian. The phrases are utilitarian, assuming that you have to make yourself understood in places where no English is spoken.

"Please" works wonders. Try to add it to the beginning or end of every question or request in the list below, and you'll see many Italian smiles and have a much better time during your visit.

Pronunciation: Every letter and syllable is sounded (except *h*). The accent is on the last syllable but one, unless otherwise shown.

Vowels: A is pronounced *ah,* e-*eh;* i-*ee;* o-*oh;* u-*ou* as in *you.* (These sounds are slightly flattened when unstressed or when followed by more than one consonant).
Double-vowels do not exist: *Austria*—ah-ou-stree-ah, *dieci*—dee-ay-chee.

Consonants: (a) **Single Consonants:** As in English, except: c—like *ch* before i or e (*cento*—chentoh; *cinque*—cheenquay); g—as in English germ before e or i. Otherwise like g in gone.
w—(occurring only in foreign words)—like English *v.*
z—like *ts:* zio—tsee-oh.

(b) **Combinations of Consonants:** Sc—like *sh* before e or i. Otherwise like *k* (*lasciare*—lashiah-reh; *scala*—scah-lah). Gl is pronounced lj: Camogli—Kahmohljee.
Read over the following words and phrases with constant reference to the above rules; then speak them slowly, clearly, and boldly, and any Italian will understand.

General

Please	Per favore
Thank you	Gràzie
Not at all	Prego
What is this called in Italian?	Come si chiama questo in Italiano?
Here	Qui
There	Li
How much?	Quanto?
My change?	Il mio resto?
Day	il giorno
Morning	la mattina
Afternoon	il pomeriggio
Evening	la sera
Night	la notte
This morning	stamani
Sunday	domenica
Monday	lunedì
Tuesday	martedì
Wednesday	mercoledì
Thursday	giovedì
Friday	venerdì
Saturday	sabato

403

January	gennaio
February	febbraio
March	marzo
April	aprile
May	maggio
June	giugno
July	luglio
August	agosto
September	Settembre
October	ottobre
November	novembre
December	dicembre

Numbers

0	zero	11	undici	22	ventidue	80	ottanta
1	uno	12	dodici	30	trenta	81	ottantuno
2	due	13	tredici	31	trentuno	90	novanta
3	tre	14	quattordici	40	quaranta	91	novantuno
4	quattro	15	quindici	41	quarantuno	100	cento
5	cinque	16	sedici	50	cinquanta	101	cento uno
6	sei	17	diciassette	51	cinquantuno	200	duecento
7	sette	18	diciotto	60	sessanta	1,000	mille
8	otto	19	diciannove	61	sessantuno	2,000	due mila
9	nove	20	venti	70	settanta	1,000,000	un milione
10	dieci	21	ventuno	71	settantuno		

By Train

I have (want) a reserved seat.	Ho (desìdero) un posto riservato.
Is there a dining car?	C'è un vagone ristorante?
What time is the first service?	A che ora è il primo servìzio?
for breakfast (lunch dinner)?	per la colazione (il pranzo, la cena)?
When does the train leave?	A che ora parte il treno?
When does the train arrive in . . . ?	Quando arriva il treno a . . . ?
What's the name of this station?	Come si chiama questa stazione?
How far is it to . . . ?	Quanto siamo lontani da . . . ?
How long do we stay here?	Quanto ci fermiamo qui?
Take this to the check room.	Porti questa al deposito bagagli al mano.
Is there a bar in the station?	C'è un bar nella stazione?
Coffee and a sandwich.	Un caffè e un panino.
A glass (bottle) of beer. . . .	Un bicchiere (una bottiglia) di birra.
. . . to take away.	. . . da portare via.
Have you English (American) newspapers?	Ha dei giornali inglesi (americani)?

By Car

Where is the office of the Automobile Club?	Dov'è l'ufficio dell' Automobile Club?
Where can I get gas (petrol)?	Dove posso trovare della benzina?
Twenty liters, please.	Venti litri, per favore.
Will you put some air in my tires?	Mi vuol gonfiare le gomme?
Is there a repair shop here?	C'è un' officina qui?
I need a tow to a garage.	Ho bisogno di essere rimorchiato fino al garage.
Where can I get spare parts for an	Dove posso trovare dei pezzi di

English (American) car?	ricambio per una macchina inglese (americana)?

Can I take this road to . . . ?	Va bene questa strada per . . . ?
I need water for my radiator.	Ho bisogno di acqua per il radiatore.
What is the name of this city (town), village?	Come si chiama questa città, questo paese?
Am I on the right road for . . . ?	Vado bene per . . . ?
Have you a road map of this region of Italy?	Ha una guida stradale di questa regione d'Italia?
One-way traffic.	Senso unico.

Hotels

Where is there a good restaurant (hotel)?	Dove c'è un buon ristorante (albergo)?
Is there anybody who speaks English?	C'è qualcuno che parla inglese?
I want a double room, a single room, for one night, two nights, with bath (telephone).	Desìdero una camera doppia, una camera a un letto, per una notte, due notti, con bagno (telefono).
How much, including all taxes?	Quanto costa, comprese tutte le tasse?
Name	Nome
Address	Indirizzo
Coming from	Provenienza
Nationality	Nazionalità
Where is . . . the bathroom? the toilet? my luggage?	Dov'è . . . il bagno? la toiletta? il mio bagàglio?
Come in!	Avanti!
Bring me soap, towels, iced water.	Mi porti del sapone, asciugamani, acqua ghiacciata.
Call us at eight (nine).	Ci chiami alle otto (nove).
Bring us morning tea (coffee).	Ci porti il tè in camera (il caffè).

Meals

Waiter, I want a table for three.	Cameriere, desìdero una tavola per tre.
Tea, coffee, tomato juice.	Tè, caffè, sugo di pomodoro.
Rolls and butter.	Panini e burro.
Bacon and eggs.	Pancetta affumicata e due uova.
A boiled egg.	Un uovo alla cocca.
Salt, pepper, oil, vinegar.	Sale, pepe, olio, aceto.
Bring me some more tea, coffee.	Mi dia ancora del tè, caffè.
The menu. Today's specialty.	Il menù. La specialità del giorno.
Hors d'oeuvre.	Gli antipasti.
What are the local dishes?	Quali sono le specialità del luogo?
Meat, lamb, beef, veal, steak, chicken, liver.	Carne, agnello, manzo, vitello, bistecca, pollo, fegato.
Potatoes (boiled, mashed, fried).	Patate (lesse, puree, fritte).
Fish, sole, trout, salmon.	Pesce, sogliola, trota, salmone.
Salad.	Insalata.
What kind of cheese have you?	Quali qualità di formaggio avete?
What is the local cheese?	Qual'e il formaggio locale?

Bring a bottle of good local wine.

Ci porti una bottiglia di buon vino locale.

The bill for the whole party.

Il conto complessivo.

See also the *Food* and *Wine* chapters, as well as the Regional Specialties in each *Practical Information* section for further words and phrases

Around Town

Where is the British (American) Consulate?

Dov'è il consolato inglese (americano)?

Will you write the address here?

Mi vuol scrivere qui l'indirizzo?

How do I get there?

Come posso andarci?

Where is the bus (tram) stop?

Dov'è la fermata dell'autobus (tram)?

Where can I get off for . . . ?

Dove scendo per . . . ?

Where is the nearest bank?

Dov'è la banca più vicina?

What is the exchange rate for the dollar (pound)?

Cos'è il cambio del dollaro (della sterlina)?

I want to change twenty dollars (pounds).

Desìdero cambiare venti dollari (sterline).

Where is . . .

Dov'è

a tobacconist?

il tabaccaio?

a pharmacy?

una farmacia?

a hairdresser?

un parrucchiere?

a barber?

un barbiere?

a post office?

un ufficio postale?

I want: razorblades, a hair cut, a shave, a shampoo, to send a telegram to England (America).

Desìdero: lamette da barba, tagliare i capelli, fare la barba, uno shampoo, mandare un telegramma in Inghilterra (in America).

How much per word?

Quanto viene per parola?

Ordinary rate

Normale

Urgent

Urgente

When will it arrive?

Quando arriverà?

Where is the opera?

Dov'è. . . . (name of the theater)?

Where can I buy tickets?

Dove posso comprare dei biglietti?

At what time is the box office open?

A che ora è aperto il botteghino?

I want three tickets for tomorrow night.

Desìdero tre biglietti per domani sera.

At what time does the performance begin (end)?

A che ora comincia (finisce) lo spettacolo?

Where can I buy a

Dove posso comprare

map of the city,

una pianta della città?

films?

una pellicola?

Where is Piazza . . . ?

Dov'è Piazza . . . ?

the Town Hall?

il municipio?

the church of . . . ?

la chiesa di . . . ?

the . . . Museum?

il museo . . . ?

Where can I get films developed?

Dove posso far sviluppare una pellicola?

I want two prints of each.

Desìdero due copie di'ognuna.

I'd like these two enlarged.

Desìdero un ingrandimento di queste due.

Trips Out of Town

How do I get to . . . ?	Come faccio ad andare a . . . ?
Where is the station?	Dov'è la stazione?
Where does the bus start from?	Da dove parte l'autobus?
We want to go to the sea, to the mountains.	Desideriamo andare al mare, in montagna.
Two first (second) class singles to . . .	Due di prima (secònda), solo andata per . . .
Three first class returns to . . .	Tre di prima classe andata e ritorno per . . .
Do we have to change trains? Where?	Dobbiamo cambiare treno? Dove?
Is there a connection?	C'è una coincidenza?
What time is the next train? the last train? for . . .	A che ora c'è il prossimo treno? l'ultimo treno? per . . .
A bathing cabin for two, a beach umbrella, three deck chairs.	Una cabina per due, un ombrellone, tre sedie a sdraio.
I want to hire a rowing-boat, sailing boat.	Desidero affittare una barca, una barca a vela.
How much per hour? per day?	.Quanto viene all' ora? Per tutto il giorno?

Feeling Ill?

I am ill.	Sono malato (malata).
My husband (my wife) is ill.	Mio marito (mia moglie) è malato (malata).
My child (my friend) is ill.	Mio bambino/a (mio amico/a) è malato (malata).
Please call a doctor.	Per piacere chiamate un medico.
Where is the hospital?	Dov'è l'ospedale?
The emergency room.	Pronto soccorso.
I need an ambulance.	Ho bisogno di un'ambulanza.
Where is the pharmacy?	Dov'è la farmacia?
Can you fill this prescription?	Può prepararmi questa ricetta?
Aspirin.	Aspirina.
Antacid.	Antiacido.
Soda bicarbonate.	Bicarbonato di soda.

Index

The letters H and R indicate hotel and restaurant listings
(See also Practical Information sections at the end of each chapter
for additional details.)

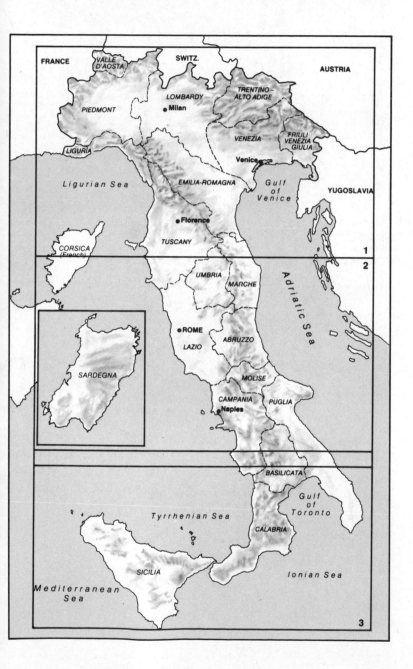

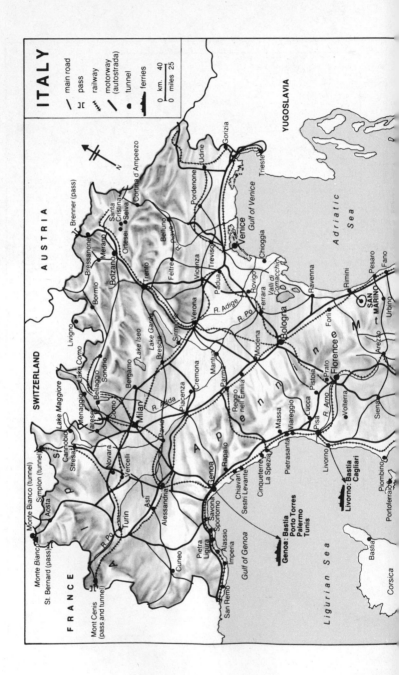

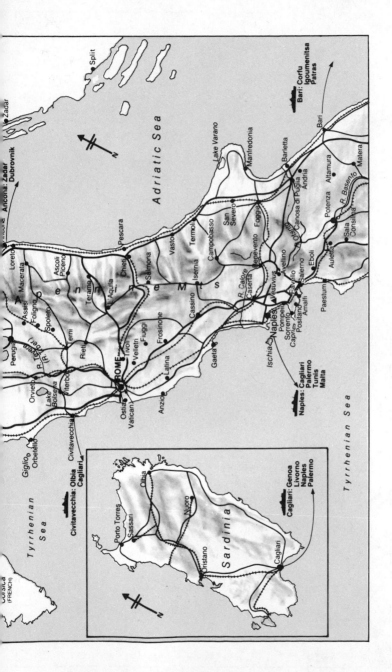

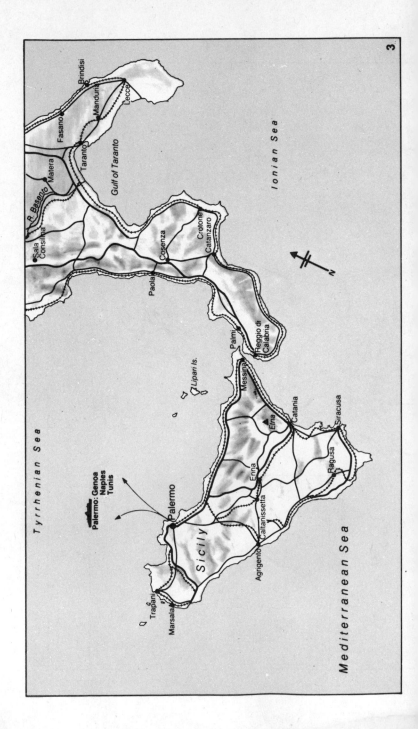

Fodor's Travel Guides

U.S. Guides

Alaska
American Cities
The American South
Arizona
Atlantic City & the
  New Jersey Shore
Boston
California
Cape Cod
Carolinas & the
  Georgia Coast
Chesapeake
Chicago
Colorado
Dallas & Fort Worth
Disney World & the
  Orlando Area

The Far West
Florida
Greater Miami,
  Fort Lauderdale,
  Palm Beach
Hawaii
Hawaii *(Great Travel
  Values)*
Houston & Galveston
I-10: California to
  Florida
I-55: Chicago to New
  Orleans
I-75: Michigan to
  Florida
I-80: San Francisco to
  New York

I-95: Maine to Miami
Las Vegas
Los Angeles, Orange
  County, Palm Springs
Maui
New England
New Mexico
New Orleans
New Orleans *(Pocket
  Guide)*
New York City
New York City *(Pocket
  Guide)*
New York State
Pacific North Coast
Philadelphia
Puerto Rico *(Fun in)*

Rockies
San Diego
San Francisco
San Francisco *(Pocket
  Guide)*
Texas
United States of
  America
Virgin Islands
  (U.S. & British)
Virginia
Waikiki
Washington, DC
Williamsburg,
  Jamestown &
  Yorktown

Foreign Guides

Acapulco
Amsterdam
Australia, New Zealand
  & the South Pacific
Austria
The Bahamas
The Bahamas *(Pocket
  Guide)*
Barbados *(Fun in)*
Beijing, Guangzhou &
  Shanghai
Belgium & Luxembourg
Bermuda
Brazil
Britain *(Great Travel
  Values)*
Canada
Canada *(Great Travel
  Values)*
Canada's Maritime
  Provinces
Cancún, Cozumel,
  Mérida, The
  Yucatán
Caribbean
Caribbean *(Great
  Travel Values)*

Central America
Copenhagen,
  Stockholm, Oslo,
  Helsinki, Reykjavik
Eastern Europe
Egypt
Europe
Europe *(Budget)*
Florence & Venice
France
France *(Great Travel
  Values)*
Germany
Germany *(Great Travel
  Values)*
Great Britain
Greece
Holland
Hong Kong & Macau
Hungary
India
Ireland
Israel
Italy
Italy *(Great Travel
  Values)*
Jamaica *(Fun in)*

Japan
Japan *(Great Travel
  Values)*
Jordan & the Holy Land
Kenya
Korea
Lisbon
Loire Valley
London
London *(Pocket Guide)*
London *(Great Travel
  Values)*
Madrid
Mexico
Mexico *(Great Travel
  Values)*
Mexico City & Acapulco
Mexico's Baja & Puerto
  Vallarta, Mazatlán,
  Manzanillo, Copper
  Canyon
Montreal
Munich
New Zealand
North Africa
Paris
Paris *(Pocket Guide)*

People's Republic of
  China
Portugal
Province of Quebec
Rio de Janeiro
The Riviera *(Fun on)*
Rome
St. Martin/St. Maarten
Scandinavia
Scotland
Singapore
South America
South Pacific
Southeast Asia
Soviet Union
Spain
Spain *(Great Travel
  Values)*
Sweden
Switzerland
Sydney
Tokyo
Toronto
Turkey
Vienna
Yugoslavia

Special-Interest Guides

Bed & Breakfast
  Guide: North America
1936...On the
  Continent

Royalty Watching
Selected Hotels of
  Europe

Selected Resorts
  and Hotels of the U.S.
Ski Resorts of North
  America

Views to Dine by
  around the World